LIFT TAKE YOUR STUDYING TO THE NEXT LEVEL.

This book comes with 1-year digital access to the *Examples & Explanations* for this course.

Step 1: Go to **www.CasebookConnect.com/LIFT** and redeem your access code to get started.

Access Code:

Step 2: Go to your BOOKSHELF and select your online *Examples & Explanations* to start reading, highlighting, and taking notes in the margins of your e-book.

Step 3: Select the STUDY tab in your toolbar to access the questions from your book in interactive format, designed to give you extra practice and help you master the course material.

Is this a used casebook? Access code already scratched off?

You can purchase the online *Examples & Explanations* and still access all of the powerful tools listed above. Please visit CasebookConnect.com/Catalog to learn more about Connected Study Aids.

PLEASE NOTE: Each access code provides 12 month access and can only be used once. This code will also expire one year after the discontinuation of the corresponding print title and must be redeemed before then. CCH reserves the right to discontinue this program at any time for any business reason. For further details, please see the Casebook Connect End User Agreement.

PIN: 9111149617

01137

D1156548

Sales

ASPEN CASEBOOK SERIES

Sales
A Systems Approach

Sixth Edition

Daniel Keating
Tyrrell Williams Professor of Law
Washington University

 Wolters Kluwer

Published by Wolters Kluwer in New York.

Wolters Kluwer Legal & Regulatory Solutions U.S. serves customers worldwide with CCH, Aspen Publishers, and Kluwer Law International products (www.WKLegaledu.com).

To contact Customer Service, e-mail customer.service@wolterskluwer.com, call 1-800-234-1660, fax 1-800-901-9075, or mail correspondence to:

Wolters Kluwer
Attn: Order Department
PO Box 990
Frederick, MD 21705

Printed in the United States of America.

2 3 4 5 6 7 8 9 0

ISBN 978-1-4548-5792-1

Library of Congress Cataloging-in-Publication Data

Names: Keating, Daniel L. (Daniel Louis), 1961- author.
Title: Sales : a systems approach / Daniel Keating, Tyrrell Williams
 Professor of Law, Washington University.
Description: Sixth Edition. | New York : Wolters Kluwer, 2016. | Series:
 Aspen casebook series
Identifiers: LCCN 2015043297 | ISBN 9781454857921
Subjects: LCSH: Sales — United States. | LCGFT: Casebooks.
Classification: LCC KF915 .K43 2016 | DDC 346.7307/2 — dc23
LC record available at http://lccn.loc.gov/2015043297

About Wolters Kluwer Legal & Regulatory Solutions U.S.

Wolters Kluwer Legal & Regulatory Solutions U.S. delivers expert content and solutions in the areas of law, corporate compliance, health compliance, reimbursement, and legal education. Its practical solutions help customers successfully navigate the demands of a changing environment to drive their daily activities, enhance decision quality and inspire confident outcomes.

Serving customers worldwide, its legal and regulatory solutions portfolio includes products under the Aspen Publishers, CCH Incorporated, Kluwer Law International, ftwilliam.com and MediRegs names. They are regarded as exceptional and trusted resources for general legal and practice-specific knowledge, compliance and risk management, dynamic workflow solutions, and expert commentary.

To my students,

who continue to make it so fun for me to teach

Summary of Contents

Contents

Preface

For this sixth edition, the primary citation for Article 1 remains revised Article 1, reflecting the reality that revised Article 1 has become the law in every state except Missouri. Because of the near-unanimity with which revised Article 1 has been adopted by the states, this edition eliminates the parallel citation to the pre-revised version of Article 1.

As with the previous editions, this book follows the format of the LoPucki/Warren/Lawless *Secured Transactions* book in three significant ways that distinguish it from previous works in the area. First, the materials are organized into 28 class-sized assignments. The approach in this book is even more flexible, however, in that the book is suitable for either a two-hour or a three-hour sales course. For those teaching a three-hour sales course, 12 of the 28 assignments have enough problems in the problem set to occupy two classes, rather than just one. For those teaching a two-hour sales course, the Teacher's Manual provides a syllabus that indicates which problems the teacher should skip in the "double-class" problem sets so that the two-hour teacher can simply teach all 28 assignments in just one class each.

Second, the materials are designed for class sessions devoted exclusively to problem-solving rather than to lecture or analysis of cases. Accordingly, the assignments contain relatively few cases. To ensure that the cases present issues of significance in current commerce, the majority of the cases come from the mid-1990s or later.

The third significant feature of the materials is the systems perspective shared with the *Secured Transactions* book, the *Law of Debtors and Creditors* casebook by Warren/Westbrook/Porter/Pottow, and *Payment Systems and Other Financial Transactions* by Ronald Mann. This perspective emphasizes the institutions and mechanisms that market participants use to conduct their transactions. This perspective is furthered in the sales material in at least three ways: (1) I conducted over three dozen extensive interviews with players in the sales system and incorporated the findings of those interviews throughout the material. (2) The material includes a number of provisions from actual sales documents and forms, which should help to give students a feel for how the system works in practice. (3) Newspaper excerpts are included in some of the assignments to give illustrations of how the sales system affects real people in the real world.

In addition, this book's coverage of sales systems encompasses not just the domestic sale of goods, but also leases, international sales, and real estate sales. These latter three systems are similar in many respects to the domestic sale of goods system, but there are some important differences that are explored in several of the assignments.

This book's goal at all points is to provide students with two things: the ability to see the grand structure of the existing systems that are covered in this book, and the ability to pick up and use new systems that develop in the years to come.

Daniel Keating

December 2015
St. Louis, Missouri

Acknowledgments

Just as with earlier editions of this casebook, I owe a debt of gratitude to those people who made helpful comments on the book: Lucas Osborn (a million thanks for his numerous helpful insights!), Michael Greenfield, Alexander Meiklejohn, and Layne Keele. I want to give a special thanks to my very able research assistant, Kelsey Laugel, who did a fantastic job with her copy-editing as well as with her many helpful substantive comments.

I do not want to forget all of the help I received previously from professors who used the casebook in its first edition. As to that edition, I received a dozen or more helpful suggestions from each of the following users, and I still wish to express my gratitude to them: Michael Greenfield, Alexander Meiklejohn, Stephen Sepinuck (who also generously agreed to share his "Active Learning Exercises" for use in my Teacher's Manual), and Paul Shupack (with whom for one semester I had at least weekly e-mail communication about his use of the book).

Other users who took the time to give me valuable ideas concerning how to improve the first edition and to whom I am also grateful include: Jean Braucher, Michael Korybut, Gary Neustadter, C. Scott Pryor, Keith Rowley, and William J. Woodward, Jr.

In addition, I wish to thank the students who took my class when I taught the first edition of the book. Their in-class answers gave me great insights on whether or not the problems were working, and some students were even kind enough to point out typos when they found them.

As to the first edition of this book, I still owe a special debt of gratitude to Ronald Mann, who not only read every assignment within 24 hours after I wrote it, but also inspired me by his own tireless example. Ronald was even so kind as to review the revised version of the first edition after he taught from the draft version, thereby serving as a priceless but unpaid editor. Also for the first edition, I thank Lynn LoPucki and Elizabeth Warren for their valuable comments and suggestions about the material. I thank my colleague Michael Greenfield for always being on-call to answer my Article 2 questions as I wrote the first edition. Four commercial law teachers besides Mann were kind enough to teach all or part of a first draft of the first edition of the book in the spring of '97 and I benefitted from their comments: Roger Billings, John Hennigan, Gary Neustadter, and Nancy Ota. Finally, I am grateful to the following individuals who took the time to give me some "real world" perspective on sales: John Dul, Anixter, Inc.; John Podczerwinski, Schnading Corp.; Mark D. Rabe, McDonnell Douglas Corp; Kenneth Hovorka, Rock-Tenn Co.; William Geary, Rock-Tenn Co.; Joseph F. Jedlicka III, Anheuser-Busch Companies, Inc.; Steve Volland, Anheuser-Busch Companies, Inc.; Brian M. Foster, Ralcorp Holdings,

Inc.; Lester Tober, Tober Industries, Inc.; Glen Horton, Washington University; Gayle G. Stratmann, Eveready Battery Company, Inc.; Richard A. Cohen, May Department Stores Co.; John K. Kane, Bryan Cave; plus a couple of dozen anonymous sources whom I interviewed for an article that I published in the year 2000 about Article 2's "battle of the forms" provision.

The following are acknowledged and thanked for granting permission to reprint:

The Associated Press for permission to reprint a portion of Harry F. Rosenthal, Justice, FTC Oppose Lawyers-Only Real Estate Closings, September 20, 1996.

The St. Louis Post-Dispatch for permission to reprint a portion of Carolyn Tuft, Title Insurance: Let Buyers Be Wary, October 1, 1995.

The St. Petersburg Times for permission to reprint a portion of Amy Ellis, Dream Car Turns Into Nightmare, November 5, 1995.

The Business Law Brief for permission to reprint a portion of Julian Harris, Acquiring Title to Goods, February 1994.

The Guardian for permission to reprint a portion of Richard Colbey, Extended Warranties Spark New Wave of Complaints, February 17, 1996.

Sales

Chapter 1.   Formation

Assignment 1:   The Role and Scope of Codes in Sales Systems

A.   Fundamental Aspects of Sales

People have been buying and selling things for just about as long as there have been things to buy and sell. In ancient times, "sales" primarily took the form of what we would think of as trades, but as currency systems developed, people began to purchase items with money rather than with other, directly useful items.

As trade became more and more sophisticated, various social and legal institutions were created to expedite and simplify transfers of ownership within sales systems. Sales "systems" include all of the people, institutions, laws, and practices that are involved in transfers of ownership for a price. Admittedly, there are different systems for different kinds of goods. But whether a sale involves a corporation buying sophisticated machinery or a consumer buying a laptop computer at Sears, sales systems generally perform four functions that facilitate the transfer of ownership from seller to buyer.

First, sales systems bring buyers and sellers together and enable them to create legally enforceable transfers of ownership. In facilitating the formation function, the systems not only provide legal rules to define when formation occurs but also provide the people and institutions that help enable formation. With higher-value items, there tends to be a layer of employees (often known as brokers) whose sole function is to encourage the formation of additional sales agreements. In the car industry, for example, sellers typically employ an army of individuals who try to convince potential buyers to become actual buyers.

Second, sales systems provide a set of standard terms that govern the transfer of ownership unless the buyer and seller choose to modify the standard terms. Often, but not always, this important gap-filling function of sales systems is performed by a code, most notably the Uniform Commercial Code (UCC, or the Code). There are other ways that sales systems can fill gaps, however, such as the common law or even the standard form contracts that are used by most players in a particular sales industry.

One important caveat at this point is not to confuse the Code with the sales system itself. Codes such as the UCC play an important role in law-related sales systems, but they are merely one cog in the bigger machine. Consider, for example, the residential real estate sales system. Here there is no universal code comparable to the UCC, but there are nevertheless institutions and practices within that system that arguably make the real estate sales system an even more sophisticated and unified system than that used for the sale of goods.

Anyone who has ever purchased a house knows that this sales transaction will usually involve a broker, an appraiser, an inspector, a title insurance company, and a mortgage lender. And at the end of it all, the purchaser will participate in a formalistic, almost ritualistic, event known as a "closing." The system is smooth and well-functioning, but it does not depend on a code to make it work.

The third function of sales systems is to facilitate performance. Sales systems facilitate performance by providing a set of delivery institutions that enable the possessory, legal, and symbolic transfer from seller to buyer. For example, the sales system provides a menu of standardized delivery terms that allow parties to select different arrangements with respect to insurance costs, delivery charges, and passage of the risk of loss from seller to buyer.

Fourth, sales systems enforce agreements to transfer ownership by giving the aggrieved buyer or seller various remedies for breach by the other. These remedies might be non-legal, such as a buyer's refusal to buy in the future from a seller that will not rectify its delivery of a defective product. Or these remedies could consist of the various damage formulas that the UCC provides in a case where informal dispute resolution breaks down and one party sues the other.

The assignments in this book are organized to correspond to sales systems' four subsystems described above: formation, terms, performance, and remedies. Each assignment will address four systems for transfers of ownership, using a hub-and-spoke approach to coverage. The hub is sales of goods, which are governed by Article 2 of the UCC.

The three spokes that will follow the Article 2 hub in each of the assignments are personal property leases, international sales of goods, and real estate conveyances. Personal property leases are included because although they do not involve sales, they do involve a very analogous system for the temporary transfer of possession. Furthermore, the rules of UCC Article 2A, which govern leases, borrow heavily from Article 2, and thus there is a particular efficiency in including the 2A spoke on a wheel whose hub is Article 2. A final reason for including coverage of leases is that it is occasionally quite difficult to distinguish a lease from a sale. Both types of transactions involve the exchange of consideration for rights in property; with leases, however, there is not only a physical transfer of the goods being leased, but also a temporal division in the ownership rights of these goods.

International sales are generally governed by the Convention on Contracts for the International Sale of Goods (CISG). This code borrows some concepts from the UCC but in other respects departs significantly from the UCC. The CISG therefore serves as a useful point of comparison that helps one to appreciate the workings of the UCC. Finally, the real estate conveyancing system, although it lacks a uniform code, nevertheless has a good deal of conceptual overlap with the sales of goods system.

B.   The Real World of Sales

This book includes excerpts from extensive interviews with over a dozen buyers and sellers in various industries. Those interviewed include officers in Fortune 50 companies, as well as owners of smaller, privately held enterprises. The primary purpose in conducting these interviews was to discover how relevant the *law* of sales is in the day-to-day operations of the sales system.

The interviews deal with issues of contract formation, the statute of frauds, parol evidence, warranties and disclaimers, commercial impracticability, acceptance and inspection, delivery practices, and remedies. For each of these areas, the interviews seek to discover what role, if any, the existing legal rules play in shaping the actual practices of buyers and sellers.

In the assignments to come there will be frequent reference to the results of these interviews, but at this point a few general observations are in order. Probably the most striking finding of this investigation is that there seem to be two, only slightly overlapping, worlds out there: the world of business practice and the world of law. In the world of business practice, law is much less significant than reputation and leverage as forces that govern the day-to-day behavior of the actors.

If a buyer or seller is not acting consistently with the expected norms in an industry, the most common response of an aggrieved party is not to sue, but rather to cease doing business with the violator. Where there is a long-term relationship at stake, both sides have an incentive to compromise and to avoid the litigation world. Even where the relationship is fairly new, the prospect of future business with the other side will often be sufficient to coax parties away from hard-line positions.

These findings about the relative dichotomy between business law and business practice are by no means revolutionary. In an often-cited article that was written more than 50 years ago, Professor Stewart Macaulay discovered the same truths in a wide-ranging empirical study concerning what he called "non-contractual relations in business." Assessing those results more than 20 years later in An Empirical View of Contract, 1985 Wis. L. Rev. 465, 467-468, Professor Macaulay mused:

> Contract planning and contract law, at best, stand at the margin of important long-term continuing business relations. Business people often do not plan, exhibit great care in drafting contracts, pay much attention to those that lawyers carefully draft, or honor a legal approach to business relationships. There are business cultures defining the risks assumed in bargains, and what should be done when things go wrong. People perform disadvantageous contracts today because often this gains credit that they can draw on in the future. People often renegotiate deals that have turned out badly for one or both sides. They recognize a range of excuses much broader than those accepted in most legal systems.

Although excerpts such as this one certainly downplay the significance of sales law in day-to-day sales practice, they do not mean to suggest that the law has no role to play in sales systems. There are at least three ways in which sales law has an impact on sales systems. First, the law of sales will be crucial in those instances where the normal business relationship breaks down and the parties end up in litigation. Although this eventuality may be slim for any particular contract, when litigation does occur the stakes tend to be high. This is also the point at which lawyers get called into the game.

Second, when parties to a sales agreement negotiate informal settlements to disputes, they will probably do so in the "shadow of the law." In one of the interviews, the general counsel of a computer hardware distributor explained that before his sales people meet with a customer to settle a dispute, they will often request from the general counsel's office "our bottom-line legal position." Although the ultimate legal position of a buyer or seller will not necessarily be the dispositive factor in the resolution of a particular dispute, the legal status of each side's position can at least be an important factor.

Finally, legal rules are important in sales systems because they help dictate the terms of the various forms that business people use in conducting trans-actions within a given sales system. Lawyers draft these forms — purchase orders, distribution agreements, and the like — and business people use them. The forms are the place where lawyers can change the default rules that would otherwise apply in the case of litigation. Forms matter not only because they could be binding in the unlikely event of litigation, but also because business people often act as if the forms are binding. Indeed, business people will some-times (but not always) change their behavior to conform to what the forms say.

Professor Russell Weintraub, who conducted an extensive survey of cor-porate general counsel concerning contract practices, noted the role of legal rules in shaping the content of contracts. In the article where he discusses the results of his survey at 1992 Wis. L. Rev. 1, 5, Professor Weintraub observed:

> Although it is a delusion to assume that commercial conduct is primarily con-trolled by what is "legal," the law should not be contrary to practices that the com-munity perceives as normal and desirable. Laws opposed to practice are unlikely to change practice, but will, when haphazardly and occasionally applied, con-demn what should be encouraged.
>
> Moreover, recognizing that legal rules do not control commercial conduct is not the same as saying that rules have no effect on practice. Central to the functional impact of contract law is the fact that legal rules affect not only the parties to litigation, but also the frequency and form of future contracts. The concern with influence on future bargains may call for different rules than if the only concern were past bargains. Once litigation has begun, the siren call for relatively simple, clear rules facilitating settlement becomes especially attractive.

C.   Functions of a Code in Sales Systems

Imagine that you are the president of a manufacturing enterprise that makes clothing of various kinds. You received a new purchase order for 20 dozen pairs of blue jeans from an independent retailer, Jeans 'R' Us. You promptly sent the jeans to the store and a week later you got a call from the store's manager, who informed you that two dozen pairs of the jeans that you had sent had zippers that did not zip.

The purchase order that the buyer sent to you said nothing about zippers having to zip. And yet you did not hesitate for a moment in apologizing to the Jeans 'R' Us owner, and you quickly sent a replacement shipment for the two dozen jeans with the defective zippers.

It so happens that this transaction was a sale of goods and therefore was covered by the UCC. It is also true that you are probably a "merchant" under the UCC with respect to these jeans and therefore you made, whether you intended to or not, a warranty of merchantability to Jeans 'R' Us. That warranty included, among other things, a promise that the jeans would be "fit for [their] ordinary purpose," and jeans with broken zippers are not fit. Thus, under the UCC, you would have been obligated in any event to repair or replace the jeans.

When you immediately agreed to make your buyer whole, to what degree do you think the requirements of the UCC were driving your behavior? Probably very little. Even in a world without the UCC, you had plenty of reasons for wanting to send two dozen new pairs of jeans to Jeans 'R' Us.

First, you might be a good person who believes that replacing bad jeans with good ones is the ethically proper thing to do. Second, even if you do not have a strong moral sense, you might have hoped that your new customer would buy more jeans from you in the future, and refusing to replace the bad jeans would reduce the prospect of later sales to this buyer. Furthermore, even if you did not care about future deals with Jeans 'R' Us, this disappointed buyer might have friends in the industry who themselves are present or prospective customers of your company. And we all know how people talk.

Finally, even if the UCC did not exist, it is very possible that the common law would imply in this sales contract something comparable to the warranty of merchantability. So even if you were not particularly ethical and did not care about your reputation, you still might get sued for breach with respect to the two dozen bad zippers (although the amount at stake seems appropriate only for a suit in small claims court).

When you think about the role of a code in sales systems, you should not overestimate its day-to-day significance on the players in the system. Doubtless there are reputational and ethical concerns that have a more powerful influence on the behavior of buyers and sellers than any code ever could. Nevertheless, a code has an important role to play in sales systems, and that is the role of gap filling.

Parties to a sales contract cannot think of every contingency in advance. Even if they could, in most sales it would not be worth the time it would take to plan for and agree about the outcome of every possible twist and turn of the sale. With sales of personal property, Article 2 fills the gaps for the parties with a convenient and fairly comprehensive set of default terms on issues such as warranties and remedies.

As hard as a code drafter might try, no code will successfully fill all of the gaps in all of the contracts that the code is intended to cover. That is where the common law comes in, as a kind of backup gap filler. Before the first uniform sales act, the common law was the primary gap filler for sales contracts. The advantage of Article 2 as a gap filler compared with the common law is that Article 2 is more predictable and generally more uniform from state to state than is the common law.

Nevertheless, even a code as comprehensive and as widely adopted as the UCC must acknowledge the role of the common law. UCC §1-103 tells us that the provisions of the Code displace any common law to the contrary, but that the common law shall continue to supplement the provisions of the Code. There are some common law doctrines, such as the parol evidence rule, that have clearly been supplanted (at least in sales of goods cases) by Article 2. UCC §2-202.

On the other hand, as we shall see in the material that follows, the common law continues to play at least three roles in law-related sales systems. First, in cases where Article 2 is merely codifying existing law, the common law can help define terms that the UCC has left undefined. For example, nowhere does the UCC define such fundamental terms as "breach," "offer," or "possession," but several UCC provisions use those terms.

Second, in some UCC sections and Official Comments the Code drafters make it clear that the UCC provision in question is not intended to affect certain related common law doctrines. Thus, parties must still look to the common law to define the parameters of those related doctrines.

Finally, there are a number of common law doctrines that are never referred to explicitly in UCC sections or Comments but that nevertheless continue to operate side by side with Code provisions. These include such concepts as mitigation of damages and frustration of purpose for a buyer, and even such related tort theories as intentional interference with contract.

One last general point to remember about the UCC is that the official version of the UCC that you might find in your statutory supplement is not necessarily "the law" in every state. Indeed, as of this writing, the official amended version of Article 2 that was promulgated in 2003 by the American Law Institute and the National Conference of Commissioners on Uniform State Laws has not been enacted in any state. Almost every state uses some form of the 1972 version of Article 2. When state legislatures enact articles of the UCC, they often include non-uniform amendments. Thus, you should always check your own state's enactment of the UCC. Furthermore, even where the UCC provision is the same from one state to another, the courts of each state may have interpreted the provision differently. Once again, you need to check the state common law that is controlling in any given case.

D.   Scope of Article 2

In any sales system there will be some set of rules that will serve as implied terms to agreements when the parties to a sale fail to specify certain terms. The rules might be those of Article 2, but they need not be in order to have a functioning system. Whatever the governing set of rules for the system, it is important that players in the system know whether they will ultimately be subject to those rules or not. The particular default rules that govern the system will affect how the players structure and shape the transactions within the system. That is why it is important to consider the question of the scope of Article 2: what's included and what's not in Article 2's world of default terms.

Our exploration into the scope of Article 2 is not to suggest that Article 2 is the only set of default rules out there in the world of sales. Article 2 is, however, the most prevalent set of default rules for sales of goods. In that respect, it is a set of default rules whose scope is worth studying.

There are some discrete sales systems that specifically shun Article 2 and its rules. Professor Lisa Bernstein has done detailed studies of two different sales industries that do not use Article 2 as their governing set of rules: the diamond industry and the grain industry. What was noteworthy to Professor Bernstein about the diamond industry was not merely the set of substantive rules that diamond traders use to govern transactions among its members, but also the private extralegal system that the industry uses to enforce agreements: "Although many of the shortcomings in the American legal system that make litigation unattractive to diamond dealers are also present in most commercial contexts, the diamond industry is unique in its ability to create and, more important, to enforce its own system of private law." Lisa Bernstein, Opting Out of the Legal System: Extralegal Contractual Relations in the Diamond Industry, 21 J. Legal Stud. 115, 116 (1992).

In Professor Bernstein's study of the grain industry, she highlighted one important contrast between how grain industry adjudicators use their own set of rules and how courts use Article 2's set of default rules. Article 2 emphasizes the importance of courts enforcing course of performance or course of dealing—that is, the actual practices used by the disputing parties before the relationship broke down—when faced with a sales dispute. The grain industry's private legal system, by contrast, does not seek to explore the actual practices between two contracting parties, or what Professor Bernstein calls "relationship-preserving norms": "[T]ransactors do not necessarily want the relationship-preserving norms they follow in performing contracts and cooperatively resolving disputes among themselves to be used by third-party neutrals to decide cases when they are in an end-game situation. . . . [W]hen courts apply the Code's usage of trade, course of dealing, and course of performance provisions, they will often be using relationship-preserving norms to resolve end-game disputes." Lisa Bernstein, Merchant Law in a Merchant Court: Rethinking the Code's Search for Immanent Business Norms, 144 U. Pa. L. Rev. 1765, 1770 (1996).

Thus, Professor Bernstein calls into question one of the fundamental premises underlying Article 2: that courts should apply the rules in litigation with reference to how the parties acted when they were not in litigation. Having to contend with this umbrella of usage of trade, course of dealing, and course of performance is at least one functional consequence of having a given sale be subject to the rules of Article 2.

Another key functional consideration of Article 2 coverage is whether or not the particular transaction will be subject to the gap filling role of the Code that was discussed previously. While there are many gap fillers in Article 2, two of them provide the most common grounds for parties' fights about whether or not Article 2 applies to their transaction: the warranty gap filler and the statute of limitations gap filler.

One of the most attractive features to a plaintiff of suing on a warranty theory is that the prima facie case is fairly easy to prove. Where the alternative is often a tort suit in negligence, the task in a warranty suit of proving merely the existence of a warranty, causation, and damages seems easy compared with having to show that elusive "lack of due care" required in a tort suit. Furthermore, if the suit is for breach of the warranty of merchantability, then the issue of warranty existence is as simple as demonstrating that this was a sale of goods and the seller was a merchant in goods of the kind.

Whereas the warranty gap filler often gives the plaintiff a reason to want Article 2 coverage, the Article 2 statute of limitations will sometimes give the plaintiff a reason to want the transaction to be deemed outside of Article 2's scope. UCC §2-725(1) gives a plaintiff four years to commence an action for breach of a sales contract, but the four years is measured from the time when the cause of action *accrued*, whether or not the plaintiff was aware of it. Many state statutes of limitations for general contract actions, by contrast, do not begin running until the plaintiff actually discovers or should have discovered the breach.

For example, imagine that a contractor agreed to assemble and install a sophisticated product assembly machine in the buyer's factory. Suppose that the machine contained a latent defect that did not manifest itself until more than four years following the sale. If the transaction were covered under Article 2, then the buyer would be barred by the statute of limitations from bringing a breach of warranty action. If the transaction were considered outside of Article 2, then the buyer could conceivably bring a breach of contract action since the general state statute of limitations would probably not begin to run until the buyer actually discovered or should have discovered the defect.

Although the gap filling function of the UCC can be very important in many cases, we should also remember that it is truly a last resort. Courts will look to the UCC gap filler only if they lack a more specific indication of what the parties must have intended with respect to the term in dispute. In other words, we should use UCC gap fillers only when there is, in fact, a gap to be filled.

There are at least four ways in which a UCC gap filler will be superseded. First, the gap filler will not apply to a particular term if the contract itself specifies what that term should be. UCC §1-302(a) makes it clear that the Code drafters desired first and foremost to give effect to private agreements, at least to the extent that those agreements are within the limits of good faith and commercial reasonableness.

Second, even where the parties' written contract is silent on a particular matter, the parties' repeated occasions for performance within that contract may establish an agreement by implication. UCC §1-303(a) calls these particular kinds of implicit terms "course of performance."

Third, where parties' past dealings with one another have established a particular way that the parties do business with one another, then such a history may establish by implication certain standard terms between the parties. UCC §1-303(b) calls such implied terms based on past contracts between the same parties "course of dealing."

Finally, if there is a custom in a particular industry concerning a performance term, that custom will prevail over the UCC gap filler whenever the two are inconsistent. The UCC calls such customs "usage of trade." UCC §1-303(c).

In addition to defining the various ways in which the UCC gap fillers can be superseded, the Code drafters also created in §1-303(e) a hierarchy among these rules: "express terms control both course of dealing and usage of trade and course of dealing controls usage of trade." On the other hand, the statement of this hierarchy begins with the admonition that whenever it is reasonable, we should seek to construe the express terms of an agreement as consistent with course of dealing or usage of trade.

Ragus Co. v. City of Chicago

628 N.E.2d 999 (Ill. App. Ct. 1993)

Rizzi, J.

This action arises out of a contract between Ragus Company (Ragus) and the City of Chicago (City). The contract called for Ragus to supply the City with a certain quantity of rodent traps. As a result of differing interpretations regarding the number of traps specified in the contract, Ragus supplied the City with only half of the rodent traps the City expected. The City refused delivery and suspended Ragus from its bidding process for six months. Ragus subsequently brought a five-count complaint against the City and three of the City's employees, Alexander Grzyb, Walter Brueggen and Mark Pofelski. . . .

The facts of this case are undisputed. In July 1991, the City announced that it was seeking bids from companies to supply the City with Gotcha Glue Boards, a brand of rodent traps. The City's announcement called for the following specifications for the traps:

150 cases of 5 1/2" × 11"; 24/case.

75 cases of 11" × 11"; 12/case.

Ragus submitted a bid offering to supply the City with the traps at a price of $30.00 a case, for a total of $6,750.00. The City awarded the contract to Ragus on August 18, 1991. On October 3 and 4, 1991, Ragus attempted to deliver to the City 150 cases each containing 24 of the bigger [sic] traps and 75 cases each containing 12 of the smaller [sic] traps. The City refused delivery because it was expecting 150 cases containing 24 pairs of the larger [sic] traps and 75 cases containing 12 pairs of the smaller [sic] traps. On October 16, 1991, the City notified Ragus that it had 10 days to cure what it perceived as a defect in Ragus' performance by delivering twice the number of traps. Ragus claimed that it was in compliance with the contract and did not tender the additional traps demanded by the City. On November 7, 1991, the City suspended Ragus from the bidding process until April 26, 1992.

Ragus then filed a five-count complaint seeking declaratory relief and money damages. In count I of the complaint, Ragus asked the court to construe the contract and declare that Ragus had complied with the contract. In count II, Ragus asked the court to declare that defendants wrongfully suspended Ragus from the City's bidding process. . . .

Defendants in turn filed a motion to dismiss the complaint pursuant to §2-619(a)(9) of the Illinois Code of Civil Procedure. A hearing was had on this motion. At the hearing defendants presented affidavits to show that usage of trade demonstrates that "24/case" refers to 24 pairs per case.

The president of the manufacturer of Gotcha Glue Boards averred that for the last 10 years Gotcha Glue Boards have been packaged in pairs. Defendant Alexander Grzyb, the City's purchasing agent, averred that once the contract was terminated with Ragus, he awarded a contract for Gotcha Glue Boards to Production Dynamics Company. That contract called for "150 cases of Gotcha Glue Boards, 5 1/2" × 11"; 24/case." Production Dynamics Company supplied the City with 150 cases each containing 24 pairs of traps. Lastly, Tony Proscia, a City employee, averred that he oversees goods shipped by various suppliers to the City. Every other case of 5 1/2" × 11" Gotcha Glue Boards he inspected contained 24 pairs of traps.

In an attempt to counter the above affidavits, Ragus presented the affidavit of its president, George L. Lowe. This affidavit, however, simply did not address the factual allegations concerning usage of trade. Accordingly, the factual averments of defendants' affidavits are admitted. . . .

Ragus next argues that the court erred when it referred to usage of trade pursuant to the Uniform Commercial Code §1-205(4) [revised §1-303(e)], in order to interpret the contract where the contract itself was unambiguous. We, however, disagree that the contract was unambiguous. The dispute focused on the interpretation of whether "24/case" and "12/case" refer to individual traps or to pairs of traps. In order to eliminate ambiguity from a contract it is necessary to exclude other reasonable interpretations. The above quoted language does not exclude the reasonable interpretation that 24 pairs and 12 pairs per case are the number of traps called for in the contract. Therefore, reference to usage of trade was proper.

Ragus also argues that defendants failed to present sufficient evidence establishing usage of trade. We disagree. Defendants presented the affidavits of three people who currently deal with Gotcha Glue Boards, including the president of the company that manufactures these traps. Taken together, the affidavits establish that the sole manufacturer of Gotcha Glue Boards packages and sells the traps in pairs, middle men purchase and resell the traps in pairs, and the City buys and receives the traps in pairs. Ragus failed to counter these factual averments. We hold that the trial court had before it sufficient evidence to find that when a party dealing in Gotcha Glue Boards spoke of "24/case" or "12/case," this meant 24 pairs and 12 pairs per case. The trial court properly construed the contract and dismissed count I of Ragus' complaint. . . .

On the issue of scope, Article 2's provisions are most deficient in their coverage of what are commonly known as "mixed contracts": those involving a combination of goods and services, or a combination of goods and something other than services. Article 2 says that it applies to "transactions in goods," UCC §2-102, and then defines goods as "all things (including specially manufactured goods) which are movable at the time of identification to the contract for sale." UCC §2-105(1). Nowhere does either of these provisions suggest how to treat a contract that includes both goods and non-goods aspects.

An example of a mixed goods-services contract would be a carpenter's contract with a homeowner for the carpenter to install new cabinets in the homeowner's kitchen. Whenever someone sells an entire business that consists in part of goods, that is an example of a contract that mixes goods and something other than services, like goodwill or customer lists.

Courts have taken two approaches to these mixed contracts. Most courts apply some version of a predominant purpose test, by which the court decides whether the predominant purpose of the transaction is to sell goods or services. If it is goods, then Article 2 applies to the whole transaction, even the services portion of it. If the predominant purpose is determined to be services, then Article 2 does not apply to any part of the transaction, not even the goods portion.

The other common approach to the mixed contract question has been called the gravamen of the action test. Under that test, the court determines whether the gravamen of the action (the source of the complaint) is with the goods or the services portion of the transaction. If the problem lies with the goods, then Article 2 applies even if the predominant purpose of the transaction is services rather than goods. If the problem lies with the services, then Article 2 does not apply to the dispute even if the predominant purpose of the transaction is goods rather than services.

Each test has its problems. Often it is quite difficult to determine whether the "predominant purpose" of a particular transaction is goods or services. While it might seem easier to decide what is the "gravamen of the action" in a particular case, even that determination can be tricky. For example, suppose you go to an eye doctor to get some medicine for your eyes. Imagine that you have specifically instructed the doctor that you are allergic to sodium-based solutions, but she gives you eye drops that contain sodium. The eye drop container *says* it contains sodium.

When you have an allergic reaction, does the gravamen of your action involve the goods or services portion of your transaction with the doctor? On one hand, you might say that the gravamen of the action was the goods, since it was the sodium in the solution that caused your allergic reaction. On the other hand, the goods were not inherently defective, and it was only because of shoddy medical services that you were given a prescription containing a substance to which you knew you were allergic.

One common sales transaction that has generated a lot of case law on the "mixed goods/services" question has been the sale of computer software and related services.

Simulados Software, Ltd. v. Photon Infotech Private, Ltd.

40 F. Supp. 3d 1191 (N.D. Calif. 2014)

DAVILA, J.

Presently before the Court is Defendant Photon Infotech Private, Ltd.'s ("Photon" or "Defendant") Motion to Dismiss Plaintiff Simulados Software, Ltd.'s ("Simulados" or "Plaintiff") Amended Complaint ("AC"). . . . Having fully reviewed the parties' papers, the Court will GRANT Defendant's motion for the reasons stated below.

I. BACKGROUND

Simulados is a Texas software development company based in Houston, Texas. Photon is a technology consulting corporation incorporated in New Jersey with its principal place of business in Chennai, India and a virtual office in San Jose, California. Simulados developed a program called Certify Teacher, which is a test simulation program used by educators to prepare for the Texas Examinations of Educator Standards ("TExES") certification exam. Simulados decided to produce a version of its product compatible with Apple Macintosh ("Mac") computers as well as an internet web application.

In early 2009, Photon called Simulados, representing Photon's ability to create a Mac-compatible product and develop a web application. Simulados and

Photon entered into a contract ("Contract") on March 31, 2009, which consisted of a Statement of Work ("SOW") and a Master Professional Services Agreement ("MPSA"). In the Contract, Photon represented that the project would start on May 20, 2009 and finish on September 17, 2009. The Contract provided that Photon would complete: CD mastering, migrating the existing source code to Real Basic, convert VB project, add Mac specific BASIC code, add support for New DB format, address performance bottlenecks in product, customize for Mac operating systems, add platform specific paths, tweak for Mac Human Interface Guidelines, provide license key generation and key validation, create a web application, create website authentication certification for downloads, upgrade to database content creator, provide support for reading the content, provide support for modifying content, migrate up to three sample products, and code review. Simulados agreed to pay $23,560 in four installments, the final of which was to be made upon delivery of a complete workable product. The Contract contained the following choice-of-law and forum selection provision: "[t]his Agreement shall be governed by and construed and enforce [sic] in accordance with the laws of the State of California."

Simulados contends that Photon never fulfilled its obligations under the Contract. On June 9, 2009, Photon communicated to Simulados that it was initiating the project, and represented that there would not be any outstanding serious or critical defects at the time of the site launch, with fewer than five medium defects and fewer than ten low defects. On August 14, 2009, Photon requested that Simulados approve completion of the project's development phase. A teleconference demonstration was held on August 19, 2009 and on September 24, 2009 Simulados received an access link for user testing and approval. During the review, Simulados found 38 low level and 8 critical issues. Simulados requested a status update on the web application and expressed dissatisfaction that the product was not complete. On May 3, 2010, Simulados gave Photon a deadline of June 3, 2012 to correct an additional 17 errors. On May 17, 2010, Photon responded to Simulados' notice, providing a link to incomplete software. To date, Photon has not provided Simulados with fully functioning web application.

Simulados filed a complaint on May 11, 2012 in the District Court for the Southern District of Texas. The case was transferred to this Court on August 20, 2012, based on the choice-of-law provision in the Contract. Simulados filed an Amended Complaint ("AC") on December 11, 2012. On December 24, 2012, Photon filed a Motion to Dismiss, which is presently before the Court. Plaintiffs have filed written opposition to this motion. The parties engaged in mediation, but failed to reach an agreement regarding arbitration. Photon re-noticed its Motion on July 23, 2013. Pursuant to Civil Local Rule 7-1(b), the Court took the motion under submission without oral argument. . . .

III.   DISCUSSION

The AC contains the following causes of action: breach of contract, fraud and fraudulent inducement, and violations of the Texas Deceptive Trade Practices Act. . . .

C.   Claims Arising Under the Uniform Commercial Code

Photon contends that Simulados' claim that it is entitled to remedies outside the contract by virtue of the UCC is implausible and must be dismissed because Article 2 of the UCC applies only to contracts for the sale of goods, not services, and the Contract between the parties is for services. Simulados argues that the Contract is for sale of software, which is considered a good, and thus the UCC applies. For the reasons outlined below, the Court will dismiss any claims arising from the UCC.

The UCC applies to the transaction of goods. Cal. Com. Code §2102. The UCC defines goods as "all things (including specially manufactured goods) which are movable at the time of identification to the contract for sale. . . ." Cal. Com. Code §2105. Applying the UCC to software poses a complex issue because transactions for software often combine elements of both goods and services. As such, courts have arrived at different decisions concerning whether software transactions are covered by the UCC.

The primary test used by courts to determine whether software is a good under the UCC is the predominant factor test, where courts look to the "essence of the agreement" on a case-by-case basis to decide how to characterize the transaction. Gross v. Symantec Corp., No. C-12-00154-CRB, 2012 WL 3116158, at *8 (N.D. Cal. July 31, 2012) (citing RRX Indus., Inc. v. Lab-Con, Inc., 772 F.2d 543, 546 (9th Cir. 1985)). Courts determine whether the predominant factor or purpose of the contract is rendition of services, with goods incidentally involved, or is rendition of goods, with labor incidentally involved.

Generally, courts have found that mass-produced, standardized, or generally available software, even with modifications and ancillary services included in the agreement, is a good that is covered by the UCC. In *RRX Industries, Inc. v. Lab-Con, Inc.*, the Ninth Circuit found that a license for mass-produced software for use in medical laboratories was covered by the UCC, even when the software contract also provided for ancillary services such as training, repair, and system upgrading. *RRX Indus.*, 772 F.2d 543 (9th Cir. 1985). The court noted, "[h]ere, the sales aspect of the transaction predominates. The [services] were incidental to sale of the soft-ware package and did not defeat characterization of the system as a good." Id. at 546. See also *Gross*, 2012 WL 3116158, at *8-9 (where a user purchased and downloaded Symantec's pre-existing software from the internet, this court deter-mined that the "essence of the agreement" was the sale of a good); Olcott Intern v. Micro Data, 793 N.E.2d 1063 (Ind. Ct. App. 2003) ("generally-available stan-dardized software" was found to be a good under the UCC); Rottner v. AVG Tech. USA, Inc., 943 F. Supp. 2d 222, 230 (D. Mass. 2013) (noting that the sale of a downloadable computer software is like a sale of tangible goods and that courts nationally have consistently classified the sale of a software package as the sale of a good for UCC purposes); Advent Sys. Ltd. v. Unisys Corp., 925 F.2d 670, 675-76 (3d Cir. 1991) (noting that the majority of academic commentary supports the view that software fits with the definition of a good under the UCC).

Software may still be considered a good even when accompanied by ancillary services, which "are not substantially different from those generally accompanying package sales of computer systems consisting of hardware and software." *Advent Sys.*, 925 F.2d at 676. Such ancillary services include installation, training, and technical support. See Dahlmann v. Sulcus Hosp. Tech. Corp., 63 F. Supp. 2d 772, 775 (E.D. Mich. 1999) (a contract for property management systems incorporating hardware, software, installation, training, and technical support services for plaintiffs' hotels was a contract for goods because the provisions for services were incidental to the agreements for the system); ePresence v. Evolve, 190 F. Supp. 2d 159 (D. Mass. 2002) (a contract for software licensing which also included services was determined to be a transaction for goods, as the software programs themselves were the essence of the parties' agreement); Wachter Mgmt. Co. v. Dexter & Chaney, Inc., 282 Kan. 365, 369, 144 P.3d 747 (2006) (even when incidental services such as modifications, corrections, maintenance, training, and consulting were provided with software, the services would have been unnecessary if the software had not been purchased, so the transaction is predominantly for a good).

Even software adapted for specific needs has been considered a good. In Micro Data Base Systems, Inc. v. Dharma Systems, Inc., 148 F.3d 649 (7th Cir. 1998), the Seventh Circuit determined that the UCC governed a contract for software where one party agreed to adapt its software program for use in the other party's system. The court noted that "labor is a service" that is part of the manufacture of every good and opined, "we can think of no reason why the UCC is not suitable to govern disputes arising from the sale of custom software." Id. 654-55. Similarly, the Third Circuit found that the software contracted for was a good where one party planned to modify its existing software and hardware interfaces for the other party's use. *Advent Sys.*, 925 F.2d 670. The court noted, "[t]he fact that some programs may be tailored for specific purposes need not alter their status as 'goods' because the Code definition includes 'specially manufactured goods.'" Id. at 675. The Third Circuit found that the advantages of applying the UCC to software transactions (namely uniformity on a range of questions) and the importance of software to the commercial world were strong policy arguments favoring the application of the UCC and that the majority of academic commentary espoused the view that software falls under the UCC. Id. at 675-76. See also Commc'ns Groups, Inc. v. Warner Commc'ns, 138 Misc. 2d 80, 83, 527 N.Y.S.2d 341 (N.Y. Civ. Ct. 1988) (determining that a contract which provided for the installation of specially designed software equipment for one party's telephone and computer systems, including recording, accounting and traffic analysis and optimizations, modules, buffer, directories and an operational user guide was a transaction of software equipment involving movable, tangible and identifiable products or goods); Waterfront Properties v. Xerox Connect, 58 UCC Rep. Serv. 2d 809, 2006 WL 266581 (W.D.N.C. 2006) (agreements for the provision of custom adapted pre-existing computer software and attendant hardware were contracts predominately for goods, which are governed by the UCC).

On the other end of the spectrum, courts in this district and beyond have determined that certain software transactions are better defined as services and therefore are not covered by the UCC. Where software is designed from scratch, or the transaction is mainly for one party's knowledge and skills in creating software, the software is often found to be a service rather than a good.

In Systems America, Inc. v. Rockwell Software, Inc., No. C-03-2232, 2007 WL 218242 (N.D. Cal. Jan 26, 2007), the agreement entered into between the parties called for development of a final software product for reproduction and distribution to one party's customers. The developing party developed new software to supplement existing software, provided the source code to an escrow agent, and retained all ownership rights to the software. The court determined that the contract was for services, not goods, because the essence of the contract was the development of software from scratch and the granting of a license for use of the software. Id. at *4. Where a contract required a party to design, develop, and implement a tailored, highly complex automated software system, that contract was deemed to be for services, not goods. State v. Lockheed Martin, No. C-036815, 2002 WL 99554, at *18 (Cal. Ct. App., Jan. 25, 2002). This district found that even in a situation where an agreement was made for production of physical prototypes, since most of the price paid was for the other party's "knowledge, skill, and ability" to develop software code and test prototypes, the agreement was for services rather than goods. TK Power v. Textron, 433 F. Supp. 2d 1058, 1062 (N.D. Cal. 2006). See also Data Processing Serv. v. L.H. Smith Oil Corp., 492 N.E.2d 314, 318-19 (Ind. Ct. App. 1986) (custom-designed accounting software is not a good because no hardware was involved and the contract bargained for the programmer's "knowledge, skill, and ability" rather than standardized software); Pearl Inv. v. Standard I/O, 257 F. Supp. 2d 326 (D. Me. 2003) (custom-made software is distinguishable from pre-existing software—even with custom modifications and upgrades—and is a service); Multi–Tech Sys. v. Floreat, No. Civ-01-1320, 2002 WL 432016, at *3 (D. Minn. March 18, 2002) ("work" toward "jointly developing" a new product is a service . . ." the UCC does not apply to an agreement to design and develop a product, even if compensation under that agreement is based in part on later sales of that product"); Wharton Mgmt. Grp. v. Sigma Consultants, Inc., 50 UCC Rep. Serv. 2d 678, 1990 WL 18360 (Del. Super. Ct. 1990) (software contract is for services where a party was hired for its skills to "design, develop, and install computer software which would meet . . . specific needs and objectives . . .").

In this instance, Photon was meant to produce a Mac-compliant version of Simulados' existing Windows-based software and an internet web application. Based on an analysis of the cases concerning the application of the UCC to software transactions, this Court determines that in this particular case, Simulados contracted for a service and the UCC does not apply to this software transaction. Following other courts, this Court uses the predominance test on a case-by-case basis to analyze a transaction that involves elements of both a good and a service. The Contract between the parties calls for Photon to provide services, skills, and knowledge to customize Simulados' existing product for sale to Simulados' customers. Although customized software may still be considered a good, here Simulados was not purchasing any software from Photon. Rather, Photon was only providing services to modify Simulados' already-existing software. As such,

Simulados was contracting only for the modifications, a service, and not for software as a separate good. Thus, the UCC does not apply to this transaction and any claims arising from it are dismissed. . . .

———————————

Some courts have assumed that a transaction's failure to qualify under Article 2's scope provision necessarily precludes application of the standards set down in Article 2. There is, however, another way of approaching the matter. Nowhere does it say that a court cannot apply the principles of Article 2 to subjects that are admittedly not within the formal scope of Article 2. Many courts have in fact heeded the admonitions of the UCC drafters, who note with favor in at least one Official Comment those courts that "have recognized the policies embodied in an act as applicable in reason to subject-matter which was not expressly included in the language of the act . . . where reason and policy so required, even where the subject-matter had been intentionally excluded from the act in general." UCC §1-103, Comment 1.

Probably the most significant Article 2 concept for a court to apply by analogy in non-goods transactions is the implied warranty of merchantability. That is the warranty that all merchants create in sales under Article 2, at least where the merchant deals in goods of the kind that are sold. UCC §2-314(1). In a nutshell, the warranty of merchantability promises the buyer that the goods will be fit for their ordinary purpose. It hardly seems radical (at least in consumer sales) for a court to suggest that even in a non-goods sale, the merchant implicitly promises that whatever it sells will be fit for ordinary uses.

While we are on the subject of the warranty of merchantability, it probably makes sense to deal here with another important scope issue within Article 2: the special default rules that apply only with respect to merchants. Merchants occupy a special place within Article 2. In many parts of the UCC, those qualifying as merchants are held to higher standards than are other players in the system.

Cook v. Downing

891 P.2d 611 (Okla. Ct. App. 1994)

HUNTER, J.

Appellant is a licensed dentist who devotes less than 50% of his practice to fitting and making dentures. Appellee, a patient, sued Appellant in small claims court because of mouth trouble she had on account of the dentures. Appellee alleged the condition was the result of ill-fitting dentures. Appellant testified that the condition was generalized and not consistent with localized sore spots which would result from ill-fitting dentures. Appellant referred Appellee to oral surgeons. The dental specialists' evidence showed that they believed the condition was due to either candidas, an autoimmune reaction or an allergy to the dental material. Although none of the dental evidence pinpointed the source of the problem, it consistently ruled out ill-fitting dentures.

After trial, the court entered judgment in favor of Appellee, setting forth that damages were awarded pursuant to Article 2 of the Oklahoma Uniform Commercial Code, §§2-104, 2-105 and 2-315, "Implied Warranty of Fitness for a Particular Purpose" and that attorney fees were awarded pursuant to 12 O.S.1991 §936. Section 2-104(1) defines merchant as "a person who deals in the goods of the kind or otherwise by his occupation holds himself out as having knowledge or skill peculiar to the practices or goods involved in the transaction or to whom such knowledge or skill may be attributed by his employment of an agent or broker or other intermediary who by his occupation holds himself out as having such knowledge or skill." Section 2-105(1) defines goods as meaning "all things (including specially manufactured goods) which are movable at the time of identification to the contract for sale other than the money in which the price is to be paid, investment securities (Article 8) and things in action. 'Goods' also includes the unborn young of animals and growing crops and other identified things attached to realty. . . ." The law of implied warranty in the commercial code is found in §2-315 which states:

> Where the seller at the time of contracting has reason to know any particular purpose for which the goods are required and that the buyer is relying on the seller's skill or judgment to select or furnish suitable goods, there is unless excluded or modified under the next section an implied warranty that the goods shall be fit for such purpose.

We agree with Appellant's position that any claim Appellee might have sounds in tort. In Oklahoma, dentists, professionals who are regulated by the state, furnish dentures. In general, dentists must use ordinary skill in treating their patients. A patient does not establish the elements of legal detriment by only showing non-success or unsatisfactory results.

A dentist is not a merchant and the Uniform Commercial Code is not the law to apply to these facts. Finding no Oklahoma law on point, we align ourselves with the reasoning stated by the Court of Appeals of North Carolina in Preston v. Thompson, 53 N.C. App. 290, 280 S.E.2d 780 (1981). In the *Preston* case, the patient determined through her research in the yellow pages that the dentist was a specialist in dentures. The patient claimed the doctor made oral assurances that the dentures would fit satisfactorily. The dentures did not fit well and subsequent attempts at correcting the problem were not successful. The patient sued the dentist on an implied warranty theory pursuant to the Uniform Commercial Code. The court held, 280 S.E.2d at 784, that the transaction was not of "goods" and that a dentist was not a "merchant" under the UCC. We adopt the rule as enunciated by the North Carolina court, 280 S.E.2d at 784, that "those who, for a fee, furnish their professional medical services for the guidance and assistance of others are not liable in the absence of negligence or intentional misconduct" (citation omitted). The court further held, 280 S.E.2d at 785, that "the fact that defendant holds himself out as specializing in the preparing and fitting of dentures does not remove him from the practice of dentistry and transform him into a merchant."

We hold that under the laws of Oklahoma, a dentist is not a merchant and dentures, furnished by a dentist, are not goods under the UCC.

A dentist could be sued for breach of contract, if such contract were alleged to exist, but that is not the fact as revealed in the record in our case. Appellee presented evidence of an advertisement guaranteeing dentures to fit, but testified that she did not see this ad until after she had begun her treatment with Appellant. The evidence does not support any breach of contract action.

As a matter of law, Appellee erroneously based her cause of action on the Uniform Commercial Code rather than negligence. The court erred in entering judgment in favor of Appellee based on this law. For this reason, we reverse the judgment of the trial court and remand the matter with directions to enter judgment in favor of Appellant.

REVERSED and REMANDED with directions.

Jones, J., dissenting:

As is typical of small claims cases, there were no pleadings here to define the issues. At trial, however, issues were raised as to dental malpractice and breach of implied warranties under the UCC. Although the trial court based its decision on a finding of a breach of the implied warranty of fitness for a particular purpose, §2-315, the trial court's decision must be affirmed if sustainable on any ground.

The decision cannot be affirmed on the basis of professional negligence as the necessary evidence of such negligence was lacking. But neither can the trial court's decision be affirmed on the basis of implied warranty of fitness for a particular purpose. There was no particular or special purpose involved as is required by §2-315. The use Appellee was to make of the dentures was their ordinary use, and that they may not have been suitable for the ordinary purpose for which they were to be used is the concept of "merchantability."

The implied warranty of merchantability is codified at §2-314 and deserves a closer look.

> "(1) . . . a warranty that the goods shall be merchantable is implied in a contract for their sale if the seller is a merchant with respect to goods of that kind. . . ."
> "(2) Goods to be merchantable must be at least such as . . ."
> "(c) are fit for the ordinary purposes for which such goods are used. . . ."
> A "merchant" is defined as:
> . . . a person who deals in goods of the kind or otherwise by his occupation holds himself out as having knowledge or skill peculiar to the practices or goods involved in the transaction or to whom such knowledge or skill may be attributed by his employment of an agent or broker or other intermediary who by his occupation holds himself out as having such knowledge or skill. §2-104(1).
> "Goods" means "all things (including specially manufactured goods) which are movable at the time of identification to the contract for sale other than the money in which the price is to be paid, investment securities . . . and things in action. §2-105(1).

"Dentists" and "dentures" appear to be included in the definitions of merchants and goods.

The transaction of a patient being fitted for and purchasing dentures from a dentist is actually a hybrid. It is not purely a sale of goods by a merchant, nor is it purely the providing of a service by a health care professional. Whether implied warranties under Article 2 of the UCC apply to such a transaction should depend on whether the predominant element of the transaction is the sale of goods or the rendering of services. If the sale of goods predominates, it would be within the scope of Article 2 and the implied warranties contained therein. However, if the service aspect predominates, there would be no implied warranties.

Although the record contains no specific findings of fact, the record does contain evidence from which it could be concluded that this transaction was principally a sale of goods and that the implied warranty of merchantability applies thereto. The evidence was also sufficient that the trier of fact could have concluded that the dentures were not fit for their ordinary purpose as required to establish a prima facie case for breach of the implied warranty of merchantability. We must affirm a law action tried to the court if there is any competent evidence to support the judgment.

In contemporary society the old distinctions separating health care professionals from other businessmen are blurring in many respects. This Court's holding that a dentist is not a merchant, and dentures, furnished by a dentist, are not goods ignores the fact that nothing excludes them from the statutory definitions of merchant and goods. It also ignores the fact that health care professionals in some instances are selling goods to their "patients," with the providing of professional services being secondary to the sale. To such transactions there is no reason Article 2 of the U.C.C should not apply.

I respectfully dissent.

The implied warranty of merchantability is perhaps the most prominent example of the special responsibility of a merchant. Another instance where more is expected of merchants than non-merchants involves Article 2's statute of frauds provision. UCC §2-201(1) provides that sales of goods for at least $500 require a writing that evidences the contract in order for the contract to be enforceable. UCC §2-201(2), however, creates an exception to the writing requirement in the case where a merchant fails to object to the written confirmation of an oral contract that is sent by another merchant. Thus, merchants who do not read their mail can lose their ability to assert the statute of frauds in some situations where similarly situated non-merchants would retain that defense.

Article 2's merchant definition section is one of those places in the UCC where the Official Comments tell us much more than the provision itself. UCC §2-104(1) tells us that a merchant is either a person "who deals in goods of the kind" or a person who "holds himself out as having knowledge or skill peculiar to the practices or goods involved in the transaction." What §2-104(1) does *not* say is that the functional consequences of being a merchant may vary depending on what kind of a merchant a person is.

Comment 2 to §2-104 introduces the concept that there are three different categories of consequences to being a merchant. The first category of consequences involves the Article 2 rules surrounding general business practices like answering the mail and giving firm offers. As the Comment explains, for this category of consequences "almost every person in business" would be considered a merchant and therefore subject to the special rules of those sections.

The second category of consequences covers mainly the implied warranty of merchantability. The Comment explains that only merchants who deal in goods of the kind get saddled with that particular responsibility. Thus, for example, a sporting goods store that made an isolated sale of paint left over after a store repainting project would not make the implied warranty of merchantability to its paint buyer.

The final category of consequences discussed in Comment 2 deals with the merchant's general duties of good faith and standards of fair dealing in the trade. Relevant sections here include those creating the special duty of the merchant-buyer to follow a seller's reasonable instructions regarding goods in the buyer's possession following rejection, as well as the heightened duty of a merchant to give adequate assurance of future performance. Just as with the first category of consequences, any person in business will be subject to the requirements of this group of special merchant provisions.

Problem Set 1

1.1.   You just graduated from law school and have taken a job as an associate at a major law firm that is known for its extensive international practice. Your firm receives a call from the Minister of Commerce of a formerly communist country that is now attempting to convert to a free-market economy. This foreign official would like your firm to serve as a consultant on the issue of whether his country should adopt a commercial code. In particular, he would like the firm to consider the following questions: What are the benefits that his country's economy can gain from enacting a commercial code as opposed to letting private agreements handle the details of all commercial dealings? For which subjects (e.g., price, quantity, place of delivery) should the code include gap fillers? To the extent the code serves a gap-filling function, how do you decide what the gap fillers should be (e.g., should the default mode for place of delivery be buyer's place or seller's place)? Because you have recently taken several UCC courses, your firm asks you to develop preliminary responses to these questions.

1.2.   a. Lumber Works, Inc., makes a contract to sell five separate shipments of lumber to Wooden Play Sets Corporation pursuant to a single contract. The place of delivery for these shipments is not specified in the single contract that governs all five shipments. For the first three deliveries, the seller delivers the lumber to the buyer's place of business. Then the seller's daughter, a first-year law student, tells the seller that the Article 2 gap filler for place of delivery says that delivery should be at the seller's place — in other words, that the buyer has to come and pick up the goods at the buyer's expense. After hearing this, the seller feels justified in trying to change the delivery mode for the final two deliveries within this contract. The buyer, understandably, is not happy. Does the seller have the right to insist on the buyer's picking up the lumber for the last two deliveries? UCC §§2-308(a), 1-201(b)(3), 1-303(a).

b. Suppose the same facts as part (a), except this time there have been no deliveries so far under this particular contract. However, this buyer and seller have done these deals with each other several times in the past. In every prior sale between these parties, the seller has delivered the goods to the buyer. The contract for this particular sale has been signed by both parties, and nowhere does it mention place of delivery. After signing the contract, but before the first delivery under this contract, the seller learns of the UCC gap filler and decides that the buyer should come and pick up the lumber this time. May the seller insist that the buyer pick up the lumber? UCC §1-303(b) and (d).

c. Suppose again the same buyer and seller of lumber, but now assume that these two parties have had no prior dealings with one another. Imagine, how-ever, that the custom in the lumber industry is that the seller always delivers the lumber to the buyer. The contract has been signed and no place of delivery is mentioned in the contract. The seller learns of the UCC gap filler and wants the buyer to come and get the lumber. May the seller insist that the buyer pick up the lumber? UCC §§1-201(b)(3), 1-303(c).

1.3. Your favorite aunt just called you because she knew you are the only attorney in the family. It seems that Aunt Millie had taken seven reels of her home movies, representing three decades of family vacations, into the local camera shop to have the shop transfer the movies from the old-fashioned reels onto DVD discs. Much to Aunt Millie's horror, she got a call from the camera shop yesterday in which the manager explained that a new clerk had messed up the transfer process and destroyed all of Aunt Millie's home movies. Aunt Millie related to you her disgust with the manager's offer to give her new blank movie reels and DVD discs to make up for the destroyed movies. As you con-template Aunt Millie's rights against the camera shop, will UCC Article 2 and its warranties be part of the picture? UCC §§2-102, 2-313, 2-314, 2-315.

1.4. Your law firm was recently retained to represent Kelleher and Associates, a limited liability partnership of optometrists who specialize in making and fitting contact lenses for the "problem wearer." Patients at Kelleher generally pay about three to four times more for their contact lenses than they would at one of the national contact lens franchises. That price, however, includes the various testing procedures that patients receive before Kelleher custom-designs the lenses. Up to this point, Kelleher has not had its patients sign any kind of contract. One of the partners at Kelleher has a daugh-ter in her second year of law school, who suggested to her dad that he might want to have patients sign in advance a form contract that disclaims all of the UCC warranties. The Kelleher partner told you that, for reasons of customer goodwill, he would just as soon not institute that procedure unless "there are compelling reasons to do so." What is your advice? UCC §§2-102, 2-105(1), 2-314(1), 2-315.

1.5. Determine whether UCC Article 2 applies to the following transactions. UCC §§2-102, 2-105(1).

a. The sale by an author of a movable paper certificate representing the author's rights to any future royalties from a book that the author has already written.

b. The sale of natural gas.

c. The sale of a CD to a consumer by a retail music store.

d. A recording artist's sale of an original recording on CD to a music producer that will produce and distribute the CD.

e. A publishing company's contract with an author to write a book.

f. A manufacturer's contract with a merchant buyer to specially manufacture and sell a custom-made machine.

g. A sculptor's contract with a patron of the arts to create and sell an original sculpture to the patron.

h. The sale of a raffle ticket in which the holder of the winning ticket gets a new car.

1.6. At your fifth law school reunion last month, you bumped into classmate Deborah Swift, a one-time law school "gunner" and currently a successful plaintiff's personal injury lawyer. After a few drinks, Deborah began bragging to you about her collection of Rolls Royces. By the end of the evening she had agreed to sell you the one she had driven that night, a used model, for just $18,000. The deal was that you were to bring her a check and pick the car up at her house at the end of the month. The day after the reunion, just to be safe, you sent Deborah a certified letter that described the terms of the bargain you had struck. Deborah did not object to or otherwise acknowledge the letter.

Yesterday, some 20 days after the reunion, you went to Deborah's house with a certified check for $18,000. Deborah, who seemed not nearly so friendly as she was to you at the reunion, answered the door and told you that the car you wanted was worth at least $35,000, and that you would have to take her to court to try to enforce the oral contract. Will you succeed? UCC §§2-201(1) and (2), 2-104(1) and (3), Official Comment 2 to §2-104.

Assignment 2:   Scope Issues with Leases, CISG, and Real Estate

A.   Scope of Article 2A

As far as the UCC goes, Article 2A is one of the new kids on the block. Whereas most of the other articles of the Code were introduced back in the late 1950s, the article on personal property leases was not approved by the American Law Institute (ALI) until 1987. Then, to make matters even more complicated, the ALI, on the recommendation of the National Conference of Commissioners on Uniform State Laws, passed a significant set of amendments to Article 2A in 1990.

Although lease transactions have been around for about as long as sales, favorable tax and accounting treatment caused a significant increase in the use of leases in the United States during the 1950s and 1960s. As the number of leases increased, the common law's long-standing lack of clarity in treating this type of transaction became more troublesome. As a result, there was a concerted effort in the early 1980s to clarify and codify the law surrounding leases, culminating in the first and second versions of Article 2A that are noted above. As of August 1, 2015, every state except Louisiana had adopted the 1990 version of Article 2A.

As we will see over the course of the next several assignments, Article 2A borrows very heavily from the language and concepts of Article 2. Indeed, the Official Comment to UCC §2A-101 says that "the [2A] drafting committee concluded that Article 2 was the appropriate statutory analogue." Most fundamentally, both Article 2 and Article 2A allow the parties to make their sale or lease contracts more or less as they wish, with gap fillers provided as backups but with very few limits on freedom of contract. UCC §1-302, Official Comment to §2A-101 ("This codification was greatly influenced by the fundamental tenet of the common law as it has developed with respect to leases of goods: freedom of the parties to contract."). Where there are significant differences between the rules of Article 2 and Article 2A, those differences stem from the fundamental distinction between a sale and a lease: that the lessor, unlike the seller, has a reasonable expectation of receiving the goods back at a time when the goods still have meaningful economic life.

It is easy enough to state in the abstract the distinction between a lease and a sale. Applying that distinction in practice, however, is another matter entirely. If you rent a car for $200 a week during your Florida spring break, everyone can see that such a transaction is a true lease. But suppose that you go to your local car dealer and it agrees to "lease" you a new car for five years, at $300 per month. Suppose further that you have no power to terminate your lease at any time during the five years. Finally, imagine that the lease includes a purchase option at the end of the lease for $500 — an option that, by all accounts, seems like it will be an offer that is too good to pass up. So, you might ask yourself, how exactly does this differ from a sale?

Courts have struggled for decades trying to determine whether any given transaction amounts to a "true lease" or "a disguised sale." Lots of different tests have been formulated throughout the years to aid judges in these determinations. The drafters of Article 2A, for their part, specifically endorsed what is known as "the economic realities test."

The economic realities test simply considers the likelihood, at the time the transaction is entered into, that the lessor will receive the goods back at a time when the goods still have meaningful economic life. If there is a reasonable likelihood that the lessor will indeed retain some residual interest in the goods, then the economic realities test deems the transaction to be a true lease. If not, the transaction is considered to be a disguised sale intended for security. A sale intended for security is one in which the seller sells the goods on credit but retains a special right to foreclose on the goods in the buyer's hands if the buyer fails to pay the price.

In endorsing the economic realities test, the drafters of Article 2A intended to reject any tests courts had used that focused on the intentions of the parties to the transaction. Some cases had concluded that as long as both parties intended a transaction to be a true lease, then it was. One of the problems with the intent test is that the characterization of a particular transaction as a lease or a sale will have consequences that transcend the two parties to the transaction. As just one example, the lease/sale characterization will determine which party, the lessor or the creditors of the lessee, has priority to the leased goods in the case of default by the lessee on its non-lease obligations.

Although the characterization of a transaction as a lease or a sale is an important first step in the analysis, ultimately the most crucial question is what are the functional consequences that attach to a true lease, on the one hand, and a disguised sale, on the other. The functional attributes of the distinction between a true lease and a disguised sale are of three types: tax/accounting-related, UCC-related, and bankruptcy-related.

Within the tax and accounting category, significant consequences attend a transaction's characterization as a lease versus a sale. For accounting purposes, the party acquiring goods can treat lease payments as periodic expenses; by contrast, a transaction that is a secured sale will require that the buyer's balance sheet show a debt for the purchase price. In the tax arena, the Internal Revenue Code allows a deduction for amounts paid or accrued to rent property that is used in a trade or business or in the production of income.

In contrast, the purchase of long-lived property is a capital expenditure that is not deductible when paid. If the property is used in a trade or business or in the production of income and it wears out over time, its cost may be deducted through depreciation allowances. These depreciation allowances are taken over statutorily prescribed periods that are generally much shorter than the useful economic life of the property. Consequently, an owner of depreciable equipment may obtain a substantial tax advantage (i.e., front-loaded cost recovery deductions) relative to a lessee. In addition, on the state and local levels, the difference between lease tax rates and sales tax rates can be meaningful.

With regard to differences in UCC treatment, the characterization of a transaction as a lease or a sale will determine whether Article 2A applies or, instead, Articles 2 and 9. Whether Article 2A applies instead of Article 2 will not necessarily bring significant consequences. The key article at stake is Article 9. If a purported lease transaction is found to be a sale, typically the "lessor" will at least want the transaction to be treated as a secured sale rather than as an unsecured sale. If the sale is an unsecured sale, then the lessor would have no special rights to the leased goods. If the sale is considered a secured sale, the lessor would have the chance to qualify for the special Article 9 rights of a secured creditor.

In order for the lessor to have the special rights of an Article 9 secured creditor, there are certain hoops that the lessor will have to jump through. If the transaction is found to be a disguised sale, the penalty to the putative lessor for failing to meet the Article 9 requirements is that the lessor may lose certain rights against the lessee as well as against third parties of the lessee. The lessor may lose the ability to repossess the goods or to seize the goods when third parties take them for collection.

Carlson v. Giachetti

616 N.E.2d 810 (Mass. App. 1993)

Gillerman, J.

Whether, under the Uniform Commercial Code, an equipment lease is to be treated as a "true lease" or as a security agreement is an issue that has been litigated extensively for more than two decades, but has yet to be discussed in any detail by a Massachusetts appellate court. We must do so now, with the benefit of the findings of fact made by a judge of the Superior Court after a bench trial.

The material facts found by the judge are these. John Carlson manufactures, sells and leases machinery used in the repair of damaged automobile bodies. In April of 1988 Carlson leased a six-tower chassis liner, a machine used in auto body shops to remove dents from damaged cars, together with a complete accessory package, to one Richard A. King, the owner of an auto body repair shop in Quincy. The lease called for a monthly payment of $572.40 for each of sixty months, with two such payments to be made in advance of delivery. The sixty payments came to a total of $34,344. King made the required advance payment for two months, and then defaulted.

In October of 1988, King went out of business and sold the chassis liner to the defendant Louis Giacchetti for $8,600. Giacchetti had no notice of Carlson's interest in the machinery, for it was not until late in December that Carlson filed financing statements in the appropriate public offices. In April, 1989, Carlson brought this action against Giacchetti, who refused to return the chassis liner to Carlson, for conversion and violation of G.L. c. 93A. If the court found the document was a "true lease" and not a security agreement subject to the provisions of article 9 of the Uniform Commercial Code, then King had no power to transfer title to the equipment, and Giacchetti may be liable for conversion.

The judge, however, resolved the issue of ownership in favor of Giacchetti by ruling that the lease agreement between the original parties was not a "true lease," but rather, a security agreement, and that Carlson's failure to perfect his security interest until December was fatal. See §9-301(1)(c) [§9-317(a) as amended]. We disagree with the trial judge and, for the reasons discussed below, we conclude that the lease was not intended as a security agreement.

We look to §§9-102 [§9-109 as amended] and 1-201(37) [§1-203 as amended with respect to the "lease" definition] to determine whether a contract, characterized by the parties as a lease, is a "true lease" or a security agreement. Article 9 applies, except as otherwise provided, to "any transaction (regardless of its form) which is intended to create a security interest in personal property or fixtures. . . ." §9-102(1)(a). Section 9-102(2) provides that article 9 applies to "security interests created by contract including . . . [a] lease . . . intended as security." §9-102(2).

The definition of a security agreement is contained in §1-201(37), which provides in relevant part: "Whether a lease is intended as security is to be determined by the facts of each case; however, (a) the inclusion of an option to purchase does not of itself make the lease one intended for security, and (b) an agreement that upon compliance with the terms of the lease the lessee shall become or has the option to become the owner of the property for no additional consideration or for a nominal consideration does make the lease one intended for security."

The lease in the case before us, the principal provisions of which we summarize in the margin, does not include an option in the lessee to purchase the equipment for no, or nominal, consideration, and thus the instrument does not fall within subparagraph (b) of section 1-201(37). On that basis, the issue which arises under both sections of the Code is whether, on all the facts, the parties intended to create a security interest.

While the Code directs the analysis to what was intended by the parties, it offers no guidelines for deciding the question (other than the rule of law, not applicable to this case, expressed in §1-201[37][b]). Obviously, the declared intention of the parties, standing alone, cannot be decisive. "No one would contend that third parties were bound by the clear intention of the contracting parties to use a device they call a lease if the effect created by the transaction is that of a sale. The test certainly must be applied in accordance with the outward appearance of the facts rather than in accordance with the intent held by one or both of the parties while creating effects contrary to those normally produced by the kind of instrument purportedly employed by the parties." Coogan, Leases of Equipment and Some

Other Unconventional Security Devices: An Analysis of UCC Section 1-201(37) and Article 9, 1973 Duke L.J. 909, 916 n.12 (1973). Professor Gilmore, in his treatise on security interests, has also written that the word "intended" in §1-201(37) "has nothing to do with the subjective intention of the parties, or either of them." Gilmore, Security Interests in Personal Property, §11.2, at 338 (1965).

The vagaries inherent in §1-201(37) have obliged the courts to resort to the "facts of each case," as directed by the terms of §1-201(37), with the effect of producing complex guidelines for adjudication which have left judicial decisions entirely unpredictable. The high water mark was reached in the decision of the Bankruptcy Court in In re Brookside Drug Store, Inc., 3 B.R. 120 (Bankr. D. Conn. 1980) where the court, in order to determine the intent of the parties, identified no fewer than sixteen separate factors, having to do with the content of the document and the factual setting of the transaction, as relevant to the ultimate determination. The factors recited by the Bankruptcy Court in *Brookside* include those that focus on whether the lease is a "net lease" (i.e., where the lessee assumes all risk of loss and pays all taxes, insurance, maintenance, and the like), whether the lease is a "full payout lease" (i.e., where the lessee pays an amount equal to or greater than the lessor's cost of the goods or their fair market value), whether the lessor is a financing agency, whether there is an acceleration clause in the lease, whether the lessor has permission to file a financing statement, and whether the lessee has an option to purchase the goods for a nominal consideration. The *Brookside* approach to the problem was adopted by the Bankruptcy Court in In re Mariner Communications, Inc., 76 B.R. 242 (Bankr. D. Mass. 1987), the decision relied upon by Giacchetti and by the trial judge in this case. We believe that a preferable approach to the problem is that proposed by the National Conference of Commissioners on Uniform State Laws and the American Law Institute, the original sponsors of the Uniform Commercial Code. The sponsors approved a revised §1-201(37) in 1987, as well as a definition, for the first time, of "lease" in a new article 2A.

The revised version of §1-201(37) (hereinafter "revised §1-201[37]") deletes all reference to the intent of the parties. It offers, instead, a straightforward economic analysis as the focal point of inquiry: if the obligations of the lessee under the lease are not subject to termination by the lessee, and if the lease is for the full economic life of the goods (or if the lessee may, without further consideration, acquire all rights in the goods for the full economic life of the goods) then a security interest is created. But if the lessor retains the reversionary interest in the goods, then the transaction is a true lease. Revised §1-201(37) also identifies four factors any of which, if included in the lease, do not create a security interest. Two of these factors bear on the facts of this case: the "full payout lease," and the "net lease."

The Legislature has not adopted revised §1-201(37), but that does not preclude this court from looking to the revised section for guidance. [In 1996, Massachusetts adopted the revised §1-201(37) and the 1990 version of Article 2A—ED.] We see nothing in the proposed revision which is inconsistent with the existing statutory provision. Construing the phrase "intended as security" to refer principally to the distribution of rights in respect of the economic life of the leased equipment will most likely reveal what was "intended" by the parties. Where, for example, the economic life of the leased equipment plainly will not have been exhausted at the end of the term of the lease, there will be little, if any, justification for the conclusion that the parties intended a security interest incident to a sale, rather than a lease. In our view, the provisions of revised §1-201(37) illuminate, but do not alter, the meaning of the existing provisions of §1-201(37). Further, it facilitates an uncomplicated analysis of the lease in dispute, and thereby enhances for practitioners the predictability of the judicial outcome.

In the document before us the lessee's obligations were non-cancellable by the lessee, and the lease contained no option to purchase by the lessee. Further, the lessee was obligated to keep the leased equipment in good repair and condition and, at the end of the term of the lease, to assemble and deliver the equipment to the lessor. Consistent with these covenants of the lessee was the judge's finding that upon the termination of the lease Carlson "would . . . be entitled to a return of the equipment which still had a significant resale value." This last finding by the judge establishes that Carlson had reserved an economically significant reversionary interest in the lease goods. That finding, in the context of the lease provisions we have just described, requires the conclusion that the lease before us is a true lease and was not intended as a security agreement.

The judge made numerous findings with regard to the terms of the lease, the cumulative effect of which was that the arrangement was found to be both a net lease and a full payout lease to Carlson's substantial benefit. But these provisions, either alone or in combination, do not call for a different result in this case. The contractual arrangements which are so distinctly in favor of Carlson do not uncommonly reflect the relative bargaining positions of the parties, the value of the credit provided by a lease, and the uniqueness of the equipment; consequently, they are as likely to appear in a "true lease" as they are in a secured transaction.

The judgment is vacated and the case remanded to the Superior Court for a trial on the issue of conversion, and, if appropriate, the assessment of the plaintiff's damages, if any.

SO ORDERED.

The property and priority rights that hinge on the characterization of a transaction as a true lease or a disguised sale will become important if the lessee fails to fulfill its obligations under the contract. When that happens, the lessee's bankruptcy filing may not be far behind. In fact, many of the legal battles that occur around the lease/sale distinction originate in a bankruptcy setting. Sometimes those battles are simply between the debtor as purported lessee and the lessor/seller. In other bankruptcy cases involving the lease/sale distinction, there are three parties: the debtor/lessee, the lessor/seller, and a third party that claims a superior interest in the goods to both of the first two parties.

In re Purdy

763 F.3d 513 (6th Cir. 2014)

Moore, C.J.

Between 2009 and 2012, Sunshine Heifers, LLC ("Sunshine") and Lee H. Purdy, a dairy farmer, entered into several "Dairy Cow Leases." Purdy received a total of 435 cows to milk, and, in exchange, he paid a monthly rent to Sunshine. Unfortunately, Purdy's dairy business faltered in 2012, and he petitioned for bankruptcy protection. When Purdy filed this petition, Sunshine moved to retake possession of the leased cattle. Citizens First Bank ("Citizens First"), however, had a perfected purchase money security interest in Purdy's equipment, farm products, and livestock, and it claimed that this perfected security interest gave Citizens First priority over Sunshine with regard to the 435 cattle. In particular, Citizens First argued that the "leases" between Sunshine and Purdy were disguised security agreements, that Purdy actually owned the cattle, and that the subsequently acquired livestock were covered by the bank's security interest. The bankruptcy court ruled in favor of Citizens First, finding that the leases were per se security agreements. Given that the terms of agreements expressly preserve Sunshine's ability to recover the cattle, we disagree, REVERSE the bankruptcy court's decision, and REMAND for further proceedings consistent with this opinion.

I.   BACKGROUND

Purdy operated his dairy farm in Barren County, Kentucky. In 2008, he entered into a loan relationship with Citizens First, using his herd of dairy cattle as collateral. Purdy refinanced his loan on July 3, 2009, executing an "Agricultural Security Agreement" in exchange for additional principal in the amount of $417,570. As part of the security agreement, Purdy granted Citizens First a purchase money security interest in "all . . . Equipment, Farm Products, [and] Livestock (including all increase and supplies) . . . currently owned [or] hereafter acquired. . . ." Id. Three days later, Citizens First perfected this purchase money security interest by filing a financing statement with the Kentucky Secretary of State. Purdy and Citizens Bank executed two similar security agreements in August 2010 and May 2012. Citizens First perfected these purchase money security interests as well.

Shortly after refinancing his loan with Citizens First in 2009, Purdy decided to increase the size of his dairy-cattle herd. He contacted Jeff Blevins of Sunshine regarding the prospect of leasing additional cattle. Sunshine was amenable to the idea, and on August 7, 2009, Purdy and Sunshine entered into the first of five contracts, three of which are relevant here: (1) a July 21, 2011 agreement, involving fifty head of cattle; (2) a July 14, 2012 agreement, rolling up two prior agreements and involving 285 head of cattle; and (3) another July 14, 2012 agreement, involving 100 head of cattle.

Each of these agreements is titled a "Dairy Cow Lease," and under their terms, Purdy received a total of 435 cattle for fifty months in exchange for a monthly rent.

The agreements prohibited Purdy from terminating the leases, and Purdy agreed to "return the Cows, at [his] expense, to such place as Sunshine designate[d]" at the end of the lease term. Additionally, Purdy guaranteed "the net sales proceeds from the sale of the Cows . . . at the end of the Lease term [would] be [a set amount between $290 and $300] per head (the 'Guaranteed Residual Value')." Purdy further promised to maintain insurance on the cattle, to replace any cows that were culled from the herd, and to allow Sunshine the right to inspect the herd. When the parties signed these contracts, they also executed security agreements, and Sunshine filed financing statements with the Secretary of State.

In the dairy business, farmers must "cull" a portion of their herd every year, replacing older and less productive cows with younger, healthier ones. Many times, dairy farmers will replace the culled cows with their calves. Purdy, in contrast, sold off the calves of Sunshine's cows and purchased more mature replacements. See In re Purdy, 490 B.R. 530, 534 (Bankr. W.D. Ky. 2013). This practice contravened the terms of the leases, but Sunshine was aware of Purdy's behavior and acquiesced in it. Nonetheless, the terms of the lease required Purdy to apply Sunshine's brand and a yellow ear tag to the original cows and their replacements. In contrast, Purdy applied a white ear tag to the cattle covered by Citizens First's security interest. In re Purdy, 490 B.R. at 535. By July 2012, Purdy had approximately 750 head of cattle on his farm. Of those cattle, 435 should have carried Sunshine's brand according to the terms of the leases.

In the fall of 2012, the price of cattle feed rose, and milk production became less profitable. Id. at 534. Purdy responded by selling off cattle, including many bearing Sunshine's brand, at a faster rate. Unfortunately, Purdy could not keep his operation above water, and on November 29, 2012, he filed a voluntary petition for Chapter 12 bankruptcy relief, and the bankruptcy court issued an automatic stay, preventing the removal of assets from the farm. Id. at 535. A week later, representatives of Citizens First and Sunshine inspected the 389 cattle still on the farm. Of the cows on the property, 289 had white ear tags (indicating that they were covered by Citizens First's security interest) and Sunshine's brand, 99 had only white ear tags, and one cow had neither a tag nor a brand. A short time later, another farmer returned forty-three cattle that had been taken in violation of the bankruptcy court's stay. Sunshine claimed that thirty-nine of those cattle bore Sunshine's brand.

Citizens First argued that Purdy owned all of these cattle and, therefore, that they were covered by the bank's perfected purchase money security interest. Sunshine contended that it maintained ownership of the cattle, that Purdy had only a leasehold interest in the cattle, and therefore that the cattle fell outside of Citizen First's security interest. Both Citizens First and Sunshine filed motions in the bankruptcy court for relief from the stay preventing the removal of the livestock.

On January 22, 2013, the bankruptcy court held a hearing on various motions. The dispute between Citizens First and Sunshine turned on whether the leases between Purdy and Sunshine were true leases or disguised security agreements. The bankruptcy court issued its decision on March 1, 2013, finding that: "The original term of the Lease was for 50 months. Clearly, 50 months is longer than the economic life of the goods [the cows]. Uncontradicted testimony indicated that a dairy herd is culled annually at an approximate rate of 30 percent. Within three years an entire herd is extremely likely to have been entirely replaced and certainly before the end of 50 months. Because [Purdy] met this term of the statute, the transaction is a per se security agreement and the Court's analysis ends here." In re Purdy, 490 B.R. at 536.

Consequently, the bankruptcy court determined that Citizens First's "prior perfected liens attach[ed] to all cows on [Purdy's] farm on the date the Petition was filed," and it denied Sunshine's motion to lift the stay. Id. at 540. The bankruptcy court eventually granted Citizens First relief from the stay, however, and the bank foreclosed on the herd. Citizens First auctioned the cattle for $402,353.54, and the bankruptcy trustee awarded these proceeds to Citizens First, which applied them toward Purdy's outstanding debt.

Sunshine appealed to the federal district court nine days after the auction sale. Because the cattle had already been auctioned, Sunshine requested a percentage of the sale proceeds equivalent to its share of the cattle sold. Ultimately, the district court affirmed the bankruptcy court's decision on September 25, 2013. Sunshine now appeals.

II. STANDARD OF REVIEW

"When reviewing an order of a bankruptcy court on appeal from a decision of a district court, we review the bankruptcy court's order directly and give no deference to the district court's decision." Hamilton v. Herr (In re Hamilton), 540 F.3d 367, 371 (6th Cir. 2008). We review de novo the bankruptcy court's conclusions of law, and we review the bankruptcy court's findings of fact for clear error. Id.

III. ANALYSIS

The main question in this case is whether the agreements between Purdy and Sunshine are "true leases" or merely "security agreements." "'A lease involves payment for the temporary possession, use and enjoyment of goods, with the expectation that the goods will be returned to the owner with some expected residual interest of value remaining at the end of the lease term.'" In re QDS Components, Inc., 292 B.R. 313, 322 (Bankr. S.D. Ohio 2002) (quoting James J. White & Robert S. Summers, Uniform Commercial Code §30-3, vol. 4 (5th ed., West 2002)). "'In contrast, a sale involves an unconditional transfer of absolute title to goods, while a security interest is only an inchoate interest contingent on default and limited to the remaining secured debt.'" Id. (quoting White & Summers, Uniform Commercial Code §30-3). If the agreements are true leases, then Sunshine has a reversionary interest in 435 head of cattle and is entitled to approximately $309,000 from the cattle auction. See James J. White, Robert S. Summers & Robert A. Hillman, Uniform Commercial Code §30-3(a)(1) (6th ed.,

West 2013) (distinguishing between reversionary interest and security interest). If the agreements represent the sale of the cattle and Sunshine's retention of a security interest, then Citizens First's perfected agricultural security interest trumps Sunshine's interest, and the bank keeps all of the proceeds from the cattle auction.

In deciding whether these "Dairy Cow Leases" are true leases or disguised security agreements, we look to the relevant state law. Butner v. United States, 440 U.S. 48, 54, 99 S. Ct. 914, 59 L. Ed. 2d 136 (1979). The agreements' choice-of-law provisions, in turn, direct us to the laws of Arizona.

Under Arizona law, "the facts of each case" dictate whether an agreement is a true lease or a security agreement, Ariz. Rev. Stat. §47-1203(A), and our fact-sensitive analysis proceeds in two steps. First, we employ the Bright-Line Test. According to this test, "[a] transaction in the form of a lease creates a security interest if the consideration that the lessee is to pay the lessor for the right to possession and use of the goods is an obligation for the term of the lease and is not subject to termination by the lessee, and . . . [t]he original term of the lease is equal to or greater than the remaining economic life of the goods." §47-1203(B). If the lease runs longer than the economic life of the goods, then the lease is a per se security agreement. See Duke Energy Royal, LLC v. Pillowtex Corp. (In re Pillowtex, Inc.), 349 F.3d 711, 717 (3d Cir. 2003) (interpreting New York's nearly identical version of the Uniform Commercial Code); see also Park W. Fin. Corp. v. Phoenix Equip. Co. (In re Phoenix Equip. Co.), No. 2:08-bk-13108-SSC, 2009 WL 3188684, at *7 (Bankr. D. Ariz. Sept. 30, 2009) (applying the same test to Ariz. Rev. Stat. §47-1203). If the goods retain meaningful value after the lease expires, however, we move to the second step and "'look at the specific facts of the case to determine whether the economics of the transaction suggest'" that the arrangement is a lease or a security interest. *Pillowtex*, 349 F.3d at 717 (quoting In re Taylor, 209 B.R. 482, 484 (Bankr. S.D. Ill. 1997)); see also *Phoenix Equip.*, 2009 WL 3188684, at *7 (applying same to Arizona statute). At all points in this analysis, the party challenging the leases bears the burden of proving that they are something else. See *Phoenix Equip.*, 2009 WL 3188684, at *7.

A.   Bright-Line Test

No one debates that Purdy lacked the ability to terminate the lease. The question is whether the lease term of fifty months exceeds the economic life of the cattle. The bankruptcy court fixated upon Purdy's testimony that he culled approximately thirty percent of the cattle each year, meaning that the entire herd would turn over in forty months. See In re Purdy, 490 B.R. at 536. As a result, the bankruptcy court concluded that the lease term exceeded the economic life of the cattle that Sunshine initially gave Purdy and, therefore, that the lease was a per se security agreement. Id. We disagree and hold that the bankruptcy court erred in its analysis of the cattle's economic life because the court focused upon the economic life of the individual cows originally leased to Purdy, instead of the life of the herd as required by the agreements.

According to the text of the agreements between Purdy and Sunshine, Purdy had a duty to return the same number of cattle to Sunshine that he originally leased, not the same cattle. . . . It made little difference to Sunshine whether it received the exact same cows that it originally leased to Purdy; according to Blevins—Sunshine's owner—"the main thing is to maintain the leasehold, the integrity of the lease numbers." In line with this understanding, the agreements took into account industry practices, such as culling, by requiring Purdy to replace any unproductive cows that he sold. Sunshine protected its interest in the herd by inspecting Purdy's operation, id., requiring Purdy to carry insurance, id., and creating a "Residual Guaranty," which stated that the actual cattle returned would be worth at least a set amount. Given these provisions and the testimony of the parties, it is clear to us that the relevant "good" is the herd of cattle, which has an economic life far greater than the lease term, and not the individual cows originally placed on Purdy's farm. Accordingly, we hold that the contracts flunk the Bright–Line Test and are not per se security agreements.

B. ECONOMICS-OF-THE-TRANSACTION TEST

The precise contours of the economics-of-the-transaction test are rather unclear, but courts have largely focused upon two particular factors: (1) whether the lease contains a purchase option price that is nominal; and (2) "whether the lessee develops equity in the property, such that the only economically reasonable option for the lessee is to purchase the goods." *Phoenix Equip.*, 2009 WL 3188684, at *10 (internal quotation marks omitted); see also *QDS Components*, 292 B.R. at 342; Addison v. Burnett, 41 Cal. App. 4th 1288, 49 Cal. Rptr. 2d 132, 137 (1996); 4 White, Summers & Hillman, Uniform Commercial Code §30-3(d). The ultimate question for us, however, is whether Sunshine kept a meaningful reversionary interest in the herd. See *QDS Components*, 292 B.R. at 340-41; *Phoenix Equip.*, 2009 WL 3188684, at *10. On the facts presented to us, we hold that Citizens First has also failed to carry its burden of establishing that the actual economics of the transactions indicate that the leases were disguised security agreements.

In this case, neither of the above-mentioned factors suggests that these agreements are something other than true leases because the contracts do not contain an option for Purdy to purchase the cattle at any price, let alone at a nominal one. In fact, the agreements explicitly state that Sunshine retains ownership in the cattle throughout the life of the lease and beyond. This lack of a purchase option distinguishes this case from others, such as Aoki v. Shepherd Machinery Co. (In re J.A. Thompson & Son, Inc.), 665 F.2d 941 (9th Cir. 1982), in which the Ninth Circuit held that a purchase option highly favorable to the lessee converted a lease into a security agreement. Id. at 945-46. Here, even if Purdy wanted to purchase the cattle at $300 per cow, there is nothing in the agreements that obligates Sunshine to sell to him. Sunshine could have retaken possession of its cows and leased them out to Purdy's competitor under the same terms, and there would have been nothing Purdy could have done under the agreement. In our view, this state of play is consistent with a lease.

Additionally, the fact that there is no purchase option also distinguishes this case from In re Buehne Farms, Inc., 321 B.R. 239 (Bankr. S.D. Ill. 2005), which the bankruptcy court relied upon heavily. In that case, the court was swayed by the fact that the purported leases allowed the lessee to purchase the cattle at the end of the lease for approximately $160 per cow. Id. at 244. The court noted that the lessee had spent approximately $500,000 in rental payments over the life of the lease and that spending just six percent of that would give the lessee title to the cows. Id. at 246. Considering that the lessee had spent significant money to replace culled cattle already, the *Buehne Farms* court reasoned that the lessee would be irrational not to exercise the purchase option. Id. This situation indicated that the "rental payments" were actually installment payments and that the "purchase option" was really a cleverly disguised final payment. In stark contrast, Purdy's rental payments were just that—payments per a lease. Purdy had no legal right to purchase Sunshine's herd; there was no purchase option that he could exercise. Under the terms of the agreements, Purdy had to return the same number of cows that he originally leased in fair condition as indicated by the Residual Guaranty. At approximately $300 per cow, this herd had a minimum value of $130,500. It sold at auction for approximately $309,000. Ownership of this herd—in our view—is a significant asset, and thus, we hold that Sunshine retained a meaningful reversionary interest.

Finally, whether the parties adhered to the terms of these leases in all facets, in our view, is irrelevant to determining whether the agreements were true leases or disguised security agreements. Neither the bankruptcy court nor the parties have sufficiently explained the legal import of Purdy's culling practices or put forward any evidence that the parties altered the terms of the leases making them anything but what they proclaim to be. Moreover, Arizona Revised Statutes §47-1203(C) clearly states that the fact that terms of the lease are unfavorable to the lessee, that the lessee assumes the risk of loss of the goods, or that the lease requires the lessee to maintain insurance on the goods is not alone grounds to find that a contract is a security agreement. As a result, we hold that Citizens First has not carried its burden of proving that the actual economics of the transaction demonstrate that the leases were security agreements.

IV.   CONCLUSION

For the foregoing reasons, we conclude that Citizens First has failed to demonstrate that the "Dairy Cow Leases" were actually security agreements in disguise. Because the bankruptcy court found to the contrary, we REVERSE and REMAND to the bankruptcy court for further proceedings consistent with this opinion.

DRAIN, D.J., dissenting.

In this case, I respectfully disagree with the majority's decision on the application of the facts to the tests to be applied. I would affirm the bankruptcy court's decision finding that the transactions involved in this case were disguised security agreements as opposed to true leases.

A. Bright-Line Test

I agree with the bankruptcy court, and find *In re Buehne Farms* instructive. That case involved a dairy farmer/debtor who argued his fifty-month cattle leases were disguised as security agreements when his lessors motioned the bankruptcy court to extend the time for the debtor to assume or reject fifty-month cattle leases. In re Buehne, 321 B.R. 239 at 240. The debtor obtained his cattle via two leases with third-party buyers. Id. at 241. The Buehne Farms leases are almost identical to Purdy's leases. Id. The *In re Buehne* court found that the average dairy farmer culls at an annual rate of twenty to thirty percent and the debtor's cows had a forty-eight month economic life. Id. at 242. The *In re Buehne Farms* court found the economic life of a dairy cow could range from thirty-six to sixty months. Id.

Sunshine argues this case is distinguishable because the leases Purdy signed did not have purchase options. Although this is true, I find this case is instructive because it offers guidance on the economic life of dairy cows given a farmer's culling practices.

We review the bankruptcy court findings of fact under the clear-error standard. B-Line, LLC v. Wingerter (*In re Wingerter*), 594 F.3d 931, 935-36 (6th Cir. 2010) (citing Behlke v. Eisen (*In re Behlke*), 358 F.3d 429, 433 (6th Cir. 2004)). Under this standard, the reviewing court must ask whether the bankruptcy court's factual findings were erroneous.

The bankruptcy court in this case heard similar testimony about cull rates and the practices on the Purdy farm. Id. at 537. The bankruptcy court determined that Purdy had a thirty percent cull rate. Id. at 533. This rate causes nearly complete herd turnover after thirty-six months. I agree with the bankruptcy court's determination that the individual heads of cattle are the good at issue. Each head of cattle was a means of production rather than part of a unit. For Purdy, each cow was a sophisticated piece of equipment that produced a product: milk. The economic life of the individual heads of cattle would not last the term of the lease. Any cows on Purdy's farm at the end of the lease term would not be the original cows because he would have culled those cows from the herd. In fact, Purdy would have culled nearly all of the cattle from Lease 1 at the time of the petition. Thus, the agreements were for a period longer than the cows' economic value to Purdy. The lease and Sunshine's testimony speak to total herd maintenance over the lease term, but this was not important to the parties. The parties did not follow these provisions of the lease. This finding was within the economic life range used by the *In re Beuhne Farms* court who heard similar testimony regarding culling practices. I find no error in the bankruptcy court's factual finding of a thirty month culling rate. Therefore, I do not agree with the majority. Unlike the majority, I would hold the Bright-Line Test is met and the leases were per se security agreements.

B.   Economic Realities of the Transaction

The majority finds that the leases fail the Bright-Line test. A lease agreement can fail the Bright-Line test, which is inevitable when the herd is the relevant good, and the court can still find that an agreement creates a security interest. See A.R.S. §47-1203(A); In re Phoenix Equip., Co., Inc., 2009 WL 3188684 at *10 (stating the facts of a case can determine whether a lease is a security agreement). It is my view that the economics of the transactions do not support a finding that the parties entered into lease agreements, and Citizens bore the burden of establishing the documents were not what they purported to be.

The UCC and its Arizona adaptation offer very little guidance to courts on how to analyze the economics of a transaction. A common factor courts use is whether the lessor has a reversionary interest in the leased goods or an option to purchase. Id. Courts are not limited to these factors. In re WorldCom, Inc., 339 B.R. 56, 72 (Bankr. S.D.N.Y. 2006). In fact, by limiting itself to these factors, the court conducts a similar analysis to the Bight-Line test. In re Phoenix Equip. Co., Inc., 2009 WL 3188684 at *10 (holding parties' course of dealings was a relevant factor in determining whether leases were security interests). Courts should focus on other relevant facts at the time of the agreements. Id.

In re Phoenix Equipment Co. Inc. is distinguishable from this matter because it also involves a purchase option. Id. at *11. The *In re Phoenix Equip. Co., Inc.* leases did not provide for an option in the language of the lease, but the court inferred the option by analyzing the parties' course of dealings. Id. When the parties could not establish whether the purchase price on the option was nominal, the *In re Phoenix Equipment Co., Inc.* court focused on the structure and effect of the parties' transactions. Id. (stating the court must consider the agreements within the context of the parties' relationship). The debtor needed capital in order to run his operation and entered into transactions in which he transferred title of equipment to his creditor in exchange for the capital. Id. The court concluded the nature of the transactions showed that the debtor did not need a lease agreement, but needed capital to continue operating. Id. at *12.

In the three relevant leases, third parties sold cattle to Purdy. Sunshine reimbursed Purdy for the cost of the cattle. Sunshine knew Purdy did not adhere to the replacement cattle provisions in its agreements, but chose to ignore his non-compliance. Sunshine was aware of Citizens' lien at the time it entered into the transactions and filed its statements. The facts of the case at the time of the transaction indicate that Purdy needed money to place cows on the farm. Sunshine, by the way it forwarded funds to Purdy, appears to have supplied Purdy with funds rather than the actual cattle. Sunshine received a lien on the cattle whose acquisition it financed. These facts indicate the parties entered into three financing transactions rather than three lease transactions.

Furthermore, the reimbursement sheds doubt on Sunshine's characterization of the leases as finance leases under Article 2A. Under Arizona's adaptation of the UCC, finance leases have three characteristics. A.R.S. 47-2A103(A)(7). First, the lessor does not select, manufacture, or supply the goods. Id. at (a). Second, the lessor acquires the goods or a right to possess and use of the goods in connection with the lease. Id. at (b). Purdy selected the cattle, and the cattle were branded in accordance with Exhibit B of the lease, which creates a presumption of ownership. Third, one of three events involving the lessee must occur. Id. at (c). The lessee must, before signing the lease, receive a copy of the contract by which the lessor acquired the goods. Id. Alternatively, lessee approval of the contract by which the lessor acquired the goods can be a condition of the effectiveness of the lease. Id. Last, the lessee, prior to signing the contract, "receives an accurate and complete statement designating the promises and warranties, and any disclaimers of warranties, limitations or modifications of remedies, or liquidated damages, including those of a third party, such as the manufacturer of the goods, provided to the lessor by the person supplying the goods in connection with or as part of the contract by which the lessor acquired the goods or the right to possession and use of the goods[.]" Id. It is not clear from the record whether any of these three instances occurred.

Purdy purchased the cattle, and there is no indication in the record Purdy approved or saw a contract or any warranties or promises the third-party buyer would have given to Sunshine. Sunshine only has invoices and bills to indicate it paid for cattle that Purdy already had on his farm. Sunshine has not shown its leases meet the statutory requirements of the finance lease. Thus, the bankruptcy court did not err by relying on the parties' post lease conduct in reaching its conclusion. Testimony reveals Sunshine acquiesced in Purdy's decision to sell the cattle, and use the funds to either purchase more cattle or deposit the sale proceeds in his Citizens' account. It was not error for the bankruptcy court to rely on the fact that Purdy acquired the cattle from third parties and Sunshine reimbursed these parties. This arrangement was tantamount to Sunshine financing the acquisition of cattle for Purdy's dairy operation. Moreover, Sunshine failed to come forward with evidence it actually owned the cattle delivered by the third party buyers, which calls into question the leases status as finance leases. I would hold the economics of the transaction support a finding that the parties entered into security agreements for the cattle rather than leases.

For these reasons, I respectfully dissent and would affirm the bankruptcy court's decision.

The UCC's definition of security interest properly concedes that "[w]hether a transaction creates a lease or a security interest is determined by the facts of each case. . . ." UCC §1-203 sounds rather unhelpful on its face. It does, however, do two useful things. First, it sets out four different scenarios in which the transaction in question *must* be considered a disguised sale. This list is not intended to be exclusive, but it at least gives us some situations in which the statute speaks with certainty on the lease/sale question.

Second, UCC §1-203 sets out a number of factors that do not by themselves necessarily create a disguised sale. For example, the subsection says that just because a lease includes a purchase option at fair market value does not of itself turn the lease into a disguised sale. It also says that just because the lessee agrees to assume the risk of loss or to pay insurance or taxes on the goods does not turn the transaction into a disguised sale. These provisions were inserted to reverse some case law that had, in the drafters' view, wrongly concluded that certain transactions were disguised sales merely because of one of the factors that §1-203 now rejects as being dispositive on the question.

In addition to providing some guidance as to the distinction between a true lease and a disguised sale, the drafters of Article 2A also created special rules for two distinct kinds of leases: the consumer lease and the finance lease. Most of the provisions in Article 2A assume a basic two-party, arm's-length lease transaction in which the parties have roughly equal bargaining power.

With respect to the consumer lease, however, the drafters did not assume equal bargaining power and therefore created some special protections for the consumer lessee. UCC §2A-103(1)(e) defines a consumer lease as a lease transaction between a lessor that is in the business of leasing and an individual lessee who leases goods for personal, family, or household use. Some of the unique benefits accorded to the consumer lessee include prohibitions against bad-faith accelerations by the lessor, special disclosure requirements, and heightened unconscionability protections. UCC §§2A-109, 2A-208(2), 2A-108(2).

The finance lease departs from the paradigm lease transaction in that it involves three parties rather than two, and the putative "lessor" is really no more than a provider of financing to the lessee. As we will see later, the drafters of Article 2A included a number of provisions that reduce the finance lessor's responsibility for the performance of the leased goods and create direct rights for the lessee against the seller, known as the "supplier."

B.   Scope of the CISG

If the task of the UCC drafters seems daunting, consider what faced those who attempted to create a commercial code that would govern transactions between parties in different countries with widely diverse cultural and legal systems. It is no wonder that the establishment of an international commercial code was tried and failed several times in the past. Yet with the dizzying increase in the pace of international trade, in the 1980s the various barriers that had previously prevented the widespread adoption of such a code were finally overcome.

In 1980, the United Nations Commission on International Trade submitted the Convention on Contracts for the International Sales of Goods (CISG) to 62 nations in Vienna. Presently over 80 countries have ratified the CISG, including such major world trade players as the United States, China, France, Germany, Canada, and Mexico. Read together, Articles 1 and 6 of the CISG say that unless the parties otherwise specify, the provisions of the CISG will apply to sales of goods contracts between parties with places of business in "Contracting States," that is, countries that have ratified the CISG. The CISG will apply, however, only if the parties have reason to know by the time of contract formation that they have places of business in different Contracting States. CISG Art. 1(2).

The CISG, which became effective in 1988, defines a party's "place of business" as the place "which has the closest relationship to the contract and its performance. . . ." CISG Art. 10(a). The CISG provides that it applies to "contracts for the sale of goods," CISG Art. 1(1), but it fails to define just what constitutes "goods." Though the CISG does not define "goods," it does specifically address the issue of mixed goods and services contracts by expressly excluding in Article 3(2) contracts where "the preponderant part of [the seller's obligation] consists in the supply of labor or other services."

Like Article 2 of the UCC, the CISG is by its terms a default mode that parties may opt out of. CISG Art. 6.

Valero Marketing & Supply Co. v. Greeni Oy & Greeni Trading Oy

373 F. Supp. 2d 475 (D.N.J. 2005)

DEBEVOISE, J.

This matter is before the Court on Plaintiff's, Valero Marketing & Supply Company ("Valero"), motion for partial summary judgment against Defendants, Greeni Oy and Greeni Trading Oy (together "Greeni"), for breach of contract. Valero is a corporation incorporated in the State of Delaware with its principal place of business in San Antonio, Texas. It is engaged in the business of blending components purchased from third parties into reformulated gasoline. Greeni Trading is a corporation incorporated in Finland with its principal place of business in Helsinki, Finland. It is engaged in the business of buying and selling petroleum products and chartering oceangoing vessels.

Valero's Complaint alleges that it suffered substantial loss resulting from Greeni's failure to deliver to it, within a certain delivery window, naphtha for which it had contracted. Valero contends it is entitled to partial summary judgment on the issue of Greeni's liability. It contends that Greeni is liable for the losses it suffered because it was unable to blend the naphtha with other components into reformulated gasoline for delivery into the cash market before September 30, 2001.

I.   BACKGROUND

A.   VALERO'S RELATIONSHIP WITH GREENI

In early August 2001, Ilkka Kokko, a petroleum trader and one of two owners of Greeni Trading, contacted its cargo broker, Cees van der Hout of Starsupply

Petroleum Feedstocks, Inc. ("Starsupply"), to advise him of the availability of a quantity of naphtha which Greeni owned and was interested in selling. Van der Hout undertook the task of selling Greeni's naphtha. Among the individuals van der Hout contacted was Stuart Burt, the trader responsible for Valero's blending operation in Perth Amboy, New Jersey. On or about August 15, 2001, Valero, as buyer, and Greeni, as seller, entered into a contract, orally through van der Hout (Greeni's standard practice), for the delivery of 25,000 metric tons ("mt") of naphtha to Valero's shore tanks in New York Harbor.

B.   The Contract Terms

Greeni agreed to sell and Valero agreed to buy 25,000mt of naphtha to be delivered between September 10-20, 2001. At the time the deal was reached, the naphtha was in stock at Hamburg, Germany and was owned by Greeni. On the same day the oral agreement was reached, van der Hout faxed a written confirmation of the deal to Burt and Kokko. The confirmation detailed the deal in terms of, *inter alia,* product, quantity, quality, timing of delivery and pricing, the fact that the vessel on which the naphtha would be shipped was subject to inspection and approval by Valero's Transportation Group and that title and risk of loss or damage to the naphtha would remain with Greeni throughout the voyage and until the product passed at the flange connection between the vessel's manifold connection and the shore line at the discharge port, New York Harbor. The confirmation also provided that English law and arbitration would govern the contract, a term to which Valero did not object or affirmatively agree to. On or about August 17, 2001, Valero sent to Greeni a written confirmation. Valero's written confirmation contained similar provisions to Greeni's, but stated that New York law and jurisdiction would apply. Greeni did not object or agree to the terms contained in Valero's confirmation.

Greeni enlisted its ship brokers to locate a vessel to transport the naphtha and shortly thereafter located the Bear G. On or about August 22, 2001, Kokko fixed the Bear G subject to charterer's approval, a subject that was set to expire on August 29, 2001. Greeni lifted the subjects to the Bear G on August 29, 2001, prior to nominating the vessel to Valero. On or about August 30, 2001, Greeni nominated the Bear G to Valero. The same day, upon receipt of Greeni's nomination, Lawrence Smith, of Valero's Transportation Group, rejected the nomination of the Bear G. Valero's reason for rejecting the Bear G was that it did not meet Valero's criteria for acceptance. Smith's review of the vessel was based on his knowledge of the vessel's history and a review of relevant reports, including a report on the Bear G made available by the Oil Companies International Marine Forum ("ILIMF"). The report stated that on November 16, 2000, the Bear G entered the Port of New York with fuel oil leaking into the ship's ballast tanks. The report also stated that the United States Coast Guard found that oxygen levels in the ballast tanks were not adequate, that a stripping line to the No. 8 cargo tank had failed and that the forward firefighting station was not adequate. Van der Hout relayed Valero's rejection of the Bear G to Kokko. Despite Valero's rejection Greeni decided to use the Bear G to transport the naphtha, noting that Valero had accepted the vessel on a recent transaction with Greeni.

The Bear G completed loading and sailed from Hamburg, Germany on September 10, 2001 (the first day of the contractual delivery window). On September 14, 2001, a second agreement was reached, under which Valero would accept delivery of the naphtha via barges (from the Bear G to Valero's dock) at Greeni's risk and expense. The agreement also stipulated that Valero would accept naphtha delivered to it before September 20, 2001 at the full contract price and that it would accept, at a discounted price, naphtha delivered to it between September 20-24, 2001.

The Bear G arrived in New York Harbor at 3:30 a.m. on September 22, 2001, 27 1/2 hours after the contractual delivery date of September 20, 2001. Greeni contends the Bear G's voyage was affected by Hurricane Gabrielle in the North Atlantic and the delivery of the naphtha was affected by the September 11, 2001 terrorist attacks in the United States. Upon the Bear G's arrival, Valero refused to permit the Bear G to unload the naphtha cargo directly to its tanks at Stolhaven Terminal. Greeni then discharged its cargo to the barges of the other receivers to whom it had sold the naphtha. Greeni did not deliver any naphtha to Valero by September 20, 2001 or by September 24, 2001.

II.   DISCUSSION

* * *

B.   Choice of Law

The choice of law question in this case is an intriguing one, dominated by the existence of the United Nations Convention on Contracts for the International Sale of Goods ("CISG" or "Convention"), 15 U.S.C. App.

The CISG was ratified by the United States on December 11, 1986 and became effective on January 1, 1988. *See* 15 U.S.C. App. at 332 (1998). The Convention strives to promote certainty among contracting parties and simplicity in judicial understanding by 1) reducing forum shopping, 2) reducing the need to resort to rules of private international law, and 3) establishing a law of sales appropriate for international transactions. Caroline Delisle Klepper, *The Convention for the International Sale of Goods: A Practical Guide for the State of Maryland and Its Trade Community,* 15 Md. J. Int'l L. & Trade 235, 237 (Fall 1991). Nations have adopted the CISG to provide for "the orderly conduct of international commerce." *Ajax Tool Works, Inc. v. Can-Eng Mfg. Ltd.,* 2003 WL 223187, *2 (N.D. Ill. 2003).

When two foreign nations are signatories to the CISG, as are the United States and Finland, the CISG governs contracts for the sale of goods between parties whose places of business are in these different nations. 15 U.S.C. App., Art. 1(1)(a); *See Supermicro Computer Inc. v. Digitechnic, S.A.,* 145 F. Supp. 2d 1147, 1151 (N.D.

Cal. 2001). The CISG applies where the contract is silent as to choice of law. *Amco Ukrservice v. Am. Meter Co.,* 312 F. Supp. 2d 681, 686 (E.D. Pa. 2004); *Supermicro Computer Inc. v. Digitechnic, S.A.,* 145 F. Supp. 2d at 1151.

The CISG has four parts. Part II of the CISG governs formation of contracts. As Valero correctly notes, the CISG doesn't govern in this matter with respect to contract formation and thus with respect to the effect to be given to Valero's confirmation designating New York law. Article 19 of Part II of the CISG addresses the addition of terms to a contract, 15 U.S.C. App. Art. 19. However, upon ratifying the CISG, Finland declared, in accordance with Article 92(1), that it would not be bound by Part II of the Convention governing formation of the contract. *Standard Bent Glass Corp. v. Glassrobots Oy,* 333 F.3d 440, 444 (3d Cir. 2003). Accordingly, because Finland is not a signatory to Part II of the CISG, the CISG does not govern the effect of the choice of law provision contained in Valero's written confirmation.

On the other hand, unless Valero has effectively opted out of the CISG by means of the provision in its confirmation that New York law is applicable, the CISG governs the rights and obligations of Valero and Greeni arising from such contract. "Although the CISG is plainly limited in its scope (15 U.S.C. App. Art. 4), the CISG nevertheless can and does preempt state contract law to the extent that state causes of action fall within the scope of the CISG." *Asante Technologies, Inc. v. PMC-Sierra, Inc.,* 164 F. Supp. 2d 1142 (N.D. Cal. 2001).

Article 6 of the CISG provides that "[t]he parties may exclude the application of the Convention or, subject to Article 12, derogate from or vary the effect of any of its provisions." 15 U.S.C. App. Art. 6. The original oral agreement, as negotiated between Valero and Greeni, contained no provision that excluded the application of the CISG. Consequently, as noted above, the CISG governed the rights and obligations of the parties. Valero contends that it effectively excluded application of the CISG by means of its written confirmation.

The court concludes, however, that Valero failed to exclude the agreement from the CISG. This conclusion can be reached by two routes, each arriving at the same destination. First, if under New Jersey law the confirmation effectively amended the original agreement, it nevertheless failed to replace the CISG with New York's UCC, because in the circumstances of this case New York itself would have applied CISG. Second, under New Jersey law, the substitution of the CISG with New York's UCC materially altered the original agreement and therefore did not become a part of that agreement.

Several federal courts have adopted the first approach, holding that to exclude the CISG a party must not only provide that the law of a particular state will apply, it must also expressly state that the CISG will not apply.

BP Oil Int'l *Ltd., v. Empresa Estatal Petroleos de Ecuador,* 332 F.3d 333 (5th Cir. 2003) concerned Petro Ecuador's purchase of gasoline from BP Oil to be transported from Texas to Ecuador. Petro Ecuador refused delivery asserting the gasoline did not meet the contract's quality specifications. The final agreement provided, among other things, "Jurisdiction: Laws of the Republic of Ecuador." The Court of

Appeals assumed that this provision unambiguously conveyed the intent to apply Ecuadorian law.

The district court, relying on its diversity jurisdiction, applied Texas choice of law rules, which recognized choice of law provisions in a contract, and determined that Ecuadorian law applied, rejecting BP Oil's contention that the CISG governed. The Court of Appeals noted that the district court also had federal question jurisdiction by virtue of the CISG, a treaty ratified by the Senate which created a private right of action in the federal court. "As incorporated federal law, the CISG governs the dispute so long as the parties have not elected to exclude its application. CISG Art. 6." 332 F.3d at 337. The Court rejected Petro Ecuador's contention that the contract's choice of law provision demonstrated the parties' intent to apply Ecuadorian domestic law instead of the CISG, because "[a] signatory's assent to the CISG necessarily incorporates the treaty as part of that nation's domestic law." *Id.* "Similarly, because the CISG is the law of Ecuador, it governs this dispute. '[I]f the parties decide to exclude the Convention, it should be expressly excluded by language which states that it does not apply and also states what law shall govern the contract.'" *Id.* at 337 (citation omitted).

Asante Techs., Inc. v. PMC-Sierra, Inc., 164 F. Supp. 2d 1142 (N.D. Cal. 2001) reached the same result. Asante, a Delaware corporation, purchased electronic components from PMC, also a Delaware corporation but having its place of business for purposes of the CISG in British Columbia, Canada. The terms and conditions that Asante submitted provided: "APPLICABLE LAW. The validity [and] performance of this [purchase] order shall be governed by the laws of the state shown on Buyer's address on this order." 164 F. Supp. 2d at 1145. PMC's terms and conditions of sale provided: "APPLICABLE LAW. The contract between the parties is made, governed by, and shall be construed in accordance with the laws of the Province of British Columbia and the laws of Canada applicable therein, which shall be deemed to be the proper law hereof." *Id.*

The district court denied Asante's motion to remand, asserting that there was federal jurisdiction on the ground that the CISG completely preempted state law to the extent that the CISG governed the contract. The court held that the parties had failed to exclude application of the CISG simply by their designation of California and British Columbia law, because the CISG is the law of British Columbia and because by virtue of the Supremacy Clause . . ." under general California law, the CISG is applicable to contracts where the contracting parties are from different countries that have adopted the CISG. In the absence of clear language indicating that both contracting parties intended to opt out of the CISG, and in view of Defendant's Terms and Conditions which would apply the CISG, the Court rejects Plaintiff's contention that the choice of law provisions preclude the applicability of the CISG." *Id.* at 1150.

Ajax Tool Works, Inc. v. Can-Eng Mfg. Ltd., 2003 WL 223187 (N.D. Ill. 2003) concerned Ajax's purchase of a furnace from Can-Eng. Ajax was an Illinois corporation, Can-Eng an Ontario, Canada corporation. The parties' contract provided that the "agreement shall be governed by the laws of the Province of Ontario, Canada." Holding that notwithstanding this provision the CISG applied, the court stated, "[o]bviously, this clause does not exclude the CISG. Further, although the parties have designated Ontario law as controlling, it is not the provincial law of Ontario that applies; rather, because the CISG is the law of Ontario, the CISG governs the parties' agreement." 2003 WL 223187 at *3.

In its reply Valero argues that because the United States has opted out of Article 1 1(b), that:

> "[the courts in] Asante and Ajax committed two basic errors in applying CISG. First, in relying on the parties' choice of law to lead to a choice of CISG, the decisions failed to recognize that the United States specifically disclaimed Article 1 1(b) of the Convention. CISG Art. 1. Article 1 1(b) applies CISG if the application of private choice of law rules (here, a contractual choice) leads to the application of the laws of a CISG signatory. Because the United States specifically refused Article 1 1(b) it is forbidden to apply CISG on the basis that the parties chose the laws of an American jurisdiction." (Valero Reply Brief at 5).

Although it is true that contracting states may elect not to adopt article 1 1(b) and the United States has opted out of that provision, Valero has misinterpreted the meaning of this opting out. The result of the United States opting out, unless the parties expressly agree otherwise, is that the CISG does not apply to contracts between a United States party and a party with a place of business in a state that has not adopted the CISG. Richard M. Lavers, *Contracts for the International Sale of Goods,* 60-NOV Wis. B. Bull. 11, 11-12 (November 1987). The United States clearly decided to apply the law of the Convention only to transactions between parties in two contracting states. The United States opting out would have an impact when one state was a contracting state and the other state was not a contracting state. "In cases where Sub 1(b) is relevant the trading partners of the Contracting States are in non-Contracting states." John Honnold, *Uniform Law for International Sales Under the 1980 United Nations Convention,* 86-89 (2d Ed.) (1991). It is clear that the Convention applies when both the buyer and seller are in contracting states, as is the case here (Finland and the United States are both contracting parties to the CISG). The United States's opting out of Article 1 1(b) of the Convention is of no relevance in the case at bar.

Applying the reasoning of *BP Oil, Asante* and *Ajax* to the present case, if Valero effectively supplemented the oral agreement to include a provision to the effect that New York law applied, the provision failed to specifically exclude application of the CISG and under New York law the courts, by virtue of the Supremacy Clause, would apply the CISG . . . .

Not all courts agree with the *Valero* court's conclusion that a choice-of-law provision designating the law of a U.S. state is insufficient to exclude application of the CISG. In *American Biophysics Corp. v. Dubois Marine Specialties,* 411 F. Supp. 2d 61 (D.R.I. 2006), the court held that a choice-of-law provision indicating that Rhode Island law would apply was enough to exclude the CISG. At least one commentator has argued that the *American Biophysics* case was wrongly decided. *See* William P. Johnson, Understanding Exclusion of the CISG: A New Paradigm of Determining Party Intent, 59 Buff. L. Rev. 213 (2011).

A comparison of the scope of the CISG with UCC Article 2 reveals at least three key matters included in UCC Article 2 but excluded from the CISG. First, the CISG does not cover the sale of consumer goods, unless the seller neither knew nor should have known that the goods were being purchased for a consumer purpose. CISG Art. 2(a). Second, Article 5 says that the CISG does not apply to the liability of the seller for death or personal injury caused by the goods sold. Finally, the CISG specifically excludes from its coverage issues regarding whether the sale to the buyer cuts off the property interests of third parties in the goods that were sold. CISG Art. 4(b).

The gap filling rules of the CISG were difficult to settle on, given the various legal cultures of the several countries that were involved in the drafting process. Unlike the case with the UCC, there is no body of "common law" to draw upon where the CISG is silent. In Article 7(1), the CISG says that "[q]uestions concerning matters governed by this Convention which are not expressly settled in it are to be settled in conformity with the general principles on which it is based or, in the absence of such principles, in conformity with the law applicable by virtue of the rules of private international law." The phrase "private international law" is a reference to the choice-of-law rules that determine whose domestic laws will govern a particular contract dispute.

C.   Real Estate

There is no widely adopted uniform code in the real estate system that plays a role comparable to that played by the UCC in the personal property system. Thus, real estate law is often a function of the geographical idiosyncrasies of particular states or regions of the country. Furthermore, since real estate by definition is not portable, the system does not have the same need for uniform rules governing interstate transactions as does the system for the sale of personal property.

Nevertheless, the common law in most states, plus some individual nonuniform state statutes, have ended up creating default terms that are analogous to some of the most important default terms found in Article 2 of the UCC. For example, these scattered statutes and the common law will read into most real estate conveyances certain implied warranties.

Later in the book there will be a discussion of the role of brokers in the real estate system, a role that includes the creation and distribution of local "form contracts" that serve as starting points for parties to various standard, small real estate transactions. These form contracts, because of their wide use in most local markets, serve a default function in that their terms will govern unless the parties agree to modify them.

Although UCC Article 2 covers the sale of personal property, it includes one provision that is worth noting in the context of real estate sales. UCC §2-107 attempts to draw a line between the personal property and real property aspects of sales that in some respects affects both. Section 2-107(1) says that a contract for the sale of things that are to be removed from realty, such as minerals, oil and gas, or structures attached to land, is covered by Article 2 if the materials are to be severed by the seller.

Section 2-107(2) covers the sale of timber as well as things not covered in subsection (1) that can be removed from realty without material harm to the realty. A contract for the sale of these readily severable items will be covered by Article 2 whether the buyer or the seller does the severing.

Problem Set 2

2.1.   Lou's Used Cars for Less both sells and leases used cars. Determine whether the following transactions, all of which purport to be leases, are in fact true leases or instead are disguised sales. UCC §2A-103(1)(j), §1-203, Official Comments 1 and 2 to §1-203.

a. Martha Keough leases a used Cadillac from Lou. The Cadillac is 3 years old and its reasonably predicted useful life is 15 years from the lease's inception. Had Martha purchased the car, the cash price would have been $20,000. The terms of the lease are that Martha will pay Lou $300 per month for the next 60 months. At the end of the lease, she has the option to purchase the car for $7,000, which is its predicted fair-market value at the time the option is to be exercised. The lease provides that Martha will pay the insurance on the car and will be responsible for paying for maintenance during the course of the lease. Martha has no option to terminate the lease before the 5-year period is up.

b. Same facts as part (a), except Martha agrees to pay Lou $600 per month for 60 months for the same car.

c. Same facts as part (a), except that the car's reasonably predicted useful life is only 5½ years from the lease's inception, and the car is expected to be worth just $500 at the end of the 5-year lease term. The purchase option is still $7,000.

d. Same facts as part (a), except that Martha has a 10-year renewal option for $10 per year at the end of the original 5-year lease.

e. Same facts as part (a), except that Martha has a 10-year renewal option for $10 per year at the end of the original 5-year lease, and she also has the right to terminate the original 5-year lease at any time.

f. Same facts as part (a), except that Martha ends up driving the car so much that the car wears out completely in only 3 years.

g. Same facts as part (a), except that the car's reasonably predicted useful life is only 5 years from the lease's inception, although Martha can terminate the lease at any time by paying a fee of $5,000.

2.2.   Brigid Rogers owns and operates a year-round amusement park. She agrees to lease a new ride, the Portable Death Watch, from Acme Fun Rides, Inc. The terms of the lease are that Brigid will pay $300 per month for 10 years, at which point the Portable Death Watch will be returned to Acme. The expected useful life of the ride is 20 years, and its cash price in a current sale would be $30,000. Brigid can terminate the lease at any time, and the lease includes a purchase option that arises 1 year into the lease for $10,000. The lease also includes a boldface provision separately signed by both Brigid and Acme that says, "BOTH PARTIES HEREBY INTEND AND AGREE THAT THIS CONTRACT CONSTITUTES A TRUE LEASE AND BOTH PARTIES HEREBY WAIVE ANY RIGHT TO CLAIM OTHERWISE AT ANY TIME."

After signing the lease and making the first payment, Brigid has the new ride delivered to her carnival grounds. Two months later a new carnival entrepreneur, Joe Bergers, moves to town and tells Brigid how impressed he is by the Portable Death Watch. Deciding she is tired of the carnival business, Brigid agrees to sell the ride to Joe for $30,000 cash. Before buying the ride, Joe checks the appropriate Article 9 files to make sure there are no recorded interests against the ride. Finding none (since Acme did not believe it needed to file notice of its interest as a lessor), Joe pays $30,000 to Brigid, who then skips town. When Brigid fails to make the next lease payment, Acme locates the Portable Death Watch in Joe's possession and demands its return. Who should prevail in a suit by Acme against Joe? UCC §§1-203, 9-317(b), 9-505(b).

2.3.   Your law firm represents Jay's Rent-to-Own Pianos, a piano retailer that sells and rents both new and used pianos. The company's owner, Jay Berringer, explained to you that for tax and accounting reasons, he wanted to be certain that all of his rent contracts qualify as true leases rather than as disguised sales. On the other hand, he said, for profit reasons he wanted to structure the rent contracts so that customers would almost always end up buying the pianos.

Jay believes his latest lease creation indeed accomplishes both ends. He calls it the "three-year special": the first month's rent is 50 percent of the piano's purchase price, and each of the remaining 35 monthly payments is just 1.5 percent of the piano's price. The customer may terminate the lease at any time after the first month and may purchase the piano either at the end of the lease or during it, with the customer getting full credit toward the purchase price for all lease payments made up to that point. The store will even extend credit, if necessary, for the first month's rent. Has Jay come up with a winner? If not, can you tinker with the "three-year special" so that Jay achieves what he is after? UCC §§1-203, 9-505(b).

2.4.   You are the junior member of the Uniform Law Commission's Article 2A revision committee, which is also examining the 1990 amendments to UCC §1-203. One of the committee's senior members, David Flanders, pulls you aside at a break during your first meeting, and he says he has a question for you that he is afraid would sound stupid to the more seasoned members of the committee.

"I don't get it," David tells you. "Section 1-203(c)(1) says that a transaction is not a disguised sale just because the lessee is obligated to make lease payments that have a present value equal to or greater than the fair market value of the goods. But it seems to me that that situation necessarily *would* be a sale, or why else would the lessee enter into a contract with those terms in the first place?"

Do you have a response for David?

2.5. We Back You Up, Inc. (WBYU), is a manufacturer of custom-designed office chairs for highly paid business executives who have back problems. WBYU has its corporate office in Detroit and its only factory in Mexico City, Mexico. Whenever a potential client calls, the WBYU corporate office sends a consultant from Detroit to visit the executive and create specifications for a specially manufactured chair. Those specs are then emailed to its Mexico City factory, which produces the chair and ships it directly to the client. When Carla Icahn, CEO of a small New York City marketing firm, orders two such chairs (one for use in her office and one for watching TV in her apartment), will that transaction be covered by the CISG? CISG Arts. 1, 10, 2, 3.

2.6. Miles Farmer lives in the city but also has a summer place in the country that consists of 10 acres of land, the original farmhouse, and several dozen apple trees. Miles is now hurting for cash and is considering selling all or part of his summer getaway. Which of the following sales by Miles would be covered by Article 2? UCC §2-107.

a. A sale of the farmhouse to be severed from the land.

b. The farmhouse (to remain attached to the land) plus all of the land.

c. Six bushels of apples to be picked from the trees on the land.

Assignment 3: The Process of Sales Contract Formation

Hill v. Gateway 2000, Inc.

105 F.3d 1147 (7th Cir. 1997)

EASTERBROOK, C.J.

A customer picks up the phone, orders a computer, and gives a credit card number. Presently a box arrives, containing the computer and a list of terms, said to govern unless the customer returns the computer within 30 days. Are these terms effective as the parties' contract, or is the contract term-free because the order-taker did not read any terms over the phone and elicit the customer's assent?

One of the terms in the box containing a Gateway 2000 system was an arbitration clause. Rich and Enza Hill, the customers, kept the computer more than 30 days before complaining about its components and performance. They filed suit in federal court arguing, among other things, that the product's shortcomings make Gateway a racketeer (mail and wire fraud are said to be the predicate offenses), leading to treble damages under RICO for the Hills and a class of all other purchasers. Gateway asked the district court to enforce the arbitration clause; the judge refused, writing that "[t]he present record is insufficient to support a finding of a valid arbitration agreement between the parties or that the plaintiffs were given adequate notice of the arbitration clause." Gateway took an immediate appeal, as is its right.

The Hills say that the arbitration clause did not stand out: they concede noticing the statement of terms but deny reading it closely enough to discover the agreement to arbitrate, and they ask us to conclude that they therefore may go to court. Yet an agreement to arbitrate must be enforced "save upon such grounds as exist at law or in equity for the revocation of any contract." 9 U.S.C. §2. Doctor's Associates, Inc. v. Casarotto, 116 S. Ct. 1652, 134 L. Ed. 2d 902 (1996), holds that this provision of the Federal Arbitration Act is inconsistent with any requirement that an arbitration clause be prominent. A contract need not be read to be effective; people who accept take the risk that the unread terms may in retrospect prove unwelcome. Terms inside Gateway's box stand or fall together. If they constitute the parties' contract because the Hills had an opportunity to return the computer after reading them, then all must be enforced.

ProCD, Inc. v. Zeidenberg, 86 F.3d 1447 (7th Cir. 1996), holds that terms inside a box of software bind consumers who use the software after an opportunity to read the terms and to reject them by returning the product. Likewise, Carnival

50

Cruise Lines, Inc. v. Shute, 499 U.S. 585 (1991), enforces a forum-selection clause that was included among three pages of terms attached to a cruise ship ticket. *ProCD* and *Carnival Cruise Lines* exemplify the many commercial transactions in which people pay for products with terms to follow; *ProCD* discusses others. 86 F.3d at 1451-52. The district court concluded in *ProCD* that the contract is formed when the consumer pays for the software; as a result, the court held, only terms known to the consumer at that moment are part of the contract, and provisos inside the box do not count. Although this is one way a contract could be formed, it is not the only way: "A vendor, as master of the offer, may invite acceptance by conduct, and may propose limitations on the kind of conduct that constitutes acceptance. A buyer may accept by performing the acts the vendor proposes to treat as acceptance." Id. at 1452. Gateway shipped computers with the same sort of accept-or-return offer ProCD made to users of its software. ProCD relied on the Uniform Commercial Code rather than any peculiarities of Wisconsin law; both Illinois and South Dakota, the two states whose law might govern relations between Gateway and the Hills, have adopted the UCC; neither side has pointed us to any atypical doctrines in those states that might be pertinent; *ProCD* therefore applies to this dispute.

Plaintiffs ask us to limit *ProCD* to software, but where's the sense in that? *ProCD* is about the law of contract, not the law of software. Payment preceding the revelation of full terms is common for air transportation, insurance, and many other endeavors. Practical considerations support allowing vendors to enclose the full legal terms with their products. Cashiers cannot be expected to read legal documents to customers before ringing up sales. If the staff at the other end of the phone for direct-sales operations such as Gateway's had to read the four-page statement of terms before taking the buyer's credit card number, the droning voice would anesthetize rather than enlighten many potential buyers. Others would hang up in a rage over the waste of their time. And oral recitation would not avoid customers' assertions (whether true or feigned) that the clerk did not read term X to them, or that they did not remember or understand it. Writing provides benefits for both sides of commercial transactions. Customers as a group are better off when vendors skip costly and ineffectual steps such as telephonic recitation, and use instead a simple approve-or-return device. Competent adults are bound by such documents, read or unread. For what little it is worth, we add that the box from Gateway was crammed with software. The computer came with an operating system, without which it was useful only as a boat anchor. Gateway also included many application programs. So the Hills' effort to limit *ProCD* to software would not avail them factually, even if it were sound legally—which it is not.

For their second sally, the Hills contend that *ProCD* should be limited to executory contracts (to licenses in particular), and therefore does not apply because both parties' performance of this contract was complete when the box arrived at their home. This is legally and factually wrong: legally because the question at hand concerns the formation of the contract rather than its performance, and factually because both contracts were incompletely performed. *ProCD* did not depend on the fact that the seller characterized the transaction as a license rather than as a contract; we treated it as a contract for the sale of goods and reserved the question whether for other purposes a "license" characterization might be preferable. All debates about characterization to one side, the transaction in *ProCD* was no more executory than the one here: Zeidenberg paid for the software and walked out of the store with a box under his arm, so if arrival of the box with the product ends the time for revelation of contractual terms, then the time ended in *ProCD* before Zeidenberg opened the box. But of course ProCD had not completed performance with delivery of the box, and neither had Gateway. One element of the transaction was the warranty, which obliges sellers to fix defects in their products. The Hills have invoked Gateway's warranty and are not satisfied with its response, so they are not well positioned to say that Gateway's obligations were fulfilled when the motor carrier unloaded the box. What is more, both ProCD and Gateway promised to help customers to use their products. Long-term service and information obligations are common in the computer business, on both hardware and software sides. Gateway offers "lifetime service" and has a round-the-clock telephone hotline to fulfil this promise. Some vendors spend more money helping customers use their products than on developing and manufacturing them. The document in Gateway's box includes promises of future performance that some consumers value highly; these promises bind Gateway just as the arbitration clause binds the Hills.

Next the Hills insist that *ProCD* is irrelevant because Zeidenberg was a "merchant" and they are not. Section 2-207(2) of the UCC, the infamous battle-of-the-forms section, states that "additional terms [following acceptance of an offer] are to be construed as proposals for addition to a contract. Between merchants such terms become part of the contract unless. . . ." Plaintiffs tell us that *ProCD* came out as it did only because Zeidenberg was a "merchant" and the terms inside ProCD's box were not excluded by the "unless" clause. This argument pays scant attention to the opinion in *ProCD,* which concluded that, when there is only one form, "sec. 2-207 is irrelevant." 86 F.3d at 1452. The question in *ProCD* was not whether terms were added to a contract after its formation, but how and when the contract was formed—in particular, whether a vendor may propose that a contract of sale be formed, not in the store (or over the phone) with the payment of money or a general "send me the product," but after the customer has had a chance to inspect both the item and the terms. *ProCD* answers "yes," for merchants and consumers alike. Yet again, for what little it is worth we observe that the Hills misunderstand the setting of *ProCD.* A "merchant" under the UCC "means a person who deals in goods of the kind or otherwise by his occupation holds himself out as having knowledge or skill peculiar to the practices or goods involved in the transaction," §2-104(1). Zeidenberg bought the product at a retail store, an uncommon place for merchants to acquire inventory. His corporation put ProCD's database on the Internet for anyone to browse, which led to the litigation but did not make Zeidenberg a software merchant.

At oral argument the Hills propounded still another distinction: the box containing ProCD's software displayed a notice that additional terms were within, while the box containing Gateway's computer did not. The difference is functional, not legal. Consumers browsing the aisles of a store can look at the box, and if they are unwilling to deal with the prospect of additional terms can leave the box alone, avoiding the transactions costs of returning the package after reviewing its contents. Gateway's box, by contrast, is just a shipping carton; it is not on display anywhere. Its function is to protect the product during transit, and the information on its sides is for the use of handlers rather than would-be purchasers.

Perhaps the Hills would have had a better argument if they were first alerted to the bundling of hardware and legal-ware after opening the box and wanted to return the computer in order to avoid disagreeable terms, but were dissuaded by the expense of shipping. What the remedy would be in such a case—could it exceed the shipping charges?—is an interesting question, but one that need not detain us because the Hills knew before they ordered the computer that the carton would include some important terms, and they did not seek to discover these in advance. Gateway's ads state that their products come with limited warranties and lifetime support. How limited was the warranty—30 days, with service contingent on shipping the computer back, or five years, with free onsite service? What sort of support was offered? Shoppers have three principal ways to discover these things. First, they can ask the vendor to send a copy before deciding whether to buy. The Magnuson-Moss Warranty Act requires firms to distribute their warranty terms on request, 15 U.S.C. §2302(b)(1)(A); the Hills do not contend that Gateway would have refused to enclose the remaining terms too. Concealment would be bad for business, scaring some customers away and leading to excess returns from others. Second, shoppers can consult public sources (computer magazines, the Web sites of vendors) that may contain this information. Third, they may inspect the documents after the product's delivery. Like Zeidenberg, the Hills took the third option. By keeping the computer beyond 30 days, the Hills accepted Gateway's offer, including the arbitration clause.

The Hills' remaining arguments, including a contention that the arbitration clause is unenforceable as part of a scheme to defraud, do not require more than a citation to Prima Paint Corp. v. Flood & Conklin Mfg. Co., 388 U.S. 395, 87 S. Ct. 1801, 18 L. Ed. 2d 1270 (1967). Whatever may be said pro and con about the cost and efficacy of arbitration (which the Hills disparage) is for Congress and the contracting parties to consider. Claims based on RICO are no less arbitrable than those founded on the contract or the law of torts. The decision of the district court is vacated, and this case is remanded with instructions to compel the Hills to submit their dispute to arbitration.

It is impossible to discuss the process of contract formation in the sales system without some reference to the context of the particular sale. If you go into your local hardware store and buy a rake, it is easy enough to articulate the how and when of contract formation. The "how" is that you take the rake from the shelf, walk it up to the cash register, and hand over your cash or credit card to the clerk. The moment of contract formation is roughly when you hand over your money and the clerk takes it.

If you decided to go out and buy a new car instead of a rake, the contract formation process would be a bit more formal. You would likely test-drive the car, haggle with the car dealer over price, and then sign a sales contract that would purport to detail the terms of your purchase. Even with this larger transaction, however, the contract formation process is still pretty straightforward.

Now suppose we have two merchants who wish to buy and sell a dozen copy machines. The two parties might sit down and draft a detailed contract that spells out all the terms of the sale. The interviews with buyers and sellers that were conducted for this book, however, suggest that this would be a rare occurrence. As one seller put it, "It usually doesn't make economic sense to try to agree in advance on all of the non-immediate boilerplate terms. In most cases, the stakes are so low and the likelihood that it will ever matter is so low that everyone is really better off ignoring the differences in boilerplate and not trying to come to an agreement on everything."

Rather than the contract being formally drafted, the sale will more likely take place on "open account." In an open account sale, the buyer will communicate in some way with the seller about what the buyer wishes to purchase. The buyer's communication might be by phone, or it might take the form of a written purchase order. The interviews with buyers and sellers suggest that buyers use purchase orders in at least two different ways.

First, the purchase order might truly serve as the "offer" to the seller. In that case, there would be no previously concluded oral contract, although there may have been inquiries by the buyer concerning whether the seller carried the goods that the buyer was interested in purchasing.

Second, the purchase order might be used by the buyer as a way to confirm an oral agreement that has already been reached in a phone call prior to the written purchase order being sent. As one clothing buyer explained, "In the phone call, we agree on the key issues: price, quantity, style, time of delivery. The purchase order will reiterate those key terms, but will also deal with less important, non-negotiated issues."

After the seller receives the buyer's order in an open account sale, the seller will check the buyer's credit with the seller's credit group. Although some parties will arrange for institutional financing that may allow the buyer to defer payment substantially, it is unusual for sellers themselves to extend credit any longer than 30 to 60 days past delivery.

If the buyer's credit is not problematic, the seller will forward the buyer's order to the seller's shipping department, which will then ship the goods to the buyer with a written invoice. Some sellers might also send the buyer an acknowledgement form prior to shipping the goods, although many sellers will not bother with this step. In any event, the buyer's purchase order and the seller's invoice and acknowledgement form will usually be standard form documents that include many boilerplate terms, in addition to spaces to insert the particulars of any single sale.

To get a sense of the difference in boilerplate between a buyer's form and a seller's form, consider the following warranty terms used by the same manufacturer, which is sometimes a seller and sometimes a buyer. When this manufacturer is a buyer, its purchase order includes the following:

> Seller warrants that the goods will conform to description and specifications and will be free from all defects in material and workmanship and all defects due to design (other than Buyer's design). . . . Upon request of Buyer, Seller, at its sole expense, shall repair, or replace f.o.b. Seller's plant, all or any part of any machinery or equipment covered by this order which proves, within one (1) year from the date it is placed in operation but no later than eighteen (18) months from date of shipment, to be defective in material or workmanship. . . . The rights and remedies of Buyer set forth in this order are not exclusive and are in addition to all other rights and remedies of Buyer.

When this manufacturer is a seller, its acknowledgement form states the following concerning warranties:

> The Company warrants to Purchaser that products furnished hereunder will be free from defects in material, workmanship and title and will be of the kind and quality specified in Seller's quotation of published documents. . . . The warranties and remedies set forth herein are conditioned upon (a) proper storage, installation, use and maintenance, and conformance with any applicable recommendations of the Company and (b) Purchaser promptly notifying the Company of any defects and, if required, promptly making the product available for correction. . . . If any product fails to meet the foregoing warranties (except title), the Company shall thereupon correct any such failure either at its option (1) by repairing any defective or damaged part or parts of the products, or (2) by making available F.O.B. Seller's plant or other point of shipment any necessary repaired or replacement parts, freight allowed to destination within the continental U.S.A. Where a failure cannot be corrected by the Company's reasonable efforts, the parties will negotiate an equitable adjustment in price.
>
> The preceding paragraph sets forth the exclusive remedies for claims based on failure of products (except title), whether claims in contract or tort (including negligence), and however instituted and, upon the expiration of the warranty period, all such liability shall terminate. Except as set forth under the heading Patents, the foregoing warranties are exclusive and in lieu of all other warranties whether written, oral, implied or statutory. NO IMPLIED WARRANTY OF MERCHANTABILITY OR FITNESS FOR PURPOSE SHALL APPLY. Seller does not warrant any products of others which Purchaser has designated. In no event will the Company be liable for consequential or special damages.

As this example demonstrates, buyers and sellers both like to write boilerplate language in their forms that is favorable to them. In the vast majority of cases, these differences simply do not matter, and business people know that. Virtually none of the buyers and sellers who were interviewed for this book actually read the other party's form beyond verifying the key terms of the deal: quantity, type, price, and delivery terms.

As the retired general counsel for a major chemical company noted, "Karl Llewellyn used to say 'nobody ever reads these forms'—he was right. The buyers and the sellers, the marketing guys that were out consummating the transaction, they didn't read the forms. . . . We spent a lot of time preparing forms, both as purchaser and as seller. And we also had seminars for marketing people on what these terms meant. But when the transactions were actually consummated, very rarely would the marketing guys, the sales people, or the purchasing agents read these forms. They were asked to bring to the company's attention any variances that were requested by the other side, the seller or buyer. Sometimes they did do that, sometimes they didn't."

An in-house attorney for a Fortune 500 manufacturing company echoed these sentiments: "It seems to me that the parties sending the forms really don't intend a certain [boilerplate] term which deals with remedies or other things like that—they never thought about it. They will just take their chances and worry about that later, if there is a problem. And a lot of business people think, 'Hey, we're going to work this out, we've got a good relationship' . . . and a couple of golf games can get a lot solved, so I don't realistically think the parties have any meeting of the minds on most of this stuff [the boilerplate terms in the forms]."

As you might have guessed by now, the question of contract formation becomes a lot stickier as more steps are added to a particular system's formation process. The drafters of UCC Article 2 intended that their rules about contract formation would be more functional and less formalistic than what the common law provided. Article 2's formation rules are contained in four consecutive sections: 2-204, 2-205, 2-206, and 2-207.

This book's interviews with buyers and sellers suggest that the issue of whether a contract is formed is typically not important for its own sake. In other words, buyers and sellers usually do not fight about whether a particular exchange of words or forms amounted to a "deal." Somehow business people know whether or not there really has been a deal, and if someone tries to escape a concluded deal they will face the non-legal sanctions of a bad industry reputation and a lack of future business. In a few high-stakes cases, parties might actually litigate whether or not a deal was truly entered into, but those instances will be the exception.

Although formation itself is usually not a fighting issue, the formation rules of Article 2 do take on some significance with respect to figuring out the terms of an agreement. That would occur in those important instances in which the parties actually litigate a "battle of the forms" case. It is difficult to utilize UCC §2-207's machinery for determining terms unless you first figure out when the contract was formally concluded.

UCC §2-204 sets out three broad principles about sales contract formation: (1) Sales contracts can be made "in any manner sufficient to show agreement," even conduct; (2) even if the exact moment a sales contract was formed cannot be pinpointed, a contract may still be found to exist; and (3) the only substantive detail that is crucial to the formation of a sales contract is that there be some basis for calculating a remedy for breach.

The broad principles of §2-204 are fleshed out somewhat by the more particular offer-and-acceptance rules set down in §2-206. This latter section says that offers to make sales contracts may be accepted "in any manner and by any medium reasonable under the circumstances." More specifically, §2-206 says that when a buyer offers to purchase goods for immediate shipment, the seller may accept such an offer either by shipping the goods or by promising to ship them. Even a shipment of non-conforming goods will count as an acceptance, unless the seller specifically indicates that the non-conforming shipment is offered merely as an accommodation to the buyer (in which case the shipment would constitute a counteroffer).

UCC §2-206 is straightforward enough. UCC §2-207 is not. Before tackling the intricacies of §2-207, however, let us consider briefly the effect of another formation provision of Article 2, §2-205. UCC §2-205 creates a limited exception to the common law rule that "firm offers" require consideration in order to be binding. Under §2-205, firm offers are binding even in the absence of consideration if the offeror is a merchant and the offer is in writing. Such a firm offer under §2-205, however, is only open for a reasonable time if no time is stated in the offer. In no event would such a gratuitous firm offer remain irrevocable for longer than three months.

At least one buyer/manufacturer interviewed for this book reported that his company regularly uses the benefits of §2-205. What this buyer does before making a major purchase of supplies is communicate its standard terms and conditions with potential suppliers. The buyer (which, incidentally, has a lot of leverage because its business is considered very lucrative by vendors) then requires potential vendors to submit "firm offers" to the buyer that incorporate the terms of the buyer's own standard purchase order.

Thus, for example, if one of these suppliers promised in writing that the manufacturer could purchase two tons of steel for a certain price, the supplier could not change its mind if the manufacturer came back the next day ready, willing, and able to make that purchase. The supplier could, of course, limit that firm offer to less than a day, in which case the manufacturer would be out of luck. But if the supplier failed to specify a time, normally a manufacturer's acceptance the next day would be considered within a "reasonable time" and thus the acceptance would be timely.

Now consider UCC §2-207. To understand the situation that §2-207 was meant to address, consider again our two merchants above who want to buy and sell a dozen copy machines. Suppose that the buyer sends a purchase order to the seller that includes, among other things, provisions indicating that the seller will make certain express and implied warranties to the buyer as part of the sale. Imagine that before shipping the machines, seller sends its own acknowledgement form to buyer that purports to disclaim all implied warranties and further says that all disputes about this sale will be settled by binding arbitration.

Is there a contract at this point? Under the common law, the answer is a clear "no." The common law's "mirror image rule" holds that unless all of the terms of the purported acceptance agree with the terms of the offer, the purported acceptance cannot operate as a "true" acceptance. This is because the purported acceptance is not a mirror image of the offer.

If the parties nevertheless proceeded to perform the contract, the purported acceptance with the different terms is considered a "counteroffer" that is accepted by virtue of the buyer's performance. Thus, the seller's form controls the terms of the contract since it is the last form sent prior to performance. This is known as the "last shot" doctrine.

UCC §2-207(1) changes that result. That subsection says that an acceptance such as the one described above can indeed count as an acceptance "even though it states terms additional to or different from" those that were offered.

Even under §2-207(1), there are still two ways in which a purported acceptance might not operate as a valid acceptance. The first is if the acceptance is not "a definite and seasonable expression of acceptance." This might be the case, for example, if the acceptance came a long time after the offer was made, or if the terms of the acceptance were wildly and fundamentally different from the terms of the offer. In other words, an offer to buy apples could not be accepted by an acceptance that agreed to sell oranges. Nevertheless, the acceptance may differ in even "material" ways from the offer and still count as an acceptance. Unfortunately, there is no easy way to draw the line between divergent but valid acceptances on the one hand, and "apples/oranges," invalid acceptances on the other.

The second way that a purported acceptance might not count as a valid acceptance under §2-207(1) is if the acceptance is "expressly made conditional on assent to the additional or different terms." This could arguably be accomplished by the offeree's including conspicuous language in its form that tracks the relevant "expressly made conditional" language of §2-207. On the other hand, if a cautious offeree truly intended not to go forward with the deal except on its own terms, the offeree probably would want to bring that fact home to the offeror in an even more direct way. For example, if the copy machine seller in our hypothetical did not want to do the deal unless there were no implied warranties, the seller ought to insist that the buyer separately sign a "no implied warranties" letter before shipping the machines. As the following case shows, it is not enough for the seller to have its desired term appear on a form that the seller has sent in numerous previous deals with the same buyer.

Belden, Inc. v. American Electronic Components, Inc.

885 N.E.2d 751 (Ind. Ct. App. 2008)

BARNES, J.

Belden, Inc., and Belden Wire & Cable Company (collectively "Belden") appeal the trial court's granting of partial summary judgment in favor of American Electronic Components, Inc. ("AEC"). We affirm.

ISSUES

Belden raises four issues, which we consolidate and restate as:

I. whether the limitation on damages on the back of Belden's order acknowledgment applies to the parties' contract; and

II. whether Belden created an express warranty based on its prior assertions to AEC.

FACTS

Belden manufactures wire, and AEC manufactures automobile sensors. Since 1989, AEC, in repeated transactions, has purchased wire from Belden to use in its sensors.

In 1996 and 1997, Belden sought to comply with AEC's quality control program and provided detailed information to AEC regarding the materials it used to manufacture its wire. In its assurances, Belden indicated that it would use insulation from Quantum Chemical Corp. ("Quantum"). In June 2003, however, Belden began using insulation supplied by Dow Chemical Company ("Dow"). The Dow insulation had different physical properties than the insulation provided by Quantum.

In October 2003, Belden sold AEC wire manufactured with the Dow insulation. AEC used this wire to make its sensors, and the insulation ultimately cracked. Chrysler had installed AEC's sensors containing the faulty wire in approximately 18,000 vehicles. Chrysler recalled 14,000 vehicles and repaired the remaining 4,000 prior to sale. Pursuant to an agreement with Chrysler, AEC is required to reimburse Chrysler for expenses associated with the recall.

In 2004, AEC filed a complaint against Belden seeking consequential damages for the changes in the insulation that resulted in the recall. In 2005, AEC filed a partial motion for summary judgment. In 2006, Belden responded and filed a cross-motion for summary judgment. The motions for summary judgment were "limited to the issues of duty and limitation of remedy and [did] not present any issues as to breach, causation, or damages." Appellant's App. p. 14. On July 6, 2006, the trial court held a hearing on the parties' motions for partial summary judgment. On July 6, 2007, the trial court entered an order granting AEC's motion for partial summary judgment and denying Belden's cross-motion. Belden now appeals.

ANALYSIS

I.   BATTLE OF THE FORMS

Belden first argues that the boilerplate language on the back of its "customer order acknowledgment" limited the damages available to AEC. Appellant's App. p. 94. The parties were involved in repeated transactions over many years. Prior to

1998, AEC sent all purchase orders by mail on a form that contained AEC's terms and conditions on the back. Beginning in 1998, AEC sent its purchase orders to Belden via fax. The faxed purchase orders only included the front of the form and omitted the terms and conditions printed on the back of the form.

On October 17, 2003, AEC sent Belden a purchase order containing the quantity, price, shipment date, and product specifications. Belden responded on October 22, 2003, with its order acknowledgment. The order acknowledgment referenced AEC's specific requests and contained boilerplate language on the back. At issue here is the language purporting to limit Belden's liability for special, indirect, incidental, or consequential damages. *See id.* at 95. The back of order acknowledgment also stated:

> 1.2 Where this Agreement is found to be an acknowledgment, if such acknowledgment constitutes an acceptance of an offer such acceptance is expressly made conditional upon Buyer's assent solely to the terms of such acknowledgment, and acceptance of any part of Product(s) delivered by Company shall be deemed to constitute such assent by Buyer. . . .

Id. Based on these exchanges, the parties dispute whether the limitation on damages is a term of their agreement.

We start our analysis with Section 2-207 of the Uniform Commercial Code ("UCC"), which provides:

> (1) A definite and seasonable expression of acceptance or a written confirmation which is sent within a reasonable time operates as an acceptance even though it states terms additional to or different from those offered or agreed upon, unless acceptance is expressly made conditional on assent to the additional or different terms.
> (2) The additional terms are to be construed as proposals for addition to the contract. Between merchants such terms become part of the contract unless:
> > (a) the offer expressly limits acceptance to the terms of the offer;
> > (b) they materially alter it; or
> > (c) notification of objection to them has already been given or is given within a reasonable time after notice of them is received.
> (3) Conduct by both parties which recognizes the existence of a contract is sufficient to establish a contract for sale although the writings of the parties do not otherwise establish a contract. In such case the terms of the particular contract consist of those terms on which the writings of the parties agree, together with any supplementary terms incorporated under any other provisions of this Act.

The parties disagree as to whether Section 2-207(2) or Section 2-207(3) applies. In Uniroyal, Inc., v. Chambers Gasket and Manufacturing Co., 177 Ind. App. 508, 380 N.E.2d 571 (1978), we addressed a strikingly similar issue. In that case, Chambers mailed a purchase order for gaskets to Uniroyal, specifying the quantity, price, and date for shipment. Uniroyal responded with an "Order Acknowledgment" stating in part, "Our Acceptance of the order is conditional on the Buyer's acceptance of the conditions of sale printed on the reverse side hereof. If buyer does not accept these conditions of sale, he shall notify seller in writing within seven (7) days after receipt of this acknowledgment." *Uniroyal*, 177 Ind. App. at 508, 380 N.E.2d at 573. Included in the conditions of sale was a limitation on damages. The gaskets were later determined to be defective, Chambers sought indemnification from Uniroyal, and the trial court entered summary judgment in favor of Chambers.

On appeal, we discussed the common law rules of contract formation and the UCC's modification of those rules:

> At common law, for an offer and an acceptance to constitute a contract, the acceptance must meet and correspond with the offer in every respect, neither falling within nor going beyond the terms proposed, but exactly meeting (those terms) at all points and closing with them just as they stand. An acceptance which varies the terms of the offer is considered a rejection and operates as a counter-offer, which may be accepted by the original offeror by performing without objection under the terms contained in the counter-offer.
>
> §2-207 was specifically designed to alter the common law "mirror-image" rule. The drafters recognized that in commercial practice, especially with the advent of printed forms, the terms of the "offer" and "acceptance" were seldom the same. They further recognized that the parties to a commercial transaction seldom were aware of the conflicting terms and conditions contained in the printed forms they exchanged. §2-207 was therefore designed to allow enforcement of an agreement despite discrepancies between offer and acceptance, if enforcement could be required without either party being bound to a material term to which he has not agreed.

Id. at 512, 380 N.E.2d at 575 (quotations and citations omitted).

Pursuant to Section 2-207, if a contract is formed under Section 2-207(1), the additional terms in the acceptance are considered proposals and become part of the contract unless Section 2-207(2) renders the proposed terms inoperative. "However, if an acceptance is expressly conditioned on the offeror's assent to the new terms, and no assent is forthcoming, the 'entire transaction aborts.'" Id. at 513, 380 N.E.2d at 575 (quoting Dorton v. Collins & Aikman Corp., 453 F.2d 1161, 1166 (6th Cir. 1972)). In other words, if an acceptance contains a clause conditioning the acceptance on assent to the additional or different terms, the writings do not form a contract. Id., 380 N.E.2d at 575. "Yet if the parties' conduct recognizes the existence of a contract by performance it is sufficient to establish a contract for sale." Id., 380 N.E.2d at 575. The terms of such a contract are those on which the writings of the parties agree, "together with any supplementary terms incorporated under any other provisions of this act."§2-207(3); see also *Uniroyal*, 177 Ind. App. at 513, 380 N.E.2d at 575.

We applied this framework in *Uniroyal* and rejected a line of cases suggesting Uniroyal's order acknowledgment was a counteroffer that Chambers accepted by taking the delivery of the goods and failing to object to the new terms. *Uniroyal*, 177 Ind. App. at 516-18, 380 N.E.2d at 577-78. We reasoned that such an application revives the "last-shot" doctrine under the common law "mirror-image" rule, the very rule that Section 2-207 was intended to avoid, by binding the offeror to additional terms upon the mere acceptance of goods. Id. at 517, 380 N.E.2d at 578. Further, we observed that the purpose of Section 2-207 would not be well-served by allowing an offeree's responsive document to state additional or different terms, and provide that the terms will be deemed accepted by the offeror's inaction, because Section 2-207 presumes that business people do not read exchanged preprinted forms and assumes that the offeror would not learn of such terms. Id., 380 N.E.2d at 578. We also reasoned:

> the clause placing the burden of affirmative objection on the original offeror is itself a modification of the offer to which the offeror should first have to assent, and absent its assent, any shipping and acceptance of the goods should be deemed to constitute the consummation of the contract under Section 2-207(3).

Id. 517-18, 380 N.E.2d at 578 (quotation and citation omitted).

We concluded that the writings exchanged by Chambers and Uniroyal did not create a contract but that the parties performed their contractual obligations so as to create a contract under Section 2-207(3). Id. at 518, 380 N.E.2d at 578; see also Continental Grain Co, v. Followell, 475 N.E.2d 318, 324 (Ind. Ct. App. 1985), trans. denied (applying Section 2-207 and *Uniroyal* to conclude that no contract was formed by the parties' writings or actions). Therefore, the terms of the contract consisted of the terms upon which the parties' writings agreed and the supplementary terms of the UCC. *Uniroyal*, 177 Ind. App. at 518, 380 N.E.2d at 578; see also §2-207(3).

As in *Uniroyal*, we agree here that Belden could not unilaterally include terms that were expressly conditional on AEC's assent. Thus, the parties' writings did not create a contract. Nevertheless, we conclude that the parties' actions were in recognition of the existence of a contract and were sufficient to establish a contract for the sale of wire. The terms of the contract are the written terms on which the parties agreed and the "supplementary terms incorporated under any other provisions of [the UCC]." §2-207(3).

The parties dispute, however, what supplementary terms are incorporated into their contract. The first question we must address is Belden's argument that the terms called for in Section 2-207(2) are included in the parties' contract based on Comment 6, which provides:

> If no answer is received within a reasonable time after additional terms are proposed, it is both fair and commercially sound to assume that their inclusion has been assented to. Where clauses on confirming forms sent by both parties conflict each party must be assumed to object to a clause of the other conflicting with one on the confirmation sent by himself. As a result the requirement that there be notice of objection which is found in subsection (2) is satisfied and the conflicting terms do not become a part of the contract. *The contract then consists of the terms originally expressly agreed to, terms on which the confirmations agree, and terms supplied by this Act, including subsection (2).* The written confirmation is also subject to Section 2-201. Under that section a failure to respond permits enforcement of a prior oral agreement; under this section a failure to respond permits additional terms to become part of the agreement.

§2-207 cmt. 6 (emphasis added).

Belden urges that, based on the emphasized language, we look to Section 2-207(2) to determine whether the terms in the order acknowledgment are included in the contract. Pursuant to Section 2-207(2), Belden contends that its additional terms became part of the contract unless they materially altered the contract—the only exclusionary provision of Section 2-207(2) that is relevant under these facts. Belden claims that the limitation on damages does not materially alter the contract.

We need not determine whether the limitation on damages is a material alteration because we believe that Belden's reading of Comment 6 is overbroad. As the Supreme Judicial Court of Massachusetts has observed, Comment 6 only applies where the terms conflict. Commerce & Industry Ins. Co. v. Bayer Corp., 433 Mass. 388, 742 N.E.2d 567, 573 (2001). Because only Belden's order acknowledgment contained a limitation on damages, there are no conflicting terms to implicate Comment 6. See id. Further:

> the criteria in [§2-207(2)] determine what "additional or different terms" will or will not be part of a contract that is formed by the exchange of writings. Where the writings do not form a contract, [§2-207(3)] states its own criteria—"those terms on which the writings agree" plus any terms that would be provided by other Code sections. One cannot turn to subsection (2) as another Code section that would supply a term when, by its express provisions, subsection (2) simply does not apply to the transaction.

Id. at 573-74; see also Coastal & Native Plant Specialties, Inc. v. Engineered Textile Prod., Inc., 139 F. Supp. 2d 1326, 1337 (N.D. Fla. 2001) ("[A] party cannot utilize section 2-207(2) to provide additional terms once a contract is formed pursuant to section 2-207(3).").

We agree with this reasoning. If we turned to Section 2-207(2) to determine the terms where the parties' writings did not create a contract, then Section 2-207(3) would be rendered meaningless. We will not do this. See City of Carmel v. Steele, 865 N.E.2d 612, 618 (Ind. 2007) ("To effectuate legislative intent, we read the sections of an act together in order that no part is rendered meaningless if it can be harmonized with the remainder of the statute."). Thus, we rely solely on Section 2-207(3) to determine what terms are included in the contract.

Belden also argues that the parties' course of dealing is a "supplementary term" to be included by Section 2-207(3). Belden contends that the parties' course of dealing acknowledges the limitation on damages and that it is therefore included as a term of the contract.

There is a split in authorities as to whether Section 2-207(3)'s reference to "supplementary terms" includes course of performance, course of dealing, and usage of trade as defined in Section 1-205 or just the standard "gap fillers" contained in the Article 2 of the UCC. Compare Coastal & Native Plant Specialties, 139 F. Supp. 2d at 1337 ("When a contract is formed pursuant to section 2-207(3), as here, the contract terms consist of the standard gap-filler provisions of the UCC as well as those sections relating to course of performance and course of dealing and usage of trade."), and Dresser Industries, Inc., Waukesha Engine Div. v. Gradall Co., 965

F.2d 1442, 1451 (7th Cir. 1992) (concluding that under the Wisconsin UCC, a court is not limited to the standardized gap-fillers of Article 2, but may utilize any terms arising under the entire UCC, including course of performance, course of dealing, and usage of trade), with C. Itoh & Co. (America) Inc. v. Jordan Int'l Co., 552 F.2d 1228, 1237 (7th Cir. 1977) ("Accordingly, we find that the 'supplementary terms' contemplated by Section 2-207(3) are limited to those supplied by the standardized 'gap-filler' provisions of Article Two."). For the sake of argument, we assume, without deciding, that the parties' course of dealing is in fact a supplementary term for purposes of Section 2-207(3).

Belden asserts that during the more than 100 transactions between the parties from 1998 to 2003, AEC never objected to the limitation on damages and, therefore, the parties' course of dealing incorporates the limitation on damages into the contract. AEC responds, "since it is undisputed that AEC never gave its express assent to Belden's terms in any prior transaction throughout the parties' fifteen-year relationship, Belden has not established a course of dealing between the parties as a matter of law." Appellee's Br. p. 27.

Pursuant to Section 1-205(1), "A course of dealing is a sequence of previous conduct between the parties to a particular transaction which is fairly to be regarded as establishing a common basis of understanding for interpreting their expressions and other conduct." Our research shows that most cases involving the repeated exchange of forms does not in and of itself establish a course of dealing between the parties that incorporates the terms of those forms into the parties' contract under Section 2-207(3). See Step-Saver Data Sys., Inc. v. Wyse Tech., 939 F.2d 91, 103-04 (3d Cir. 1991) ("While one court has concluded that terms repeated in a number of written confirmations eventually become part of the contract even though neither party ever takes any action with respect to the issue addressed by those terms, most courts have rejected such reasoning." (footnote omitted)); see also PCS Nitrogen Fertilizer, L.P. v. Christy Refractories, L.L.C., 225 F.3d 974, 982 (8th Cir. 2000) ("Moreover, the fact that Christy repeatedly sent its customer acknowledgment form to PCS does not establish a course of dealing; the multiple forms merely demonstrated Christy's desire to include the arbitration clause as a term of the contract.").

We agree with the reasoning set forth in *Step-Saver*:

> For two reasons, we hold that the repeated sending of a writing which contains certain standard terms, without any action with respect to the issues addressed by those terms, cannot constitute a course of dealing which would incorporate a term of the writing otherwise excluded under §2-207. First, the repeated exchange of forms by the parties only tells Step-Saver that TSL *desires* certain terms. Given TSL's failure to obtain Step-Saver's express assent to these terms before it will ship the program, Step-Saver can reasonably believe that, while TSL desires certain terms, it has agreed to do business on other terms—those terms expressly agreed upon by the parties. Thus, even though Step-Saver would not be surprised to learn that TSL desires the terms of the box-top license, Step-Saver might well be surprised to learn that the terms of the box-top license have been incorporated into the parties' agreement.
>
> Second, the seller in these multiple transaction cases will typically have the opportunity to negotiate the precise terms of the parties' agreement, as TSL sought to do

> in this case. The seller's unwillingness or inability to obtain a negotiated agreement reflecting its terms strongly suggests that, while the seller would like a court to incorporate its terms if a dispute were to arise, those terms are not a part of the parties' commercial bargain. For these reasons, we are not convinced that TSL's unilateral act of repeatedly sending copies of the box-top license with its product can establish a course of dealing between TSL and Step-Saver that resulted in the adoption of the terms of the box-top license.

Step-Saver, 939 F.2d at 104 (footnote omitted). Belden's repeated sending of the order acknowledgment containing the same limitation on damages and same requirement of assent by AEC does not in and of itself establish a course of dealing between the parties showing that the parties agreed to Belden's terms and conditions of sale. At best, it shows that Belden wanted AEC to assent to its terms and conditions, which AEC never did.

Belden also asserts that AEC's acceptance of a credit or refund in other instances of alleged non-conformity establishes the parties' course of dealing regarding damages. In other words, Belden argues that by forgoing consequential damages in the past, the parties have established a course of dealing in which AEC is precluded from seeking consequential damages for this alleged breach.

A course of dealing is limited to "previous conduct between the parties." §1-205(1). Thus, the parties' conduct after the October 2003 transaction is not relevant to establish their course of dealing for purposes of the October 2003 transaction. With this in mind, we refer to the five "material return notices" from AEC to Belden cited by Belden. These forms state the material being rejected, the reason for rejection, and AEC's request for a credit. Appellant's App. pp. 67-75.

These forms do not expressly establish that AEC has forfeited its right to seek additional damages. They simply show that AEC requested a credit for non-conforming wire. Further, that AEC did not previously claim lost profits or consequential damages does not conclusively show that AEC agreed to forgo such remedies in the future. Belden has not established a course of dealing in which AEC agreed to Belden's limitation on remedies as a matter of law.

In sum, we agree with the trial court's conclusion that Section 2-207(3) applies to this case and that Section 2-207(3), not Section 2-207(2), controls the terms of the parties' agreement. We also conclude that Section 1-205 does not establish a course of dealing in which AEC agreed to the limitation on damages. The trial court properly granted summary judgment in favor of AEC as to the issue of the applicability of Belden's limitation on damages.

While we are on the subject of §2-207(1), you should note one drafting glitch in that subsection. The subsection begins by saying that "[a] definite and seasonable expression of acceptance *or a written confirmation which is sent within a reasonable time* operates as an acceptance . . ." (emphasis added). It makes little sense to say that a confirmation can ever operate as an acceptance. A confirmation by definition presupposes that there has already been a valid offer and acceptance; otherwise, how could there be a preexisting contract to confirm? Presumably what the drafters meant here is that, for purposes of deciding how to treat additional or different terms that appear in a confirmation, §2-207 is the controlling section. That, in turn, leads us to §2-207(2).

Each of the subsections of §2-207 plays a specific role. As we just explored, §2-207(1) determines when a writing with different terms nevertheless constitutes an acceptance. The purpose of §2-207(2) is to tell us what to do with new terms in the acceptance. UCC §2-207(3), which we will consider shortly, covers the situation in which the buyer and seller act as if there is a contract even though the purported written acceptance does not qualify as a valid written acceptance under §2-207(1).

Now let us see how §2-207(2) operates in practice. To consider again our example of the copy machine sale, suppose that the seller sends the acknowledgement form with the arbitration clause and the "no implied warranties" clause, and then ships the machines. The buyer accepts the machines and begins using them. At some later point, the buyer has complaints about the performance of the machines. Both buyer and seller need to know at this point whether seller has made any implied warranties and whether buyer must bring its complaints to arbitration.

Just like §2-207(1), §2-207(2) suffers from drafting problems. By its terms, §2-207(2) purports to cover only "additional" terms in the acceptance. Official Comment 3 to 2-207, however, says that "[w]hether or not additional or different terms will become part of the agreement depends upon the provisions of subsection (2)" (emphasis added). The arbitration clause, as an "additional" term, is clearly covered by §2-207(2). Such additional terms, we are told, are "mere proposals" except that between merchants these additional terms will automatically become part of the contract unless: (1) the offer has clearly limited acceptance to the terms of the offer, (2) the additional terms amount to a material alteration of the offer, or (3) the offeror has objected in advance to the additional terms or objects to them within a reasonable time.

There is a lot of litigation about which additional terms do or do not amount to material alterations of an offer. The various examples of material and non-material additional terms that are provided in Official Comments 4 and 5 to §2-207 have not been very successful in clarifying the issue. Ultimately, much will depend on whether the additional term is common in the buyer's and seller's industry. The arbitration clause in the copy machine seller's form, for example, might or might not amount to a material alteration of the buyer's purchase order depending on whether arbitration is a common mode of dispute resolution in that industry.

The treatment of different terms is perhaps even more of a mess than the treatment of additional terms. If you believe what Comment 3 says, as some courts do, then different terms as well as additional terms are handled by §2-207(2). If that is true, however, then the different terms in an acceptance should never become part of the contract. This is because the mere fact of their being contrary to a particular term in the offer should mean that the offeror has in effect objected to them in advance.

Most courts handle different terms using what has been called the "knock-out rule," which has no particular statutory basis but which apparently strikes the majority of courts as the proper result. Under the knockout rule, the court will "knock out" the different terms and use the UCC to fill the gap left by the knocked-out terms. In our copy machine sale, you may recall, our buyer's form said "implied warranties" and our seller's form said "no implied warranties." Under the knockout approach, both terms would drop out and the UCC gap filler—that there are implied warranties—would fill the gap. Thus, in that case, the gap filler would end up giving the buyer what the buyer wanted: implied warranties.

The final subsection of §2-207, subdivision (3), covers a situation just like we saw in the *Belden* case: Suppose that our copy machine buyer's purchase order had said something like "seller must accept all of the terms of this offer or there will be no contract." Imagine also that seller's acknowledgement form, besides including additional and different terms, also included the conspicuous statement that "this acceptance is expressly made conditional on buyer's assent to the additional or different terms contained herein."

Suppose that, despite these terms, the seller shipped the machines and the buyer accepted them. Imagine that a few months following the sale, the buyer began having trouble with the machines and wanted to sue the seller on a breach-of-implied-warranty theory. The buyer now needs to know whether there is an implied warranty and whether the warranty claim needs to be brought to arbitration.

This is where §2-207(3) comes in. Where, as in this case, the purported acceptance cannot qualify as a true acceptance even under the liberal standards of §2-207(1), then there is no contract by the exchange of writings. Even where the writings get "kicked out" of §2-207(1), there may nevertheless be conduct by both parties that, in the words of §2-207(3), "recognizes the existence of a contract." In this case, there would seem to be such conduct: seller shipped the machines, and buyer accepted them and paid for them. Thus, §2-207(3) would conclude that there is a contract here "although the writings of the parties do not otherwise establish a contract."

In the §2-207(3) case of a contract by "conduct only," we end up with a rule that virtually replicates the judicially created "knockout rule" for different terms under §2-207(2): Use the terms on which the writings agree, and add to them the UCC gap fillers for the terms on which the writings do not agree. The only way that §2-207(3)'s statutory knockout rule differs from the judicially created knockout rule for §2-207(2) is in its treatment of additional terms: the §2-207(3) rule "knocks out" additional terms, whereas under §2-207(2) additional terms between merchants will become part of the contract unless one of the three exceptions in §2-207(2) applies.

Thus, in our copy machine sale, under §2-207(3) the buyer comes out looking like a winner with respect to both the additional term and the different term: the seller's arbitration clause gets tossed out, and as to implied warranties, the UCC gap filler says that they will exist.

On the subject of §2-207(3), there is a very common conceptual mistake that you should seek to avoid. Where the two parties have exchanged forms and then have proceeded to perform the contract, you should not immediately jump to §2-207(3) to determine the contract's terms. There is a clear temptation to do so: you know that there is sufficient conduct to create a contract, and besides, you think to yourself, wouldn't it be great to avoid altogether having to contend with §2-207(1) and (2)?

Yet the language of §2-207(3) is clear that you should apply that section only when "the writings of the parties do not otherwise establish a contract." This means that to get to §2-207(3), you must first decide either that the purported acceptance was not a "definite and seasonable expression of acceptance" or that the acceptance was "expressly made conditional on assent to the additional or different terms." Otherwise, you do have a contract by the writings and you must determine its terms under §2-207(2) rather than §2-207(3).

As of August 2015, all states except for Illinois, New York, and Washington had adopted the Uniform Electronic Transactions Act (UETA). The contract formation rules of UETA recognize the formation of sales contracts by the interaction of electronic agents of the parties or by the interaction of an electronic agent and an individual acting on the individual's own behalf or for another person. Thus, for example, the fact that an individual buyer makes its contract by interacting with a website does not make the contract any less binding on either side than if the buyer had interacted directly with an individual seller.

In addition, at the federal level the Electronic Signatures in Global and National Commerce Act ("E-Sign") was signed into law on June 30, 2000. Much like UETA, the federal E-Sign law provides that signatures or contracts are not to be denied legal effect merely because they are in electronic form. Thus, electronic signatures should continue to grow in popularity as a means for effecting contract formation under Article 2 of the UCC. Keep in mind, however, that neither UETA nor E-Sign requires a party to agree to use or accept an electronic signature. The two statutes simply make it clear that parties to a contract can choose to proceed by electronic means if they so desire.

An increasing number of merchants have begun transacting their open account sales with a system known as Electronic Data Interchange (EDI). The EDI system transmits the standard purchase order/invoice information by use of electronic mail. In at least some cases a buyer or seller's decision to use EDI with a particular customer also provides an occasion to actually sit down and work out the terms and conditions of the sale with that customer. In some industries, the hard work of creating standard terms that are fair to both buyers and sellers has been accomplished by industry trade associations that include both buyer and seller representation.

Standard EDI forms have been created thus far for grocers, for warehouses, and for general merchandise transactions. By use of these standard forms, the buyer needs merely to fill in certain blanks in the form that are peculiar to the buyer's specific order: the parties, the merchandise, the quantity, the price, and the delivery terms. As noted above, these standard forms will be the product of negotiating between industry representatives for both buyers and sellers. From the buyer's perspective, they will not be as favorable as the buyer's standard purchase order; from the seller's perspective, they will not be as favorable as the seller's standard acknowledgement form.

One obvious business advantage of EDI is that it reduces costs by eliminating the need for the sending and storage of the paper documentation that accompanies traditional open-account transactions. A second clear advantage to EDI is speed: the buyer's purchase order on EDI can be transmitted to the seller in a matter of moments instead of hours or days. Yet these advantages of EDI can be captured even without sitting down and working out all of the terms and conditions of a particular sale. In industries where there are no standard EDI terms and conditions, parties can still get the benefits of EDI without agreeing on terms and conditions.

Several of the buyers and sellers that were interviewed for this book indicated that they use EDI to transact business with certain customers even though they have not worked out the terms and conditions of the sale with those customers. Before conducting sales by EDI, a buyer and seller will enter into what is known as an EDI "trading partner agreement." That agreement might include negotiated terms and conditions, or it might simply beg the question by indicating both that "buyer's standard terms and conditions will govern" and that "seller's standard terms and conditions govern," even though both parties know full well that those terms and conditions are quite inconsistent with one another.

While an EDI trading agreement might provide the impetus for a buyer and seller to negotiate terms and conditions, the use of EDI is neither a necessary nor a sufficient condition to resolving the battle of the forms. Buyers and sellers who are involved in either a large single transaction or a long-term series of sales may well conclude that it is worth the sunk cost to work out all of the terms and conditions of their deal. Yet parties can and sometimes do make this investment of time even in cases where no EDI is involved. On the other hand, as noted above, parties that want the time- and paper-saving efficiencies of EDI can capture those even when they decide it is not in their interests to negotiate all of the terms and conditions of sale.

In the final analysis, there may be no "solution" to the battle of forms. Rather, the decision of buyers and sellers not to sit down and negotiate all of the terms and conditions of a particular sale may well be the most economically rational course to take, even though there will be a small percentage of these deals where, in hindsight, this failure will prove costly and time-consuming.

Problem Set 3

3.1.   a. Suppose that in the *Gateway 2000* case at the beginning of this assignment, the terms and conditions that the Hills failed to read closely also included the following: (1) that the buyers agreed not to use any other printer with the computer except a special Gateway printer (whether or not any other printers were actually compatible), (2) that the seller was not responsible for any consequential damages suffered by the buyers from defects in the computer, and (3) that the buyers' only remedy for any defects in the computer is that buyers would receive a special Gateway baseball cap for their troubles. Would these clauses be just as enforceable against the buyers as the arbitration clause? UCC §§2-206, 2-204, 2-207; Official Comment 1 to §2-207; Official Comment 1 to §2-719.

b. Suppose that in *Gateway 2000,* following the phone conversation in which the Hills placed their order (and in which the seller promised to send the computer), the seller called the Hills back a week later and said, "We've decided that we cannot sell the computer to you at the price you ordered it; you must agree to pay 10 percent more than that or we won't ship it." Would the seller be able to enforce such a condition on the sale?

3.2.   a. Your law firm took on a new client last month, an exercise equipment manufacturer called Heavy Metal, Inc. You were assigned to meet with Heavy Metal's president, Arlene Ledger, to discuss her various legal concerns about certain sales by this company, which she founded herself. Arlene's first concern relates to a major order of stair climber machines that her company filled last month for Fit for Life, a national health club chain.

Fit for Life's purchase order, which Arlene had not read until recently, indicated that "seller will be liable for all remedies available under the UCC." Heavy Metal's acknowledgement form, by contrast, disclaimed in boldface language all consequential damages. One other thing troubled Arlene about this transaction: she had meant to send the acknowledgement form before shipping the stair climbers, but instead she had shipped the machines and only later did she send the acknowledgement form. Arlene said that she is extremely worried about having all those stair climbers out there for which her company might be liable for unlimited consequential damages. Are Arlene's fears well grounded? UCC §§2-204, 2-206, 2-207.

b. Same facts as part (a), except that instead of shipping the stair climbers that were requested in Fit for Life's purchase order, Heavy Metal ships an order of super-incline treadmills to Fit for Life but never sends an acknowledgement form. "We were out of stair climbers, but I felt like these treadmills would probably work for them instead," reasoned Arlene. Arlene did not warn Fit for Life in advance about the change in product. When Fit for Life receives the treadmills, is there an enforceable contract? If so, on whose terms? UCC §§2-204, 2-206, 2-207.

c. Same facts as part (a), except that Heavy Metal neither ships the goods nor sends an acknowledgement form for three months, because the original purchase order got lost on Arlene's desk. When Arlene finds it three months later, she sends an acknowledgement form in response by overnight mail. When Fit for Life receives the belated acknowledgement form, is there an enforceable contract? UCC §§2-204, 2-206, 2-207.

d. Same facts as part (a), except that Fit for Life's purchase order includes a clause within that form's boilerplate language that says, "This purchase order can only be accepted by an acknowledgement form that agrees with all of the terms contained in this purchase order. If the acknowledgment form varies in any way from the terms of this purchase order, then there is no contract." If Heavy Metal has not yet sent the stair climbers and responds to this purchase order with its standard acknowledgement form, is there an enforceable contract? UCC §§2-204, 2-206, 2-207.

3.3. a. Another recent situation that Arlene wants to ask about relates to a purchase order the company just received from Sportlife, a regional sporting goods chain, to buy a dozen 580XL circuit trainer weight machines for current shipment. In this case, Arlene said, immediately after receiving the purchase order she did send Sportlife an acknowledgement form *before* shipping the machines. In fact, although she sent the acknowledgement, she still has not shipped the machines to Sportlife. What bothers Arlene about this order is that she had a phone conversation yesterday with a friend in the industry, who strongly advised Arlene not to do business with Sportlife. "They're more trouble than they're worth," her friend had told her. "They make your life miserable by complaining about problems with the orders that don't even exist."

Arlene wants to know whether it is too late to get out of this contract. In looking at the purchase order and the acknowledgement form, you notice that Heavy Metal's acknowledgement form requires that all disputes be brought to binding arbitration. The purchase order says nothing about the mode of dispute resolution. Can Arlene still avoid this deal? UCC §§2-204, 2-206, 2-207. Could she have avoided it under the common law?

b. Same facts as part (a), except that Heavy Metal's acknowledgement form purports to accept Sportlife's offer to buy a dozen Lifecycle stationary bikes rather than a dozen 580XL circuit trainer weight machines. Prior to shipment by Heavy Metal, is there a contract at all? UCC §§2-204, 2-206, 2-207.

c. Same facts as part (a), except that Heavy Metal's acknowledgement form also says. "THIS ACCEPTANCE IS EXPRESSLY MADE CONDITIONAL ON BUYER'S ASSENT TO ANY ADDITIONAL OR DIFFERENT TERMS CONTAINED IN THIS FORM." Prior to shipment of the goods, can Arlene still avoid this deal? UCC §§2-204, 2-206, 2-207.

d. Same facts as part (a), except that Heavy Metal's acknowledgement form also says, "THIS ACCEPTANCE IS EXPRESSLY MADE CONDITIONAL ON BUYER'S ASSENT TO ANY ADDITIONAL OR DIFFERENT TERMS CONTAINED IN THIS FORM," and Arlene has both shipped the goods and accepted payment for them. Now is there a contract? If so, will disputes be subject to arbitration? UCC §§2-204, 2-206, 2-207. What would the answers to those two questions be under the common law?

3.4. a. The next problem Arlene wants to talk about stems from her company's sale of an industrial-level weight machine to a local Gold's Gym franchise. It turns out that one of the cables on the machine broke during use and severely injured one of the Gold's Gym patrons. The Gold's Gym manager called Arlene last week and told her that if his patron sued the gym, Gold's Gym would make Heavy Metal responsible for all of the damages.

This transaction involved a purchase order from Gold's, an acknowledgement form from Heavy Metal, and then shipment of the machine from Heavy Metal to Gold's. Gold's purchase order specifically reserved all of its remedies and mentioned nothing about the mode of dispute resolution. Heavy Metal's acknowledgement form had a conspicuous disclaimer of consequential damages and a provision that all disputes would be subject to binding arbitration (but no "expressly made conditional" language). Is there a contract at all? Will the consequential damages disclaimer hold? Will disputes be subject to arbitration? UCC §§2-204, 2-206, 2-207.

b. Same facts as part (a), except suppose that Heavy Metal has sold various weight machines to this Gold's Gym franchise during the past several months, with each side always using the same forms. Imagine that when this relationship between buyer and seller began, the manager of the Gold's franchise actually read Heavy Metal's acknowledgement form. At that time, he noticed the arbitration clause, called Arlene, and told her that he didn't like the arbitration clause in her form. Arlene replied, "Take it or leave it." The Gold's manager said, "Well, I guess so." Now Arlene wants to cite that one-time conversation to make the following argument: as far as the arbitration clause goes, this isn't a §2-207 case at all, since the buyer in fact specifically assented to this additional term on Arlene's acknowledgement form. Will this argument work for Arlene?

c. Same facts as part (a), except that this transaction had begun with an oral contract between Arlene and the Gold's manager. The terms of the oral contract included the fact that Heavy Metal would not be responsible for consequential damages. Following the oral contract, Gold's sent Arlene a written confirmation. That confirmation stated the terms of the oral contract, including type of machine and price, but it said that the seller *would* be responsible for consequential damages. Further, the confirmation said, "THIS ACCEPTANCE IS EXPRESSLY MADE CONDITIONAL ON SELLER'S ASSENT TO THE ADDITIONAL OR DIFFERENT TERMS CONTAINED IN THE CONFIRMATION." Unlike in part (a), there has been no performance yet by either side. Arlene comes to you and says that she wants to enforce the oral contract, but only if she is not responsible for consequential damages. (1) What effect, if any, should be given to the "expressly made conditional" clause contained in the confirmation? UCC §§2-204, 2-206, 2-207. (2) At this point, can Arlene enforce the sale according to the terms of the oral contract (i.e., no consequential damages)? UCC §§2-204, 2-206, 2-207. (3) What if Gold's confirmation had included not only a different term (seller's responsibility for consequential damages), but also an additional term (e.g., "delivery must take place on a Thursday")? Would the additional term become part of the contract? UCC §§2-204, 2-206, 2-207.

3.5.   Arlene tells you that she is tired of talking about mistakes she may have made in the past. She now wants to know how she can avoid problems in the future. In particular, she wants to know if there is something else she should include in her form or if there is some procedure she should follow to ensure that her "exclusion of consequential damages" clause becomes a valid term of every sale that she makes. Do you have any suggestions for her? UCC §§2-204, 2-206, 2-207.

Assignment 4: Formation with Leases, International Sales, and Real Estate

A. Formation of Contracts for Leases

The difference between the formation provisions of UCC Article 2 and those of Article 2A reflects the difference in practice between how sales are formed, on one hand, and how leases are formed, on the other. For one thing, commercial leases will rarely be created through the exchange of forms, in contrast to the case of a merchant-to-merchant sale of goods on open account. Any large commercial lease will likely be the product of a negotiated contract. Because of the lessor's residual interest, it will typically make sense for the two sides to sit down and work out all of the terms and conditions of the lease in advance of entering into the lease. The most important consequence of this difference is that Article 2A has no "battle of the forms" section or even anything that looks remotely like UCC §2-207.

Although the Article 2A drafters did not feel compelled to create a lease analogue to §2-207, they did borrow liberally (and literally, in some cases) from the sales formation rules of §§2-204, 2-205, and 2-206. UCC §§2A-204 and 2A-205 directly steal from their Article 2 cousins, aside from plugging in the phrase "lease contract" where the phrase "sales contract" appears in Article 2. Thus, in §2A-204 the general formation rules for leases have the same flexible principles that guide formation for sales: lease contracts may be formed in any manner that shows agreement; we do not need to know exactly when a lease contract is formed in order to conclude that it has been formed; and the only substantive detail needed in a lease contract is "a reasonably certain basis for giving an appropriate remedy." UCC §2A-205 creates for leases the same limited exception to the common law unenforceability of firm offers without consideration as is found in §2-205.

UCC §2A-206 represents a modest reworking of §2-206. The lease version of the offer and acceptance section contains the same proviso that unless otherwise clearly indicated, an offer to make a lease should be construed as inviting acceptance "in any manner and by any medium reasonable in the circumstances." What is missing from §2A-206 are the parts of §2-206 that refer to purchase orders and shipment. Just like the absence of a clone to §2-207, the absence in Article 2A of the §2-206 shipping provisions is a translation of

Article 2 that, in the words of the Official Comment to §2A-206, "reflect[s] leasing practices and terminology."

B. Formation of Contracts for International Sales

Whereas Article 2A of the UCC did not include §2-207 because leasing formation practices make those issues largely irrelevant, the CISG drafters did not include the rules of §2-207 because they must not have agreed with them. In international sales, just as in domestic sales, there will often be purchase orders and acknowledgement forms. And sometimes these forms will have terms that do not agree.

The way the CISG handles the "battle of the forms" is something of a cross between UCC §2-207 and the common law "mirror image" rule. On one hand, CISG Article 19(1) says that purported acceptances that contain additions or modifications are not acceptances, but are instead counteroffers. That sounds like the common law mirror-image rule. On the other hand, Article 19(2) says that purported acceptances that contain additional or different terms *do* count as valid acceptances as long as the new terms are not material alterations and the offeror does not object to the discrepancy "without undue delay." That sounds a lot like UCC §2-207(1). Yet the CISG's definition of what constitutes a material alteration is fairly broad: any additional or different terms "relating among other things, to the price, payment, quality and quantity of the goods, place and time of delivery, extent of one party's liability to the other or the settlement of disputes." CISG Art. 19(3).

There are a number of significant differences between UCC §2-207 and CISG Article 19. The first is that §2-207 will clearly allow an acceptance that contains even material alterations of the offer. Second, there is nothing in Article 19 that is quite analogous to the offeree's ability in §2-207(1) to make its acceptance "expressly . . . conditional on assent to the additional or different terms."

Finally, Article 19 does not contain an analogue to §2-207(3) that tells us exactly what happens when a purported acceptance that *does* contain materially different terms is not objected to and then is followed by conduct by both sides that indicates a contract. The apparent result under the CISG in such a scenario would be a return to the common law's "last-shot" doctrine, by which the party who sent the last form would see its terms control as long as buyer and seller both proceeded to act as if there were a contract. Under CISG Article 19(1), the purported acceptance with the materially different terms will be a counteroffer. Under CISG Article 18(1), the original offeror's proceeding to perform under the contract would constitute conduct by which the original offeror will be deemed to have accepted the "counteroffer."

The following is one of the few reported cases so far that has had to deal with the "battle of the forms" in an international context.

Roser Technologies, Inc. v. Carl Schreiber

2013 WL 4852314 (W.D. Pa. 2013)

Schwab, J.

I.   INTRODUCTION

This is a breach of contract action involving a contract for the manufacture and sale of copper molding plates. Plaintiff Roser Technologies, Inc. ("RTI") alleges that Defendant Carl Schreiber GmbH d/b/a CSN Metals ("CSN") breached its supply contract when CSN insisted that RTI expedite payment or secure a letter of credit. CSN filed a Second Amended Counterclaim alleging that RTI breached the contract by repudiation.

RTI filed a Motion for Judgment on the Pleadings with respect to CSN's breach of contract counterclaim. CSN filed a Cross-Motion for Judgment on the Pleadings with respect to its breach of contract claim and with respect to the original RTI Complaint, which asserted a claim for breach of contract. After careful consideration of the Cross-Motions for Judgment on the Pleadings, Briefs in support thereof, Briefs in opposition, and Replies, RTI's Motion for Judgment on the Pleadings will be DENIED, and CSN's Cross-Motion for Judgment on the Pleadings will be GRANTED.

II.   FACTUAL BACKGROUND

This case revolves around two exchanges of documents for the manufacture and sale of copper mold plates. The first document exchange began on May 11, 2011, when CSN provided quotation 714257 to RTI. On August 9, 2011, RTI sent purchase order 6676, which was "per CSN quote 714257," to CSN. On October 8, 2011, CSN sent order confirmation 17507 to RTI. The order confirmation listed RTI's order number as 6676.

The second document exchange began on August 11, 2011, when CSN provided quotation 714576 to RTI. On August 23, 2011, RTI sent purchase order 6761, which was "per CSN quote 414576," to CSN. On August 25, 2011, CSN sent order confirmation 17579 to RTI, which listed the order number as "6761."

The first page of CSN quotations 714257 and 714576 included the following language, "According to our standard conditions of sale to be found under www.csnmetals.de, we have pleasure in quoting without engagement as follows[.]" The second page of both quotations included the following language, "If we have offered a payment target, a sufficient coverage by our credit insurance company is assumed. In case this cannot obtained we have to ask for equivalent guarantees or payment in advance."

The first page of CSN order confirmations 17507 and 17579 stated, "We thank you for your purchase order. This order confirmation is subject to our standard conditions of sale as known (www.csnmetals.de)." CSN's standard conditions of sale provide, among other things, that "supplies and benefits shall exclusively be governed by German law. The application of laws on international sales of moveable objects and on international purchase contracts on moveable objects is excluded."

On October 4, 2011, CSN emailed RTI. CSN informed RTI that "Cofoaca USA cut the credit line complete." CSN informed RTI that "the best options are to change into 'payment in advance' or L/C (letter of credit)." On October 17, 2011, CSN emailed RTI offering a third option: "[I]n order to minimize our risk we can also offer you to change the delivery to partial shipments. The second shipment would leave as soon as the payment for the first shipment has been transferred to us etc." RTI sent CSN a letter dated October 24, 2011, advising that because of CSN's refusal to perform, RTI would procure the requested copper from an alternate supplier. . . .

IV.   DISCUSSION

A.   CHOICE-OF-LAW

1.   Applicable Standard

For the reasons discussed infra, this Court has jurisdiction pursuant to 28 U.S.C. §§1331 and 1332. The Court must apply the choice-of-law rules of the forum state, Pennsylvania. Totalplan Corp. of Am. v. Colborne, 14 F.3d 824, 832 (2d Cir. 1994) (citing Klaxon Co. v. Stentor Elec. Mfg. Co., Inc., 313 U.S. 487, 488, 61 S. Ct. 1020, 85 L. Ed. 1477 (1941)). "Pennsylvania applies the flexible, interests/ contacts methodology to contract choice-of-law questions." Pac. Employers Ins. Co. v. Global Reinsurance Corp. of Am., 693 F.3d 417, 432 (3d Cir. 2012) (internal quotation marks and ellipsis omitted) (quoting Hammersmith v. TIG Ins. Co., 480 F.3d 220, 226-27 (3d Cir. 2007)).

"The first step in the analysis is to identify the . . . laws [that] might apply." Id. The parties agree that the choice is between the Uniform Commercial Code ("UCC"), and the United Nations Convention for the International Sale of Goods ("CISG"). Next, the Court must "determine whether or not an actual conflict exists. . . . That is done by examining the substance of the potentially applicable laws to determine whether there is distinction between them." Maniscalco v. Bro. Int'l (USA) Corp., 709 F.3d 202, 206 (3d Cir. 2013) (internal quotation marks and citations omitted).

The main issue before the Court is which, if any, of CSN's standard conditions are included as part of the contracts that are the subject of this litigation. RTI argues that there is no choice-of-law issue because the UCC and CISG do not differ with respect to the issue before the Court. Doc. No. 41, 12 n.1. CSN argues that there is a difference and that the CISG applies. Doc. No. 45, 13-15. Thus, the Court will discuss the approaches of the UCC and the CISG with respect to this situation, commonly referred to as a battle of the forms, to determine if there is a conflict that needs to be resolved.

2. Uniform Commercial Code

"The UCC addresses the sad fact that many sales contracts are not fully bargained, not carefully drafted, and not understandingly signed by both parties. In these cases, [the Court] appl[ies] UCC section 2-207 to ascertain the terms of an agreement." Standard Bent Glass Corp. v. Glassrobots Oy, 333 F.3d 440, 444 (3d Cir. 2003) (ellipsis, internal quotation marks, and citations omitted). In circumstances such as the case at bar, under the UCC,

> [t]he parties'[ ] performance demonstrates the existence of a contract. The dispute is, therefore, not over the existence of a contract, but the nature of its terms. When the parties'[ ] conduct establishes a contract, but the parties have failed to adopt expressly a particular writing as the terms of their agreement, and the writings exchanged by the parties do not agree, UCC §2-207 determines the terms of the contract.

Step-Saver Data Sys., Inc. v. Wyse Tech., 939 F.2d 91, 98 (3d Cir. 1991).

In this case, the standard conditions that CSN seeks to have included as part of the contract are merely referenced in the documents that were exchanged. Under the UCC, a provision will not be incorporated by reference if it would result in surprise or hardship to the party against whom enforcement is sought." *Standard Bent Glass*, 333 F.3d at 448. Furthermore, "[u]nder UCC section 2-207(2)(b), absent objection, additional terms become part of the contract unless they materially alter it. A material alteration is one that would result in surprise or hardship if incorporated without express awareness by the other party." Id. at 448 n.12 (internal quotation marks and citation omitted). Thus, under the UCC, whether the standard conditions are incorporated into the contract between the parties depends upon whether incorporation would result in surprise or hardship to RTI.

3. Convention for the International Sale of Goods

a. Additional Terms

Additional terms are governed by Article 19 of the CISG, which provides that:

> (1) A reply to an offer which purports to be an acceptance but contains additions, limitations or other modifications is a rejection of the offer and constitutes a counter-offer.

(2) However, a reply to an offer which purports to be an acceptance but contains additional or different terms which do not materially alter the terms of the offer constitutes an acceptance, unless the offeror, without undue delay, objects orally to the discrepancy or dispatches a notice to that effect. If he does not so object, the terms of the contract are the terms of the offer with the modifications contained in the acceptance.

(3) Additional or different terms relating, among other things, to the price, payment, quality and quantity of the goods, place and time of delivery, extent of one party's liability to the other or the settlement of disputes are considered to alter the terms of the offer materially.

i.   American Court Decisions

Few American courts, either state or federal, have interpreted Article 19. In Claudia v. Olivieri Footwear Ltd., 1998 WL 164824 (S.D.N.Y. Apr.7, 1998), the United States District Court for the Southern District of New York held that Article 19 embodies the mirror image rule. Id. at *7 n.6 (citing Larry A. Dimatteo, *An International Contract Law Formula: The Informality of International Business Transactions Plus the Internationalization of Contract Law Equals Unexpected Contractual Liability*, 23 Syracuse J. Int'l L. & Com. 67, 108 (1997); Legal Analysis of the United Nations Convention on Contracts for the International Sale of Goods, (1980), commentary on Article 19). In Travelers Prop. Cas. Co. of Am. v. Saint-Gobain Technical Fabrics Canada Ltd., 474 F. Supp. 2d 1075 (D. Minn. 2007), the United States District Court for the District of Minnesota noted that "Article 19 embodies a mirror image rule." Id. at 1082. Likewise, the United States District Court for the Southern District of Ohio has stated that "the CISG applies the common law concept of mirror image." Miami Valley Paper, LLC v. Lebbing Eng'g & Consulting Gmbh, 2009 WL 818618, *4 (S.D. Ohio Mar. 26, 2009); see also CSS Antenna, Inc. v. Amp hen ol-Tuchel Elecs., GmbH, 764 F. Supp. 2d 745, 752-53 (D. Md. 2011) (applying Article 19 in a fashion consistent with the mirror image rule).

ii.   Other Authorities

"When [American Courts] interpret treaties, [they] consider the interpretations of the courts of other nations." Negusie v. Holder, 555 U.S. 511, 537, 129 S. Ct. 1159, 173 L. Ed. 2d 20 (2009) (Stevens, J. concurring in part and dissenting in part) (citing Zicherman v. Korean Air Lines Co., 516 U.S. 217, 226-28, 116 S. Ct. 629, 133 L. Ed. 2d 596, (1996)). German Courts have interpreted Article 19 as embodying a mirror image rule. See Bundesgerichtshof [BGH] [Federal Supreme Court] Jan. 9, 2002 (Powdered milk case), 2002 BGH Report 265, English translation available at http://www.cisg. law.pace.edu/cisg/wais/db/cases2/020109gl.html (last accessed Sept. 10, 2013); Oberlandesgericht [OLG] [Appellate Court Frankfurt am Main] June 26, 2006 (Printed goods case), English translation available at http:// cisgw3. law.pace.edu/cases/060626gl.html (last accessed Sept. 10, 2013) (noting that "the silence of [Buyer] to [Seller]'s order confirmations is not to be considered as an affirmation of [Seller's standard terms referred to."); Amtsgericht Kehl [AG Kehl] [Petty District Court] Oct. 6, 1995 (Knitware case), English translation available at http://cisgw3.law.pace.edu/cases/951006gl.html (last accessed Sept. 10, 2013)

("Assuming that [seller] had sent its General Conditions to the [buyer], this would have constituted a counteroffer in the sense of CISG Article 19(1).").

Finally, it is appropriate to consider commentaries when interpreting treaties. Cf. United States v. Alvarez-Machain, 504 U.S. 655, 659, 112 S. Ct. 2188, 119 L. Ed. 2d 441 (1992) (discussing Justice Miller's examination of commentary regarding the interpretation of a treaty). Commentators have noted that Article 19 is an embodiment of the mirror image rule. Anelize Slomp Aguiar, *The Law Applicable to International Trade Transactions with Brazilian Parties: A Comparative Study of the Brazilian Law, the CISG, and the American Law About Contract Formation*, 17 Law & Business Review of the Americas 487, 527 (2011) ("the CISG in fact adopts the old common law 'Mirror Image Rule'"); Ernest E. Smith & Owen L. Anderson, *Oil and Gas Marketing in Latin America*, Rocky Mountain Mineral Law Special Institute (1994) ("the CISG essentially adopts the 'mirror image' rule").

Thus, with respect to the battle of the forms, the determinative factor under the CISG is when the contract was formed. The terms of the contract are those embodied in the last offer (or counteroffer) made prior to a contract being formed. Once the contents of the original contract are determined, both parties must affirmatively assent to any amendment to the terms of the contract for such amendment to become part of the contract. See Chateau des Charmes Wines Ltd. v. Sabate USA Inc., 328 F.3d 528, 531 (9th Cir. 2003). Furthermore, standard conditions are only incorporated into an offer if the other party had proper notice.

"[N]o provision of the [CISG] creates such diametrical opposition to the [UCC] rule as does Article 19 in its clear adoption of the 'mirror image' rule. . . ." Ronald A. Brand, *Fundamentals of International Business Transactions: Volume I*, 75 (2013). Under the UCC, standard conditions in an acceptance that materially alter the terms of the agreement are disregarded. Under the CISG, an acceptance with different standard conditions is not actually an acceptance, but rather is a rejection and counteroffer.

b.   Incorporation of Standard Conditions

i.   American Court Decisions

The United States District Court for the District of Maryland addressed the incorporation of standard conditions in CSS Antenna. The Court considered the fact that there was "no evidence on the record to show that [buyer] had actual knowledge of [seller's] General Conditions." *CSS Antenna*, 764 F. Supp. 2d at 754. The Court also considered that the parties had never previously discussed the standard conditions in negotiations as weighing heavily against inclusions of the general conditions in the contract. Id.

Former Chief Judge Lancaster also addressed the incorporation of standard conditions under the CISG in Tyco Valves & Controls Distribution GmbH v. Tippins, Inc., 2006 WL 2924814 (W.D. Pa. Oct.10, 2006). He found factors to be considered when determining if standard conditions have been properly incorporated include whether the other party actually received the standard conditions and whether there is evidence that the other party read the standard conditions (such as initials next to the standard conditions). Id. at *5.

ii.   Other Authorities

Under the CISG, "[i]t is . . . required that the recipient of a contract offer that is supposed to be based on general terms and conditions have the possibility to become aware of them in a reasonable manner." Bundesgerichtshof [BGH] [Federal Supreme Court] Oct. 31, 2001 (Machinery case), 2001 BGHZ No. 149, English translation available at http://www.cisg.law.pace.edu/cisg/wais/db/cases2/011031gl.html (last accessed Sept. 10, 2013). As the German Supreme Court stated:

> [I]t is easily possible to attach to his offer the general terms and conditions, which generally favor him. It would, therefore, contradict the principle of good faith in international trade as well as the general obligations of cooperation and information of the parties to impose on the other party an obligation to inquire concerning the clauses that have not been transmitted and to burden him with the risks and disadvantages of the unknown general terms and conditions of the other party.

Id. (internal citations omitted).

In other words, "[i]t is accepted by legal practice that the other party must have the possibility to easily take note of the General Terms and Conditions." Oberlandesgericht [OLG] [Appellate Court Dusseldorf] Apr. 21, 2004 (Mobile car phones case), English translation available at http://www.cisg .law.pace.edu/cisg/wais/db/cases2/040421g3.html (last accessed Sept. 10, 2013).

Thus, UCC Section 2-207 also differs in a significant manner from CISG Articles 8 and 14 with respect to the incorporation of standard conditions. Under the UCC, standard conditions are incorporated unless they would cause surprise or hardship to the other party. Under the CISG standard conditions are only incorporated if one party attempts to incorporate the standard conditions and the other party had reasonable notice of this attempted incorporation. Accordingly, a conflict exists between the UCC and CISG, and the Court must determine which law applies to the instant case.

4.   Applicability of CISG

As mandated by Article VI of the United States Constitution, Pennsylvania's choice-of-law principles recognize that international treaties to which the United States is a contracting state, when applicable, are controlling. See Sinha v. Sinha, 834 A.2d 600, 603 (Pa. Super. 2003). The CISG "applies to contracts of sale of goods between parties whose places of business are in different States . . . when the States are Contracting States." Forestal Guarani S.A. v. Daros Int'l, Inc., 613 F.3d 395, 397 (3d Cir. 2010) (ellipsis in original) (quoting CISG Article l(l)(a)). "The United States ratified the CISG on December 11, 1986." Id. Germany is also a contracting state to the CISG. See It's Intoxicating, Inc. v. Maritim Hotelgesellschaft mbH, 2013 WL 3973975, *17 (M.D. Pa. July 31, 2013). The parties' places of business were in different states, as is required by Article 1(2) of the CISG. E.g. doc. no.

3-1, 12 (listing RTI's place of business as Titusville, PA and CSN's place of business as Neunkirchen, Germany).

"Because both the United States [and Germany] are signatories to the CISG and the alleged contract at issue involves the sale of goods . . . the CISG governs." *Forestal Guarani,* 613 F.3d at 397. However, just because the CISG governs does not necessarily mean that it applies in this case. Under Article 6 of the CISG, the parties may choose to exclude application of the CISG. In order for the contract to exclude the CISG it must include language which affirmatively states that the CISG does not apply. BP Oil Int'l, Ltd., v. Empresa Estatal Petroleos de Ecuador, 332 F.3d 333, 337 (5th Cir. 2003); It's International, 2013 WL 3973975 at *2 (citing American Mint LLC v. GOSoftware, Inc., 2005 WL 2021248, *2 (M.D. Pa. Aug.16, 2005)); Cedar Petrochemicals, Inc. v. Dongbu Hannong Chem. Co., 2011 WL 4494602, *3 (S.D.N.Y. Sept. 28, 2011); Hanwha Corp. v. Cedar Petrochemicals, Inc., 760 F. Supp. 2d 426, 430 (S.D.N.Y. 2011); Belcher-Robinson, L.L.C v. Linamar Corp., 699 F. Supp. 2d 1329, 1335 n.4 (M.D. Ala. 2010); Zhejiang Shaoxing Yongli Printing & Dyeing Co. v. Microflock Textile Group Corp., 2008 WL 2098062, *2 (S.D. Fla. May 19, 2008); Ajax Tool Works, Inc. v. Can-Eng Mfg. Ltd., 2003 WL 223187, *2 (N.D. Ill. Jan.30, 2003); Asante Techs., Inc. v. PMC-Sierra, Inc., 164 F. Supp. 2d 1142, 1150 (N.D. Cal. 2001).

In this case, CSN attempted to exclude the CISG in its standard conditions, which stated, "Supplies and benefits shall exclusively be governed by German law. The application of laws on international sales of moveable objects and on international purchase contracts on moveable objects is excluded." Doc. No. 3-1, 10. Even if the standard conditions are incorporated into the parties' contract, this attempted exclusion is ineffective. It does not explicitly reference the CISG. Furthermore, CSN's standard conditions attempt to exclude international law on the sale of "moveable objects." The CISG does not use the term "moveable objects." The only use of the word "objects" is as a synonym for the word "protests" not as a synonym for the word "goods."

Furthermore, the parties' positions in this litigation demonstrate that they believe exclusion was ineffective. Neither party argues that German law is applicable. Instead, they argue for either the CISG or the UCC. The papers that were exchanged between the two parties do not mention the UCC, or Pennsylvania law. If the exclusion included in CSN's standard conditions had been effective, German law would be the applicable law as the standard conditions reference German law in the same section as the attempted exclusion. RTI's statement that "CSN can't create a scenario where the CISG applies" is unconvincing. Doc. No. 38, 5. Further, RTI's argument that the UCC applies is without merit. The attempted exclusion is ineffective, and the CISG is the applicable law with respect to the instant contract dispute.

B. Contract Formation

Having determined that the CISG is the applicable law, the Court turns to the formation of a contract between RTI and CSN. CSN argues that RTI's purchase orders were offers and that CSN's order confirmations were rejections and coun-teroffers under the CISG. Alternatively, CSN argues that if its order confirma-tions are considered acceptances, that the purchase orders (the offers) included CSN's standard conditions via reference to CSN's quotations. RTI on the other hand, argues that its purchase orders were offers that did not include by refer-ence CSN's standard conditions and that CSN's order confirmations were in fact acceptances of the offers.

1. RTI's Purchase Orders

CSN's standard conditions are part of the contract under any theory being advanced by the parties if RTI's purchase orders incorporated by reference CSN's standard conditions. CSN's quotations included the following language, "According to our standard conditions of sale to be found under www.csnmetals.de, we have pleasure in quoting without engagement as follows." Doc. No. 3-1, 2, 20. RTI's purchase orders were "per CSN quote" followed by the respective quotation num-bers. Id. 12-15, 23-30.

CSN relies upon Citisteel USA, Inc. v. Gen. Elec. Co., 78 F. App'x 832 (3d Cir. 2003), in support of its argument that a purchase order that references a quo-tation incorporates the standard conditions of that quotation. CSN's reliance is misplaced. As discussed supra, the CISG governs this contract dispute. In *Citisteel*, "[t]he parties agree[d] that Delaware law applie[d.]" Id. at 836 n.5. Under Delaware law, "reliance on . . . subjective intent is misplaced." Id. at 836 n.6. However, "the CISG expresses a preference that the offeror's intent be considered subjectively." *Hanwha*, 760 F. Supp. 2d at 432 Thus, *Citisteel* is not dispositive.

The parties do not cite, and the Court is not aware of, any decisions from courts in the United States addressing whether, under the CISG, an offer that references a document, which references standard conditions, incorporates those standard conditions in the offer. However, the Court finds instructive a decision from the Austrian Supreme Court. Oberster Gerichtshof [OGH] [Supreme Court] (Tantalum powder case), Dec. 17, 2003, English translation available at http://cisgw3.law.pace.edu/cases/031217a3.html (last accessed Sept. 10, 2013) (citing CISG Articles 8 & 14). The Court held that "standard terms, in order to be applicable to a con-tract, must be included in the proposal of the party relying on them as intended to govern the contract in a way that the other party under the given circumstances knew or could not have been reasonably unaware of this intent."

In this case, RTI did not intend the standard conditions to apply to the con-tract. This fact is plain from the face of the purchase orders. The purchase orders included terms that were different from those included in CSN's standard condi-tions. For example, the purchase orders state that the orders are FOB destination while CSN's standard conditions state that the orders are FOB origin. Furthermore, the quotations state that payment is due within 90 days (with important excep-tions discussed infra), while the purchase orders state that payment would be due within 60 days. Thus, RTI did not have the requisite intent to incorporate the standard terms that were referenced in CSN's quotations. See Tantalum pow-der case ("It requires an unambiguous declaration of the provider's intent."). Accordingly, the Court finds that RTI's purchase orders did not incorporate CSN's quotations.

2. CSN's Order Confirmations

a. Standard Conditions

Having determined that RTI's purchase orders did not incorporate CSN's standard conditions referenced in its quotations, the Court must determine whether CSN's order confirmations constituted acceptances under the CISG or constituted rejections and counteroffers. The Court has detailed the manner in which the CISG treats the battle of the forms, supra.

The first page of CSN's order confirmations stated, "We thank you for your purchase order. This order confirmation is subject to our standard conditions of sale as known (www.csnmetals.de)." As discussed supra, CSN's standard conditions were not incorporated into the RTI purchase orders. Therefore, if the standard conditions were properly incorporated into the order confirmations, the order confirmations would constitute counteroffers and not acceptances.

The Court finds persuasive *CSS Antenna*. In that case, an order confirmation included the following language: "According to our general conditions . . . [which] can be viewed at . . . our homepage. . . ." *CSS Antenna*, 764 F. Supp. 2d at 754. The Court held that language to be "ambiguous at best." Id.

In the case at bar, all of the factors that weigh against a finding that CSN's standard conditions were properly incorporated into the contract are present while none of the factors that weigh in favor of incorporation are present. The language included on the order confirmations was ambiguous at best, as the language merely directs the other party to a website which needs to be navigated in order for the standard conditions to be located. See *CSS Antenna*, 764 F. Supp. 2d at 754. There is no evidence that RTI had actual knowledge of the attempted inclusion of CSN's standard conditions. See id. There is no evidence that the parties had discussed incorporation of the standard conditions during contract negotiations. See id. There is no evidence that RTI actually received CSN's standard conditions. *Tyco*, 2006 WL 2924814 at *5. Further, no employee of RTI initialed next to the statement attempting to incorporate the standard conditions. Id.

Typically, when considering Motions for Judgment on the Pleadings, the Court would find further discovery on this issue appropriate. However, both parties agree that there are no further documents which would aid in the Court's determination of whether the standard conditions apply. See doc. no. 38, 6-8 (stating on the record that no discovery was necessary regarding contract formation). Thus, the Court finds that, when considering all of the evidence, CSN's reference to its standard conditions did not suffice to incorporate those terms into the order confirmations. Therefore, CSN's standard conditions are not part of the contract as they were not a part of either the purchase orders or order confirmations.

b.   Payment Target Language

As former Chief Judge McLaughlin stated, "there is one sub-issue [relating to the incorporation of CSN's standard conditions.]" Doc. No. 38, 4. The order confirmations stated that, "If we have offered a payment target, a sufficient coverage by our credit insurance company is assumed. In case this cannot be obtained we have to ask for equivalent guarantees or payment in advance."

The Court finds that this language was properly incorporated into both order confirmations. It was in regular print on the front of both order confirmations. Id. The language did not reference any other document but rather was an independent additional term under Article 19 of the CISG. Furthermore, the additional term was material under CISG Article 19(3), as it related to payment terms for the goods.

RTI's sole argument against this additional term under the CISG is that the additional term did not impose any duty on RTI but merely gave CSN the ability to ask for equivalent guarantees or advance payment. This argument is without merit. The word "ask" can mean "to expect or demand." The American Heritage Dictionary of the English Language, Fourth Edition (2000). When considered in the context that it was used, this is the natural meaning of the word "ask" in the order confirmations. The same sentence that the word "ask" appears in also uses the term "guarantees," evidencing the mandatory nature of the term ask. Furthermore, it is illogical to include in a contract a provision by which one party would request another party provide something as important as a guarantee regarding payment and then be fully satisfied if the other party refused to provide such a guarantee or advance payment. Any reasonable businessperson reading such a statement would have recognized that this term was a requirement if CSN did not obtain sufficient coverage from its insurance carrier.

The additional term that was properly incorporated into CSN's order confirmations was material under Article 19. Thus, the order confirmations were not in fact acceptances but rather constituted counteroffers.

3.   RTI's Acceptance

The final step in determining if a contract was formed between RTI and CSN is consideration of the emails that were exchanged between the parties in August 2011. CSN argues that these emails were acceptances by RTI and therefore a valid contract was formed between the parties.

On August 9, 2011, RTI emailed CSN purchase order 6676. Doc. No. 29-7, 4. On August 10, 2011, CSN replied, stating:

> [T]hanks again for the new purchase order. Please find attached our order confirmation as per e-copy for your best service. In case you would realize anything wrong or

feel something important is missing on it, please let us know as it's most important for us to make sure about best customer service and support. * * *VERY IMPORTANT: * * * As you know we need "FULLY APPROVED DRAWINGS", original format. Please provide to us ASAP. As per our ISO-manual and strict management advise [sic] our mould-line-mgmt. can only schedule the order having these dwgs. (dwgs. actually in our hands are stated "confidential, quote only, uncontrolled drawing".

Id., 3-4.

CSN then followed-up on August 15, 2011, asking for an approximate date that it would receive the drawing from RTI. Id., 3. RTI responded that same day stating that "The approved drawings went out UPS today, and you should receive them Wednesday, 8/17/11." Id. CSN then acknowledged receipt of those drawings on August 17, 2011. Id., 2.

On August 23, 2011, RTI emailed CSN purchase order 6761. Doc. No. 29-11, 3. On August 25, 2011, CSN replied, stating:

[T]hanks for being a little sort [sic], but today's almost same crazy as yesterday. Please find our order confirmation attached. To play safe, let's have the usual crosscheck: In case you would realize anything wrong or feel something important is missing on it, please let us know as it's most important for us to make sure about best customer service and support. If there's any question about it from your side, please feel welcome to contract any time you need. Please send the fully approved, original format drawings over to us ASAP, so that we proceed on our end.

Id., 2-3.

Later on August 25, 2011, RTI replied stating that "After reviewing your order confirmation, please proceed with the manufacture of these plates." Id., 2. On August 26, 2011, CSN sent an email that stated "ok . . . thanks for the quick reply. Still make sure to the the [sic] order drawings to us. (fully approved, original format.)" Id.

Article 18(1) of the CISG provides that "A statement made by or other conduct of the offeree indicating assent to an offer is an acceptance." RTI's acceptance of CSN's counteroffer with respect to purchase order 6761 is evident from the email exchange. RTI stated that it had reviewed CSN's order confirmation and that CSN could "proceed with the manufacture of these plates." Doc. No. 29-11, 2. This was an affirmative statement indicating assent to the counteroffer, the order confirmation, without any reservation or attempted alteration. Thus, with respect to purchase order 6761, a contract was formed by RTI's email to CSN that stated manufacture could go forward. The terms of the contract were those set forth in CSN's order confirmation, including the term relating to advance payment. However, CSN's standard conditions were not incorporated into the contract that was entered into between the parties for the reasons set forth supra.

Although not as explicit as the conduct relating to purchase order 6761, RTI also accepted CSN's counteroffer with respect to purchase order 6676. CSN's emails of August 10, 2011, and August 15, 2011, made clear that they needed RTI's drawings in order to proceed with the order. RTI then took affirmative action and followed the directions that were set forth in CSN's emails by sending via UPS the drawings for CSN's use. RTI then made an affirmative statement to CSN regarding the mailing of the drawings to CSN. Thus, RTI accepted CSN's counteroffer, at the very latest, on August 17, 2011, when CSN received the drawings. RTI made no statement in any email to CSN that it was not accepting the additional term that CSN included in its counteroffer, the order confirmation. Thus, a valid contract under the CISG was also formed with respect to purchase order 6676. The terms of the contract were those set forth in CSN's order confirmation, including the term relating to advance payment. However, CSN's standard conditions were not incorporated into the contract that was entered into between the parties for the reasons set forth supra.

C.   Breach of Contract

Having determined the parties' obligations under the contract, the Court now turns to whether either party breached its obligations under the contract. CSN argues that RTI repudiated the contract and therefore was in material breach. Article 71 of the CISG provides that: "A party may suspend the performance of his obligations if, after the conclusion of the contract, it becomes apparent that the other party will not perform a substantial part of his obligations as a result of . . . his conduct in preparing to perform or in performing the contract." In this case, there is no dispute that RTI refused to perform on the contract. RTI sent a letter to CSN on October 24, 2011, stating that it would procure the requested copper from an alternate supplier. On October 25, 2011, RTI sent an email to CSN stating that "P.O.'s 6676 and 6761 are cancelled immediately due to CSN's inability to conform to RTI's terms listed on the P.O.'s." CSN responded stating that "please be informed the cancellation of the order is NOT ACCEPTED by CSN." RTI then sent a follow-up letter to CSN on October 28, 2011, stating that it would not fol-low through with its obligations relating to advance payment or other forms of guarantee. On November 4, 2011, RTI sent yet another letter confirming it was canceling the purchase orders.

It is hard to imagine a clearer repudiation. RTI sent repeated notices to CSN over an 11 day period setting forth its reasons for not performing the contract. In short, RTI believed that the terms of the contract were different than they actually were. Thus, RTI breached its contractual obligations to CSN.

V.   CONCLUSION

This contract dispute demonstrates the confusion that can arise in a battle of the forms, particularly when the applicable law is disputed. For the reasons set forth above, the CISG governs this contract dispute. RTI's purchase orders did not incor-porate CSN's standard conditions via reference to CSN's quotations. CSN's order confirmations did not incorporate its standard conditions. However, CSN did include within its counteroffer a term relating to payment if CSN's insurer refused to cover the transaction. Thereafter, CSN affirmatively invoked that term. After its invocation by CSN, RTI breached its contractual obligations by repudiating the contract. Therefore, RTI's Motion for Judgment on the Pleadings will be DENIED and CSN's Cross-Motion for Judgment on the Pleadings will be GRANTED.

———————————

Besides the different way that the CISG handles the "battle of the forms" that was discussed in *Roser Technologies*, there are a couple of other distinctions worth noting between the CISG formation rules and the Article 2 rules. First, the CISG provides in Article 18(2) that acceptances are effective only when actually received by the offeror, not when they are sent to the offeror, as is true under the UCC.

Second, CISG Article 16(2) contains an even more liberal exception than does UCC §2-205 to the common law rule that firm offers are not binding unless they are given for consideration. CISG Article 16(2) says that offers which indicate that they are irrevocable may not be revoked for the time stated by the offeror. Unlike the conditions of UCC §2-205, the irrevocability of a firm offer under CISG Article 16(2) is not a function of the offer being in writing and is not limited to a period of three months.

C.   Formation of Real Estate Contracts

Understanding the formation of real estate contracts is simplified by the fact that the process typically does not involve the exchange of inconsistent forms, a common problem with commercial sales of goods. What complicates the real estate formation process is that there are typically one or more brokers serving as agents or subagents of the seller and, in many cases, the buyer.

With significant commercial real estate sales, the contract formation process will be fairly straightforward. Both buyer and seller will normally be represented by lawyers, and the two sides will hammer out a sales contract that will detail as many of the terms as the two sides can think of and care to resolve.

From a systems perspective, perhaps the most interesting real estate formation process occurs in the context of residential real estate sales. With residential sales, there is a very elaborate and developed system in place that includes real estate brokers as key players in the process. Indeed, it is safe to say that the vast majority of residential real estate contracts in this country are formed only with the intervention of real estate brokers.

Until the 1990s, real estate brokers who worked with buyers like the Shaughnessys, described below, were almost always working as subagents of the seller, since even an agent working with a buyer would get paid out of the seller's proceeds from the purchase price. As it became increasingly clear that most buyers did not understand this nuance of agency law and its implications for their agents' duty of loyalty, states began to get stricter about mandating disclosures by any agent or broker working with or for a buyer in a residential home purchase. Today most states offer a residential home buyer an array of different agency relationships, with the key point of most state legislation being adequate disclosure to the buyer of the home. In other words, the real estate agent must have the buyer sign in advance a written disclosure in which the agent makes clear whether the agent is working for the buyer, the seller, or even a traditional "dual agency" where the agent purports to work for both.

Consider a typical residential real estate scenario: Steve and Karen Shaughnessy were married soon after they both graduated from law school, and now the two of them would like to buy a house. A classmate who has lived in the area all his life recommends to them a "great real estate agent," Patty Schaner. Steve and Karen approach Patty, who agrees to "work with" them.

Patty then learns what the Shaughnessys are looking for in a house and how much they can afford. She begins taking the couple to "showings" of houses on the market that seem to meet the couple's specifications and budget. Patty's ability to quickly find houses on the market that meet the Shaughnessys' requirements will be enhanced by her access to the local multiple listing service (MLS). The MLS is typically formed by the local real estate brokers group for the purpose of sharing listings. The MLS consists of a computer database that can display home listings according to such parameters as price, location, and number of rooms. In most areas, over 90 percent of homes that are listed with brokers will have a description included in the MLS.

After several dozen showings, the Shaughnessys finally find their "dream home." The home they wish to buy is owned by the Garners, a growing family that has just purchased a new and larger home. When the Garners decided to put their home on the market, they entered into a 90-day "exclusive listing agreement" with Bob Erker, a neighbor who also happened to be a real estate agent. The listing agreement provides that Bob will receive a six percent commission upon closing of the sale, even if the Garners decide to ditch Bob during the 90-day period and sell their house through another agent, or even if the Garners are able to sell their house with no agent.

The Shaughnessys tell Patty that they would like to make an offer to the Garners for the house's full asking price, $200,000. Patty supplies the Shaughnessys a form contract on which to make that offer. The contract was drafted as a cooperative effort between the local bar association and the local association of realtors. It contains several boilerplate provisions, plus some blanks for the particulars of this deal and any contingencies that either side would like to insert. The Shaughnessys ask Patty to insert contingencies providing that they will not be obligated to close unless they obtain specified financing and unless the house is found to be in good repair by an inspector to be hired by the Shaughnessys.

Patty brings the signed offer with the financing and inspection contingencies to the Garners. If the Garners choose to accept and sign the Shaughnessys' offer, then a residential sales contract, albeit one with contingencies, will have been formed. If the contract survives all the way through closing, Bob will not end up with as much money as you might think: Bob's 6 percent commission is first split between the listing agent (Bob) and the selling agent (Patty). In most cases, Bob and Patty then split their 3 percent with their respective home offices. Thus, in this $200,000 home sale, Bob, Patty, and each of their offices end up with $3,000 apiece.

Typically the two common contingencies of financing and inspection will give the buyer a lot of leeway to escape the contract even after it has been signed. However, as the following case shows, sometimes buyers who believe that one of these contingencies has excused their performance of a signed purchase contract will learn that they are mistaken.

Shimrak v. Goodsir

2014 WL 4244313 (Ohio App. 2014)

STEWART, J.

This is an appeal on questions of law concerning the interpretation of a financing contingency clause in a residential property purchase agreement. The seller of the property alleged that after the buyers were neither approved nor denied financing for the purchase within a certain period of time, the contingency clause in the agreement gave the buyers two options: either request that the seller grant a written extension of time to obtain financing or remove the contingency in writing. The seller maintained that the buyers did not request an extension of time nor did they waive the financing contingency in writing, so the buyers breached the purchase agreement by not going forward with the purchase. The buyers claimed that a failure to obtain financing under the terms of the contingency clause rendered the purchase agreement null and void. The court agreed with the buyers and this appeal followed.

On May 24, 2006, defendant-appellant Susan Goodsir, the successor trustee to the William Meyer Trust and seller, agreed with plaintiffs-appellees Peter and Patricia Shimrak, buyers, to a purchase agreement for the sale of a house that was an asset of the trust. The Shimraks paid $2,000 in earnest money and the parties set a closing date of August 24, 2006, for the transaction.

Paragraph E of the purchase agreement contained the following financing contingency:

> This transaction is conditioned upon BUYER obtaining a commitment for a first mortgage loan (the "Loan") from Howard Hanna Mortgage Services or such other lending institution chosen by BUYER in the amount set forth in D(3) above, or in a lesser amount acceptable to BUYER. BUYER agrees to apply in writing for the loan within five (5) Days, as defined in Section Q, after the date of Acceptance, to cooperate fully

with the lender's requests for information and to use good faith efforts to obtain the Loan. If BUYER's loan application is neither approved nor denied within 30 days after the date of Acceptance, then BUYER may either request a written extension or remove this contingency in writing.

If BUYER's loan application is denied, or if SELLER refuses an extension and BUYER does not remove this contingency, then this agreement ("AGREEMENT") shall be null and void, neither BUYER, SELLER, nor any REALTOR(S) involved in this transaction shall have any further liability or obligation to each other, and both BUYER and SELLER agree to sign a mutual release whereupon the earnest money shall be returned to BUYER.

The uncontested facts show that the Shimraks applied for financing, but were unable to obtain a commitment from a lender. On August 4, 2006, Goodsir first learned about the Shimraks's difficulties in obtaining financing and that the Shimraks might be requesting a delay in closing. On August 7, 2006, the Shimraks were told that their lender would approve financing only upon the sale of their house. They asked Goodsir to amend the purchase agreement to add a new contingency making their purchase of Goodsir's house contingent upon the Shimraks selling their home. Goodsir formally rejected the proposed amendment of the purchase agreement. With no financing forthcoming because they had yet to sell their home, the Shimraks notified Goodsir on August 18, 2006, that they would be withdrawing from the transaction. Goodsir then relisted the house for sale, eventually agreeing with another buyer in May 2007 to sell the house for $65,000 less than what the Shimraks had agreed to pay.

The Shimraks initiated this action in the Rocky River Municipal Court seeking return of the $2,000 they paid as earnest money for the purchase. Goodsir then counterclaimed for breach of contract relating to the Shimraks' failure to perform as outlined in the purchase agreement. She also sought a declaratory judgment of her rights under the purchase agreement. With Goodsir's counterclaim exceeding the monetary jurisdiction of the municipal court, the case was transferred to the court of common pleas. The court of common pleas then released the earnest money to the Shimraks without objection from Goodsir.

The court conducted a hearing on the declaratory judgment action. Goodsir argued at the hearing, as she does in this appeal, that the financing contingency in Paragraph E gave the Shimraks one of two options in the event they were neither approved nor denied financing within 30 days after she accepted the purchase agreement: either request a written extension of time or remove the contingency in writing. She maintained that the Shimraks offered a third option by proposing to amend the purchase agreement to make it contingent on the sale of their house. Goodsir argued that the Shimraks' proposal was not an option authorized by the purchase agreement and that their failure to exercise one of the two options stated in the purchase agreement meant that they were obligated to complete the purchase and their failure to do so was a breach of the purchase agreement.

The Shimraks argued that the two options contained in Paragraph E—either make a request for a written extension of time or remove the financing contingency—were discretionary courses of action for them, neither of which superseded their right to walk away from the purchase agreement if they were not approved for financing after the 30-day period.

In a written opinion, the court found that Paragraph E's use of the word "may" when referring to the two options available to a buyer in the event the loan application was neither approved nor denied meant that those options were discretionary. The court stated:

> As the Court reads the Agreement, if after thirty (30) days, approximately June 24, 2006, [Shimrak] was unable to secure the financing then [Shimrak] has the option to do at any point in time, one or none of the following: 1. Request an additional extension; 2. Remove the contingency. Furthermore, if at whatever point [Shimrak] requested such an extension and [Goodsir] denied said extension, then the Agreement was null and void.
>
> Here, at the end of the thirty (30) day time period, [Shimrak] was unable to secure the financing. Some ninety (90) days after the Agreement was entered into, in August 2006, [Shimrak] requested an extension pursuant to Section E. [Goodsir] denied the request for an extension. Upon that denial, the Agreement was null and void pursuant to Section E. [Shimrak] should not be punished here for [Goodsir's] use of a poorly written contract that failed to specify a time frame for the request for an extension or removal of the clause.

R.C. 2721.03 states that any person interested in a contract may have determined any question of construction arising under the contract. The interpretation of a contract is a question of law for the court. In re All Kelley & Ferraro Asbestos Cases, 104 Ohio St. 3d 605, 2004 Ohio-7104, 821 N.E.2d 159, ¶ 28. The court must give the words used in a contract their plain and ordinary meaning in order to ascertain the intent of the parties to the contract, Penn Traffic Co. v. AIU Ins. Co., 99 Ohio St. 3d 227, 2003-Ohio-373, 790 N.E.2d 1199, ¶ 9, unless the common words result in a "manifest absurdity or some other meaning is clearly evidenced from the face or overall contents" of the agreement. Alexander v. Buckeye Pipe Line Co., 53 Ohio St. 2d 241, 374 N.E.2d 146 (1978), paragraph two of the syllabus.

The court's ruling made three points: first, that the options set forth in Paragraph E of the agreement were discretionary; second, that the agreement imposed no time limitations on when those options were to be exercised; and third, that the request to add a contingency for the sale of the Shimraks' home constituted a request for an extension that Goodsir denied, thus rendering the contract null and void. Goodsir argues that the court erred on all three points. We agree.

The disputed language of Paragraph E states: "If BUYER's loan application is neither approved nor denied within 30 days after the date of Acceptance, then BUYER may either request a written extension or remove this contingency in writing." (Emphasis added.)

The court made the error of construing the word "may" in isolation from the word "either." We interpret the disputed sentence to mean that if the buyer's application for financing is neither approved nor denied within 30 days of the seller accepting an offer to purchase the property, the buyer must exercise one of the two stated options: and the buyer has the discretion to choose which of the two options to exercise. In other words, we do not read the discretionary word "may" in isolation, but as "may either"—the word "either" being mandatory and the word "may" being discretionary as to which of the two required options the buyer must exercise. Admittedly, the language used in Paragraph E is not a model of clarity, but to interpret it as the court did (that the Shimraks could invoke "one or none" of the options listed) would render the clause completely meaningless: agreements are made to evoke performance, not to encourage the lack thereof. Courts must employ the construction of a contract that makes the agreement fair and reasonable and gives the agreement meaning and purpose. See GLIC Real Estate Holdings, LLC v. Bicentennial Plaza Ltd., 2012-Ohio-2269, 971 N.E.2d 404, ¶ 10 (10th Dist.). The court's interpretation of Paragraph E inserted a new option that had no basis in the overall context of the agreement.

In Perhavec v. Rosnack, 11th Dist. Lake No.2003-L-157, 2005-Ohio-138, the court of appeals construed identical language to mean that should a loan application be neither approved nor denied within a stated number of days after the date of acceptance, the buyers "should request a written extension of this contingency or request this contingency be removed from the contract." Id. at ¶ 15. The court of appeals' use of the word "should" suggested that the options provided were mandatory and the seller's discretion extended only as far as deciding which option to exercise. Compare State v. James, 4th Dist. Ross No. 13CA3371, 2013-Ohio-5322 (stating that when a plea bargain, which is governed by the law of contract, is violated by the state, the court "may either" allow the negotiated plea to be withdrawn or require the state to fulfill its end of the bargain, but nonetheless must choose one of those two options).

Our conclusion is reinforced by the nature of the options available to the buyer in the event the buyer's application for financing is neither approved nor denied within 30 days of the seller accepting the purchase offer. Those options—requesting an extension of time to obtain financing or removing the contingency—put the obligation solely on the buyer after the 30-day period had expired. The only time that Goodsir had the obligation to act was if the Shimraks exercised the option of seeking an extension of time to obtain financing. If the Shimraks had requested an extension of time to obtain financing, the onus would have shifted to Goodsir to either grant the extension or deny it, making the purchase agreement null and void. The Shimraks did not pursue this option and cannot complain that Goodsir somehow failed to act as required by the purchase agreement.

Contrary to the court's conclusion, there is no option that simply allows the buyer to walk away from the purchase agreement with impunity, nor could that option be inferred under the circumstances. Having offered to purchase the property, the buyers "cannot defeat the contract by their own fault" and "must make a bona fide effort" to obtain financing. Graham-Chrysler Plymouth, Inc. v. Warren, 9th Dist. Summit No. 9222, 1979 Ohio App. LEXIS 9939 (Aug. 15, 1979). While the parties agree that the Shimraks acted in good faith to obtain financing, the fact remains that the Shimraks had performance obligations under the terms of the agreement and could not unilaterally withdraw from the purchase agreement.

It is important to acknowledge that this is not a case where the Shimraks were denied financing yet were forced to go through with the purchase. The purchase agreement made it clear that had financing been denied, the purchase agreement would become null and void. The Shimraks' request for financing was neither approved nor denied, leaving them in limbo, but not without recourse. They could have requested an extension of time to obtain financing and shifted the burden of action to Goodsir, who could either grant the request and allow the contract of sale to continue on or deny the request and void the purchase agreement. The Shimraks could also have removed the financing contingency to allow the sale to continue to closing. What they could not do was simply take no action after the 30-day time period had expired, not act as required by Paragraph E, and then renege on their promise to buy the property.

Having found that the purchase agreement required the Shimraks to choose one of two options in the event their application for financing was neither approved nor denied, we next consider the court's ruling that the Shimraks "did elect one of the enumerated options" under Paragraph E. Judgment entry at 5. The court considered the Shimraks' proposed addendum dated August 7, 2006, to make the purchase agreement contingent upon the sale of their house, to be an option under the agreement.

The court erred by finding that the Shimraks elected one of the enumerated options available under Paragraph E. The purchase agreement provides only two options in the event a buyer's application for financing is neither approved nor denied within 30 days after the date of acceptance: request a written extension or remove the financing contingency. The Shimraks did not elect one of these options, but instead offered a third: they requested an addendum to the purchase agreement making the purchase agreement contingent on the sale of their house.

The court erroneously equated the Shimraks' request to add a contingency relating to the sale of their home as being the same thing as a request for an extension of time to obtain financing. A contingency is very different from an extension. In a contract, a "contingency" is a condition precedent that must occur for the parties' promises to be binding. Hussey v. Daum, 2d Dist. Montgomery No. 14246, 1994 Ohio App. LEXIS 2338 (June 1, 1994). If the stated contingency does not occur, there is no duty to perform under the terms of the contract. An extension of time to perform the obligations of a contract does not excuse performance, but merely delays it. The proposed addendum was not a request for an extension of time, but a fundamental change to the purchase agreement.

In addition, the court's conclusion that Goodsir "denied the request for an extension," judgment entry at 4, is wholly contradicted by the Shimraks' evidence. In a letter dated August 18, 2006, Peter Shimrak responded to Goodsir's contention that the Shimraks breached the purchase agreement by noting that "I have not signed anything removing the contingency, and I have not asked you for an extension. . . ." See Plaintiff's exhibit No. 6. With the Shimraks having conceded in writing that they did not request an extension of time even though their financing had been neither approved nor denied, the court erred by finding that Goodsir denied a request for an extension of time and thus rendered the purchase agreement null and void.

Although we have found that the court incorrectly concluded that the Shimraks did employ one of the options set forth in Paragraph E of the purchase agreement, the court nonetheless concluded that there were no time limitations on when an option had to be exercised. Goodsir argues that this finding gave the Shimraks an unstated additional option under the purchase agreement: do nothing. Goodsir argues that by so ruling, the court made the 30-day time period in which to obtain financing meaningless and allowed the Shimraks to wait until just before the time of closing to inform her that they had not obtained financing.

Paragraph E sets forth two time frames: (1) within five days after acceptance of the offer to purchase, the Shimraks had to apply in writing for a commitment for a first mortgage loan; and (2) if the Shimraks' loan application was neither approved nor denied within 30 days after the date Goodsir accepted the Shimraks' offer to purchase the property, the Shimraks had to elect to either request a written extension in which to obtain financing or remove the financing contingency in writing. The question we must resolve then is when did the Shimraks have to elect one of the options after their loan application was neither approved nor denied within the 30-day time frame.

At the outset, we find the court erred by concluding that Paragraph E's failure to state a time frame for when the Shimraks had to elect which option to pursue was the fault of Goodsir, who used a "poorly written contract that failed to specify a time frame for the request of an extension or removal of the [financing contingency] clause." Judgment entry at 4. The undisputed evidence showed that the Shimraks' real estate agent prepared the offer using an "Offer to Purchase Real Estate and Acceptance" form prepared on her company's letterhead. Not only did Goodsir's real estate agent not prepare the offer submitted by the Shimraks, Goodsir's real estate agent worked for a different real estate company. The evidence showed that the Shimraks selected the form on which they offered to purchase the property, so the court should not have blamed Goodsir for the use of a "poorly written contract." To the extent that the court believed the Shimraks were being "punished" by the terms of the purchase agreement, that punishment was their own doing.

Finding that Paragraph E of the purchase agreement should have been construed against the Shimraks begs the question of whether the contract is ambiguous. Silence in a contract is not the same as an ambiguity. E. Ohio Gas Co. v. Akron, 81 Ohio St. 33, 54-55, 90 N.E. 40 (1909). Paragraph E omitted any reference to a time frame in which a buyer whose application for financing is neither approved nor denied must elect one of the provided options. Unlike an ambiguity that exists when contract language is susceptible of more than one interpretation, State ex rel. Toledo Edison Co. v. Clyde, 76 Ohio St. 3d 508, 513, 668 N.E.2d 498 (1996), the purchase agreement was simply silent on when the Shimraks had to exercise the options provided in Paragraph E. Absent any ambiguity, the court should not have endeavored to construe that part of the purchase agreement in favor of either party, let alone in favor of the Shimraks.

With the purchase agreement silent on when a buyer was required to elect one of the two options available under Paragraph E, we employ the rule that if a contract is silent on a point, "[t]he parties to a contract are required to use good faith to fill the gap." Burlington Res. Oil & Gas Co. v. Cox, 133 Ohio App. 3d 543, 547, 729 N.E.2d 398 (4th Dist. 1999). "'Good faith' is a compact reference to an implied undertaking not to take opportunistic advantage in a way that could not have been contemplated at the time of drafting, and which therefore was not resolved explicitly by the parties." Ed Schory & Sons v. Francis, 75 Ohio St. 3d 433, 443-444, 662 N.E.2d 1074 (1996), quoting Kham & Nate's Shoes No. 2, Inc. v. First Bank of Whiting, 908 F.2d 1351, 1357-1358 (7th Cir. 1990). "What the duty of good faith consists of depends upon the language of the contract in each case which leads to an evaluation of reasonable expectations of the parties." Fultz & Thatcher V. Burrows Group Corp., 12th Dist. Warren No. CA2005-11-126, 2006-Ohio-7041, ¶ 34, citing B-Right Trucking Co. v. Interstate Plaza Consulting, 154 Ohio App. 3d 545, 2003-Ohio–5156, 798 N.E.2d 29, ¶ 32 (7th Dist.). The court therefore erred by concluding as a matter of law that there was no particular time frame in which the Shimraks had to elect one of the options available under Paragraph E.

It is unnecessary in this case for us to establish a bright-line rule under which the Shimraks had to exercise one of the options under Paragraph E because we find as a matter of law that, based on the facts of this case, the Shimraks did not act within a reasonable period of time after the expiration of the 30-day period to inform Goodsir that their application for financing had neither been approved nor denied. The 30-day period for obtaining financing expired on June 24, 2006, yet the Shimraks waited until August 7, 2006 to inform Goodsir that their application had been neither approved nor denied. Nothing in the evidence showed why the Shimraks could not have communicated with Goodsir immediately after the 30-day period or shortly thereafter. Indeed, the Shimraks appeared unconcerned about the consequences of any delay to Goodsir: when Goodsir's attorney pointed out to Peter Shimrak that August 7, 2006 (the date on which the Shimraks proposed to amend the purchase agreement) was well beyond the 30-day time period set forth in Paragraph E, Peter Shimrak responded, "Whatever." Tr. 30.

The consequence of the Shimraks' failure to timely exercise one of the options set forth under Paragraph E of the purchase agreement was manifest. The Shimraks knew that Goodsir had received at least one other offer on the house — the existence of another bidder is what prompted the Shimraks to offer the list price for the house. When the bank neither approved nor denied their application for financing within 30 days of applying for financing, the Shimraks did nothing. Surely it was their hope that their house would sell and they would have the funds to purchase the Goodsir property. By their own admission, the Shimraks "really wanted the place[.]" But by waiting so long after the expiration of the 30-day period, the Shimraks must have known that any chance Goodsir had to entertain and/or accept other offers on the house was stifled. From the time the Shimraks' offer was accepted to the time when they formally withdrew their offer, almost three months had elapsed. It was highly unlikely that any potential buyer who tendered a competing offer would wait that long and renew the same offer previously made. Under the circumstances, their action was untimely and unreasonable.

Despite our finding that the Shimraks did not timely exercise one of two options available to them under Paragraph E when their lender had neither approved nor denied their application for financing, a final question remains: was the Shimraks' loan application ultimately denied so as to render the purchase agreement null and void?

The plain language of the purchase agreement states that a denial of a loan application renders the agreement null and void. The Shimraks argue that the August 7, 2006 email sent by their bank stating that it would "provide financing to Peter Shimrak . . . once his current home sells" was a denial of financing that rendered the purchase agreement null and void.

Even if we assume that the Shimraks are correct that their lender making financing contingent upon the sale of their house constituted a denial of financing, we must reject the Shimraks' argument because they were already in breach of the purchase agreement by failing to timely exercise one of the options listed in Paragraph E of the agreement when they were informed of their claimed denied financing. They cannot rely on a subsequent denial of their loan application to purge an earlier breach.

In any event, the Shimraks try to have it both ways when they argue that their lender denied their loan application on August 7, 2006, by telling them that it would approve financing only if they sold their home. If that was truly the case, their application for financing would have been denied within 30 days of making their application for financing because the same situation existed. Yet at that point in time, the Shimraks plainly did not consider their application for financing rejected and the purchase agreement null and void. They concede in their appellate brief that their "loan application was not approved or denied within 30 days after Goodsir's acceptance." Appellee's brief at 6. Having conceded that point, they cannot argue that their lender rejected their application for financing by setting forth a condition that had existed all along.

In fact, it was disingenuous for the Shimraks to argue that their lender's August 7, 2006 notice that it would approve financing only upon the sale of the Shimraks' home was the first time that they were aware this would be a condition of financing. The record suggests that the Shimraks knew all along that their application for financing would be approved only upon the sale of their house. In his testimony before the court, Peter Shimrak testified that he and his wife had suffered certain financial reversals and needed financing to buy the Goodsir property. He was asked:

> Q. Did you apply for financing by May 30th, 2006?
> A. Of course we did.
> Q. Okay.
> A. But we were never able to get financing because we couldn't sell our home.

Tr. 20.

The above testimony was consistent with other testimony by Peter Shimrak; namely, that he did not remove the financing contingency after the 30-day window for obtaining financing closed because "I had to have financing." Tr. 28. And in response to a question of why the Shimraks had not made the purchase agreement contingent on the sale of their house, Peter Shimrak testified it was "[b]ecause I was convinced we were going to sell our home and buy this nice home, and it just didn't work out." Tr. 29. Based on this testimony, the Shimraks knew at the time they entered into the purchase agreement that they would have to sell their home in order to obtain financing for the Goodsir property. They could not credibly argue that August 7, 2006 was the first time they learned that their loan application would be approved only on the condition that they sell their home. What is more, it is apparent from the circumstances that the Shimraks did not consider their application for financing to have been denied at the time they were obligated to exercise one of the options listed under Paragraph E. Indeed, having conceded that point, they cannot argue that their lender rejected their application for financing by setting forth a condition that had existed all along. To hold otherwise would allow a buyer to indefinitely string along a seller and then walk away from an agreement, leaving the seller with no recourse.

In conclusion, we find that the court erred as a matter of law by granting judgment to the Shimraks. The assigned errors are sustained. This matter is reversed and remanded to the trial court with instructions to enter judgment for Goodsir. . . .

Problem Set 4

4.1. a. You were working out at your fitness center after work one night last week, when who should you run into again but your one-time law school classmate Deborah Swift (from Problem 1.6). Deborah told you that she was feeling bad about the "misunderstanding" the two of you had at your fifth law school reunion a few weeks ago. She also told you that since the reunion she has quit her job as a lawyer and has started her own business selling and leasing Rolls Royces. In any event, to make amends Deborah said that she would offer to lease you that same used Rolls Royce for two years, for just $250 per month. To avoid any confusion, Deborah said that this time she would put the offer in writing and would keep it open for five months.

You agreed to pay Deborah $200 for "tying up" this car for five months, and she said she would even apply this money toward the first month's lease payment should you choose to lease the car. After you paid Deborah and got her signed writing, you remembered that your Uncle Harry, the auto buff, was due to visit you in four months. You are also a little suspicious about the great lease rate for Deborah's car. Are you safe to wait until Uncle Harry comes and looks at the car before exercising your option? UCC §2A-205.

b. Same facts as part (a), except that you do not pay anything for Deborah's signed writing promising the same lease deal. Are you safe now to wait until Uncle Harry comes to town? UCC §2A-205.

c. What if under the facts of part (b), you did wait four months for Uncle Harry and then Deborah said that the offer was no longer open. Could you come up with another theory of enforcement outside of §2A-205? UCC §1-103.

4.2.   Recall the facts of Problem 3.4(a): Gym franchise sends purchase order to weight machine seller; seller responds with acknowledgement form that includes a different term (no consequential damages) and an additional term (arbitration); buyer and seller perform without discussing differences in forms, but later those differences become relevant when a gym patron is injured by the machine. Suppose now that the Gold's Gym franchisee in that problem had been based in Toronto, Canada, rather than in the United States. Suppose also that the consequential damages suffered by the buyer were purely economic rather than stemming from a patron's personal injury (cf. CISG Art. 5). How would your answers to the three questions in Problem 3.4(a) change? Is there a contract at all? Will the consequential damages disclaimer hold? Will disputes be subject to arbitration? CISG Arts. 1(1), 18(1), 19.

4.3.   The following letter appeared in the syndicated real estate column of Robert Bruss:

"Dear Bob: I am selling a house I inherited. I told the Realtor to advertise it 'as is' because it's a fixer-upper. A buyer made a purchase offer I accepted. It contained a contingency for a professional inspection. That was fine with me. But the inspection revealed many defects, as I knew it would. Now the buyer refuses to complete the purchase unless I give her a $7,500 credit for repairs. To me, this looks like a $7,500 price reduction. Can the buyer force me to pay for these repairs?"

Assume that the inspection contingency read as follows: "Buyer's purchase offer is contingent on the buyer's approval of a professional inspection report, which the buyer will arrange to have prepared within 14 days of this offer." What would your answer be if you were Robert Bruss?

4.4.   Recall our hypothetical home buyers, the Shaughnessys. On the recommendation of some friends, they approached real estate agent Patty Schaner, who agreed to "work with" them in their quest to purchase a house. Imagine that when the Shaughnessys found their "dream home," listed by the Garners at $200,000, the Shaughnessys asked Patty if she could advise them on how little they could offer and still get the house. Patty then had a discussion with Bob Erker, the Garners' agent, who told Patty that the Garners had said from the start that though they were listing the home at $200,000, they would be thrilled to get $180,000 for it. In light of this conversation with Bob, what can Patty advise the Shaughnessys concerning their question to her about what offer to make? How would your answer differ depending on whether Patty was a "true buyer's agent" or just a subagent of the seller?

Assignment 5:   Statute of Frauds with Sales of Goods

When most non-lawyers think of legally enforceable contracts, they think of a writing. The fact is, of course, that under the common law most contracts do not have to be in writing in order to be legally enforceable. In that respect, the requirement of a writing for enforceability is the exception rather than the rule in the world of contracts. The writing requirement has, nevertheless, been made a feature of the system for the sale of goods.

Just because there is a legal rule stating that sales contracts must be contained in a signed record or writing to be enforceable, however, does not mean that buyers and sellers will necessarily find it in their interests to put every sales contract in writing. Putting a sales agreement in writing takes time and effort, and sometimes the benefits gained do not justify the time and effort spent.

As one furniture manufacturer interviewed for this book put it, "For us, putting contracts into writing is a costly way to do business. We occasionally have buyers back out by claiming that they never made an order when we know they did, but that's still a small enough percentage of our orders that we still don't feel it's worth it to have every contract put in writing."

Another seller, a manufacturer of plastics, described how his company's system for purchasing raw materials from suppliers does not include formalizing their deals with a signed writing: "I handle our buying of raw materials from suppliers, things like rosin and colors. When we need a certain raw material I'll call three or four suppliers to find out whether they've got it and how much they'll sell it for. After that I'll call back the supplier I want and I'll do an oral order for the amount that we need. In that conversation, we'll settle on type, price, quantity, and delivery terms. I'll write that down and send the information to our warehouse people, who will then know what to expect and when to expect it. I never follow these phone calls with a written purchase order, but that's never been a problem. Probably 80 percent of the suppliers we deal with don't bother to send acknowledgement forms, either. If anyone ever tried to renege on one of these oral contracts, we would just stop doing business with them."

The decision of whether or not to include a writing component in one's purchasing system will also be a function of the size of the particular sale, as described by an in-house lawyer at a Fortune 100 company: "There are some purchases where we will deliberately choose not to use a writing, namely when the size of the purchase is small and it's a regular customer. In fact, we have a certain dollar threshold below which we will not insist on a signed writing from the seller, and still a lower threshold below which we won't even bother to send our own signed confirmation. The stakes are low enough in those cases and the likelihood of a problem low enough that we're willing to take our chances just so that we can conduct business more quickly. Besides, we have the business leverage of refusing to buy from a particular supplier in the future."

The above examples demonstrate that many sophisticated buyers and sellers decide that it is not in their interests to put every contract in writing, despite the statute of frauds rule. There are, however, many buyers and sellers who do follow a firm policy of having every sales contract memorialized in a writing. As one lawyer from a major clothing retailer put it, "Although our contracts to purchase clothes from wholesalers or manufacturers are probably formed on the phone, we insist that our purchasing people always follow with a signed written purchase order for at least two reasons: first, for purposes of our internal recordkeeping, and second, because it makes me feel comfortable as a lawyer to think that we have something in writing."

In situations where a buyer and seller are engaged in a series of ongoing sales, one approach that is often taken to the writing requirement is that the two parties negotiate and sign at the beginning of their relationship one "master agreement" that outlines all of the terms and conditions of each sale that will take place in the future. All future sales are then conducted without the benefit of individual signed writings, and often the master agreement will specifically state that both parties agree to waive their ability to assert the statute of frauds as a bar to enforceability.

A lawyer who advises several natural gas suppliers described the use of this type of arrangement to handle what are known as "day trades" in the gas industry:

> Contracts that best reflect the reality of the hyperactive day-trading business address management approval through recognition of oral contracts. Because of the current Uniform Commercial Code ("UCC") requirement found at 2-201, there may be an issue as to the enforceability of any contract for the sale of goods in excess of $500 which is not evidenced by writing. . . . On the other hand, for a day trade, a company may make the decision to forgo a written contract because of simple economics — the risk of loss for one day's flow of gas may not justify the necessary administration costs.
>
> In order to avoid the potential problems that could result by flowing gas without a written contract, the following language may be used in any master gas contract for swing/interruptible/day-trading activities: "The Parties agree by their execution hereof that transactions will be entered into orally. No written confirmation will be required prior to the time Gas flows under such transaction and, unless otherwise agreed, each Party shall be responsible for making its own communications necessary to effect the flow of Gas. However, for billing and payment purposes, [Buyer][Seller] will provide a written confirmation of any such oral transaction to [Seller][Buyer] prior to the date specified herein for billing."
>
> The master contract also would have language indicating that the entire "Contract" is made up of the terms and conditions in the master contract as well as all transactions entered into under the terms of the master contract, whether

oral or written. An example of a clause of this type is: "The contract contemplated by this agreement shall include all transactions entered into by the parties, whether oral (as provided for in the preceding paragraph) or written; and the provisions of this Master Contract and all such transactions shall form a single Contract between the parties." An additional protection would be to allow tape recording of the oral contracts. ("Emphasis on Oral Commitments Advocated for Short-Term Deals," Gas Transactions Report, Vol. 3, No. 11 (1995).)

Buyers and sellers that use Electronic Data Interchange, as described in Assignment 3, can similarly use the master EDI trading partner agreement to address questions about whether electronic orders are sufficient to satisfy the statute of frauds. Most EDI trading partner agreements will include acknowledgements to the agreement by both sides that each electronic order constitutes a signed writing that is sufficient to satisfy Article 2's statute of frauds requirement.

The goals of the Article 2 drafters in formulating UCC §2-201 were apparently to reconcile two competing dangers: on one hand, not requiring any writing increases the risk that a party might fabricate the existence of an oral contract that never really existed; on the other hand, creating any writing requirement as a prerequisite for enforceability increases the risk that parties who enter into bona fide oral agreements might renege on them. The way that the drafters attempt to reconcile this tension is to require some tangible evidence that a contract exists, but not too much. In addition, §2-201 provides four different circumstances in which a sales contract is enforceable even without a writing. Under the UCC approach, then, it would still be difficult for a party to enforce a contract that never existed, but it would not be too onerous to enforce a less-than-fully-documented contract that really did exist.

The Article 2 writing requirement does not apply at all where the contract for the sale of goods is for less than $500. Even when the requirement does apply, the required writing need contain just three elements under §2-201(1): (1) a sufficient indication that the contract for sale has been made, (2) the signature of the party who is trying to avoid the contract, and (3) a quantity term.

Even where the party seeking to enforce the contract cannot muster the fairly minimal writing that is required by §2-201(1), §2-201 provides other ways in which the writing requirement might be met. One way that is set out in §2-201(3)(a) is for the seller to show that it relied to its detriment on the existence of an oral contract in beginning the manufacture of specially manufactured goods according to that contract. For this exception to operate, the seller must also show that the special manufacture began "under circumstances which reasonably indicate that the goods are for the buyer."

A second and more troublesome exception that is found in §2-201(3)(b) allows enforcement of the sales contract despite the lack of a writing where the party seeking to avoid the contract "admits in his pleading, testimony or otherwise in court that a contract for sale was made." This exception is problematic for a couple of reasons. First, it rewards those who are willing to lie under oath and punishes those who are not. If the whole idea of the statute of frauds is that contracts that are not in writing are unenforceable, shouldn't a party seeking to avoid such a contract be able to freely admit, "Yes, I made this oral agreement, but the system says I don't have to honor it since I never signed anything"?

A second reason that the "admission exception" is troublesome is that it is never clear just how far a plaintiff who does not have a writing should be able to take its case before having its claim rejected. Given the admission exception, a plaintiff could argue that its case must go to trial just so that the plaintiff can have an opportunity to get the defendant to admit in open court that the oral contract did exist. The defendant, on the other hand, can contend that as long as it denies the existence of the oral contract at the pleading stage, there is little point in forcing the defendant to have to deny it again at a later stage in the case. This is particularly true, the defendant might say, given that one of the likely purposes of having a writing requirement is to avoid wasting a court's time litigating about the existence of contracts that are not supported by a writing.

DF Activities Corp. v. Brown

851 F.2d 920 (7th Cir. 1988)

Posner, J.

This appeal in a diversity breach of contract case raises an interesting question concerning the statute of frauds, in the context of a dispute over a chair of more than ordinary value. The plaintiff, DF Activities Corporation (owner of the Domino's pizza chain), is controlled by a passionate enthusiast for the work of Frank Lloyd Wright. The defendant, Dorothy Brown, a resident of Lake Forest (a suburb of Chicago), lived for many years in a house designed by Frank Lloyd Wright—the Willits House—and became the owner of a chair that Wright had designed, the Willits Chair. This is a stark, high-backed, uncomfortable-looking chair of distinguished design that DF wanted to add to its art collection. In September and October 1986, Sarah-Ann Briggs, DF's art director, negotiated with Dorothy Brown to buy the Willits Chair. DF contends—and Mrs. Brown denies—that she agreed in a phone conversation with Briggs on November 26 to sell the chair to DF for $60,000, payable in two equal installments, the first due on December 31 and the second on March 26. On December 3 Briggs wrote Brown a letter confirming the agreement, followed shortly by a check for $30,000. Two weeks later Brown returned the letter and the check with the following handwritten note at the bottom of the letter: "Since I did not hear from you until December and I spoke with you the middle of November, I have made other arrangements for the chair. It is no longer available for sale to you." Sometime later Brown sold the chair for $198,000, precipitating this suit for the difference between the price at which the chair was sold and the contract price of $60,000. Brown moved under Fed. R. Civ. P. 12(b)(6) to dismiss the suit as barred by the statute of frauds in the Uniform Commercial Code. See UCC §2-201. (The Code is, of course, in force in Illinois, and the substantive issues in this case are, all agree, governed by Illinois law.) Attached to the motion was Brown's affidavit that she had never agreed to sell the chair to DF or its representative, Briggs. The affidavit also denied any recollection of a conversation with Briggs on November 26, and was accompanied by both a letter from Brown to Briggs dated September 20 withdrawing an offer to sell the chair and a letter from Briggs to Brown dated October 29 withdrawing DF's offer to buy the chair.

The district judge granted the motion to dismiss and dismissed the suit. DF appeals, contending that although a contract for a sale of goods at a price of $500 or more is subject to the statute of frauds, the (alleged) oral contract made on November 26 may be within the statutory exception for cases where "the party against whom enforcement is sought admits in his pleading, testimony or otherwise in court that a contract for sale was made." UCC §2-201(3)(b). DF does not argue that Brown's handwritten note at the bottom of Briggs' letter is sufficient acknowledgment of a contract to bring the case within the exemption in §2-201(1).

At first glance DF's case may seem quite hopeless. Far from admitting in her pleading, testimony, or otherwise in court that a contract for sale was made, Mrs. Brown denied under oath that a contract had been made. DF argues, however, that if it could depose her, maybe she would admit in her deposition that the affidavit was in error, that she had talked to Briggs on November 26, and that they had agreed to the sale of the chair on the terms contained in Briggs' letter of confirmation to her.

There is remarkably little authority on the precise question raised by this appeal—whether a sworn denial ends the case or the plaintiff may press on, and insist on discovery. In fact we have found no authority at the appellate level, state or federal. Many cases hold, it is true, that the defendant in a suit on an oral contract apparently made unenforceable by the statute of frauds cannot block discovery aimed at extracting an admission that the contract was made, simply by moving to dismiss the suit on the basis of the statute of frauds or by denying in the answer to the complaint that a contract had been made. There is also contrary authority. . . . We need not take sides on the conflict. When there is a bare motion to dismiss, or an answer, with no evidentiary materials, the possibility remains a live one that, if asked under oath whether a contract had been made, the defendant would admit it had been. The only way to test the proposition is for the plaintiff to take the defendant's deposition, or, if there is no discovery, to call the defendant as an adverse witness at trial. But where as in this case the defendant swears in an affidavit that there was no contract, we see no point in keeping the lawsuit alive. Of course the defendant may blurt out an admission in a deposition, but this is hardly likely, especially since by doing so he may be admitting to having perjured himself in his affidavit. Stranger things have happened, but remote possibilities do not warrant subjecting the parties and the judiciary to proceedings almost certain to be futile.

A plaintiff cannot withstand summary judgment by arguing that although in pretrial discovery he has gathered no evidence of the defendant's liability, his luck may improve at trial. The statement in a leading commercial law text that a defense based on the statute of frauds must always be determined at trial because the defendant might in cross-examination admit the making of the contract, see White & Summers, Handbook of the Law Under the Uniform Commercial Code 67 (1980), reflects a misunderstanding of the role of summary judgment; for the statement implies, contrary to modern practice, that a party unable to generate a genuine issue of fact at the summary judgment stage, because he has no evidence with which to contest an affidavit of his adversary, see Fed. R. Civ. P. 56(e), may nevertheless obtain a trial of the issue. He may not. By the same token, a plaintiff in a suit on a contract within the statute of frauds should not be allowed to resist a motion to dismiss, backed by an affidavit that the defendant denies the contract was made, by arguing that his luck may improve in discovery. Just as summary judgment proceedings differ from trials, so the conditions of a deposition differ from the conditions in which an affidavit is prepared; affidavits in litigation are prepared by lawyers, and merely signed by affiants. Yet to allow an affiant to be deposed by opposing counsel would be to invite the unedifying form of discovery in which the examining lawyer tries to put words in the witness's mouth and construe them as admissions.

The history of the judicial-admission exception to the statute of frauds, well told in Stevens, Ethics and the Statute of Frauds, 37 Cornell L.Q. 355 (1952), reinforces our conclusion. The exception began with common-sense recognition that if the defendant admitted in a pleading that he had made a contract with the plaintiff, the purpose of the statute of frauds—protection against fraudulent or otherwise false contractual claims—was fulfilled. (The situation would be quite otherwise, of course, with an oral admission, for a plaintiff willing to testify falsely to the existence of a contract would be equally willing to testify falsely to the defendant's having admitted the existence of the contract.) Toward the end of the eighteenth century the courts began to reject the exception, fearing that it was an invitation to the defendant to perjure himself. Later the pendulum swung again, and the exception is now firmly established. The concern with perjury that caused the courts in the middle period to reject the exception supports the position taken by Mrs. Brown in this case. She has sworn under oath that she did not agree to sell the Willits Chair to DF. DF wants an opportunity to depose her in the hope that she can be induced to change her testimony. But if she changes her testimony this will be virtually an admission that she perjured herself in her affidavit (for it is hardly likely that her denial was based simply on a faulty recollection). She is not likely to do this. What is possible is that her testimony will be sufficiently ambiguous to enable DF to argue that there should be still further factual investigation—perhaps a full-fledged trial at which Mrs. Brown will be questioned again about the existence of the contract.

With such possibilities for protraction, the statute of frauds becomes a defense of meager value. And yet it seems to us as it did to the framers of the Uniform Commercial Code that the statute of frauds serves an important purpose in a system such as ours that does not require that all contracts be in writing in order to be enforceable and that allows juries of lay persons to decide commercial cases.

The methods of judicial factfinding do not distinguish unerringly between true and false testimony, and are in any event very expensive. People deserve some protection against the risks and costs of being hauled into court and accused of owing money on the basis of an unacknowledged promise. And being deposed is scarcely less unpleasant than being cross-examined—indeed, often it is more unpleasant, because the examining lawyer is not inhibited by the presence of a judge or jury who might resent hectoring tactics. The transcripts of depositions are often very ugly documents.

Some courts still allow the judicial-admission exception to be defeated by the defendant's simple denial, in a pleading, that there was a contract; this is the position well articulated in Judge Shadur's opinion in the *Triangle Marketing* case. To make the defendant repeat the denial under oath is already to erode the exception (as well as to create the invitation to perjury that so concerned the courts that rejected the judicial-admission exception altogether), for there is always the possibility, though a very small one, that the defendant might be charged with perjury. But, in any event, once the defendant has denied the contract under oath, the safety valve of §2-201(3)(b) is closed. The chance that at a deposition the defendant might be badgered into withdrawing his denial is too remote to justify prolonging an effort to enforce an oral contract in the teeth of the statute of frauds. If Dorothy Brown did agree on November 27 to sell the chair to DF at a bargain price, it behooved Briggs to get Brown's signature on the dotted line, posthaste.

AFFIRMED.

FLAUM, J., dissenting.

Because I disagree with the majority's holding that additional discovery is prohibited whenever a defendant raises a statute of frauds defense and submits a sworn denial that he or she formed an oral contract with the plaintiff, I respectfully dissent. Neither would I hold, however, that a plaintiff is automatically entitled to additional discovery in the face of a defendant's sworn denial that an agreement was reached. Rather, in my view district courts should have the authority to exercise their discretion to determine the limits of permissible discovery in these cases. This flexibility is particularly important where, as here, the defendant's affidavit does not contain a conclusive denial of contract formation. While district courts have broad discretion in discovery matters, I believe the district court abused that discretion in the present case.

The purpose of the statute of frauds "is to protect a party from the fraudulent and perjurious claim of another that an oral contract was made and not to prevent an oral contract admittedly made from enforcement." URSA Farmers Coop. Co. v. Trent, 58 Ill. App. 3d 930, 16 Ill. Dec. 348, 350, 374 N.E.2d 1123, 1125 (1978) (citing Cohn v. Fisher, 118 N.J. Super. 286, 287 A.2d 222 (1972)). The statute is also designed to protect innocent parties from the expense of defending against allegations that they breached a contract that is not evidenced by a writing. As the majority notes, there is no Illinois case law conclusively deciding a plaintiff's right to obtain further discovery when a defendant denies the existence of an oral contract in a sworn affidavit. Relevant case law in other jurisdictions is split between the position that the majority adopts today and a rule permitting additional discovery (and in some cases full trials) in statute of frauds cases.

Although it is difficult to give full effect to both the statute of frauds and the admissions exception thereto, that is what we must attempt to do. In my view, these provisions can best be reconciled by allowing district courts to exercise their discretion to determine when additional discovery is likely to be fruitful and when it is being sought just to improperly pursue a defendant who is clearly entitled to the protection of the statute of frauds.

If a denial is a complete bar to additional discovery, the exception to the statute of frauds for admissions made in a "pleading, testimony or otherwise in court that a contract for sale was made" would be rendered virtually meaningless. In Illinois involuntary admissions can satisfy the admissions exception to the statute of frauds. Such involuntary admissions will be almost impossible under the majority's rule because the plaintiff will never have an opportunity to examine the defendant in order to elicit an involuntary admission. Either the defendant will make a fatal admission in his or her affidavit and the statute of frauds exception will be satisfied without resort to the testimony component, or the defendant will deny the contract in his or her pleadings and the case will be dismissed before a testimonial admission is possible. A blanket rule prohibiting any further discovery once the defendant denies under oath that a contract was formed is therefore too inflexible.

Similarly, I would not adopt a rule that requires district courts to allow additional discovery in every one of these cases. I would leave the decision to the discretion of the district judge. In cases where a defendant does not explicitly deny under oath that an oral contract was reached, or where there is some indication that the statute of frauds is being used to perpetrate a fraud, it would be permissible to allow the plaintiff to question the defendant under oath to ensure that he or she personally denies that the parties formed an oral contract. This does not mean, however, that summary judgment is never appropriate when the statute of frauds is raised as an affirmative defense. If a defendant who conditionally denies contract formation in his or her pleadings or affidavit specifically denies that an agreement was reached in a deposition, summary judgment might well be appropriate at that stage of the litigation. A simple denial in an affidavit, however, should not trigger foreclosure of further discovery in every case.

In the present case I think the district court abused its discretion by disallowing any additional discovery once Brown filed her motion to dismiss and accompanying affidavit. The majority argues that it would be futile for DF Activities Corporation ("DF") to take Brown's deposition. Brown is unlikely to admit any facts from which a reasonable trier of fact could conclude that an oral contract was formed because, in the face of her affidavit, such admissions would leave her exposed to perjury charges. In my view, this overstates the content of Brown's affidavit. While Brown denied that any oral or written agreement was reached in both her answer and motion to dismiss, such a blanket denial is curiously missing from her affidavit. Rather, in her affidavit Brown stated only that she did not accept any offer from Domino's Farms or Sarah Briggs for the sale of the Willits chair and that she does not recall having a conversation with Sarah Briggs on November

26, 1988. Deposing Brown therefore would not necessarily be a futile effort. It is possible that under questioning during a deposition Brown would remember the November 26 conversation during which Briggs claims she and Brown reached an agreement for the sale of the chair. Although any convenient prior memory lapse might be viewed with suspicion if a deposition elicited additional information, it is highly unlikely that it would lead to perjury charges. On the facts of this case, I believe the district court abused its discretion when it refused to allow DF to take Brown's deposition.

I share the majority's concern that one of the purposes of the statute of frauds is to protect litigants from the cost of defending breach of contract claims based on alleged agreements that are not supported by written documentation. The statute of frauds, however, contains a specific exception for cases in which a party admits in a pleading, testimony, or otherwise in court that an oral contract was reached, and that provision must be given some effect. The testimonial admissions provision would be virtually meaningless if a district court could never exercise its discretion to permit additional discovery in the face of a defendant's sworn denial in an affidavit.

Because in my view the district court abused its discretion when it prohibited further discovery, I would remand this case to the district court with instructions to permit discovery to continue at least to the point where DF is given an opportunity to depose Brown. If Brown then denies under oath during her deposition that any oral contract was made, summary judgment might well be appropriate at that time.

Courts and commentators do not agree on just how far a plaintiff without a writing or writing substitute to satisfy the statute of frauds should be able to take its case before being dismissed. Most, but not all, courts believe that a plaintiff should at least get to conduct some discovery before having its case dismissed for lack of a writing. Comment 6 to §2-201 says that the writing need not be delivered in order to satisfy the statute, suggesting that plaintiffs ought to at least be able to discover documents in the possession of the defendant that may satisfy the writing requirement of the statute.

A third and more straightforward exception to the writing requirement in §2-201 is what is known as the "part performance" exception. This exception, found in §2-201(3)(c), simply says that, to the extent that either the seller receives and accepts payment for the goods or the buyer receives and accepts the goods, neither party can deny the existence of the oral contract. As Official Comment 2 to §2-201 puts it, "[r]eceipt and acceptance either of goods or of the price constitutes an unambiguous overt admission by both sides that a contract actually exists."

Easily the most litigated exception to the writing requirement in §2-201 is the so-called merchant's exception found in §2-201(2). As the next case demonstrates, it is not always clear what kind of writing will qualify as a "confirmation" to trigger the merchant's exception.

General Trading Int'l v. Wal-Mart Stores

320 F.3d 831 (8th Cir. 2003)

BOWMAN, J.

General Trading International, Inc. (GTI), sued Wal-Mart Stores, Inc., for breach of contract, action for goods sold, and action on account in a dispute arising out of Wal-Mart's alleged failure to pay for large numbers of decorative "vine reindeer" sold to Wal-Mart for resale to the public during the 1999 Christmas season. Wal-Mart counterclaimed for breach of contract and for fraud. According to Wal-Mart, most of the reindeer, manufactured in Haiti, were "scary-looking" and unsuitable for sale as Christmas merchandise. Wal-Mart claims that GTI orally agreed to absorb $200,000 of the purchase price because of Wal-Mart's dissatisfaction with the quality of the product. GTI, denying the existence of the alleged oral agreement, filed a motion for partial summary judgment, seeking an award of $200,000 of the unpaid balance, by arguing that the alleged oral agreement was unenforceable and violated the statute of frauds. The District Court granted partial summary judgment in favor of GTI and submitted the remaining claims to a jury, which returned a verdict in GTI's favor. Subsequently, the District Court denied Wal-Mart's motion for judgment as a matter of law or for a new trial and GTI's request for attorney fees. Wal-Mart appeals the grant of partial summary judgment and the denial of its motion for a new trial. GTI cross appeals the denial of attorney fees. We affirm.

Although the factual history of this dispute is set forth in detail in the partial summary-judgment opinion of the District Court, see Mem. Op. at 1-17 (Jan. 15, 2002), we will summarize some of the major events, especially as they relate to Wal-Mart's claims on appeal. In February 1999, Beth Gitlin, a seasonal buyer for Wal-Mart, began negotiating with Patrick Francis, the president of GTI (a company that sells seasonal craft items to large retailers) for the purchase of 250,000 vine reindeer for resale to Wal-Mart customers during the 1999 Christmas season. In March 1999, GTI executed Wal-Mart's standard vendor agreement. The vendor agreement provided that any changes in the agreement must be in writing and executed by both parties. Wal-Mart issued separate purchase orders, covering price and quantity terms, to GTI for the purchase of the reindeer.

In mid-August 1999, Wal-Mart noticed serious defects with the reindeer when the first shipments began arriving at its stores and warehouses. Gitlin estimated that, at that time, at least seventy percent of the reindeer were of poor quality. A Wal-Mart employee described the reindeer as "[m]oldy, broken grapevines, shapes that no more resembled a deer than they did a rabbit . . . scary-looking." Id. at 3 (quoting Estes Dep. at 19). During the next few weeks, Gitlin communicated with Francis about quality problems with the product. On September 13, 1999, Wal-Mart directed GTI to cancel all further shipments of the reindeer.

On September 23, 1999, Gitlin met with Francis and Jeff Kuhn, a GTI representative, to discuss the slow sales and quality problems. During that meeting, Wal-Mart agreed to accept delivery of any reindeer GTI had already manufactured (approximately 25,000), but at a lower price than the prior purchase orders. In addition, Gitlin requested that GTI agree to Wal-Mart's withholding of $400,000 owed to GTI for potential claims for defective merchandise. Finally, according to Wal-Mart, GTI orally agreed, at some point before September 30, to reduce the total amount due from Wal-Mart by $200,000 because of Wal-Mart's price mark-down of the reindeer at its stores in view of their poor quality. On September 30, 1999, Gitlin sent Francis and Kuhn an e-mail stating that sales of the reindeer were "too low" and that Wal-Mart would take a price markdown on the product within the next two weeks. E-mail from Gitlin to Francis and Kuhn (Sept. 30, 1999) (Gitlin's Sept. 30 e-mail). In that e-mail, Gitlin also stated that she was "also con-cerned about the defective percentage and claims at the end of the season. You say they normally run less than 10%. I'm going to be conservative and estimate 20%. I'm going to change the reserve on the account to $600,000 and will release the rest of the payments." Id. Gitlin did not receive a response to this e-mail from Francis or Kuhn.

On November 12, 1999, Kuhn sent Gitlin an e-mail stating GTI's frustration in obtaining payment from Wal-Mart on past-due invoices for the reindeer. In that e-mail, Kuhn noted that Gitlin said Wal-Mart was "going to hold $400,000 against future defective claims." E-Mail from Kuhn to Gitlin (Nov. 12, 1999). Gitlin replied three days later asking Kuhn to call her to discuss the matter. Gitlin and Kuhn spoke on November 19, 1999, and Gitlin sent Kuhn an e-mail that same day in which she stated, "As we both agree, we have $600,000 on hold now. $200,000 was to go to Markdowns and $400,000 was to cover claims. If you are willing to do this, then I will be able to consider reducing the amount on hold from $600,000 to $500,000." E-mail from Gitlin to Kuhn (Nov. 19, 1999) (Gitlin's Nov. 19 e-mail). Counsel for GTI sent Gitlin a facsimile letter that day demanding payment of the entire balance owed to GTI. Kuhn replied to Gitlin on November 22 and stated that "GTI would accept Wal-Mart withholding the amount of $400,000.00 for present and future charge backs." E-mail from Kuhn to Gitlin (Nov. 22, 1999). Kuhn sent Gitlin another e-mail on November 24 and stated that "[t]he principals [sic] of GTI's position is unwavering and non-negotiable. We want a check for $521,429 next week and on 1/15-2/1/2000 the $400,000 reserve will be revisited and adjusted accordingly." E-mail from Kuhn to Gitlin (Nov. 24, 1999). Thereafter, during the next several weeks, Gitlin and Kuhn continued to exchange e-mails, which can be characterized primarily as GTI continuing to demand immediate payment of outstanding invoices, or some settlement thereof, and Wal-Mart reit-erating its position that GTI agreed to Wal-Mart's retention of funds for defective merchandise claims and $200,000 for price markdowns. GTI never acknowledged the $200,000 for price markdowns in any of its correspondence with Wal-Mart.

In December 2000, GTI sued Wal-Mart for breach of contract, action for goods sold, and action on account, alleging that GTI had shipped Wal-Mart 176,217 vine reindeer at an agreed price of $1,839,777.96, of which Wal-Mart had only paid $1,444,093.79. Wal-Mart counterclaimed for fraud and breach of contract. On October 1, 2001, GTI filed a motion for partial summary judgment, seeking an award of $200,000 of the unpaid balance, by arguing that the vendor agree-ment precluded any oral modifications and that the statute of frauds barred the alleged oral agreement to deduct $200,000 for price markdowns. The District Court granted GTI's motion on January 15, 2002, concluding that both the terms of the vendor agreement and the provisions of the statute of frauds barred the oral agreement to reduce $200,000 from the amount owed to GTI. The jury heard the remaining claims the next month and returned a verdict in favor of GTI on its breach of contract claim, awarding GTI $63,280, and in favor of GTI on Wal-Mart's counterclaim for breach of contract. Subsequently, the District Court denied Wal-Mart's motion for judgment as a matter of law or new trial and GTI's request for an award of attorney fees. On appeal, Wal-Mart contends the District Court erred in granting partial summary judgment to GTI on the $200,000 claim and abused its discretion in denying Wal-Mart's motion for a new trial on the ground that the erroneous grant of partial summary judgment prejudiced Wal-Mart in the trial of the remainder of the case. GTI cross appeals, arguing the denial of its request for attorney fees was an abuse of discretion. . . .

Wal-Mart first argues the District Court erred when it granted partial summary judgment in favor of GTI by holding that the oral agreement to reduce $200,000 from the amount owed to GTI for price markdowns was barred by the statute of frauds. Subject to certain limited exceptions, the statute-of-frauds provision of the Arkansas version of the Uniform Commercial Code (UCC) renders unenforceable any unwritten contract for the sale of goods with a value of more than $500 "unless there is some writing sufficient to indicate that a contract for sale has been made between the parties and signed by the party against whom enforcement is sought." Ark. Code Ann. §4-2-201(1) (Michie 2001). Both parties agree the case is governed by the so-called "merchants' exception" to the statute of frauds. Under the merchants' exception, a confirmatory writing setting forth the terms of the agreement is sufficient if the recipient of the writing knows its contents and fails to object in writing within ten days. See §4-2-201(2) (Michie 2001). Here, Wal-Mart claims GTI did not object within ten days of Wal-Mart's sending GTI a confirmatory writing of the oral agreement for the $200,000 allowance. Specifically, Wal-Mart argues Gitlin's September 30 e-mail as well as her other e-mails to Kuhn and Francis are confirmatory memoranda to which GTI did not object in writing.

The question of whether a writing constitutes a confirmation of an oral agreement sufficient to satisfy the statute of frauds is a question of law for the court. See Vess Beverages, Inc. v. Paddington Corp., 886 F.2d 208, 214 (8th Cir. 1989) (whether document satisfies the statute of frauds is a question of law) (applying Missouri UCC). In this case, the District Court concluded that as a matter of law none of Wal-Mart's e-mails were sufficient. We agree.

We turn first to Gitlin's September 30 e-mail to Francis and Kuhn. In that e-mail, Gitlin stated that she was "going to change the reserve on the account to $600,000." Gitlin's Sept. 30 e-mail. According to Wal-Mart, this e-mail clearly indicates that Wal-Mart believed the original contract had been changed. Moreover, Wal-Mart argues that "although the breakdown of the $600,000 into a $400,000 reserve allowance for defective merchandise claims and a $200,000 for a markdown allowance is not explicit, it is strongly implied by the text of the e-mail." Br. of Appellant at 34. GTI does not dispute that it never responded to this e-mail.

Instead, GTI argues that Gitlin's September 30 e-mail is not a confirmatory writing under §4-2-201(1).

While the merchants' exception does not require a confirmatory writing to be signed by the party to be charged, see §4-2-201(2), the writing still must satisfy the dictates of §2-201(1). See St. Ansgar Mills, Inc. v. Streit, 613 N.W.2d 289, 294 (Iowa 2000) ("[A] writing is still required [under §2-201(2)], but it does not need to be signed by the party against whom the contract is sought to be enforced."); Howard Constr. Co. v. Jeff-Cole Quarries, Inc., 669 S.W.2d 221, 227 (Mo. Ct. App. 1983) ("[C]ourts have found that the §2-201(2) confirmatory memorandum must satisfy the 'sufficient to indicate' requirement of §2-201(1)"). Under the UCC, "[a]ll that is required [for a writing to indicate a contract for sale has been made under §2-201(1)] is that the writing afford a basis for believing that the offered oral evidence rests on a real transaction." UCC §2-201, cmt. 1. Most courts that have interpreted the "sufficient to indicate" requirement "have required that the writing indicate the consummation of a contract, not mere negotiations." *Howard Constr. Co.*, 669 S.W.2d at 227. Thus, writings that contain language evincing a tentative agreement or writings that lack language indicating a binding or complete agreement have been found insufficient. Id.; cf. M.K. Metals, Inc. v. Container Recovery Corp., 645 F.2d 583, 591 (8th Cir. 1981) (concluding that the terms of the agreement were so specifically geared to the desires of the party to be charged that the agreement reflected a complete contract) (applying Missouri UCC).

Based upon our review of Gitlin's September 30 e-mail, we agree with GTI that this e-mail fails sufficiently to indicate the formation or existence of any agreement between the parties through inference or otherwise. This e-mail is simply devoid of any language concerning an agreement on the issue of $200,000 for markdowns. While the e-mail references a $600,000 reserve, it does not state what, if any, portion of that amount was agreed to be set aside for markdowns. At most, the e-mail shows Wal-Mart's unilateral effort at taking a markdown on the reindeer and changing the reserve, e.g., "I will be taking a MD on this either next week or the following. . . . I'm going to change the reserve on the account to $600,000." Gitlin's Sept. 30 e-mail. In summary, the language in the e-mail does not constitute a sufficient writing for purposes of the statute of frauds because it does not evince any agreement between the parties on price markdowns. See R.S. Bennett & Co. v. Econ. Mech. Indus., 606 F.2d 182, 186 (7th Cir. 1979) (a §2-201(2) writing must "indicate [] that the parties have already made a deal or reached an agreement") (applying Illinois UCC).

Wal-Mart next argues that even if the September 30 e-mail is not a sufficient writing, Gitlin's subsequent e-mails to Kuhn and Francis constitute confirmatory memoranda. In particular, Wal-Mart points to Gitlin's e-mail to Kuhn on November 19 in which she stated, "As we both agree, we have $600,000 on hold now. $200,000 was to go to Markdowns and $400,000 was to cover claims. If you are willing to do this, then I will be able to consider reducing the amount on hold from $600,000 to $500,000." Gitlin's Nov. 19 e-mail. GTI does not directly refute that this or subsequent e-mails from Gitlin could constitute confirmatory memorandums. Instead, GTI argues that it filed timely objections to these writings.

Specifically, Kuhn replied on November 22 and 24 and offered to sign a letter authorizing Wal-Mart to retain $400,000 for defective merchandise claims, but he also demanded immediate payment on all outstanding invoices, noting that GTI's position was not negotiable.

Section 4-2-201(2) does not prescribe any particular form for an objection to a confirmatory writing. Nonetheless, both parties agree that courts require an unequivocal objection to a confirmatory writing alleging an oral agreement. See, e.g., *M.K. Metals, Inc.,* 645 F.2d at 592 (holding response to a purchase order was not an adequate objection under §2-201(2) because it did not challenge the price term in the purchase order, but rather stated that "there was someone who was willing to pay more than the amount stated in the purchase order") (applying Missouri UCC). Here, Wal-Mart argues that GTI did not unequivocally object to its confirmatory writing because GTI failed specifically to object to the $200,000 for price markdowns in its November 22 and 24 e-mail responses to Gitlin's e-mails. In analyzing these e-mails, the District Court concluded that GTI's "reply e-mails including different terms and containing demands for payment of the amount due on the invoices, less a reserve, constitute objections under §2-201(2)." Mem. Op. at 26. Though GTI failed to mention the $200,000 in its responses, it is clear when viewing the responses as a whole that GTI never agreed to Gitlin's assertion that they had reached an agreement on markdowns. Instead, GTI's responses, with a demand for full payment, less a reserve for defective merchandise claims, can only be characterized as unequivocal objections to any agreement on markdowns.

On the facts of this case, the merchants' exception to the statute of frauds has not been satisfied. Accordingly, we find the District Court did not err in granting partial summary judgment in favor of GTI on its claim for $200,000 of the unpaid balance of the reindeers' purchase price. . . .

———

There is one subtle but crucial point worth noting about the operation of the Article 2 writing requirement: the difference in the consequences of meeting versus not meeting that requirement will tend to make courts liberal in finding that the requirement has been met. If the plaintiff is unable to meet the requirement, that fact spells death for the plaintiff's case — it's all over. On the other hand, if the plaintiff does meet the requirement, all that happens is that the plaintiff gets to continue attempting to prove the enforceability of the contract. Given this difference in stakes, it is easy to see why in a close case courts might be inclined to find that the requirement has been met.

Problem Set 5

5.1. a. Mike Sims and Sara McCarthy are both in the furniture business. The two of them met at an industry convention where Mike alleges that they made an oral contract in which Mike agreed to sell Sara eight antique oak desks for $12,000 each, delivery to be made in five weeks to Sara's out-of-state place of business. Two days after the oral contract, Mike sent Sara a confirming memorandum on his company's letterhead that outlined the terms of their deal, including quantity. Consistent with normal practice, there was no signature on the memo. When Sara received the confirmation, she immediately called Mike and said, "You promised me that you could send me the desks in three weeks, not five. As far as I'm concerned, our deal is off." If Sara does nothing more, can Mike enforce the oral contract with Sara? UCC §§2-201, 1-201(b)(37); Official Comment 37 to §1-201.

b. Same facts as part (a), except Sara sends her objection in writing (the contents of which are as quoted in part (a)). Can Mike enforce the oral contract with Sara? UCC §2-201.

c. Same facts as part (a), except that Mike does not send a confirmation, but Sara sends Mike a check for $20,000, with "downpayment for desk deal" marked on the memo line. To what extent may Mike enforce the oral contract with Sara? UCC §2-201, Official Comment 2 to §2-201.

d. Same facts as part (a), except that Mike does not send a confirmation. When Mike eventually files a complaint in federal court to enforce the contract, Sara responds with a F.R.C.P. 12(b)(6) motion that states, "Even if everything alleged in plaintiff's complaint is true, the contract is still unenforceable for lack of a writing." Should the trial judge dismiss Mike's complaint at this point? UCC §2-201.

e. Same facts as part (a), except that Mike does not send a confirmation. However, shortly after his oral contract with Sara, Mike enters into a written contract with another furniture seller to buy eight antique oak desks (of the type promised to Sara) for $10,000 each. Now can Mike enforce the oral contract with Sara? UCC §§2-201, 1-103.

5.2. Arlene Ledger (from Problem 3.2) is back at your law office to ask you about a couple of difficulties she has had with certain customers of her exercise equipment company, Heavy Metal. Several weeks ago, she had met with Tom Lauder, director of Monticello Senior Center, to discuss the possibility of Heavy Metal manufacturing three identical multi-station weight machines that would be custom-made for the special needs of the residents of his senior center. In particular, the weight stack would have lighter increments than normal and each of the stations on the machine could be used even by residents who were wheelchair-bound.

Arlene said that Lauder had later called her and told her to go ahead and make the three special machines, which the two had agreed would cost $8,000 each. When Heavy Metal had nearly finished the first of these three machines, Lauder called Arlene again and left a message that said, "We won't need the machines after all. So sorry to trouble you." Arlene sheepishly admits to you that she never put this deal in writing. Now, she tells you, she is stuck with one special machine that no other buyer may want, plus a $3,000 bill from a consultant who had helped to draft the plans for the prototype for these three machines. Will Arlene be in a position to enforce this contract with Monticello

Senior Center? If so, can she enforce it just for the one machine in process or for all three? UCC §2-201, cf. Official Comment 2 to §2-201.

5.3.   Your law firm just took on a new client, Max Swain, an independent grocery store owner. Max was at an independent grocers' convention last week and he heard a lot about his colleagues' use of Electronic Data Interchange. Max concedes that he is a traditionalist at heart, but he said that he would not mind eliminating all of the paperwork involved with the current method by which he orders groceries from his various suppliers. Max tells you that he thinks he is ready to "take the plunge" and buy a special computer that will enable him to transmit orders via the EDI system. He wants to know if this new method of doing business has any increased risks over the old-fashioned way, and whether there are ways that he might reduce those risks. What do you advise him? UCC §§2-201, 1-201(b)(37), 1-201(b)(43).

Assignment 6: Parol Evidence with Sales of Goods

In the case where parties to a sales contract do decide to memorialize their agreement with a writing, they are thereby limiting their ability to enforce terms that are not contained in that writing. Whereas the UCC's statute of frauds rule hinders the enforceability of certain contracts, the parol evidence rule bars the introduction into evidence (and therefore the enforceability) of certain terms that are not put into writing.

In the sales system as it operates in practice, whether or not parties create "side deals" that are not contained in the relevant writing or writings will be a function of how formal they intend for the writing or writings to be. If the particular sales contract is documented by a purchase order alone, or by a purchase order and an acknowledgement form, there may well be nontrivial terms that are not contained in writing.

As one steel manufacturer explained, "Sometimes our sales people will enter into non-written special deals with certain buyers as to matters such as a lower-than-list price or longer-than-usual credit terms. These side deals are noted in our files but we never then formally acknowledge them in writing."

If a particular sale is significant enough for the two sides to sit down and negotiate a full-blown written contract, that contract will almost always include a standard merger clause that reads something like this: "This Agreement constitutes the complete and final agreement and understanding among the parties relating to the subject matter hereof, and supersedes all prior proposals, negotiations, agreements, and understandings relating to such subject matter. In entering into this Agreement, Buyer acknowledges that it is relying on no statement, representation, warranty, covenant, or agreement of any kind made by the Seller or any employee or agent of the Seller, except for the agreements of Seller set forth herein."

The idea behind the merger clause is that if the two parties are going to spend the sunk cost to sit down and work out all of the terms of their agreement, then it doesn't make sense to leave room for "side deals" that go beyond what the parties agreed to in writing. After all, if "side deals" were going to be the order of the day, then why waste the time to think about and reduce to writing the terms that are to govern the transaction?

Druckzentrum Harry Jung GmbH & Co. v. Motorola Mobility LLC

774 F.3d 410 (7th Cir. 2014)

Sykes, C.J.

A German printing company sued Motorola Mobility LLC, the cell-phone manufacturer, alleging that it breached a supply contract for printing services. In early 2008 Motorola agreed to make a good-faith effort to purchase 2% of its cell-phone user-manual needs from Druckzentrum Harry Jung GmbH & Co., a printer based in northern Germany. Halfway through the two-year contract period, Motorola's cell-phone sales contracted sharply. In response to the downturn, Motorola decided to consolidate its cell-phone manufacturing and distribution operations in China and buy all related print products there. Motorola notified Druckzentrum of the shift, and the two companies continued to do business together for a few more months during the transition.

The loss of Motorola's business did Druckzentrum in; the printer entered bankruptcy in Germany and brought this suit against Motorola alleging breach of contract and fraud in the inducement of the contract. Among other things, Druckzentrum claimed that the contract gave it an exclusive right to all of Motorola's user-manual printing business for cell phones sold in Europe, the Middle East, and Asia during the two-year contract period. The district judge rejected this claim on the pleadings and later entered summary judgment for Motorola on the rest of the case, finding no evidence to support either a claim of breach of contract or fraud.

We affirm. The parties' written contract contains no promise of an exclusive right to all of Motorola's printing business in Europe, the Middle East, and Asia. And because the contract is fully integrated, Druckzentrum cannot use parol evidence of prior understandings to upset the bargain the parties put in writing. Moreover, although Motorola promised to make a good-faith effort to purchase 2% of its cell-phone user-manual printing needs from Druckzentrum for a two-year period, the contract listed several reasons Motorola might justifiably miss the target. These included business downturns of the sort Motorola experienced, and there is no evidence that it acted in bad faith by moving its printing and distribution activities away from Europe. Finally, the evidence is insufficient to create a jury issue on the claim that Motorola fraudulently induced Druckzentrum to enter into the contract or continue performing under it.

I.   BACKGROUND

Druckzentrum is a printer based in Flensburg, Germany. Motorola is based in Illinois but maintains operations globally. In 1995 Motorola began using Druckzentrum to print user manuals for its cell-phone products marketed in Europe, the Middle East, and Asia—a marketing area apparently known in the trade as the "EMEA" region. During this time period, Motorola manufactured its phones in China and shipped them to a distribution facility in Flensburg, where they were packaged with user manuals printed by Druckzentrum and distributed for sale throughout the EMEA region.

In 2007 Motorola embarked on a program to improve the way it purchased products from vendors. At workshops conducted in fall 2007, Motorola educated vendors on the new process by which they could bid for contracts. Vendors first had to sign a "Corporate Supply Agreement" with a stated effective date of October 1, 2007. Druckzentrum was among the vendors invited to participate. After signing the agreement, Druckzentrum representatives attended a workshop in Illinois.

The materials distributed during the workshop made it clear that vendors would bid for a particular product "segment"—e.g., printed materials, cardboard boxes, plastic packaging, and so forth. It was less clear whether vendors were bidding for a particular region as well. Although the bidding materials contain many references to regions and vendors were supposed to state a bid in reference to a particular region, it is not clear whether Motorola would actually award work on a regional basis.

During the bidding process, Motorola shared its sales forecasts with vendors. Bidders needed to know what sales volume they could expect in order to set prices and ensure that they had capacity to meet demand. Motorola told Druckzentrum that it expected to sell 37 million mobile phones in the EMEA region in 2008 and made other rosy projections.

After bidding for the print segment in the EMEA region, Druckzentrum was given an "Initial Award" consisting of a "base share" of 2% and a "swing share" of 8%, meaning that Motorola made a "commitment" to buy 2% of print products from Druckzentrum and could, at its option, buy another 8% of print products from the company. The percentages were stated on the basis of global spending; thus, 2% of print means 2% of global print purchases, not 2% of EMEA print purchases. But there was no "commitment" in an absolute sense; rather, Motorola promised only to make a good-faith effort to hit the target and identified various commercial factors that might lead it to miss. All of this was embodied in a Notice of Initial Award, which the parties refer to as the "NIA" but we will simplify and just call "the contract."

Motorola sent a signed copy of the contract to Druckzentrum on January 23, 2008, although the previously executed Corporate Supply Agreement, which was incorporated by reference, stated an effective date of October 1, 2007. Another quirk is that the parties did not finalize prices until after Motorola awarded Druckzentrum the contract. As a result Motorola purchased nothing from Druckzentrum for the first few months of the contract. As the parties negotiated over prices during the winter and early spring of 2008, Motorola regularly sent updated sales forecasts to Druckzentrum. The updated forecasts showed revised downward sales projections, but they were in a different format than the earlier forecasts; Druckzentrum's fraud claim centers on the change in formatting.

After finalizing pricing, Druckzentrum countersigned the contract in April 2008, and Motorola started placing orders. By its terms, the contract was good through September 30, 2009, "unless terminated earlier." Among various other grounds for early termination, Motorola could terminate the contract "for convenience" on 90 days' written notice.

Throughout calendar year 2008, Motorola's cell-phone sales in the EMEA region dropped precipitously, and by November of that year, Motorola decided to shutter its German operations in favor of a "direct ship" model. Under the new model, everything would happen in China, including the printing of user manuals. Motorola orally notified Druckzentrum of this decision by phone on November 4, 2008. On November 18 Motorola's purchasing agent in Germany notified Druckzentrum by email that all business would conclude by the end of the first quarter of 2009. Motorola and Druckzentrum continued to do business during this transition period. When orders ceased, Druckzentrum sent a notice of cancellation dated April 24, 2009. On July 1, 2009, Motorola faxed a formal letter terminating the contract.

Sometime after losing Motorola's printing business, Druckzentrum entered bankruptcy in German courts. Druckzentrum then sued Motorola in federal court in the Northern District of Illinois alleging claims for breach of contract and fraud. First, Druckzentrum alleged that it had a two-year exclusive right to all of Motorola's print business for cell-phone products destined for the EMEA market, and by moving the work to a Chinese vendor, Motorola breached the contract. Another theory of breach centered on Motorola's failure to meet the 2% purchasing target. On the fraud claim, Druckzentrum alleged that Motorola fraudulently misrepresented its sales prospects during the bidding process, inducing Druckzentrum to bid at lower prices and continue performing to its detriment.

The district court dismissed the exclusivity claim on the pleadings, holding that the contract did not give Druckzentrum an exclusive right to Motorola's printing business in the EMEA region. Following extensive discovery, Motorola moved for summary judgment on the remaining claims, and the court granted the motion. The judge explained that the contract required that Motorola make a good-faith effort to hit the purchasing target but also provided that changes in commercial circumstances would excuse a miss. Because there was no evidence of bad faith—Motorola had moved its operations to China in response to plummeting sales—the judge concluded that there was no breach. The judge also held that Motorola gave proper notice of termination by emailing Druckzentrum on November 18, 2008, saying that business would cease and the Flensburg facility would close by the end of the first quarter 2009.

Finally, Druckzentrum's fraud claim rested on an argument that the sales forecasts Motorola provided during the bidding process were misleading. The judge rejected this claim as well, holding that there was no evidence that Motorola "knowingly misled [Druckzentrum] about its sales forecasts in an attempt to induce [it] to reduce pricing or otherwise enter into an agreement." After resolving a few other disputes not relevant here, the judge entered final judgment for Motorola, and Druckzentrum appealed.

II.   DISCUSSION

A. Breach of Contract

Druckzentrum argues that it had an exclusive right to all of Motorola's user-manual printing business for cell phones marketed in the EMEA region during the two-year contract period. If that's true, then Motorola broke its exclusivity promise by moving its printing business to a Chinese vendor halfway through the contract period.

Druckzentrum admits, as it must, that the written contract does not contain an express exclusivity promise. Rather, Druckzentrum contends that Motorola made the promise during the bidding process. This argument requires resort to parol evidence, which is foreclosed by the contract's integration clause. The contract contains an "Entire Agreement" provision clearly stating that "[t]his Agreement is the entire understanding between the parties concerning this Initial Award and supersedes all earlier discussions, agreements and representations regarding this Initial Award."

The Uniform Commercial Code, as adopted in Illinois, provides as follows:

> §2-202 Final written expression: parol or extrinsic evidence.
> Terms with respect to which the confirmatory memoranda of the parties agree or which are otherwise set forth in a writing *intended by the parties as a final expression of their agreement* with respect to such terms as are included therein *may not be contradicted by evidence of any prior agreement or of a contemporaneous oral agreement but may be explained or supplemented*
> (a) by course of performance, course of dealing, or usage of trade . . . ; and
> (b) *by evidence of consistent additional terms unless the court finds the writing to have been intended also as a complete and exclusive statement of the terms of the agreement.*

810 Ill. Comp. Stat. 5/2-202 (emphases added).

Druckzentrum tries to fit the facts of this case into subsection (b), which permits the importation of consistent terms from prior agreements but only if the contract is not fully integrated. Id. §5/2-202(b); see also id. cmt. 1. Motorola counters that the contract is in fact fully integrated and cannot be supplemented by parol evidence of prior agreements. In the words of the Illinois statute, the contract was "intended . . . as a complete and exclusive statement of the terms of the agreement." Id. §5/2-202(b) (emphasis added).

The contract language supports Motorola's position. The integration clause plainly states that "[t]his Agreement is the entire understanding between the parties . . . and supercedes all earlier discussions, agreements and representations. . . ." (Emphases added.) In an effort to overcome this unambiguous text, Druckzentrum argues that because the contract incorporates extrinsic materials by reference, it cannot reasonably be understood to be an exclusive statement of the parties' agreement despite the presence of an apparently conclusive integration clause. This argument backfires. When a contract expressly incorporates specific extrinsic materials by reference, the proper inference is that other, unmentioned extrinsic agreements are not part of the contract.

Moreover, the rule in Illinois is that "[i]f the additional terms are such that if agreed upon, they would certainly have been included in the document in the view of the court, then evidence of their alleged making must be kept from the trier of fact." 810 Ill. Comp. Stat. 5/2-202 cmt. 3 (explaining when a contract is fully integrated). Druckzentrum's claim of exclusivity in the EMEA region suggests that it considers this to be one of the key benefits of the deal. If the parties truly contemplated that Motorola was making such a critical promise, they certainly would have included it in the written contract.

Finally, Druckzentrum argues that the contract award is ambiguous and the presence of ambiguity means that the contract cannot be fully integrated. Even if the factual premise of this argument is correct, the legal conclusion does not follow. The existence of contractual ambiguity may allow consideration of extrinsic evidence to clarify those portions of the contract that are unclear. But it does not warrant a conclusion that the contract is not fully integrated such that evidence of prior agreements can be used to import entirely new terms.

And indeed the factual premise is not correct. Druckzentrum's argument about contractual ambiguity hinges on an implausible interpretation of the structure of the initial award. By its terms, the contract awarded Druckzentrum "2% of Base Share for the Print Segment with up to an additional 8% Swing Spend." Druckzentrum points out that 2% + 8% = 10%, and notes that 10% just happens to be the percentage of Motorola's worldwide print spending attributable to the EMEA region. Druckzentrum suggests that by stating the award in this way, Motorola promised exclusivity in the EMEA region, and parol evidence would confirm that interpretation.

It's true that the award is stated in technical terms. But it is not unclear. Motorola did not promise Druckzentrum 10% of its worldwide print spend; it promised 2% of its worldwide print spend with another 8% constituting a "swing spend" that it could award at its discretion. Because the contract is fully integrated and unambiguous (or at least unambiguous on this point), Druckzentrum cannot use parol evidence to prove up an enforceable promise of exclusivity in the EMEA region.

Druckzentrum also argues that Motorola breached the contract by failing to meet the 2% target during the contract period based solely on its own commercial interests. There is obviously no dispute that Motorola missed the target after it ceased doing business with Druckzentrum at the end of the first quarter of 2009. Motorola responds that it promised only a good-faith effort to meet the purchasing target, and the contract specified that the actual purchases would vary based on a number of commercial factors, including changes in business conditions.

More specifically, the contract provides as follows:

Motorola will use good faith efforts to award Products to Druckzentrum Harry Jung that in the aggregate, are reasonably likely to achieve the target percentage identified in the Initial Award. However, the actual percentage realized by Druckzentrum Harry Jung may vary from the target percentage due to a variety of factors, including but not limited to the following: i) one or more Motorola products in which Products are used does not achieve the level of success in the marketplace that was expected by Motorola; ii) one or more products in which Products are used, or the Products themselves, launches late, has a quality problem, is delayed in qualification, experiences a production interruption, is rejected by a Motorola customer, or is cancelled for whatever reason; iii) divestiture or other major change in Motorola's business; or iv) factors outside of Motorola's reasonable control that impact the percentage realized. Motorola is not liable, and Druckzentrum Harry Jung will have no claim against

Motorola, for any percentage variance from the target percentage identified in the Initial Award.

Read fairly and in context, this provision means that Motorola will not be liable for breach if, despite its good-faith efforts, one of the listed circumstances or something comparable prevented it from meeting the 2% purchasing target. In other words, Motorola did not assume an absolute duty to meet the purchasing target during the contract period; rather, it assumed a duty to make a good-faith effort to meet the target. Certain adverse business circumstances—including a drop in the level of success of Motorola's products in the marketplace—might excuse a miss.

And the evidence is undisputed that Motorola implemented its direct-ship distribution model in response to plummeting sales in the EMEA region. This entailed moving its user-manual printing business to China, where its cell phones were manufactured. A falloff in sales is specifically listed in the contract as one of the circumstances that would justify missing the 2% purchasing target. "Contract law does not require parties to behave altruistically toward each other. . . ." Original Great Am. Chocolate Chip Cookie Co. v. River Valley Cookies, Ltd., 970 F.2d 273, 280 (7th Cir. 1992). Rather, bad faith occurs when "a provision [is] invoked dishonestly to achieve a purpose contrary to that for which the contract had been made." Id. Motorola's promise to make a good-faith effort to meet a purchasing target did not require it to adhere to a business model that protected Druckzentrum's interests even in the face of a significant downturn in its cell-phone sales. To the contrary, the contract specifically contemplated that Motorola might miss the target if its products were less successful than anticipated or in the event of a "major change in [its] business."

The situation might be different if Motorola had switched to a cheaper print vendor in China while retaining its original distribution model; if that were the case, it might be possible for a jury to find that Motorola acted in bad faith. The situation would also be different if Motorola's switch to the direct-ship model was motivated specifically by a desire to ditch Druckzentrum as a vendor. And the situation would certainly be different if Motorola had retained its existing business model and simply switched to a cheaper print vendor in Germany. But these are not the facts here. Motorola's decision to cease purchasing from Druckzentrum was part of a broader change in its business model undertaken in response to a significant downturn in sales. Druckzentrum points to no evidence of bad faith.

Finally, Druckzentrum complains about the form of Motorola's termination notice. The contract provided that "Motorola may terminate for convenience upon ninety (90) days prior written notice to Supplier." Druckzentrum argues that the November 18, 2008 email was not sufficient because it was not a "written notice." Druckzentrum also notes that the email did not comply with other contractual formalities; a formal notice of termination was not sent until July 1, 2009. For its part, Motorola insists that the email sufficed as formal written notice of termination.

We don't need to resolve this skirmish. Druckzentrum is not arguing that the claimed inadequacy of the November 18 notice is an independent basis on which to find a compensable breach of contract. Instead, the dispute about the sufficiency of the notice relates only to the proper measure of damages. In other words, if the November 18 email sufficed as a notice of termination, then any damages for Motorola's failure to meet the 2% purchasing target would stop accruing 90 days after that date. Because there was no breach of contract in the first place, the dispute about the emailed termination notice is immaterial. . . .

For the foregoing reasons, the record supports neither a fraud claim nor a breach-of-contract claim. The district court properly entered summary judgment for Motorola.

AFFIRMED.

Most of the buyers and sellers interviewed for this book indicated that if a particular sale was important enough to warrant its own separate contract, then it also made sense to include a merger clause. However, one lawyer who oversees procurement practices in a Fortune 100 company said that there are some situations where it is not in his company's interest to include a merger clause in a long-term contract with a supplier:

> When we do single large contracts, we may or may not want a merger clause. Sometimes certain of our suppliers give us a lot of side services that we couldn't hope to fully describe or capture in a writing. Frankly, sometimes they'll do a lot more than they're legally obligated to do just to keep us happy as a customer. Therefore, it's not always in our interest to put the merger clause in because it's probably better for us to be able to insist on a supplier's "customary and ordinary" services rather than a laundry list of particulars in the writing. We're afraid if we undertake to try to list everything and then we leave something out, the supplier might decide only to do those things for us that we specifically outlined in the contract.

Whether or not particular extrinsic evidence is admissible under UCC §2-202 is a function of both the nature of the evidence sought to be introduced and the status of the writing that would serve to keep the evidence out. As tricky and nebulous as §2-202 can be, there are nevertheless three categorical statements that can be made about the issue that section covers.

First, if the writing that seeks to keep evidence out is not intended by both parties to be a final expression of the parties' agreement with respect to the terms included therein, then it will not serve to keep out any parol evidence. Thus, while a confirmation sent by one party, an offer sheet, and a purchase order are all writings that contain terms, none of these is a writing that is intended by both parties to be a final expression of the parties' agreement as to the terms contained in the writing.

Second, even where there is a writing intended by both parties to be a final expression of their agreement, parties may always introduce evidence of side agreements that occurred *after* the writing in question. This is just another way of saying that parties are always free to modify earlier agreements that they made, no matter how comprehensive and final the earlier agreement seemed to be at the time. UCC §2-209.

A third categorical statement that can be made about parol evidence in the sales system is that even where there is a writing intended by both parties to be a final expression of their agreement, a party may always introduce evidence of usage of trade, course of dealing, or course of performance to explain or supplement the writing. The one exception to this statement is that these terms may not explain or supplement a writing if the writing has "carefully negated" that possibility, in the words of Official Comment 2 to §2-202. Even this exception is probably limited to the careful negation of a particular usage of trade, course of dealing, or course of performance; it would seem nearly impossible for a court to read any sales agreement in the complete absence of context to the particular parties' prior dealings and the industry in which they deal.

Cravotta v. Deggingers' Foundry, Inc.

215 P.3d 636 (Kan. Ct. App. 2010)

HILL, J.

In this case, Deggingers' Foundry, Inc., of Topeka, promised in a settlement agreement to manufacture and deliver some chandeliers and other items to the plaintiff, Mark Cravotta, in Dallas, Texas, by a certain date. The foundry failed to do so. During the trial of this matter, when Tim Degginger claimed Cravotta's failure to forward important electrical system information stopped the foundry from making a timely delivery, the district court ruled the Uniform Commercial Code's statute of frauds barred Degginger from successfully raising such a defense. We must reverse and remand this case because the trial court failed to consider the contract in the commercial context from which it arose, as the Code requires. By relying only on the statute of frauds and not considering the parol evidence statute in the Code, the court erred.

Cravotta engaged the Deggingers' Foundry to make some chandeliers, sconces, and lanterns for installation in a mansion in Texas in April 2003. Cravotta wanted the foundry to make 3 nickel-bronze chandeliers, 8 nickel-wall sconces, and 16 silicone-bronze lanterns. The cost for these items was $106,000, and the parties anticipated a production time of 90 days.

The parties signed a concise two-page contract drawn on Deggingers' letterhead. The essence of their agreement provided a 10-step list of how the parties intended to complete the project:

> "By way of outline this contract shall be implemented by:
>
> "1. Contract.
> "2. Final shop drawings prepared by Degginger's Foundry, Inc.
> "3. Final engineering review of the shop drawings.
> "4. Patterns.

"5. Prototypes.
"6. Owner Approval.
"7. Aesthetic sample submittals.
"8. Production.
"9. Product approval.
"10. Shipping to job site."

The rest of the agreement contained terms concerning method of payment and other matters not pertinent to this appeal.

Matters did not go smoothly for the parties, and on June 20, 2005, Cravotta filed a breach of contract lawsuit against Degginger in Shawnee County. Cravotta alleged he had already paid $79,500 under the contract and Degginger had breached their contract by failing to manufacture the products. Cravotta sought $79,500 in damages plus interest. In response, Degginger admitted it made the contract with Cravotta but alleged the original contract had been modified by a series of subsequent communications and acknowledgments from both sides.

Despite the lawsuit, the parties were still working toward a common goal. For example, Degginger delivered the 16 lanterns to Cravotta even after Cravotta filed the petition. But, we note those lanterns had no wiring or glass. Tension between the parties apparently eased since, instead of going forward with the breach-of-contract case, Cravotta and Degginger reached an agreement to settle the lawsuit and complete the project.

On February 3, 2006, the district court held a hearing so a record could be made of the parties' agreement. Cravotta appeared at the hearing, but only counsel was present on behalf of Degginger. Cravotta's attorney stated the parties had agreed that Degginger currently owed $62,478.22 to Cravotta under the April 7, 2003, contract. Degginger agreed to complete the eight sconces and three chandeliers. These items would be completed in a manner satisfactory to Cravotta and delivered to him by April 15, 2006. Once the items were completed and delivered to Cravotta, Degginger would be credited $62,478.22 and, for completing the work, Cravotta would pay Degginger the remaining balance owed to the foundry under the contract. Finally, Degginger agreed to pay Cravotta $6,000 for legal fees.

Unfortunately, Degginger did not deliver the sconces and chandeliers to Cravotta by April 15, 2006. Therefore, on May 12, 2006, Degginger filed several motions alleging Cravotta had prevented the foundry from completing the sconces and chandeliers on time because Cravotta failed to provide vital information needed to complete the wiring of the items. Thus, Degginger asked the district court to find that Cravotta had breached the settlement agreement and asked the court to order Cravotta to pay $27,000 to Degginger for completing at least part of the contract. In turn, Cravotta denied the allegations and asked for judgment against Degginger. The question then became which party first breached their settlement agreement.

The district court tried the dispute in April 2008. Tim Degginger, President of Deggingers' Foundry, Inc., testified about all of the work the foundry had completed in compliance with the contract. Because Cravotta could not provide acceptable models or patterns, the foundry had to hand-sculpt some patterns and machine-sculpt the remaining patterns used to create the chandeliers and sconces. After months of discussions and submissions of many drawings, the parties finally agreed on a design that was acceptable to the owner of the house in Texas. Degginger pointed out that for 1 chandelier, the foundry made 33 parts from lost-wax castings, each hand sculpted. The remaining 53 other parts were sand-cast, meaning they were hand carved as well. He said the chandeliers and sconces are at the foundry, essentially complete. The only remaining work to be done on them is wiring and the final polishing. According to Degginger, wiring is the problem.

From the start of the project until the trial to the court, Degginger sought information from Cravotta about the "stepdown transformers" inside the house where the items were going to be placed. According to Degginger, Cravotta never provided this information. In the foundry's view, this information was crucial in order to ensure that the sconces and chandeliers were properly wired and safe to use inside the house. Degginger stated the house in Texas has a very unusual electrical system for a residence—480-volt, three-phase power, and current at 600 watts. He pointed out that the foundry uses a similar electrical system to melt bronze, 300 pounds in 15 minutes. Such electrical power is very dangerous, potentially lethal. The stepdown transformers lower the current to 220 or 110 volts, single phase. Therefore, wiring of the chandeliers and sconces required expert design assistance, what Degginger referred to was an electrical engineer's stamp of approval on the wiring plans.

In support, the foundry introduced as an example of the parties ongoing communication, a February 28, 2005, e-mail to Cravotta from Janet Zoble, who was hired by Degginger to work with Cravotta in designing the items to be created. It stated:

> "Electrical drawings are nearly complete on the chandelier. Detailing will require input from the electrical engineer. I'm sure he will want to know the wattage you intend as well as the size of the breakers dedicated to the chandeliers and sconces. There are 18 bulbs per chandelier; at 25 watts that's 450W each or 900W for the two living room units; at 40W that would be 750W each or 1500W for two. Would you intend any more than that?"

In addition, Degginger introduced an April 11, 2006, letter written by its attorney and sent to Cravotta's attorney stating: "Mr. Degginger advises me that we have completed our part of the metal work and Mr. Cravotta still has some decisions to make."

Degginger also stated that all the work the foundry could perform to finish the sconces and chandelier was finished by mid-March 2006. He acknowledged that under the settlement agreement the foundry was to complete the chandeliers and sconces and deliver them by April 15, 2006. Cravotta did not put on any evidence to rebut Degginger's testimony.

In ruling on this case, the district court was troubled by the fact that neither the April 7, 2003, contract nor the settlement agreement of February 3, 2006, explicitly mentioned Cravotta had a duty to provide electrical information to Degginger.

The district court believed that if the need of such information was so significant, the parties should have stated so explicitly in the agreements. Ultimately, the court concluded that if Cravotta had such a duty, the statute of frauds found in K.S.A. 84-2-201 required that it be put in writing and signed by Cravotta. Because that was not done, the district court ruled the statute prevented it from finding that Cravotta had such a duty under the agreements. Thus, the district court found that because Degginger did not complete and deliver the sconces and chandeliers by April 15, 2006, it breached the settlement agreement. Therefore, the court granted judgment to Cravotta in the amount of $62,478.22 (plus interest) and $6,000 in attorney fees. . . .

Since this case involves the sale of goods, the Uniform Commercial Code applies. The Code, in many ways, directs parties and the courts to view commercial transactions within the context of the marketplace. One of the Code's purposes is "to permit the continued expansion of commercial practices through custom, usage and agreement of the parties." K.S.A. 84-1-102(b). In other words, the Code tries to promote commerce, not inhibit it. Even the section of the Code used by the trial court, K.S.A. 84-2-201(1), points out that some writing is essential, but "a writing" is enforceable even if it omits an agreed upon term:

> "Except as otherwise provided in this section a contract for the sale of goods for the price of $500 or more is not enforceable by way of action or defense unless there is some writing sufficient to indicate that a contract for sale has been made between the parties and signed by the party against whom enforcement is sought or by his authorized agent or broker. *A writing is not insufficient because it omits or incorrectly states a term agreed upon but the contract is not enforceable under this paragraph beyond the quantity of goods shown in such writing.*" (Emphasis added.)

The next section of the Code, K.S.A. 84-2-202, which deals with parol evidence, instructs that commercial contracts must be viewed in conjunction with the parties' course of dealing and the common practices of a particular trade:

> "Terms with respect to which the confirmatory memoranda of the parties agree or which are otherwise set forth in a writing *intended by the parties as a final expression of their agreement with respect to such terms as are included therein* may not be contradicted by evidence of any prior agreement or of a contemporaneous oral agreement but may be explained or supplemented
>
>> "(a) by course of dealing or usage of trade (section 84-1-205) or by course of performance (section 84-2-208); and
>> "(b) by evidence of consistent additional terms unless the court finds the writing to have been intended also as a complete and exclusive statement of the terms of the agreement."

(Emphasis added.) K.S.A. 84-2-202.

As with any set of statutes dealing with a common subject, the Uniform Commercial Code must be interpreted in a harmonious fashion. The statute of frauds in Sales Article 2 must be read in tandem with the parol evidence statute.

The first deals with the creation of the bargain, the second shows the court what bargain can be enforced.

Both parties admit they entered into a contract for the sale of goods. They also agreed on the quantity of goods to be sold. There was simply no dispute between them about whether there is a binding contract. Therefore, the statute of frauds in K.S.A. 84-2-201 has little bearing when deciding the merits of this case. See K.S.A. 84-2-201(1) and (3)(b) (a contract is not enforceable beyond the quantity of goods shown in the writing or admitted to by the party); *Wendling v. Puls,* 227 Kan. 780, 788, 610 P.2d 580 (1980) (because the parties admitted the existence of the contract in court, K.S.A. 84-2-201 did not prevent the contract from being enforced). Actually, the only dispute between the parties was whether Cravotta had a contractual duty to provide electrical information to Degginger so it could complete construction of the chandeliers and sconces and deliver them to Cravotta by April 15, 2006.

In our view, K.S.A. 84-2-201, as a matter of law, certainly did not prevent the district court from finding that Cravotta had such a duty, even though the parties did not put it in writing. The statute states: "A writing is not insufficient because it *omits* or incorrectly states a term agreed upon but the contract is not enforceable under this paragraph beyond the quantity of goods shown in such writing." (Emphasis added.) K.S.A. 84-2-201(1). The Official UCC Comment 1 to K.S.A. 84-2-201 states: "The required writing *need not contain all the material terms of the contract* and such material terms as are stated need not be precisely stated. All that is required is that the writing afford a basis for believing that the offered oral evidence rests on a real transaction." (Emphasis added.) In other words, K.S.A. 84-2-201 does not prevent a court from finding that, based on extrinsic evidence, a written contract contains a term not explicitly stated within it. But before the court ruled the statute of fraud prevented Deggingers' Foundry from presenting its defense, the court should have first determined if the parties intended their settlement agreement to be their total agreement. In other words, the court should have decided if the contract was integrated.

We turn again to the Code. If contracting parties intend a writing to be a final expression of their agreement with respect to such terms stated within that writing, then under K.S.A. 84-2-202 such a writing is considered integrated. This means the terms cannot be contradicted by evidence of any prior agreement or contemporaneous oral agreement. But, even so, the terms of an integrated writing may be supplemented by evidence of consistent *additional* terms. Going further, if a writing is completely integrated (*i.e.*, the parties intended the writing to be a *complete and exclusive* statement of the terms of their agreement), the writing cannot be contradicted or supplemented by extrinsic any evidence. A writing is considered completely integrated if the additional terms sought to be added to the writing are such that, if agreed upon, they would have certainly been included in the original contract. See K.S.A. 84-2-202, Kansas Comment 1996, 1-2. In order to determine this, the district court here must make additional findings.

Whether the parties intend a writing as a final expression of their agreement or a complete and exclusive statement of the terms of their agreement are questions of fact for the district court to decide. See K.S.A. 84-2-202, Kansas Comment 1996, 2. In *Blair Constr., Inc. v. McBeth,* 273 Kan. 679, 686, 44 P.3d 1244 (2002), the court said: "Intent is a question of fact to be determined from examining the written instruments and from the facts and circumstances surrounding their execution. [Citations omitted.]" In *Betaco, Inc. v. Cessna Aircraft Co.,* 32 F.3d 1126, 1131 (7th Cir. 1994), under K.S.A. 84-2-202[b], the court concluded the determination of whether a contract is completely integrated is primarily a factual determination that "'goes beyond the four corners of the contract.'" In *Transamerica Oil Corp. v. Lynes, Inc.,* 723 F.2d 758, 763 (10th Cir. 1983), the court held that under K.S.A. 84-2-202, whether the parties intended a writing to be a final expression of their agreement is a question of fact for the district court to decide.

Furthermore, whether extrinsic evidence constitutes a course of dealing, a usage of trade, or a course of performance is a factual inquiry that the district court must undertake. See K.S.A. 84-1-205, Kansas Comment 1996, 2-3; K.S.A. 84-2-208, Kansas Comment 1996, 1; *Aero Consulting Corp. v. Cessna Aircraft Co.,* 867 F. Supp. 1480, 1489-91 (D. Kan. 1994) (determining whether plaintiff's evidence established "course of dealing" under K.S.A. 84-1-205[1]).

Much in the record supports the court finding the duty existed. The course of dealing of the parties highlights their transaction. The original contract of April 7, 2003, recited that one of the agreed steps of production would be "final engineering review of the shop drawings." Degginger's testimony revealed that the parties were almost continuously negotiating about the materials and design of the finished products. Professional drafting was employed. Prototypes would be fashioned and either accepted or rejected. The foundry created models that it either modified or adopted during this manufacturing process. Naturally, safety was also a concern. The chandeliers are massive metal structures that will overhang whatever or whoever may be beneath them. Cravotta intended to install them in a house with a very unusual and potentially dangerous electrical system. We point out the Official UCC Comment to K.S.A. 84-2-202 advises: "[T]he course of actual performance by the parties is considered the best indication of what they intended the writing to mean."

Finally, whether a party's duty under a contract was based on a condition precedent is a question for the finder of fact to decide. *Source Direct, Inc. v. Mantell,* 19 Kan. App. 2d 399, 407, 870 P.2d 686 (1994).

The district court here made no such analysis, nor did it make findings that would determine the applicability of K.S.A. 84-2-202 in this case. An appellate court cannot make such findings. See *Dragon v. Vanguard Industries,* 282 Kan. 349, 356, 144 P.3d 1279 (2006) (appellate court may remand for more specific factual findings when it concludes that lack of findings precludes meaningful review); *In re Estate of Cline,* 258 Kan. 196, 206, 898 P.2d 643 (1995) (appellate court may remand for additional findings when record on review does not support a presumption that the district court found all facts necessary to support its judgment).

Affirmed in part and reversed in part. We remand with directions for the district court to determine if the parties intended their settlement agreement to be integrated, either fully or partially, if the parties made some enforceable subsequent agreement, or if the course of dealing, course of performance between the parties, trade custom, or some trade usage modified the parties' settlement agreement.

Affirmed in part, reversed in part, and remanded with directions.

———

Another issue with the introduction of usage of trade is what constitutes permissible "explaining or supplementing" versus impermissible "contradicting." Some courts have been very lenient in their definition of "explaining or supplementing." One court allowed a defendant to introduce usage of trade to the effect that, in this particular industry, a stated quantity really does not mean a stated quantity but instead means whatever the buyer in fact happens to need. This, the court said, did not "contradict" an express term in the contract (the stated quantity), but instead merely explained or supplemented it. Columbia Nitrogen Corp. v. Royster Corp., 451 F.2d 3 (4th Cir. 1971).

Beyond these categorical statements about certain kinds of writings or certain kinds of evidence, the general rule about parol evidence in the sales of goods system is this: Prior consistent additional terms may be introduced to explain or supplement any writing except where the writing is intended by both parties to be a complete and exclusive statement of all the terms of the contract. The "complete and exclusive" nature of the writing might be proven, for example, by the existence of a well-drafted and conspicuous merger clause that screams out the completeness and exclusivity of the writing.

A corollary to the general rule that "consistent additional terms" may be introduced as evidence is that "contradictory" terms may not be. Sometimes the difference between these two kinds of terms is less than obvious. For example, suppose that the seller of a used car told the buyer orally that the buyer could return the car for any reason during the first six months after the sale and receive a full refund. Suppose that this statement were made prior to the execution of a written contract that was found to be a final expression of the parties' agreement, at least with respect to the terms included therein. The writing said nothing about the buyer's right to return the car for a refund.

Is the pre-writing oral statement about buyer's right to return the car a "consistent additional term" or a "contradictory" one? On one hand, this statement does not directly contradict anything contained in the writing, since the writing is silent about the buyer's right to return the car for a full refund. On the other hand, the common understanding in the absence of anything said to the contrary is that all sales are final, and therefore a right of the buyer to return the car for up to six months would contradict that unstated assumption.

Problem Set 6

6.1. a. Arlene Ledger (from Problem 3.2) is having difficulty with her company's steel supplier, Wilson Steel. Jake Wilson, president of Wilson Steel, had negotiated a contract with Arlene by which Arlene had agreed to purchase all of her company's requirements for steel over the next year from Wilson at a stated price per ton. In getting Arlene to sign this contract, Jake had assured Arlene that he was so confident of how low his price was, that if she happened to find a lower price during the next year she could buy her steel requirements from the lower-priced competitor. Arlene admits to you that she never did read the contract closely before signing it. Now, Arlene tells you, just two months after signing this contract, she has found a lower-priced steel supplier.

As you look at the contract Arlene signed with Wilson, you notice two things: (1) the contract says nothing about this "low-price guarantee," and (2) the contract does not contain a merger clause. What do you advise Arlene about her ability to buy her steel requirements from the lower-priced competitor to Wilson? UCC §2-202, Official Comment 3 to §2-202.

b. Same facts as part (a), except that the contract does contain a merger clause, and Jake gave Arlene the price guarantee *after* the two had signed the contract. In a suit to enforce the contract, may Arlene introduce evidence of Jake's price guarantee? UCC §§2-202, 2-209(1).

c. Same facts as part (a), except that the contract does contain a merger clause, and Jake and Arlene have done these requirements contracts several times in the past. In all of these prior deals, Jake has made the same oral assurances concerning the price guarantee, but Arlene has never had to exercise her rights under the guarantee. In a suit to enforce the contract, may Arlene introduce evidence of Jake's price guarantee? UCC §§1-303, 2-202.

d. Same facts as part (a), except that the contract does contain a merger clause, and the custom in this industry is that for requirements contracts like this one, the price is typically the lowest price that the buyer could get from any other source at the time it requires each steel shipment. In a suit to enforce the contract, may Arlene introduce evidence of Jake's price guarantee? If not, may she nevertheless introduce evidence of the price custom in the industry, which in fact is identical to what Jake guaranteed orally? UCC §§1-303, 2-202.

6.2. You have finally learned your lesson about doing business with your one-time law school classmate and Rolls Royce collector Deborah Swift (from Problem 1.6). Unfortunately, one of your friends has not. Justin Roberts, a non-lawyer and neighbor of yours, comes to you for some friendly advice about a problem that he is having with Deborah. Justin, himself a car buff, had gone with a friend to Deborah's house and had done a "handshake deal" with Deborah to buy Deborah's four '89 Rolls Royces for $17,000 each. According to this oral agreement, Justin was to pick the cars up in 30 days.

The day after Justin's visit to Deborah's house, he received a signed letter from her purporting to confirm their agreement. Deborah's letter, however, said that their agreement was for Justin to purchase just two of her '89 Rolls Royces, and for $25,000 each instead of $17,000. Following receipt of that letter, Justin tried for two weeks to reach Deborah to clear up what he thought might have been an honest mistake on her part about the terms of their deal.

When Justin finally did reach her, Deborah insisted that it was "her way or the highway," even though Justin's friend was willing to swear that Justin's version of the oral agreement was correct.

If you represent Justin, for what quantity and price will you be able to enforce his deal with Deborah? UCC §§2-201, 2-202, 2-207.

Assignment 7: Requisites to Formalization in Leases, International Sales, and Real Estate Sales

A. Requisites to Formalization in Leases

When it comes to requisites for formalizing a contract, the system for leases is roughly parallel to that for sales. The rules governing extrinsic evidence for lease contracts in §2A-202 are precisely the same as those found for sales of goods in §2-202. However, the rules on the necessity for a writing in lease deals, found in §2A-201, differ in a few notable respects from the comparable rules for sales.

First, the necessity for a writing with leases does not kick in unless the total lease payments are at least $1,000. Some states, including California and Florida, have added a non-uniform amendment to §2A-201 that requires consumer leases to be in writing in order to be enforceable, no matter how small the amount of total lease payments.

Second, when a writing is required in a lease deal, that writing has a couple of additional requirements compared to the writing that §2-201(1) requires for sales of goods. Not only does the lease writing in §2A-201(1) need to include a signature of the party to be charged and an indication that a lease contract has been made, it must also "describe the goods leased and the lease term."

The statutory exceptions to the writing requirement for leases also depart slightly from those available for sales of goods contracts. The main difference is that there is no "merchant's exception" to the writing requirement in the case of leases. The rationale for that omission, we are told by the drafters in the Official Comment to §2A-201, is that "the number of such transactions involving leases, as opposed to sales, was thought to be modest." This echoes the rationale mentioned in Assignment 4 for why Article 2A does not include a "battle of the forms" section: lessors and lessees do not typically exchange purchase orders and acknowledgement forms, as do buyers and sellers. Instead, lessors and lessees normally both sign a single written contract that spells out the terms of their lease agreement.

The other difference in the exceptions to the writing requirement between leases and sales is the absence in §2A-201(3) of the exception for payment received and accepted by the lessor. As to this change from the sales counterpart, the drafters of Article 2A note in the Official Comment to §2A-201 that the payment typically tendered in a lease deal is only for a relatively small portion of the total lease payments. In light of this reality, the drafters believed that "as a matter of policy, this act of payment is not a sufficient substitute for the required memorandum."

B.   Requisites to Formalization in International Sales

In international sales, the requisites to formalization are few and far between. There is no default rule in the CISG that bars the introduction of extrinsic evidence. Instead, CISG Article 8(3) tells us that "due consideration is to be given to all relevant circumstances of the case including the negotiations, any practices which the parties have established between themselves, usages and any subsequent conduct of the parties."

Of course, parties in an international sales contract may always choose to override the CISG default term on that score and create by contract their own parol evidence rule. A standard merger clause that deems a particular writing to be complete and exclusive would seem to do the trick. CISG Article 6 is clear on the ability of parties to "derogate from or vary the effect of any of [the CISG's] provisions."

TeeVee Toons, Inc. v. Gerhard Schubert GmbH

2006 WL2463537 (S.D.N.Y. 2006)

CASEY, J.

TeeVee Toons, Inc. and its affiliate Steve Gottlieb, Inc. ("Plaintiffs") brought this action against Gerhard Schubert GmbH ("Schubert"), claiming that Schubert improperly manufactured a packaging system commissioned by TeeVee Toons, Inc. ("TVT") and alleging breach of contract, fraud, and negligence. Schubert moves for an order granting summary judgment in Schubert's favor on Plaintiffs' claims. For the following reasons, Schubert's motion is GRANTED in part and DENIED in part.

I.   BACKGROUND

In the early part of the 1990s, TVT record-company president and founder Steve Gottlieb ("Gottlieb") invented and patented a biodegradable-cardboard "flip-top" packaging called the "Biobox," which was designed to provide a secure, environmentally friendly way to package audio and video cassettes. (See United States Patent 5,361,898.) In 1994, Gottlieb began searching for a company that could develop a system capable of mass-producing the Biobox, and he settled on the German firm Schubert. At the time, Schubert marketed its products in the United

States through an exclusive agency agreement with Rodico, Inc. ("Rodico"), a New Jersey-based company.

After protracted negotiations, TVT and Schubert entered into a written contract in February 1995 for Schubert to build a Biobox-production system ("February 1995 Quotation Contract"). Shortly thereafter, problems started accumulating. First, Schubert experienced delays that set the project back nearly two years. In 1997, when the Biobox-production system ("Schubert System") was finally finished and delivered to Cinram, Inc. ("Cinram")—the production facility in Richmond, Indiana that TVT had contracted with—the system malfunctioned frequently and severely.

Eventually, upset with the lack of progress made in curing the Schubert System's defects, TVT and its affiliate Steve Gottlieb, Inc. ("SGI") commenced this action in July 2000, asserting various contract and tort claims and claiming that they suffered millions of dollars in damages, including money paid to Schubert for the system and repairs, money spent on other technicians and equipment to try to fix or replace components, money spent to set up its production facility, money that will have to be spent to replace the facility, money spent on administration of the Biobox project, and lost profits. On March 28, 2002, the Court denied Schubert's motion to dismiss Plaintiffs' Complaint. TeeVee Toons, Inc. v. Gerhard Schubert GmbH, No. 00 Civ. 5189 (RCC), 2002 WL 498627, at *9 (S.D.N.Y. Mar. 29, 2002). Schubert now moves for an order granting summary judgment in Schubert's favor on Plaintiffs' contract and tort claims.

II. DISCUSSION

* * *

C.   TVT's Contract Claims

1.   Choice of Law

TVT's contract claims are governed by the United Nations Convention on Contracts for the International Sale of Goods, Apr. 11, 1980, S. Treaty Doc. No. 98-9 (1983), 1489 U.N.T.S. 3, 19 I.L.M. 668 (1980) ("CISG" or "Convention"), which "applies to contracts of sale of goods between parties whose places of business are in different States . . . when the States are Contracting States." CISG art. 1(1)(a), 19 I.L.M. at 672. TVT's place of business is in the United States (in New York) and Schubert's place of business is in Germany (in Crailsheim). Both the United States and Germany are contracting states. See United Nations Comm'n on Int'l Trade Law (UNCITRAL), Status: 1980 United Nations Convention on Contracts for the International Sale of Goods (2005), at http://www.uncitral.org/unci tral/en/uncitral _texts/sale_ goods/1980CISG_status.html (last visited Aug. 16, 2006) (listing the parties to the CISG, including the United States and Germany); see also St. Paul Guardian Ins. Co. v. Neuromed Med. Sys. & Support, GmbH, No. 00 Civ.

9344 (SHS), 2002 WL 465312, at *3 (S.D.N.Y. Mar. 26, 2002) (noting that "both the U.S. and Germany are Contracting States" to the CISG and that "Germany has been a Contracting State since 1991").

Further, none of the exceptions to CISG applicability is present. Article 2 of the CISG provides that the "Convention does not apply to sales: (a) of goods bought for personal, family or household use . . . ; (b) by auction; (c) on execution or otherwise by authority of law; (d) of stocks, shares, investment securities, negotiable instruments or money; (e) of ships, vessels, hovercraft or aircraft; [or] (f) of electricity." CISG art. 2, 19 I.L.M. at 672. None of the enumerated exceptions of Article 2 exists here. Article 3 provides that the "Convention does not apply in contracts in which the preponderant part of the obligations of the party who furnishes the goods consists in the supply of labour or services," CISG art. 3(2), 19 I.L.M. at 672, but "the preponderant part of the obligations" here pertains to the manufactured Schubert System, not labor or other services. Article 5's prohibition against CISG application to actions sounding in personal injury likewise does not block CISG application in this matter. See CISG art. 5, 19 I.L.M. at 673 ("This Convention does not apply to the liability of the seller for death or personal injury caused by the goods to any person."). Article 6 provides that "[t]he parties may exclude the application of this Convention or, subject to article 12, derogate from or vary the effect of any of its provisions," CISG art. 6, 19 I.L.M. at 673, but neither party chose, by express provision in the contract at issue, to opt out of the application of the CISG. See also Delchi Carrier SpA v. Rotorex Corp., 71 F.3d 1024, 1028 n.1 (2d Cir. 1995) (holding that when an "agreement is silent as to choice of law, the Convention applies if both parties are located in signatory nations" unless the parties have "by contract chose[n] to be bound by a source of law other than the CISG, such as the Uniform Commercial Code" (citing CISG, arts. 1, 6)); St. Paul Guardian Ins. Co., 2002 WL 465312, at *3 (holding that the CISG governed the transaction in that case "because (1) both the U.S. and Germany are Contracting States to that Convention, and (2) neither party chose, by express provision in the contract, to opt out of the application of the CISG").

TVT asserts its contract claims under Articles 35 and 36 of the CISG. (See Compl. ¶¶60-76 (first claim for relief for failure to conform with respect to fitness for ordinary or particular purpose under Article 35(2)(a)-(b) of the CISG); id. ¶¶77-88 (second claim for relief for failure to conform with respect to model or sample under Article 35(2)(c) of the CISG); id. ¶¶89-99 (third claim for relief for breach of guarantee under Article 36(2) of the CISG).)

2.   Failure to Conform Under the United Nations Convention on Contracts for the International Sale of Goods Under Article 35

Article 35 provides in pertinent part, that a "seller must deliver goods which are of the quantity, quality and description required by the contract and which are contained or packaged in the manner required by the contract." CISG art. 35(1),

19 I.L.M. at 679. Goods do not conform with the contract, except where the parties have agreed otherwise, unless they:

> (a) are fit for the purposes for which goods of the same description would ordinarily be used;
> (b) are fit for any particular purpose expressly or impliedly made known to the seller at the time of the conclusion of the contract, except where the circumstances show that the buyer did not rely, or that it was unreasonable for him to rely, on the seller's skill and judgment; [and]
> (c) possess the qualities of goods which the seller has held out to the buyer as a sample or model. . . .

CISG art. 35(2)(a)-(c), 19 I.L.M. at 679.

a.   Fitness for Ordinary or Particular Purpose Under Article 35(2)(a)-(b)

1.   Fitness for Ordinary or Particular Purpose: Breach

TVT alleges that the Schubert System "was not fit for the ordinary purpose of an automatic erecting, loading, and closing system for a flip-top cassette carton, and it was not fit for the particular purpose for which it was ordered and purchased, namely, the rapid and reliable production of Biobox packaging cartons" in violation of Article 35(2)(a)-(b). (Compl. ¶68.)

There is no genuine issue of material fact with respect to the Schubert System's failure to produce Bioboxes at the proper rate and of the proper quality. (See, e.g., Gottlieb Decl. Opp'n Ex. T (three-page list of Biobox "line problems" encountered by Cinram maintenance staff dated Dec. 6, 1997); id. Ex. V (memorandum from Cinram to Gottlieb dated July 16, 1999 regarding "Biobox Machine Problems"); id. Ex. W (letter from Gottlieb to Rodico dated Oct. 29, 1997 outlining speed and quality problems and noting that Cinram was "extremely concerned given the performance of the machine"); id. Ex. X (letter from Gottlieb to Rodico dated Nov. 13, 1997 indicating Gottlieb's concerns "that Schubert understand how far the machine is away from being operational per the original specifications" with respect to speed and quality); id. Ex. Y (letter from Gottlieb to Schubert dated Nov. 24, 1997 reporting "that the Biobox project has come to a screeching halt" because of the speed and quality problems with the Schubert System); id. Ex. Z (memorandum from Rodico to TVT dated Dec. 18, 1997 discussing problems with the Schubert System); id. Ex. BB (inter-Schubert facsimile dated July 26, 1999 summarizing problems with the Schubert System).) And the record makes clear that TVT notified Schubert of this nonconformity as early as October 1997. (See Gottlieb Decl. Opp'n Ex. W (letter from Gottlieb to Schubert agent Neuber at Rodico dated Oct. 29, 1997 outlining speed and quality problems.) In the Court's view, the time interval from the Schubert System's "late August 1997" delivery (Compl. ¶40) to the October 1997 notification was "reasonable" as required by CISG Article 39(1).

Schubert argues, however, that provisions in the "Terms and Conditions" attached to the February 1995 Quotation Contract effectively disclaim all or part of the relevant Article 35 warranty. (Def.'s Mem. Supp. at 17-18, 21; see also Gottlieb Decl. Opp'n Ex. E (February 1995 Quotation Contract) at 32 ("Please refer to the attached Terms and Conditions.").) TVT counters that "there was an express oral understanding reached between TVT and Schubert's agent that the onerous boilerplate language [of the Terms and Conditions] would *not* apply to [the Biobox] project." (Pls.' Mem. Opp'n at 12.) There exists an issue of fact as to whether the attached "Terms and Conditions" are excluded from February 1995 Quotation Contract.

Unlike American contract law, the CISG contains no statute of frauds. See, e.g., Atla-Medine v. Crompton Corp., No. 00 Civ. 5901 (HB), 2001 WL 1382592, at *5 n.6 (S.D.N.Y. Nov. 7, 2001) ("Where applicable, the CISG may render enforceable agreements not evidenced by a writing and therefore subject to the Statute of Frauds."); Larry DiMatteo et al., The Interpretive Turn in International Sales Law: An Analysis of 15 Years of CISG Jurisprudence, 24 Nw. J. Int'l L. & Bus. 299, 437 n.872 (2004) (explaining how CISG Article 11 does away with the writing requirement). According to CISG Article 11, "[a] contract of sale need not be concluded in or evidenced by writing and is not subject to any other requirement as to form[, but] may be proved by any means, including witnesses." CISG art. 11, 19 I.L.M. at 674. In particular, it may be proved by oral statements between the parties; the CISG, unlike American contract law, includes no parol-evidence rule, and "allows all relevant information into evidence even if it contradicts the written documentation." Claudia v. Olivieri Footwear Ltd., No. 96 Civ. 8052 (HB) (THK), 1998 WL 164824, at *4-*5 (S.D.N.Y. Apr. 7, 1998). CISG Article 8 explains how such oral evidence should be interpreted:

> (1) For the purposes of this Convention statements made by and other conduct of a party are to be interpreted according to his intent where the other party knew or could not have been unaware what that intent was.
> (2) If the preceding paragraph is not applicable, statements made by and other conduct of a party are to be interpreted according to the understanding that a reasonable person of the same kind as the other party would have had in the same circumstances.
> (3) In determining the intent of a party or the understanding a reasonable person would have had, due consideration is to be given to all relevant circumstances of the case including the negotiations, any practices which the parties have established between themselves, usages and any subsequent conduct of the parties.

CISG art. 8, 19 I.L.M. at 673; see also MCC-Marble Ceramic Ctr. v. Ceramica Nuova D'Agostino, S.P.A., 144 F.3d 1384, 1388-89 (11th Cir. 1998) (noting that Article 8(1) "requires a court to consider . . . evidence of the parties' subjective intent" and that Article 8(3) "is a clear instruction to admit and consider parol evidence regarding the negotiations to the extent they reveal the parties' subjective intent").

Under the CISG, therefore, any statements made between Schubert (or its representatives) and TVT (or its representatives) that contradict the written "Terms and Conditions," or that indicate that the "Terms and Conditions" section as a whole is not part of the final agreement between the parties, must be considered in deciding what is part of the February 1995 Quotation Contract. Some of the relevant statements, for example, tend to indicate that the entire "Terms and Conditions" section does not apply. In particular, TVT contends that a Schubert agent told TVT, in the course of conversations occurring between February 3, 1995 (the date that the February 1995 Quotation Contract was drafted) and February 13, 1995 (the date that TVT sent its acceptance of the February 1995 Quotation Contract), that TVT should "'not worry' about the fine print" and "that the boilerplate fine print [comprising the Terms and Conditions section attached to the February 1995 Quotation Contract] was meaningless on this project." (Gottlieb Decl. Opp'n ¶11.) TVT also claims that the Schubert agent "said everything necessary to comfort [TVT] and assure [TVT] that those pages were *inapplicable* to this deal" and that TVT "could *ignore* the fine print." (Id. ¶12; Pls.' R. 56.1 Resp. ¶2 (alleging that Gottlieb was told by Schubert's agent that "he could ignore the fine print").) Because CISG Article 8(3) explicitly permits the Court to consult "subsequent conduct" in determining intent, it is relevant to point to Gottlieb's statement that "[i]f [he] had ever thought that Schubert could enforce the ["Terms and Conditions"] . . . [he] would *never* have gone forward with Schubert; and [Schubert's agent] and those he represented in Germany certainly knew that." (Gottlieb Decl. Opp'n ¶13.) Schubert's agent claims, however, that he said that he merely told TVT "not to worry about or over-emphasize the fine print." (Neuber Decl. Opp'n ¶5.) In particular, he claims that he did not use the word "ignore." (Id.) Although this language, without more, is not strong enough to completely confirm TVT's interpretation that the "Terms and Conditions" section is unenforceable, it is strong enough to raise a genuine factual question regarding whether Schubert's agent "could not have been unaware" that TVT was interpreting his words and conduct as doing away with the boilerplate "Terms and Conditions."

The matter is made more complex because one of the provisions in the "Terms and Conditions" section is a merger clause, which extinguishes all prior oral agreements:

> This quotation comprises our entire quotation. On any order placed pursuant hereto, the above provisions entirely supersede any prior correspondence, quotation or agreement. There are no agreements between us in respect of the product quoted herein except as set forth in writing and expressly made a part of this quotation.

(February 1995 Quotation Contract, Terms & Conditions, Merger Clause.)

The question of whether, under the principles of the CISG, a prior oral agreement to disregard boilerplate language itself containing, *inter alia,* a merger clause, trumps the written merger clause itself appears to be a question of first impression for (at the very least) American courts. Indeed, "U.S. federal caselaw interpreting and applying the CISG is scant." Usinor Industeel v. Leeco Steel Prods., 209 F. Supp. 2d 880, 884 (N.D. Ill. 2002). Although the Eleventh Circuit's decision in *MCC-Marble* contains nearly identical facts to this case, see generally 144 F.3d 1384, the merger-clause issue was notably absent in that case, see id. at 1391 & n.19 (noting that parties may be able to avoid parol-evidence issues by including a merger clause extinguishing any prior understandings not expressed in the writings, but notably not discussing whether a prior oral agreement to disregard boilerplate language that includes a merger clause trumps the written merger clause itself).

The Court thus turns to the text of the CISG, as interpreted by the CISG Advisory Council. See Delchi Carrier, 71 F.3d at 1027-28 ("Because there is virtually no case-law under the Convention, we look to its language and to 'the general principles' upon which it is based." (quoting CISG art. 7(2))). The CISG Advisory Council has noted that "extrinsic evidence [such as the oral dealings between Schubert and TVT representatives] should not be excluded, unless the parties actually intend the Merger Clause to have this effect" and that "Article 8 requires an examination of all relevant facts and circumstances when deciding whether the Merger Clause represents the parties' intent." See CISG-AC Opinion no. 3 ¶4.5 (Oct. 23, 2004). That is, to be effective, a merger clause must reflect "the *parties'* intent." Id. (emphasis added). This suggests that if either party had a contrary intent, the merger clause between them would have no effect; only if both Schubert and TVT shared the intent to be bound by the Merger Clause contained in the "Terms and Conditions" is the Merger Clause operative.

There exists a genuine issue of material fact as to whether Schubert and TVT shared the intent to be bound by the "Terms and Conditions" portion of the February 1995 Quotation Contract or the written Merger Clause contained therein. If the final writing evinces the shared intent of TVT and Schubert (by their agents) to proceed with a meaningful Merger Clause, then the "Terms and Conditions" section is part of the February 1995 Quotation Contract such that the liability limitations apply, see CISG art. 6, 19 I.L.M. at 673 (allowing contracting parties to "derogate from or vary the effect of any of [the CISG's] provisions"), meaning that the warranty provision in the "Terms and Conditions" section would override the protections of CISG Article 35 and undermine TVT's Article 35 cause of action. If, however, there was no shared intent of TVT and Schubert (by their agents) to be bound by either the "Terms and Conditions" section or Merger Clause, then the "Terms and Conditions" section and Merger Clause would drop out, and TVT would be entitled to the full panoply of implied warranties offered by the CISG, including the Article 35 provisions forming the basis of this contract claim.

Summary judgment is inappropriate on TVT's Article 35(2)(a)-(b) claim because there is a genuine issue of material fact regarding the parties' intent to incorporate the "Terms and Conditions" section and Merger Clause therein. Under the guidelines set forth herein, the finder of fact in this case will be required to determine the subjective intent of Gottlieb, on behalf of TVT, and Neuber, on behalf of Schubert, at the time Schubert's offer was accepted by TVT. Nevertheless, TVT is barred from recovering certain categories of damages under the Article 35(2)(a)-(b) claim as a matter of law. Thus, on this contract claim, summary judgment for Schubert is DENIED except with respect to certain categories of damages, as the Court will now explain. . . .

CISG Article 11 indicates that there is no writing requirement in international sales contracts. This is in accordance with the continental approach and has the practical advantage of avoiding the need for transnational discovery of documents necessary to satisfy a writing requirement if there were one.

The drafters of the CISG did, however, create a compromise provision for those countries believing that it was important for there to be a statute of frauds. Article 96 allows a country to make a declaration that there *will* be a statute of frauds requirement in any contract involving parties that have their principal place of business in that country. The United States has not chosen to make such a declaration, and therefore international sales contracts involving U.S. parties will not be subject to the UCC statute of frauds rules.

C. Requisites to Formalization in the Real Estate System

Although real estate sales will not be governed by the writing requirement of UCC §2-201, most states have some form of writing requirement for the sale of real estate, either through a statute or through the common law. This is hardly surprising, given that the sale of real estate was the first category of sales under the law to require some kind of writing to be enforceable.

The writing requirement for the enforceability of real estate sales tends to be stricter than that for the sale of goods. Whereas the Article 2 rules require very little in the way of terms that must be in writing, most of the state statutes of frauds for real estate require that the writing include the "material terms" of the sale. Sometimes the statute will specify which terms are material, and these will typically include party names, identification of the property, the nature of the title to be conveyed, and the price.

Where a party to a real estate contract has not satisfied the statute of frauds, there remains the argument that the plaintiff detrimentally relied on the oral promises made by the defendant. Although not all courts accept this argument, equitable estoppel is one of the commonly accepted exceptions to the usual requirement that a contract to sell real estate must be in writing.

A second common exception to the real estate statute of frauds, which is in some sense a subset of equitable estoppel, is part performance. With the part performance exception, the buyer takes some action in part performance (payment, possession, or improvements) that substitutes for the missing writing.

Richard v. Richard
900 A.2d 1170 (R.I. 2006)

WILLIAMS, C.J.

This appeal comes to us from the Family Court concerning the divorce of Jennifer M. Richard (Jennifer) from Gregory J. Richard (Gregory). The appellant, Norman

Richard (Norman), Gregory's father, is aggrieved by a decree of the Family Court ordering him to convey certain real property, located at 99 Montgomery Street in Tiverton (Tiverton property), to Gregory and Jennifer, his former daughter-in-law, in accordance with the terms of a purported oral contract. . . .

Gregory and Jennifer were married in October 1995. Earlier that same year, Gregory and Jennifer had moved into the Tiverton property, then owned by Norman, as lessees, paying between $110 and $150 per week to Norman. According to Gregory and Jennifer, the parties had discussed the couple's acquisition of the Tiverton property from Norman since 1997.

Jennifer testified that in the fall of 2000 Norman first agreed to sell the Tiverton property to the couple for a total price of $70,000. Gregory placed the date of this agreement closer to June 2001. Norman testified that he did have a discussion with Gregory regarding the Tiverton property, but denies that he agreed to sell it for $70,000. This agreement was never memorialized in writing.

The substance of that discussion is in dispute. Norman claims that he approached Gregory to discuss selling the Tiverton property. He said that Gregory informed him that the bank would lend Gregory the money to purchase the Tiverton property only if he could come up with 35 percent of the purchase price. Norman calculated this figure at $70,000. Norman testified that he agreed to help his son and Jennifer realize home ownership by acting as a bank to facilitate the young couple's savings: Gregory and Jennifer would pay him $140 per week, which he would keep, record, and amass until the $70,000 down payment amount was reached. Once the couple had attained the down payment amount, he presumably would release the funds so that a bank loan could be obtained. Norman testified that Gregory and Jennifer also paid $100 per week in rent in addition to the $140 payments.

The story offered by Jennifer and Gregory differed immeasurably. They insisted that Norman, in fact, offered to sell them the Tiverton property for a total purchase price of $70,000. Although the value of the home was stipulated to be in excess of $200,000, any additional consideration was found by the trial justice to be based on family affection. According to Jennifer, beginning in June 2001, she began paying Norman either $200 or $250 per week pursuant to the oral contract. Norman testified, and the record reflects, that payments of $140, and later $100, were recorded in two ledgers—one kept at the Tiverton property and one kept at Norman's home. One of the ledgers subtracted the payments from the $70,000 purchase price. These notations were made in Norman's hand. According to Jennifer, the remaining amount of each week's payment was applied toward property taxes and homeowner's insurance.

Sometime after the agreement, Gregory and Jennifer undertook to improve the Tiverton property. Gregory testified that these improvements were done with Norman's approval. And the upgrades were extensive: the front of the home was landscaped; exterior lights were added; a new front door was installed; the front entry was retiled; an oak banister was installed; the living room was renovated; the kitchen was upgraded; three rooms were given new carpet and paint; several light fixtures and ceiling fans were added; and a sun porch was completed, which included the addition of French doors, drywall, and windows. On cross-examination, Jennifer testified that the tile in the front entry, the front door, the banister, the master bedroom, the last door in the sun porch, and one other bedroom were completed "after the actual purchase of the home," which she indicated was in March 2001.

In April 2002, Norman took out a $30,000 mortgage on the Tiverton property to pay bills. Earlier that month, Gregory had borrowed from him a total of $8,000 to buy a vehicle and a boat motor. Norman subtracted the $8,000 indebtedness from the $30,000 mortgage, leaving $22,000. Norman then subtracted the $22,000 from the remaining balance noted in the Tiverton property ledger. Jennifer testified that the $22,000 was deducted from the balance of the purchase price of the home because it was a lien on the property. Norman disagreed in part; while acknowledging the lien, he also explained the deduction as an incentive to encourage Gregory and Jennifer to achieve their savings goal.

In October 2002, Gregory moved from the Tiverton property; he and Jennifer had separated. Once the divorce proceedings had commenced, Jennifer's relationship with Norman also deteriorated. The Tiverton property ledger revealed that payments to Norman ceased on October 4, 2002, which payment brought the outstanding balance to $38,100; Norman's personal ledger, however, showed payments made by Jennifer until November 1, 2002, at which point Norman made the notation "on hold."

A trial on whether the Tiverton property could be considered in the distribution of marital assets was held on several dates between July 2003 and April 2004. On March 26, 2004, the trial justice issued a bench decision, which was followed by a written judgment. The trial justice found by clear and convincing evidence that an oral agreement between Norman and the couple to convey the Tiverton property existed and was enforceable. The trial justice found that "in reliance on the agreement, [Jennifer] and [Gregory] made substantial improvements to the property and had possession of the property the entire time right up until the present date." The trial justice was persuaded that Norman agreed to sell the Tiverton property for $70,000, citing the fact that he had subtracted the balance of the $30,000 equity loan from the couples' outstanding balance. In addition, the trial justice found incredible Norman's explanation that he was holding the couple's payments for an eventual down payment, when the couple simply could have opened their own bank account. As to credibility, the trial justice found that Jennifer and Gregory were "forthright and truthful and candid in their testimony." Conversely, he found Norman to be "lacking in credibility and quite frankly untruthful." In fact, the trial justice found Norman's testimony "to be devoid of believability and bordering on perjury."

The trial justice imposed a constructive trust on the Tiverton property, requiring Norman to convey the land to Jennifer and Gregory in exchange for the outstanding balance of $38,100, plus $7,800 in back rent. He also ordered that the couple would take the property subject to the equity loan taken out by Norman. Norman appealed to this Court pursuant to G.L. 1956 §14-1-52(a) challenging the trial justice's findings concerning ownership of the Tiverton property.

On appeal, Norman argues that the trial justice erred as a matter of law by concluding there existed an enforceable oral contract between Norman and the couple under the doctrine of part performance. Norman adds other claims as well . . . .

General Laws 1956 §9-1-4 sets forth this state's statute of frauds. It provides, in pertinent part, as follows:

> "No action shall be brought:
>
> "(1) Whereby to charge any person upon any contract for the sale of lands, tenements, or hereditaments, or the making of any lease thereof for a longer time than one year;
>
> . . .
>
> "unless the promise or agreement upon which the action shall be brought, or some note or memorandum thereof, shall be in writing, and signed by the party to be charged therewith, or by some other person by him or her thereunto lawfully authorized."

One exception to this statute is that of part performance: When a party seeking enforcement of an oral contract "has performed to such an extent that repudiation of the contract would lead to an unjust or fraudulent result, the court will disregard the requirement of a writing and enforce an oral agreement." *R.W.P. Concessions, Inc. v. Rhode Island Zoological Society,* 487 A.2d 129, 131 (R.I. 1985). A court generally will enforce an alleged oral contract pursuant to the doctrine of part performance only if a party can adequately demonstrate, in reliance on said agreement, possession of the property, improvements thereon, or payment of a substantial part of the purchase price. *Pearl Brewing Co. v. McNaboe,* 495 A.2d 238, 242 (R.I. 1985) ("[t]aking possession of property . . . together with making improvements or paying a substantial part of the purchase price, is generally sufficient to avoid the bar of the statute of frauds"); *R.W.P. Concessions, Inc.,* 487 A.2d at 131 ("the terms of the agreement must be clear and the possession or improvements in reliance thereon must be substantial and clearly shown"). "[P]art payment of the purchase price, possession or making improvements severally might not be sufficient to remove the case, yet a combination of all may be." *Najarian v. Boyajian,* 48 R.I. 213, 215, 136 A. 767, 768 (1927). We note, however, that the statute of frauds is not to be taken lightly, and any partial performance must unequivocally indicate the existence of the purported oral agreement. *See Messner Vetere Berger McNamee Schmetterer Euro RSCG, Inc. v. Aegis Group PLC,* 93 N.Y.2d 229, 689 N.Y.S.2d 674, 711 N.E.2d 953, 956 (1999) ("Part performance alone, of course, is not sufficient. The performance must be unequivocally referable to the agreement."); 4 *Corbin on Contracts* (Statute of Frauds) §18.11 (rev. ed. 1997).

Norman first argues that the trial justice erred in finding that Jennifer and Gregory satisfied the requisite possession prong of the part performance exception. He claims that Jennifer and Gregory took possession of the Tiverton property pursuant to an oral agreement to *rent* the premises long before the alleged oral promise for conveyance; therefore, Norman suggests, the possession could not have been pursuant to an oral contract to purchase the property.

Although the commencement of a possession contemporaneous to an alleged oral agreement typically might satisfy the possession requirement, a continued or existing possession will not necessarily preclude application of the part performance doctrine. In fact, the authorities are largely in accord that the operative inquiry is whether a possession adequately indicates the existence of an oral contract:

> "The continuance in possession by a purchaser who is already in possession may, in a proper case, be sufficiently referable to the parol contract of sale to constitute a part performance thereof. There may be additional acts or peculiar circumstances which sufficiently refer the possession to the contract. So, a prior possession by the purchaser is not an absolute bar to proof of a change in the character of the possession after the making of a parol contract of sale, although it may cast upon the purchaser the burden of showing that his continued possession is referable to the contract." *Herbstreith v. Walls,* 147 Neb. 805, 25 N.W.2d 409, 411 (1946) (quoting 49 Am. Jur. *Statute of Frauds* §442 at 748); *see also Sutton v. Warner,* 12 Cal. App. 4th 415, 15 Cal. Rptr. 2d 632, 637 (1993) (adopting the rationale of *Herbstreith*); *Boesiger v. Freer,* 85 Idaho 551, 381 P.2d 802, 805 (1963) ("Competent evidence may clearly show that [a prior] possession, [continued] after the making of an oral contract, was definitely referable to the contract."); 4 *Corbin on Contracts* §18.14 at 538; Restatement (Second) *Contracts* §129 (1981).

In the present matter, sufficient competent evidence was presented to support a finding that the continued possession of the Tiverton property by Gregory and Jennifer adequately indicated the existence of the purported oral contract to constitute a part performance thereof. First, the ledger notations made in Norman's own hand begin on June 1, 2001, and indicate receipt of regular $140 payments, and later $100 payments, from Gregory and Jennifer, which were deducted from a $70,000 figure in one ledger. Both Gregory and Jennifer testified that this $70,000 figure represented the negotiated sale price of the Tiverton property. Jennifer testified that the remaining portion of the money paid weekly to Norman was applied to property taxes and insurance. Taken together, this is strong evidence that the nature of the possession of the Tiverton property had changed on or about the dates Jennifer and Gregory claimed as the date of actual contract formation.

Furthermore, many of the improvements were made to the property after the agreement. Norman's own son, Gregory, testified, in the face of contrary evidence from his father, that Norman permitted these improvements because the house rightfully belonged to Gregory and Jennifer. In light of this evidence, we think the possession of the Tiverton property by Gregory and Jennifer satisfied this element of the part performance doctrine.

Norman next challenges the trial justice's findings regarding improvements made to the Tiverton property. Under the part performance doctrine, improvements to land purportedly made in reliance upon an oral contract must indicate the existence of the contract in such a way that the improvements "would have been improvident to make in the absence of some such contract, so that they are strong circumstantial evidence of its existence." 4 *Corbin on Contracts* §18.15 at

541. Improvements in reliance on an alleged oral contract ordinarily must be permanent. *R.W.P. Concessions, Inc.,* 487 A.2d at 132.

Norman first argues that the trial justice committed reversible error in deeming the improvements made to the Tiverton property to be "substantial" enough to trigger the part performance exception. He contends that the total cost of the improvements made after the agreement—which he values between $2,075 and $2,375—constituted slightly more than 1 percent of the stipulated value of the property, and thus could not be "substantial." Without even reaching whether Norman's assessment of the value of the improvements is factually accurate, we cannot agree with his argument.

First, we note that this Court has never held that the question of whether improvements suffice to constitute part performance turns upon their cost in relation to the total value of the improved property. In *R.W.P. Concessions, Inc.,* 487 A.2d at 131, 132, this Court did recognize that even a substantial expenditure of time and money was insufficient to constitute part performance when improvements to ready a concession stand were easily removable "at the termination of the operating relationship." Yet this is certainly not the case in the present matter, where Jennifer and Gregory imbued the Tiverton property with significant "sweat equity." Specifically, the addition of new doors and a banister, the replacement of floors, and the renovation of bedrooms—all of which Norman concedes took place after the agreement—are improvements not easily removable from the premises, and therefore would have been improvident absent an enforceable contract for the sale of the Tiverton property.

Norman also argues that the trial justice erred by considering certain improvements to the Tiverton property made *prior* to the alleged oral agreement. We disagree. The trial justice enumerated the following as improvements supporting the application of the part performance doctrine: French doors were installed, a sun room was appended, the front entry was tiled, a new front door was added, the kitchen was completely overhauled, the bedrooms were refurbished, and the landscaping was improved. When cross-examined, however, Jennifer offered a different, but still substantial, list of improvements rendered after the "actual purchase of the home": The tile in the front entry was laid, the front door was replaced, the new oak banister was installed, the last door in the sun room was hung, and both the master and another bedroom were renovated. We are of the opinion that even this second, albeit less comprehensive, list is sufficient evidence to indicate the existence of an oral agreement.

Finally, even if the improvements by themselves were insufficient to constitute part performance, some combination of improvements, substantial payment of the purchase price, or possession can be enough. *Najarian,* 48 R.I. at 215, 136 A. at 768. An independent review of the evidence presented in this case leads us to conclude that the oral contract should be honored. Jennifer and Gregory paid Norman $140 per week from June 1, 2001, until April 12, 2002, when the couple reduced the weekly payments to $100; all these payments were deducted from a $70,000 figure, as evidenced by a ledger kept by Norman. Both Jennifer and

Gregory testified that this $70,000 was the negotiated purchase price of the property. The purchase price was later reduced by $22,000 to account for a $30,000 home equity loan taken out by Norman, less an $8,000 private loan from Norman to Gregory and Jennifer. We hold that these payments toward the purchase price of the Tiverton property and the several permanent improvements made thereon, together with the continued possession, sufficiently constitute part performance of the oral contract.

We did not easily or quickly conclude that there was sufficient part performance in this case. This was a close and difficult case for this Court. We would advise bench and bar that we consider the statute of frauds to be as important as it is venerable. We shall continue to look with some degree of skepticism upon the claims of any party who seeks to escape from the statutory mandate by invoking an exception.

CONCLUSION

For the reasons stated herein, the decision of the Family Court is affirmed. Norman shall convey said property to Jennifer and Gregory for the balance due on the purchase price. Because of a mathematical error, the Family Court judgment shall be amended to indicate that the balance due on the purchase price is $39,100. In addition to this amount, Jennifer and Gregory shall pay Norman $7,800 for back rent pursuant to an order of the Family Court entered on February 7, 2003, for a total amount of $46,900. In accord with the Family Court's final judgment, Jennifer and Gregory shall take title to the Tiverton property subject to the outstanding equity loan, for which Jennifer and Gregory will be jointly and severally liable. The record shall be remanded to the Family Court.

Regarding real estate law's treatment of parol evidence, the rule looks an awful lot like the one in UCC §2-202. The reason for this similarity is that the UCC parol evidence rule was essentially just a codification of the parol evidence rule that governs real estate contracts as well as any other contracts under the common law. In some minor respects, the common law version of the parol evidence rule can be slightly more restrictive than the UCC version regarding which parol evidence is admissible, depending on which state's common law is at issue.

For example, some courts under the common law parol evidence rule have required that the contract be "ambiguous" with respect to the term that a party seeks to explain or supplement by the introduction of parol evidence. The UCC rule, by contrast, does not require ambiguity as a prerequisite to a party's ability to explain or supplement a partially integrated writing with "consistent additional terms."

Problem Set 7

7.1. a. Jay Berringer, owner of Jay's Rent-to-Own Pianos (Problem 2.3), is back in your office with more questions. It seems that one of Jay's brand new workers, Sam Clark, did not realize that Jay's policy was that all of his store's leases were to be in writing. As a result, Sam entered into an oral lease contract with Bonnie Kilgen. The terms of that "handshake deal" were that Bonnie would lease a used Steinway upright piano for $75 per month for one year, with an option for $150 to renew the lease for one more year on the same terms. Jay wants to know to what extent this oral lease contract will be enforceable if Bonnie decides she does not want to go forward with it. What do you advise? UCC §2A-201.

b. Same facts as part (a), except that the oral contract required that the first year's rent would be $100 per month and would all be paid up-front in one $1,200 payment, which Bonnie has already made. The one-year lease renewal option is for $50 per month, rent to be paid at the start of each month. To what extent is this oral lease agreement enforceable by Bonnie? UCC §2A-201, Official Comment to §2A-201.

c. Same facts as part (a), except that the first year's rent was $100 per month and Jay's has delivered the piano to Bonnie, who accepted it and began using it. Two months later, however, before any written lease contract is executed, Bonnie enters into a written contract with a neighbor by which Bonnie purports to lease the piano to the neighbor for $200 per month for one year. Jay learns about this and decides that he would like to rent the piano to the neighbor for $200 per month instead of to Bonnie for $100 per month. May Jay void Bonnie's oral lease so that he may enter into a new lease with her neighbor? UCC §2A-201.

7.2. a. Susan Heil, an authorized sales agent for Ford Motor Co. of Detroit, entered into an oral contract on behalf of Ford Motor with Toronto Ford, a Canadian car dealership. The two sides agreed orally that Ford Motor Co. would sell Toronto Ford 36 Taurus station wagons at the manufacturer's standard dealer price, delivery to take place in one month. The two sides also agreed orally that Michigan law (excluding the CISG) would govern the transaction. Shortly before delivery, Toronto Ford indicates to Susan that it wants out of the deal. Susan eventually files a lawsuit in Detroit to enforce the oral contract. Toronto Ford moves for summary judgment, pleading the statute of frauds defense and attaching a signed affidavit denying that it ever entered into a contract with the plaintiff. If you are the trial judge, should you grant the summary judgment motion? CISG Arts. 1(1), 6, 11; UCC §2-201.

b. Same facts as part (a), except that the two parties do have a written sales contract. The contract, which has no merger clause, mentions all of the relevant terms except the fact that Michigan law (excluding the CISG) will govern the transaction. The choice-of-law provision was an oral side agreement that the two parties entered into before the writing was signed. Now Toronto Ford has breached the contract, and Susan Heil would like to avail her company of the UCC's remedy provisions rather than the CISG's. Will Susan be able to successfully introduce evidence of the side agreement on choice of law? CISG Arts. 1(1), 6, 8(3); UCC §2-202, Official Comment 3 to §2-202.

7.3.   a. When Pete Smarz's daughter, Denise, got married two years ago, Pete decided that he would help out the newlywed couple by letting them rent his second home in West Virginia. Pete told Denise and her husband, Bill, that the two of them could rent the house for two years at $500 per month. All of the parties agree with that portion of the facts. Denise and Bill claim that Pete also told the two of them that if they were still married and had a child at the end of the two years, Pete would let them buy the house for its appraised value minus the total of the rent payments they had made for two years. Pete denies that he ever gave the couple this purchase option. Denise tells you that her father is just angry because he and Bill had a falling out, and her father just wants to get back at Bill by kicking both of them out of the house. It has now been two years since the lease began, Denise and Bill have a six-month-old son, and the house has been appraised at $150,000. Denise asks you whether she can enforce the purchase option and buy the house from her father for $138,000, which is the appraised value minus the rent payments made. What do you advise her?

b. Same facts as part (a), except that Denise and Bill added a two-story addition to the back of the house during their second year in the house, for a total cost of $40,000. To what extent does this help their case for enforcement of the purchase option?

Assessment Questions for Chapter 1

Example 1: Buyer and Seller, who have never done business with each other before, enter into an installment contract in which Seller agrees to ship to Buyer a series of 10 installments of 100 widgets in each installment. The contract says that Seller will deliver each installment to Buyer's place of business. For the first eight installments, Buyer picks up the widgets at Seller's place of business. Immediately prior to the date for performance of the ninth installment of widgets, Buyer calls Seller and insists that Seller deliver the widgets to Buyer's place of business. Which of the following statements is most accurate?

(A)   Seller must deliver the widgets, because express terms of the contract control course of dealing.

(B)   Seller must deliver the widgets, because express terms of the contract control course of performance.

(C)   Seller must deliver the widgets, because express terms of the contract control usage of trade.

(D)   Buyer must pick up the widgets, because course of performance controls express terms.

(E)   Buyer might have to pick up the widgets, because course of performance is relevant to showing waiver of an express term.

Question 1 Answer: The correct answer is (E). Although §1-303(e)(1) says that express terms prevail over course of performance, §1-303(f) says that course of performance "is relevant to show a waiver or modification of any term inconsistent with the course of performance." (A) is wrong because what is relevant in this question is the relationship between express terms and course of performance, not the relationship between express terms and course of dealing. (B) is wrong because it ignores the waiver possibility given in §1-303(f). (C) is wrong because it refers to "usage of trade," which is not relevant in this question. (D) is wrong because as a general proposition, course of performance does not control express terms, unless the course of performance suggests a waiver of the express terms.

Question 2: Which of the following contracts is least likely to be governed by UCC Article 2?

(A) A contract with an artist to buy one of his original sculptures.
(B) A contract to sell the original Mona Lisa painting by a seller who has not even acquired it yet from the museum that owns the painting.
(C) A contract between a retail buyer and a retail bookstore for the sale of a book.
(D) The sale of a raffle ticket in which the winning prize is a computer.
(E) A contract for the sale of natural gas.

Question 2 Answer: The correct answer is (D). The sale of a raffle ticket is not a transaction in goods that is governed by UCC Article 2 because although the ticket is "movable," the ticket is not in itself "goods" but rather a "thing in action" (i.e., a right to recovery, even if contingent, such as with a raffle ticket). Section 2-105(1) specifically excludes "things in action" from its definition of "goods" even if the thing in action takes a movable form such as the raffle ticket. (A) is wrong because even though a lot of intellectual property and labor goes into the creation of the sculpture, the resulting movable thing has a significance beyond simply as a repository of the intellectual property that is behind it. (B) is wrong because a contract for the sale of goods does not require that the seller currently have possession or ownership of the goods to be sold in order for the contract to be covered by Article 2. (C) is wrong because even though a book represents the author's intellectual property, the seller here is a retailer and it's not the retailer's intellectual property that is being sold. (E) is wrong because even though we can't hold gas in our hands, it is nevertheless "movable" and therefore counts as "goods" under §2-105(1).

Question 3: Car Dealership decides to repaint its buildings for the first time in five years. Because it does not do this very often, it mistakenly ends up buying about twice as much paint as it needs for the job. Car Dealership then decides to sell the excess paint to a furniture warehouse down the street. Which of the following statements is most accurate?

(A) Car Dealership makes an implied warranty of merchantability regarding the paint, because Car Dealership is a merchant by virtue of its knowledge of business practices generally.

(B) Car Dealership makes an implied warranty of merchantability regarding the paint, because Car Dealership is not a consumer.

(C) Car Dealership makes no implied warranty of merchantability regarding the paint, because although Car Dealership is a merchant generally, in selling the paint Car Dealership is not acting in its mercantile capacity.

(D) Car Dealership makes no implied warranty of merchantability regarding the paint, because Car Dealership is not a merchant.

(E) Car Dealership makes no implied warranty of merchantability regarding the paint, because this is an isolated sale of paint for Car Dealership.

Question 3 Answer: The correct answer is (E). Even though Car Dealership is a merchant with respect to cars and with respect to business practices generally, it is not a merchant with respect to paint and therefore does not make the implied warranty of merchantability in an isolated sale of paint. See Official Comment 2 to §2-104. (A) is wrong because although Car Dealership is a merchant with respect to business practices generally, that is not enough for it to make an implied warranty of merchantability with respect to paint. (B) is wrong because not all non-consumer sellers make implied warranties of merchantability with respect to every sale that they make. (C) is wrong because the reason why Car Dealership does not make an implied warranty of merchantability here is not that Car Dealership is not acting in its mercantile capacity, but because it is not in the business of selling paint. (D) is wrong because clearly Car Dealership is a merchant more generally, even if not a merchant specifically with respect to selling paint.

Question 4: Lessor and Lessee agree to a lease of a used Ford automobile that has, at the time of the lease's inception, a remaining useful life of 12 years. The car is currently worth $16,000, and Lessee has no option to terminate the lease. The lease is for four years at $400 per month and Lessee is responsible for maintenance and insurance. At the end of the lease period, Lessee has an option to purchase the car for an amount equal to its fair market value at the time of the purchase option. Which of the following statements about the lease is most accurate?

(A) This is probably not a true lease, since it is inconsistent with the nature of a true lease that Lessee, rather than Lessor, should be responsible for maintenance and insurance.

(B) This is probably not a true lease, since a fair-market value purchase option is so attractive that Lessee is almost certain to exercise it and thus will almost certainly become the owner of the car at the end of the lease period.

(C) This is probably not a true lease, since Lessee will end up paying lease payments that exceed the value of the car and thus would be crazy to walk away from the lease at the end of its term after investing that much money in lease payments.

(D) This is probably a true lease, since there appears to be a reasonable likelihood that Lessor will receive the car back at a time when it still has a meaningful residual value.

(E) This is probably not a true lease, since Lessee has no right to terminate the lease and therefore this case fits within one of §1-203's categories of "definite disguised sales."

Question 4 Answer: The correct answer is (D). Under the "economic realities test," a transaction counts as a true lease if there is a reasonable likelihood that a lessor will receive the goods back at a time when they still have a meaningful residual value. In this case, the remaining useful life of the goods well exceeds the lease term, and while there is a purchase option at the end of the lease, it is not for a nominal price. (A) is wrong because §1-203(c)(3) says that a lessee's obligation to be responsible for maintenance and insurance is not enough by itself to create a disguised sale. (B) is wrong because §1-203(c)(6) says that a fair-market-value purchase option is not enough by itself to create a disguised sale. (C) is wrong because §1-203(c)(1) says that we do not have a disguised sale merely because the lessee is obligated to pay a total amount of lease payments that equals or exceeds the value of the leased goods. (E) is wrong because in order to fit within one of §1-203(b)'s categories of "definite disguised sales," the lease needs at least one of four other features in addition to the lessee having no right to terminate the lease, and this lease has none of those four features.

Question 5: Same facts as Question 4, except that the lease provides that Lessee has a purchase option of $100 at the end of the four-year lease, and one year into the lease the car is destroyed when a tree falls on top of it. The lease contract provides that Lessee has risk of loss, and Lessee has failed to get insurance. Which of the following statements about the lease is most accurate?

(A) This contract is probably a disguised sale, since the destruction of the car guarantees that Lessor will never get the car back at a time when the car has a meaningful residual value.

(B) This contract is probably a disguised sale, since this lease now fits within one of §1-203's "definite disguised sale" categories.

(C) This contract is probably a true lease, since we need to measure at the inception of the contract the Lessor's likelihood of ever getting the car back, and at the inception of the contract nobody knows that the car is going to be destroyed.

(D) This contract is probably a true lease, since risk of loss principles dictate that Lessor rather than Lessee should have had the risk of loss.

(E) This contract is probably a true lease, since used goods can never be the subject of a disguised sale since some of their residual value has already been spent even prior to the making of the contract.

Question 5 Answer: The correct answer is (B). Because Lessee has no right to terminate this lease and the lease contains a nominal purchase option at the end of it, the lease is a definite disguised sale under §1-203(b)(4). (A) is wrong because the point at which we measure whether a transaction is a true lease is at the inception of the lease, not at a later point with the benefit of hindsight. (C) is wrong because even without knowing that the car will be destroyed, we still know at the inception of the contract that the Lessor is unlikely to get the car back due to the nominal purchase option. (D) is wrong because even if the default rule is that Lessor normally has risk of loss, §1-302 provides that most default rules in the UCC can be varied by agreement and this lease contract says that Lessee has risk of loss. (E) is wrong because nowhere does §1-203 indicate that used goods cannot be the subject of a disguised sale.

Question 6: In a true lease transaction, Lessor leases a pinball machine to Lessee for five years at $3,000 per year. Just to be safe, Lessor files a financing statement in the appropriate place to give notice of its interest in the machine. One year into the lease, Lessee sells the machine to Buyer, a good-faith purchaser, for $25,000. Lessor learns about the sale and sues Buyer for return of the machine. When Lessor sues Buyer, Lessor will

(A) win, because lessors in true leases generally defeat even the rights of subsequent good-faith purchasers for value.

(B) win, because Lessor was smart enough to give notice to the world of its ownership interest by filing the financing statement and thus cured the "apparent ownership problem."

(C) win, because the lease agreement did not include a provision in the lease that said that Lessee was not allowed to sell the pinball machine.

(D) lose, because by filing the financing statement, Lessor is indicating to anyone who searches the files that maybe this is not a true lease after all.

(E) lose, because a paramount policy of the UCC is that we must protect good-faith purchasers in the ordinary course of business.

Question 6 Answer: The correct answer is (A). As a general proposition, a seller can only transfer whatever title that the seller has to goods, and Lessee here was not the owner of this pinball machine. Therefore, Lessee cannot transfer good title to Buyer since this was a true lease rather than a disguised sale. (B) is wrong because in a true lease like this one, the Lessor is not even required to file a financing statement and cure the apparent ownership problem. (C) is wrong because even if the lease did not include a prohibition against the lessee selling the pinball machine, Lessee still would not have had the power to transfer good title to Buyer. (D) is wrong because §9-505(b) says that the mere filing of a financing statement is not a factor in deciding whether a particular transaction is a true lease or a disguised sale. (E) is wrong because generally even good-faith purchasers in the ordinary course of business cannot take good title from a seller who lacks good title.

Question 7: Canadian Seller, whose sole place of business is in Toronto, custom-designs computers and makes a contract with Buyer, a Detroit lawyer, for the sale of a $10,000 computer. Seller believes that the computer is for Buyer's law practice, but in fact it's for Buyer's son, who loves computer games and needs a high-end computer to run the latest games. Seller has no reason to know this. Buyer has no reason to know that he is dealing with a seller whose place of business is Canada. The sales contract says nothing about choice of law. This contract

(A) will not be governed by the CISG, since the CISG does not cover sales to consumers, even if the seller has no reason to know that the sale is for a consumer purpose.

(B) will not be governed by the CISG, since Buyer has no reason to know from the circumstances that he is dealing with a Seller whose place of business is Canada.

(C) will be governed by the CISG, since Seller thinks that it is selling the computer for Buyer's business and has no reason to know otherwise.

(D) Both A and B are true.

(E) None of the above are true.

Question 7 Answer: The correct answer is (B). According to Article 1 of the CISG, the CISG will only apply if both parties have reason to know by the time of contract formation that they have places of business in different Contracting States. Because Buyer has no reason to know that Seller's place of business is Canada, then this contract will not be governed by the CISG according to Article 1(2). (A) is wrong because according to Article 2(a), the CISG will not cover sales of consumer goods unless Seller has no reason to know that the sale is for a consumer purpose. (C) is wrong because according to Article 1(2), the CISG will only apply if both parties have reason to know by the time of contract formation that they have places of business in different Contracting States. (D) is wrong because (A) is not true. (E) is wrong because (B) is true.

Question 8: Which of the following sales would not be covered by Article 2 of the UCC?

(A) Six bushels of pears from the seller's orchard to be picked by the seller.

(B) Six bushels of pears from the seller's orchard to be picked by the buyer.

(C) A house (but not the land on which it sits) to be severed by the buyer and moved to the buyer's land.

(D) A house (but not the land on which it sits) to be severed by the seller and moved to the buyer's land.

(E) Both C and D.

Question 8 Answer: The correct answer is (C). Section 2-107(1) says that a contract for sale of a structure to be removed from realty is covered by Article 2 only if the structure is to be severed by the seller. Therefore, this sale of a house to be severed by the buyer is not covered by Article 2. (A) is wrong because §2-107(2) says that a contract for the sale of growing crops apart from the land on which they sit will be covered by Article 2 whether the buyer or the seller does the severing. (B) is wrong for the same reason that (A) is wrong. (D) is wrong because in this contract the house is to be severed by the seller and therefore is covered by Article 2. (E) is wrong because (D) is wrong.

Question 9: Merchant Buyer (Buyer) sends a purchase order to Merchant Seller (Seller) for two dozen widgets at Seller's standard price to be delivered in one month to Buyer's place of business. Buyer's purchase order says that all of the UCC remedies, including consequential damages, will be available to Buyer in the event of a breach by Seller. Seller sends a timely acknowledgment form that purports to accept Buyer's offer. However, Seller's form conspicuously disclaims any consequential damages, adds a term saying that all disputes will be subject to arbitration, and then closes with a boldface clause that says that "Seller's acceptance of Buyer's offer is expressly made conditional on Buyer's assent to any different or additional terms contained in this acceptance." Neither Buyer nor Seller reads the other side's form closely, and Seller ships the two dozen widgets to Buyer the next month. Buyer accepts and pays for the widgets. Do Buyer and Seller have a contract at this point?

(A) Yes, and the contract was formed at the point when Seller sent Buyer the acknowledgment form, despite the different and additional terms that were included in Seller's form.

(B) Yes, and the contract was formed at the point when Seller shipped the widgets, since that act by Seller served as a clear acceptance (through conduct) of Buyer's offer to purchase the widgets.

(C) Yes, but the contract was not formed until Buyer accepted and paid for the widgets.

(D) No, because Seller's form was clear that Buyer had to assent to Seller's different and additional terms, and Buyer did not in fact assent.

(E) No, because if we enforce this contract, we are simply returning to the common law's "last-shot" doctrine.

Question 9 Answer: The correct answer is (C). Because Seller included the proper language in its "expressly made conditional" clause in its acknowledgment form, then no contract was formed by the writings alone according to §2-207(1). However, once Seller shipped the widgets and Buyer accepted and paid for them, then the two parties formed a contract by conduct under §2-207(3). (A) is wrong because Seller's "expressly made conditional" language prevented formation of the contract by the writings. (B) is wrong because in order to have a contract by conduct under §2-207(3), we need to have conduct by both parties that recognizes the existence of a contract. (D) is wrong because even though the exchange of writings did not form a contract, the later conduct be each side did form a contract under §2-207(3). (E) is wrong because the "last shot" doctrine (rejected by §2-207(3)) focuses on which terms govern rather than on whether a contract has been formed.

Question 10: Same facts as Question 9. If there is a problem with the widgets, will Buyer be eligible to recover from Seller for consequential damages?

(A) No, because Seller made it clear that its acceptance of Buyer's offer was expressly conditional on Buyer's assent to any different or additional terms in Seller's offer, and Seller's consequential damages disclaimer was clearly a different term.

(B) No, because even though Buyer and Seller are both merchants, Seller's disclaimer of consequential damages was a material alteration of Buyer's offer and therefore does not become part of the contract.

(C) No, because after knocking out both Buyer's and Seller's terms on remedies, we are left with the UCC gap-filler term, which does not allow Buyer to recover consequential damages.

(D) Yes, because Seller's conduct in shipping the widgets was an implicit acceptance of all the terms of Buyer's offer, including Buyer's right to recover consequential damages.

(E) Yes, because Buyer's and Seller's forms do not agree on remedies, and therefore we go with the UCC gap filler on remedies, which does allow consequential damages for Buyer.

Question 10 Answer: The correct answer is (E). Since we have a contract only by conduct and not by the writings of the two parties, we determine the terms of the contract under §2-207(3). That subsection tells us that the terms consist of those terms on which the two writings agree, plus UCC gap fillers where the writings do not agree. Here the writings do not agree on remedies, and the UCC gap filler is that all remedies, including consequential damages, are available to the aggrieved buyer. (A) is wrong because Buyer's lack of assent becomes irrelevant to formation of the contract once the two parties form a contract by conduct. (B) is wrong because §2-207(2) is only relevant for deciding terms when we have a contract by the writings under §2-207(1) rather than a contract by conduct under §2-207(3) as we have here. (B) is also wrong because even if we were under §2-207(2) in this case, the knockout rule would apply and Buyer would be eligible to recover consequential damages. (D) is wrong because it uses the common law's "last shot" doctrine, which §2-207(3) rejects.

Question 11: Same facts as Question 9. If there is a problem with the widgets, will Seller's arbitration clause be effective?

(A) No, because Buyer's form did not have an arbitration clause, and the UCC gap filler for dispute resolution does not restrict the aggrieved party to arbitration.

(B) No, because this was a contract between merchants, and Seller's additional term of arbitration was a material alteration of Buyer's offer.

(C) Yes, because when Buyer accepted and paid for the widgets, Buyer was thereby accepting all of the terms in Seller's acknowledgment form, including the arbitration clause.

(D) Yes, because Seller's form could not have been more clear that Seller was conditioning its acceptance on Buyer's assent to any additional or different terms in Seller's form, and the arbitration clause was an additional term in Seller's form.

(E) Yes, because even though Buyer's form did not include an arbitration clause, the UCC gap filler for dispute resolution says that an aggrieved buyer must arbitrate its claims against a breaching seller.

Question 11 Answer: The correct answer is (A). Because this was a contract formed by conduct rather than by the exchange of writings, the terms will be governed by §2-207(3). That subsection says that the terms will consist of those terms on which the writings of the parties agree, plus UCC gap fillers where the writings do not agree. Seller's arbitration term was an additional term and therefore does not become part of the contract. The UCC's gap filler for dispute resolution does not restrict aggrieved parties to arbitration. (B) is wrong because it suggests that §2-207(2) applies here in order to determine terms, but §2-207(2) only applies when we have a contract by the exchange of forms, or where there is a single written confirmation following an oral contract. (C) is wrong because it suggests an application of the common law's "last shot" doctrine, which §2-207(3) rejects. (D) is wrong because although Seller's "expressly made conditional" clause prevented formation of a contract by the exchange of writings, that same clause will not affect the terms of a contract that is later formed by the conduct of both parties. (E) is wrong because the UCC gap filler for dispute resolution does not restrict an aggrieved buyer to arbitration.

Question 12: Merchant Buyer (Buyer) sends a purchase order to Merchant Seller (Seller), who is located in a different country. Both countries are CISG signatories. Buyer's purchase order requests three dozen widgets for a specific price, states that all remedies for breach will be available to Buyer (including consequential damages), and says nothing about the mode of dispute resolution. Seller responds with an acknowledgment form that agrees on price, quantity, and delivery terms, but purports to disclaim consequential damages and, in addition, requires arbitration as the mode of dispute resolution. Which of the following statements best describes the legal state of affairs at this point under the CISG?

(A) There is a contract, and Seller's terms will control since the CISG follows the common law's "last shot" doctrine.

(B) There is a contract, but Seller's consequential damages disclaimer and arbitration clause will not become part of the contract since both terms would be considered by the CISG to be "material alterations" of Buyer's offer.

(C) There is a contract, but whether Seller's additional and different terms will control will depend on whether Buyer makes a timely objection to those terms.

(D) There is no contract, even though there would be one at this point if this case were handled under UCC §2-207.

(E) There is no contract, just as there would be no contract if this case were handled under UCC §2-207.

Question 12 Answer: The correct answer is (D). CISG Article 19(1) more or less follows the common-law "mirror image" rule in requiring that in order for an exchange of forms to create a contract, the terms on the acceptance must not contain any additional or different terms that are material. A disclaimer of consequential damages and an arbitration clause would both be considered material under CISG Article 19(3). This is a different result than we would get under UCC §2-207(1), where we can have a contract formed by the exchange of writings even when there are additional or different terms in the acceptance that are material alterations of the terms of the offer. (A) is wrong because even though the CISG follows the common law's "last shot" doctrine, this doctrine will not apply in a case where there has been an exchange of forms by two parties but no conduct by either party beyond that. (B) is wrong for the same reason, even though (B) is right that Seller's two new terms would both be considered "material" by the CISG. (C) is wrong for the same reason, and wrong also for suggesting that Buyer would need to object to terms in an acceptance that constitute material alterations to the terms of the offer. (E) is wrong because it misstates the result under UCC §2-207(1), which is that there would be a contract by the writings in this case.

Question 13: Same facts as Question 12, except that after receiving Seller's acknowledgment form, Buyer sends full payment in advance to Seller for the widgets without objecting to any of Seller's terms in the acknowledgment form. Seller has not yet shipped the goods. Which of the following statements best describes the legal state of affairs at this point under the CISG?

(A) There is no contract yet, because Seller still has not shipped the goods and we need conduct by both sides in order to have a contract here under the CISG.

(B) There is a contract, and Buyer's terms will control since Buyer's payment was the "last shot" in this battle of forms and conduct.

(C) There is a contract, and Seller's terms will control since Seller's acknowledgment form constituted an acceptance of Buyer's offer that will bind Buyer as to any additional or different terms that appeared in Seller's form.

(D) There is a contract, and whether Seller's terms will control will depend on whether Buyer objects to Seller's additional and different terms prior to Seller shipping the goods to Buyer.

(E) None of the above statements is correct.

Question 13 Answer: The correct answer is (E). Seller's acknowledgment with materially different terms constituted a counteroffer under CISG Article 19(1) that was accepted by Buyer's conduct in paying under CISG Article 18(1). For that reason, Seller's terms will control this contract. All of the other four choices are wrong. (A) is wrong because under CISG Article 18(1) conduct by either side can create a contract when there is an offer or counteroffer outstanding. (B) is wrong because the "last shot" in the "last shot" doctrine refers to the last form that was sent if the forms do not create a contract by the writings; in this case, Seller's acknowledgment form with the materially different terms was the "last shot" that was accepted by Buyer's conduct of paying. (C) is wrong because it says that Seller's acknowledgment form constituted an acceptance of Buyer's offer, when in fact CISG Article 19(1) would make Seller's form a counteroffer because of the materially different terms in that form. The acceptance here was Buyer's conduct in paying for the goods, and that acceptance was of Seller's counteroffer continued in Seller's acknowledgment form. (D) is wrong because once Buyer accepts Seller's counteroffer with Buyer's conduct, it is too late for Buyer to object to any of the terms in Seller's counteroffer that Buyer accepted.

Question 14: Merchant Buyer ("Buyer") and Merchant Seller ("Seller") enter into an oral contract for the sale of six red widgets for a total of $60,000, delivery to take place in two months. Two days following that oral agreement, Buyer sends Seller a signed confirmation letter that contains all of the terms of the oral agreement, including price and quantity, but says that the widgets are to be blue. Seller reads the confirmation letter two days after it is received and remembers that the oral agreement required red widgets. At this point in time, which of the following statements describes the legal state of affairs?

(A) Neither side can enforce the contract because of the statute of frauds.

(B) Seller can enforce the contract, but not Buyer.

(C) Buyer can enforce the contract, but not Seller.

(D) Both sides can enforce the contract.

(E) Neither side can enforce the contract because the terms in Buyer's confirmation are not completely correct.

Question 14 Answer: The correct answer is (B). Seller can enforce this oral contract because it now has a writing signed by the party against whom enforcement is sought. Section 2-201(1) says that the writing is not "insufficient" merely because it incorrectly states a term agreed upon, here the color of the widgets. (A) is wrong because Seller can enforce this oral contract. (C) is wrong because Seller can enforce this contract, but Buyer cannot because Buyer lacks a signed writing from Seller at this point. (D) is wrong because Buyer cannot enforce the contract. (E) is wrong because §2-201 does not require that the terms in the writing all be included or all be correct.

Question 15: Same facts as Question 14, except that two weeks after receiving Buyer's signed confirmation, Seller sends Buyer a signed writing in which Seller says, "I object to your confirmation because the terms you included are not consistent with what we had talked about." Buyer receives Seller's signed writing and reads it. At this point in time, which of the following statements describes the legal state of affairs?

(A) Neither side can enforce the contract because of the statute of frauds.

(B) Seller can enforce the contract, but not Buyer.

(C) Buyer can enforce the contract, but not Seller.

(D) Both sides can enforce the contract.

(E) Neither side can enforce the contract because following Seller's written objection, it is clear that there was no meeting of the minds.

Question 15 Answer: The correct answer is (D). Both sides can now enforce the contract because Seller has Buyer's signed writing that meets §2-201(1)'s requirements even though the color indicated in the signed writing is incorrect. Buyer can now also enforce the oral contract because Seller failed to object within 10 days to Buyer's signed confirmation that was sent between merchants. Buyer therefore qualifies for the §2-201(2) exception to the statute of frauds. (A) is wrong because as noted above, both sides can now enforce this contract. (B) is wrong because Buyer can now enforce the contract thanks to the §2-201(2) exception. (C) is wrong because Seller can enforce the contract due to Buyer's signed writing. (E) is wrong because there was a meeting of the minds even if Buyer failed to remember the proper color that was agreed to in their oral contract.

Question 16: Merchant Buyer (Buyer) and Merchant Seller (Seller) make an oral contract for the sale of an industrial-size drill press machine for use in Buyer's manufacturing facility. The terms agreed upon in the oral contract include price, delivery terms, warranties, and a promise from Seller to Buyer that for two years Seller will service the machine at Buyer's facility once each month for no extra charge. Prior to shipping the machine, Seller sends Buyer a signed written confirmation of their oral agreement for purchase and sale of the machine. The confirmation includes price, delivery terms, and warranties, but is silent on Seller's oral promise to service the machine for no extra charge. Buyer receives the confirmation and files it away without reading it. Seller ships the machine and Buyer pays for it. When Buyer asks Seller to come out and service the machine, Seller says that this was not a part of their contract. In a lawsuit against Seller, will Buyer be allowed to introduce evidence of Seller's promise to service the machine for no extra charge?

(A) No, because that is the kind of term that if agreed upon would certainly have been included in Seller's written confirmation.
(B) No, unless a court determines that this is a consistent additional term.
(C) Yes, unless the confirmation contained a conspicuous merger clause.
(D) Yes, but only if this term is a usage of trade in this industry.
(E) Yes, even if the confirmation did contain a conspicuous merger clause and even if this term is not a usage of trade in this industry.

Question 16 Answer: The correct answer is (E). Seller's confirmation was not intended by both parties to be a final expression even of the terms included therein since Buyer did not sign that confirmation. As a result, under §2-202 the confirmation will not serve to exclude any parol evidence in this case. (A), (B), (C), and (D) are all wrong for this reason.

Question 17: Same facts as Question 16, except that instead of sending the signed confirmation, Seller has Buyer sign a written contract along with Seller that includes the very same terms that were in the confirmation described in

Question 16. Assume for this question that the written contract did not include a merger clause. In a lawsuit against Seller, will Buyer be allowed to introduce evidence of Seller's promise to service the machine for no extra charge?

(A) Yes, as long as a court determines that this is a consistent additional term.

(B) Yes, but only if this is the kind of term that if agreed upon would certainly have been included in the written contract.

(C) Yes, but only if this term is a usage of trade in this industry.

(D) No, even if this term is a usage of trade in this industry.

(E) No, because this term was only an oral promise by Seller and therefore runs afoul of the statute of frauds.

Question 17 Answer: The correct answer is (A). Because this writing did not include a merger clause, it is highly unlikely that a court would conclude that it was intended as a complete and exclusive statement of all the terms of the contract. As a result, §2-202(b) says that the writing may be supplemented by evidence of consistent additional terms. (B) is wrong because if this is the kind of term that if agreed upon would certainly have been included in the written contract, then that is a reason why Buyer should not be allowed to introduce evidence of that term. (C) is wrong because under §2-202(b), evidence of consistent additional terms would be allowed in this case even if those terms were not part of the usage of trade in this industry. (D) is wrong because if this term were a usage of trade in this industry, that would be an additional reason to allow Buyer to introduce evidence of such term under §2-202(a). (E) is wrong because the statute of frauds affects the overall enforceability of contracts, not the enforceability of individual terms (other than quantity).

Question 18: Merchant Buyer (Buyer) and Merchant Seller (Seller) agree orally to the sale of a dozen widgets at a price of $20,000 and with stated delivery terms. Buyer is located in Chicago, and Seller is located in Montreal. Buyer and Seller agree orally that Illinois law and not the CISG will apply to their contract. After concluding the oral agreement, Buyer sends Seller a written and signed confirmation which repeats all of the terms of their oral contract, but states that the CISG will apply rather than Illinois law. Seller comes to you and says that he does not want to perform this contract unless Illinois law rather than the CISG will apply to the contract. Can Seller enforce the oral contract as originally agreed to, including the application of Illinois law?

(A) No, because Illinois law would prohibit introduction of the parol evidence concerning the orally agreed-to choice of law provision.

(B) No, because the CISG would prohibit introduction of the parol evidence concerning the orally agreed-to choice of law provision.

(C) No, because Illinois law's statute of frauds rule would require Seller to rely on the confirmation as its writing to satisfy the statute of frauds, and that confirmation says that the CISG will apply.

(D) Yes, because neither the CISG's nor Illinois' parol evidence rule would bar introduction of that oral term on choice of law, nor would either law's statute of frauds rule prohibit the enforcement of this oral contract by Seller.

(E) None of the above.

Question 18 Answer: The correct answer is (D). The CISG does not have a parol evidence rule that would prevent the term on choice of law from being introduced. The UCC's parol evidence rule of §2-202 would not apply because the written confirmation here is not a final expression of both parties' agreement even with respect to the terms contained therein. The CISG does not have a statute of frauds that would prevent enforcement by Seller of this oral contract. The UCC's statute of frauds provision could be satisfied by Seller under the merchant's exception of §2-201(2). (A) is wrong because the written confirmation sent by Buyer does not serve as a final expression of both parties' agreement that would bar evidence of any terms by Seller. (B) is wrong because the CISG does not have a parol evidence rule. (C) is wrong because even if Seller must rely on Buyer's written confirmation to satisfy the UCC statute of frauds, under §2-201(2) Seller will not be bound by the terms of that confirmation except for quantity. (E) is wrong because (D) is true.

Question 19: Lessor and Lessee enter into a five-year oral lease agreement of a residential house in which Lessee agrees to pay rent of $2,000 per month to occupy the house. The terms of this oral lease are that Lessee is responsible for all maintenance of the house during the course of the lease period, reflecting the below-market lease payment of $2,000 for this house. Lessor also grants Lessee as part of this oral lease an option to purchase the house no sooner than three years into the lease and no later than by the end of the five-year lease period. The purchase price of this oral option is an amount that is equal to the then-fair-market-value of the house (as determined by a third-party appraiser) minus the total of any lease payments made by Lessee up to that point. After four years of occupying the house, making lease payments, and maintaining the house, Lessee seeks to exercise the option to purchase. Lessor has changed his mind and denies ever having offered the purchase option as part of the oral lease agreement. Will Lessee likely prevail if Lessee seeks to enforce the purchase option?

(A) No, because the common law statute of frauds would require that Lessee get such a promise in writing in order to enforce it.

(B) No, because the common law parol evidence rule would prevent Lessee from introducing evidence of the purchase option.

(C) No, for both of the reasons stated in (A) and (B).

(D) Yes, because in this case Lessee's payments of $2,000 each month were in fact payments towards the purchase price and therefore constituted part performance of the purchase option.

(E) Yes, because in this case Lessee's maintenance of the property was detrimental reliance that creates an exception to the common law statute of frauds.

Question 19 Answer: The correct answer is (A). The common law requires contracts for the sale of real estate to be in writing in order to be enforceable. There is a part-performance exception to this requirement, but here the "part performance" of payment and maintenance was in fact consistent with a pure lease transaction. (B) is wrong because there is no writing here that would trigger the parol evidence rule. (C) is wrong because (B) is wrong. (D) is wrong because the $2,000 per month payment here was perfectly consistent with a pure lease transaction. (E) is wrong because the maintenance being performed here by Lessee could be explained not as detrimental reliance on the purchase option, but rather to reflect the below-market lease payments.

Chapter 2.   Terms

Assignment 8:   Warranties with Sales of Goods

A.   The Effects of Warranty Law on Business Practice

From the buyer's perspective, a key feature of any sales transaction is trying to ensure that the goods being purchased will work the way they are supposed to. UCC Article 2 contains a number of provisions that define the nature and scope of the promises the seller makes concerning the quality of goods that the seller is transferring to the buyer. Some of these provisions deal with explicit promises made by the seller, whereas other provisions create certain implicit promises that will become part of the deal unless the seller does something affirmative to disclaim them.

Players in the system generally are not thinking too much about the various warranty rules of Article 2 when they conduct purchase and sale transactions. They are, however, focusing very much on the issue of quality for the sake of future business.

As the president of a medium-sized shoe manufacturer put it, "Nobody bargains over warranties, because it's really pretty simple: Either the shoes are what they are supposed to be, or they're not. If they're not, you're not going to be in business very long. As seller, our incentive [to sell a quality product] is not driven by legal warranties, it's driven by business necessity."

The general counsel for a computer hardware distributor echoed these sentiments: "The warranties we give to retailers are whatever we get from the manufacturers, which is typically limited to repair, replacement, or refund of the hardware. Our real incentive, though, is never the warranty that we give but our philosophy of serving our customers. That's the reason, not warranties, that we try to make something right if one of our buyers gets a bad shipment."

The owner of a medium-sized air tool manufacturer explained how, as a seller, he stands behind his products, but he also expects his own suppliers to do the same: "One time a company in Cleveland, Ohio, made some needle tubes not dimensionally correct and they were going to charge us to correct the problem. And they stood by their position, which was that there was a blueprint that did not have that particular dimension on it. And our position was that we are a long-time customer of [theirs], and I've known [their president] for probably 20 years. So I wrote to their president and said, 'Al, fix your own problems, and correct those problems and get those needle tubes to us.' I did that over the fax machine, and they complied with my request."

There are two major issues regarding warranty creation that tend to command the attention of buyers and sellers in the sales system: (1) sellers feel the need for an outside time limit on warranties, but buyers who resell do not want any time limits to begin until their resale; and (2) middlemen do not like to give greater warranties to their buyers than they're getting from their own sellers.

As to outside time limits on warranties, sellers prefer that their responsibility for a particular sale not be completely open-ended. Sellers at least want to know that after a certain passage of time, the goods delivered are in fact acceptable. A furniture manufacturer related a problem that his company had a couple of years ago along these lines: "In a disturbing number of cases the ultimate buyer, the consumer, would ask the retailer to take the furniture back two or three years after the consumer had purchased it. Our retailers, figuring we would take it from them, would agree to do so for the sake of their own business and then would expect us to make them whole. We now make it clear that our warranties run 12 months from the time the retailer gets it from us; we'll honor the warranty within that time period even if the true claimant is the consumer rather than our buyer."

Although sellers may want to cap the length of their exposure for warranty problems, buyers who resell do not want warranty time limits to begin until the goods leave their own hands. One manufacturer described this tension between the desire of the seller for liability that is not open-ended and the desire of the buyer who resells not to get stuck with a warranty problem caused by its supplier: "For reasons of certainty, many of our suppliers want to cap the time during which we can complain about a problem. But the reality is that sometimes a problem won't manifest itself until the product has reached our buyer, and that could take some time. So we always want the warranty to start running from the time when our buyer gets the finished product, not when we get the raw material."

Beyond the timing issues, buyers who resell are very careful as a general matter to make certain that the warranties that they give to their buyers are no greater than the warranties that they are receiving from their own sellers. Otherwise, wholesalers can get stuck in the unenviable position of being responsible to their buyers for problems created by the manufacturer, with no recourse against the manufacturer. As one Fortune 100 manufacturer noted, "Our biggest warranty issue is that we need to make sure that the warranties we're getting from our suppliers are the same warranties that we will have to give to the government when we sell the finished product to it. In fact, we will put clauses in our purchase contracts to that effect, and it's not something that we'll negotiate about since we can't afford to be stuck with a problem in our sale that was created by one of our suppliers."

B.   The Basic UCC Quality Warranties

How the above-described warranty tensions end up being reconciled is typically a product of the leverage and negotiating skills of the players in each discrete transaction. The actual scope of the quality promises that are made in each case are thus more likely to come down to business realities than to legal rules. The legal rules of Article 2 are important, though, in that they provide the structure within which these negotiations take place. In most cases, the default rules of Article 2 provide the starting point for negotiations.

The UCC provides two implied warranties that relate to the performance of the goods sold. There is also an implied title warranty, which will be discussed in Assignment 16. Of the two implied warranties of quality, the more important is the implied warranty of merchantability found in UCC §2-314. Unless disclaimed or modified, this implied warranty arises in every sale of goods where the seller is a merchant with respect to goods of the kind being sold. UCC §2-314(1). The two key promises within the implied warranty of merchantability are that the goods being sold are at least as good as other, similar goods in the trade, and that the goods are fit for the ordinary purposes for which goods of that description are used. UCC §2-314(2)(a) and (c).

With the implied warranty of merchantability under Article 2, the buyer's complaint about the goods would typically relate to the quality of what was received. However, sometimes the buyer's breach of implied warranty action focuses not on quality as such, but on the absence of certain features that the buyer believes the product should contain in order to be merchantable.

Phillips v. Cricket Lighters

883 A.2d 439 (Pa. 2005)

Cappy, C.J.

This is an appeal by allowance. We are asked to resolve whether the Superior Court properly reversed the trial court's entry of summary judgment, thus allowing the breach of warranty and punitive damages claims to proceed in this matter. For the reasons that follow, we now reverse.

On the night of November 30, 1993, two year old Jerome Campbell ("Jerome") retrieved a Cricket disposable butane cigarette lighter which belonged to his mother, Robyn Williams ("Robyn"). It is uncontested that this butane lighter lacked any child-resistant feature. Jerome was able to use the lighter to ignite some linens. The fire that resulted killed Jerome, Robyn, and another minor child of Robyn's; one minor child, Neil Williams ("Neil"), survived.

Gwendolyn Phillips ("Appellee"), as administratrix of the estates of the three decedents and as guardian of Neil, instituted this action against the manufacturers and distributors of the Cricket lighter (collectively, "Appellants"). In her complaint, Appellee raised, *inter alia,* claims of design defect sounding in both strict liability and negligence, negligent infliction of emotional distress, breach of the implied warranty of merchantability, and punitive damages. These claims were all predicated on Appellee's allegations that Appellants should have manufactured and distributed a lighter that had childproof features.

Appellants filed for summary judgment. The trial court found in favor of Appellants, and dismissed all claims against them.

On appeal, Appellee presented five issues to the Superior Court, claiming that summary judgment should not have been entered on her breach of warranty, punitive damages, negligent infliction of emotional distress, or design defect claims sounding in strict liability or negligence. The Superior Court reversed the trial court's entry of summary judgment on all five of these claims.

Appellants then appealed to this court, and we granted allocatur. Following argument, we affirmed in part, reversed in part, and vacated in part the order of the Superior Court. See Phillips v. Cricket Lighters, 576 Pa. 644, 841 A.2d 1000 (2003) ("*Phillips I*"). As fully detailed in our *Phillips I* decision, we affirmed that portion of the Superior Court's order reinstating Appellee's negligence and negligent infliction of emotional distress claims. We reversed that portion of the Superior Court's order reinstating the strict liability design defect claim, finding that Appellee could not make out a strict liability claim in this matter as Jerome, a two-year-old child, was not the "intended user" of the lighter. We also vacated that portion of the Superior Court's order regarding the breach of warranty claim and reversed the Superior Court with regard to its decision on the punitive damages issue; we remanded this matter to the Superior Court for it to reconsider the punitive damages and breach of warranty claims.

On remand, the Superior Court once again reversed the trial court's entry of summary judgment in favor of Appellants with regard to the breach of warranty and punitive damages claims. Phillips v. Cricket Lighters, 852 A.2d 365 (2004). As to the breach of warranty claim, the Superior Court concluded that a reasonable jury could find that the Cricket lighter was not merchantable and thus the trial court erred in entering summary judgment in favor of Appellants on the breach of warranty claim. The Superior Court emphasized that the fact that a two-year old child was an unintended user of the lighter was not fatal to the warranty claim. The Superior Court stated that per 13 Pa. C.S. §2318, implied breach of warranty protections extend to all members of the buyer's household with no limitations being placed on whether the person who had used the product was the intended user.

With regard to the punitive damages claim, the Superior Court found that Appellee had presented evidence sufficient to create a jury question as to whether Appellants' actions exhibited reckless indifference to the interests of others. It therefore found that the trial court erred when it entered summary judgment on this claim.

Appellants filed a petition for allowance of appeal. We granted allocatur. For the reasons that follow, we now reverse.

In reviewing this matter, we must determine whether the Superior Court correctly reversed the trial court's entry of summary judgment. "[A]n appellate court may reverse the entry of summary judgment only where it finds that the trial court erred in concluding that the matter presented no genuine issue as to any material fact and that it is clear that the moving party was entitled to a judgment as a matter of law." *Phillips I*, 841 A.2d at 1005 (citing Pappas v. Asbel, 564 Pa. 407,

768 A.2d 1089 (2001)). In conducting this analysis, we are directed to resolve "all doubts as to the existence of a genuine issue of material fact . . . against the moving party." Ertel v. Patriot-News Co., 544 Pa. 93, 674 A.2d 1038, 1041 (1996). As the questions raised in this matter are solely ones of law, our review is *de novo.*

The first issue which we will address is the Superior Court's determination that the trial court erred in granting summary judgment on Appellee's breach of warranty claim. The statute defining implied warranty of merchantability states that in order for goods to be considered "merchantable," they must be at least such as:

(1) pass without objection in the trade under the contract description;
(2) in the case of fungible goods, are of fair average quality within the description;
(3) are fit for the ordinary purposes for which such goods are used;
(4) run, within the variations permitted by the agreement, of even kind, quality and quantity within each unit and among all units involved;
(5) are adequately contained, packaged, and labeled as the agreement may require; and
(6) conform to the promises or affirmations of fact made on the container or label if any.

13 Pa. C.S. §2314. In the matter *sub judice,* the focus is on whether Appellee can establish that the Cricket lighter was not fit for the ordinary purposes for which such goods are used. See 13 Pa. C.S. §2314(3). In analyzing this question, we note that "[t]he concept of merchantability does not require that the goods be the best quality or the best obtainable but it does require that they have an inherent soundness which makes them suitable for the purpose for which they are designed. . . ." Gall by Gall v. Allegheny County Health Dep't, 521 Pa. 68, 555 A.2d 786, 789-90 (1989) (internal citations omitted).

Appellee argues that she can establish that the Cricket lighter was unmerchantable. Echoing the analysis of the Superior Court below, she states that 13 Pa. C.S. §2318 dictates that she can recover on her §2314 claim. Section 2318 states, in pertinent part, that the warranty pursuant to §2314 "extends to any natural person who is in the family or household of his buyer or who is a guest in his home if it is reasonable to expect that such person may use, consume or be affected by the goods and who is injured in person by breach of the warranty." Appellee reasons that as Jerome was a family member of Robyn, the purchaser of the Cricket lighter, and as it was reasonable for Appellants to anticipate that a small child such as Jerome would use the Cricket lighter, then a breach of warranty claim will lie against Appellants.

Appellee's analysis is inapt. Section 2318 does not define when a breach of warranty has occurred. Rather, by its plain language, it spells out who may recover when a breach of warranty under §2314 has indeed occurred. 13 Pa. C.S. §2318 (stating that the warranty protections extends to a certain class of people "who [are] injured in person *by breach of the warranty*"). This plain reading of the statute is bolstered by the official Comments to section 2318; those Comments state that the purpose of this provision was to make clear that the ancient concepts of privity would not bar a modern breach of warranty claim. In essence, §2318 was adopted to broaden the class of people who could recover when a product is found to be unmerchantable. This section does not, however, expand upon or in any fashion provide further elucidation of what constitutes a breach of warranty.

To answer this question, we turn again to §2314's requirement that to be merchantable, the goods must be fit for their "ordinary purposes." The word "ordinary" is readily understood to mean "common" or "average." See American Heritage Dictionary of the English Language 925 (1981). In the context of this matter, it is apparent that the ordinary purpose of the Cricket lighter was to allow an adult user to produce a flame. Its ordinary purpose certainly was not to be a two-year old child's plaything. The fact that the product was tragically misused in such a way does not alter the ordinary purpose of the product. As the lighter was fit for its ordinary purpose, it was merchantable; Appellee's contention to the contrary must fail. Accordingly, the Superior Court erred when it reversed the trial court's order granting summary judgment in favor of Appellants on the breach of warranty claim.

The next issue we address is whether the Superior Court correctly determined that Appellee had adduced enough evidence regarding her punitive damages claim such that a jury issue was created.

Our case law makes it clear that punitive damages are an "extreme remedy" available in only the most exceptional matters. See Martin v. Johns-Manville Corp., 508 Pa. 154, 494 A.2d 1088, 1098 n.14 (Pa. 1985), *rev'd on other grounds sub nom.* Kirkbride v. Lisbon Contractors, Inc., 521 Pa. 97, 555 A.2d 800 (1989). Punitive damages may be appropriately awarded only when the plaintiff has established that the defendant has acted in an outrageous fashion due to either "the defendant's evil motive or his reckless indifference to the rights of others." *Martin*, 494 A.2d at 1096; see also Hutchison v. Luddy, 870 A.2d 766, 770 (Pa. 2005) (finding that punitive damages may be appropriately awarded only when the plaintiff has established that the defendant has acted in a fashion "so outrageous as to demonstrate willful, wanton or reckless conduct"). A defendant acts recklessly when "his conduct creates an unreasonable risk of physical harm to another [and] such risk is substantially greater than that which is necessary to make his conduct negligent." Id. at 771 (citation omitted). Thus, a showing of mere negligence, or even gross negligence, will not suffice to establish that punitive damages should be imposed. SHV Coal, Inc. v. Continental Grain Co., 526 Pa. 489, 587 A.2d 702, 705 (1991). Rather, the plaintiff must adduce evidence which goes beyond a showing of negligence, evidence sufficient to establish that the defendant's acts amounted to "intentional, willful, wanton or reckless conduct. . . ." Id. at 704 (citation omitted).

What is clear from these cases is that there is a distinction between negligence and punitive damages claims, with a plaintiff being required to meet a far lesser burden to establish a negligence claim than that which is imposed in connection with a punitive damages claim. This distinction is an important one. Damages awarded in a negligence action compensate a plaintiff for his or her losses. Punitive damages, in contrast, are not awarded to compensate the plaintiff for her damages but rather to heap an additional punishment on a defendant who is found to have acted in a fashion which is particularly egregious. G.J.D. by G.J.D. v. Johnson, 552 Pa. 169, 713 A.2d 1127, 1129 (1998). Such a punishment should not be meted out to every defendant who is found to have acted negligently; rather, it should be reserved for those cases in which the defendant has acted in a particularly outrageous fashion.

We now turn to applying these principles to the matter *sub judice.* In support of her punitive damages claim, Appellee points to evidence she adduced showing that fires caused by children playing with butane lighters resulted in the deaths of 120 people per year, with an additional 750 people being injured in these fires. Expert Report and Affidavit of John O. Geremia, Ph.D. ("Geremia Affidavit") at 7 (citing the Consumer Product Safety Commission's report on child-resistant cigarette lighters, 53 Fed. Reg. 6833-01 (March 3, 1988)). Furthermore, evidence introduced by Appellee established that the estimated annual cost of child-play butane lighter fires to be between $300-375 [sic] million, or 60 to 75 cents per lighter sold. Id.

Appellee also relies on the deposition testimony of Rene Frigiere, Ph.D. ("Frigiere"), an employee of Appellants. Frigiere stated that Appellants knew of the dangers posed by young children playing with butane lighters. Deposition testimony of Rene Frigiere, 1/16/1998, at 68-70. Frigiere also admitted that Appellants could have placed child resistant features on their butane lighters; Appellee emphasizes that Frigiere indicated that Appellants chose not to place such features on their lighters unilaterally as they feared that their adult customers would opt not to buy such a product. Id. at 47. As noted by Appellee, Appellants came to this conclusion, in part, after test-marketing such a product in France where they discovered that their adult customers disliked the lighter with the child resistant features as such a lighter was more difficult to use. Id. at 118-20. Appellee focuses on this testimony as she apparently believes that Appellants' weighing of financial factors is a resounding indictment of Appellants and assuredly shows that their conduct was outrageous.

As we found in *Phillips I,* Appellee had adduced enough evidence to create a jury question on whether Appellants acted negligently in selling a butane lighter which lacked child safety devices. *Phillips I,* 841 A.2d at 1008-10. Yet, the question with which we are now presented is not whether this evidence could support a finding of negligence. Rather, we must determine whether Appellee has adduced evidence sufficient to show that Appellants had an evil motive or were recklessly indifferent to the rights of others by creating a risk of harm which is substantially greater than that which is necessary to make his conduct negligent. *Martin,* 494 A.2d at 1097 n.11.

It is readily apparent that the evidence does not show that Appellants had some evil motive such as intentionally manufacturing a lighter with the express wish that children misuse it and start fires. Thus, the narrow question here is whether Appellants acted with reckless indifference of a risk of harm which is substantially greater than that which is necessary to make their conduct negligent. After careful review, we conclude that Appellee has not shown that Appellants' conduct was so outrageous that the risk of harm here can be said to be "substantially greater" than that which would be posed by negligent conduct.

We base our conclusion on many factors. First, the allegedly dangerous aspect of this product did not arise out of intended use of Appellants' product. Rather, it arose when the product was improperly utilized as a toy by a young child. While failure to mitigate and prevent a danger posed by misuses can give rise to liability in negligence, such a failure looks far less wanton than if the alleged danger arose in connection with the normal use of the product. Second, as acknowledged by both Appellee and Appellants, at the time this butane lighter was sold, it complied with all safety standards. Of course, compliance with safety standards does not, standing alone, automatically insulate a defendant from punitive damages; it is a factor to be considered in determining whether punitive damages may be recovered. Finally, we flatly reject Appellee's assertion that Appellants' weighing of financial concerns in determining whether to incorporate additional safety features into its product on a unilateral basis establishes that Appellants acted wantonly. Rather, it shows simply that Appellants were considering all of the myriad elements that affect decisions a for-profit entity must make in manufacturing and marketing commercial products. Thus, we conclude that as a matter of law, Appellee has not adduced evidence sufficient to establish that Appellants' conduct was so outrageous so as to support an award of punitive damages.

For the foregoing reasons, we reverse the order of the Superior Court. . . .

Even used goods, as long as they are sold by merchants, come with an implied warranty of merchantability. Of course, that does not mean that used goods are warranted to perform as if they were new goods. As noted by Official Comment 3 to §2-314, "A contract for the sale of second-hand goods, however, involves only such obligation as is appropriate to such goods for that is their contract description."

The other implied warranty is the warranty of fitness for a particular purpose. This implied warranty arises in much more limited circumstances than the warranty of merchantability. Unless disclaimed or modified, the fitness warranty is implied whenever the seller knows that the buyer is buying the goods for a particular purpose and is relying on the seller's expertise to select or furnish the goods. UCC §2-315. The fitness warranty promises that the goods are indeed fit for the buyer's particular purpose. A common situation in which the fitness warranty arises is where the buyer furnishes to the seller certain specifications indicating the particular purpose for which the buyer is purchasing the goods. For example, suppose that a farmer goes to a farm-supply store and tells the clerk that he needs a plow for the very rocky soil on his farm. If the clerk suggests to the farmer a particular plow, then there may be an implied warranty that this plow is fit for using in rocky soil.

Buyers sometimes confuse the two implied warranties by wrongly believing that an implied warranty of fitness arises even in a case where the buyer's contemplated use of the goods is an ordinary one rather than a "particular" purpose. Yet Official Comment 2 to §2-315 makes it clear that the implied warranty of fitness was not intended for the buyer whose use of the goods is ordinary: "For example, shoes are generally used for the purpose of walking upon ordinary ground, but a seller may know that a particular pair was selected to be used for climbing mountains."

Leal v. Holtvogt

702 N.E.2d 1246 (Ohio App. 1998)

FAIN, J.

. . . Joseph and Claudia Holtvogt owned and operated Shady Glen Arabians, a horse barn in Miami County, Ohio. They were experienced in Arabian horse training, breeding, boarding, selling, and showing. In 1992, the Leals, novices in the equine industry, decided to begin raising horses. In April 1993, Ferdinand Leal began visiting Shady Glen Arabians regularly to learn how to ride and handle horses. Before long, a friendship developed between the Holtvogts and Leals, and Ferdinand Leal began spending three to four days each week at the Holtvogts' barn helping Joseph Holtvogt with the horses.

In late 1993, the Leals decided they wanted to start a breeding program by purchasing a stallion to breed with a mare they owned. At first, they were interested in purchasing Procale, a stallion owned by John Bowman. After talking to Mr. Holtvogt about Procale, the Leals decided not to buy him. The Holtvogts then offered the Leals a one-half interest in McQue Jabask, an Arabian stallion that the Holtvogts owned. At trial, the Leals testified that before they agreed to invest in McQue Jabask, Mr. Holtvogt made a number of statements regarding the stallion, such as McQue Jabask was a national top-ten champion in three categories; he was an all-around winning stallion; he earns $20,000 per year in stud fees; he is capable of attaining national show titles again; and his foals were selling for $6,000 to $10,000 each (these statements will be referred to hereinafter as "the five contested statements").

In January 1994, the Leals and Holtvogts entered into a contract of sale for a one-half interest in McQue Jabask for $16,000. The contract also established a partnership agreement, which called for the parties to share equally in the expenses and profits arising from their joint ownership of McQue Jabask.

There was expert testimony that prior to January 1994, McQue Jabask had been treated for lameness and was suffering a chronic lameness condition in his right rear and fore fetlocks. Mr. Holtvogt testified that he had taken the stallion for lameness treatments numerous times. He also stated that he did not disclose this information to the Leals.

By July 1994, the Leals were dissatisfied with the partnership and indicated to the Holtvogts that they wanted either a refund of their money or a remedy for their concerns. In March 1995, the mortality insurance on McQue Jabask lapsed when neither the Leals nor the Holtvogts paid the insurance premium.

Mary Leal, a former Dayton police officer, was unhappy with the partnership. She began making disparaging remarks about Joseph Holtvogt's honesty and integrity to the past and present customers of Shady Glen Arabians. As a result of these remarks, Joseph Holtvogt testified that he suffered from depression, had visited some medical doctors, and was on medication. The Holtvogts did stipulate, however, that they could not prove any business or economic damages due to Mary Leal's remarks.

On January 17, 1996, McQue Jabask died from stomach ulcer complications. Since neither party had renewed the stallion's mortality insurance, McQue Jabask was uninsured. . . .

. . . In its entry, the trial court found the following:

> "[T]he information the [Holtvogts] failed to apprise the [Leals] of was the lameness of the horse at the time the contract was executed in January 1994."
>
> "The [Leals] suffered damages in the amount of $16,000.00 as a result of this negligent misrepresentation."
>
> "The *same set of facts* establishes a cause of action for breach of express warranty *on the condition of the horse for the purposes intended*." (Emphasis added.)

In its entry, the trial court did not just say that an express warranty was breached, but rather said that an "express warranty *on the condition of the horse for the purposes intended*" was breached. (Emphasis added.) We conclude that the trial court intended to say that an implied warranty of fitness for a particular purpose was breached. Our conclusion is supported by the trial court's statement that the same set of facts establishes claims for both a breach of express warranty on the condition of the horse for the purposes intended and negligent misrepresentation. We note that the elements of a claim for negligent misrepresentation and breach of an implied warranty of fitness for a particular purpose are quite similar, while the elements of negligent misrepresentation and breach of an express warranty are not similar. Thus, we conclude that the trial court, in its conclusions of law, intended to say that an implied warranty of fitness for a particular purpose was given and breached by the Holtvogts when they failed to disclose McQue Jabask's lameness to the Leals.

An implied warranty of fitness for a particular purpose is covered by the Uniform Commercial Code, Sales, R.C. 1302.28, which provides:

> "Where the seller at the time of contracting has reason to know any particular purpose for which the goods are required and that the buyer is relying on the seller's skill or judgment to select or furnish suitable goods, there is unless excluded or modified under section 1302.29 of the Revised Code an implied warranty that the goods shall be fit for such purpose."

Ohio courts have set forth the following test to determine whether an implied warranty of fitness for a particular purpose has been created: (1) the seller must have reason to know of the buyer's particular purpose; (2) the seller must have reason to know that the buyer is relying on the seller's skill or judgment to furnish or select appropriate goods; and (3) the buyer must, in fact, rely upon the seller's skill or judgment. Hollingsworth v. The Software House, Inc. (1986), 32 Ohio App. 3d 61, 65, 513 N.E.2d 1372, 1375-1376; Delorise Brown, M.D., Inc. v. Allio (1993), 86 Ohio App. 3d 359, 362, 620 N.E.2d 1020, 1021-1022.

The first element requires that Mr. Holtvogt knew why the Leals decided to buy an interest in McQue Jabask. From our review of the record, we see that Mr. Holtvogt clearly knew that the Leals wanted to buy an interest in the stallion to start a breeding program. Mr. Holtvogt testified:

> ". . . [The Leals] had explained what type of horse they were looking for [and] it seemed to me that [McQue] Jabask fit the bill [of] what they were looking for and that's why I mentioned to them, uh, to Ferdinand that there might be a possibility that we would be interested in selling part interest in him."
>
> ". . . [T]he things that they were saying, . . . those things were, were present in, in [McQue] Jabask." . . .
>
> ". . . [I]t just, it made sense that, you know, in the fact that the Leals could breed to [McQue] Jabask. . . . Um, we could, uh, with the experience and the reputation that we had we could help market their foals, um, it was, I really felt that it was something that could work."

Thus, evidence of the first element of an implied warranty of fitness for a particular purpose was presented at trial.

The second element requires that Mr. Holtvogt had reason to know that the Leals were relying on his skill and judgment to select or furnish the appropriate goods. Evidence presented at trial shows that Mr. Holtvogt knew, or at least should have known, that the Leals were relying on his judgment when they purchased an interest in the stallion. The relationship between Mr. Holtvogt and Mr. Leal was like that of a teacher and student. Mr. Leal spent a great deal of time at the Holtvogts' barn, helping Mr. Holtvogt with the horses and learning from Mr. Holtvogt. Mr. Holtvogt testified that he was an expert trainer and breeder with Arabian horses, and the evidence shows that he knew Mr. Leal knew very little about horses. Furthermore, the Leals testified that they were interested in purchasing another horse, Procale, but that Mr. Holtvogt steered them away from that horse, saying that horse was not the type of horse that the Leals wanted to buy. Mr. Holtvogt even testified that he mentioned McQue Jabask to the Leals because the stallion was the type of horse that they were looking for. Thus, evidence of the second element of an implied warranty of fitness for a particular purpose was presented at trial.

The third element requires that the Leals actually did rely upon Mr. Holtvogt's skill and judgment when they purchased an interest in the stallion. The trial court found that the Leals justifiably relied upon the Holtvogts' representations regarding the stallion. This finding is not against the manifest weight of the evidence. As stated earlier, there was competent and credible evidence presented at trial to support this finding, as both Leals were novices in the horse industry and they testified that they trusted Mr. Holtvogt and considered him to be the expert. Thus, evidence of the third element was presented at trial.

Because all three elements were proven at trial, we conclude that an implied warranty of fitness for a particular purpose was given by the Holtvogts to the Leals at the time of the sale. There must be evidence that the warranty was breached if the Leals are to recover. Delorise Brown, M.D., Inc., 86 Ohio App. 3d at 363, 620 N.E.2d at 1022. "Whether a warranty has failed to fulfill its essential purpose is ordinarily a determination for the fact finder." Id.

The trial court found that a warranty was breached by the Holtvogts because the horse was lame. As stated above, competent and credible evidence was presented to support the trial court's finding that McQue Jabask suffered from chronic lameness at the time of the sale. At trial, Dixie Gansmiller testified that even though a lame stallion could stand for stud, its lameness would affect her decision whether to breed her mares with it. Thus, we conclude that competent and credible evidence in the record does demonstrate that McQue Jabask was not fit for the particular purpose intended by the Leals when they invested in him. . . .

In addition to outlining the terms and conditions of implied warranties, Article 2 also describes the various ways in which express warranties are created. Express warranties must be affirmatively created by the seller to the immediate buyer through affirmations of fact, promises, descriptions, samples, or models, as long as any of these become "part of the basis of the bargain." UCC §2-313(1). In order to create an express warranty a seller need not use any magic words like "guarantee" or "warranty," but if a seller is merely giving its opinion of the goods, then such statements are considered "puffing" and do not give rise to a warranty. UCC §2-313(2).

The determination of whether a particular statement by a seller amounts to a true express warranty or mere "puffing" is very fact-specific. There are a number of particular factors that may be relevant to the inquiry. First, specific language is much more likely to be deemed an express warranty than is vague language. For example, "this car gets 32 miles to the gallon" is much more likely to be an express warranty than "this is a wonderful car."

Second, all other things being equal, a written statement is more likely to be considered an express warranty than is an oral statement. Third, the context in which the seller's statement was made will normally be important in deciding whether the statement is an express warranty rather than puffing. For example, in a context where the seller makes a statement in response to the buyer's request that the seller give his opinion of the product, that context is at least a factor that weighs in favor of the seller's statement being considered puffing.

Ultimately, the express warranty/puffing determination comes down to the reasonableness of the buyer's reliance on the seller's statement. If the buyer's reliance on the seller's statement was reasonable under the circumstances, that tips the balance in favor of an express warranty rather than puffing. If the buyer's reliance was not reasonable, it is more likely the seller's statement will be characterized as puffing. As Comment 8 to §2-313 puts it, "Concerning affirmations of value or a seller's opinion or commendation under subsection (2), the basic question remains the same: What statements of the seller have in the circumstances and in objective judgment become part of the basis of the bargain?"

At this point, you should note an interesting anomaly between the law on the books regarding express warranties and the sales system as it actually operates. UCC §2-313 is very clear about the requirement that the seller's promises about the goods be at least "part of the basis of the bargain" in order to qualify as express warranties. Yet the reality is that in most sales transactions, whether commercial or consumer, the buyer does not even bother to read the terms of the written "warranty" until some point after paying for the goods, if at all.

Does this mean that the written warranty does not in fact amount to a valid express warranty, since the purchaser cannot claim reliance on promises that were not even read before the sale was concluded? In other words, how can something that the buyer never reads be "part of the basis of the bargain" for purposes of UCC §2-313? In practice, it would be rare for a seller to attempt to escape the terms of a written warranty on the grounds that the buyer never read it. Could an unscrupulous seller avoid liability on that basis if it wanted?

An in-house lawyer for a Fortune 100 clothing retailer, which does a significant amount of buying from wholesale clothing vendors, made the following argument for the legal enforceability of such unread warranties: "It's true that nobody dickers over the terms of warranties. We have fairly extensive warranties in our purchase orders about merchantability, fitness, flammability, and the like. Although nobody reads those before agreeing to sell, our regular vendors get these forms time and time again so they know when we enter into each contract that we are going to be expecting the usual warranties. In that sense we are relying on the existence of those warranties as a basis of our bargain with them."

Whenever a defect in a product causes personal injury, the plaintiff will often bring suit both on a UCC warranty theory and on the tort theories of negligence and strict products liability. The advantage of the warranty theory is that the plaintiff does not need to show lack of due care, as the plaintiff must in a negligence action. On the other hand, the tort plaintiff does not have to contend with certain privity problems that can sometimes prevent otherwise viable warranty suits. Furthermore, the tort plaintiff is not subject to the strict notice requirements of UCC §2-607(3)(a), nor does the tort plaintiff need to show the reliance element that is necessary for an express warranty claim.

C. Extended Warranties and Maintenance Agreements

In the last few decades there has been a proliferation of so-called extended warranties or maintenance agreements. The basic idea behind these instruments is that the manufacturer's warranty may be limited in either duration or scope, and the extended warranty provides a relatively cheap form of insurance for the buyer in case there is a problem that is not covered by the basic warranty. Extended warranty programs are most commonly available with big-ticket consumer items such as a car or a major home appliance.

It is not difficult to understand the increased availability of extended warranties. The profit margins on extended warranties are huge, given that about 80 percent of those that are sold go unused. Consumer Reports said in a recent study, "Warranty sales often bring in more profit than the merchandise, because for every dollar a retailer makes on a warranty, it spends an average of just 4 to 15 cents fixing the product. Only 12% to 20% of those who buy warranties ever use them."

What the consumer may not realize is that some extended warranties are largely duplicating what the customer is already getting from the manufacturer's warranty. As the purchasing officer for a major university noted, "The big thing now is maintenance agreements. But I tell my departments not to go right out and buy the maintenance agreement until the original warranty is about to run. If the equipment has problems during the original period, some of the manufacturer's warranties will automatically be extended."

Another surprise that consumers may encounter in purchasing extended warranties is that those warranties are often serviced by a third party that has no formal connection to the seller of the goods. The same university purchasing officer quoted above also noted the importance to his organization of the warranty being serviced by the seller itself rather than some third party: "Once we were buying a multi-million-dollar machine from a major manufacturer and they wanted to put the warranty immediately with a third party, but we just wouldn't let them do it. Our people here don't always read the warranties closely before they buy something, but at least if the product doesn't work and we don't get satisfaction, we can threaten not to do business with the seller again. It becomes a much more complicated scenario when you're not even dealing with the seller anymore."

Consumers who end up buying extended warranties that are serviced by third parties quickly come to realize that these third-party servicers have a vested interest in coming up with reasons why claims should not be paid. Like primary-care physicians in health maintenance organizations, third-party warrantors are gatekeepers that attempt to screen out as many complaints as possible before they even reach the paying stage.

Richard Colbey, a British barrister, described his personal experience with a third-party warrantor as follows:

> The words "take out Coverplan Plus and you need only make one simple phone call to ensure a prompt skillful repair" still bring my blood close to boiling point three years after I misguidedly took out a policy on a fax machine I bought from Dixons.
>
>   I reasoned it was worth paying a bit extra to be spared the aggravation if the fax did go wrong. When it did, my first attempt to make that phone call resulted in

me being cut off. When I finally got through I was told to ring another number to arrange an appointment with a firm of independent engineers. Their number was perpetually engaged. Eventually I gave up and bought a new fax.

Dixons, although willing to refund the insurance premium, needed to be persuaded that I was serious about the threat of legal proceedings before coughing up a further pounds 150 compensation. (Richard Colbey, "Extended Warranties Spark New Wave of Complaints," *The Guardian,* City page, February 17, 1996.)

Yet another problem consumers have encountered with third-party warrantors is when the warrantor has an arrangement with the seller whereby the seller agrees to pay the warrantor for each repair that the warrantor completes. In cases where the seller has stopped paying the third-party servicer, the servicer may force the customer to pay for the servicer's repair and then instruct the customer to bill the seller directly. This is exactly what happened to Silo customers who had purchased extended warranties when that store stopped paying its third-party servicer.

In the final analysis, it is impossible to say that extended warranties are never a good idea. Like all forms of insurance, they are a gamble, but consumers are often not fully aware of all of the risks involved with that gamble:

> An extended warranty or service contract is actually [product] repair insurance. It's a gamble that will pay off only if [the product] needs repairs that cost more than the price of the contract, if the repairs are not already covered under the manufacturers' warranty, and if the warranty company stays in business and agrees that the repairs are covered. (Judy Garnatz Harriman, "A Close Look at Extended Warranties," *St. Petersburg Times*, 2D, March 13, 1995.)

Problem Set 8

8.1.   a. You just sold your law school classmate a computer that you had owned for three months. A week after the sale, your classmate complains that the characters on the screen fade noticeably after about 20 minutes. You had never noticed this when you used the computer. Have you breached the implied warranty of merchantability? UCC §2-314.

b. Same facts as part (a), except that you knew about the fading problem and did not mention it prior to the sale. Have you breached the implied warranty of merchantability? Are you liable on some other theory? UCC §§2-314, 1-304, 1-201(b)(20); Official Comment 3 to §2-314.

c. Same facts as part (a), except that you knew about the fading problem and not only did you not mention it, you told your classmate that this computer was "super." Have you breached an express warranty? Are you liable on some other theory? UCC §2-313, Official Comments 3 and 8 to §2-313, §1-103.

d. Same facts as part (a), except your law school classmate bought the used computer from your law school, which holds an annual sale of used computers. Has the law school breached the implied warranty of merchantability?

UCC §2-314, Official Comment 3 to §2-314, §2-104(1), Official Comment 2 to §2-104.

8.2.   a. Bob Sinclair owns a used-car lot, Bob's Affordable Wheels. You just graduated from college and visit Bob's with an eye to finding a car in the $10,000 price range. You spot a used Honda Accord for $9,900 and ask Bob about the car. "She's a humdinger, all right," says Bob. If you purchase the Accord, has Bob made an express warranty? If so, what is its content? UCC §2-313.

b. Same facts as part (a), except that you are particularly concerned about gas mileage, so you ask Bob what kind of mileage the used Accord gets. "You know those Accords," says Bob. "They're like camels." If you purchase the Accord, has Bob made an express warranty? If so, what is its content? UCC §2-313.

c. Same facts as part (a), except that you bring your mother with you to Bob's, because your mother knows a lot more about cars than you do. Your mother tells you that the used Accord is a good bet because it gets such good gas mileage. Just to be sure, you ask Bob about this particular Accord's gas mileage, and he gives you the "like camels" line. Has Bob made an express warranty? UCC §2-313.

d. Same facts as part (a), except that as soon as you come in, you tell Bob that the most important thing for you is to buy a car that gets good gas mileage. "Then I've got just the car for you, young man," Bob tells you, and shows you the used Accord. Has Bob made an express warranty to you? UCC §2-313. Has he made any other type of warranty? UCC §2-315.

e. Same facts as part (a), except that right after you give Bob the check for $9,900 but before you leave his lot, you tell him, "By the way, I forgot to ask you about gas mileage. That's extremely important to me. Does this car get good mileage?" Bob replies, "Son, I promise that this car will give you at least 30 miles per gallon in the city." Has Bob made an express warranty? UCC §§2-313, 2-209; Official Comment 7 to §2-313.

f. Same facts as part (a), except that before buying the car you ask Bob whether it comes with a warranty. "You bet, son," says Bob, who then hands you a six-page warranty that you do not bother to read on the spot. Two days later, as you read the warranty, your eyes light up when you get to the part about gas mileage. "Great," you tell yourself, "this says that the car will get at least 30 miles per gallon in the city." Has Bob made an express warranty concerning the gas mileage? UCC §2-313.

8.3.   a. Carol Campbell owns a clothing store, Dress for Success, that sells a variety of men's and women's business attire. Paul Wofsey selected a new suit there, had it altered by the store, bought it, and took it home. When he tried the suit on two weeks later, he sat down and discovered to his painful surprise that someone had sewn a rusty tack into the seat of the pants. Is Carol's store liable for breach of warranty? UCC §2-314.

b. Same facts as part (a), except that Carol has her workers examine all of the inventory thoroughly every night to make sure there are no foreign objects such as pins stuck in the clothes. Will this evidence be useful for Carol if nobody knows how or when the rusty tack got into the pants? UCC §2-314, Official Comment 13 to §2-314.

c. Same facts as part (b). Will this evidence be useful for Carol if it is established as a fact that an angry customer placed the rusty tack in the pants a half-hour before Paul bought them? UCC §2-314, Official Comment 13 to §2-314.

8.4.   You just began your first job after graduation as in-house counsel for a major beer manufacturer. Your initial project involves a lawsuit that was filed against your company by a 62-year-old man who developed cirrhosis of the liver after several decades of heavy beer drinking. One of the theories of his suit, the one that you have been asked to focus on, is that your company breached its implied warranty of merchantability because beer that causes cirrhosis of the liver is not fit for its ordinary use. Your general counsel asked you to think about different arguments that your company can make in response to this warranty claim. What statutory arguments can you come up with as to why your company should not be liable on an implied warranty theory? UCC §2-314(2), Official Comment 13 to UCC §2-314.

8.5.   Your law firm was just retained to represent a car manufacturer that was sued by a woman who was a passenger in one of your client's newer models that the woman had purchased. The woman, who was seriously injured in a car accident, claims that the manufacturer's failure to include side airbags as a standard feature in the car she bought amounted to a breach of the implied warranty of merchantability. The car, which was one of the manufacturer's economy models, did have standard front airbags for both the driver and passenger. What are the strongest Article 2 arguments your firm can muster to defend against this lawsuit? How generally should a court decide when the implied warranty of merchantability must include a particular safety feature? UCC §2-314(2).

8.6.   Consider the following actual news story that appeared in the *St. Louis Post-Dispatch*:

> Dairy Industry Sued Over Man's Ill Health (SEATTLE) (AP) — Norman Mayo, 61, is suing the dairy industry, claiming drinking whole milk contributed to his clogged arteries and a minor stroke. He said he might have avoided the problems if he had been warned on milk cartons about fat and cholesterol. The federal lawsuit names Safeway and the Dairy Farmers of Washington as defendants. Mayo wants warnings on dairy products. "If tobacco products can be required to have warning labels, why not dairy products?" said Mayo, a former smoker. "I think milk is just as dangerous as tobacco."

Suppose Mr. Mayo's implied warranty theory is not lack of fitness for ordinary use, as in Problem 8.4, but instead that the whole milk was not "adequately contained, packaged, and labeled" because of its lack of a warning about health risks. Should Mr. Mayo prevail on this theory? UCC §2-314(2)(e).

8.7.   Consider Carol Campbell again, and in particular the facts of Problem 8.3(c), where even her nightly inspections are not enough to catch the angry customer who sewed the rusty tack into the seat of Paul's pants. Carol now wants to defend by saying that the cost of avoiding this particular harm would not be worth the benefit, since Carol's workers would have needed to do clothes inspections every 15 minutes to avoid this harm. Therefore, says Carol, she should not be liable for an unavoidable harm. Will this defense work?

Assignment 9: Notice and Privity

The preceding discussion focused on how the three major Article 2 quality warranties are formed. However, it is not nearly enough for a plaintiff to demonstrate that the seller made a particular Article 2 warranty. In order to recover on a warranty theory, a plaintiff needs to show a number of things: (1) that the warranty was made; (2) that the warranty was breached; (3) that the breach of warranty caused the harm complained of; (4) the extent of damages; and (5) that the plaintiff can fend off any possible affirmative defense, including disclaimers, statutes of limitations, lack of notice, lack of privity, and assumption of the risk.

Causation between breach and harm might seem like an easy fact to establish, but in many cases the seller can legitimately allege that the injury complained of by the buyer was caused by factors other than the product's defect. And, in some cases, even though the product is proven to be defective, the seller might allege that the product's defect was caused by the buyer following the purchase, and therefore there was no breach of warranty at all.

When the buyer does discover a defect in the goods, it must notify the seller within a reasonable time or lose all right to a remedy for the breach. Indeed, UCC §2-607(3)(a) makes it clear that the buyer that wishes to preserve its remedies must notify the seller of any defect within a reasonable time after the buyer "should have discovered any breach." Thus, for example, if a buyer fails to follow customary inspection procedures for a given industry and only later learns of a defect that could have been discovered sooner, the buyer might waive the right to recover from the seller for breach.

Regarding §2-607's notice requirements, the general counsel of an international electronics manufacturer observed, "[F]or those of us on the sales side, we sure as heck like §2-607. Many a buyer has run up on that rock and failed to give timely notice of breach. I've had a couple of cases in which that's been a real meat ax. You know, you just failed to give me my notice. Once was in the case of an infringement situation. I think I find that too often lawyers representing buyers, and even lawyers representing sellers, are just terribly careless when it comes to looking at the Code and doing what the Code says to do."

Hebron v. American Isuzu Motors, Inc.

60 F.3d 1095 (4th Cir. 1995)

NIEMEYER, C.J.

In June 1991, Rachel E. Hebron was driving her 1991 model Isuzu Trooper truck on Interstate 395 in Alexandria, Virginia, when she was "cut off" without warning

185

by a vehicle entering her lane directly in front of her. Hebron braked and turned the steering wheel to the right to avoid a collision. Her truck swerved and then rolled over, causing Hebron to sustain permanent injuries. The driver of the other vehicle failed to stop and has never been identified.

Two years later, in June 1993, after the Isuzu truck had been disposed of, Hebron sued American Isuzu Motors, Inc., for $750,000 in damages, giving American Isuzu its first notice of her claim on July 12, 1993, when it received a copy of her complaint. The complaint alleged that the Isuzu truck was not safe "to drive upon the public highways" and that American Isuzu breached the implied warranty of merchantability given when its dealer sold Hebron the truck in December 1990.

On the eve of trial, after discovery had been completed, American Isuzu renewed an earlier-filed motion for summary judgment based in part on Hebron's failure to provide American Isuzu with "reasonable notice" of her claim in violation of Virginia's Uniform Commercial Code, §8.2-607(3)(a) of the Virginia Code. The district court granted the motion, observing that Hebron failed to provide notice for over two years without any explanation and during that period disposed of the truck, thus "depriving [American Isuzu] of any opportunity to inspect the vehicle to prepare its defense." The court explained that even though the reasonableness of notice is usually a factual question, in this case "Hebron's two-year delay before notifying [American Isuzu] of the alleged breach of warranty is unreasonable as a matter of law." The court relied on two cases in which merchant buyers were found, as a matter of law, to have given insufficient notice: Smith-Moore Body Co. v. Heil Co., 603 F. Supp. 354, 358 (E.D. Va. 1985) (seven-month delay in giving notice held to be unreasonable), and Begley v. Jeep Corp., 491 F. Supp. 63, 66 (W.D. Va. 1980) (delay of two years and five months held to be unreasonable). In both cases, the seller was deprived of an opportunity to investigate the accident in a timely manner and to inspect the allegedly defective product.

On appeal, Hebron contends that §8.2-607(3)(a) of the Virginia Code applies only to a contractual relationship between "commercial parties," and that the district court erred in failing to recognize that hers is a personal injury claim made by a retail buyer. She argues that "the notice requirement of the Uniform Commercial Code was not enacted to control product liability personal injury litigation," relying primarily on Hill v. Joseph T. Ryerson & Son, Inc., 165 W. Va. 22, 268 S.E.2d 296 (1980) (holding that defense of lack of notice is unavailable in product liability actions for personal injuries under West Virginia Uniform Commercial Code provision). However, Hebron cannot provide any authority from Virginia in support of this contention.

Section 8.2-607(3)(a) of the Virginia Code, which remains consistent with the language of §2-607 of the Uniform Commercial Code, provides:

> (3) Where a tender has been accepted
> (a) the buyer must within a reasonable time after he discovers or should have discovered any breach notify the seller of breach or be barred from any remedy; . . .

The term "buyer" is defined as "a person who buys or contracts to buy goods." Va. Code §8.2-103(1)(a). The word "person" in that definition is not restricted to commercial parties or merchants, and the definition does not explicitly exclude retail consumers. Since "merchant" is a defined term under the Uniform Commercial Code, see Va. Code §8.2-104(1), that term surely would have been used in the notice provision in §8.2-607 if such a restrictive application were intended. Any doubt about whether the term "buyer" in §8.2-607(3)(a) includes both retail consumers and merchant buyers is resolved by the official comment to §8.2-607(3)(a), which addresses both merchant buyers and retail buyers. Comment 4 provides in part:

> The time of notification is to be determined by applying commercial standards to a *merchant buyer*. "A reasonable time" for notification from a *retail consumer* is to be judged by different standards. . . .

Va. Code §8.2-607(3)(a), cmt. 4 (emphasis added). Thus, even though the requirement of reasonable notice may be more strictly applied to merchant buyers than to retail consumers, the term "buyer" as used in §8.2-607(3)(a) clearly applies both to merchant buyers and retail consumers. Retail consumers are, under the plain meaning of the word, "persons" who buy or contract to buy goods. See Va. Code §8.2-103(1)(a). See also Ronald A. Anderson, Anderson on the Uniform Commercial Code §2-607:27, at 137 (3d ed. 1983) ("When the buyer sues the seller for *personal injuries* based upon a breach of warranty it is necessary that he had complied with the notice provision." (emphasis added)); Chestnut v. Ford Motor Co., 445 F.2d 967, 969 (4th Cir. 1971) (observing generally that lack of notice of a breach is a defense to a warranty claim) (dictum); Belton v. Ridge Tool Co., No. 90-1406, 1990 WL 116783 (4th Cir. June 4, 1990) (unpublished) (Va. Code §8.2-607(3)(a) bars any remedy for personal injuries when notice is delayed 19 months without explanation).

In the absence of any indication that §8.2-607(3)(a) was intended to apply only to merchant buyers, we hold that it applies to all buyers of goods, including retail consumers.

Hebron also contends that the question of whether she gave American Isuzu reasonable notice of the breach of warranty is a question of fact reserved for the jury. She correctly notes that a question of reasonableness is ordinarily one of fact. But this is so only within a limited range of factual circumstances. The district court, recognizing the general rule, found that in this case the two-year unexplained delay in giving notice, coupled with the plaintiff's disposal of critical evidence, was unreasonable as a matter of law. We agree.

Hebron waited two years to notify American Isuzu of her claim, and when she did, she had already disposed of the vehicle. Moreover, she produced no evidence about her vehicle or any claimed defect. She took no pictures, had no inspection conducted, and retained nothing from the vehicle after the accident. Finally, she has offered no explanation for the delay, despite having been invited to do so in response to the motion for summary judgment. One of the important functions of the summary judgment process is to elicit the positions of the parties and have them tested under applicable law. In the circumstances of this case, we hold that a two-year delay in giving notice under §8.2-607(3)(a) is unreasonable as a matter of law where no explanation for the delay is provided and actual prejudice is sustained. The prejudice caused to American Isuzu goes to the heart of the statute's purpose.

The essence of Hebron's claim is that implied as part of the sale of the Isuzu truck was an implied promise that the truck was fit for the ordinary purposes for which such goods are used. See Va. Code §8.2-314(2)(c). But also implied, through the same commercial code that grounds her claim, is the requirement that when the buyer has reason to believe that this promise was breached, she must notify the seller within a reasonable time. This obligation is made a condition of any remedies. See Va. Code §8.2-607(3)(a). Since Hebron chose to sue only for breach of implied warranty of merchantability and thus elected only to invoke rights arising out of her contractual relationship with American Isuzu, she was required, as a condition to enforcing the warranty, to give "reasonable notice" after the breach was discovered. Such notice serves the important functions of promoting the voluntary resolution of disputes and minimizing prejudice to the seller from the passage of time. (Another function of the notice rule, which is not implicated here, is enabling the seller to cure the breach. This policy relates principally to commercial transactions where losses from defective goods can be minimized.) As stated in comment 4:

> The notification which saves the buyer's rights under this Article need only be such as informs the seller that the transaction is claimed to involve a breach, and thus opens the way for normal settlement through negotiation.

Va. Code §8.2-607(3)(a), cmt. 4. These purposes were defeated by Hebron's failure to give reasonable notice to American Isuzu in this case.

Accordingly, we affirm the judgment of the district court.

AFFIRMED.

Lack of privity is another hurdle that many would-be warranty plaintiffs must struggle to overcome. In theory, because warranty law is based in contract law, a warrantor is directly liable only to the party with which it has a contract. Thus, a manufacturer has no direct warranty liability to the consumer who purchases the manufactured goods from a retailer rather than from the manufacturer. Similarly, the manufacturer has no direct warranty liability to a retailer who purchases the manufactured goods through a third-party distributor.

In practice, most manufacturers will treat their warranties as if they run directly to the ultimate purchaser. As an in-house lawyer for a major beer manufacturer described it, "We don't even mention anything about warranties or disclaimers in our distribution agreement, because we're always going to stand behind our beer and step into the shoes of whoever is getting sued. Our philosophy is that if there's a problem with the product, it's generally going to be our responsibility ultimately. The one exception to that is that we do require our wholesalers to ensure that the retailers don't sell overaged beer, which is a function of making sure that the retailers rotate out the old beer on a first-come, first-served basis."

Even if a manufacturer is not willing to step forward and defend a warranty suit brought against a seller further down the chain of distribution, Article 2 provides a mechanism by which the seller being sued can "vouch in" its own seller to defend the suit. In a case where a buyer is sued for an obligation for which its seller should be responsible, the buyer may give the seller written notice of the litigation. If the seller refuses to come in and defend for its buyer, then the seller will be bound by any finding of fact in the first litigation to the extent that its buyer later sues it. UCC §2-607(5)(a).

Thus, suppose a wholesale beer distributor is sued by a retailer for return of the purchase price paid for 100 cases of beer that was alleged to be flat. Imagine that after receiving notice of that litigation from its wholesaler, the beer manufacturer refused to enter the litigation and defend. If, in the retailer's suit against the wholesaler, the court found as a fact that the beer was flat, then the manufacturer would be bound by that finding of fact in a later suit by the wholesaler against the manufacturer for breach of warranty.

In situations like these, the issue is one of vertical privity: the ability of a buyer to sue a seller other than its immediate seller. Even when the manufacturer is not "vouched in," most states provide by common law that when consumers are personally injured by a manufacturer's product, the manufacturer cannot escape warranty liability due to lack of vertical privity.

There is a separate privity issue, however, known as horizontal privity: the ability of a non-buyer who uses or is affected by a product to sue a seller for breach of warranty. Once again, the lack of "privity" is evident. A non-buyer who uses a product has no contractual connection even to the immediate seller of the product. Nevertheless, there may be occasions in which non-buyers are injured by products and cannot, for procedural or other reasons, successfully recover from the seller on a negligence or strict products liability theory.

This is where UCC §2-318 comes in. Section 2-318 is the only Article 2 section that offers states three different alternatives for adoption. A majority of states have adopted Alternative A to §2-318, although some states have adopted Alternative B or Alternative C. Alternative A removes the horizontal privity barrier for family members or household guests of the buyer in cases where the non-buyers have suffered personal injury due to the seller's breach of warranty.

Thus, for example, suppose that the father of three teenage boys living at home purchases a new car that comes with a three-year, 36,000-mile warranty. Suppose that four months after that purchase one of the buyer's sons is driving the car and the car catches fire due to a faulty engine-cooling system. Imagine that the son suffers burns as a result of the fire. Even though that son lacks horizontal privity with the car dealer, Alternative A of UCC §2-318 allows an action in warranty by the son against the car dealer.

The two other alternatives in §2-318, B and C, remove the horizontal privity problem for an even broader class of plaintiffs than does Alternative A. Alternative B gives the privity-removing benefit to "any natural person who may reasonably be expected to use, consume, or be affected by the goods" and who suffers personal injury by the seller's breach of warranty, rather than just to family members and household guests of the seller. Alternative C is the most generous of the three alternatives, removing the requirement of Alternative B that the injury suffered be a personal injury. Thus, Alternative C would seem to allow its beneficiaries to recover even for property damage or economic loss.

Interestingly, one Alternative C jurisdiction, Virginia, has held that §2-318 does not allow recovery of purely economic loss for third-party beneficiaries. In Beard Plumbing and Heating v. Thompson Plastics, 152 F.3d 313 (4th Cir. 1998), the United States Court of Appeals for the Fourth Circuit certified this question to the Virginia Supreme Court and was directed not to allow recovery for economic loss on a breach of implied warranty theory. The Virginia Supreme Court noted that such a result was consistent with the prohibition of recovering purely economic loss in tort. Furthermore, the court reasoned that §2-715(2)(b)'s allowance of consequential damages for economic loss was premised on the existence of privity between the parties, and that this privity requirement should supersede the more general language of §2-318 Alternative C. What the court did not discuss was that §2-318 and its three alternatives were specifically designed to create exceptions to the usual requirement of privity for recovery of *any* damages on a warranty theory. Therefore, to observe that Alternative C was inconsistent with the requirements in §2-715(2)(b) seems to miss the whole point of §2-318.

Crews v. W.A. Brown & Son, Inc.

416 S.E.2d 924 (N.C. Ct. App. 1992)

Greene, J.

The plaintiffs appeal from an order entered 14 January 1991 allowing Foodcraft Equipment Company's (Foodcraft) motion for summary judgment.

In mid-1984, Foodcraft, a corporation, sold a walk-in freezer to Calvary Baptist Church (Church). Foodcraft was not in the business of manufacturing freezer equipment and did not manufacture the walk-in freezer that it sold to Church. In July, 1984, Foodcraft contracted with W.A. Brown & Son, Inc. (Brown) for the purchase of the parts needed to "field assemble" a walk-in freezer. Brown maintained its principal place of business in Rowan County, North Carolina. Brown shipped all the necessary parts to Foodcraft on 25 October 1984. Included in this shipment was a pre-assembled door. The inside of the door to the freezer contained a label stating:

YOU ARE NOT LOCKED IN!

The manufacturer of this unit has equipped it with a STANDARD-KEIL EASY ACTION latch assembly. You cannot be locked in, even if the door closes behind you and the cylinder is locked. By pushing the inside release on the inside of this unit, you may operate the latch and open the door.

No Foodcraft employee removed this label from the door.

Installed in the door by Brown was a Standard-Keil door latch assembly with inside and outside releases. Foodcraft did not adjust this door latch assembly or alter it in any way. When Foodcraft received the freezer parts, Foodcraft employees took them to the church, assembled the freezer, and tested it to be sure that it operated properly. After the Foodcraft employees assembled the freezer, they tested the door latch assembly to be sure that the freezer could be opened from the inside by pressing the red release button. They concluded that the door latch assembly worked properly, and according to Jack Kroustalis, an officer with Foodcraft, "[a]t the time we received and hung the door, there was no indication that the Standard-Keil easy action latch assembly of the door to the walk-in freezer was defective or that the seal and/or door latch assembly in the door of the walk-in freezer was improperly installed in any fashion." Furthermore, Harry Gallins, vice-president of Foodcraft, installed a "heated pressure release port" in the freezer to prevent a vacuum from being created inside the freezer whenever the door is closed.

Vickie Ann Buchanan Crews (Crews), a thirteen-year-old member of Church, was working at the church on the evening of 2 July 1985 as a volunteer managing the registration desk to the Family Life Center at the church. As a registration desk volunteer, Crews signed people in and out of the church gymnasium, signed equipment in and out to those people using the gym, and answered the telephone. At approximately 8:45 p.m., Crews went into the church's kitchen to get some ice for a soft drink. She was wearing shorts and a shirt, but no shoes. Once inside the kitchen, Crews heard a noise which she thought came from the walk-in freezer. She went to the freezer, opened the door, and stepped inside. When she did, the freezer door closed behind her. She pushed on the red release button on the inside of the door, but the door would not open. She continued to try to open the door, but she could not open it. She banged on the door with her hands and feet, she pushed on the door with her shoulder, and she screamed. After about an hour of unsuccessful attempts, Crews became tired and sat down on a small rack. She had lost all feeling in her feet which were now completely white. Despite being tired, she continued to kick the door. At approximately 10:00 p.m., someone discovered Crews in the freezer. By that time, however, she had suffered severe frostbite to her feet, legs, and buttocks. Paramedics took her to a nearby hospital where she remained for approximately two months and where she underwent approximately five separate operations. During the first operation, doctors removed nine and one-half of her toes. During the remaining operations, doctors performed, among other things, skin grafts.

Crews later recalled noticing a thick, white substance resembling frost on the inside of the release button. According to the plaintiffs' expert, Crews was unable to open the door from the inside because frost had accumulated inside the release mechanism. The expert opined that the frost had accumulated inside the release mechanism through the seal that separates the plastic cover of the latch assembly from the metal of the freezer door "and that this was caused by improper installation of the seal and/or latch assembly in the door of the walk-in freezer."

Crews and her mother filed a complaint against Brown, Foodcraft, and Church. Crews sought recovery for, among other things, the loss of her toes and her pain and suffering, and her mother sought recovery for Crews' medical expenses. With regard to Foodcraft, the plaintiffs alleged that Foodcraft was negligent in failing to assemble, install, and inspect the freezer properly and in failing to provide adequate warnings on the freezer. The plaintiffs also alleged breach of warranty claims against Foodcraft including breach of express warranties and breach of the implied warranties of merchantability and fitness for a particular purpose. . . .

The issues are whether (I) there is a genuine issue of material fact as to whether Foodcraft assembled and installed the freezer with reasonable care and inspected it for latent defects with reasonable care; and (II) Foodcraft's alleged express and implied warranties extend to members of Church who suffer personal injury while on church property. . . .

The plaintiffs argue that the trial court erred in granting Foodcraft's summary judgment motion on their breach of express and implied warranties claims. Foodcraft argues that the trial court properly granted its motion because the plaintiffs' claims are barred by a lack of privity with Foodcraft.

Except where the barrier of privity has been legislatively or judicially removed, the absence of a contractual relationship between the seller or manufacturer of an allegedly defective product and the person injured by it continues to preclude products liability actions for breach of express and implied warranties. To determine whether the barrier has been removed, a court must examine the basis for the breach of warranty action and determine whether the defendant in the action is the seller or the manufacturer.

"Where the cause of action is based on breach of express warranty, directed by the manufacturer to the ultimate purchaser, lack of privity between the plaintiff-purchaser and the defendant-manufacturer is not a bar." Daye & Morris, supra, §26.33; Kinlaw v. Long Mfg., 298 N.C. 494, 499-500, 259 S.E.2d 552, 556-57 (1979). This rule applies when the express warranty addressed to the ultimate consumer is written as well as when the manufacturer makes oral representations to a retailer which "are intended to be communicated to remote buyers to induce them to buy a product." Alberti v. Manufactured Homes, Inc., 329 N.C. 727, 737, 407 S.E.2d 819, 825 (1991). Furthermore, by statute, not only may the ultimate purchaser sue the manufacturer for breach of express warranty, but "any natural person who is in the family or household of his buyer or who is a guest in his home if it is reasonable to expect that such person may use, consume or be affected by the goods and who is injured in person by breach of the warranty" may sue the manufacturer for breach of its express warranty.

Where the cause of action against the manufacturer is based on breach of implied warranty, the Products Liability Act (Act) eliminates the privity requirement where the claimant "is a buyer, as defined in the Uniform Commercial Code, of the product involved, or . . . is a member or a guest of a member of the family of the buyer, a guest of the buyer, or an employee of the buyer. . . ."

Where, however, the products liability action is brought against the seller for breach of either express or implied warranty, the privity barrier has been removed legislatively to the same extent as it has been removed in actions against manufacturers for breach of express warranty. N.C.G.S. §25-2-318. Accordingly, assuming the existence of express and implied warranties, N.C.G.S. §25-2-318 extends those warranties beyond the buyer but only to natural persons suffering personal injury who are in the buyer's family or household or who are guests in the buyer's home and only if it is reasonable to expect such persons may use, consume, or be affected by the goods. The statute does not extend warranty coverage to persons beyond those specifically enumerated. This construction is consistent with the legislative intent behind N.C.G.S. §25-2-318, which was to eliminate the doctrine of privity as to the buyer's family, household, and guests, but not to abolish the doctrine as it relates to strangers to the contract. Furthermore, this Court has applied N.C.G.S. §25-2-318 consistently with this legislative intent. This Court has previously held that because N.C.G.S. §25-2-318 "specifically limits actions on warranties, either express or implied," an employee of a buyer of a dangerous chemical was barred by a lack of privity from suing the seller for breach of implied warranty.

The plaintiffs have brought against Foodcraft claims for breach of express and implied warranties. Because the plaintiffs do not contend either that Foodcraft was owned in whole or significant part by Brown or that it owned Brown in whole or significant part, and because Foodcraft assembled the freezer after it had sold it to Church, Foodcraft is not the manufacturer of the freezer under the Act but rather the seller. Furthermore, Foodcraft is properly classified as the seller of the freezer under the Uniform Commercial Code as enacted in North Carolina as Chapter 25 defines "seller" to include corporations which sell goods. Neither party disputes that Foodcraft, as a merchant, sold goods to Church.

Assuming the existence of express and implied warranties, however, those warranties do not extend to the plaintiffs. Because a church does not have a "family" or a "household" in the ordinary meanings of those terms, Crews cannot be classified as a member of Church's "family" or "household" under N.C.G.S. §25-2-318. Because a church is not a "home" within the ordinary meaning of that term, Church cannot be classified as a "home." Accordingly, because Crews was not in the buyer's "family" or "household," and because she was not a guest in the buyer's "home," N.C.G.S. §25-2-318 does not extend the coverage of Foodcraft's warranties to the plaintiffs.

Furthermore, because the plaintiffs did not allege in their complaint any facts indicating that they were third-party beneficiaries of Foodcraft's contract with Church, we will not consider whether to imply privity in this case. Accordingly, because N.C.G.S. §25-2-318 does not extend the coverage of Foodcraft's warranties to the plaintiffs, the trial court's order allowing Foodcraft's summary judgment motion is affirmed.

Problem Set 9

9.1.   a. Judi Pierce is an independent truck driver who just purchased a new truck from the Mack Company, a retail truck seller. Five months after the sale, the Mack Company gets the following fax from Judi: "Your new truck stinks. It broke down three months ago and I've lost six jobs since then because my truck has been sitting in my driveway. I'm going to sue you for breach of warranty." Does the Mack Company have a good defense to such a suit? UCC §2-607(3)(a), Official Comment 4 to §2-607.

b. Same facts as part (a), except that Judi ordered the truck for delivery on July 1. The truck did not ultimately arrive until October 1 of the same year. Although Judi had said nothing during the delay, on October 5 she fired off the following fax to the Mack Company: "You guys stink. How do you expect me to make a living when you deliver your truck three months late? Thanks to you guys, I lost six jobs that I could have had. I'm going to sue you for breach of contract." Does the Mack Company have a good defense to such a suit? UCC §2-607(3)(a), Official Comment 4 to §2-607.

c. Same facts as part (a), except Judi gives immediate notice of the problem to the Mack Company. Later, though, when the Mack Company goes bankrupt, she decides that she had better sue the manufacturer, Acme Truck, for breach of warranty. Is Acme entitled to the same notice as Mack? Should Judi's notice to Mack also count for Acme? UCC §§2-607(3)(a), 2-607(5)(a).

d. Same facts as part (a), except that the truck's defect causes Judi to swerve off the road, hitting pedestrian Michael Baker. Michael spends two months in the hospital, and then a year later hires a lawyer to sue the Mack Company for breach of warranty. The complaint filed by the lawyer is the first the Mack Company learns of Michael's injury, although Judi did complain about the truck's defect to the Mack Company shortly after the accident. Does the Mack Company have a good defense against Michael? UCC §2-607(3)(a), Official Comment 5 to §2-607.

9.2.   a. A manufacturer of commercial lawn mowers brought your law firm a new case. The case involves an industrial-sized rider mower that had been built by this manufacturer and then sold to the ultimate buyer, Jack Reilly, by a separate retailer. Jack's nephew, Tom, was driving the mower while working for his uncle's lawn service when the brakes on the mower failed and Tom smashed into the client's garage. Tom was hurt and incurred hospital bills of over $20,000. Although the mowing client, Erin Clark, was not hurt, her garage suffered damages of $6,000. Tom, who is uninsured, is suing the retailer on a breach of implied warranty theory (the tort statute of limitations has expired, but the UCC statute of limitations has not), seeking to recover both for his personal injury and for the property damage to Erin Clark's garage, which her lawsuit is asking him to pay. How should this case come out in a jurisdiction that has adopted Alternative A to §2-318? UCC §2-318, Alternative A; Official Comment 3 to §2-318. How about in an Alternative B jurisdiction? UCC §2-318, Alternative B.

b. Same facts as part (a), except that Tom is suing the manufacturer for breach of warranty. How should this case come out in an Alternative A jurisdiction? How about an Alternative B jurisdiction? Official Comment 3 to §2-318.

c. Same facts as part (a), except that Erin Clark also suffered personal injury. Can Erin recover from the retailer in an Alternative A jurisdiction? How about an Alternative B jurisdiction?

d. Would your answers to part (a) change if the written warranty included a boldface clause stating that the various warranties ran only to the purchaser of the mower and not to any third parties? Official Comment 1 to §2-318.

e. Would your answers to part (a) change if the written warranty included a boldface clause stating that the implied warranty of merchantability was being disclaimed completely? Official Comment 1 to §2-318.

f. Same facts as part (a) (Erin's garage was damaged but she was not hurt), except that there was a warranty disclaimer stating that all of the retailer's warranties, including merchantability, extended only to the immediate buyer of the mower. Can Erin recover from the retailer in an Alternative B jurisdiction? In an Alternative C jurisdiction? UCC §2-318, Alternatives B and C.

Assignment 10: Magnuson-Moss

One warranty law that has had a significant impact on warranty practice is the Magnuson-Moss Act. Though we normally think of warranty law as contract law, and we think of contract law as state law, Magnuson-Moss is a federal statute that is intended to protect consumers from unscrupulous warrantors. Although Magnuson-Moss's greatest impact has probably been in the area of warranty disclaimers (which will be discussed in Assignment 13), the statute has also had a significant impact on warranty creation and enforcement.

As to warranty creation, Magnuson-Moss is something of a truth-in-labeling law for consumer warranties. Magnuson-Moss sets down a number of federal minimum warranty standards that relate to remedies, the duration of implied warranties, and the like, and then requires consumer product warrantors either to meet those minimum standards or to conspicuously designate the warranty as a "limited warranty." 15 U.S.C. §§2303, 2304. If a warrantor's warranty does meet these minimum standards, the warrantor must designate the warranty as a "full warranty," but it must also indicate in the heading a statement of the duration of the full warranty, for example, "Full Two-Year Warranty."

The Magnuson-Moss Act includes a fairly extensive definition of what does and does not constitute a "consumer product." Section 101(1) of Magnuson-Moss defines a consumer product as tangible personal property that is normally used for personal, family, or household purposes. Nevertheless, there are still cases that raise the question of whether a particular sale comes within the terms of Magnuson-Moss.

Forcellati v. Hyland's, Inc.

876 F. Supp. 2d 1155 (C.D. Calif. 2012)

King, D.J.

This matter is before us on Defendants Hyland's, Inc. ("Hyland's"), Standard Homeopathic Laboratories, Inc., and Standard Homeopathic Company's (collectively, "Defendants") Motion to Dismiss Complaint ("Motion"). We have considered the papers filed in support of and in opposition to this Motion and deem this matter appropriate for resolution without oral argument. L.R. 7-15. As the Parties are familiar with the facts, we will repeat them only as necessary. Accordingly, we rule as follows.

I. BACKGROUND

On a motion to dismiss, we accept the allegations of the Complaint as true and construe them in the light most favorable to the plaintiff. Cousins v. Lockyer, 568 F.3d 1063, 1067 (9th Cir. 2009). Plaintiff Enzo Forcellati ("Plaintiff"), a New Jersey resident, states that Defendants "represent [ ] that [their] homeopathic Cold and Flu Remedies offer children 'Fast acting,' 'Safe & Effective,' 'Multi-symptom' relief from cold and flu symptoms, including runny noses, sore throats, coughs, head-aches, body aches, flu and congestion." (Class Action Complaint ("CAC") ¶2). Plaintiff asserts, however, that Defendants' products are "nothing more than sweet-ened, flavored water with only highly diluted concentrations of the products' so-called 'active ingredients.'" (Id.). On the basis of these allegations, Plaintiff asserts the following claims: (1) Violation of Magnuson-Moss Act, 15 U.S.C. §§2301 et seq.; (2) Unjust Enrichment; (3) Breach of Express Warranty; (4) Breach of Implied Warranty; (5) Violation of the New Jersey Consumer Fraud Act, N.J.S.A. §§58:8-1 et seq. ("NJCFA claim"); (6) Violation of the Consumer Legal Remedies Act, Cal. Civ. Code §§1750 et seq. ("CLRA claim"); (7) Violation of the False Advertising Law, Cal. Bus. & Prof. Code §§17500 et seq. ("FAL claim"); and (8) Violation of the Unfair Competition Law, Cal. Bus. & Prof. Code 17200 et seq. ("UCL claim"). Plaintiff brings the first, second, third, and fourth claims individually and on behalf of a nationwide class and New Jersey sub-class; the fifth claim on behalf of a New Jersey sub-class; and the sixth, seventh, and eighth claims on behalf of a nation-wide class.

Defendants move to dismiss the CAC for the following reasons: First, Defendants argue that based on the Ninth Circuit's opinion in Mazza v. Am. Honda Motor Co., 666 F.3d 581 (9th Cir. 2012), Plaintiff "lacks standing to assert claims under California's consumer protection laws, for himself or on behalf of a putative nation-wide class." (Mot. 1). Second, Defendants argue, also pursuant to Mazza, that "Plaintiff cannot certify a nationwide class for alleged violations of consumer protection laws." (Id. at 2). Third, Defendants argue that Plaintiff lacks standing to assert claims regarding any products that he did not use. Fourth, Defendants argue that Plaintiff's warranty claims fail because "Plaintiff has not alleged any statements that create any actionable express or implied warranties." (Id. at 1-2). Defendants further argue that Plaintiff's Magnuson-Moss Act claim fails because their over-the-counter medications are not "consumer products" within the mean-ing of Magnuson-Moss. Fifth, Defendants argue that Plaintiff's purported unjust enrichment claim fails because unjust enrichment is a remedy, rather than a claim. Sixth, Defendants argue that Plaintiff's NJCFA claim is deficient because he does not allege that Defendants engaged in any unlawful conduct or that Plaintiff suf-fered an ascertainable loss. . . .

III. DISCUSSION

* * *

3. MAGNUSON-MOSS ACT CLAIM

Defendants' argue that Plaintiff's Magnuson-Moss Act claim fails because the Act only applies to "consumer products," and their over-the-counter homeopathic medications are not "consumer products" as defined by the Act. Defendants acknowledge that Magnuson-Moss does not specifically enumerate what products fall within the definition of "consumer products." However, they note that the Consumer Product Safety Act expressly states that "drugs, devices, or cosmetics" as defined in the Food, Drug, and Cosmetics Act, 21 U.S.C. §301 et seq. ("FDCA") are not "consumer product[s]." Thus, they contend, citing the California Court of Appeal's decision in Kanter v. Warner-Lambert Co., 99 Cal. App. 4th 780, 798, 122 Cal. Rptr. 2d 72 (2002), that a drug regulated by the FDCA (which Defendants' products are) is not a "consumer product" under Magnuson-Moss.

The Magnuson-Moss Act defines "consumer product" as "any tangible personal property which is distributed in commerce and which is normally used for personal, family, or household purposes (including any such property intended to be attached to or installed in any real property without regard to whether it is so attached or installed)." 15 U.S.C. §2301(1). While the Act does not enumerate any particular "consumer products," numerous courts have discussed FTC regulations articulating such examples as "boats, photographic film and chemicals, clothing, appliances, jewelry, furniture, typewriters, motor homes, automobiles, mobile homes, vehicle parts and accessories, stereos, carpeting, small aircraft, toys, and food." Kemp v. Pfizer, Inc., 835 F. Supp. 1015, 1024 (E.D. Mich. 1993) (quoting Magnuson-Moss Warranty Act: Implementation and Enforcement Policy, 40 Fed. Reg. 25,721, 25,722 (1975)); accord Boelens v. Redman Homes, Inc., 748 F.2d 1058, 1062 n.6 (5th Cir. 1984); Russo v. NCS Pearson, Inc., 462 F. Supp. 2d 981, 998 (D. Minn. 2006). Although over-the-counter cold and flu medications are not enumerated in FTC regulation examples, they certainly appear to fit within the broad definition contained in the Magnuson-Moss Act—tangible goods that are "normally used for personal, family, or household purposes."

In *Kanter*, the case cited by Defendants, the plaintiffs sued the manufacturers of an over-the-counter head lice treatment and alleged "that the product labels contain false and misleading statements about the effectiveness of the drugs." 99 Cal. App. 4th at 784, 122 Cal. Rptr. 2d 72. The plaintiffs asserted, inter alia, a claim for breach of warranty under the Magnuson-Moss Act. The California Court of Appeal cobbled together three statutes to conclude that the defendants' products were not "consumer products" within the meaning of the Magnuson-Moss Act:

> Magnuson-Moss applies only to "consumer product[s]," defined as "any tangible personal property which is distributed in commerce and which is normally used for personal, family, or household purposes. . . ." The act does not otherwise enumerate

> products within the scope of the definition. The federal Consumer Product Safety Act, however, expressly states that "drugs, devices, or cosmetics" as defined in the FDCA are not "consumer product[s]." Reading these statutes together, at least two courts have concluded that a medical device regulated by the [FDCA] is not a consumer product within the meaning of Magnuson-Moss. [Goldsmith v. Mentor Corp., 913 F. Supp. 56, 63 (D.N.H. 1995); Kemp v. Pfizer, Inc., 835 F. Supp. 1015 (E.D. Mich. 1993).] By parity of reasoning, a drug regulated by the FDCA is also not a consumer product within the meaning of Magnuson-Moss.

Id. (some citations omitted). We respectfully disagree with the California Court of Appeal that parity of reasoning requires the two statutes, with different definitions, to be interpreted similarly. First, the cases upon which the court relied discussed products that could not reasonably be considered goods that are "normally used for personal, family, or household purposes." 15 U.S.C. §2301(1). In *Goldsmith*, the court discussed whether a testicular prosthesis was a "consumer product" under the Magnuson-Moss Act. 913 F. Supp. at 57. *Goldsmith* relied on *Kemp*, which contemplated whether a prosthetic heart valve was a "consumer product" covered by Magnuson-Moss. 835 F. Supp. at 1024. Notably, the court in *Goldsmith* concluded that such a product was not a "consumer product" covered by the Magnuson-Moss Act because it was "not the type of product normally used for consumer purposes by the general public. Goods that are not customarily available to the ordinary person are not consumer products." Id. While these courts discussed the FDCA's definition of consumer product, it is difficult to imagine how they possibly could have concluded that medical prostheses could have been covered by the Magnuson-Moss Act irrespective of their express exclusion from the FDCA's definition. As the court noted in *Kemp*, such products are certainly not "normally used" within a household.

Second, we do not consider the FDCA's definition of "consumer product" to be conclusive, or even compelling for determining whether a good is a "consumer product" under Magnuson-Moss. The FDCA defines "consumer product," in pertinent part, as follows:

> The term "consumer product" means any article, or component part thereof, produced or distributed (i) for sale to a consumer for use in or around a permanent or temporary household or residence, a school, in recreation, or otherwise, or (ii) for the personal use, consumption or enjoyment of a consumer in or around a permanent or temporary household or residence, a school, in recreation, or otherwise; but such term does not include—
>
> (A) any article which is not customarily produced or distributed for sale to, or use or consumption by, or enjoyment of, a consumer,
>
> (C) motor vehicles or motor vehicle equipment (as defined by section 30102(a)(6) and (7) of Title 49),
>
> (G) boats which could be subjected to safety regulation under chapter 43 of Title 46; vessels, and appurtenances to vessels (other than such boats), which could be subjected to safety regulation under title 52 of the Revised Statutes or other marine safety statutes administered by the department in which the Coast Guard is operating; and equipment (including associated equipment, as defined

in section 2101(1) of Title 46) to the extent that a risk of injury associated with the use of such equipment on boats or vessels could be eliminated or reduced by actions taken under any statute referred to in this subparagraph,

(H) drugs, devices, or cosmetics (as such terms are defined in sections 201(g), (h), and (i) of the Federal Food, Drug, and Cosmetic Act [21 U.S.C.A. §321(g), (h), and (i)]), or

(I) food. The term "food", as used in this subparagraph means all "food", as defined in section 201(f) of the Federal Food, Drug, and Cosmetic Act [21 U.S.C.A. §321(f)], including poultry and poultry products (as defined in sections 4(e) and (f) of the Poultry Products Inspection Act [21 U.S.C.A. §453(e) and (f)]), meat, meat food products (as defined in section 1(j) of the Federal Meat Inspection Act [21 U.S.C.A. §601(j)]), and eggs and egg products (as defined in section 4 of the Egg Products Inspection Act [21 U.S.C.A. §1033]).

15 U.S.C. §2052(a)(5). Accordingly, "consumer product" is defined much differently in the FDCA than the Magnuson-Moss Act, and it expressly excludes products that clearly fall within Magnuson-Moss. For example, the FDCA excludes food, boats, and motor vehicles—products that are expressly included as consumer products in the FTC's regulations interpreting Magnuson-Moss. Therefore, a product's express exclusion from the definition of "consumer product" in the FDCA does not compel a similar interpretation of the Magnuson-Moss Act where the product is otherwise a good "normally used for personal, family, or household purposes."

Third, there may be very good reasons for "consumer product" to be defined differently in Consumer Product Safety Act (as part of the FDCA) and the Magnuson-Moss Act. The Consumer Product Safety Act is primarily concerned with the safety of various products, and thus it may make sense to exclude products whose safety is regulated by agencies other than the Consumer Product Safety Commission—products like vehicles, food, and drugs. This helps to prevent conflicting or inconsistent regulatory requirements. In contrast, Magnuson-Moss is less focused on safety and more focused on ensuring that products do not have misleading claims as to the efficacy of those products. Thus, it may not be a significant concern if goods considered "consumer products" under Magnuson-Moss are regulated by other agencies with regard to those products' safety. This is perhaps evidenced by the FTC's interpretation of Magnuson-Moss as including vehicles and food, even though the safety of those products are regulated by other acts. Accordingly, Defendants have provided no compelling reason for why we should interpret these two different definitions to be coterminous, and there appear to be very good reasons not to (not the least of which is the fact that FTC regulations expressly include products that are excluded from the definition in the FDCA).

Defendants have not engaged in a sufficiently comprehensive analysis of these two statutes, their interpretive regulations, and the regulatory structure of the agencies governing over-the-counter medications for us to conclude that over-the-counter homeopathic medications are not "consumer products" under

Magnuson-Moss. Accordingly, they have not borne their burden at this stage of litigation of demonstrating that Plaintiff's Magnuson-Moss Act claim should be dismissed as a matter of law. We hereby DENY Defendants' motion inasmuch as it seeks dismissal of Plaintiff's Magnuson-Moss Act claim. . . .

If you stop and take a look at the warranty for any consumer product that you have purchased recently, you can see the impact of the Magnuson-Moss Act in the warranty's description. Just how many consumers have been protected from otherwise misleading warranty headings is anybody's guess. At least, however, sellers of consumer products can no longer use bold "Full Warranty" headings above warranties that are in fact providing no real recourse for the consumer. As a matter of practice, the vast majority of consumer products today come with a "Limited" rather than a "Full" warranty.

Probably the most significant part of the Magnuson-Moss Act is its provisions regarding the recovery of attorneys' fees for successful consumer warranty suits. Congress realized that one problem in enforcing consumer warranty actions was that the typically small amounts in controversy usually made it unlikely that individual consumers could avail themselves of the court system to vindicate their warranty rights.

Magnuson-Moss alleviates this problem by providing that courts may allow for the recovery of costs and attorneys' fees by plaintiffs who prevail in actions brought under Magnuson-Moss. 15 U.S.C. §2310(d).

McNiff v. Mazda Motor of America, Inc.

892 N.E.2d 598 (Ill. App. Ct. 2008)

TURNER, J.

In August 2005, plaintiff, Courtney McNiff, brought suit to recover damages against defendants, Mazda Motor of America, Inc. (Mazda), and Sam Leman Mazda, for breach of written warranty and breach of implied warranty of merchantability. The parties eventually settled. In March 2007, plaintiff filed a petition for an award of costs and attorney fees. In May 2007, the trial court awarded plaintiff's two attorneys a total of $26,015.50 in fees and costs. Defendant Mazda and plaintiff filed motions to reconsider, both of which the court denied.

On appeal, defendant Mazda argues the trial court (1) erred in awarding attorney fees on an hourly basis when plaintiff entered into a contingency-fee agreement with her attorneys and (2) abused its discretion in compensating the attorneys. In her cross-appeal, plaintiff argues the trial court erred (1) in refusing to award attorney fees for her response to the motion for reconsideration and (2) by awarding her attorney a lower rate. We affirm in part, reverse in part, and remand with directions.

I. BACKGROUND

In May 2004, plaintiff's grandfather purchased a new 2004 Mazda RX-8 from Sam Leman Mazda for the list price of $30,854 and immediately gifted the car to plaintiff. The car developed mechanical difficulties rendering it unreliable. Plaintiff asked for a refund but received a second engine instead. Thereafter, the vehicle continued to have difficulties.

In August 2005, plaintiff filed a two-count complaint against defendants, alleging breach of written warranty and breach of implied warranty of merchantability under the Magnuson-Moss Warranty—Federal Trade Commission Improvement Act (Magnuson-Moss Act) (15 U.S.C. §§2301 through 2312 (2000)). Plaintiff retained Attorneys Daniel Deneen and William Hutul to represent her in the lawsuit against defendants. In October 2005, defendants filed their answer to the complaint. Ultimately, the parties agreed to a settlement, and defendant Mazda repurchased the vehicle for $30,000. The settlement did not include attorney fees.

In March 2007, plaintiff filed a petition for an award of costs and attorney fees pursuant to the Magnuson-Moss Act. Deneen attached an invoice for services showing a total of $13,650 due for 56.25 hours of work. Deneen indicated he charged a premium rate of $225 per hour for fiduciary-fraud and consumer-fraud litigation through mid-May 2006 and $250 per hour thereafter. His standard rate was $175 per hour until May 2006 when it increased to $200 per hour. The petition also stated Hutul's time records showed 45.4 hours of work from August 11, 2005, through February 6, 2007. At Hutul's rate of $325 per hour, the fees amounted to $14,755. In April 2007, Deneen filed a supplemental petition asking for, *inter alia,* $1,875 in fees for preparing and filing the fee petition.

Defendants filed a response in opposition to plaintiff's fee petition. Defendants argued plaintiff and her attorneys entered into a contingency-fee agreement, whereby counsel agreed attorney fees would be equal to one-third of all amounts collected or recovered in the case. As the parties settled for $30,000, defendants argued plaintiff's request for fees should be capped at $10,000. Defendants also contended counsels' time sheets failed to provide sufficient evidence of the reasonableness of the hourly rate and hours expended.

In May 2007, the trial court filed its order on the petition for fees. The court found Deneen's reasonable rate of compensation to be $200 per hour. Based on 65.25 hours of work, the court ordered defendant Mazda to pay Deneen $13,530.50 for his fees, which included $480.50 in costs. The court also found Hutul's reasonable rate of compensation to be $275 per hour. Based on 45.4 hours of work, the court ordered defendant to pay Hutul $12,485 for his fees.

In June 2007, defendant Mazda filed a motion to reconsider. Defendant argued the relationship between plaintiff and her counsel was controlled by the contingency-fee agreement and the trial court could not award attorney fees in excess of $10,000. Defendant also argued the time sheets submitted by plaintiff's counsel lacked specific detail, consisted of block billing, did not correlate with one another, and contained duplicate time entries. In July 2007, plaintiff filed a response and a motion to reconsider, asking, *inter alia,* the court to award attorney fees for prosecuting the fee petition, including the motion to reconsider.

In August 2007, the trial court entered an order denying the motions to reconsider. As to defendant, the court found a contingency-fee agreement did not impose a cap on a fee award. As to plaintiff, the court found it "considered the reasonableness of the time expended in preparing and prosecuting the fee petition and did not exclude that time from its order of fees." Defendant Mazda filed an appeal, and plaintiff filed a cross-appeal.

II. ANALYSIS

A. DEFENDANT'S APPEAL

1. Standard of Review

"Illinois follows the 'American Rule,' which provides that absent statutory authority or a contractual agreement, each party must bear its own attorney fees and costs." Negro Nest, L.L.C. v. Mid–Northern Management, Inc., 362 Ill. App. 3d 640, 641-42, 298 Ill. Dec. 436, 839 N.E.2d 1083, 1085 (2005). If a statute or contractual agreement expressly authorizes an award of attorney fees, the court may award fees "so long as they are reasonable." Career Concepts, Inc. v. Synergy, Inc., 372 Ill. App. 3d 395, 405, 310 Ill. Dec. 61, 865 N.E.2d 385, 394 (2007). "A trial court's decision whether to award attorney fees is a matter within its discretion and will not be disturbed absent an abuse of that discretion." Central Illinois Electrical Services, L.L.C. v. Slepian, 358 Ill. App. 3d 545, 550, 294 Ill. Dec. 844, 831 N.E.2d 1169, 1173 (2005).

2. Magnuson-Moss Act

Consumers often require the assistance of counsel to enforce their rights under the Magnuson-Moss Act. Melton v. Frigidaire, 346 Ill. App. 3d 331, 339, 281 Ill. Dec. 954, 805 N.E.2d 322, 327 (2004). Section 2310(d)(2) of the Magnuson-Moss Act provides for the recovery of costs and attorney fees to a prevailing consumer as follows:

> "If a consumer finally prevails in any action brought under paragraph (1) of this subsection, he may be allowed by the court to recover as part of the judgment a sum equal to the aggregate amount of cost and expenses (including attorneys' fees based on actual time expended) determined by the court to have been reasonably incurred by the plaintiff for or in connection with the commencement and prosecution of such action, unless the court in its discretion shall determine that such an award of attorneys' fees would be inappropriate." 15 U.S.C. §2310(d)(2) (2000).

This fee-shifting provision was enacted "to vindicate the rights of a consumer who was injured by a party such as defendant and [was] intended to encourage consumers to pursue their legal remedies by providing them with access to legal assistance." State Farm Fire & Casualty Co. v. Miller Electric Co., 231 Ill. App. 3d 355, 359, 172 Ill. Dec. 890, 596 N.E.2d 169, 171 (1992). "The plain language of section 2310(d)(2) of the Magnuson-Moss Act provides that an award of attorney fees to a prevailing plaintiff is within the sound discretion of the trial court and will not be disturbed on review absent an abuse of discretion." Cannon v. William Chevrolet/Geo, Inc., 341 Ill. App. 3d 674, 685, 276 Ill. Dec. 593, 794 N.E.2d 843, 852 (2003).

In the case *sub judice,* defendant concedes plaintiff was a prevailing party under the Magnuson-Moss Act. However, defendant claims plaintiff could not be awarded attorney fees in excess of the amount agreed on by plaintiff and her attorneys in the contingency-fee agreement. The fee agreement stated, in part, as follows:

> "Client agrees that the attorneys shall receive a contingent fee equal to one[-]third, or thirty-three and one-third percent (33.33%) of all amounts collected or otherwise recovered, whether by suit, trial, or out[-]of[-]court settlement. . . .
>
> Client understands that this litigation may involve laws and/or statutes which provide for an award of attorneys' fees to the attorneys, as against the [d]efendants, based on the actual time spent on this case by the attorneys. Client understands and agrees that any such fee award by the [c]ourt against [d]efendants shall go to Daniel Deneen and William Hutul. The amount of any such award that is collected by the attorneys shall be credited against the contingent fee, and the contingent fee shall be reduced by the amount of court[-]awarded fees collected by the attorneys."

Because of the $30,000 settlement, defendant argues plaintiff's award of attorney fees should have been limited to $10,000, and the trial court's award over and above that amount was an abuse of discretion.

The Magnuson-Moss Act gives the trial court the discretion to award attorney fees that were reasonably incurred in the prosecution of the action. "[A] contingency[-]fee agreement can be a relevant factor in determining reasonableness." Rath v. Carbondale Nursing & Rehabilitation Center, Inc., 374 Ill. App. 3d 536, 544, 312 Ill. Dec. 722, 871 N.E.2d 122, 130 (2007). In *Blanchard v. Bergeron,* 489 U.S. 87, 109 S. Ct. 939, 103 L. Ed. 2d 67 (1989), the United States Supreme Court was confronted with a district court's discretionary award of reasonable attorney fees to a prevailing party in a federal civil-rights action. The Supreme Court found "a contingent-fee contract does not impose an automatic ceiling on an award of attorney's fees." *Blanchard,* 489 U.S. at 93, 109 S. Ct. at 944, 103 L. Ed. 2d at 75. Instead, "[t]he presence of a pre-existing fee agreement may aid in determining reasonableness." *Blanchard,* 489 U.S. at 93, 109 S. Ct. at 944, 103 L. Ed. 2d at 75; see also *Rath,* 374 Ill. App. 3d at 544, 312 Ill. Dec. 722, 871 N.E.2d at 130.

Here, defendant Mazda agreed to pay plaintiff $30,000, not including her attorney fees. The contingency-fee agreement indicated plaintiff's required payment for attorney fees would be reduced by any credits for court-awarded attorney fees. The presence of a fee agreement does not impose a ceiling on the award of fees. See Keller v. State Farm Insurance Co., 180 Ill. App. 3d 539, 557, 129 Ill.

Dec. 510, 536 N.E.2d 194, 206 (1989) (finding the trial court erred in concluding it was constrained by the contingency-fee agreement in awarding attorney fees when the insurance statute provided for the payment of "reasonable" attorney fees). Further, nothing in the Magnuson-Moss Act requires that any contingency-fee agreements control over a trial court's award of fees. Thus, the fees awarded must be reasonable, and the trial court found the requested fees to be reasonable in this case.

We note the cases cited by defendant are distinguishable. The facts in *Career Concepts*, 372 Ill. App. 3d at 406, 310 Ill. Dec. 61, 865 N.E.2d at 394-95, did not involve a fee-shifting provision. In Majcher v. Laurel Motors, Inc., 287 Ill. App. 3d 719, 732, 223 Ill. Dec. 683, 680 N.E.2d 416, 425 (1997), the plaintiff and her counsel entered into a contingency-fee agreement whereby the client would pay one-third of all amounts recovered and attorney fees awarded by the court would be in addition to the fees payable by the client. The Second District did not allow counsel to collect a contingent fee, as well as an hourly fee, as it would amount to double payment and violate the Rules of Professional Conduct. *Majcher*, 287 Ill. App. 3d at 732, 223 Ill. Dec. 683, 680 N.E.2d at 425. Here, however, the fee agreement did not provide for double payment as counsel will not collect the contingent fee. Instead, the amount plaintiff would have been required to pay was reduced by the trial court's award of attorney fees. Accordingly, defendant is not entitled to a reduction in the award of attorney fees based on plaintiff's contingency-fee agreement.

3. Amount of Compensation

In the alternative, defendant argues the trial court abused its discretion in awarding Deneen 65.25 hours of compensation and Hutul 45.4 hours of compensation. Defendant claims (1) Deneen's time records were "glaringly void of any detail" and (2) Hutul's time records were undated, vague and ambiguous, redundant, and excessive.

To help the trial court in assessing whether an attorney's fees are reasonable, "the petitioner must provide sufficient information, including detailed time records that were kept throughout the proceeding." Richardson v. Haddon, 375 Ill. App. 3d 312, 314, 313 Ill. Dec. 946, 873 N.E.2d 570, 573 (2007).

"When assessing the reasonableness of fees, a trial court may consider a variety of factors, including the nature of the case, the case's novelty and difficulty level, the skill and standing of the attorney, the degree of responsibility required, the usual and customary charges for similar work, and the connection between the litigation and the fees charged." *Richardson*, 375 Ill. App. 3d at 314-15, 313 Ill. Dec. 946, 873 N.E.2d at 573.

In this case, we find no abuse of discretion. Deneen's time records are of the type this court routinely sees on appeal in cases concerning the proper amount of attorney fees. The records show the date the services were rendered, a description of the services, the hours, the fee rate, and the total dollar amount. While defendant argues the description of services should have been more detailed, the records provide an adequate list to allow the trial court to determine whether the fees were reasonably incurred in this case.

Hutul's records also provide sufficient information for the trial court to determine the reasonable amount of fees. Hutul's entries are handwritten, and at times are difficult to read, but they describe the services rendered and the time expended. Although evidence suggested a range of rates for Hutul's services, the trial court found $275 per hour to be a reasonable rate of compensation "in this specific matter." We find no abuse of discretion. . . .

III.   CONCLUSION

For the reasons stated, we reverse the trial court's judgment insofar as it denied plaintiff's request for attorney fees incurred in responding to defendant's motion to reconsider; we otherwise affirm, and we remand the case to the trial court for consideration of attorney fees and costs incurred on appeal and the motion to reconsider.

For an action to be brought under Magnuson-Moss, the plaintiff must have been damaged by the failure of a seller to comply with its obligations under a warranty or service contract with respect to a consumer product. Courts are split on whether it is necessary that the seller make a "written warranty" as that term is defined by Magnuson-Moss in order to bring a Magnuson-Moss action, or whether instead an implied warranty of merchantability is alone sufficient for a plaintiff to get the benefits of Magnuson-Moss.

McCurdy v. Texar, Inc.
575 So. 2d 299 (Fla. Dist. Ct. App. 1991)

LETTS, J.

Involved here is the purchase of an allegedly defective boat and the purchaser's attempts to seek redress under the Magnuson-Moss Warranty Act, 15 U.S.C. §2310(d) (1982). The trial judge held the act inapplicable because the boat manufacturer gave no written warranties "as is required" by the act. We reverse.

There is a paucity of cases on this subject. Two federal courts have discussed the matter and appear to believe that the Magnuson-Moss Act is only applicable where there are written warranties. Skelton v. General Motors Corp., 500 F. Supp. 1181 (N.D. Ill. 1980), and Skelton v. General Motors Corp., 660 F.2d 311 (7th Cir. 1981), cert. denied, 456 U.S. 974, 102 S. Ct. 2238, 72 L. Ed. 2d 848 (1982). Yet, the latter decision, which is an appellate version of the former, was actually engaged in explaining the nature of a written warranty and its applicability is questionable.

Causes of action for implied warranties appear to be sanctioned by 15 U.S.C. §2310(d)(1), which provides:

> (d)(1) Subject to subsections (a)(3) and (e) of this section, a consumer who is damaged by the failure of a supplier, warrantor, or service contractor to comply with any obligation under this chapter, or under a written warranty, implied warranty, or service contract, may bring suit for damages and other legal and equitable relief—
>
> > (A) in any court of competent jurisdiction in any State or the District of Columbia; or
> >
> > (B) in an appropriate district court of the United States, subject to paragraph (3) of this subsection.
>
> (2) If a consumer finally prevails in any action brought under paragraph (1) of this subsection, he may be allowed by the court to recover as part of the judgment a sum equal to the aggregate amount of cost and expenses (including attorneys' fees based on actual time expended) determined by the court to have been reasonably incurred by the plaintiff for or in connection with the commencement and prosecution of such action, unless the court in its discretion shall determine that such an award of attorneys' fees would be inappropriate.

This quoted section, quite clearly, encompasses implied warranties which are obviously not in writing and this very court has also noted the appropriateness of such a cause of action.

In another federal district case, no express warranty was pled, only a breach of the implied warranties. Feinstein v. Firestone Tire & Rubber Co., 535 F. Supp. 595 (S.D.N.Y. 1982). The court dismissed the consumer's cause of action because there were no damages incurred, not because there were no written warranties.

Further support for our conclusion is found in footnote 10 in Annotation, Consumer Product Warranty Suits Under Magnuson-Moss Warranty Act, 59 A.L.R. Fed. 461, 470 (1982), which provides:

> Under 15 [U.S.C.A.] §2310(d), a consumer must be damaged by a supplier's, warrantor's, or service contractor's failure to comply with "any obligation" under the Act, or under a written warranty, implied warranty, or service contract, in order to obtain federal jurisdiction to bring a suit for damages or other legal and equitable relief in the federal courts. This provision has not only provided a means of enforcing the substantive requirements of the Act, but also has established a federal cause of action for breach of an implied warranty which has arisen under state law even if no written warranty was involved.

Two law review assessments are also of this view. Miller and Kanter, Litigation Under Magnuson-Moss: New Opportunities in Private Actions, 13 UCC L.J. 10, 13 (Summer 1980); Denicola, The Magnuson-Moss Warranty Act: Making Consumer Product Warranty a Federal Case, 44 Fordham L.R. 273 (1975). See also Reitz, Consumer Product Warranties Under Federal & State Laws, §10.02 (2d ed. 1987). . . .

McNamara v. Nomeco Building Specialties, Inc.

26 F. Supp. 2d 1168 (D. Minn. 1998)

ERICKSON, Mag.

. . . The Plaintiffs are homeowners, who live on Pike Lake in Duluth, Minnesota. They were in the process of remodeling their lake home, when they contacted Donald E. Bergeson ("Bergeson"), who is a Nomeco sales representative, in order to discuss the replacement of their Pella-manufactured bay window. The window, which faces the lake, had a tendency to fog over with exterior condensation in the Summer months, due to climatological conditions.

The Plaintiffs told Bergeson that they wanted to replace the bay window with one that would be condensation-free throughout the Summer. A fog-free replacement window was critical to the Plaintiffs' as their current condensation problems were obscuring their view of the lake. Bergeson met with the Plaintiffs at their residence, in order to further assess the condensation problem. Bergeson claims to have relayed the Plaintiffs' problem to Keith Rudd ("Rudd"), who is a Pella representative. Rudd does not recall, however, having been contacted by Bergeson, or having made any product recommendations to him. . . . After having purportedly discussed the situation with Rudd, Bergeson told the Plaintiffs that Rudd had recommended the installation of Pella's "Smart Sash III" window as a replacement for the problematic bay window.

The Plaintiffs asked Bergeson if the Smart Sash III windows would experience the same condensation difficulties, and Bergeson responded that, based upon what he had learned from Pella, there would be no condensation difficulties with the new bay window. According to the Plaintiff Michael McNamara, Bergeson "guaranteed us verbally that the . . . new Pella window would not have that condensation problem." . . . Based upon Bergeson's oral representation, that the windows would be fog-free, the Plaintiffs purchased the Smart Sash III bay window, which their contractor then installed. Nomeco did not issue any written warranty, to the Plaintiffs, in connection with the sale of the Pella window. . . .

Notwithstanding Bergeson's alleged representation to the Plaintiffs, the new window experienced the same condensation problems that had plagued their old window. Apparently, the Plaintiffs are now trying, again, to replace their bay window. They have testified that, in retrospect, they do not believe that Bergeson lied to them, but only parroted misinformation which had been provided to him by Pella. . . . To recover their claimed losses, the Plaintiffs commenced this action in which they allege claims for a breach of contract, a breach of an express warranty, a violation of the Uniform Commercial Code, a violation of the Minnesota Consumer Fraud Act, a violation of the Minnesota Consumer Protection Act, a violation of Magnuson-Moss, and a right to attorney's fees for the consumer fraud claim. Nomeco has moved to dismiss, or to be awarded Summary Judgment on, the consumer fraud and related attorney's fees claims, and on the Magnuson-Moss claim. . . .

The viability of the Plaintiffs' claim under Magnuson-Moss, as it relates to Nomeco, turns on whether the protections of the Act apply to implied warranties which are not attendant to any form of written warranty. As we have noted, the Plaintiffs have conceded that Nomeco did not issue a written warranty in connection with the sale of the bay window, and Nomeco urges that the existence of a written warranty is a condition precedent to any action for a breach of implied warranty under Magnuson-Moss.

In a Section entitled "Remedies in consumer disputes," Magnuson-Moss provides for civil actions, by aggrieved consumers, as follows:

> [A] consumer who is damaged by the failure of a supplier, warrantor, or service contractor to comply with any obligation under this chapter, or under a written warranty, implied warranty, or service contract, may bring suit for damages and other legal and equitable relief—
>> (A) in any court of competent jurisdiction in any State or the District of Columbia; or
>> (B) in an appropriate district court of the United States. Title 15 U.S.C. §2310(d).

By its express terms, the provision allows actions to be commenced for any violation of the substantive portions of the Act, which regulate both written and implied warranties, and for the breach of an implied warranty. This provision creates "a federal private cause of action for consumers injured by the violation of (1) any obligation under the Act, (2) any warranty subject to the extensive regulatory requirements of the Act, or (3) any implied warranty the deceptive and unconscionable limitation of which was a major focus of the Act's regulatory provisions." Skelton v. General Motors Corp., 660 F.2d 311, 320 (7th Cir. 1981), cert. denied, 456 U.S. 974, 102 S. Ct. 2238, 72 L. Ed. 2d 848 (1982). Given this broad language, the Plaintiffs argue that they are entitled to enforce an implied warranty, notwithstanding the absence of a written warranty from Nomeco.

As to implied warranties, Magnuson-Moss specifically provides as follows:

> No supplier may disclaim . . . or modify any implied warranty to a consumer with respect to such consumer product if (1) such supplier makes any written warranty to the consumer with respect to such consumer product, or (2) at the time of the sale, or within 90 days thereafter, such supplier enters into a service contract with the consumer which applies to such consumer product. Title 15 U.S.C. §2308(a).

A facial reading of Sections 2310(d) and 2308(a) reveals some tension between their respective intendments. Read in a vacuum, Section 2310(d) would appear to allow the sort of claim that the Plaintiffs have present here; namely, a free standing cause of action, under Magnuson-Moss, for the alleged breach of the implied warranty of fitness for a particular purpose. See, Minnesota Statute Section 336.2-315. Section 2308, however, reflects that an action for the breach of implied warranty would not lie, under Magnuson-Moss, in the absence of a written warranty, on the same product, from the supplier.

Notwithstanding the apparent conflict in these provisions, there is a dearth of authority on the precise question we now face. There is some authority which suggests that, as confirmed by the Act's legislative history, its provisions were intended only to protect consumers from the unconscionable and deceptive use of written warranties, and not to create a Federal cause of action for every implied warranties which could arise under State law. In Skelton v. General Motors, 500 F. Supp. 1181 (N.D. Ill. 1980), for example, the District Court explained:

> The statute was not designed completely to supplant the state law of warranties and sales, but rather was intended primarily to regulate transactions involving written, usually formal, warranties under the narrow definition of §101(6). Further, in such transactions the Act not only regulates the contents and effect of the warranty document itself, but is also designed to provide a basic level of honesty and reliability to the entire transaction. Therefore, the Act requires certain written representations, generally the "paper with the filigree border," which trigger the Act's protections. Other written promises presented in connection with the same transaction should also be enforceable as part of the "written warranty." Id. at 1190 [footnotes omitted].

In reversing the District Court's decision, the Seventh Circuit did not address the lower Court's assumption that the issuance of a written warranty was a prerequisite to a Federal claim but, instead, overturned the Court's interpretation of what constituted a written warranty. See, Skelton v. General Motors Corp., supra at 322. As a consequence, the District Court's construction of Magnuson-Moss is well short of controlling.

In Robin Towing Corp. v. Honeywell, Inc., 859 F.2d 1218, 1222-23 (5th Cir. 1988), the Court of Appeals for the Fifth Circuit explained that the Act "prevents a supplier of a consumer product from avoiding an implied warranty if the supplier 'makes any written warranty' or 'enters into a service contract' with the consumer." The Court held that a homeowner could not maintain a claim under the Act, for the avoidance of an implied warranty, because "the conditions [i.e., the existence of a written warranty] are not present that would prevent Honeywell from disclaiming any implied warranty." Id. at 1223. The decision is also not squarely on point, however, since Honeywell had prospectively disclaimed the implied warranties of merchantability and fitness in the contract itself, and not as an after-the-fact means of avoiding UCC liability. Id. at 1220 n.1. As a result, the Court directed the focus of its analysis to Section 2308(a), and did not squarely address the meaning of Section 2310(d). Here, in contrast to the circumstances in Robin Towing, we confront a claimed breach of implied warranty, and not a prospective disclaimer of the warranty.

On the other side of the spectrum, there is a smattering of case authority, and academic commentary, which suggests that the Plaintiff's claim is cognizable under Magnuson-Moss. Most directly on point is McCurdy v. Texar, Inc., 575 So. 2d 299, 300 (Fla. Dist. Ct. App. 1991), which held that a plaintiff could pursue a claim under the Act, even though no written warranty was issued by the supplier. As the Court explained:

> Under 15 [U.S.C.A.] §2310(d), a consumer must be damaged by a supplier's, warrantor's, or service contractor's failure to comply with "any obligation" under the Act,

or under a written warranty, implied warranty, or service contract, in order to obtain federal jurisdiction to bring a suit for damages or other legal and equitable relief in the federal courts. This provision has not only provided a means of enforcing the substantive requirements of the Act, but has also established a federal cause of action for breach of an implied warranty which has arisen under state law even if no written warranty was involved.

Id. at 300-01 [emphasis added] [alteration in original], quoting Consumer Product Warranty Suits in Federal Court Under Magnuson-Moss Warranty, 59 A.L.R. Fed. 461, 470 n.10 (1982), and citing Miller and Kanter, Litigation Under Magnuson-Moss: New Opportunities in Private Actions, 13 UCC L.J. 10, 13 (Summer 1980), Denicola, The Magnuson-Moss Warranty Act: Making Consumer Product Warranty in a Federal Case, 44 Fordham L.R. 273 (1975), Reitz, Consumer Product Warranties Under Federal & State Laws, §10.02 (2d ed. 1987).

Nevertheless, the Court, in *McCurdy*, did not so much as advert to Section 2308(a), let alone attempt to reconcile its clear conflict with the broadly phrased language of Section 2310(d).

Other decisions are noteworthy only for what they do not state. In Feinstein v. Firestone Tire & Rubber Co., 535 F. Supp. 595, 601-02 (S.D.N.Y. 1982), the District Court denied certification to a class of tire purchasers claiming the breach of an implied warranty, without any written warranty, not because of the absence of a written warranty, but because the majority of the plaintiffs' claims failed on the merits. See also, Stones v. Sears, Roebuck & Co., 251 Neb. 560, 558 N.W.2d 540, 547-48 (Neb. 1997) (affirming dismissal of free-standing Magnuson-Moss implied warranty claims by purchasers of propane grills, on the merits); Hyler v. Garner, 548 N.W.2d 864, 876 (Iowa 1996) (affirming motor home buyer's recovery for breach of implied warranty of fitness under Section 2310(d)). Of course, none of these cases addressed the issue before us, and their implicit acceptance of the Plaintiffs' position, without the issue having been actually disputed, bears inappreciable precedential weight.

Given the paucity of controlling or persuasive authority, we address the issue as, largely, one of first impression which evokes an issue of pure statutory construction. Of course, the starting point for any statutory interpretation is the plain language of the statute itself. Good Samaritan Hosp. v. Shalala, 508 U.S. 402, 409, 113 S. Ct. 2151, 124 L. Ed. 2d 368 (1993). If the intent of Congress is clearly expressed in the terms of the statute, our inquiry is at an end, for we "must give effect to the unambiguously expressed intent of Congress." Chevron U.S.A. v. Natural Resources Def. Council, 467 U.S. 837, 842-43, 104 S. Ct. 2778, 81 L. Ed. 2d 694 (1984). In ascertaining the intent of Congress from a plain reading of a statute, it is fundamental that "'a statute should be interpreted so as not to render one part inoperative.'" Mountain States Tel. & Tel. Co. v. Pueblo of Santa Ana, 472 U.S. 237, 249, 105 S. Ct. 2587, 86 L. Ed. 2d 168 (1985), quoting Colautti v. Franklin, 439 U.S. 379, 392, 99 S. Ct. 675, 58 L. Ed. 2d 596 (1979).

As noted, Section 2310(d), by its terms, appears to generally authorize an action for a breach of an implied warranty. The Act defines an "implied warranty" as "an implied warranty arising under State law (as modified by Sections 2308 and 2304(a) of this title) in connection with the sale by a supplier of a consumer product." Title 15 U.S.C. §2301(7). In turn, Section 2308, as pertinent, makes it unlawful for a supplier to "disclaim" any implied warranty if there is a conjoined written warranty. Quite clearly, Section 2308 does not encompass all "implied warranties," but only those relating to products which have an accompanying written warranty. While the Act does not define the term "disclaim," as used in its ordinary sense, the term means: "1. To deny or renounce any claim to or connection with; disown; 2. To deny the validity of; repudiate; 3. Law. To renounce one's right or claim to." American Heritage Dictionary, p.530 (3d ed. 1992). Given the ordinary meaning of the term "disclaim," Section 2308(a) prohibits a supplier from denying liability on an implied warranty, only where there is an accompanying written warranty on the same consumer product. Accordingly, we believe that an implied warranty is "disclaimed" where, as here, the warranty is disowned, repudiated, or renounced. In legal effect, Nomeco has denied the Plaintiffs' entitlement to an implied warranty and, in that respect, Nomeco has "disclaimed" any such implied warranty.

If one were to afford Section 2310(d) the breadth of coverage advocated by the Plaintiffs, then the limitation prescribed in the definition "implied warranty," and the limitation in Section 2308(a) itself, would be rendered superfluous, as any implied warranty would be actionable under the Act, and not merely one that has been coupled with a written warranty. In contrast, in construing Section 2308(a) as mandating the presence of a written warranty as a condition precedent to a Federal implied warranty claim under Magnuson-Moss, no statutory term or provision is abrogated, or nullified. Therefore, we find the latter interpretation, which reconciles the conflicting provisions, to render an accurate interpretation of Congress' intent.

The sensibility of this reading is confirmed by the Act's underlying purpose, as evidenced by its legislative history. As the Seventh Circuit has explained, the drafters were concerned with "deceptive warranty practices," and "believed that consumer product warranties often were too complex to be understood, too varied to allow meaningful comparisons and too restricted to provide meaningful warranty protection." Skelton v. General Motors Corp., supra at 313-14, citing S. Rep. No. 93-151, 93d Cong., 1st Sess. 6-8 (1973), H.R. Rep. No. 93-1107, 93d Cong., 2d Sess. 22-29, reprinted in (1974) U.S. Code Cong. & Ad. News 7702, 7705-11. According to Congress, deceptive warranty practices were most likely to occur when a written warranty was issued. The Report of the House Committee on Interstate and Foreign Commerce reflects this motivating concern:

> [T]he paper with the filigree border bearing the bold caption "Warranty" or "Guarantee" was often of no greater worth than the paper it was printed on. Indeed, in many cases where a warranty or guarantee was ostensibly given the old saying applied "The bold print giveth and the fine print taketh away." For the paper operated to take away from the consumer the implied warranties of merchantability and fitness arising by operation of law leaving little in its stead.

H.R. Rep. No. 93-1107, 93d Cong., 2d Sess. 13, reprinted in (1974) U.S. Code Cong. & Ad. News 7706.

While not conclusive, we find the intentions of Congress, as reflected in the available indicia of legislative intent, to be corroborative of the construction of the Act that we here have drawn. Significantly, we have found no evidence that Congress intended a Federal replication, or preemption, of the State's regulation of implied warranties through the UCC, and related consumer sales enactments. Of course, adopting the Plaintiffs' construction would necessarily create a second tier of implied warranty claims, as emanating from Federal law. We think that Congress' adoption of a State law standard, for the definition of "implied warranty" reveals Congress' rejection of a wholesale, Federal regulation of implied warranties which have not been accompanied by a written warranty.

Accordingly, since we conclude that a party may not bring an implied warranty claim under Magnuson-Moss, in the absence of an adjoining written warranty, we recommend that Nomeco's Motion for Summary Judgment on the Plaintiffs' Magnuson-Moss claim be granted. . . .

There is one other potential benefit for consumers who sue under the Magnuson-Moss Act. In a case where the party injured by the consumer product is not the buyer, Magnuson-Moss's definition of "consumer" allows a plaintiff to overcome the horizontal privity problem. Magnuson-Moss allows a "consumer" to sue a warrantor, and then defines "consumer" to include not only the purchaser of the product, but also "any person to whom such product is transferred during the duration of an implied or written warranty (or service contract) applicable to the product." 15 U.S.C. §2301(3).

If a consumer is suing for breach of a written warranty as that term is defined by Magnuson-Moss, the consumer should also be able to overcome vertical privity problems and sue directly a remote seller such as a manufacturer. If a written warranty exists but the consumer is suing for breach of an implied warranty, however, courts are split as to whether Magnuson-Moss does away with the need for vertical privity. In a jurisdiction that follows the holding in *McCurdy*, this same issue should arise even in the absence of a written warranty.

Courts that do not allow direct suits by consumers against remote sellers for breach of implied warranties emphasize that Magnuson-Moss defines an implied warranty with reference to state law. Thus, these courts reason, if state law would not allow a direct suit against a remote seller for breach of an implied warranty, then neither should Magnuson-Moss. *See, e.g.*, Walsh v. Ford Motor Co., 588 F. Supp. 1513 (D.D.C. 1984). Courts that do allow direct suits against remote sellers for breach of implied warranty (where a written warranty is also present) point to the language in Magnuson-Moss §110(d) that allows a consumer to sue a "supplier," which includes a manufacturer, for breach of a "written warranty, implied warranty, or service contract." 15 U.S.C. §2310(d). *See, e.g.*, Ventura v. Ford Motor Corp., 433 A.2d 801 (Supr. Ct. App. Div. 1981).

Even though Magnuson-Moss is a federal statute, Congress did not wish to flood the federal courts with a series of nickel-and-dime consumer warranty suits. Accordingly, the jurisdictional provisions of Magnuson-Moss allow suits to be brought under the statute in any state court while federal jurisdiction is limited to cases where the amount in controversy is at least $50,000. 15 U.S.C. §2310(d)(3).

A separate rule, the FTC Used Motor Vehicle Trade Regulation Rule, is similar to Magnuson-Moss in its emphasis on full disclosure to consumers. The FTC rule, which applies only to used-car sales, requires that used-car dealers post a prominent "Buyer's Guide" in the window of each used car that it intends to sell. The Buyer's Guide indicates to the consumer whether or not the car is being sold with a warranty and, if so, whether the warranty is a full warranty or a limited warranty. 16 C.F.R. §455.2.

Problem Set 10

10.1.   a. You are working as a summer intern at your city's Legal Aid Bureau. Your first client is a college student who feels that he has been ripped off by one of the local computer stores. The student explains to you that when he bought his new computer, which cost $3,000 and has proven to be a disaster, the store did not even give him a written warranty on it. Is that a violation of Magnuson-Moss? 15 U.S.C. §2302.

b. Same facts as part (a). Even in the absence of a written warranty, how can Magnuson-Moss help your client? 15 U.S.C. §§2310(d), (a)(3), and (e), 2301; UCC §2-314. If you are suing under Magnuson-Moss, can you bring your suit in federal district court? 15 U.S.C. §2310(d)(1), (d)(3), (b), and (c)(1).

c. Same facts as part (a), except that your client tells you that he lent his computer to a classmate a couple of weeks after buying it. While the classmate was using the computer in the classmate's dorm room, the computer malfunctioned and destroyed an expensive custom-designed video game that the classmate had on a hard disk. Your client's classmate would like to recover from the retail seller of the computer for the $200 in damages represented by the destroyed video game. In an Alternative A jurisdiction, may your client's classmate recover against the retailer through a UCC warranty action? UCC §2-318, Alternative A.

d. Same facts as part (c). May your client's classmate recover against the retailer for his destroyed video game in a Magnuson-Moss action? 15 U.S.C. §§2310(d), 2301(3), 2301(7).

e. Same facts as part (c), except that the retailer had included a full written warranty promising that the computer would run defect-free for at least two years. To what extent does this help the classmate's cause of action for damages under Magnuson-Moss? 15 U.S.C. §§2310(d), 2301(3), 2301(6).

f. Same facts as part (c), except that when the computer wrecked the classmate's video game, that malfunction also disabled the computer and caused it $1,000 worth of damage. Now your client wants to sue both the retailer and the manufacturer for breach of the implied warranty of merchantability. May the manufacturer be joined in a suit under the UCC in an Alternative A jurisdiction? UCC §2-318, Alternative A.

g. Same facts as part (f). May the manufacturer be joined in a suit under Magnuson-Moss? 15 U.S.C. §§2310(d)(1), 2301(4). Would it make any difference if the manufacturer had made a written warranty? 15 U.S.C. §2310(f).

Assignment 11: Lease, International, and Real Estate Warranties

A. Lease Warranties: The Case of Finance Leases

Like so many other parts of UCC Article 2A, the provisions on lease warranties strongly resemble the comparable provisions in Article 2 for sales of goods. There is, however, one notable exception to the general pattern of lease warranty provisions mimicking the provisions of sale warranties: a leasing device known as the "finance lease."

A finance lease is a lease transaction that involves three parties: the supplier, the lessor, and the lessee. Functionally, a finance lease is very similar to a sale of goods from the supplier to the lessee, and the warranty provisions of Article 2A treat a finance lease very much as if it were a sale from the supplier to the lessee. As explained in the Official Comment to §2A-103, most sale-leaseback transactions will qualify as finance leases. Official Comment g to §2A-103.

In a finance lease, the "supplier" is the party that supplies the goods that will be leased to the lessee. The "lessor" in a finance lease is more functionally a financier, typically a bank or other financial institution. In a finance lease, the lessor has nothing to do with the selection, manufacture, or supply of the leased goods, which the lessor purchases (or leases) from the supplier solely in connection with the particular finance lease. The lessee in a finance lease is the party that identifies the goods to be leased, and the lessee will also have an opportunity to review the purchase (or lease) contract between the supplier and the lessor. UCC §2A-103(1)(g).

Leaf Financial Corp. v. ACS Services, Inc.

2010 WL 1740884 (Del. Sup. Ct. 2010)

BRADY, J.

INTRODUCTION

Leaf Financial Corporation ("Leaf") moves for summary judgment in a claim of breach of a finance lease contract against ACS Services, Inc. ("ACS") and William Adams, Jr. ("Adams") (Adams and ACS collectively, "Defendants").

Upon reviewing the Motion, responses thereto, and additional submissions filed subsequent to oral arguments, this Court is fully advised on the matter and is prepared to issue its decision.

FACTS

On January 11, 2006, Leaf and ACS contracted for Leaf to purchase a "managed service program" system (the "System") from N-Able. Leaf leased the System to ACS in exchange for a monthly lease payment. Adams executed the Lease as Personal Guarantor, and therefore, guaranteed to remit all payments pursuant to the payment schedule. In accordance with the Lease, Leaf purchased the system, and it was delivered to ACS. Defendants maintain that the System did not function properly. ACS expended over one hundred hours trouble-shooting and working with N-Able to fix the issues before "scrap[ping] the failed relationship" in July 2006. ACS did not make any payments under the Lease.

Leaf is a finance and asset management company which lends money to businesses to purchase commercial equipment. Leaf does not manufacture, distribute, or supply the equipment it finances. Leaf also expressly disclaims any warranty, express or implied, in the merchantability or fitness of the equipment it finances. The first page of the Lease contains an explicit waiver of all warranties:

> The Equipment is being leased to you "as is." You acknowledge that we do not manufacture the Equipment and that you have selected the Equipment and the supplier based on your own judgment. WE MAKE NO WARRANTIES, EXPRESS OR IMPLIED, INCLUDING WARRANTIES OF MERCHANTABILITY OR FITNESS FOR A PARTICULAR PURPOSE IN CONNECTION WITH THE EQUIPMENT THAT IS THE SUBJECT OF THIS AGREEMENT. WE SHALL NOT BE RESPONSIBLE FOR ANY CONSEQUENTIAL OR INCIDENTAL DAMAGES. WE SHALL NOT BE LIABLE FOR ANY LOSS OF INJURY TO YOU OR TO ANY THIRD PERSON FOR PROPERTY, INCLUDING DIRECT, INDIRECT, CONSEQUENTIAL, INCIDENTAL AND SPECIAL DAMAGES CAUSED BY THE USE, OWNERSHIP, LEASE OR POSSESSION OF THE EQUIPMENT. You agree to continue making Lease payments to us under this Lease, regardless of any claims you may have against the manufacturer or the supplier. We transfer to you for the term of this Lease any warranties made by the manufacturer or the supplier. No representation or warranty by the manufacturer or supplier is binding on us nor shall breach of any warranty relieve you of your obligation to us as provided herein.

There is another Lease Provision which is prominently titled "ARTICLE 2A RIGHTS AND REMEDIES" which states: "You agree that this Lease is a finance lease as that term is defined in Article 2A of the Uniform Commercial Code ("UCC"). You hereby agree to waive any and all rights and remedies granted to you by sections 2A-508 through 2A-522 of the UCC." UCC Sections 2A-508 through 2A-522 specify lessee defenses in light of a default by a lessor and are the precise sections that the Defendants rely upon in attempting to evade liability under the Lease.

According to the Lease, ACS's payment obligations were absolute and unconditional regardless of any problems with the quality of the leased goods. The Lease provides that if ACS defaulted on their payment obligations, the full balance could be immediately demanded. In addition, the parties separately executed an Addendum to the Equipment Lease Agreement which specified that the Defendants have no right to assert failure of the underlying software in any action by Leaf to enforce the Lease:

> (a) This is an irrevocable Lease for the full term and cannot be cancelled for any reason. (b) Lessee's obligation to make the Lease payments is absolute, unconditional and independent and is not subject to any abatement, set-off, defense or counterclaim for any reason whatsoever, including equipment or systems failure, damage, loss or any other cause or problem. (c) the Equipment is leased "as is"; Lessor makes no representation, guarantee, express warranty or implied warranty, including without limitation an implied warranty of merchantability or fitness for a particular purpose; if the equipment does not operate as represented by the Vendor or is unsatisfactory for any other reason, Lessee shall make any such claims solely against the Vendor and not Lessor; and no representation, guarantee or warranty by the Vendor is binding on Lessor nor shall any breach thereof relieve Lessee of its obligations to Lessor hereunder or under the Lease.

THE PARTIES' CONTENTIONS

Defendants oppose Leaf's Motion for Summary Judgment. Specifically, Defendants argue the following: (1) under the Uniform Commercial Code, Article 2A, Defendants are relieved from all obligations under the transaction because the merchandise was defective; (2) Leaf is not entitled to assert a finance lease under Article 2A because the parties formed a partnership relationship and/or ACS did not accept the goods; (3) alternatively, Defendants revoked acceptance of the computer system; (4) further discovery is needed; and (5) Plaintiff has requested an excessive amount of attorney's fees.

Leaf argues that Defendants have no valid grounds to defend against the breach of contract action. Leaf contends that it effectively disclaimed all implied warranties of merchantability and fitness for a particular purpose in the warranty language contained in the lease, and that Defendants waived their defense of non-acceptance or revocation of acceptance when they signed the lease. Leaf contends it relied on this waiver provision in entering into this transaction and advancing funds which enabled the Defendants to purchase the software. Additionally, Leaf argues that Defendants agreed that they would have no right to assert failure of the underlying software in any action by Leaf to enforce the Lease and specifically agreed to make payments required under the Lease whether or not the software operated as expected. Defendants agreed that any remedies available for defects in the software would be asserted solely against N–Able, the software vendor.

Leaf argues that Defendants' understanding as to whether a partnership agreement was created is irrelevant, as it is based solely on parol evidence, which should not be considered and that the plain and unambiguous terms of the Lease indicate that no such partnership was contemplated by the parties.

STANDARD OF REVIEW

The standard for granting summary judgment is high. Summary judgment may be granted where the record shows that there is no genuine issue as to any material fact and that the moving party is entitled to judgment as a matter of law. "In determining whether there is a genuine issue of material fact, the evidence must be viewed in a light most favorable to the non-moving party." "When taking all of the facts in a light most favorable to the non-moving party, if there remains a genuine issue of material fact requiring trial, summary judgment may not be granted."

ANALYSIS

1. THE PARTIES ENTERED INTO A FINANCE LEASE

A finance lease is a three-party transaction in which the lessee selects goods from a supplier or manufacturer. The lessee then contracts to have a third party lessor purchase the goods and lease them to the lessee. Delaware adopted Article 2A of the UCC, which defines finance leases and how they are created. Finance leases are created either within the parameters of 6 Del. C. §2A-103 or by agreement of the parties.

Defendants claim the Lease is not a finance lease because they were never provided with a copy of the Lease as required by 6 Del. C. §2A-103(g)(iii)(A). Defendants also argue that a finance lease was not formed because a finance lease must be based upon the premise that the lessor has no participation in the underlying relationship between the supplier and the seller. Defendants, however, do not provide any Delaware case law to support this assertion. Defendants contend that N-able established a "partnership" relationship between itself, its customers (including ACS) and the funding source, Leaf. Defendants rely upon Adams's Affidavit, brochures, and other documents to support the argument that a partnership relationship existed.

Defendants' argument that the Lease is not a finance lease because they were never provided with a copy overlooks the fact that 6 Del. C. §2A-103 (g)(iii) only requires that one of the four listed elements be satisfied in order to create a finance lease lease. The statutory language indicates the following elements:

> "Finance lease" means a lease with respect to which: (i) The lessor does not select, manufacture or supply the goods; (ii) The lessor acquires the goods or the right to possession and use of the goods in connection with the lease; and (iii) One of the following occurs: (A) The lessee receives a copy of the contract by which the lessor acquired the goods or the right to possession and use of the goods before signing the lease contract; (B) The lessee's approval of the contract by which the lessor acquired

the goods or the right to possession and use of the goods is a condition to effectiveness of the lease contract; (C) The lessee, before signing the lease contract, receives an accurate and complete statement designating the promises and warranties, and any disclaimers of warranties, limitations or modifications of remedies, or liquidated damages, including those of a third party, such as the manufacturer of the goods, provided to the lessor by the person supplying the goods in connection with or as part of the contract by which the lessor acquired the goods or the right to possession and use of the goods; or (D) If the lease is not a consumer lease, the lessor, before the lessee signs the lease contract, informs the lessee in writing: (1) Of the identity of the person supplying the goods to the lessor, unless the lessee has selected that person and directed the lessor to acquire the goods or the right to possession and use of the goods from that person, (2) That the lessee is entitled under this Article to the promises and warranties, including those of any third party, provided to the lessor by the person supplying the goods in connection with or as part of the contract by which the lessor acquired the goods or the right to possession and use of the goods, and (3) That the lessee may communicate with the person supplying the goods to the lessor and receive an accurate and complete statement of those promises and warranties, including any disclaimers and limitations of them or of remedies.

The Court finds that the statutory requirements for creating a finance lease exist in this case. First, Leaf did not select, manufacture or supply the goods. Second, Leaf acquired the goods or the right to possession and use of the goods in connection with the Lease. Leaf would not have otherwise acquired the software from N-Able. Third, ACS ordered the software from N-able.

Even if a lease does not meet Delaware's statutory definition of a finance lease, the parties may create such a lease by agreement. In this case, this Lease was signed by Adams and explicitly states the following language under subheading Article 2A Rights and Remedies:

> You agree that this Lease is a finance lease as that term is defined in Article 2A of the Uniform Commercial Code ("UCC"). You hereby agree to waive any and all rights and remedies granted to you by Sections 2A-508 through 2A-522 of the UCC.

The Court finds that a valid finance lease was formed between ACS and Leaf that the parties explicitly agreed to create such a Lease, and further, that they understood, at the time of signing that they were, in fact, creating such a lease.

2.   There Was No Partnership

The Court rejects Defendants' argument that a partnership relationship was formed. Defendants rely upon Adams's Affidavit which indicates that "from the beginning, N-Able promoted a partnership relationship between itself, its customers, and its funding source, Leaf." The plain and unambiguous terms of the Lease indicate that no partnership relationship was contemplated by the parties. ACS signed the lease agreement which expressly identified the parties to the lease and the nature of the lease as a finance lease. Further, to find a partnership, the Court must consider parol evidence. The Lease provides it is a fully integrated agreement, and therefore the Court will not consider parol evidence.

The contract language is a clear and unambiguous expression of agreement which should be upheld on its face. Finally, the attempt to contradict the integrated agreement's terms represented in the Lease is forbidden under the UCC.

3. The Defendants' Promises Under the Lease Became Irrevocable After Accepting the Goods

Under 6 Del. C. §2A-515, a lessee's promises, in a non-consumer finance lease, become irrevocable upon acceptance of the goods. This so-called waiver of defense clause is strictly enforceable as a matter of law for three reasons. First, in a finance lease, the lessor's sole obligation is financial; the lessee should look to the supplier for any problems with the product. Secondly, once the lessor pays for the goods, the lessor's obligation is fulfilled. Finally, waiver of defense clauses are essential to the equipment leasing industry as a guaranteed means of security for the lessor's loan.

Here, Defendants argue that they are relieved from all obligations under the Lease because the merchandise was defective. Defendants argue they are authorized to rely upon the warranty sections of the UCC, Sections 6 Del. C. §2A-21225 and 6 Del. C. §2A-213.26 Defendants also argue that they are authorized to rely upon the acceptance and revocation provisions of the UCC, Sections 6 Del. C. §2A-508, 6 Del. C. §2A-509 and 6 Del. C. §2A-517.27

The Court, however, finds that Defendants are not entitled to rely upon the warranty provisions in UCC Sections 6 Del. C. §2A-212 and 6 Del. C. §2A-213 because the Lease, which was signed by the parties, includes an explicit waiver of all warranties. Under 6 Del. C. §2A-214, equipment lessors may disclaim all implied warranties:

> 2) Subject to subsection (3), to exclude or modify the implied warranty of merchantability or any part of it the language must mention "merchantability," must be in writing, and must be conspicuous. Subject to subsection (3), to exclude or modify any implied warranty of fitness the exclusion must be by a writing and be conspicuous. Language to exclude all implied warranties of fitness is sufficient if it is in writing, is conspicuous and states, for example, "There is no warranty that the goods will be fit for a particular purpose".

> 3) Notwithstanding subsection (2), but subject to subsection (4),

> (a) unless the circumstances indicate otherwise, all implied warranties are excluded by expressions like "as is," or "with all faults," or by other language that in common understanding calls the lessee's attention to the exclusion of warranties and makes plain that there is no implied warranty, if in writing and conspicuous. . . .

The language in the Lease is bold, capitalized, and conspicuously presented in a section entitled "NO WARRANTY." The language informs the lessee that it is taking the equipment "as is" specifically without any warranty. This language also transfers to the lessee all warranty claims which may exist against the manufacturer or supplier.

Defendants are also not entitled to rely upon UCC Sections 6 Del. C. §2A-508, §2A-509 and §2A-517 because they specifically waived these rights to do so under the Lease. There is a provision in the Lease prominently titled "ARTICLE 2A RIGHTS AND REMEDIES" which states that ACS "hereby agree[s] to waive any and all rights and remedies granted to [ACS] by Sections 2A-508 through 2A-522 of the UCC." Defendants have cited no authority which would support relieving them of their obligation to comply with this term. Furthermore, Defendants separately executed an addendum to the equipment lease, which includes the provision that Defendants would have no right to assert failure of the underlying software in any action by Leaf to enforce the Lease. Given these waiver provisions, the circumstances or terms of acceptance are irrelevant. Defendants specifically agreed to make payments under the Lease whether or not the software operated as expected.

In addition to waiving their right to rely upon the non-acceptance provisions under the UCC, ACS failed to notify Leaf that it rejected the goods within the timeframe established by the Lease. The Lease provided that the "lease term will commence when the Equipment is delivered and installed. Unless you notify us otherwise in writing within 7 days of installation, you unconditionally accept the equipment." The software was delivered on January 16, 2006. The installation date was scheduled for February 9, 2006. Defendants contend additional time was required beyond that date because the program had to be installed at client sites as well to assure the product worked properly. However, ACS did not notify Leaf that it rejected the goods until July 11, 2006. Even if some accommodations were made to expand the term "installation" to include other sites, Defendants were aware long before July 11, 2006 that there were difficulties and could have made proper notification. Therefore, ACS accepted the goods under the terms of the Lease.

The Court requested additional information from the parties on August 25, 2009 regarding: (1) the date on which the product was delivered to ACS by N-Able; (2) whether ACS notified Leaf in writing within seven days after delivery that it did not accept the goods; and (3) whether Leaf required ACS to provide Leaf with a signed delivery and acceptance certificate. While the parties could, or would, not agree on any of the above, the record is sufficiently established to allow the Court to determine the date of delivery was at least more than seven days prior to any notification in writing, to Leaf, of any problems. Additionally, it appears Leaf may not have required a signed delivery and acceptance certificate. While Leaf did not require such a certificate, the right to require one belonged to Leaf, and the Lease affords no remedies to the Defendants.

CONCLUSION

The Court finds that the Lease was clearly a finance lease. Defendants waived all warranty claims and any and all rights and remedies, granted to Defendants,

Here, defendant contends that a reasonable inspection did not occur prior to purchase because the defect would have been easily discoverable by a trained person, engaged in the business of home inspection. Indeed, Rushing testified that such an inspection by a trained person, had that person measured the depth of material and analyzed the mixture, would have indicated "rather quickly" the existence of the defects in the stucco installation.

However, Rushing also testified that a lay person would not "key in on any of these problems until they started to appear the way they are now," and plaintiff testified he made a lay person's inspection of the home prior to purchase. The trial court found that, at the time of the purchase, "there [were] few cracks in the stucco of a normal nature," and "only from 1987 would a reasonable purchaser have been put on any kind of notice that a disastrous problem lay hidden beneath the exterior stucco and paint."

We disagree with defendant's contention that a "reasonable inspection" must include, as one of its components, an inspection by an expert or professional home inspection service to scrutinize the house for internal defects prior to purchase. Rather, under the policies stated in *Columbia* and *Powercraft,* an implied warranty should be voided for lack of a "reasonable inspection" only if the defect could have been discovered during an inspection made by the average purchaser, not an expert.

The rule of caveat emptor applies generally to the sale of real estate. However, the general rule is not applied to the construction of residential houses because of the public policy favoring the protection of innocent home purchasers and the accountability of home builders. In *Columbia,* we recognized the disparity between the expertise of the home builder and the average home purchaser:

> Many firms and persons . . . hold themselves out as skilled in home construction and are in the business of building and selling to individual owners. . . . Building construction by modern methods is complex and intertwined with governmental codes and regulations. The ordinary home buyer is not in a position, by skill or training, to discover defects lurking in the plumbing, the electrical wiring, the structure itself, all of which is usually covered up and not open for inspection.

122 Ariz. at 32, 592 P.2d at 1298, quoting Tavares v. Horstman, 542 P.2d 1275, 1279 (Wyo. 1975). The same recognition was extended to subsequent purchasers in *Powercraft*:

> Home builders should anticipate that the houses they construct will eventually, and perhaps frequently, change ownership. The effect of latent defects will be just as catastrophic on a subsequent owner as on an original buyer and the builder will be just as unable to justify improper or substandard work. Because the builder-vendor is in a better position than a subsequent owner to prevent occurrence of major problems, the costs of poor workmanship should be his to bear. 139 Ariz. at 245, 678 P.2d at 430.

Admittedly, the "reasonable inspection" requirement for subsequent purchasers is necessary to avoid a windfall to the purchaser who negotiates a reduction in the purchase price based upon defects and then subsequently seeks damages from the builder for the same defects. However, a requirement that the "reasonable inspection" made prior to purchase be done by an expert rather than by the purchaser would negate the policy considerations for recognizing an implied warranty in the first place. In declining to adopt such a rule, we agree with the observations of the Colorado Supreme Court:

> An experienced builder who has erected and sold many houses is in a far better position to determine the structural condition of a house than most buyers. Even if a buyer is sufficiently knowledgeable to evaluate a home's condition, he rarely has access to make any inspection of the underlying structural work, as distinguished from the merely cosmetic features.

Duncan v. Schuster-Graham Homes, Inc., 194 Colo. 441, 578 P.2d 637, 638-39 (1978).

The evidence in this case clearly established that the average purchaser would not have discovered the defect upon reasonable inspection and that plaintiff made such an inspection. We thus find no error in the trial court's finding that plaintiff met the reasonable inspection requirement necessary to an implied warranty of habitability or proper workmanship.

Defendant also contends that the trial court's extension of an implied warranty more than twelve years after completion of construction is unreasonable, and fails to meet the limitations on the warranty set forth by the supreme court in *Powercraft* and followed by Division Two of this court in Sheibels v. Estes Homes, 161 Ariz. 403, 778 P.2d 1299 (App. 1989).

In *Powercraft,* the supreme court adopted the standard of reasonableness first articulated by the Indiana Supreme Court in Barnes v. Mac Brown & Co., 264 Ind. 227, 342 N.E.2d 619 (1976):

> The standard to be applied in determining whether or not there has been a breach of warranty is one of reasonableness in light of surrounding circumstances. The age of a home, its maintenance, the use to which it has been put, are but a few factors entering into this factual determination at trial.

Powercraft, 139 Ariz. at 245, 678 P.2d at 430, quoting *Barnes,* 342 N.E.2d at 621. . . .

[T]he duration that an implied warranty will exist is a factual determination that will depend, in part, on the life expectancy of the questioned component in a non-defective condition. In making this determination, a fact finder need not decide the outside limits of that life expectancy, but only whether liability is reasonable at the point of the breach under the particular facts of the case.

In this case, the trial court heard expert testimony that a stucco exterior has a normal life expectancy in the Arizona desert of thirty to fifty years, and defendant conceded that the stucco process applied to plaintiff's house could be reasonably expected to last more than the twelve years that it did. The evidence also established that the damage from the defective stucco application was gradual and progressive, occurring over a period of at least ten years, and was not discoverable by reasonable inspection until it actually was discovered. Under these circumstances, we find no error in the trial court's conclusion that, based on the expected life of the defective component of the house, twelve years was not an unreasonable period for an implied warranty of habitability and workmanship to exist.

Based on the foregoing, we affirm the judgment of the trial court. . . .

With the sale of used homes, as noted above, states are split on whether the original builder's warranty of habitability can ever run to subsequent purchasers. Beyond this possibility of a suit against the original builder, there are generally no implied warranties that are given by the homeowner/seller himself or herself, and used homes are effectively sold "as is" in the absence of express warranties. That is why with residential resale transactions most buyers use a professional home inspector to inspect the house before committing to purchase it. A typical home inspection contingency clause in a residential real estate sales contract looks something like this:

> Buyer and Seller agree that the property is being sold in its present, "as is" condition, with no warranties, express or implied, and that conditions of the property that are visible on a reasonable inspection by a prospective Buyer should either be taken into account by the Buyer in the purchase price, or the Buyer should make correction of these conditions by Seller a requirement of the contract. Within fifteen (15) days after the "Acceptance Deadline" date of the sale contract, Buyer, at his option and expense, has the right to obtain written inspection reports from a qualified and reputable engineer, contractor, or home inspection service of the property and improvements limited to structural defects, environmental hazards, termite or other type of infestation and damage, plumbing, wells and sewer systems and equipment, roof, heating, and/or air conditioning systems and equipment, electrical systems and equipment, swimming pool and equipment, exterior drainage, basement leaks, and mechanical equipment including appliances, and shall furnish a copy thereof to Seller or listing agency stating in writing any defects unacceptable to Buyer.

The clause would then go on to state that, in the event of such defects, the parties have 10 days to agree on who will pay for and correct the defects, or to agree instead to a price adjustment in lieu of correction. If those attempts fail, then the contingency clause provides that the deal is off.

2.   Third-Party Home Warranties

Just as discussed in Assignment 8 with regard to consumer products, there has been an increase in the last couple of decades in the use of home warranties in the sale of both new and used homes. Unlike the case with the sale of goods, in the home sale market the warranty programs are serviced almost exclusively by third parties rather than by the seller itself.

Once more it is important to distinguish between new-home sales and used-home sales. Resale home warranty plans, when they are part of a sale, are typically offered by the seller as an enticement for the buyer. These resale warranties generally consist of a one-year service contract providing for repair or replacement of a home's major systems and appliances if any of those fail during the life of the warranty.

Unlike extended warranties on consumer products, resale home warranties are actually used by the buyer fairly frequently. One survey indicated that the average buyer with a resale home warranty made two uses per year of the warranty. The popularity of resale home warranties varies significantly from state to state. In Texas only about 6 percent of recent home resales included home warranties. In California, by contrast, the figure has been as high as 76 percent.

New home warranties are normally longer in duration of coverage than resale home warranties, and sometimes can last as long as 10 years on certain systems in the house. Partly because of this, some new home warrantors have run into financial difficulty resulting in their inability to pay claims in some cases. The most prominent example of a new-home warrantor overextending itself is HOW Insurance Company, a Virginia-based firm that was forced into receivership by Virginia insurance regulators on the grounds that it had not set aside sufficient reserves to pay future claims. As a result of the action by the Virginia insurance regulators, HOW Insurance Company was barred from writing any new policies. Furthermore, pending claims by homeowners against the company are being paid at just 40 cents on the dollar so that there will be some money left for future claimants.

Even when the new-home warrantor is solvent, the policies come with limits:

> Indeed, new-home warranties are sharply limited. Homes with major structural defects, for instance, must be deemed unsafe, unsanitary or unlivable to qualify for repair under most warranties — and it is the warranty company that makes the judgment. Even when claims are declared legitimate, payouts can be months, even years, in coming. And warranty companies frequently provide quick fixes rather than permanent cures for even major problems, such as faulty foundations. (Karen Blumenthal, "Insured warranties attacked; some owners say policies worthless," *The Cincinnati Enquirer*, H4, January 22, 1995.)

Problem Set 11

11.1.   a. First National Bank has a leasing division, First National Leasing, that leased a dozen trailers to a trucking firm, Standard Delivery. Prior to entering the lease, Standard determined the kind of trailer it wanted and identified for First National a company, Billings Equipment Co., that sold this type of trailer. First National then purchased a dozen custom-built trailers from Billings after having Standard sign off on the terms of First National's purchase agreement with Billings, which included various express warranties. Following Standard's approval of the sale terms, First National signed a 10-year lease agreement with Standard. One year into the lease, two of the trailers began leaking when it rained. What rights does Standard have against First National Leasing as to the defective trailers? UCC §§2A-103(1)(g), 2A-212(1), 2A-213(1), 2A-407, Official Comment (g) to §2A-103.

b. Same facts as part (a), except that the leasing officer at First National tells the Standard officer in charge of this deal, "I highly recommend that we get the trailers from Billings Equipment Co. We've dealt with them before and their trailers have always been first-rate." Would Standard now have rights against First National Leasing as to the defective trailers? UCC §§2A-103(1)(g), 2A-210, 2A-407(1), Official Comment 2 to §2A-407.

c. Same facts as part (a). What rights does Standard have against Billings Equipment as to the defective trailers? UCC §§2A-209(1), 2-313, 2-314; Official Comment 1 to §2A-209. What if the sales contract contained warranty disclaimers—would those be effective? UCC §2A-209(1).

d. Same facts as part (a), except that the Standard officer told the Billings salesman prior to the sale, "We make a lot of deliveries over rugged mountain roads. So we need trailers with good shocks." The Billings salesman then replied, "Might I recommend our Rover XXL model?" It turned out that the Rover XXL had shock absorbers no better than those on the typical trailer, and so the shocks failed on a number of the trailers within the first year of the lease. The written sales contract between Billings and First National said nothing about the durability of the shocks. Does Standard have any rights against Billings regarding the shocks? UCC §§2-315, 2A-213, 2A-209(1).

11.2.   In your capacity as in-house counsel for First National Bank, the leasing division has asked you to take a look at the form lease that it uses whenever the bank engages in a finance lease. The leasing officers who do these deals on a regular basis tell you that it's very important that these transactions get characterized as finance leases so that the bank can get all of the benefits of being a finance lessor. What kinds of clauses will you make sure are included in the contract? UCC §2A-103(1)(g); Official Comment (g) to §2A-103; §§2A-212(1), 2A-213, 2A-407(1).

11.3.   Steve Stern is a construction worker whose job sometimes takes him out of state for a few weeks at a time. He and his wife, Sandra Werner, have been looking for a few months to buy a house after living in an apartment for the first three years of their marriage. When Sandra found a 4-year-old house in an established neighborhood of 80-year-old houses, she decided to make an offer on the house on the spot, even though Steve was out of town on a job. She included an inspection contingency clause in the contract, which was accepted by the seller. Sandra figured that Steve could do the inspection himself, but he was so exhausted from traveling and working the out-of-town job that he told Sandra she could do a walk-through on her own. Sandra did not notice anything in her admittedly superficial inspection, and she and her husband purchased the house. Two months after moving in, Steve was fixing the gutters when he noticed something peculiar about the way in which the roof shingles were attached. Upon closer inspection, Steve could see (because of his extensive experience in the construction industry) that the roof work was incredibly shoddy, and he estimated it would cost nearly $5,000 to get the roof done right. May Sandra and Steve recover against the original builder for the cost of the roof repairs?

Assignment 12:   Reducing or Eliminating Warranty Liability: Basics

A.   Warranty Reduction with Sales of Goods

There is a recurring tension that characterizes the issue of warranty disclaimers and limitations in the sales system. On one hand, all sellers have an incentive to stand behind the quality of their goods because such an assurance helps future sales either with repeat buyers or with new customers who learn of the seller's good reputation. On the other hand, having unlimited warranty liability can be a very expensive proposition, even if the goods being sold are generally fit for their ordinary purpose.

When it comes to warranty disclaimers, there is a tendency for commercial sellers to care more about the long-term relational aspects of a sale than about the money saved by enforcing a warranty disclaimer in a particular context. The one limitation that even commercial sellers will fight for, however, is a disclaimer of consequential damages. Consequential damages, you may recall from your contracts class, are damages a buyer suffers that go beyond any damage to the product itself. Consequential damages, for example, might include a consumer's personal injuries from a defective product or a business's economic loss from a poorly designed machine.

Sellers are particularly wary of accepting unlimited consequential damage liability when the product they are selling is a relatively inexpensive item. An in-house lawyer for an industrial products manufacturer explains, "When we offer a component of small value that will be put in a much more expensive product, we can't have the potential liability all out of whack with the potential return. It would damage our business. So we're going to take a pretty strong position there. Look, we understand that our little part fails. You may have some significant damages, but you know, we've got to go forward with the understanding we're going to do the best we can and to supply you a good product. But if we don't, we can't have liability that's all out of whack with potential return."

Just as sellers of commercial goods are reluctant to accept the possibility of consequential damages, buyers of commercial goods will not lightly bargain away that category of recovery. As the in-house counsel for a major beer manufacturer put it, "Our equipment suppliers will often want to limit remedies to repair or replacement of defective parts, but we'll resist those efforts because sometimes we will have important and legitimate consequential damages to claim. For example, if a filtration system that we've been sold doesn't work and we lose a lot of beer because of that, we'll want to be reimbursed for the lost beer by the seller who sold us the filtration system. Whether or not the consequential damages disclaimer stays or goes will depend mainly on commercial leverage. In that respect, it has helped us a lot that we're a big company."

Sellers of consumer goods often care about reputational concerns just as much as sellers of commercial goods. There is nevertheless a large class of consumer sales — those in which the size of each transaction is large but repeat business is low, such as used-car sales — where it may be in the seller's interest to care more about the short-term dollar cost of broad warranty protection for its buyers than about the longer-term reputational cost of very limited warranty protection. To complicate the workings of the system even further, the employees of the seller that deal directly with the buyer are often sales people whose incentives are geared almost exclusively toward closing the deal. Even when these sales people are required to sell goods that have very little warranty protection, there is a strong temptation for them to make oral promises about quality to the potential buyer that may or may not become enforceable terms of the sales contract.

The Consumers Digest "Used-Car Buying and Selling Guide" describes the following scenario along these lines:

> Dishonest dealers may tell consumers that "as is" refers to the equipment or options that come with the car, or that it reflects any warranty terms that may have been offered verbally. Neither is true. More commonly, a dishonest dealer will offer to fix a problem you might discover while examining the vehicle, have you sign the contract that contains the "as is" clause, and then refuse to honor the oral promise after the car changes hands. Although an oral promise technically constitutes an express warranty, it is difficult to prove. In most states, under what's known as the "parol evidence rule," terms in a written agreement always override inconsistent spoken promises. To avoid this pitfall, get all promises in writing. (Consumers Digest, Vol. 35, No. 4 (1996).)

As the following story from Florida demonstrates, situations like the "as is" used-car sale described above are by no means limited to the proverbial "$500 special." Indeed, scenarios like these can even happen with much higher-end used car sales:

> It was the best looking vehicle Diana Smith had ever owned. The shiny red, used Jeep Grand Cherokee was no steal at $25,300, but Smith pulled together enough for a down payment and traded in her 1988 Ford Thunderbird. Her kids loved it. And Smith, a single mother who works as a secretary in Lecanto, was thrilled to finally have something nice to shuttle them around in. Now, five months after she bought the 2-year-old Jeep at a tent sale in Dunnellon, Smith says she would love nothing more than to have her old car back. That's because the Jeep, sold to her by Rallye Dodge of Ocala, was apparently in a wreck before she bought it.
>
> Smith doesn't have the money to repair the bent frame, flattened brake lines, buckled roof and other damage the Jeep suffered. She said she still drives the car,

even though she is concerned about its safety, because she has no choice. Because she signed a contract with a warranty disclaimer, or "as is" clause, the dealership's general manager told her there is nothing he can do. "I am just heartbroken," said Smith, 39. "My 15-year-old won't even get in it. I thought it was the nicest thing I had ever owned. Now, the thrill is completely gone. . . . "

[Smith] said the salesman told her that the vehicle had been repainted only because someone had scratched it. "I asked him specifically if it had been in a wreck because I noticed there was a bubble in the paint," she said. "Nobody can convince me that they didn't lie to me about it." Smith first learned of the damage when she brought the Jeep into Crystal Chevrolet-Geo in Crystal River for minor repairs after another driver rear-ended her. The manager of the body shop told her about the previous repair work that had been done, including plastic body filler applied to the roof and frame. All together, 15 separate repairs were listed as needed to return the Jeep to pre-wreck condition.

Smith has notified Chrysler Corp., the Florida Department of Consumer Affairs, the Department of Highway Safety and Motor Vehicles and 60 Minutes. A letter from the motor vehicles division states that, because Smith signed an "as is" clause, she has no legal recourse other than a civil suit. A representative from Chrysler told her a complaint would be filed in the company's data base, but beyond that, nothing could be done. The representative told Smith that she should have had the car checked before she bought it. Smith said she believes there are plenty of things she should have done—like shopped at a different dealership. "I figured it was a reputable place," she said. "If Lee Iacocca were still around, I bet he'd do something about this." (Amy Ellis, "Dream Car Turns into Nightmare," *St. Petersburg Times*, November 5, 1995.)

Perhaps because of stories like the one above, there is significant regulation at both the state and federal levels governing the mechanics of warranty disclaimers and limitations. At the state level, there is Article 2 of the UCC, which contains a number of provisions setting down specific requirements that must be met in order for warranty disclaimers to be effective.

In addition, nearly all states have some form of "lemon law" that covers the sale of new (and in some cases used) cars. The primary type of abuse targeted by state lemon laws are car manufacturers' attempts to limit a buyer's remedy to repair or replacement of defective parts. The problem with such a remedy limit, as most car buyers know, is that with some cars this would mean having to bring the car back for adjustments practically every month. In those cases, what the buyer really wants is a different car. One of the key features of state lemon laws is a limit on the number of repair attempts that must be made before a car seller is required to offer the buyer either a new car or a refund of the purchase price.

At the federal level, the Magnuson-Moss Act includes some regulations that limit the ability of consumer product sellers to disclaim the implied warranty of merchantability. Furthermore, as noted in Assignment 10, the FTC Used Car Rule mandates conspicuous disclosure of a used car's warranty protections and limitations in plain view of any prospective purchaser.

Before looking in greater detail at these various statutory limits on a seller's ability to disclaim or reduce warranty liability, there is a more general point that needs to be made about this area: When it comes to enforcing warranty limitations, courts will be very tough on the seller, particularly where the buyer is a consumer. This is not to suggest, of course, that properly worded and clearly written warranty disclaimers will never work to do what their drafters intended. Rather, the lesson is, as the following case shows, that any ambiguity in the language of a warranty disclaimer is likely to be construed strictly against the seller that drafted it.

Wilbur v. Toyota Motor Sales, U.S.A.

86 F.3d 23 (2d Cir. 1996)

OAKES, SENIOR C.J.

Appellant Nicolyn S. Wilbur ("Wilbur") appeals from an order entered on March 27, 1995, by the United States District Court for the District of Vermont, Franklin S. Billings, Jr., Senior Judge, granting summary judgment to Appellee Toyota Motor Sales, U.S.A., Inc. ("Toyota"). Wilbur sued Toyota for violating the Magnuson-Moss Warranty-Federal Trade Commission Improvement Act and the Vermont Consumer Fraud Act ("VCFA"), by refusing to honor its new car warranty on her Toyota Camry. On appeal, Wilbur argues that the district court erred in finding as a matter of law that the warranty excluded damage done to the car before it was purchased. We agree with Wilbur that the damage occurring prior to the date the dealer listed the car as "in service" was not excluded from warranty coverage. Accordingly, we reverse the summary judgment in favor of Toyota and remand to the district court. . . .

On May 18, 1992, Wilbur bought a 1992 Toyota Camry for $18,600 from Tri-Nordic Toyota ("Tri-Nordic") in White River Junction, Vermont. The car had been used as a demonstrator by the dealership and had roughly 5,800 miles on the odometer. Wilbur's Bill of Sale identified the car as a "New Camry Demo."

Before Wilbur bought the car, Tri-Nordic informed her that the car had been in an accident requiring almost $4,000 in repairs. The accident, a rear-end collision, occurred in October 1991 when one of Tri-Nordic's employees was using the car to look at New Hampshire's fall foliage with his relatives. Tri-Nordic told Wilbur that the car had been fully repaired and had sustained no structural damage.

At the time of purchase, Wilbur received a copy of Toyota's "New Vehicle Limited Warranty," which stated that the warranty went into effect "on the date the vehicle is first delivered or put into use (in-service date)." Tri-Nordic filled in the in-service date as 5/18/92, the date Wilbur bought the car. The warranty further stated that "repairs and adjustments required as a result of . . . accident . . . are not covered."

In June 1992, Wilbur drove the Camry to California for the summer. On the way, she discovered that the car's ABS braking system did not work, that the trunk had a major leak, and that the rear of the car made a creaking noise. When she brought the car to a Toyota dealer in California for repairs, the dealer told her that the repairs were excluded from warranty coverage because the vehicle had sustained structural damage in an accident. After making visits to several other dealerships, all of which refused to honor her Toyota warranty, Wilbur obtained an estimate of approximately $9,500 for the repairs. She also had the car appraised and learned that a potential buyer who knew of its condition would not have paid more than $10,000 for it.

Wilbur reported the repair estimate to Tri-Nordic, which offered to make the repairs if Wilbur agreed to split the cost of transporting the car back to Vermont. After refusing to do so, Wilbur made numerous complaints about the denial of warranty coverage to Toyota, Tri-Nordic, and the Attorney General of Vermont.

Wilbur brought suit in Vermont state court against Tri-Nordic and Toyota in February 1994, alleging that Toyota had violated the MMWA, that Tri-Nordic had violated the Vermont Motor Vehicle Manufacturers, Distributors and Dealers Franchising Practices Act, and that both parties had violated the VCFA. The district court held that because the damage from the accident was excluded from coverage under the warranty as a matter of law, Toyota did not violate the MMWA or the VCFA when it refused to repair Wilbur's car. This appeal followed. . . .

Before discussing the merits, it will be helpful to explain how the parties refer to certain aspects of Toyota's warranty. When referencing the date on which the warranty commenced, the parties mean the date that starts the period in which exclusions spelled out in the warranty apply. Though they sometimes speak as if the warranty is not even applicable to the period before it commenced, they do not mean this literally: if a defect resulted from damage that occurred while the vehicle was being manufactured, for example, the warranty would apply to such a defect. Thus, when Toyota contends that the accident occurred during the warranty period and Wilbur says it did not, Toyota means that the accident exclusion in the warranty applied and relieved Toyota of liability, while Wilbur means that the accident exclusion did not apply and that therefore the warranty entitled her to compensation.

In this case, both sides agree that the warranty would cover a defect resulting from an accident that occurred before delivery to Tri-Nordic and would not cover a defect resulting from an accident that occurred after Wilbur bought the car. They dispute whether the warranty covers an accident that occurred during the period the car was used by Tri-Nordic as a demo.

The district court found that the warranty, with its accident exclusion, went into effect at the start of the demo period, that Wilbur "assumed the remainder of the limited factory warranty" when she bought the Camry and that the accident in October "occurred during the course of the warranty," i.e., at a time when the warranty's accident exclusion was applicable. Because the warranty specifically excluded repairs resulting from accidents, the district court concluded that the damage to Wilbur's car was not covered. The MMWA mandated this conclusion, the district court reasoned, because the accident exclusion was clearly and conspicuously disclosed in accordance with the law.

The central issue in this case is whether the warranty, with its accident exclusion, applied to the period before the in-service date when the car was being used as a demo. The district court found, and Toyota argues on appeal, that the warranty had already begun to run when the accident happened, over seven months before Wilbur purchased the car. A review of the warranty in light of the requirements of the MMWA, however, leads us to a different result.

The Toyota New Vehicle Limited Warranty issued to Wilbur at the time of purchase stated that "[t]he warranty period begins on the date the vehicle is first delivered or put into use (in-service date)." The in-service date was filled in by Tri-Nordic as May 18, 1992—the day Wilbur bought the car. It seems evident, then, that the warranty had not commenced when the accident occurred and that therefore the repairs were not excluded from warranty coverage.

Despite these facts, Toyota claims that a later section of the warranty book entitled "California Emission Control Warranty" makes clear that the warranty period begins on the date the vehicle is first delivered to the ultimate purchaser; or, if the vehicle is first placed into service as "demonstrator" or "company car" prior to delivery, on the date it is first placed into service.

Toyota urges us to treat this isolated language, appearing ten pages later in the warranty book as part of a wholly separate warranty, as a clear indication to Wilbur that the New Vehicle Limited Warranty had commenced at the time of the accident. We are unwilling to do so.

The MMWA grants relief to a consumer "who is damaged by the failure of a . . . warrantor . . . to comply with any obligation . . . under a written warranty." 15 U.S.C. §2310(d)(1) (1994). When drafting a written warranty, Toyota must "fully and conspicuously disclose in simple and readily understood language [its] terms and conditions." 15 U.S.C. §2302(a) (1994). The accompanying regulations define one such term as "[t]he point in time or event on which the warranty term commences, if different from the purchase date." 16 C.F.R. §701.3(a)(4) (1995).

Facially, Toyota's New Vehicle Limited Warranty appears to fulfill the MMWA's clarity requirements: the warranty commences on the in-service date, which is filled in by the dealer when the car is sold. Failure to repair damage sustained before the in-service date therefore puts Toyota in violation of MMWA for breach of warranty. Moreover, Toyota's suggested addition of the California Emission Control Warranty's language renders the time of the warranty's commencement ambiguous at best: Is the "in-service date" the date the car is put into use by the buyer or by the dealer? Under Toyota's own construction, then, the warranty would violate the MMWA because it would not "fully and conspicuously disclose" its commencement date.

Toyota is thus placed in a somewhat uncomfortable position. If it subscribes to a straight reading of its New Vehicle Limited Warranty, it must concede that Wilbur's warranty had not commenced when the accident occurred and that its refusal to repair her car is a breach of warranty. If Toyota stands by the warranty construction it has pressed upon us here, its warranty must be deemed cryptic and unclear. In either case, Wilbur may recover damages under the MMWA.

Concededly, it was the actions of Tri-Nordic, not Toyota, which resulted in the damage to the car that in turn led to this lawsuit. But Toyota provided Wilbur with a new car warranty and gave its dealer the authority to fill in the in-service date. The MMWA, by requiring any warrantor to draft clear warranty terms and conditions, simply incorporates the well-established contract principle of contra proferentem by which a drafting party must be prepared to have ambiguities construed against it. We therefore find that Wilbur's claim under the MMWA cannot be defeated on Toyota's motion for summary judgment and must be allowed to proceed to trial.

Because the district court based its decision in this case on the warranty's accident exclusion and did not address the warranty's commencement date, the court erred in granting summary judgment to Toyota on the MMWA claim. Thus, the district court's grant of summary judgment on Wilbur's state claim, based on its finding that the absence of liability under the MMWA removed any basis for recovery under the VCFA, was also in error. We reverse and remand both claims for reconsideration by the district court.

The preceding case is a good example of a recurring tension that courts are often forced to resolve in cases involving warranty disclaimers: was the loss complained of by the buyer due to a conscious allocation of risk by both parties at the time of contracting (in which case the seller should win), or was the buyer's loss due instead to unfair oppression by the seller (in which case the buyer should win)?

The drafters of Article 2 were well aware of this tension when they put together the various rules governing sales warranties and disclaimers. The only problem was that these UCC drafters apparently also wanted to be both pro-freedom of contract and anti-oppression at the same time. Consider the following examples of the Code's inconsistency on this issue.

From Official Comment 1 to §2-302 (unconscionability): "The principle is one of the prevention of oppression and unfair surprise, and not of disturbance of allocation of risk because of superior bargaining power."

From Official Comment 4 to §2-313 (express warranties): "This is not intended to mean that the parties, if they consciously desire, cannot make their own bargain as they wish. But in determining what they have agreed upon good faith is a factor and consideration should be given to the fact that the probability is small that a real price is intended to be exchanged for a pseudo-obligation."

From Official Comment 3 to §2-719 (limitation of remedies): "Subsection (3) recognizes the validity of clauses limiting or excluding consequential damages but makes it clear that they may not operate in an unconscionable manner. Actually such terms are merely an allocation of unknown or undeterminable risks."

Unfortunately, the Article 2 drafters were better at identifying this tension between freedom of contract and anti-oppression than they were at outlining specific factors to resolve it. When courts are faced with a case highlighting this tension, they tend to consider the following factors either explicitly or implicitly:

1.   The relative bargaining power and sophistication of the parties — is the buyer a consumer or a business person?

2. The price paid—did it appear that the buyer chose to sacrifice greater warranty protection by paying a lower than usual price?
3. Usage of trade, course of dealing, and course of performance—these all provide some clues as to what the parties probably had in mind when they struck their deal.
4. What the words of the contract actually said, including how clearly the limitation of the usual warranty protection was brought home to the buyer, and how well the provisions complied with the technical requirements of Article 2 on disclaimers and limitations of warranty.

B. Warranty Reduction with Leases

For the most part, the provisions in UCC Article 2A concerning a seller's ability to reduce its liability for warranties were directly borrowed from Article 2. In that respect, §2A-214 reads almost like a carbon copy of §2-316. There are, however, two notable differences between §2-316 and §2A-214.

The first difference is that, whereas under §2-316(2) a seller can disclaim the implied warranty of merchantability with a properly worded oral disclaimer, under §2A-214(2) a lessor can disclaim the implied warranty of merchantability only by using a conspicuous written disclaimer. In both §2-316(2) and §2A-214(2), the disclaimer must mention the word "merchantability" to be effective. If the seller chooses to use a written disclaimer of the implied warranty of merchantability under §2-316(2), the disclaimer must be conspicuous, which is consistent with the written disclaimer requirements of §2A-214(2).

The second difference between §2-316 and §2A-214 is the example that each provision gives for properly disclaiming the implied warranty of fitness for a particular purpose. Both provisions provide that such a disclaimer must be in writing and must be conspicuous. The example of a sufficient disclaimer of the fitness warranty given in §2-316(2) is the fairly general statement: "There are no warranties which extend beyond the description on the face hereof." Section 2A-214(2), by contrast, provides an example of a sufficient fitness disclaimer that is much more specific: "There is no warranty that the goods will be fit for a particular purpose."

C. Warranty Reduction with International Sales

As in so many areas, the CISG ends up in much the same place as the UCC with respect to warranty reduction, except that it uses a lot fewer words. The CISG manages to include in one place, Article 35, virtually all of its rules on both warranty creation and warranty reduction.

There are two places within CISG Article 35 where warranty reduction rules can be found. The first is in the introductory clause to Article 35(2). Subsection 35(2) describes four different warranties that arise in a sale of goods covered by the CISG, including the implied warranties of merchantability and fitness for a particular purpose. These obligations of the seller will not arise, however, "where the parties have agreed otherwise." The just-quoted language is the clause that begins subsection (2) of Article 35 and therefore conditions the seller's liability for the warranties subsequently outlined in Article 35(2).

The second part of Article 35 that is relevant for warranty reduction purposes is subsection (3). That subsection is similar in many respects to UCC §2-316(3)(b), which says that a seller is not liable for defects that a buyer ought to have discovered in an examination of the goods, if the buyer either actually examined the goods before purchasing them or refused to do so. CISG Article 35(3) provides, much along the same lines, that a seller is not liable for any nonconformity in the goods if prior to the formation of the sales contract "the buyer knew or could not have been unaware of such lack of conformity." In comparing these two standards of buyer waiver, note that the CISG does not, in contrast to the UCC, impose a duty on the buyer to investigate the goods at the risk of losing warranty rights even if the seller were to make a demand of the buyer.

In general, the CISG seems much more likely to defer to freedom of contract in the realm of warranty reduction, and also seems much less protective of the buyer on this score than is the UCC. That difference is perfectly understandable if you remember from Assignment 2 that the CISG, unlike the UCC, excludes from its scope the sale of goods to consumers. CISG Art. 2(a). The UCC drafters, by contrast, had consumers primarily in mind when they set out to articulate which hoops a seller would need to jump through in order to successfully reduce the seller's usual warranty obligations to the buyer.

D.   Disclaiming the Real Estate Implied Warranty of Habitability

As discussed in Assignment 11, most states have created either by statute or by common law an implied warranty of habitability for buyers of new homes that are built by professional builders. Unlike the comparable context of sales of goods under Article 2, there is no uniform set of rules in the real estate realm that dictate whether and how a home builder might successfully disclaim this implied warranty of habitability.

There is, however, one general observation that can be made about disclaiming the implied warranty of habitability: the builder's only hope for such a disclaimer to work is to put the disclaimer in clear and unmistakable terms. Anything less, as the following case demonstrates, will cause a court to deem the disclaimer ineffective.

Axline v. Kutner

863 S.W.2d 421 (Tenn. Ct. App. 1993)

FARMER, J.

This is an action by a home buyer against the seller/contractor. The trial court granted [the seller's] motion for partial summary judgment. . . .

The implied warranty rule [is] as follows:

> "[w]e hold that in every contract for the sale of a recently completed dwelling, and in every contract for the sale of a dwelling then under construction, the vendor, if he be in the business of building such dwellings, shall be held to impliedly warrant to the initial vendee that, at the time of the passing of the deed or the taking of possession by the initial vendee (whichever first occurs), the dwelling, together with all its fixtures, is sufficiently free from major structural defects, and is constructed in a workmanlike manner, so as to meet the standard of workmanlike quality then prevailing at the time and place of construction; and that this implied warranty in the contract of sale survives the passing of the deed or the taking of possession by the initial vendee." [Hartley v. Ballou 208 S.E.2d 776 (1974).]

Dixon, 632 S.W.2d at 541.

The court in *Dixon* further said that this warranty is implied only when the written contract is silent. Builder-vendors and purchasers are free to contract in writing for a warranty upon different terms and conditions or to expressly disclaim any warranty. The written contract contained no reference as to the quality of workmanship.

Defendants contend that the implied warranty doctrine is not applicable here because of the provision in *Dixon* that the warranty is implied only when the written contract is silent, and that this contract limits the warranty to one (1) year. [We have] held:

> Because the buyer is completely relying on the skills of the vendor-builder in this situation, we think that in order to have a valid disclaimer of the implied warranty, it must be in clear and unambiguous language. The buyer must be given adequate notice of the implied warranty protections that he is waiving by signing the contract. In addition, such a "disclaimer" must be strictly construed against the seller. This is generally the law in other jurisdictions which have adopted this, or a comparable, implied warranty of good workmanship and materials.

Plaintiffs contend that the term "one year builder's warranty" is meaningless because there is no indication what the builder is warranting. Construing strictly against the builder/seller, we are inclined to agree.

Appellees further rely upon the following handwritten language to the contract: "PURCHASER ACCEPTS PROPERTY IN ITS EXISTING CONDITION, NO WARRANTIES OR REPRESENTATIONS HAVING BEEN MADE BY SELLER OR AGENT WHICH ARE NOT EXPRESSLY STATED HEREIN." This exact language was contained in the agreement before the court in Dewberry v. Maddox wherein this court said:

We do not think that this provision is adequate to disclaim the implied warranty. . . . In the setting of the marketplace, the builder or seller of new construction—not unlike the manufacturer or merchandiser of personalty—makes implied representations, ordinarily indispensable to the sale, that the builder has used reasonable skill and judgment in constructing the building. On the other hand, the purchaser does not usually possess the knowledge of the builder and is unable to fully examine a complete house and its components without disturbing the finished product. Further, unlike the purchaser of an older building, he has no opportunity to observe how the building has withstood the passage of time. Thus, he generally relies on those in a position to know the quality of the work to be sold, and his reliance is surely evident to the construction industry.

We conclude that the trial court erred in granting partial summary judgment in this matter and that judgment is reversed. This cause is remanded to the trial court for further proceedings consistent with this opinion.

———————

Another way to view the *Axline* case is as a situation involving the cumulation and conflict of warranties. In other words, when a seller gives both express and implied warranties, how should those warranties be construed in relationship to one another? Although real estate law lacks a widely adopted uniform code like that for sales, one would suspect that courts considering real estate cases would be guided generally by the cumulation and conflict principles set down in UCC §2-317: (1) whenever it is reasonable to do so, warranties should be construed as consistent with one another and therefore as cumulative; and (2) whenever it is unreasonable to construe warranties as consistent with one another, express warranties displace inconsistent implied warranties except for the implied warranty of fitness for a particular purpose.

If the issue in *Axline* had been framed as a case of cumulation and conflict, the builder no doubt would have argued that a one-year express warranty is inherently inconsistent with a more open-ended implied warranty of habitability. Thus, the builder would argue, the one-year express warranty must displace the inconsistent implied warranty of habitability.

The buyers, on the other hand, could have argued that there is nothing inconsistent with cumulating the one-year express warranty, which provides certain rights for a certain length of time, with the lengthier implied warranty of habitability, which provides other rights for a longer period of time. In other words, the buyer could argue that it is not unreasonable to "stack" a limited-duration express warranty with a longer-duration implied warranty.

Problem Set 12

12.1.   Fresh out of law school, you have just opened up your own law practice in a storefront in the neighborhood where you grew up. One of your first clients is Mrs. McGillicudy, your former next-door neighbor, who remembers you back when "you just barely came up to my knees." It turns out that Mrs. McGillicudy had just bought a used Cadillac from the local used-car lot, Lou's Used Cars for Less. Three weeks after the purchase, the Cadillac was giving Mrs. McGillicudy a host of problems that she wanted Lou's to repair. When she brought the car back in, Lou pulled out the contract that she had signed and pointed out a clause that said there were no warranties included with the sale of this car. You take a look at the contract, which includes the following clause in very fine print: "There are no warranties, express or implied, that are included as a part of this sale." You ask Mrs. McGillicudy if she read that clause before purchasing the car. "Of course, dear," she says. "I always read everything carefully before I sign something." Is there still hope for Mrs. McGillicudy in having her car repaired by Lou's? UCC §§2-316, 1-201(b)(10).

12.2. It seems that Lou's Used Cars for Less is going to be a steady source of business for your fledgling law practice. Another dissatisfied customer of Lou's comes to you for advice. Deborah Swift (from Problem 1.6), your erstwhile law school classmate and a current personal-injury lawyer, asks for your advice concerning a recent transaction she had with Lou's. Deborah purchased a used Jeep Cherokee from Lou's a few weeks ago, and she discovered only yesterday that the vehicle has a serious engine problem. When Deborah brought the Jeep back to Lou's for repair, he pointed out to her that he had asked her to check out the Jeep before buying it and she had refused. "I was in a hurry," Deborah told you. "If I had spent a lot of time examining the car, I might have been able to discover the problem, but that's only because I tinker with used cars as a hobby." Does Deborah have a reasonable basis for demanding that Lou repair her Jeep? UCC §2-316(3)(b), Official Comment 8 to §2-316.

12.3. After you have won several cases against Lou's Used Cars for Less, Lou has convinced his big law firm, Dewey, Cheatem & Howe, to hire you to work for them. Now Lou wants you to look at his standard sales contract with an eye toward re-drafting it. Based on a couple of your previous victories against him, Lou knows that he needs to increase the prominence of his implied warranty disclaimer and to use the word "merchantability." Lou wonders if there is any mileage (no pun intended, he says) in including a prominent disclaimer of express warranties as well. "You know those sales people," he says. "They'll say darn near anything to sell a car, bless their souls." What do you advise Lou? Are there other clauses you recommend including in the contract to prevent the sales people from "giving away the store"? UCC §§2-316(1), 2-202, Official Comment 2 to §2-316.

12.4. Since joining Dewey, Cheatem & Howe, you seem to be getting as many cases for Lou's Used Cars for Less as you used to get against him when you were on your own. Your next defense for Lou involves a buyer who bought a used Ford Taurus wagon from Lou's. A month after the purchase, the brakes failed on the car and the buyer was seriously injured, although the car was not damaged. Lou's contract for that sale involved a conspicuous limitation of remedy to repair or replace defective parts. Lou says he is happy to repair the car's brakes, but he doesn't feel like paying thousands of dollars in hospital bills. Lou asks you whether the exclusive remedy will be effective here. He also wants to know if it would have helped him in this case if he had included a prominent "AS IS" clause instead of the exclusive remedy. What do you say to Lou on these two questions? UCC §§2-719, 2-316(3)(a), 2-302; Official Comment 2 to §2-316, Official Comments 1 and 3 to §2-719.

12.5. Dan and Carol Pontello, who had a new home built by Cannon Construction Co. six years ago, recently came to see you in your law office. Their home had come with a written "Builder's Warranty" providing that "Builder warrants that the home will be free of defects in material and workmanship for a period of five years on the foundation and for a period of two years on all other parts of the home. The five-year foundation warranty includes a warranty against any cracks or water seepage." The contract also contained a merger clause, separately signed by both buyer and seller, which said, "This contract is the complete and final understanding of the agreement between the parties and supersedes any and all other agreements or rights implied by law that are not contained within the four corners of this agreement." Six years after the signing of this contract, the foundation suddenly developed significant cracks, leading to costly basement flooding. The Pontellos point out to you that most of their friends who had new houses built got 10-year foundation warranties and, further, that most foundations in new houses around this area last without problems for at least 10 years. The Pontellos want to know if they have a good cause of action against Cannon Construction for the cracks in their foundation. What do you tell them?

Assignment 13: Reducing or Eliminating Warranty Liability: Advanced

Perhaps the most efficient way to analyze the major state and federal regulations concerning warranty limitations is to consider those regulations in the context of an actual warranty disclaimer provision. Consider the following clause, which is the warranty provided on a consumer swingset:

FULL 90-DAY WARRANTY ON MISSING OR DEFECTIVE PARTS

Seller will promptly supply without charge any missing part provided that a description of the missing part and the model number of the product is given to Seller during the 90-day warranty period, which begins on the date of purchase. Seller will promptly repair or replace without charge any defective part provided the part is returned to Seller during the 90-day warranty period, which begins on the date of purchase. The warranty does not apply to defects discovered after purchase which were caused by damage (not resulting from defects) or which were caused by unreasonable use. SELLER MAKES NO OTHER WARRANTIES, EXPRESS OR IMPLIED, WITH RESPECT TO ITS PRODUCTS, THEIR MERCHANTABILITY, OR FITNESS FOR A PARTICULAR PURPOSE. IN NO CASE SHALL SELLER BE LIABLE FOR ANY INCIDENTAL OR CONSEQUENTIAL DAMAGES FOR BREACH OF THIS OR ANY OTHER WARRANTY, EXPRESSED OR IMPLIED, WHATSOEVER, EXCEPT THAT DAMAGES FOR PERSONAL INJURIES SHALL NOT BE PRECLUDED. SOME STATES DO NOT ALLOW THE EXCLUSION OR LIMITATION OF CONSEQUENTIAL OR INCIDENTAL DAMAGES, SO THE ABOVE LIMITATIONS OR EXCLUSIONS MAY NOT APPLY TO YOU.

Let us now walk through this warranty, part by part, to consider what warranty laws are implicated.

"FULL 90-DAY WARRANTY ON MISSING OR DEFECTIVE PARTS." This heading is in direct response to the Magnuson-Moss Act's "truth in labeling" provisions that were discussed in Assignment 10. Magnuson-Moss §103(a)(1) requires that if the written warranty meets the federal minimum standards set down in §104(a), then the warranty shall conspicuously be designated as a "full (statement of duration) warranty." Note the 90-day "statement of duration."

"Seller will promptly supply without charge any missing part. . . . Seller will promptly repair or replace without charge any defective part. . . ." Here the seller is making explicit what Magnuson-Moss would require it to do anyway as a seller that makes a full warranty. 15 U.S.C. §2304(a)(1). Note, too, that at the end of these two sentences the seller makes clear that the 90-day durational limit on the full warranty begins on the date of purchase, rather than on, say, the date of first use by the consumer.

"The warranty does not apply to defects discovered after purchase which were caused by damage (not resulting from defects) or which were caused by unreasonable use." Here the seller is stating that which would be true even in the absence of this statement: the seller is not responsible for defects that arise following the buyer's purchase that are caused either by the buyer's own misuse or by external forces that are unrelated to a defect in the product. This is because the normal obligation of a warrantor does not include acting as an insurer of the goods warranted, nor does Magnuson-Moss require such an obligation on the part of the warrantor.

"SELLER MAKES NO OTHER WARRANTIES, EXPRESS OR IMPLIED, WITH RESPECT TO ITS PRODUCTS, THEIR MERCHANTABILITY, OR FITNESS FOR A PARTICULAR PURPOSE." Here the seller attempts in one fell swoop to disclaim all three Article 2 quality warranties: the express warranty, the implied warranty of merchantability, and the implied warranty of fitness for a particular purpose.

To the seller's credit, it is not purporting to disclaim the express warranties it made in the words immediately above this sentence; it is instead purporting to disclaim any "other" express warranties that may have been made. The general rule about disclaiming express warranties is that once express warranties are made, they cannot be disclaimed. UCC §2-316(1). If the express warranty is oral, however, the parol evidence rule may prevent the statement from being introduced into evidence. UCC §2-202.

As for the implied warranties of merchantability and fitness, the seller seems to have done all of the right things under Article 2 to make these disclaimers effective. UCC §2-316(2). To disclaim the implied warranty of merchantability, the seller's language must specifically mention "merchantability," and if the disclaimer is in writing, the writing must be conspicuous. Id. To disclaim the implied warranty of fitness for a particular purpose, the disclaimer must be in writing and must be conspicuous. Id. Alternatively, the seller could exclude all implied warranties under Article 2 by simply using the phrase "as is" or similar language "which in common understanding calls the buyer's attention to the exclusion of warranties and makes plain that there is no implied warranty." UCC §2-316(3)(a).

There is just one problem with the swingset seller's attempt to disclaim the two implied warranties: Magnuson-Moss says that any such disclaimer by a full warrantor, such as this seller, will be ineffective. In particular, Magnuson-Moss says at §108(a) that "[n]o such supplier may disclaim or modify (except as provided in subsection (b) of this section) any implied warranty to a consumer with respect to such consumer product if (1) such supplier makes any written warranty to the consumer with respect to such consumer product. . . ." Section 108(c) then says that "[a] disclaimer, modification, or limitation made in violation of this section shall be ineffective for purposes of this [Act] and State law."

There are at least two possible explanations for why this seller bothered to attempt something that Magnuson-Moss says it cannot do: (1) Even if the disclaimer is legally ineffective, the average consumer may not know this and therefore may fail to pursue remedies because of the erroneous assumption that the disclaimer is effective. (2) The written warranty provided here does not apply to the "product" but merely to the product's "missing or defective parts." Therefore, the §108(a) prohibition of implied warranty disclaimers does not kick in at all here, since §108(a) governs only those suppliers that have made written warranties with respect to the consumer "product." As a matter of statutory interpretation, this argument seems dubious at best. Thus, as §108(c) of Magnuson-Moss provides, the attempted disclaimer of the implied warranty of merchantability should be ineffective.

Before leaving the subject of Magnuson-Moss, it should be noted that sellers who make "limited" rather than "full" written warranties are similarly prevented from disclaiming the implied warranties completely, but they are (unlike "full warrantors") authorized to limit the duration of the implied warranties. 15 U.S.C. §2308(b). Thus, for example, a seller that has made a "Limited 90-Day Warranty" would be authorized by Magnuson-Moss to limit the duration of the implied warranties to a period no shorter than 90 days. A seller making a "Full 90-Day Warranty" is not allowed to limit the duration of the implied warranties.

"IN NO CASE SHALL SELLER BE LIABLE FOR ANY INCIDENTAL OR CONSEQUENTIAL DAMAGES FOR BREACH OF THIS OR ANY OTHER WARRANTY, EXPRESS OR IMPLIED, WHATSOEVER, EXCEPT THAT DAMAGES FOR PERSONAL INJURIES SHALL NOT BE PRECLUDED." One effective way for sellers to reduce their warranty exposure is to limit the remedies available to the buyer in the event that the seller does breach a warranty. Article 2 authorizes a seller to create certain remedies that will be the buyer's exclusive remedies, such as repair or replacement of defective parts. UCC §2-719(1)(a). In order for the exclusive remedy provision to be effective, the seller must make clear to the buyer the exclusivity of the stated remedy. UCC §2-719(1)(b).

Any exclusive remedy may be invalidated if the court determines that circumstances caused the remedy to "fail of its essential purpose." UCC §2-719(2). This might be the case, for example, where a car seller limits the buyer's remedy to repair or replacement of defective parts, and the whole car is damaged badly due to the malfunction of one small part. In that case, the buyer would justifiably argue that the purpose of the limited remedy was to give the buyer a car that ran consistently. If the seller is allowed to replace only the one small defective part, the buyer can argue that unforeseen circumstances (the damage caused to the rest of the car) caused this limited remedy to fail of its essential purpose. When an exclusive or limited remedy fails of its essential purpose, then "remedy may be had as provided in this Act." UCC §2-719(2).

Although at the beginning of the swingset warranty quoted above this seller mentioned repair or replacement of defective parts, the seller did not attempt to make that the buyer's exclusive remedy for breach of warranty. The seller did, however, later include the separate exclusion of consequential damages. UCC §2-719(3) allows such exclusions of consequential damages unless the exclusion is "unconscionable"; the subsection goes on to state that "[l]imitation of consequential damages for injury to the person in the case of consumer goods is prima facie unconscionable. . . ." This explains why the seller included the phrase "DAMAGES FOR PERSONAL INJURIES SHALL NOT BE PRECLUDED." If the seller had not included this qualification concerning recovery for personal injuries, a court could well have voided as unconscionable the entire consequential damages disclaimer, even as it applies to consequential damages for things other than personal injury. UCC §2-302(1) (when a court finds a term or an entire contract to be unconscionable, it may "refuse to enforce the contract, or it may enforce the remainder of the contract without the unconscionable clause, or it may so limit the application of any unconscionable clause as to avoid any unconscionable result").

Although Magnuson-Moss creates limits on a consumer product seller's ability to disclaim implied warranties, Magnuson-Moss does not contain many restrictions on the seller's ability to limit the buyer's remedies. If a seller makes a full written warranty, then Magnuson-Moss creates two minor restrictions on a seller's ability to limit the buyer's remedies for breach of warranty. First, the seller must make conspicuous on the face of the warranty any exclusions or limitations of consequential damages, 15 U.S.C. §2304(a)(3) (even with a limited warranty, Magnuson-Moss requires an exclusion of consequential damages to be conspicuous, but the exclusion does not have to appear on the face of warranty, 16 C.F.R §701.3(a)(8)); and second, the seller must allow the buyer to get a replacement or a full refund for a defective product when the seller is unable to remedy malfunctions in the product after a reasonable number of attempts, 15 U.S.C. §2304(a)(4).

One last point to note about this warranty concerns privity, a subject explored first in Assignment 9. If this warranty is being given by the consumer's direct seller, privity will not be a problem. If, however, the warranty is being provided indirectly by the manufacturer, then the aggrieved buyer will have to overcome lack of vertical privity in a warranty suit against the manufacturer. The reason that the distinction could matter here is that the Magnuson-Moss prohibition of implied warranty disclaimers will not mean much to a remote seller that is not responsible for an implied warranty to the ultimate buyer in the first place. As we saw in Assignment 10, however, courts are split as to whether Magnuson-Moss removes a consumer's need for vertical privity in an implied warranty suit against a manufacturer.

Whenever a direct seller gives a written warranty or service contract to a consumer buyer, that seller has precluded its ability to disclaim the implied warranties of merchantability because of Magnuson-Moss. As the next case demonstrates, this will hold true even when the seller is selling used consumer goods on an "as is" basis.

Ismael v. Goodman Toyota

417 S.E.2d 290 (N.C. Ct. App. 1992)

WELLS, J.

Plaintiff instituted this action to recover damages he allegedly suffered as a result of his purchase of a used car from defendant. Plaintiff claimed that the defendant breached its implied warranty of merchantability because the car was unroadworthy, was not repairable at the time of purchase and was therefore unfit for its particular purpose. The case was heard by the trial court without a jury.

Plaintiff's evidence tended to show the following facts and circumstances. On 13 April 1989, plaintiff purchased a used 1985 Ford Tempo, with recorded mileage of 58,810, from defendant. The purchase price was $5,054.00. Additionally, plaintiff simultaneously purchased from defendant a Vehicle Service Agreement for $695.00, which was to cover the car for 24 months or 24,000 miles, whichever first occurred. Plaintiff testified that defendant assured him the service agreement would cover the car's engine, transmission, axles, brakes and air conditioning among other things. Plaintiff traded in a 1985 Ford Escort wagon valued at $1,600.00 in exchange for the Tempo and service agreement. Plaintiff financed the remaining purchase price of $4,626.44. The total cost of the Ford Tempo, including finance charges, was $7,414.60.

Plaintiff testified that he and his wife noticed the car "shook" during their test drive on the night of their purchase. Defendant's salesman assured them that the car "probably just needed a tune-up and that Goodman would repair anything that was found wrong with the car at no charge." Plaintiff admitted he purchased the car "as is" but contended he did so only because of the salesman's assurance of repair and because of the vehicle service agreement he purchased to cover the car.

On the day after plaintiff purchased the car, he returned it to defendant for repair because "the engine kept cutting off, the engine light stayed on, and the car pulled from side to side, shook badly and made loud noises." During the first four months of his ownership, plaintiff had to return the car to defendant for repairs on at least six occasions. Defendant did not charge for these repairs, and did not file claims under the service agreement. Each time defendant returned the car to plaintiff, plaintiff was assured it was fixed. However, plaintiff was never able to keep the car for more than three days before having to return it to defendant again for repair. Defendant kept the car one to three weeks every time plaintiff returned the car. Plaintiff had use of the car for less than two weeks of his first four months of ownership.

Plaintiff finally decided to stop taking the car back to defendant for repairs. Plaintiff testified that defendant told him that the car could not be repaired and that the problems he was experiencing with the car were normally experienced with used 4-cylinder cars. Plaintiff then spent in excess of $900.00 trying to have the car repaired by various Ford dealer service departments and auto mechanics to no avail. Plaintiff was told the car was not repairable due to sludge in the engine. The car has not been driven since December 1989. However, plaintiff continued to make payments of $193.82 on the car each month up to the time of trial in order to protect his credit record. From April 1989 to the time of trial, plaintiff was able to drive the car a total of only 700 miles.

Defendant offered evidence in the form of testimony by David Goodman. Defendant's evidence tended to show that all of the used cars on defendant's lot are in varying conditions. Further, defendant sells all of its used cars "as is" and the "purchase price is adjusted according to the car's worth and its mileage." Goodman further testified that the Tempo's mileage was very high when plaintiff purchased the car and that plaintiff had not maintained the car in a clean fashion.

In its judgment, the trial court made findings of fact, entered conclusions of law and denied any relief to plaintiff. The trial court concluded that plaintiff had purchased the vehicle in used "as is" condition and defendant "assumed and bore no responsibility for subsequent repair of the vehicle or its roadworthiness." The trial court further concluded defendant was not liable to plaintiff "for negligence or breach of warranty, as the duty and warranty obligations in this matter ran to the General Warranty company under the service contract and not to Defendant dealership." The trial court held that plaintiff was not entitled to have and recover damages from defendant. Plaintiff appealed from this judgment.

On appeal, plaintiff contends, inter alia, that the trial court erred in making the following conclusions of law:

CONCLUSIONS OF LAW

. . .

2. Due to the purchase of the subject vehicle in used "as is" condition, the Defendant dealer assumed and bore no responsibility for subsequent repair of the vehicle or its roadworthiness.

3. Defendant also bore no responsibility for repairing the vehicle, notwithstanding any alleged verbal promises and agreements made subsequent to the purchase of the vehicle in "as is" condition.

4. Defendant is not liable to Plaintiff for negligence or breach of warranty, as the duty and warranty obligations in this matter ran to the General Warranty company under the service contract and not to defendant dealership.

The underlying premise of plaintiff's contention is that defendant violated the Magnuson-Moss Warranty Act and is therefore liable for damages plaintiff suffered as a result of that violation.

We first point out that on appeal the trial court's conclusions of law are reviewable de novo. After a thorough review of the record in this case, we agree with plaintiff's foregoing contention for the reasons set forth below.

In 1975, Congress passed the Magnuson-Moss Warranty-Federal Trade Commission Improvement Act (hereinafter the "Act"), 15 U.S.C.A. §§2301 et seq. (West 1982), which applies to consumer products manufactured after 4 July 1975. 15 U.S.C.A. §2312(a). The Act was passed in an attempt to make warranties on consumer products more understandable and enforceable and further to establish a more effective procedural mechanism for consumer claims which typically involve a small amount of damages and for which a remedy may otherwise be unavailable. . . .

In order for this plaintiff to have established his entitlement to relief under the Act, he must have shown he was damaged by the defendant's failure to comply with an obligation under the Act, the service contract, and/or an implied warranty. 15 U.S.C.A. §2310(d)(1). Defendant contends that since the uncontradicted evidence proved the car was sold "as is," all express and implied warranties were effectively disclaimed pursuant to our Uniform Commercial Code, specifically N.C. Gen. Stat. §25-2-316(3)(a), and therefore plaintiff had no claim for breach of an implied warranty. Defendant also contends that since no express or implied warranties were given, the Act does not apply in this case. We disagree.

"Implied warranty" as defined by the Act is "an implied warranty arising under State law (as modified by sections 2308 and 2304(a) of this title) in connection with the sale by a supplier of a consumer product." 15 U.S.C.A. §2301(7). Under our Uniform Commercial Code, an implied warranty of merchantability arises in a contract for the sale of goods by a merchant unless excluded or modified. Furthermore, our courts have specifically held that an implied warranty of merchantability arises upon the sale of a used car by a dealer.

Defendant correctly contends that, as a general rule, the implied warranty of merchantability is excluded by an "as is" sale. N.C. Gen. Stat. §25-2-316(3)(a). However, the Act significantly limits a supplier's ability to modify or disclaim implied warranties. 15 U.S.C.A. §2308(a). If, at the time of sale or within 90 days thereafter, a supplier enters into a service contract with the consumer which applies to such consumer product, the supplier may not disclaim or modify any implied warranty with respect to that product. Id. Furthermore, a disclaimer made in violation of §2308(a) is ineffective for purposes of the Act and State law. 15 U.S.C.A. §2308(c).

The Act defines the term "service contract" as "a contract in writing to perform, over a fixed period of time or for a specified duration, services relating to the maintenance or repair (or both) of a consumer product." 15 U.S.C.A. §2301(8). Further, in its "Rules, Regulations, Statements and Interpretations Under the Magnuson-Moss Warranty Act," the FTC gave examples of what was meant by the term "service contract" as used in the Act. The FTC stated, inter alia, that "an agreement which calls for some consideration in addition to the purchase price of the consumer product, or which is entered into at some date after the purchase of the consumer product to which it applies, is a service contract." 16 C.F.R. §700.11(c).

In this case, the evidence that plaintiff and defendant, at the time of sale, entered into a written service contract for repair of the Tempo was undisputed. The agreement was a service contract within the meaning of the Act because it was in writing and defendant agreed to perform certain repairs for a specified duration (24,000 miles) or fixed period of time (24 months). Further, the plaintiff paid defendant an additional $695.00 for the contract. Therefore, under §2308(a)(2) of the Act, defendant was prohibited from disclaiming the implied warranty of merchantability which arose in the contract of sale under State law and the "as is" sale was ineffective as a disclaimer of this warranty.

We conclude that plaintiff could properly seek relief under §2310(d)(1) of the Act because defendant violated the Act when he failed to comply with §2308.

Furthermore, plaintiff could pursue a claim for breach of the implied warranty of merchantability which arose upon this sale since the disclaimer was ineffective for purposes of the Act and State law. Accordingly, we hold that the trial court's conclusions of law numbered 2 and 3 were erroneous. . . .

For the reasons set forth above, we hold that the trial court erred in concluding that (1) defendant bore no responsibility for subsequent repair of the vehicle or its roadworthiness, (2) defendant bore no responsibility for repairing the vehicle notwithstanding any agreements made subsequent to the purchase of the vehicle in "as is" condition, (3) defendant is not liable to plaintiff for breach of warranty, and (4) plaintiff is not entitled to recover any money from defendant.

Since, as stated earlier, plaintiff conclusively established his entitlement to relief, the only issue remaining to be resolved is the amount of damages to which plaintiff is entitled. Following a partial new trial on the issue of damages, the trial court shall enter an appropriate judgment consistent with this opinion. Since the issues above are dispositive of this appeal, we decline to address plaintiff's other assignments of error.

REVERSED AND REMANDED.

Problem Set 13

13.1.   a. Because his car lot's reputation for quality has been going downhill lately, Lou (of Lou's Used Cars for Less) is thinking of offering a new warranty for all of his used cars. He would title it in big bold letters as a "Full One-Year Warranty." However, he would also like to include as part of the warranty the following limitations: a complete disclaimer of the implied warranty of merchantability or at least some limit on its duration, an exclusive remedy to repair or replacement of defective parts, and a separate exclusion of consequential damages. If Lou creates the Full One-Year Warranty, which of his proposed limitations will be allowable, and what issues might arise in his attempts to include these warranty limitations? 15 U.S.C. §§2304(a) and (e), 2308.

b. How would your answer change if Lou's warranty were a "Limited One-Year Warranty"?

13.2.   Imagine that you get a call from a friend who purchased the swingset that carries the warranty printed earlier in this assignment. Four months after this purchase, your friend's son was injured when the chain snapped on the swing he was using. Your friend wonders whether he can recover damages for his son's injuries despite the warranty. (Put aside tort possibilities for the purposes of this problem.) What is your advice to him? UCC §§2-314(2)(c), 2-316(2), 2-317, 2-719(3); 15 U.S.C. §2308.

13.3.   a. Acme Advertising Agency enters into a contract with Hard Drive Computer Co. for the purchase of an office computer system. The price is $38,000. The contract says in boldface that the seller, Hard Drive, makes no warranties except that the goods are merchantable, and even with respect to that warranty, notice of breach must be given within four months of the sale or the buyer has no remedy. Five months after the sale, the computer system breaks down. Acme gives Hard Drive notice of the problem, but Hard Drive says it is simply too late for Acme to make a claim for breach. The Acme president complains, "Wait, that's not fair. I gave you notice of this problem as soon as I discovered it. And there was just no way I could have discovered it until right now, five months after the sale." Hard Drive refuses to fix the system, and Acme sues for breach of the warranty of merchantability. If you were the judge on these facts, in whose favor would you rule? UCC §§2-607(3)(a), 1-302(b); Official Comment 1 to §1-302; §2-316, Official Comment 1 to §2-316; §§2-317, 2-719.

b. Same facts as part (a), except now suppose that a computer system like this (without a specific time limit on notice of breach) normally would sell for $80,000 rather than the $38,000 that this seller sold it for. Now how would you rule?

Assignment 14: Commercial Impracticability

A. Commercial Impracticability with Sales of Goods

From the perspectives of the buyer and the seller, every agreement to transfer goods for a price involves various elements of risk. The seller is gambling that it can actually deliver the goods, either by producing the goods itself or by obtaining them from some third party. The seller is also taking the risk that the price for which it has agreed to sell the goods will not prove to be unduly low in light of later market shifts.

The buyer, in turn, accepts the risk that it will not want the goods by the time they are to be delivered. The buyer is also taking on the risk that the price it has agreed to pay will not prove to be unreasonably high in light of any post-bargain but pre-performance market movements.

Events don't always turn out the way that the parties to a sales contract want them to. Sometimes the seller is unable to obtain the goods that it thought it could; sometimes the price of goods shifts significantly in a way that makes the original deal very unprofitable for either the buyer or the seller. As a general matter, the sales system says that's just too bad for the unlucky buyer or seller. The very nature of a sales contract is that both parties are assuming certain risks, which risks inherently constitute some of the consideration being extended by each side to the deal.

Nevertheless, some contingencies are thought to be so far out of the realm of what either party could reasonably anticipate that the occurrence of one of these contingencies might excuse performance by the adversely affected party. These special contingencies generally fall into two categories: an unexpected failure of seller's source of supply or a dramatic price fluctuation. The first category would be a basis only for a seller's excuse. The second category might excuse either buyer or seller.

At this point it makes sense to try to clarify two common sources of confusion with respect to the doctrine of commercial impracticability. The first confusing issue is the distinction between the scope of §2-613, Casualty to Identified Goods, and the scope of the more general impracticability provision, §2-615. Section 2-613 applies only where "the contract *requires* for its performance goods identified when the contract is made" (emphasis added), and the goods are damaged or destroyed through no fault of either party before risk of their loss has passed to the buyer. In such a case, the seller is excused from performance although the buyer will then have a specific opportunity to buy the damaged goods at a reduced price.

For a case to qualify under §2-613, it is not enough that the seller happened to identify particular goods for the buyer that end up being destroyed. The nature of the contract must be such that the contract requires for its performance certain goods that are identified when the contract is made: "I'll buy that painting"; "I'll sell you my Prince tennis racket." If a seller earmarks certain fungible goods for the buyer and they end up being destroyed, the seller's only hope for excuse must come from §2-615 rather than §2-613.

Once it is determined that §2-613 applies, that section sets out two possibilities. First, if the loss is "total," then the contract is avoided completely. Second, §2-613(b) says that if the loss is "partial," then "the buyer may nevertheless demand inspection and at his option either treat the contract as avoided or accept the goods with due allowance from the contract price for the deterioration." For example, suppose you contracted to sell your car to a buyer for $5,000 and your car suffered a $1,000 dent prior to your tendering the car to the buyer. Per §2-613(b), your buyer would have the option to either avoid the contract or to buy the car for $4,000 rather than $5,000, with the new price reflecting a "due allowance" for the dent.

The second common source of confusion in the excuse area is the functional consequence of a seller qualifying for excuse when goods are destroyed while in the seller's care. Here one must distinguish between risk of loss, on one hand, and excuse from performance, on the other. If the seller in this case qualifies for excuse, that does not change the risk of loss: the seller still owned the goods at the time of destruction and, therefore, the seller suffered an economic loss to that extent.

Yet, even though the seller still suffers the risk of loss, qualifying for excuse means that the seller will not suffer a further loss: paying damages to the buyer for seller's delay or nonperformance. These damages might include such things as loss of a good bargain for the buyer or consequential damages that the buyer suffers. These are all items that go beyond the cost of the destroyed goods themselves.

The UCC is not especially helpful in defining what circumstances excuse a party from its performance obligations. The relevant sections, 2-613 to 2-616, speak strictly in terms of a seller's ability to be excused. However, Official Comment 9 of §2-615 suggests that a buyer may also be covered by that section in the case of a requirements or outputs contract. Furthermore, some courts have been willing to consider a buyer's defense of excuse in a sale of goods case simply by reference to the common law of excuse. Whether it is a buyer or seller claiming excuse, the doctrine can only apply in a case where the sales contract has not already been fully performed.

Turbines Ltd. v. Transupport, Inc.

825 N.W.2d 767 (Neb. 2013)

STEPHAN, J.

Turbines Ltd. (Turbines), a Nebraska corporation, purchased a replacement part for a helicopter engine from Transupport, Incorporated, a New Hampshire corporation, intending to use the part to fill an order Turbines had received from a customer in Singapore to be shipped to Malaysia. When Turbines learned that filling the order could subject it to criminal liability under federal law, Turbines attempted to return the part to Transupport and obtain a refund of the $30,000 purchase price. Transupport refused to refund the payment, and Turbines brought this action in the district court for Cuming County, seeking rescission of the purchase order. Although served with summons and notice of the proceedings, Transupport failed to appear at both a pretrial conference and the trial. After receiving evidence, the district court entered judgment in favor of Turbines. Eight days later, Transupport appeared through counsel and filed motions for new trial and to vacate the judgment. The district court overruled those motions, and Transupport appealed. The Nebraska Court of Appeals determined that the district court did not err in overruling the posttrial motions. But the Court of Appeals reversed the default judgment against Transupport and ordered that Turbines' complaint be dismissed, reasoning the evidence adduced at trial did not support rescission as a matter of law. We granted Turbines' petition for further review and now affirm the judgment of the Court of Appeals.

BACKGROUND

FACTS

Turbines, owned by Marvin Kottman, is in the business of helicopter sales and support. Sometime in late 2006 or early 2007, Monarch Aviation (Monarch) contacted Turbines' office in Singapore seeking to purchase a turbine nozzle. Turbines did not have the nozzle in its inventory, so it approached Transupport, a turbine engine parts supplier with which it had done business since the mid-1980s. Turbines told Transupport that it wanted the nozzle for a customer in Singapore, whom it did not otherwise identify, and e-mail correspondence between Transupport and Turbines reflects a discussion about the customer's requests and requirements. Kottman testified that the customer referred to in the e-mails was Monarch and that Transupport was aware of Turbines' plans to ship the nozzle to Malaysia.

Turbines purchased the nozzle from Transupport for $30,000 and tendered payment with the purchase order. Under the "Remarks" section, the purchase order states, "Subject to Inspection and acceptance by customer." Kottman testified he inserted this language to document that he had explained to Transupport that he had no use for the nozzle and that if it was unacceptable to his customer, he would return the nozzle to Transupport. But additional text on the purchase order stated: "Turbines . . . is Transupport's customer, acceptance/rejection is always at customer." Kottman testified that this notation was not on the purchase order when it was sent to Transupport.

Transupport shipped the nozzle to Turbines with an accompanying invoice showing that the purchase price had been prepaid. The invoice stated that Transupport was not the "USPPI" for the item. Kottman explained that USPPI is a customs term for U.S. principal party of interest; a USPPI is required for all exports of goods. Boilerplate language at the bottom of the invoice states that the sale may include munitions list items or commerce-controlled list items and indicates that a license may be required for export. The back of the invoice includes Transupport's return policy: "NO RETURNS WITH OUT [sic] PRIOR AUTHORIZATION. NO RETURNS AFTER 90 DAYS." Kottman testified that he never agreed to this return policy.

Turbines attempted to ship the nozzle to Malaysia as directed by Monarch. The nozzle was seized in February 2007 by U.S. Customs and Border Protection (U.S. Customs), which claimed that a license from the U.S. Department of State was required to ship the nozzle overseas. After several appeals, it was determined that no license was required, and the nozzle was returned to Turbines sometime after January 2009. Turbines kept Transupport informed of the status of the nozzle during the contested seizure by U.S. Customs.

During the time that U.S. Customs retained the nozzle, Turbines learned that Monarch was redirecting goods to Iran, a prohibited destination, and that a person associated with Monarch had become the subject of a federal indictment. The indictment was unsealed in August 2007, 6 months after the parties' transaction was completed. Under federal law, if Turbines shipped the nozzle to Monarch after learning this information, it was subject to criminal penalties. Thus, after receiving the nozzle from U.S. Customs, Turbines returned it to Transupport and requested that the purchase price be refunded. Transupport refused to do so and eventually shipped the nozzle back to Turbines' counsel. . . .

COURT OF APPEALS' OPINION

Transupport appealed, and assigned and argued to the Court of Appeals that the district court erred in (1) striking its answer, (2) overruling its motion to vacate judgment and motion for new trial, and (3) determining Turbines was entitled to rescission. The Court of Appeals determined that the district court did not err in striking Transupport's purported answer, reasoning Foote was not a member of the Nebraska Bar and therefore his letter was a nullity. The Court of Appeals determined the district court did not abuse its discretion in overruling Transupport's motion to vacate judgment, reasoning Transupport failed to protect its own interests by ignoring the district court's orders and failing to appear for trial. The Court of Appeals also upheld the district court's ruling on Transupport's motion for new trial, determining that the motion did not set out any statutory grounds for a new trial as specified in §25-1142, but instead alleged statutory grounds for a motion to vacate.

But ultimately, the Court of Appeals found Transupport was entitled to relief because the evidence did not support rescission of the contract. It found that Neb. UCC §2-615 (Reissue 2001) did not support rescission, because that section excuses a seller from timely delivering goods, and Transupport had delivered the nozzle. The court also found the doctrine of supervening frustration did not support rescission, because it was "impossible to say that a 'basic assumption' of the contract was Turbines' ability to export the nozzle to Monarch." Lastly, the Court of Appeals concluded that a unilateral mistake did not permit rescission, reasoning that enforcement of the contract would not be unconscionable. Turbines timely filed a petition for further review, which we granted. . . .

ANALYSIS

* * *

Generally, grounds for cancellation or rescission of a contract include fraud, duress, unilateral or mutual mistake, and inadequacy of consideration. Turbines' complaint does not identify any specific legal grounds for rescission and does not include any allegations of fraud or duress on the part of Transupport. In its brief filed in the Court of Appeals, Turbines relied on §2-615 and "common law contractual principles related to supervening impracticability" as its legal grounds for rescission. The Court of Appeals examined the record and concluded that the pleadings and evidence did not provide a legal basis for rescission under §2-615, the doctrines of supervening impracticability or supervening frustration, or unilateral mistake. On further review, Turbines argues that the Court of Appeals erred in its analysis of these theories and failed to consider others.

UNIFORM COMMERCIAL CODE §2-615

Section 2–615 provides:

> Except so far as a seller may have assumed a greater obligation and subject to the preceding section on substituted performance:
>
> (a) Delay in delivery or nondelivery in whole or in part by a seller who complies with paragraphs (b) and (c) is not a breach of his duty under a contract for sale if performance as agreed has been made impracticable by the occurrence of a contingency the nonoccurrence of which was a basic assumption on which the contract was made or by compliance in good faith with any applicable foreign or domestic governmental regulation or order whether or not it later proves to be invalid.
>
> (b) Where the causes mentioned in paragraph (a) affect only a part of the seller's capacity to perform, he must allocate production and deliveries among his customers but may at his option include regular customers not then under contract as well as his own requirements for further manufacture. He may so allocate in any manner which is fair and reasonable.

(c) The seller must notify the buyer seasonably that there will be delay or nonde-livery and, when allocation is required under paragraph (b), of the estimated quota thus made available for the buyer.

Comment 1 to §2-615 states that it "excuses a seller from timely delivery of goods contracted for, where his or her performance has become commercially impracticable because of unforeseen supervening circumstances not within the contemplation of the parties at the time of contracting." The Court of Appeals reasoned that §2-615 was inapplicable because there was no failure on the part of the seller, Transupport, to deliver the nozzle to Turbines.

Relying upon comment 9 to §2-615, which states that under certain circumstances, it "may well apply" to the performance of a buyer under a "requirements" or "supply" contract, Turbines argues that it applies here. But this case does not involve such a contract. More important, it is not an action for breach of contract. Section 2-615 specifies circumstances under which nonperformance or delayed performance of a sales contract will not constitute a breach. Here, there is no issue of breach, because the contract was fully performed by each party in that Transupport shipped the nozzle to Turbines and Turbines remitted the purchase price to Transupport. We agree with the Court of Appeals that §2-615 does not provide a legal basis for rescission on the facts presented here.

In *Cleasby v. Leo A. Daly Co.*, we determined that business necessity justified an international architectural consulting firm's termination of a project manager's assignment at an overseas jobsite when an illness caused the manager's prolonged absence from the country where the work was being performed. In reaching this conclusion, we relied in part upon Restatement (Second) of Contracts §§261 and 265.13 Section 261, entitled "Discharge by Supervening Impracticability," provides:

> Where, after a contract is made, a party's performance is made impracticable without his fault by the occurrence of an event the non-occurrence of which was a basic assumption on which the contract was made, his duty to render that performance is discharged, unless the language or the circumstances indicate the contrary.

Section 265, entitled "Discharge by Supervening Frustration," provides:

> Where, after a contract is made, a party's principal purpose is substantially frustrated without his fault by the occurrence of an event the non-occurrence of which was a basic assumption on which the contract was made, his remaining duties to render performance are discharged, unless the language or the circumstances indicate the contrary.

The Court of Appeals concluded that §265 could not provide a legal basis for rescission because it was "impossible to say that a 'basic assumption' of the contract was Turbines' ability to export the nozzle to Monarch." But we believe that there is a more basic question of law, namely, whether the doctrine of supervening frustration can serve as the basis for rescinding a contract that has been fully performed. In *Kunkel Auto Supply Co. v. Leech*, the buyer purchased automotive equipment from the seller and gave a promissory note in payment. Both parties believed that the equipment would allow the buyer to operate a state testing station under a statute which they understood to require mandatory vehicle testing. That understanding was incorrect, and the statute was eventually repealed. When sued on the note, the buyer alleged that it was void under various theories, including the doctrine of commercial frustration derived in part from a previous version of the Restatement of Contracts on which §265 is based. We held as a matter of law that this defense was not viable because the contract, so far as the seller was concerned, was fully performed before the defense arose. We noted that the doctrine of commercial frustration "applies to executory contracts alone."

In *Mobile Home Estates v. Levitt Mobile Home*, the Arizona Supreme Court relied in part on our decision in *Kunkel Auto Supply Co.* in holding that the doctrine of commercial frustration could not be utilized as a basis for rescinding a fully performed contract. In that case, a mobile home dealer purchased and paid for several modular duplex dwelling units with the intention of reselling them. Resale proved difficult if not impossible because the units did not comply with subsequently adopted standards. The purchaser sought rescission of the contract and recovery of the purchase price under the Arizona doctrine of "commercial frustration," which provided that "when, due to circumstances beyond the control of the parties the performance of a contract is rendered impossible, the party failing to perform is exonerated.' . . . " Citing *Kunkel Auto Supply Co.* and other authorities, the court concluded: "It would be contrary to logic and common sense to hold that a contract was rendered impossible to perform when, in fact, it had already been performed."

We find this analysis applicable to §265 of the Restatement, which clearly contemplates an executory contract by providing that a party's "remaining duties to render performance are discharged" by the occurrence of an event which substantially frustrates the party's principal purpose. Each of the illustrations which follow the statement of the rule involve circumstances where a party's obligation to perform an executory contract is discharged by the occurrence of an event which frustrates that party's purpose in entering into the contract. We therefore conclude as a matter of law that the doctrine of discharge by supervening frustration as set forth in §265 of the Restatement cannot serve as the basis for rescission of a contract that has been fully performed. And although the Court of Appeals did not specifically discuss the doctrine of discharge by supervening impracticability under §261 of the Restatement, we conclude that the same reasoning applies. Like §265, §261 defines circumstances under which a party's obligation to perform a contract may be discharged. Neither contemplates the circumstances of this case, in which the contract was fully performed. . . .

CONCLUSION

Turbines fulfilled its contractual obligation to pay in advance for the nozzle which it ordered from Transupport. In turn, Transupport fulfilled its contractual obligation

to ship the nozzle to Turbines. The contract did not contemplate the circumstances which subsequently prevented Turbines from shipping the nozzle to Monarch. But the occurrence of those circumstances did not constitute a basis for rescinding the fully performed contract. Thus, although Transupport clearly ignored the district court's orders and failed to appear for trial, the district court abused its discretion in entering default judgment in favor of Turbines, because the uncontroverted facts provide no legal basis for rescission, and to allow such a judgment to stand would be untenable. Accordingly, although our reasoning differs in some respects, we affirm the judgment of the Court of Appeals.
AFFIRMED.

In practice, buyers and sellers tend to write their own excuse provisions into their contracts, at least when the stakes are fairly high. Such provisions supersede the applicable UCC sections on the subject, although in many cases these "force majeure" clauses end up providing no more guidance on the excuse issue than does the fuzzy UCC standard.

Consider the following force majeure clause in a long-term natural gas supply contract:

Suspension for Event of Force Majeure. Except with regard to Buyer's or Seller's obligations to make payments due under this Agreement, in the event that either Party is rendered unable, wholly or in part, by an event of Force Majeure to carry out its obligations under this Agreement, it is agreed that upon such Party's giving notice and full particulars of such event of Force Majeure to the other Party as soon as reasonably possible, such notice to be confirmed in writing, then the obligations of the Party giving such notice, so far as they are affected by such event of Force Majeure, from its inception, shall be suspended during the continuance of any inability so caused. The cause of the Force Majeure event shall be remedied with all reasonable dispatch. Each party shall give the other Party notice of its ability again to perform after the event of Force Majeure has been remedied, and upon such notice, the Parties shall resume their performance as if the Force Majeure had not occurred.

Definition of Force Majeure. In this Agreement the term force majeure ("Force Majeure") means any event which is not within the control of the Party claiming suspension and which by the exercise of due diligence such party could not have prevented and is unable to overcome. It is expressly agreed that neither Buyer's nor Seller's ability to obtain a more favorable price for Gas than the price for Gas purchased under this Agreement shall constitute an event of Force Majeure hereunder.

Third Party Force Majeure. Force Majeure shall include any event of Force Majeure validly claimed by Buyer's Transporter or Seller's Transporter to the extent that such event affects Seller's ability to deliver or Buyer's ability to take delivery of the Gas. Force Majeure shall not include any other curtailment or interruption of service by pipelines or other third parties, including third party producers and suppliers.

The clause above tracks in many respects the default rule that is given in UCC §2-615. The gas supply clause first mentions the duty of the party claiming excuse to give notice to the other side. In §2-615(c), the seller who wishes to claim excuse is required to notify the buyer of any delay or non-delivery occasioned by a justifiable excuse.

UCC §2-615(a) says that for the seller that qualifies for excuse, a delay in delivery or a complete non-delivery is not a breach of the seller's duty under the contract. The gas supply clause, by comparison, speaks in terms of the excused party's performance being "suspended" during the continuance of the force majeure event.

The definition of force majeure that is provided in the contractual clause emphasizes the fact that the event was not within the control of the party claiming excuse. UCC §2-615(a), by contrast, focuses on the foreseeability of the supervening event: that event must be "a contingency the non-occurrence of which was a basic assumption on which the contract was made." UCC §2-615(a) also mentions specifically the seller's good-faith compliance with applicable governmental regulations as a permissible basis for excuse.

The gas supply clause explicitly notes that either party's ability to get a better price from some other party cannot be an event of force majeure. Although §2-615 itself does not address price fluctuations as a justification for non-performance, Official Comment 4 to §2-615 does, albeit in a very inconclusive way:

> Increased cost alone does not excuse performance unless the rise in cost is due to some unforeseen contingency which alters the essential nature of the performance.

Finally, note that the contractual force majeure clause specifically addresses the issue of supplier problems as a basis for excuse. Essentially, it says that if the buyer's or seller's immediate carrier has a valid commercial impracticability defense, then so will the buyer or seller. Official Comment 5 to §2-615 speaks to the issue of the seller's source of supply failing unexpectedly. That Comment suggests that unless both buyer and seller had reason to believe that a particular source of supply was to be seller's exclusive source of supply, then the seller should not be able to rely on the inability of a particular supplier as a basis for its own excuse. Thus, the clause as written seems to broaden the buyer's and seller's ability to claim excuse beyond that which they would get from the default rule of Article 2.

In practice, commercial buyers tend not to be as harsh as Comment 5 might suggest they could be when it comes to excusing their seller's inability to deliver goods due to the seller's supply problems. As an in-house lawyer for a Fortune 100 clothing retailer put it, "Whether or not we would let some vendor off the hook when they said that they couldn't supply to us because it was impossible would depend on whether they were somehow able to supply the same goods to one of our competitors. Also, it would depend on the length and nature of our relationship with them and whether we thought they were acting in good faith."

The general counsel for a computer hardware distributor echoed these sentiments as applied to his company's capacity as a seller: "There will often be occasions in which we aren't able to fulfill an order, but our buyers will always believe us after they try to go to other manufacturers and suppliers only to realize that there really is nobody out there from whom they can get the item."

As the following case demonstrates, a buyer's willingness to accept supplier-related excuses from the seller may be significantly diminished when the buyer's dealings with the seller do not constitute a long-term relationship but rather are a one-shot proposition.

Alamance County Bd. of Educ. v. Bobby Murray Chevrolet

465 S.E.2d 306 (N.C. Ct. App. 1996)

JOHN, J.

Defendant Bobby Murray Chevrolet, Inc. ("Bobby Murray") appeals the trial court's entry of summary judgment in favor of plaintiffs, a number of North Carolina school boards ("plaintiffs"; "school boards"), on their respective claims for breach of contract. Defendant contends application of N.C.G.S. §25-2-615 (1995) regarding commercial impracticability operates under the facts of the case sub judice to excuse its performance under the contracts with plaintiffs. We disagree.

Pertinent factual and procedural information is as follows: Bobby Murray, a General Motors franchisee, received an invitation on or about 7 April 1989 to bid on approximately 1200 school bus chassis from the North Carolina Department of Administration's Division of Purchase and Contract ("the Division"). . . .

After consulting with the GMC Truck Division ("GM Truck") of defendant General Motors Corporation ("GM") regarding prices and availability, Bobby Murray proposed to supply several different sizes of chassis at specified prices. The chassis were described as "Chevrolet" brand in the bid, but were to be manufactured by GM Truck. . . .

On 26 July 1990, the Environmental Protection Agency (EPA) enacted Federal Emissions Standards changes for heavy duty diesel engines, thereby rendering the 8.2N diesel engine described in Bobby Murray's bid out of compliance with the regulations effective 1 January 1991. . . .

On 10 August 1990, Bobby Murray received a message from GM through its Dealer Communication System ("DCS"), a computer network linking GM with its dealers, setting the final chassis buildout date at the week of 10 December 1990, but warning that estimated production dates could be pushed back due to a potential shortage of the requisite brand of automatic transmission (Allison automatic transmissions). On 24 August 1990, in a DCS message to Bobby Murray, GM reiterated that due to "the uncertainty of major component availability," no further orders for school bus chassis would be accepted.

On 30 November 1990, another DCS message to Bobby Murray indicated that the chassis orders placed between 1 August and 14 August 1990 would not be filled due to unavailability of Allison automatic transmissions. Bobby Murray contacted GMC Truck on or about 11 December 1990 and learned that none of the chassis were to be built prior to the end of December because the Allison transmissions would not be provided until February or March 1991. At that point, however, installation of the 8.2N diesel engines would be illegal in consequence of the modified EPA regulations. On or about 11 December 1990, Bobby Murray notified the Division the chassis could not be supplied.

On or about 23 January 1991, the Division informed Bobby Murray the chassis were being purchased from another source, and that it intended to hold Bobby Murray liable for any excess in cost. The substitute chassis were later obtained by plaintiffs, who subsequently filed suit against Bobby Murray for a total of $150,152.94, representing the difference between the bid prices and the actual amounts expended by plaintiffs in purchasing similar chassis. In its answer and third-party complaint against GM, Bobby Murray claimed, inter alia, that GM breached its contract with Bobby Murray to provide the chassis at issue and that Bobby Murray had merely been acting as an agent of GM. Thereafter, both the plaintiffs and GM filed motions for summary judgment.

Summary judgment was entered against Bobby Murray and in favor of plaintiffs 18 April 1994 by Judge F. Fetzer Mills in the amount of $150,152.94 plus interest at 8% per annum from 11 December 1990 until paid. . . .

Bobby Murray asserts two arguments based upon [UCC §2-615]. It contends the failure of GM to supply the bus chassis was "a contingency the nonoccurrence of which" was a basic assumption of the underlying contracts between Bobby Murray and plaintiffs. Second, Bobby Murray claims governmental regulation prohibiting the installation of the 8.2N engine after 1 January 1991 was an intervening factor which should operate as an excuse. . . .

In order to be excused under §2-615, a seller of goods must establish the following elements:

(1) performance has become "impracticable";
(2) the impracticability was due to the occurrence of some contingency which the parties expressly or impliedly agreed would discharge the promisor's duty to perform;
(3) the promisor did not assume the risk that the contingency would occur;
(4) the promisor seasonably notified the promisee of the delay in delivery or that delivery would not occur at all[.]

Utilizing the foregoing criteria as well as the official commentary to §2-615 and case law from other jurisdictions, we now consider Bobby Murray's arguments on appeal.

Initially, Bobby Murray contends an implied condition of its contract with plaintiffs was the ability of GM to manufacture and supply the ordered bus chassis. We agree that when an exclusive source of supply is specified in a contract or may be implied by circumstances to have been contemplated by the parties, failure of that source may excuse the promisor from performance. N.C.G.S. §25-2-615, Official Comment 5. However, neither contingency is reflected in the record herein.

Bobby Murray insists in its brief that "[a]ppellant disclosed in the bid that the chassis would be manufactured by Chevrolet and Plaintiff-Appellees had knowledge that Appellant's sole source of supply was General Motors." However, Bobby Murray points to no record evidence of such knowledge on the part of plaintiffs, and appears to rely solely upon its status as a GM franchisee to support its assertion.

By contrast, we note that the "General Contract Terms and Conditions" on Form TC-1, incorporated into the bid document, contain the following section entitled "MANUFACTURER'S NAMES":

> Any manufacturers' names, trade names, brand names, information and/or catalog numbers used herein are for purpose(s) of description and establishing general quality levels. Such references are not intended to be restrictive and products of any manufacturer may be offered.

Further, no clause in the contract between plaintiffs and Bobby Murray conditioned the latter's performance on its ability to obtain bus chassis from its manufacturer. See William H. Henning & George I. Wallach, The Law of Sales Under the Uniform Commercial Code, ¶5.10[2], S5-4 (1994 Supplement) (generally, where seller fails to make contract with buyer contingent on adequate supply, courts reluctant to excuse seller). Plaintiffs aptly point to Richard M. Smith and Donald F. Clifford, Jr., North Carolina Practice, Uniform Commercial Code Forms Annotated, Vol. 1, §2-615, Form 3 (1968), which indicates a seller of goods may limit its liability by inclusion of the following "Single Source Clause":

> It is expressly understood that the seller has available only one source, [name of single source], of [address], for the [name or identify the raw materials obtained by the seller from the single source] used by the seller in the manufacture of the goods for the buyer under this contract. In the event of any interference or cessation of the supply from the seller's source of supply, the seller shall be temporarily, proportionately, or permanently relieved of liability under this contract, depending upon whether the interruption of the source of supply is a temporary interruption, a reduced delivery of materials, or a permanent cessation of supply. . . .

We next examine Bobby Murray's contention its performance should be excused in consequence of intervening governmental regulations. Generally, governmental regulations do not excuse performance under a contract where a party has assumed the risk of such regulation. The contract between the parties sub judice, in its "General Contract Terms and Conditions," Form TC-1, provided as follows:

> GOVERNMENTAL RESTRICTIONS: In the event any Governmental restrictions may be imposed which would necessitate alteration of the material, quality, workmanship or performance of the items offered on this proposal prior to their delivery, it shall be the responsibility of the successful bidder to notify this Division at once, indicating in

his letter the specific regulation which required such alterations. The State reserves the right to accept any such alterations, including any price adjustments occasioned thereby, or to cancel the contract.

Bobby Murray, by terms of the parties' agreement, accepted responsibility for keeping abreast of governmental regulations bearing upon the contract.

In addition, Bobby Murray was on notice 26 July 1990 that new emissions standards would preclude, effective 1 January 1991, production of bus chassis using the 8.2N engine specified in its bid. Nothing in the record indicates that this information was conveyed to plaintiffs. Bobby Murray was further notified 10 August 1990 that production dates could be pushed beyond December 1990. The record contains no evidence that Bobby Murray explored with plaintiffs, or otherwise, alternative methods of meeting its contractual obligations. Under these circumstances, equity dictates that excuse by governmental regulation be unavailable to Bobby Murray. . . .

In sum, taking the evidence presented in the light most favorable to Bobby Murray, we hold there exists no genuine issue of material fact as to plaintiffs' respective claims of breach of contract against Bobby Murray, and Bobby Murray's arguments to the contrary are unavailing. The trial court thus properly granted plaintiffs' summary judgment motion.

AFFIRMED.

In the *Bobby Murray* case above, the seller is claiming excuse as to its entire ability to perform. (The seller was also suing GM in a separate action for breach of GM's contract to provide the chassis to the seller.) Often when a seller has problems obtaining adequate supply, those problems affect only a portion of seller's ability to perform. Or sometimes a seller has several buyers under contract for the same type of goods but has the capacity to satisfy only some of those buyers.

In cases where a seller that is claiming excuse under §2-615 has more than one buyer and has a limited capacity to perform, §2-615(b) requires that the seller allocate production and delivery among its customers in a "fair and reasonable" manner. Section 2-615(b) does not give very much guidance as to what constitutes a fair and reasonable allocation; §2-615(b) does, however, provide that a seller may "include regular customers not then under contract as well as his own requirements for further manufacture."

The rules about a seller's allocation in times of shortage became significant in the mid-1970s, when there were widespread shortages in the chemical industry. Professor James J. White surveyed 30 people at 10 chemical and pharmaceutical companies in the summer of 1977 to determine whether companies that were faced with shortages actually followed the limited allocation guidance given by §2-615(b).

Professor White's first surprise in conducting these surveys was that none of the companies he surveyed had a formal written policy for handling allocations to buyers in a time of shortage. His second surprise was that the informal practices of these companies often deviated in significant and suspicious ways from a pro rata distribution among buyers that were under contract. As Professor White noted:

> The inarticulate premise of section 2-615 is that a seller should not be free in time of shortage to disregard his long term commitments and favor short term buyers who will pay higher prices. Although it is clear the seller may treat himself as a customer, section 2-615 forbids giving himself an additional, unjustified share. Rarely could one justify the addition of new customers under section 2-615 in time of shortage. Discussions with chemical company lawyers, before and during the interviewing process, disclosed that they were well aware of those problems. The written materials furnished by some lawyers indicate they were careful to point out those difficulties to their sellers. Nevertheless, I received a surprising number of admissions that sellers had engaged in non–pro rata distributions which almost certainly were in violation of section 2-615. In two cases, these admissions were made in the presence of company lawyers who were surprised and obviously discomfited by the admissions. (James J. White, Contract Law in Modern Commercial Transactions: An Artifact of Twentieth Century Business Life?, 22 Washburn L.J. 1 (1982).)

Professor White identified a number of questionable ways in which sellers deviated from a pro rata distribution in their allocations during a time of shortage. First, most sellers admitted to diverting a greater than pro rata share to their internal uses. A second deviation from pro rata distribution was that some sellers sold to new customers despite their failure to fulfill all of their obligations to customers already under contract. Third, most sellers admitted to giving a greater than pro rata share to certain favored customers.

Ten years after Professor White's empirical study was published, Professor Russell Weintraub conducted a survey of general counsel at several dozen major U.S. companies that shed still more light on the operation of the commercial excuse doctrine in actual practice. Russell J. Weintraub, A Survey of Contract Practice and Policy, 1992 Wis. L. Rev. 1. Among other topics, Professor Weintraub's survey focused on the willingness of companies to grant a customer's request for a price modification. Professor Weintraub found that 95 percent of the companies surveyed would at least sometimes grant such requests for deviations from the contractually agreed-to price. The most common reasons given for granting such requests were that the request was reasonable in the trade and that the customer was a long-time, valued customer.

In another part of Professor Weintraub's survey, he posed a hypothetical that involved a long-term supply contract and a price fluctuation that would put the seller out of business if the contract were enforced against the seller at the original price. Professor Weintraub's question to the general counsel in his survey was what outcome the law ought to require in this case.

Forty-six percent of respondents said that the court should adjust the price so as to avoid ruinous loss to the seller but still give the buyer a significant savings over the current market. Some 35 percent of respondents said that the contract should be enforced according to its original terms even if that would put the seller out of business; 14 percent of respondents said that the seller should be completely excused from performing.

Perhaps "splitting the baby" and having a court rewrite the contract is the most intuitively attractive approach in the case of a significant price fluctuation with a long-term contract. Nevertheless, American courts rarely consider it within their power to adjust the terms of a contract in a case where one party claims excuse on the basis of commercial impracticability.

Not all Western court systems share the American judiciary's aversion to rewriting the parties' contract:

> German law is perhaps the best example of a system that allows the courts to revise a contract based upon impossibility of performance of the existing contract. The origins of the current willingness of the German courts to revise contracts for the parties are found in the economic dislocation caused by World War I and the tremendous inflation that resulted. Initially, the contract revisions were limited to situations in which parties were simply unable to perform their monetary obligations because of the inflation in the German currency. Based upon the German concept of "good faith" found in the civil code and examination of *gerschaftsgrundlage*, "foundation of the transaction," German law has evolved today to the point where courts now will revise many types of contracts. Today, the standard doctrine of the German courts is to revise by court order those contracts "whose foundations have been destroyed by unexpected events or discoveries" rather than to rescind them. (Daniel T. Ostas & Burt A. Leete, Economic Analysis of Law as a Guide to Post-Communist Legal Reforms: The Case of Hungarian Contract Law, Am. Bus. L.J., Feb. 1, 1995.)

There are several criticisms to the German approach to contract reformulation. First, judges often lack a sense for the industry for which they will be rewriting the contract. Second, even if a judge knows something about a particular industry, it is doubtful that the judge would know much about the particular context in which the individual contract was negotiated. Finally, the specter of judges rewriting contracts would introduce an element of randomness or uncertainty into the prospect of contract enforcement that would likely complicate the contract formation process.

If judicial contract reformulation is not a viable approach to unexpected price increases, the only other approaches to the price increase problem would seem to be (1) never allow any price increase to be the basis for commercial excuse, or (2) allow only very significant price increases to be the basis for excuse.

The second approach allowing excuse only for sufficiently severe price increases, has serious theoretical problems. For example, suppose a judge determined that the appropriate threshold for allowing a seller's excuse is a 100 percent price increase. This would mean that, in a case in which the price increased just 95 percent, the seller would end up assuming all of the risk. Yet in a case in which the price increased 105 percent, the seller would end up assuming none of the risk.

As a way around the theoretical problems suggested here, the judge could, of course, determine that the seller would be responsible for the first 100 percent price increase and the buyer would be responsible for anything greater than that. The problem with this approach is that the judge is then merely rewriting the contract, a technique that was discussed and criticized earlier.

Perhaps the most powerful reason for a court to refuse to allow price fluctuation as a basis for excuse in a long-term contract is one articulated by Professor Weintraub:

> Only three respondents [in his survey], one of whom sold only services, did not provide some contract protection against market shifts during the performance of long-term contracts. This response suggests that when a contract that is to be performed over a period of more than a year does not contain provisions protecting the parties from market changes, either the parties have acted imprudently when tested by industry standards or the price has taken account of the risk. In either circumstance, a frustration argument based solely on market shift, when there is no reasonable attempt to draft protection into the contract, should not be favorably received. (Weintraub, 1992 Wis. L. Rev. at 51.)

B.   Commercial Impracticability with Leases

The drafters of Article 2A borrowed almost verbatim from Article 2 the rules on commercial impracticability. The lease analogue to §2-613 on casualty to identified goods is found in §2A-221, the lease version of §2-615 on excused performance is found in §2A-405, and Article 2A's provision covering the procedure on excused performance is found in §2A-406 rather than §2-616.

Probably the only difference in the lease sections from the comparable sales sections, apart from minor language changes "to reflect leasing practices and terminology," is the special treatment of nonconsumer finance lessees. Under Article 2, buyers that have contracts with sellers who are excused from performance are given the option to demand a partial performance from the seller at a reduced price. Under §2-613(b), the buyer can choose to accept damaged goods from the seller with "due allowance" against the original purchase price to reflect the damage; similarly, §2-616(1)(b) lets a buyer take its "available quota in substitution" where the seller is unable to make complete delivery.

Lessees under §§2A-221 and 2A-406 are generally given options that are comparable to those available to aggrieved buyers under Article 2. Those options, however, are not available to the nonconsumer finance lessee, whose only choice in these situations is to either terminate the contract or go forward with the contract with no reduction in rent. UCC §§2A-221(b), 2A-406(1)(b).

The reason that the finance lessee is not given the option to continue the lease contract, albeit at a reduced rent, is that such a right would be inconsistent with the policy behind the automatic "hell or high water clause" of §2A-407(1). Official Comment to §2A-406. That clause, as you may recall from Assignment 11, makes the nonconsumer finance lessee's promises "irrevocable and independent upon the lessee's acceptance of the goods." To give the non-consumer finance lessee the right to insist on the lessor's partial performance with reduced rent would mean that the finance lessee's obligation to pay full rent upon acceptance would no longer be "irrevocable and independent."

If the nonconsumer finance lessee in the case of lessor excuse wants to call off the whole contract prior to acceptance, it still may do that. But if the nonconsumer finance lessee wants to go forward with the lease contract in a case where the lessor's original performance has been excused, the lessee's decision to accept partial performance will not obviate its usual obligation following acceptance to pay full rent to the finance lessor.

C.   Commercial Impracticability with International Sales

Article 79 of the CISG sets down the principles of commercial impracticability in international sales. Those principles are similar to the UCC's Article 2 approach in most respects but are different in a couple of ways.

Raw Materials, Inc. v. Manfred Forberich GmbH & Co.

2004 WL 1535839 (N.D. Ill. 2004)

FILIP, J.

Plaintiff Raw Materials, Inc. ("RMI" or "Plaintiff"), an Illinois corporation that deals in used railroad rail, has brought suit against Defendant Manfred Forberich GmbH & Co., KG ("Forberich" or "Defendant"), a German limited partnership that sells such rail, alleging breach of contract and fraud relating to Defendant's undisputed failure to meet its contractual obligation to deliver 15,000-18,000 metric tons of used railroad rail to Plaintiff. Plaintiff has moved for summary judgment on its breach of contract claim. Defendant has defended on *force majeure* grounds. For the reasons stated below, Plaintiff's motion is denied.

RELEVANT FACTS

RMI is located in Chicago Heights, Illinois. Its primary business is purchasing, processing, and selling used railroad rail which is eventually reheated and rerolled into new products, such as fence posts or sign posts. (D.E. 21 at 1-2.) Forberich is located in Germany and is in the business of selling used railroad rail. Forberich generally obtains its rail from the former Soviet Union. (D.E. 23 at 1.)

On February 7, 2002, RMI entered into a written contract with Forberich in which Forberich agreed to supply RMI with 15,000-18,000 metric tons of used Russian rail. (D.E. 21 at 3.) The rail was to be shipped from the port in St.

Petersburg, Russia. It takes approximately three to four weeks for ships loaded with rail to travel from St. Petersburg, Russia to the United States. (D.E. 21 at 14.) The contract provides for "Delivery by: 6-30-2002," "F.O.B. Delivered Our Plant, Chicago Heights, IL," and "Shipping Instructions: RMI, INC. c/c Chicago Heights Steel, Chicago Heights, IL 60411." (D.E. 19, Ex. 7, at MF0027.)

The parties agree that in June 2002, Forberich sought an extension of its time for performance under the contract. (D.E. 23 at 4.) However, the circumstances surrounding the extension request are disputed. Forberich maintains that, pursuant to its normal practice, it had "earmarked" a particular supplier, Imperio Trading ("Imperio"), to provide it with rails that it would use to fulfill its contract with RMI. (D.E. 23 at 2-3.) In late June 2002, Imperio defaulted on its contractual obligation to provide rail to Forberich. (D.E. 23 at 4.) Forberich claims that it requested an extension from RMI because of this breach. (Id.) RMI disputes that Forberich intended to use rail from Imperio to fulfill Forberich's contract with RMI. (Id.) RMI also asserts, without citing any record evidence, that Forberich's request for an extension was based on a false representation that Forberich was unable to obtain a supply of rail from any source sufficient to meet its obligations to RMI by June 30, 2002. (D.E. 18 at 7, 9.)

Whatever the reasons Forberich may have given in seeking its extension, the parties do not dispute that RMI agreed (apparently in a telephone conversation between Mr. Forberich and RMI Vice President Ron Owczarzak, (D.E. 21, Ex. O)), to extend in some manner the time for Forberich to perform the contract. (D.E. 23 at 4.) However, the parties dispute the terms of the extension. RMI contends that it agreed to extend the delivery date (meaning delivery at RMI's place of business) to a date "later in the calendar year," but that the delivery date was never fixed due to Forberich's failure to attend a planned meeting in Chicago to discuss the extension. (D.E. 23 at 4; D.E. 21, Ex. O; D.E. 19, Ex. 3, at 55.) For purposes of its motion for summary judgment, "RMI has assumed that had Forberich delivered the contracted goods to RMI's plant by December 31, 2002, the Contract would have been satisfied." (D.E. 22 at 4 n.1.) Mr. Owczarzak testified that he "would have been satisfied had the 15,000 to 18,000 tons, metric tons of rail, been delivered to a port in the United States as of December 31st, 2002," and that he conveyed this to Mr. Forberich, though he did not specify when or how (orally or by letter). (D.E. 19, Ex. 3 at 55.) Mr. Forberich's declaration states that he understood that Forberich "had until December 31, 2002 to load the rails and execute the bill of lading to be in compliance with the contract." (D.E. 21, Ex. C, ¶11.)

Although it is undisputed that Forberich "has never delivered the contracted goods to RMI," (D.E. 21 at 5), the question of whether Forberich was required to deliver the rails to RMI's place of business by December 31, 2002 or merely was obligated to load the rails on a ship by that date is nevertheless significant because it bears on the viability of Forberich's contention that its failure to perform should be excused. Forberich asserts that its failure to perform should be excused because it was prevented from shipping the rail by the fact that the St. Petersburg port unexpectedly froze over on approximately December 1, 2002. (D.E. 22 at 4-5.) According to RMI, on the other hand, the port did not freeze over until mid-December 2002, and, since it takes 3-4 weeks for a ship carrying rail to travel from St. Petersburg to the United States, Forberich would have had to have shipped out the rail before the port froze in order for the shipment to arrive by the December 31, 2002 deadline. (D.E. 22 at 7-8.) Thus, RMI contends that Forberich's failure to perform under the contract could not have been due to the freezing of the port. (Id.) In other words, according to RMI, regardless of whether the port froze in mid-December 2002, Forberich would have breached the contract in any event because it did not load its ships early enough so that they would arrive by the December 31, 2002 deadline. If, however, Forberich was merely required to load the rail by December 31, 2002, then the freezing over of the port could have prevented Forberich from shipping the rail regardless of whether the port froze on December 1 or in mid-December.

The parties do not dispute that, in a typical winter, the St. Petersburg port does not freeze over until late January, and such freezing does not prevent the vessels from entering and exiting the port. (D.E. 23 at 6.) Mr. Forberich testified that ice breakers are normally used to allow for shipping. (D.E. 21, Ex. F, at 106.) He further testified that the winter of 2002 was the worst winter in St. Petersburg in almost sixty years and that ice interfered with shipping at the end of November and that even the icebreakers were stuck in the ice. (Id.) He also testified that these were "unexpected weather conditions." (Id. at 77.) In relation to issues concerning the freezing of the port, Forberich also submitted the declaration of Mikahil Nikolaev, who works at the St. Petersburg port. (D.E. 21, Ex. P.) Mr. Nikolaev's declaration essentially states the same facts that Mr. Forberich testified to regarding the freezing of the port, except that the declaration states that the port was frozen over on December 1, 2002, that such early freezing had not occurred since 1955, and contains the conclusion that no one could have predicted the early freezing of the port. (Id., ¶¶7, 10.) Without citation to the record, RMI's counsel states in RMI's brief in support of summary judgment that "it hardly could come as a surprise to any experienced shipping merchant (or any grammar school geography student) that the port in St. Petersburg might become icy and frozen in the Russian winter months." (D.E. 18 at 12.) One of Forberich's ships left the St. Petersburg port on approximately November 20, 2002. (D.E. 22 at 7-8, citing (D.E. 21 at 13.).) No evidence has been presented that any ships left the St. Petersburg port until months after November 20, 2002. On January 10, 2003, Mr. Forberich sent Mr. Owczarzak a letter stating that Forberich could not ship the rails because "[s]ince the last 3 weeks the port is as well as frozen and nothing is possible." (D.E. 19, Ex. 8.)

DISCUSSION

As set forth above, it is undisputed that Forberich was contractually obligated to ship 15,000 to 18,000 metric tons of rail to RMI and that it failed to do so. Thus, Forberich's ability to avoid summary judgment is dependent on whether it has presented sufficient evidence to support its affirmative defense of *force majeure* based on the theory that it was prevented from performing by the freezing over of the

St. Petersburg port. For the reasons explained below, the Court denies Plaintiff's motion for summary judgment.

A.   APPLICABLE LAW

The parties agree that their contract is governed by the Convention on Contracts for the International Sale of Goods ("CISG"). (D.E. 18 at 5; D.E. 20 at 9.) Although the contract does not contain an express *force majeure* provision, the CISG provides that:

> A party is not liable for failure to perform any of his obligations if he proves that failure was due to an impediment beyond his control and that he could not reasonably be expected to have taken the impediment into account at the time of the conclusion of the contract or to have avoided or overcome its consequences.

CISG Art. 79. RMI asserts that "[w]hile no American court has specifically interpreted or applied Article 79 of the CISG, caselaw interpreting the Uniform Commercial Code's ("UCC") provision on excuse provides guidance for interpreting the CISG's excuse provision since it contains similar requirements as those set forth in Article 79." (D.E. 18 at 8 n.5.) This approach of looking to caselaw interpreting analogous provisions of the UCC has been used by other federal courts. See, e.g., Delchi Carrier SpA v. Rotorex Corp., 71 F.3d 1024, 1028 (2d Cir. 1995) ("caselaw interpreting analogous provisions of Article 2 of the Uniform Commercial Code ('UCC') may also inform a court where the language of the relevant CISG provisions track that of the UCC"); Chicago Prime Packers, Inc. v. Northam Food Trading Co., No. 01-4447, 2004 WL 1166628, at *4 (N.D. Ill. May 21, 2004) (same). Furthermore, Forberich does not dispute that this is proper and, in fact, also points to caselaw interpreting the UCC. (D.E. 20 at 9 n.6.) Accordingly, in applying Article 79 of the CISG, the Court will use as a guide caselaw interpreting a similar provision of §2-615 of the UCC.

Under §2-615 of the UCC, "three conditions must be satisfied before performance is excused: (1) a contingency has occurred; (2) the contingency has made performance impracticable; and (3) the nonoccurrence of that contingency was a basic assumption upon which the contract was made." Waldinger Corp. v. CRS Group Engineers, Inc., 775 F.2d 781, 786 (7th Cir. 1985). The third condition turns upon whether the contingency was foreseeable; "[i]f the risk of the occurrence of the contingency was unforeseeable, the seller cannot be said to have assumed the risk. If the risk of the occurrence of the contingency was foreseeable, that risk is tacitly assigned to the seller." Id. RMI does not dispute that the freezing over of the port in St. Petersburg was a contingency. Rather, RMI essentially argues that it is entitled to summary judgment because the second and third conditions do not apply inasmuch as the undisputed facts show that the frozen port did not prevent Forberich from performing the contract and that the freezing of the port was foreseeable. Based on the record material cited by the parties, the Court respectfully disagrees.

B. Whether the Frozen Port Could Have Prevented Performance

As mentioned above, RMI contends that the frozen port could not have prevented Forberich from performing because the port did not freeze over until mid-December 2002, and, since it takes 3-4 weeks for a ship carrying rail to travel from St. Petersburg to the United States, Forberich would have had to have shipped out the rail before the port froze in order for the shipment to arrive by the December 31, 2002 deadline. (D.E. 22 at 7-8.) RMI's argument is premised on its contention that it has established beyond genuine dispute that Forberich was obligated to ship the materials so that they would arrive by December 31, 2002 (rather than just load the ships by that date, as Forberich contends). In this regard, RMI asserts that Forberich's admission in its answer that it "promised to deliver the aforementioned goods at RMI's place of business on or before June 30, 2002," (D.E. 9 at 2), is a judicial admission. While the Court agrees that this statement in RMI's answer is a judicial admission that establishes beyond contention the fact that Forberich initially promised to deliver the rail at RMI's place of business on or before June 30, 2002, see Solon v. Gary Community School Corp., 180 F.3d 844, 858 (7th Cir. 1999) ("That Gary Schools admitted the length of Bohney's service in its answer was not simply evidence as to this eligibility criterion, but a judicial admission which removed this point from the realm of contested issues"), this does not establish the inapplicability of the *force majeure* defense for at least two independent reasons.

First, even assuming that Forberich was obligated to deliver the rails by December 31, 2002, Forberich has nonetheless presented evidence (which the Court must construe in the light most favorable to Forberich) that the frozen port prevented it from meeting this obligation. In particular, Mr. Forberich testified that ice interfered with shipping not just in mid-December, but as early as the end of November. (D.E. 21, Ex. F, at 106.) The fact that a Forberich ship left the port on approximately November 20, 2002 is not inconsistent with the port freezing in the remaining ten days or so of that month. Furthermore, as noted above, no conclusive evidence has been presented that any ships left the St. Petersburg port until months after November 20, 2002. In light of the undisputed fact that delivery to a port in the U.S. from St. Petersburg takes at least 3-4 weeks and Mr. Owczarzak's testimony that he "would have been satisfied had the 15,000 to 18,000 tons, metric tons of rail, been delivered to a port in the United States as of December 31st, 2002," (D.E. 19, Ex. 3 at 55), Forberich has presented evidence that it would have been in position to meet a December 31, 2002 deadline for delivery to the U.S. by shipping out rail in the last week or so of November or the first few days of December but was prevented from doing so by the frozen port. Thus, for this reason alone, there is a disputed question of fact as to whether the frozen port prevented Forberich from performing its contractual obligations.

The second reason RMI has failed to demonstrate that the frozen port did not prevent Forberich's performance is that although it is established beyond contention that Forberich promised in the February 7, 2002, written agreement that Forberich would deliver the rail at RMI's place of business on or before June 30,

2002, an issue of fact exists regarding the nature of the extension Mr. Owczarzac orally agreed to for the time for performance of the contract. Neither side has presented evidence of what exactly was said by Mr. Owczarzak and Mr. Forberich during the initial telephone conversation in which Mr. Owczarzak agreed to an extension. On June 27, 2002, Mr. Owczarzak sent Mr. Forberich a letter stating "[w]ith reference to our telephone conversation of Wednesday, [sic] Jun 26, 2002, RAW MATERIALS, INC. has agreed to extend the delivery date from June 30, 2002 until a later date during this calendar year on CONTRACT FORB 3464/02. This later date will be confirmed sometime during your visit to Chicago in July of this year." (D.E. 23 at 4; D.E. 21, Ex. O.) However, this letter contemplates further discussions and, although the parties apparently did not meet in Chicago in July, Mr. Owczarzak testified that they did have further discussions, though he did not testify to the content of these discussions in detail. (D.E. 19, Ex. 3, at 55.) Mr. Owczarzak also testified that he conveyed to Mr. Forberich that delivery to any port in the U.S. by December 31, 2002 would be satisfactory but he did not specify when or how (orally or by letter) he made this communication. (Id.) In his declaration, Mr. Forberich stated that his understanding was that Forberich was given an extension "until December 31, 2002 to load the rails and execute a bill of lading to be in compliance with the contract." (D.E. 21, Ex. C, ¶11.)

Given that the original contract obligated delivery to RMI's place of business in Chicago Heights by June 30, 2002, it appears unlikely that Mr. Owczarzak would have done more than agree to extend the delivery date to December 31, 2002, and change the delivery location to any U.S. port, but the evidence is unclear and contradictory and it is not the Court's role in deciding a summary judgment motion to weigh evidence. See, e.g., Anderson v. Liberty Lobby, Inc., 477 U.S. 242, 255, 106 S. Ct. 2505, 91 L. Ed. 2d 202 (1986); see also David Copperfield's Disappearing, Inc. v. Haddon Advertising Agency, Inc., 897 F.2d 288, 292 (7th Cir. 1990) (stating that "the intent of the parties to an oral contract is generally a question of fact"). Thus, a question of fact exists as to whether Forberich was obligated to deliver the rail to the U.S. by December 31, 2002 or whether Forberich was merely required to load the rail by that date. Consequently, since it cannot yet be determined whether Forberich would have met its contractual obligations by shipping rail from the port at the end of December, a question of fact exists as to whether the port's freezing prevented Forberich from performing its obligation, even assuming the port froze in mid-December.

C.   Foreseeability

RMI's sole basis for its contention that the early freezing of the port was foreseeable is the assertion, without citation to the record, in its brief in support of summary judgment, that "it hardly could come as a surprise to any experienced shipping merchant (or any grammar school geography student) that the port in St. Petersburg might become icy and frozen in the Russian winter months." (D.E. 18 at 12.) However, Forberich presented evidence that the severity of the winter in 2002 and the early onset of the freezing of the port and its consequences were far from ordinary occurrences. It is undisputed that although the St. Petersburg port does usually freeze over in the winter months, this typically does not happen until late January, and such freezing does not prevent the vessels from entering and exiting the port. (D.E. 23 at 6.) More to the point, Mr. Forberich testified that although ice breakers are normally used to allow for shipping, the winter of 2002 was the worst winter in St. Petersburg in almost sixty years and that ice interfered with shipping at the end of November and that even the icebreakers were stuck in the ice. (D.E. 21, Ex. F, at 106.) He also testified that these were "unexpected weather conditions." (Id. at 77.) Whether it was foreseeable that such severe weather would occur and would stop even the icebreakers from working is a question of fact for the jury. In so holding, the Court notes that the freezing over of the upper Mississippi River has been the basis of a successful *force majeure* defense. See Louis Dreyfus Corp. v. Continental Grain Co., 395 So. 2d 442, 450 (La. Ct. App. 1981). In sum, because questions of fact exist as to whether the early freezing of the port prevented Forberich's performance and was foreseeable, Forberich's *force majeure* affirmative defense may be viable and summary judgment would be inappropriate.

CONCLUSION

For the foregoing reasons, Plaintiff's motion for summary judgment is denied.

The gist of the UCC and CISG approaches to excuse is essentially the same: CISG Article 79 excuses a party from performance where the inability was due "to an impediment beyond his control," as long as the impediment was unavoidable and the excused party could not reasonably have been expected to account for the impediment at the time of contract formation. This concept is much like what we see in UCC §2-615(a). Another similarity between CISG Article 79 and UCC §2-615 is that both provisions require the excused party to notify the other side of the basis for the excuse and of its effect on the excused party's ability to perform.

There are, however, differences between the CISG approach to commercial impracticability and the UCC approach. The CISG excuse rules are broader than the UCC's in two ways, but narrower in another way. The CISG excuse approach is broader in that it applies by its terms to both buyers and sellers rather than just to sellers, as is the case under UCC §2-615. Second, the CISG excuse rules cover a party's failure to perform "any of his obligations," whereas UCC §2-615(a) allows excuse only with respect to a seller's "[d]elay in delivery or non-delivery in whole or in part."

Practically speaking, neither of these differences should matter much. As we saw earlier in this assignment, most courts will allow buyers to claim excuse in the UCC context, either by assuming that §2-615 must also apply to buyers or by looking to the common law of excuse. Furthermore, there won't be many cases where breach of the seller's obligation is something other than either delay in delivery or non-delivery of the goods in whole or in part.

The one respect in which the CISG excuse approach is arguably stingier than UCC §2-615 arises in the case where a seller's assumed source of supply fails to deliver to the seller, thereby preventing the seller from performing its obligations to the buyer. Under the UCC, Official Comment 5 to §2-615 suggests that, as long as the seller's source of supply is assumed by both parties to be the seller's exclusive source, then the seller will be excused when the seller's source fails to deliver. Under CISG Article 79(2), by contrast, a party like the seller above is excused by the failure of a third-party source only when the third-party source itself has a valid basis of excuse.

Thus, in a case where the seller's supplier fails to deliver to the seller for no valid reason, the CISG would not excuse the seller's obligation to its own buyer even if both the seller and the buyer assumed that the seller would be getting its goods from this particular supplier. Under the UCC, however, the seller would be off the hook due to its supplier's breach, and the buyer would have to settle for the seller "turning over to the buyer . . . his rights against the defaulting source of supply to the extent of the buyer's contract in relation to which excuse is being claimed." UCC Official Comment 5 to §2-615.

D. Commercial Impracticability with Real Estate

In the case of real estate sales, there is no "real estate–specific" doctrine of commercial impracticability that has either been codified in state statutes or that has developed in the common law. Instead, parties to a real estate sales contract that wish to claim excuse from their contractual obligations must look to the general common law of impossibility, which presumably was covered in your contracts course and which (you may recall) sounds a lot like UCC §2-615.

Problem Set 14

14.1. In your capacity as an associate at Dewey, Cheatem & Howe, you were just handed another case from one of your firm's most active clients, Lou's Used Cars for Less (from Problem 2.1). One of Lou's sales people, "Slick Rick" Newman, explained to you that he had a contract to sell a used Cadillac convertible for $15,000 to a very demanding customer, Kristi Aiken. Kristi really wants this particular car because it was once driven by Tiger Woods. After the customer paid the price and signed the contract, she arranged to pick up her Cadillac from Lou's the very next day. That evening a terrible hailstorm damaged the body of the Cadillac so badly that it would cost $18,000 to repair it. The car now has a scrap value of $500. Kristi insisted that Lou's should pay for whatever body work it would take to put the car back in the condition it was when she signed the contract. Rick says he wants to know what his obligations and his options are with respect to Kristi's demands. UCC §§2-613, 2-509(3); Official Comment 3 to §2-509.

14.2.   a. Arlene Ledger, president of Heavy Metal, Inc. (from Problem 3.2), is back in your office. Heavy Metal, as you may recall, is a manufacturer of exercise equipment. Arlene explains to you that last month she agreed to fill a large order for a new local Gold's Gym franchise that is planning its grand opening late next week. The order to Gold's Gym is supposed to be delivered tomorrow. The problem, Arlene says, is that a heavy rain late last week caused a flood in the basement of Heavy Metal's building, which is where Arlene had been storing the exercise machines that were earmarked for Gold's Gym. Now those machines are rusty and unsuitable for delivery. As soon as Arlene discovered the problem she notified the president of Gold's Gym, Cory Haney. Cory, however, has told Arlene that Gold's Gym cannot afford to open late, given all of the advance publicity she has generated so far about the grand opening. Arlene asks you whether she will be able to claim an excuse for a delay in delivering the equipment to Gold's Gym. Arlene says that it would take a few weeks for her company to manufacture replacement equipment for Gold's. Arlene admits that she can buy the same equipment immediately from another manufacturer, but at a price that would cause her to lose money on her Gold's Gym contract. In reading the sales contract, you see that it says nothing either about force majeure or about source of supply. What do you tell Arlene? UCC §§2-613, 2-615; Official Comment 5 to §2-615.

b. Same facts as part (a), except the reason for Arlene's failure to perform is that Arlene's steel supplier, which was designated in Arlene's contract with Gold's Gym as Arlene's exclusive source of steel for this contract, reneged on its contract with Arlene. The steel supplier's failure to deliver was due to the destruction of its plant by a fire that was negligently caused by several of its own employees. Will Arlene be excused from her obligations to Gold's Gym? UCC §2-615, Official Comment 5 to §2-615. Would your answer change if this contract were governed by the CISG? CISG Art. 79.

c. Same facts as part (a), except that there were 60 machines in the basement, only 30 of which were ruined by the flood. The Gold's Gym order was for 40 machines, but Big Jake's Gym across town also had an order from Heavy Metal for 20 machines for his grand opening on the same day. Arlene would like to allocate 20 of the 30 good machines to Jake's and just 10 to Gold's Gym for at least two reasons: first, because she thinks it is better to have at least one happy customer rather than no happy customers; and second, because she heard from her friends in the industry that Jake's will soon be opening up lots more local branches, which she would love to supply with machines. Can Arlene justify her proposed allocation? UCC §2-615(b).

d. Same facts as part (c), except Arlene chooses to allocate the good machines in a pro rata fashion: Jake's gets 10 and Gold's gets 20. When Arlene gives Gold's Gym notice of the problem and of Gold's share of the good machines, Cory Haney of Gold's says, "We'll take the 20 you have for us right now, and we'll just wait to take the remaining 20 whenever you can make some new ones for us. We don't want to lose that great price we got." Arlene has to admit that she did undersell herself when she originally made the contract with Gold's; Arlene's strong preference would be to give Cory her fair allocation of 20 machines and be finished for good with the Gold's contract. May Arlene condition her allocation of 20 machines to Gold's on Gold's agreeing to forget the rest of the contract? UCC §§2-615, 2-616(1). Would your answer change if this contract were governed by the CISG? CISG Art. 79.

14.3.   The president of Golden Dairy, Ben Able, comes to your office to discuss a long-term supply contract that he is negotiating with a new retirement center. The directors of the retirement center would like to enter into a five-year deal in which Golden Dairy supplies all of the milk for the center's cafeteria. The center would very much like to negotiate a set price for the milk, even if that fixed price increases during each of the five years of the contract. Ben is not averse to that approach, but he is concerned about his dairy's exposure if there is a significant milk shortage during the five-year contract period. Ben would like you to suggest some ways in which the contract could give price certainty to the retirement center, but still limit the dairy's risk in the event that milk prices go through the ceiling. In light of Ben's stated desire, consider the following three possibilities: (1) completely fixed pricing, (2) completely variable pricing that ties the price to some objective market measure, and (3) variable pricing with specific price floors or ceilings. Which option would you recommend? Are there other options you can think of? Official Comments 4 and 8 to §2-615.

Assignment 15: Unconscionability

A. Unconscionability with Sales of Goods

The concept of unconscionability is one of the most amorphous features of the sales system. Like the doctrine of impossibility, unconscionability is a basis by which a party to an otherwise enforceable sales agreement may avoid that agreement. Whereas the impossibility excuse tends to be used most successfully by the commercial seller, the unconscionability excuse tends to be used by the consumer buyer.

Although the drafters of Article 2 chose to include a section on unconscionability, they were not able to agree upon a definition of the term. Section 2-302, the basic unconscionability section, does not even pretend to define the concept. Official Comment 1 to §2-302 gives us some hints as to a definition of unconscionability, but at times the Comment lapses into tautology: "the basic test is whether, in light of the commercial background and the commercial needs of the particular trade or case, the clauses involved are so one-sided as to be unconscionable under the circumstances existing at the time of the making of the contract. . . ." Probably the best we get from Comment 1 in the way of definition is as follows: "the principle is one of the prevention of oppression and unfair surprise and not of the disturbance of allocation of risks because of superior bargaining power. . . . "

When courts today are faced with claims of unconscionability, they tend to use the definition first set down in Williams v. Walker-Thomas Furniture, 350 F.2d 445 (D.C. Cir. 1965): "an absence of meaningful choice on the part of one of the parties together with contract terms which are unreasonably favorable to the other party." Professor Arthur Leff, in a famous article on the subject of unconscionability, echoed the *Walker-Thomas Furniture* definition by noting that a successful unconscionability defense should require that the defendant was the victim of both procedural unconscionability ("an absence of meaningful choice") and substantive unconscionability ("unreasonably favorable terms"). Arthur Leff, Unconscionability and the Code — The Emperor's New Clause, 115 U. Pa. L. Rev. 485 (1967). Although most courts today require both procedural and substantive unconscionability, some believe that either one or the other will suffice for a finding of unconscionability.

Although UCC §2-302 does not bother to define unconscionability, the section does give us several useful pieces of information about how the doctrine of unconscionability is to operate in practice. First, §2-302(1) tells us that the unconscionability determination is a matter of law, thus taking this consumer-friendly defense out of the hands of what would likely be a consumer-friendly jury.

Second, §2-302(1) indicates that the appropriate time for measuring the unconscionability of a contract or a clause in the contract is when the contract was made rather than in light of later events. Therefore, the fact that a particular contract turned out to be, in retrospect, a terrible deal for the buyer should not be sufficient grounds for finding substantive unconscionability.

Third, and perhaps most significant, §2-302(1) indicates the functional consequences of a judge finding that a contract or a clause in the contract was indeed unconscionable. A judge who makes a finding of unconscionability has three options: (1) refuse to enforce the contract at all, (2) enforce the remainder of the contract without the unconscionable clause, or (3) limit the application of any unconscionable clause to avoid an unconscionable result.

The final contribution that §2-302 makes to our understanding of unconscionability is to require in §2-302(2) that there be a hearing afforded to the parties that gives them "a reasonable opportunity to present evidence as to its commercial setting, purpose and effect to aid the court in making the [unconscionability] determination." The idea here seems to be that unconscionability is very much contextual and, therefore, the parties ought to have a specific opportunity to present evidence about the context surrounding the making of the contract.

Although unconscionability claims rarely succeed, §2-302 is by no means a dead letter. As the following case demonstrates, the defense is most likely to be successful in a case involving the combination of an unsophisticated consumer buyer, on the one hand, and an aggressive seller with onerous terms, on the other. As is true in this case, it is not at all uncommon for the "substantive unconscionability" to consist in part of credit terms that strike the court as overreaching.

Maxwell v. Fidelity Financial Services, Inc.

907 P.2d 51 (Ariz. 1995)

FELDMAN, C.J.

. . . The facts, taken in the light most favorable to Maxwell, against whom summary judgment was granted, are that in December 1984, Elizabeth Maxwell and her then husband, Charles, were approached by Steve Lasica, a door-to-door salesman representing the now defunct National Solar Corporation ("National"). Lasica sold the Maxwells a solar home water heater for a total purchase price of $6,512. Although National was responsible for installation, the unit was never installed properly, never functioned properly, and was eventually declared a hazard, condemned, and ordered disconnected by the City of Phoenix. Thus, although the unit may have been intrinsically worthless, the question of unconscionability is determined as of the time the contract was made.

Financing for the purchase was accomplished through a loan to the Maxwells from Fidelity Financial Services, Inc. ("Fidelity"). The sale price was financed for a ten-year period at 19.5 percent interest, making the total cost nearly $15,000.

At the time of the transaction, Elizabeth Maxwell earned approximately $400 per month working part-time as a hotel maid and her husband earned approximately $1,800 per month working for the local paper. At Fidelity's request, an appraisal was made of the Maxwells' South Phoenix home, where they had resided for the preceding twelve years. The appraisal showed that the Maxwells lived in a modest neighborhood, that their 1,539 square foot home was in need of a significant amount of general repair and maintenance, and that its market value was approximately $40,000.

In connection with the financing transaction, Elizabeth Maxwell signed numerous documents, including a loan contract, a deed of trust, a truth-in-lending disclosure form, and a promissory note and security agreement. The effect of these documents was not only to secure the deferred purchase price with a lien on the merchandise sold, but also to place a lien on Maxwell's house as additional security for payment on the water heater contract. The forms and their terms were unambiguous and clearly indicated that Maxwell was placing a lien on her house. . . .

Despite the fact that the water heater was never installed or working properly, Maxwell made payments on it for approximately three and one-half years, reducing the deferred purchase balance to $5,733. In 1988, Maxwell approached Fidelity to borrow an additional $800 for purposes unrelated to the original loan. In making this second loan, Fidelity required Maxwell to again sign a bundle of documents essentially identical to those she signed in 1984. Instead of simply adding $800 to Maxwell's outstanding balance on the 1984 contract, Fidelity created a new contract that included the unpaid balance of $5,733 on the 1984 loan, a term life insurance charge of $313, as well as the new $800 loan. In all, Maxwell financed the sum of $6,976 with this second loan. The terms of this latest loan also included interest at 19.5 interest and payments for a period of six years, making Maxwell's new payments, including interest, total nearly $12,000. The combined amount Maxwell would pay under the two contracts for a non-functioning water heater and the additional $800 loan thus totals approximately $17,000, or nearly one-half the value of her home.

Maxwell continued to make payments until 1990, when she brought this declaratory judgment action seeking, inter alia, a declaration that the 1984 contract was unenforceable on the grounds that it was unconscionable. . . . Many courts, perhaps a majority, have held that there must be some quantum of both procedural and substantive unconscionability to establish a claim, and take a balancing approach in applying them. Other courts have held that it is sufficient if either is shown. . . .

[W]e conclude that under A.R.S. §47-2302, a claim of unconscionability can be established with a showing of substantive unconscionability alone, especially in cases involving either price-cost disparity or limitation of remedies. If only procedural irregularities are present, it may be more appropriate to analyze the claims under the doctrines of fraud, misrepresentation, duress, and mistake, although such irregularities can make a case of procedural unconscionability. However, we leave for another day the questions involving the remedy for procedural uncon- scionability alone.

We conclude further that this case presents a question of at least substantive unconscionability to be decided by the trial court. From the face of it, we certainly cannot conclude that the contract as a whole is not unconscionable, given the $6,500 price of a water heater for a modest residence, payable at 19.5 percent interest, for a total time-payment price of $14,860.43. These facts present at least a question of grossly-excessive price, constituting substantive unconscionability. This contract is made even more harsh by its security terms, which, in the event of non-payment, permit Fidelity not only to repossess the water heater but foreclose on Maxwell's home. The apparent injustice and oppression in these security provi- sions not only may constitute substantive unconscionability but also may provide evidence of procedural unconscionability. . . .

Therefore, we vacate the court of appeals' opinion, reverse the trial court's judg- ment, and remand to the trial court for proceedings consistent with this opinion and A.R.S. §47-2302.

Justice Martone, one of the concurring judges in *Maxwell*, indicated in his concurring opinion that he would not have merely remanded the case to the trial court for an unconscionability determination; he would have held the contracts in question to be unconscionable as a matter of law:

> The facts as outlined by the majority lead to one inescapable conclusion: one of unconscionability. If these contracts are not unconscionable as a matter of law, what contract would be? . . . On the undisputed facts, the commercial setting, purpose and effect of the contracts are tragically plain. The commercial setting: a "now defunct" entity took advantage of a limited person living on the margin of human existence. The purpose: to extract "$17,000" from a "hotel maid" who earned "$400 per month." The effect: to subject a marginal person to the risk of loss of her home, all for a hot water heater that "was never installed properly, [and] never functioned properly."

In dealing with concepts as subjective as unconscionability, it is hard to contend that the personal views of the judge will have nothing to do with the outcome in a particular case. For example, if you were representing a consumer defendant and were attempting to assert the unconscionability defense, con- sider whether it would matter to you whether your case were being decided by the likes of Justice Martone, whose concurrence is excerpted above, or instead by Judge Richard Posner of the Seventh Circuit Court of Appeals, who wrote an opinion on unconscionability that included the following observations:

> There can be no objection to using the one-sidedness of a transaction as evidence of deception, lack of agreement, or compulsion, none of which has been shown

here. The problem with unconscionability as a legal doctrine comes in making sense out of lack of "meaningful choice" in a situation where the promisor was not deceived or compelled and really did agree to the provision that he contends was unconscionable. Suppose that for reasons unrelated to any conduct by the promisee the promisor has very restricted opportunities. Maybe he is so poor that he can be induced to sell the clothes off his back for a pittance, or is such a poor credit risk that he can be made (in the absence of usury laws) to pay an extraordinarily high interest rate to borrow money that he wants desperately. Does he have a "meaningful choice" in such circumstances? If not he may actually be made worse off by a rule of nonenforcement of hard bargains; for, knowing that a contract with him will not be enforced, merchants may be unwilling to buy his clothes or lend him money. Since the law of contracts cannot compel the making of contracts on terms favorable to one party, but can only refuse to enforce contracts with unfavorable terms, it is not an institution well designed to rectify inequalities in wealth. (Amoco Oil Co. v. Ashcraft, 791 F.2d 519, 522 (7th Cir. 1986).)

Whether or not you buy into Judge Posner's worldview generally, it is certainly the case that the unconscionability doctrine is not one that courts use lightly. If unconscionability were routinely allowed as a basis for escaping contract liability, the entire sales system would suffer from the effects of the uncertainty that would ensue. Consider the following observations from a couple of scholars considering the role that excuse doctrines such as unconscionability ought to play in the Hungarian contracts system:

> Finally, contract law reduces transaction costs by assuring propriety in the contract negotiation process. Doctrines of fraud, undue influence, and unconscionability provide the paradigms. In a typical case, one party will assert that a contract reflects a voluntary agreement worthy of judicial enforcement, and the other party will seek to be excused from performing. The court must be alert to two forms of opportunism. Perhaps the first party has misled the second into signing a contract the second did not fully understand. On the other hand, the second party may simply be trying to excuse itself from its own bad bargain. Either type of opportunism increases the costs of conducting exchanges. A court following an economic logic will decide such cases so as to minimize the potential for these two types of costly opportunism, and thereby provide an incentive structure that encourages future parties to bargain more effectively. (Ostas & Leete, Am. Bus. L.J., Feb. 1, 1995.)

B.   Unconscionability with Leases

The unconscionability provision of Article 2A, UCC §2A-108, essentially mimics most of the key provisions of §2-302, with a couple of additions that were modeled after the Uniform Consumer Credit Code. There are two major differences between §2A-108 and §2-302. First, §2A-108(2) refers to a lease contract or a clause in a lease contract being induced by "unconscionable conduct," and also grants relief where there is unconscionable conduct in the collection of a claim. Section 2-302 does not use the phrase "unconscionable conduct," nor does it regulate collections of claims.

Pantoja-Cahue v. Ford Motor Credit Co.

872 N.E.2d 1039 (Ill. App. 2007)

KARNEZIS, J.

Plaintiff Mario Pantoja-Cahue filed a six-count complaint seeking damages from defendant Ford Motor Credit Company for Ford's alleged breach of the peace and "illegal activities" in repossessing plaintiff's automobile from his locked garage. The trial court granted Ford's motion to dismiss four of the counts pursuant to section 2-615 of the Illinois Code of Civil Procedure (735 ILCS 5/2-615 (West 2004)). Plaintiff appeals, arguing the court erred in granting Ford's motion to dismiss because he sufficiently alleged Ford committed a breach of the peace when a repossession agent, at Ford's behest, broke into plaintiff's locked garage to take his vehicle in violation of (1) sections 5/2A-108 and 2A-525 of the Illinois Uniform Commercial Code (the Code) (810 ILCS 5/2A-108, 2A-525 (West 2004)); (2) plaintiff's contract with Ford; and (3) section 2 of the Illinois Consumer Fraud and Deceptive Business Practices Act (Consumer Fraud Act) (815 ILCS 505/ 2 (West 2004)). He also argues he sufficiently alleged Ford ordered the repossession knowing that the issue of the vehicle's ownership was pending before a court, in violation of section 2 of the Consumer Fraud Act.

We affirm in part, reverse in part and remand.

BACKGROUND

In August 2000, plaintiff purchased a 2000 Ford Explorer from auto dealer Webb Ford. Plaintiff, a native Spanish speaker, negotiated the purchase with a Spanish-speaking salesperson at Webb. Plaintiff signed what he thought was a contract for the purchase and financing of the vehicle, with monthly installment payments to be made to Ford. The contract was in English. Some years later, plaintiff discovered the contract was actually a lease, not a purchase agreement. Plaintiff brought suit against Ford and Webb on August 22, 2003, alleging fraud. Ford brought a replevin action against plaintiff asserting plaintiff was in default on his obligations under the lease. In the late night/early morning hours of March 11-12, 2004, repossession agents entered plaintiff's locked garage and removed the car.

On May 18, 2004, the court dismissed plaintiff's claims against Ford without prejudice. On December 1, 2004, the court entered an order settling plaintiff's case against Webb. Pursuant to the settlement, Webb repurchased the car from Ford and tendered it back to plaintiff.

On May 17, 2005, plaintiff filed a complaint against Ford and "Doe Repossession Company/Agent," an as yet unknown repossession agent acting on Ford's behalf.

On December 16, 2005, plaintiff filed the second amended complaint at issue here. Plaintiff sought damages for Ford and Doe's "unlawful activities surrounding the wrongful repossession of Plaintiff's vehicle." He alleged Ford and Doe's breaking into plaintiff's locked garage to effectuate the repossession and Ford's repossession of the vehicle knowing that title to the car was the subject of ongoing litigation variously violated section 2A-525(3) of the Code (count I against Ford), the Fair Debt Collection Practices Act (15 U.S.C. §1692 et seq. (2000)) (count II against Doe), the unlawful trespass statute (count III against Ford and Doe), section 2 of the Consumer Fraud Act (count IV against Ford and Doe), Ford's contract with plaintiff (count V against Ford) and section 2A-108 of the Code (count VI against Ford and Doe).

Ford filed a section 2-615 motion to dismiss counts I, IV, V and VI. The court granted the motion with prejudice on April 10, 2006. The court made its order final and appealable pursuant to Supreme Court Rule 304(a) (210 Ill. 2d R. 304(a)) and granted plaintiff's request to stay all pending matters pending appeal of its decision. Plaintiff timely filed his notice of appeal on April 26, 2006, arguing the court erred in granting Ford's motion to dismiss pursuant to section 2-615.

ANALYSIS

A motion to dismiss filed pursuant to section 2-615 is based on the pleadings rather than the underlying facts. Neppl v. Murphy, 316 Ill. App. 3d 581, 584, 249 Ill. Dec. 736, 736 N.E.2d 1174, 1178 (2000). It admits all well-pleaded facts appearing on the face of the complaint and attacks the legal sufficiency of the complaint, alleging only defects on the face of the complaint. *Neppl*, 316 Ill. App. 3d at 584, 249 Ill. Dec. 736, 736 N.E.2d at 1178; Elson v. State Farm Fire & Casualty Co., 295 Ill. App. 3d 1, 6, 229 Ill. Dec. 334, 691 N.E.2d 807, 811 (1998). Viewing the complaint in the light most favorable to the nonmoving party, here plaintiff, we must determine whether it alleges sufficient facts to state a cause of action upon which relief may be granted. Ziemba v. Mierzwa, 142 Ill. 2d 42, 46-47, 153 Ill. Dec. 259, 566 N.E.2d 1365, 1366 (1991). In making that determination, we must take as true all well-pleaded facts of the complaint, draw all reasonable inferences therefrom in favor of the nonmoving party, and disregard mere conclusions of law unsupported by specific factual allegations. Krueger v. Lewis, 342 Ill. App. 3d 467, 470, 276 Ill. Dec. 720, 794 N.E.2d 970, 972 (2003); *Ziemba*, 142 Ill. 2d at 47, 153 Ill. Dec. 259, 566 N.E.2d at 1366. We do not consider the merits of the case. *Elson*, 295 Ill. App. 3d at 5, 229 Ill. Dec. 334, 691 N.E.2d at 811. Our standard of review is de novo. *Neppl*, 316 Ill. App. 3d at 583, 249 Ill. Dec. 736, 736 N.E.2d at 1178. . . .

UNIFORM COMMERCIAL CODE SECTION 2A-108

In count VI, plaintiff alleged the lease agreement was unconscionable because it was formed in violation of section 2N of the Code (815 ILCS 505/2N (West 2004)).

Plaintiff does not quote section 2N or explain how the agreement violates section 2N. Instead, he quotes section 2A-108 of the Code, as follows:

> (2) With respect to a consumer lease, if the court as a matter of law finds that a lease contract or any clause of a lease contract has been induced by unconscionable conduct or that unconscionable conduct has occurred in the collection of a claim arising from a lease contract, the court may grant appropriate relief.
>
> (3) Before making a finding of unconscionability under subsection (1) or (2), the court, on its own motion or that of a party, shall afford the parties a reasonable opportunity to present evidence as to the setting, purpose, and effect of the lease contract or clause thereof, or of the conduct." 810 ILCS 5/2A-108(2), (3).

He then, in "violation one" under count VI, alleges the lease was made in violation of section 2N because it was negotiated in Spanish but he was only given a copy of the contract in English; he could not read the contract and, as a result, Webb Ford was able to trick him into signing a lease, rather than a purchase agreement; such contract was induced by unconscionable conduct; and, because it was illegal, the contract was unenforceable.

This allegation is insufficient to state a cause of action against Ford under section 2A-108. Even taking as true plaintiff's allegation that Webb Ford tricked him into signing the lease agreement, this allegation is insufficient to state a cause of action against Ford for unconscionable conduct in violation of section 2A-108. First, Ford is an entirely different entity than Webb Ford and plaintiff does not assert otherwise. Nor does plaintiff assert that Webb Ford was acting as Ford's agent in inducing plaintiff to sign the lease. Plaintiff asserts no basis on which Ford can be found liable for something Webb Ford did. Second, there is no allegation as to how the contract violates section 2N, merely the legal conclusion that it does, as well as the unsupported legal conclusion that a violation of section 2N is necessarily unconscionable.

Plaintiff's count VI "violation two" is similarly deficient. Plaintiff alleges that Ford knew plaintiff had filed suit alleging the contract was unenforceable and, despite this knowledge, "effectuated a repossession of the subject vehicle, where such repossession involved unconscionable conduct, namely, a breach of the peace. As a result, [Ford] committed unconscionable conduct in its collection of a claim arising from the lease agreement." Taking as true the assertion that Ford knew plaintiff was contesting the validity of the contract when it repossessed the car, we cannot determine how this fact is relevant to Ford's alleged unconscionable conduct in breaching the peace during the repossession. Ford had a statutory right to repossess the car upon default and plaintiff does not allege (explain) how or why performing such repossession with the knowledge that plaintiff had filed a suit contesting the lease agreement was unconscionable in the context of section 2A-108. Nor is there a well-pleaded allegation of why a "breach of the peace," presumably the breaking into the garage referred to elsewhere in the complaint, is to be considered unconscionable in the context of section 2A-108. The court did not err in dismissing count VI. . . .

The second key difference between §2-302 and §2A-108 is §2A-108(4), which allows for the possibility of attorneys' fees to be awarded to the prevailing consumer in an unconscionability action. Section 2A-108(4) also allows for the possibility of attorneys' fees being awarded against the consumer if the consumer's unconscionability action not only loses but is also deemed groundless by the court. Section 2-302 does not provide for attorneys' fees.

The key similarity between the sales and lease provisions in the UCC concerning unconscionability is that in both sections, it is extremely difficult for a plaintiff to prevail.

BMW Financial Services v. Smoke Rise Corp.

486 S.E.2d 629 (Ga. Ct. App. 1997)

Pope, P.J.

In this action to enforce an excess mileage provision in a motor vehicle lease, the plaintiff lessor appeals from the trial court's denial of its motion for summary judgment. Because there is no question of material fact regarding plaintiff's right to enforce the provision, we granted its application for interlocutory appeal and now reverse.

Defendant Smoke Rise Corporation leased a BMW automobile from plaintiff, and the corporation's president, defendant William Probst, personally guaranteed the lease. The lease, as modified in an extension agreement, provided that at the end of the lease term defendants could purchase the vehicle for $16,863.75, the estimated end-of-term wholesale value of the vehicle. It also provided that if defendants returned the vehicle rather than exercising their option to purchase it, they would have to pay a charge of "up to 15 cents" for each mile the vehicle had been driven in excess of 85,011 miles. Defendants chose not to purchase the vehicle and returned it with an odometer reading of 180,409 miles, but they refused to pay for the excess mileage. Plaintiff seeks $14,309.70, which is 15 cents times 95,398 (the difference between 180,409 and 85,011 miles), plus attorney fees.

In their defense, Smoke Rise and Probst contend the excess mileage provision is unconscionable because the $14,309.70 charge is almost as much as the projected end-of-term value of the car, and is considerably more than their experts say the actual value of the car is with 180,409 miles. Unconscionability is evaluated by looking at the circumstances at the time the contract was originally made, however, and determining whether, in light of the commercial needs of the particular trade involved, the agreement is one which "'no sane man not operating under a delusion would make and . . . no honest man would take advantage of.' [Cits.]" R.L. Kimsey Cotton Co. v. Ferguson, 233 Ga. 962, 965-66(3), 214 S.E.2d 360 (1975); accord Zepp v. Mayor & Council of Athens, 180 Ga. App. 72, 79(2), 348 S.E.2d 673 (1986). See also OCGA §11-2A-108. In the context of a corporation leasing a luxury vehicle, an excess mileage charge of 15 cents a mile is not unreasonable and certainly does not shock the conscience. Such a charge serves the necessary commercial function of compensating for out-of-the-ordinary usage which will affect the residual value of the car. If at the end of the term defendants discovered the excess mileage charge was too high relative to the value of the car, they could have exercised their option to purchase it. But they did not do so, and now they cannot complain about a charge they agreed to pay.

Defendants' argument that the provision is too indefinite to enforce is also without merit. Plaintiff is entitled to anything up to 15 cents a mile, and that includes 15 cents a mile. And the fact that it was willing to take less earlier in the dispute does not undermine its right to 15 cents a mile.

The excess mileage provision is clear and unambiguous, and must be enforced as written. Accordingly, the trial court erred in denying plaintiff's motion for summary judgment.

JUDGMENT REVERSED.

C. Unconscionability with International Sales

Although the CISG contains a provision governing commercial impracticability, it does not include any provision that recognizes a doctrine of unconscionability. This is perhaps not too surprising, since the UCC unconscionability section, 2-302, is generally applied to consumer sales and the CISG specifically excludes from its scope the sale of goods to consumers. CISG Art. 2(a). Further, the CISG says that it does not concern itself with the "validity of the contract or of any of its provisions. . . ." CISG Art. 4(a). Thus, it would seem unlikely that a court would recognize an unconscionability argument raised in a sales contract covered by the CISG.

D. Unconscionability with Real Estate

There are no statutory or common law unconscionability doctrines that are peculiar to real estate sales. On the other hand, the common law of contracts generally recognizes the concept of unconscionability. Therefore, parties to real estate sales contracts should be able to avail themselves of that doctrine. The common law doctrine is essentially the same as what UCC §2-302 provides. There should not be much difference, then, between a party's ability to claim unconscionability in a sales of goods context and a party's ability to do so in a real estate context.

Problem Set 15

15.1. Lou's Used Cars for Less is at it again. "Slick Rick" Newman comes to your office to ask you whether a recent customer of his can void a sale that Rick just entered into with her. A newly arrived immigrant, Mary Salvino, came into Lou's last week with the man for whom she cleans house, Paul Leske. Paul is a good friend of Rick, so when Mary asked Paul where she might buy a used car, Paul suggested Rick. Mary paid $8,000 cash for a used Honda Accord. That was the posted price, although most customers of Lou's end up negotiating about 25 percent off of the posted price. Paul read Mary the sales contract before she signed it, since Mary still does not read English well. That contract included a prominent "AS IS" disclaimer on the face of it. The car broke down three days after Mary bought it, and now a legal aid lawyer is threatening to sue Lou's Used Cars for Less unless Mary gets her money back. The legal aid lawyer said he will argue unconscionability. Will he likely succeed? UCC §2-302.

15.2.   a. Another of Lou's top salesman, "Fast Eddie" Turner, comes to see you to ask about a recent lease deal that he entered into with Joe Schafer. Joe, it turns out, had a horrible credit record and no other car dealer in town would sell or lease to him on credit. Joe, however, desperately wanted to lease a used purple Cadillac for "fun cruising." Fast Eddie found a used purple Cadillac on which he entered into a four-year lease with Joe for $500 per month, twice the rate that would be charged to a lessee with good credit. Further, Fast Eddie put in a special clause in which Joe granted Lou's a security interest in Joe's trailer home in the event that Joe missed a lease payment. The lease also included an acceleration clause, which would cause all future rent payments to accelerate in the event of a single missed payment. Three months into the lease, Joe missed two consecutive payments and is nowhere to be found. Now Fast Eddie wants to accelerate the lease payments and foreclose on Joe's trailer home (where Joe's wife and six hungry children are currently residing). Do you see any problem with Fast Eddie enforcing his lease contract as written? §2A-108. Does it make any difference here whether the contract with Joe is a true lease or a disguised sale?

b. Same facts as part (a), except Joe had a great credit rating. However, Joe did confide to Fast Eddie when he walked into Lou's that he (Joe) had never leased a car before. Because of this information, Fast Eddie offered Joe what Fast Eddie characterized as a "special first-time lessee's rate" of $750 per month for four years. What Fast Eddie did not tell Joe was that the typical rate for a Cadillac this old was only $250 per month. Much to Eddie's amazement, Joe signed the lease with the "special rate," mumbling something about the fact that he just wasn't a "shop-around guy." If Joe learns later that he got a bum deal, should he be able to void it? UCC §2A-108.

c. Same facts as part (b), except Joe wants to lease not a purple Cadillac, but a down-and-dirty used Ford Pinto for the sole purpose of having a car so that he can drive to work. For that deal, Fast Eddie's "first-time lessee's rate" of $150 is triple the usual $50 per month lease payment for a car like this. If Joe learns later that he got a bum deal, should he be able to void it? UCC §2A-108.

d. Same facts as part (c), except Fast Eddie gives Joe the usual rate of $50 per month on the Ford Pinto. However, a couple of months after the lease is entered into, an investigative report in Consumer Digest asserts that the model of Pinto Joe has leased contains a gas tank that explodes on impact. In light of that information, the market rate of a lease on a Pinto like Joe's drops to $5 per month. Joe wants to escape the contract on the grounds of unconscionability. May he? UCC §2A-108.

Assignment 16:   Title with Sales of Goods

The ultimate aim of a sales contract is to transfer ownership of the goods sold from seller to buyer. Sellers, however, ordinarily cannot transfer ownership of that for which they do not have good title. One of the key default terms that Article 2 implies in any sales contract is a warranty by the seller that it has good title to the goods being transferred to the buyer.

The warranty of title is probably the broadest implied warranty created by Article 2, since it is a warranty that attaches to a sale by any seller rather than, as with the warranty of merchantability, just to sales by sellers who are merchants in goods of that kind. UCC §2-312(1). The seller is strictly liable when it breaches the title warranty; it does not matter whether the seller was completely ignorant of the title problems. In any sale of goods, the seller warrants that the title of the thing sold is good, that its transfer is rightful, and that the goods are delivered free of any third-party lien or encumbrance of which the buyer is unaware. UCC §2-312(1).

Interestingly, even though the title warranty is in fact an implied warranty, the seller may not disclaim it in the ways that would suffice to disclaim other implied warranties such as merchantability or fitness for a particular purpose. Except in unusual circumstances, a seller that wishes to disclaim the warranty of title must use very specific language to that effect. UCC §2-312(2). In the alternative, there are certain special circumstances, such as a sheriff's sale, where the title warranty will be excluded by implication. UCC §2-312(2).

With personal property, good title tends to be correlated with possession but need not be. The most obvious example of a situation where title does not correlate with possession is when a thief steals a true owner's goods. The thief has possession but clearly does not have good title. Even the innocent buyer who unwittingly purchases goods from a thief will not have good title, since we are told in UCC §2-403(1) that "[a] purchaser of goods acquires all title which his transferor had. . . ." In other words, this provision is the sales law version of property law's shelter principle: a purchaser takes what the seller has.

The rules of UCC §2-403 are ultimately concerned with the question of how to allocate between two innocent parties the risk of chasing a wrongdoer who is often absent or insolvent. In the classic example, a thief steals the goods from the true owner. Then a later, innocent party comes into possession of the stolen goods with no inkling of their stolen character. Of course, all would agree that the thief in this scenario should be responsible for the loss. But in a case where the wrongdoer is either judgment-proof or not available, which innocent party (the original owner or the later possessor of the goods) should get stuck with the loss?

As suggested above, the answer is that the later possessor of the goods has to take the loss. Although nothing in §2-403 explicitly says that a thief in the chain of title prevents any later party from having good title, courts have read §2-403 to mean just that. In one case, for example, innocent purchasers of paintings from an art dealer had to surrender the paintings to the original owner because there was a thief earlier in the chain of title. See Erisoty v. Rizik, 1995 WL 91406, *9 (E.D. Pa.) (restating general principle that a "bona fide purchaser [of a chattel] from a thief gets nothing").

Any party that acquires goods after a thief has stolen them is said to have "void title," which is the same thing as saying "no title." Interestingly, UCC §2-403 is not content to create the polar opposite categories of "good title" and "void title." Instead, that section adds an intermediate (and more complex) title classification known as "voidable title."

A seller who has "voidable title" does not itself have good title but nevertheless has the power to transfer good title to a good-faith purchaser for value. Sellers who have voidable title are those who have somehow tricked the true owner into voluntarily transferring possession of the goods to them. UCC §2-403(1). They might have done so by posing as someone they were not or by otherwise defrauding the true owner. Probably the most common situation in which a party ends up with "voidable title" is when a buyer purchases goods from the true owner with a worthless check.

West v. Roberts

143 P.3d 1037 (Colo. 2006)

BENDER, J.

I.   INTRODUCTION

We review on certiorari an appellate decision from the district court, which construed Colorado Revised Statute section 18-4-405. We hold that this statute, which permits the rightful owner of stolen property to recover that property from the possession of another person, does not apply when the rightful owner intends to part with the property.

Kenneth James West relinquished his car in exchange for a cashier's check that appeared valid, but which thereafter proved to be a worthless counterfeit. When he later located the car in the possession of a subsequent purchaser, Tammy Roberts, West sued to recover the car under section 18-4-405. However, the trial court found that section 18-4-405 does not apply to situations, like this case, in which an owner voluntarily relinquishes the property, even if he is defrauded into doing so. Instead, the trial court applied Uniform Commercial Code (UCC) section

2-403, as enacted in Colorado as section 4-2-403, C.R.S. (2006). The trial court found that the UCC provision entitled Roberts, as a good faith purchaser for value, to retain ownership of the car. On appeal, the district court, acting as an appellate court, upheld the trial court's decision.

We agree with the district court's conclusion and hold that, although "theft" in our criminal code includes theft by deception, UCC section 2-403 abrogates section 18-4-405 so that "theft" in that provision does not include theft in which an owner voluntarily relinquishes property to a thief under a transaction of purchase.

Thus we affirm the district court and hold that Tammy Roberts, as a good faith purchaser for value, obtained good title to the car under C.R.S. section 4-2-403.

II.   FACTS AND PROCEEDINGS BELOW

West agreed to sell his car, a 1975 Corvette, to a man representing himself as Robert Wilson. In exchange for a cashier's check, West signed over the Corvette's title to Wilson and gave him the car. Ten days later, when West learned that the cashier's check was a forgery, he filed a stolen vehicle report with police. However, the police did not locate Wilson or the Corvette, and the case grew cold. Nearly two and a half years later, West asked the police to run a check on the Corvette's vehicle identification number. The check yielded the name and address of Tammy Roberts. Roberts, who holds certificate of title to the Corvette, had purchased the vehicle from her brother, who, in turn, had purchased it in response to a newspaper ad. West filed suit against Roberts in county court to establish legal ownership of the Corvette under Colorado's stolen property statute, C.R.S. section 18-4-405.

The trial court determined that the stolen property statute did not apply in this case. Instead, the court found that the UCC, specifically C.R.S. section 4-2-403, governed the transaction and that Roberts was the rightful owner.

In reaching the conclusion that section 2-403 of the UCC applies in this case and that Roberts was the rightful owner of the Corvette, the trial court relied on Keybank Nat'l Ass'n v. Mascarenas, 17 P.3d 209 (Colo. App. 2000). In *Keybank,* the court of appeals held that a theft in which the owner willingly entrusts his property to another is different than "ordinary theft," in which the owner is unaware of the taking and does not intend to part with the property. Id. at 214. The trial court found that, under the *Keybank* holding, theft by deception or fraud is not covered under the stolen property statute if the theft involves a transfer of goods in which the seller voluntarily parts with the goods in exchange for something else. Accordingly, the trial court held that the UCC applies in this case and that, because title can be legally transferred to a bona fide purchaser even if the transferor did not have proper authority to do so, Roberts possessed good title to the Corvette.

On appeal, the district court, acting as an appellate court, upheld the trial court's decision on two grounds. First, the court considered whether a theft had occurred for the purposes of the stolen property statute. Citing *Keybank,* the court found that a theft has not taken place if, as in this case, the owner was aware of a taking and had intended to part with the property. Thus, the court found the stolen property statute does not apply in this case. Second, the court found that the trial court correctly applied section 2-403 of the UCC. Even though the cashier's check from Wilson was later dishonored, the court held that Roberts was a bona fide purchaser and acquired a full property interest in the Corvette.

We accepted certiorari to reconcile the apparent conflict between the two statutes—section 2-403 of the UCC and the stolen property statute—and to determine which statute applies in this case. We first examine the stolen property statute and UCC section 2-403 and determine whether either statute applies in this case. We then reconcile the apparent conflict between the two statutes.

III. ANALYSIS

THE STOLEN PROPERTY STATUTE

We begin by examining whether the stolen property statute applies in this case. Matters of statutory interpretation are questions of law, which we review de novo. E.g., Ryals v. St. Mary-Corwin Reg'l Med. Ctr., 10 P.3d 654, 659 (Colo. 2000). When interpreting a statute, we look first to its plain language. E.g., Spahmer v. Gullette, 113 P.3d 158, 162 (Colo. 2005).

The stolen property statute permits the rightful owner of stolen property to recover that property from the possession of another person. §18-4-405, C.R.S; Cedar Lane Invs. v. Am. Roofing Supply of Colorado Springs, Inc., 919 P.2d 879, 882 (Colo. App. 1996). For the stolen property statute to apply, "the owner of the property must prove that the taker . . . committed acts constituting at least one of the statutory crimes" listed within the statute. Itin v. Ungar, 17 P.3d 129, 134 (Colo. 2000). However, the statute itself does not define theft. Id. at 133. Because the stolen property statute is contained in the Colorado Criminal Code, terms contained in that statute may be defined within the scheme of the statutory framework. Id. The criminal code defines theft as "knowingly obtain[ing] or exercis[ing] control over anything of value of another without authorization, *or by threat or deception,* and . . . [i]ntend[ing] to deprive the other person permanently of the use or benefit of the thing of value." §18-4-401(1)(a), C.R.S. (2006) (emphasis added). Theft by deception as set forth in subsection 18-4-401(1)(a) requires proof that the victim relied on a swindler's misrepresentations, which caused the victim to part with something of value. People v. Warner, 801 P.2d 1187, 1189-90 (Colo. 1990).

The language of the stolen property statute states that the statute applies to property obtained by theft and that even a good faith purchaser of such property may be divested of it. The definition of theft contained in section 18-4-401 is clear. Use of the word "or" in a statute is presumed to be disjunctive. Armintrout v. People, 864 P.2d 576, 581 (Colo. 1993) (citations omitted). Thus, though a theft may occur when one takes property without the owner's authorization, the use of the word "or" indicates that a theft may also occur if the property is taken by deception, even with the owner's authorization.

The trial court found that Wilson deceived West into relinquishing the Corvette and its title in exchange for a fraudulent cashier's check and, accordingly, that Wilson could be charged with theft. A theft therefore occurred for the purposes of the stolen property statute. Hence, based upon the plain language of the stolen property statute and section 18-4-401, we determine that the stolen property statute appears to apply in this case.

Having analyzed the stolen property statute, we now examine section 2-403 of the UCC.

THE UNIFORM COMMERCIAL CODE

West asserts that the trial and district courts should not have applied section 2-403 of the UCC in this case. He offers two primary arguments in support of his position: (1) the entrustment provisions of section 2-403 only protect those who purchase from merchants; and (2) subsection 2-403(1) is also inapplicable because West did not pass voidable title to Wilson, the initial purchaser of the Corvette. We address each argument in turn.

West argues that, because Wilson was not a merchant, no entrustment occurred under section 2-403 and, therefore, Roberts did not acquire valid title to the car. We agree that an entrustment did not occur, which calls upon us to clarify the statute's relevance in merchant and non-merchant transactions.

We again turn to the statutory language as the starting point in our analysis. E.g., *Spahmer*, 113 P.3d at 162. The language of section 2-403 does not indicate that all transactions falling within the statute's purview must involve a merchant; indeed, subsection (2) is the only portion of the statute that mentions the word "merchant."

Comments to a statute are relevant in its interpretation. See People v. Yascavage, 101 P.3d 1090, 1092 (Colo. 2004). As such, we turn to the official comments to section 2-403 for additional guidance in determining whether the statute applies to transactions involving non-merchants. The language of the official comments to section 2-403 strongly suggests that subsections (2), (3), and (4) apply specifically to merchant transactions, while subsection 2-403(1) is applicable to non-merchant transactions. Comment 2 states that subsections (2), (3), and (4) serve to protect persons who buy "in ordinary course out of inventory." The UCC defines a "buyer in ordinary course of business" as someone who buys "from a person . . . in the business of selling goods of that kind." §4-1-201(9), C.R.S. (2006). Comment 4 indicates that the rights of purchasers who are not buyers in ordinary course—thus including those who did not buy from a merchant—are addressed in subsection (1) of the statute.

Comment 1, which applies to subsection (1), states that the provision protects "good faith purchaser[s] for value." Within the context of the UCC, the concept of good faith purchaser for value does not appear to require that the purchaser buy from a merchant or dealer. Several provisions of the UCC must be combined to define good faith purchaser for value. The UCC defines good faith as "honesty in fact and the observance of reasonable commercial standards of fair dealing." §4-1-201(19), C.R.S. A purchaser is one who "takes by purchase." §4-1-201(30), C.R.S. Purchase, in turn, means "taking by sale, lease, discount, negotiation, mortgage, pledge, lien, security interest, issue or reissue, gift, or any other voluntary transaction creating an interest in property." §4-1-201(29), C.R.S. And a person gives value, generally, by providing "consideration sufficient to support a simple contract." §4-1-204(4), C.R.S. (2006). The Kentucky Court of Appeals offered a more concise definition of good faith purchaser for value in the context of section 2-403 as "one who takes by purchase getting sufficient consideration to support a simple contract, and who is honest in the transaction of the purchase." United Rd. Machinery Co. v. Jasper, 568 S.W.2d 242, 244 (Ky. Ct. App. 1978).

When a Colorado statute is patterned after a model code, this court may draw upon outside authority in interpreting the provision. E.g., Szaloczi v. John R. Behrmann Revocable Trust, 90 P.3d 835, 838-39 (Colo. 2004). Leading treatises on the UCC support an interpretation of subsection 2-403(1) as applying beyond merchant transactions. The Uniform Commercial Code Series explains that, under subsection (2), a protected purchaser must be a buyer in the ordinary course of business, which is different than the type of purchaser addressed in subsection (1):

> It should be noted that [a buyer in the ordinary course of business] is not the equivalent of the common law "bona fide purchaser" or the concept of "good faith purchaser for value" used in the voidable title situations addressed by Section 2-403(1). The principal difference between "buyer in the ordinary course of business" and these other terms lies [in] the fact that the buyer in the ordinary course must buy goods from a merchant in the business of selling goods of that kind and must buy them in the usual way in which such items of inventory are bought.

2 William D. Hawkland, Uniform Commercial Code Series §2-403:7 (1982).

White & Summers's treatise also suggests that subsection (1) applies to non-merchant transactions. As its title implies, section 2-403 addresses three separate topics: (1) "the general powers of a transferor of goods to transfer title or interests [in subsection (1)]"; (2) "the title of a good faith purchaser of goods [in subsection (1)]"; and (3) "the rights of a buyer in ordinary course *from a merchant* to whom goods have been entrusted [in subsections (2) and (3)]." 1 James J. White & Robert S. Summers, Uniform Commercial Code §3-12 (4th ed. 1995) (emphasis added). According to another treatise, for subsection 2-403(1), "the good faith of the purchaser is the focus of inquiry." Robert A. Hillman et al., Common Law and Equity Under the Uniform Commercial Code ¶5.04[1] (1985). In contrast, Hillman's analyses of subsections 2-403(2) and (3) indicate that they apply to merchant transactions. For example, Hillman explains that the purpose of subsection 2-403(2) is "'to enhance the reliability of commercial sales by merchants.'" Id. ¶5.04[2] (quoting Porter v. Wertz, 53 N.Y.2d 696, 439 N.Y.S.2d 105, 421 N.E.2d 500 (1981)).

Finally, we note that courts in other jurisdictions have applied UCC section 2-403 to non-merchant sales transactions. E.g., Cooper v. Pac. Auto. Ins. Co., 95 Nev. 798, 603 P.2d 281 (1979); Dartmouth Motor Sales, Inc. v. Wilcox, 128 N.H.

526, 517 A.2d 804 (1986); Atlas Auto Rental Corp. v. Weisberg, 54 Misc. 2d 168, 281 N.Y.S.2d 400 (N.Y. Civ. Ct. 1967); Creggin Group, Ltd. v. Crown Diversified Indus. Corp., 113 Ohio App. 3d 853, 682 N.E.2d 692 (1996).

Because subsection 2-403(1) does not refer to merchant transactions or buyers in ordinary course, because the definition of good faith purchaser for value does not require purchase from a merchant or dealer, and because the official comments to UCC section 2-403 indicate that only subsections (2), (3), and (4) apply solely to merchant transactions, we conclude that subsection 2-403(1) applies to non-merchant transactions. Thus, we continue our analysis to determine whether subsection 2-403(1) applies in this case.

West also contends that, because the Corvette was stolen, he did not pass voidable title to the initial purchaser-cum-thief, Wilson. Thus, argues West, Roberts could not have obtained good title under subsection 2-403(1). West's primary argument in support of his assertion that he did not pass voidable title is that no purchase took place because he relinquished title to the car in exchange for a worthless cashier's check. We disagree.

Subsection 2-403(1) protects good faith purchasers for value. The provision requires that goods be "delivered under a transaction of purchase." §4-2-403(1), C.R.S. (2006). As we have noted, under the UCC, a purchase is broadly defined as "taking by sale, lease, discount, negotiation, mortgage, pledge, lien, security interest, issue or reissue, gift, or *any other voluntary transaction creating an interest in property.*" §4-1-201(29), C.R.S. (emphasis added). Voluntary means "proceeding from the will or from one's own choice or consent." Merriam-Webster's Collegiate Dictionary 1402 (11th ed. 2004). West freely chose to deliver the car and its title to Wilson. And he chose to do so even though he had neither attempted to cash the cashier's check nor obtained contact information for Wilson. Hence, we conclude that West's transfer of the Corvette and its title in exchange for a cashier's check, even though a worthless counterfeit, constitutes a voluntary transaction that is subject to subsection 2-403(1).

Indeed, the plain language of the statute itself bolsters this conclusion. Subsection 4-2-403(1) provides, in pertinent part, that "[w]hen goods have been delivered under a transaction of purchase, the purchaser has such power [to transfer good title to a good faith purchaser for value] even though . . . [t]he delivery was in exchange for a check which is later dishonored, or . . . [t]he delivery was procured through fraud punishable as larcenous under the criminal law." §4-2-403(1)(b), (d), C.R.S. This language indicates that a transaction of purchase is not thwarted simply because a purchaser failed to provide payment that met the seller's expectation. To employ West's rationale that exchanging goods for a fraudulent cashier's check does not constitute a delivery under a transaction of purchase would render the provision meaningless.

The addition of subsection 1.5 by the legislature to Colorado's UCC statute also indicates that a transaction of purchase could encompass a fraud-based exchange. The General Assembly added subsection 1.5, which is not part of the UCC model code, in 1975. That provision specifies that, if a seller of livestock has not received payment, the purchaser "does not have power to transfer good title to a good faith purchaser for value until payment is made." §4-2-403(1.5), C.R.S. We deem it significant that subsection 1.5 demarcates livestock transactions; its only effect is to require payment before a buyer has power to transfer title. This amendment to the Colorado UCC statute suggests that, by requiring payment before the power to transfer can attach, livestock transactions are to be treated differently than other transactions controlled by the statute. Therefore it is logical to conclude that a purchaser of non-livestock goods possesses the power to transfer those goods upon receipt of the goods from the seller, even if the purchaser's payment is invalid.

Various authorities provide additional support for our conclusion. "[T]he general rule seems to be that the physical delivery of the goods to a transferor-purchaser by the true owner sufficiently empowers that transferor-purchaser to transfer good title to a good faith purchaser for value even though the delivery was in exchange for a check which was later dishonored." 3 Patricia F. Fonseca & John R. Fonseca, *Williston on Sales* §23:38 (5th ed. 1994). "Subsection 1(d) of 2-403 provides that even where delivery was procured through criminal fraud, voidable title passes." White & Summers, supra, §3-12(b). The argument that the term "transaction of purchase" indicates that the true owner did not intend to enter such a fraudulent transaction fails "in light of the clear policy of Section 2-403(1) to enable the good-faith purchaser to prevail." Hillman, supra, ¶5.04[2] n.95 (citing 3A R. Dusenberg & L. King, Sales & Bulk Transfers Under the Uniform Commercial Code §10.06[1] (1982)).

We note that courts in other jurisdictions have applied subsection 2-403(1) to similar types of fraudulent, though voluntary, transactions. "A transfer that is fraudulently induced . . . is considered a 'purchase' under the Code, and meets the threshold of being 'voluntary.'" *Demoulas v. Demoulas*, 428 Mass. 555, 703 N.E.2d 1149, 1164 (1998) (invoking subsection 2-403(1) to determine whether defendants were bona fide purchasers in a case in which a stock owner was defrauded into voluntarily transferring the stock). Accord *Cooper*, 603 P.2d at 283 (finding implicitly that a man who purchased a car with an invalid cashier's check obtained voidable title); *Kenyon v. Abel*, 36 P.3d 1161, 1165-66 (Wyo. 2001) (explaining that subsection 2-403(1)(d) effectively provides that "voidable title is created whenever the transferor voluntarily delivers goods to a purchaser even though that delivery was procured through fraud" in ultimately holding that no voluntary transfer had occurred); *Creggin Group, Ltd.*, 682 N.E.2d at 696-97 (holding that an exchange in which a man purchased an airplane using an invalid check was a transaction of purchase sufficient to confer voidable title to the purchaser regardless of the purchaser's larcenous intent).

Having concluded that West delivered the Corvette under a transaction of purchase, we continue our examination of subsection 2-403(1) in order to determine if Roberts obtained good title to the Corvette. The provision allows a person with voidable title to transfer good title to a good faith purchaser for value even under certain conditions, including when the transferor paid in cash or with a check that was later dishonored, or when the transferor otherwise procured the delivery through fraud punishable under criminal law. §4-2-403(1), C.R.S. Specifically, subsection (1)(d) states that a good faith purchaser may obtain good title to property even if the transferor acquired the property "through fraud punishable as larcenous under the criminal law." We begin by noting that West does not dispute that Roberts is a good faith purchaser for value.

Section 18-4-403 of the Colorado Criminal Code provides that any Colorado law referring to larceny "shall be interpreted as if the word 'theft' were substituted therefore." As the trial court found, Wilson could be charged with theft for deceiving West into relinquishing the Corvette and its title in exchange for a fraudulent cashier's check. Accordingly, Wilson procured the Corvette through fraud punishable as larcenous under the criminal law. Because he obtained the car under a transaction of purchase, Wilson obtained voidable title to the car despite the fact that he paid with a fraudulent cashier's check. As such, Roberts, a subsequent good faith purchaser for value, obtained good title to the Corvette under subsection 2-403(1)(d). This result is opposite of that reached under the stolen property statute, which, pursuant to our earlier analysis, would allow West to recover the car from Roberts.

IV.   APPLICATION

Because both the stolen property statute and subsection 2-403(1) of the UCC appear to apply in this case, we must next determine which statute prevails. When two statutes conflict, this Court favors a construction that avoids conflict between the provisions. People v. Mojica-Simental, 73 P.3d 15, 17-18 (Colo. 2003). If we cannot reconcile statutes passed at different legislative sessions, the statute with the latest effective date controls. §2-4-206, C.R.S. (2006); Slater v. McKinna, 997 P.2d 1196, 1199 (Colo. 2000). And the more specific provision generally prevails over the more general provision. See §2-4-205, C.R.S. (2006); People v. Smith, 971 P.2d 1056, 1058 (Colo. 1999).

The General Assembly enacted the UCC in 1965. The first version of the stolen property statute, which is effectively identical to the current provision, was enacted in 1861 as a territorial law. The UCC provision, which addresses in detail several types of scenarios, is more specific than the stolen property statute. We therefore hold that UCC section 2-403 prevails over the stolen property statute.

Further analysis bolsters our holding. The general rule, embodied in the stolen property statute, is that "[a] thief has no title and can pass none, not even to a buyer in the ordinary course." Fonseca & Fonseca, supra, §23:35. See also, e.g., Thomas M. Quinn, Uniform Commercial Code Commentary and Law Digest ¶2-403[A][5] (1978) ("Where the goods are stolen from the original owner, both the common law and the Code preserve the original owner's ownership rights . . . notwithstanding subsequent sales."). However, UCC section 2-403 provides an exception to that general rule. Comment 1 to section 2-403 hints at such an exception in the context of subsection (1), explaining that "subsection (1) provides specifically for the protection of the good faith purchaser for value in a number of specific situations which have been troublesome under prior law." §4-2-403 official cmt. 1, C.R.S. Each of the specific situations listed in subsection

2-403(1) involves a voluntary transfer of goods, even though the intent to transfer the goods may have been induced by fraud. The language of the statute leads to the conclusion that goods delivered under a transaction of purchase, even when the seller is fraudulently induced to do so, can then be validly sold to a good faith purchaser for value, whereas goods that are stolen but not delivered under a transaction of purchase cannot.

Again, treatises on the UCC support this conclusion. White and Summers explain that theft by fraud should be distinguished from robbery-type theft because the original seller has a better opportunity to prevent that type of theft:

> In general voidable title passes to those who lie in the middle of the spectrum that runs from best faith buyer at one end to robber at the other. These are buyers who commit fraud, or are otherwise guilty of naughty acts (bounced checks), but who conform to the appearance of a voluntary transaction; they would never pull a gun or crawl in through a second story window. Presumably these fraudulent buyers get voidable title from their targets, but second story men get only void title because the targets of fraud are themselves more culpable than the targets of burglary.

White & Summers, supra, §3-12(b). See also Quinn, supra, ¶2-403[A][5] ("Where the original owner parts with the goods voluntarily in circumstances which, while deplorable, do not constitute outright theft, there is always the chance that the transferee will acquire apparent ownership or 'voidable title' and, thanks to this altered state, may be able to pass along better title to a good faith purchaser than he himself may have."). By relinquishing possession of the goods to the buyer, even when fraudulently induced to do so, the original seller cloaks the "thief" with the apparent authority to sell the goods. Fonseca & Fonseca, supra, §23:35.

We note that other jurisdictions have distinguished theft by fraud that results in a voluntary transfer of the stolen property from theft by wrongful taking. E.g., *Kenyon,* 36 P.3d at 1165-66; *Demoulas,* 703 N.E.2d at 1164. This Court has also hinted at that distinction, explaining that the stolen property statute "allows an owner to regain only property 'obtained by theft, robbery, or burglary' rather than any property that has been 'wrongfully taken or detained.'" In re Marriage of Allen, 724 P.2d 651, 656 (Colo. 1986). Indeed, our court of appeals made this distinction in the context of section 2-403 in *Keybank,* upon which the trial and district courts relied in finding that Roberts acquired good title to the Corvette. Our decision today serves to extend the *Keybank* distinction beyond the context in which it was rendered—the entrustment provisions of subsections 2-403(2) and (3)—to transactions under subsection 2-403(1). However, we disagree with the *Keybank* rationale to the extent that it suggests that a distinction between theft and fraud exists within our criminal code.

We therefore hold that, although "theft" in our criminal code includes theft by deception, UCC section 2-403 abrogates the stolen property statute so that "theft" in that provision does not include any theft in which an owner voluntarily relinquishes property to a thief under a transaction of purchase.

We acknowledge that such a rule can, as in this case, result in loss to an innocent party. But a determination that West is entitled to recover the car would also be a determination that Roberts, another innocent party, must relinquish a vehicle that she purchased in good faith. The policy behind subsection 2-403(1) is to protect the party least able to protect herself—the good faith purchaser for value.

> Where an owner has voluntarily parted with possession of his chattel, even though induced by a criminal act, a bona fide purchaser can acquire good title, under the theory that where one of two innocent parties must suffer because of the wrongdoing of a third person, the loss must fall on the party who by his conduct created the circumstances which enabled the third party to perpetuate the wrong.

Anderson Contracting Co., Inc. v. Zurich Ins. Co., 448 So. 2d 37, 38 (Fla. Dist. Ct. App. 1984). The original seller is better positioned to take precautions to prevent loss than a later purchaser. For example, West could have insisted upon cash or ensured that the check would clear before relinquishing the car and title. On the other hand, to place the onus on the good faith purchaser to fully investigate every purchase in order to determine whether it originated in fraud would unduly burden trade. See, e.g., Fonseca & Fonseca, supra, §23:47. We have acknowledged that this tenet "is in accord with the overall policy of the UCC's entrustment provision: to restrict impediments to the free flow of commerce when buyers in the ordinary course of business are involved." Cugnini v. Reynolds Cattle Co., 687 P.2d 962, 967 (Colo. 1984). It is equally applicable to good faith purchasers for value under subsection 2-403(1).

V.   CONCLUSION

For the reasons stated, we affirm the judgment of the district court acting as an appellate court.

It is somewhat curious that the UCC drafters saw fit to draw such a significant distinction between a "true thief" in the chain of title, after which no one other than the true owner can have good title, and a mere con artist in the chain, which does not necessarily break the chain of title. Courts and commentators often justify the "voidable title" concept as grounded in a policy of protecting the innocent purchaser for value. Yet if that were the driving force behind the voidable title rules, then it would seem just as sensible to protect the good-faith purchaser for value even in a case where there was a "true thief" earlier in the chain of title.

A more coherent justification for the distinction that the American sales system draws between "void title" and "voidable title" would focus on the relative fault of the true owner who lost possession of the goods. Perhaps the thinking is that where the true owner has not voluntarily relinquished possession, the true owner should not be punished because it had no role in causing the title problem with which the current purchaser finds itself. In all cases of "voidable title," by contrast, the true owner has allowed itself to be duped into voluntarily relinquishing possession. As between the completely innocent good-faith purchaser and the somewhat negligent (or at least blameworthy) true owner, maybe it makes sense in the various voidable title scenarios that the law chooses to favor the good-faith purchaser.

Or, to put this another way, in situations involving voidable title the true owner is presumptively in a better position than the good-faith purchaser to prevent the loss resulting from the title problem. While one may argue that the same is often true even where a "true thief" steals the item, we know for certain that for voidable title to arise the true owner must have been duped in some way.

In determining whether a particular transferee has "void" rather than "voidable title," one useful test is to ask whether the transferor intended at the time of the exchange to transfer title to the goods. If the answer is "yes," then the transferee will have at least voidable title, if not good title. If the answer is "no"—that is, if the transferor did not intend to transfer title to the goods—then the transferee will necessarily have void title. That, of course, would include the case where the "true thief" simply steals the goods from the owner.

A close conceptual cousin to the voidable title doctrine is the doctrine of entrustment. UCC §2-403(2) provides that "[a]ny entrusting of possession of goods to a merchant who deals in goods of that kind gives him power to transfer all rights of the entruster to a buyer in ordinary course of business." Entrusting includes any delivery or acquiescence of possession by the true owner "regardless of any condition expressed between the parties to the delivery or acquiescence." UCC §2-403(3).

Thus, suppose you bring your computer in for repairs to a computer dealer that both sells and repairs computers. When you leave the computer at the dealer's, you entrust it to him for purposes of §2-403. Accordingly, if the dealer mistakenly (or even intentionally) sells the computer to a buyer in the ordinary course of business, that buyer's title to the computer would be superior to yours. You would have an action for conversion against the computer dealer, but you would have no recourse against the new owner of the computer.

Great American Insurance Co. v. Nextday Network Hardware Corp.

2014 WL 7365805 (D. Maryland 2014)

CHUANG, D.J.

This case arose after Defendant Nextday Network Hardware Corp. ("Nextday") bought hundreds of thousands of dollars' worth of information technology ("IT") equipment from an individual who stole the equipment from his employer, Vectren Corporation ("Vectren"). Plaintiff Great American Insurance Company ("Great American"), Vectren's insurer, filed suit against Nextday; the president of Nextday, Donald Banyong; and ten unidentified Nextday employees who participated in the sale (collectively, "Defendants"). The Complaint asserts claims for conversion, aiding and abetting conversion, and civil conspiracy. Presently pending is Defendants' Motion to Dismiss for Failure to State a Claim. ECF No. 7. The Motion is ripe for disposition, and no hearing is necessary to resolve the issues. See Local Rule 106.5 (D. Md. 2014). For the reasons that follow, the Motion is DENIED.

BACKGROUND

The following facts are described as alleged in the Complaint. ECF No. 1. Christopher Brian Crowe was an Associate Network and Telecommunications Analyst at Vectren. In November 2012, Vectren discovered that Crowe had been stealing new and slightly used IT equipment from Vectren data centers and other locations. The fair market value of the stolen IT equipment totaled $919,338.05. Crowe then sold the stolen IT equipment through online auction website eBay.com to Nextday for $228,609.15. Great American alleges that Banyong and ten unidentified Nextday employees participated in purchasing the equipment from Crowe, including setting the purchase price and providing the shipment information.

Crowe was eventually arrested by the Evansville Police Department ("EPD") in Indiana and charged with two counts of theft. He later pleaded guilty to the charges. In March 2013, the EPD informed Nextday that the IT equipment it purchased from Crowe was stolen. Despite the EPD's attempts to make arrangements for the equipment's return to Vectren. Banyong resisted and told the EPD that he planned to sell the remaining equipment he bought from Crowe. Great American paid Vectren for the loss and, on April 30, 2014, filed suit against Defendants. Defendants now move to dismiss.

DISCUSSION

* * *

II.   Conversion

Great American sufficiently states a plausible claim for conversion by alleging that Defendants purchased goods that Crowe had stolen from Vectren, then sold them to other buyers. Under Maryland law, conversion involves any distinct act of dominion or control "'exerted by one person over the personal property of another in denial of his right or inconsistent with it.'" Allied Inv. Corp. v. Jasen, 354 Md. 547, 731 A.2d 957, 963 (1999) (quoting Interstate Ins. Co. v. Logan, 205 Md. 583, 109 A.2d 904, 907 (1954)). In Inmi-Etti v. Aluisi, 63 Md. App. 293, 492 A.2d 917 (Md. Ct. Spec. App. 1985), the Maryland Court of Special Appeals found Pohanka Oldsmobile-GMC, Inc. ("Pohanka") liable for conversion where

Pohanka had purchased a car from an individual who had taken possession of the car without the owner's authorization. Id. at 918-19, 923. Particularly where Great American has alleged that Nextday sold the equipment it purchased from Crowe after it had been notified by the police that the property was stolen, Compl. ¶15, it has successfully pleaded a cause of action for conversion.

Defendants argue that the entrustment provision of the Commercial Law Article of the Maryland Code, which adopts a provision of the Uniform Commercial Code ("UCC"), precludes any conversion claim. This provision provides that "[a]ny entrusting of possession of goods to a merchant who deals in goods of that kind gives him power to transfer all rights of the entruster to a buyer in ordinary course of business." Md. Code Ann., Com. Law §2-403(2) (West 2014). The entrustment provision is meant to safeguard unsuspecting buyers who purchase goods from merchants in good faith. See Lakes Gas Co. v. Clark Oil Trading Co., 875 F. Supp. 2d 1289, 1304-05 (D. Kan. 2012); 2 William D. Hawkland et al., Uniform Commercial Code Series §2-403:4 (2014). Thus, if a party entrusts its goods to a "merchant," a "buyer in the ordinary course of business" who purchases those goods from the merchant cannot be liable for conversion even if the entrusting party later disputes whether the merchant had authority to make the sale. See Robison v. Gerber Prods. Co., 765 F.2d 431, 433 (4th Cir. 1985) (applying the identical UCC provision under South Carolina law).

For the entrustment provision to apply, (1) there must be an entrustment of goods; (2) that entrustment must be to a "merchant who deals in goods of that kind"; and (3) the transfer must be to a buyer in the ordinary course of business who purchases in good faith, without knowledge that the sale violates ownership rights. Id. Here, Defendants argue that the entrustment provision applies because Crowe entrusted the stolen IT equipment to Nextday, Nextday is a merchant who deals in goods of that kind, and Nextday was a buyer in the ordinary course of business. Defs.' Mem. Supp. Mot. Dismiss at 11-13. This argument, however, suffers from three fundamental deficiencies. First, the entrustment provision inherently requires three separate parties—an owner, a merchant, and a buyer—as it only applies when a rightful owner attempts to sue a buyer after the buyer purchases goods from a merchant. Nextday cannot be both the merchant and the buyer in this scenario.

Second, the entrustment provision leaves the merchant potentially liable for conversion. See 2 William D. Hawkland et al., Uniform Commercial Code Series §2-403:4 (noting that, although the entrustment provision protects the buyer from suit, the owner "will have rights against the merchant who sold the goods for conversion or other common law remedies as appropriate"). Thus, if the provision applies here and Nextday is the merchant, as Nextday claims, then the entrustment provision would not protect Nextday from suit. Instead, the provision would protect only the subsequent buyers to whom Nextday sold the stolen IT equipment.

Third, the entrustment provision does not apply where the "entrusting" party stole the goods. At its core, the entrustment provision works by giving the merchant "power to transfer all rights of the entruster to a buyer in ordinary course of business." See Md. Code Ann., Com. Law §2-403(2). In *Inmi-Etti*, the court explained that only a person with "voidable" title has the power to entrust goods under this provision. Id. at 920 (citing Md. Code Ann., Com. Law §2-403(1) ("A person with voidable title has power to transfer a good title to a good faith purchaser for value.")). "Voidable" title is obtained where the owner voluntarily transfers the goods. Id. at 923. If the goods are stolen, only "void" title is obtained, and the thief cannot pass along good title to a good faith purchaser. Id. at 921, 923. Where, as here, the "entrusting" party, Crowe, had stolen the equipment, he had only void title and therefore had no rights in the goods to transfer to the merchant, who then could not lawfully transfer any rights to the buyer. See *Inmi-Etti*, 492 A.2d at 923 ("If the goods are stolen otherwise obtained against the will of the owner, only void title can result."); 2 Wilham D. Hawkland et al., Uniform Commercial Code Series §2-403:4 ("[I]f the entruster has no rights, such as when the entruster is a thief, the buyer in ordinary course of business also gets no rights.").

The facts of *Inmi-Etti* illustrate the inapplicability of the entrustment provision to Nextday. There, the plaintiff had allowed an acquaintance, David Butler, to receive her new car; Butler then convinced the Motor Vehicle Administration to issue him a certificate of title in his name and sold the car without her authorization to Pohanka, a car dealer, which in turn sold it to a third-party customer. *Inmi-Etti*, 492 A.2d at 918-19. The court held that §2-403, which includes the entrustment provision, did not apply because Butler had void title when he sold the car to Pohanka, and that as a result, Pohanka had "obtained no title, and its sale of the vehicle constituted a conversion."2 Id. at 923. The court rejected Pohanka's claim that it was not liable because Butler had presented a "duly issued certificate of title in his name," such that Pohanka was a "good faith purchaser for value." Id. Rather, under the court's conclusion, the entrustment provision cannot apply "where the seller had no title at all." Id. at 924.

Notably, the *Inmi-Etti* court reached that conclusion even though it was unclear whether Butler had stolen the car. See id. ("[T]he record is not sufficient for us to decide whether Butler actually stole the [plaintiff's] vehicle."). Here, where Great American expressly alleges that Crowe stole the IT equipment, Compl. ¶9, the facts more strongly indicate that Crowe obtained void title and could not convey good title to Nextday as the merchant. Even then, as discussed above, the entrustment provision would protect only the buyers of the goods from Nextday, not Nextday itself.

Even if Nextday were viewed as the "buyer in the ordinary course of business," the entrustment provision still would not apply. Under that analysis, Vectren would be the owner; Crowe, the merchant; and Nextday, the buyer. The provision would not apply because Vectren did not entrust the IT equipment to Crowe. *Robison*, 765 F.2d at 433. "Entrusting" under the provision includes "any delivery and any acquiescence in retention of possession regardless of any condition expressed between the parties to the delivery or acquiescence and regardless of whether the procurement of the entrusting or the possessor's disposition of the goods have been such as to be larcenous under the criminal law." Md. Code Ann., Com. Law

§2-403(3). "Delivery," in turn, means "voluntary transfer of possession." §1-201(b)(15). So for the entrustment provision to apply, the transfer of possession of goods from the owner to the merchant must be voluntary. Here, because Crowe stole the IT equipment from Vectren, Compl. ¶9, the transfer of possession was not voluntary, so there was no entrustment. See *Inmi-Etti*, 492 A.2d at 923.

Furthermore, there is no basis to find that Crowe was a "merchant who deals in goods of that kind." *Robison*, 765 F.2d at 433. Great American alleges that Crowe was an Associate Network and Telecommunications Analyst at Vectren. Compl. ¶8. Although the Complaint does not contain allegations describing Crowe's job responsibilities in detail, there is nothing to indicate that a telecommunications analyst is a legitimate merchant dealing in the purchase and sale of new and slightly used IT equipment. Because the entrustment provision does not apply, Great American has sufficiently alleged a conversion claim against Defendants. . . .

There are two differences between the voidable title rule and the entrustment rule. First, the entrustment rule operates only when the goods are entrusted to a merchant who deals in goods of that kind. By contrast, any party—merchant or not—who dupes the owner into delivering possession of the goods may achieve voidable title.

The second difference between entrustment and voidable title is that the voidable title rule requires that there be a good-faith purchaser for value, whereas the entrustment rule requires the slightly narrower category of a buyer in the ordinary course of business. A buyer in the ordinary course of business must buy in the ordinary course from a person who is in the business of selling goods of that kind and must not have knowledge that the sale violates the ownership rights of a third party. UCC §1-201(b)(9). For purposes of this definition, a pawnbroker does not qualify as a person in the business of selling goods of a particular kind. Thus, one cannot be a buyer in the ordinary course of business when purchasing from a pawnbroker.

Lest you think that it is self-evident why the American system allocates the risk of fraud and theft between the original owner and the innocent purchaser in the way that it does, consider the following excerpt about the United Kingdom government's struggle with these very issues:

> The UK government wants to improve the legal position of the innocent buyer of goods. . . . At present, the general rule is that an innocent buyer of goods cannot acquire good title to them if the seller acquired them by illegitimate means in the first place. There are various exceptions to this, such as "market overt" (below).
>
> The main proposal is that the Sale of Goods Act 1979 should extend protection to innocent buyers who find that they are the victims of fraud, theft or mistake. As a general principle, where the owner of goods has entrusted them to, or acquiesced in their possession by, another person, an innocent buyer of those goods should acquire good title.

This principle would involve the repeal of certain sections of the Sale of Goods and Factors Acts and would apply where possession was given under a sale contract, conditional sale contract, hire purchase agreement or leasing contract. It would apply when possession had been given under a purported contract even where there was a mistake as to identity, and to sales where a voidable title had been voided without the knowledge of the possessor of the goods. . . .

The consultation document proposes that the ancient rule of market overt should be abolished. Since medieval times, buyers of goods in certain markets established by statute or custom have acquired good title regardless of the seller's title. It is felt that these markets should conform with the law as it applies to other retail premises, even though this would leave the innocent buyer with little or no chance of redress, given the nature of markets. Room has been left to debate the converse proposition — that all retail premises should convert to the market overt principle — but it is unlikely that this course of action would be adopted. . . . ("Acquiring Title to Goods," Business Law Brief, March 3, 1994.)

A quick comparison of the UCC system with the UK system existing at the time of this discussion suggests two things. First, in the case of entrustment, the traditional UK system, unlike the UCC system, did not allow the innocent buyer to prevail against the unfortunate entruster. Second, there were certain markets in the UK in which the innocent buyer always won the title battle, even where it could be shown that there was a true thief earlier in the chain of title. These differences indicate that title rules are often more arbitrary than policy-driven; one can just as easily make categorical arguments for the good-faith purchaser over the original owner, and vice versa.

As final food for thought on the title issue in the sales system, consider the following story, also from the United Kingdom (here, England), which demonstrates again how the law on the books does not always translate into the law as it works in practice. In this case, a woman chose to buy back her stolen car from a good-faith purchaser who had unwittingly bought her car from a thief:

"I was told that if we attempted to take the car back, we would be arrested for theft," she said. So, faced with a lengthy legal battle, she agreed to buy it back for £120 — her own car! A detective on Greater Manchester's stolen vehicle squad commented: "It's a classic car-theft scenario. She still had the title to the car but could be arrested for theft if she took it away. The man who bought it in good faith was not allowed to drive it because it was stolen." ("Motoring: Whose Car Is It Anyway — When It's Been Nicked?," *London Daily Telegraph*, May 20, 1995.)

Problem Set 16

16.1.   a. Your law firm has a new client, Pierre LaClede, who owns an art and framing gallery in the trendy part of town. As the firm's UCC expert, you end up getting to counsel Pierre. He first confides to you that he really dislikes lawyers, but his shop has been having so many problems with title issues lately that he had no choice but to seek legal advice in order to sort things out. The first situation Pierre asks you about involves his gallery's recent sale of a $70,000 abstract painting entitled Pain. The painting was purchased by a man who identified himself only as "the Critic" and who paid for Pain with a suitcase containing 700 $100 bills. The problem is, the bills turned out to be counterfeit and "the Critic" is nowhere to be found. Pierre did, however, discover Pain at Lucy's, a competitor gallery down the street. Lucy Fenton, the owner of that gallery, said that she had purchased the painting for $20,000 from a stranger who called himself "the Critic." Pierre wants to know whether he should be able to recover the painting from Lucy's. What is your advice? UCC §§2-403(1), 1-201(b)(20), 2-103(1)(b), 1-204.

b. Same facts as part (a), except instead of selling Pain to the Critic, Pierre lends the painting to a friend who is not an art dealer, and the friend later sells the painting to Lucy. Under this scenario could Pierre recover the painting from Lucy? UCC §2-403(1).

16.2. a. Pierre's next question deals with a $40,000 painting (with frame) entitled Peace. Pierre had bought and then custom-framed that painting himself, and Lucy from down the street had asked Pierre to bring Peace by her shop so that she could look at the frame job. Pierre did as Lucy requested, but later that same day one of Lucy's clerks mistakenly sold Peace to Frank Baebler, a new customer, for just $30,000 (reflecting Lucy's customary 25 percent "new customer" discount). Frank paid for the painting with a personal check that was later returned for insufficient funds, but he said that this was just an oversight and that he would be happy to make good on that check with a $30,000 cashier's check. Before Frank makes good on that check, however, Pierre discovers the problem and demands that Frank return the painting. Should Pierre be able to get it? UCC §§2-403(1)-(3), 1-201(b)(9), 1-204.

b. Same facts as part (a), except Frank quickly gives Lucy the cashier's check for $30,000 after Pierre demands the painting back but before Pierre actually takes the painting from Frank. Should Pierre be able to get it back? UCC §2-403.

c. Same facts as part (a), except Frank quickly gives Lucy the cashier's check for $30,000 before Pierre even demands the painting from him. Now should Pierre be able to retrieve the painting from Frank? UCC §2-403.

d. Same facts as part (a), except Frank never gives Lucy a bad check but instead a cashier's check from the beginning. Now should Pierre be able to retrieve the painting from Frank? UCC §2-403.

e. Same facts as part (a). What rights does Pierre have against Lucy, assuming that Pierre cannot recover the painting from Frank? UCC §1-103.

16.3. a. The next painting Pierre wants to discuss is Rustic Simplicity, a $50,000 impressionistic work by a hot new artist. Here is what Pierre tells you about the whereabouts of Rustic Simplicity: Pierre sold that painting to George Daly, who purchased it with a bad check. George then sold it for $40,000 cash to George's family friend, Carla Stone. Carla in turn gave Rustic Simplicity to George Daly Jr. as a birthday gift. George Jr., who is 23, still lives with George

Sr. and is aware that his dad never made good on the bounced check to Pierre. Does Pierre have recovery rights against just one Daly or against both of them? UCC §§2-403(1), 1-201(b)(29), 1-201(b)(20).

b. Same facts as part (a), except that George Jr. was not only aware of George Sr.'s bounced check, but was party to a scam that was intended to "wash the title clean" of the Rustic Simplicity painting. Does Pierre have recovery rights against George Jr.? UCC §1-103.

c. Same facts as part (a), except that after George Sr. purchased the painting with a bad check, he gave the painting to George Jr. for a birthday gift. Does Pierre have recovery rights against George Jr.? UCC §2-403(1).

d. Same facts as part (a), except that after George Sr. purchased the painting with a bad check, he gave the painting to George Jr. for a birthday gift. George Jr. then sold the painting for cash to Carla Stone, a bona fide purchaser for value. Does Pierre have recovery rights against Carla Stone? UCC §2-403(1).

e. Same facts as part (a), except that George Sr. steals the painting from Pierre rather than purchasing it with a bad check. George Sr. then sells it for cash to Carla Stone, a bona fide purchaser for value. Carla then sells the painting to George Jr., who pays for it with a bad check. Finally, George Jr. sells the painting to Harvey Nichols, a bona fide purchaser for value. Does Pierre have recovery rights against Harvey? UCC §2-403(1).

16.4. Pierre's next question has to do with a rare foreign painting known as La Cucaracha, which Pierre himself purchased for $63,000 from a local art dealer. That sale was expressly agreed by the parties to be "as is." It turns out that the dealer who sold to Pierre, Jules Locke, purchased the painting from the original owner, Mr. Delgado, with a $30,000 check that bounced. Now Mr. Delgado has come to Pierre's insisting that Pierre give the painting back to him, or Mr. Delgado will sue Pierre for its return. Must Pierre relinquish La Cucaracha? Does Pierre have any recourse against Jules? How would you advise Pierre to disclaim the warranty of title if he ever wished to do so with a particular sale? UCC §§2-403(1), 2-312(1) and (2), 2-316(3); Official Comments 1 and 6 to §2-312; §2-607(5)(a).

Assignment 17: Title with Leases, International Sales, and Real Estate

A. Title with Leases

Given the fundamental difference between a sale and a lease in terms of the ownership interest that is being transferred, it should come as no surprise that the title rules for leases differ significantly from those for sales. Whereas the sales title warranty promises that the title conveyed is good, the comparable lease warranty promises merely that no third party holds a claim or interest in the goods being leased that arose from an act or omission of the lessor that will interfere with the lessee's enjoyment of the leased goods. UCC §2A-211(1).

Besides this warranty of "quiet possession" that is given by all lessors, lessors that are merchants dealing in goods of the kind also warrant that the leased goods are delivered free of any rightful claims of infringement by third parties. UCC §2A-211(2). This second implied warranty does not exist in the case of a finance lease.

The chain of title rules found in §§2A-304 and 2A-305 essentially mimic those that appear in §2-403 except that they put those rules into the lease context. Section 2A-304 covers the cases in which a lessor with an existing lease makes a subsequent lease of the same goods to a different lessee. In effect, §2A-304(1) says that the subsequent lessee must take subject to the existing lease contract. This means that generally speaking, the existing lessee has a right to possession of the goods that is superior to the right of the subsequent lessee, at least during the period of the existing lessee's lease term. The one exception to this rule, found in §2A-304(2), comes into play when the lessor is a merchant with respect to goods of the kind and the existing lessee entrusts the goods back to its own lessor during the course of the existing lease. In this case, if the lessor leases to a new lessee in the ordinary course of business, the new lessee's right to possession of the goods is superior to that of the existing lessee.

Section 2A-304(1) also contains provisions about voidable title in the lease arena. A lessee who tricks the true owner of the goods into delivering possession to the lessee has "voidable title" to the goods, but only for the duration of the lease. This means that the initial lessee has a limited power to transfer a good leasehold interest to a subsequent lessee for value. The rights of the true owner who was tricked, while still superior to those of the initial lessee, become subordinate to the leasehold interest of the good-faith subsequent lessee. However, the rights of the subsequent lessee to possession of the goods can be no greater than the term of the lease entered into by the initial lessee.

So, for example, suppose that the initial lessee tricks the true owner with a bad check into delivering possession of the owner's goods for a one-year lease. The initial lessee then purports to lease the goods to a good-faith subsequent lessee for a three-year lease. In that case, §2A-304(1) provides that the subsequent lessee gets to retain possession of the goods as against the true owner who was tricked, but only for one year (the term of the initial lessee's lease with the true owner) rather than for three years (the purported term of the lease entered into between the initial lessee and the good-faith subsequent lessee). For that one year, the true owner (rather than the initial lessee) would be entitled to rent from the subsequent lessee, since the true owner's rights are still superior to the initial lessee that delivered a bad check. At the end of one year, the true owner would be entitled to get the goods back from the subsequent lessee. That is because the initial lessee's "voidable title" power under §2A-304(1) to create a new leasehold interest with a subsequent lessee is limited to a period that is no longer than the one-year lease that it entered into with the true owner.

Section 2A-305 governs the sale or sublease of goods by an existing lessee. The basic rule in §2A-305(1) is that a buyer or sublessee from an existing lessee can only have rights to the goods that are no better than those of the existing lessee. Thus, if an existing lessee is leasing a machine for two years and purports to sell it, at most the "buyer" is entitled to possession of the goods for two years, and even then only if the terms of the lease (including rent payment) continue to be met. The one exception to this rule, found in §2A-305(2), is where the lessee is a merchant that deals in goods of the kind to whom the goods were entrusted by the lessor. In that case, the lessee has the ability to give to a buyer or sublessee in the ordinary course of business all of the lessee's and lessor's rights to the goods, free of the existing lease contract.

In re M & S Grading, Inc.

457 F.3d 898 (B.A.P. 8th Cir. 2006)

Venters, J.

This is an appeal of the bankruptcy court's determination that the Plaintiff's interest in certain personal property in the Debtor's possession is superior to the Debtor's interest in that property and that the Debtor must relinquish possession to the Plaintiff. . . .

The issue on appeal is purely legal; the facts are straightforward and undisputed. In March 1999 the Plaintiff, The CIT Group/Equipment Financing, Inc. ("CIT"), leased two pieces of equipment ("Equipment") to Fehrs Nebraska Tractor & Equipment Co. ("Fehrs"). The parties agree that the Equipment is subject to the Nebraska Certificate of Title Act. In September 2000, Fehrs sold the Equipment to the Debtor. Fehrs executed a bill of sale, and the Debtor executed a promissory note promising to pay Fehrs the full amount of the sales price on an installment basis. Fehrs did not, however, deliver the certificate of title for the Equipment to the Debtor because Fehrs did not have it, nor did Fehrs have a right under Fehrs's lease agreement with CIT to request it. At the time of the transfer, Fehrs had not made all of the payments under the lease and the lease term had not expired. Shortly after the sale, Fehrs went out of business, and CIT received no further payments under the lease.

Almost two years later, in May 2002, the Debtor filed a chapter 11 bankruptcy and listed the Equipment as property of the bankruptcy estate. Sometime in late 2003, CIT became aware of the Debtor's claim of ownership in the Equipment. When the Debtor refused to relinquish possession of the Equipment, CIT initiated this adversary proceeding to obtain an order requiring the Debtor to turn over the Equipment.

The adversary proceeding was tried on October 3, 2005, and on December 21, 2005, the court issued a memorandum opinion in which it held that, under Nebraska UCC § 2A-305, CIT held a superior interest in the Equipment because the Debtor did not obtain a certificate of title to the Equipment when it purchased the Equipment from Fehrs. Rather, CIT still held the title to the Equipment.

The sole issue on appeal is whether the bankruptcy court properly interpreted and applied Nebraska UCC §2A-305. Section 2A-305, entitled "Sale or sublease of goods by lessee," provides in pertinent part:

> (1) Subject to the provisions of section 2A-303, a buyer or sublessee from the lessee of goods under an existing lease contract obtains, to the extent of the interest transferred, the leasehold interest in the goods that the lessee had or had power to transfer, and except as provided in subsection (2) and section 2A-511(4), takes subject to the existing lease contract. . . .
>
> (2) A buyer in the ordinary course of business or a sublessee in the ordinary course of business from a lessee who is a merchant dealing in goods of that kind to whom the goods were entrusted by the lessor obtains, to the extent of the interest transferred, all of the lessor's and lessee's rights to the goods, and takes free of the existing lease contract.
>
> (3) A buyer or sublessee from the lessee of goods that are subject to an existing lease contract and are covered by a certificate of title issued under a statute of this state or of another jurisdiction takes no greater rights than those provided both by this section and by the certificate of title statute.

The bankruptcy court carefully analyzed each provision of this statute. It explained that section (1) states the general rule that a buyer receives only the interest that the lessee had and takes subject to the existing lease contract; section (2) provides an exception to that general rule, permitting a lessee who also happens to be a merchant dealing in the goods leased to transfer both the lessee's and the lessor's rights in the goods to a buyer in the ordinary course of business; and section (3) provides an exception to the exception whereby the interest transferred to the buyer is limited by the certificate of title statute, even if the lessee is a merchant dealing in the goods and the buyer is a buyer in the ordinary course of business.

Applying the statute to the Debtor's purchase of the Equipment from Fehrs, the bankruptcy court found that the Debtor was a buyer in the ordinary course of business and that Fehrs was a merchant dealing in goods of the same kind as the Equipment, but that the Debtor did not obtain title to the Equipment because the Debtor did not receive the certificate of title from Fehrs, and under the certificate of title statute, Neb. Rev. Stat. §60-105, the holder of the certificate of title, CIT, holds a superior interest in the Equipment.

The Debtor contends that the court misinterpreted §2A-305, arguing that §2A-305 is analogous to Nebraska UCC §2-403, which the Nebraska Supreme Court held in *Dugdale of Nebraska, Inc. v. First State Bank,* does not require a buyer in the ordinary course to obtain a certificate of title in order to obtain title to certificated goods. In further support of this argument, the Debtor cites the official comment to §2A-305, which in turn references the comment to a neighboring code section, §2A-304. The comment to § 2A-304 states that § 2A-304 should be interpreted consistently with the Nebraska Supreme Court's construal of the relationship between the certificate of title statute and Nebraska UCC §2-403. The Debtor maintains that this is a reference to *Dugdale* and that it applies equally to §2A-305.

We find no error in the court's interpretation or application of § 2A-305. Whether interpreting federal or state law, a federal court's analysis of a statute must begin with the plain language. "[A] court's primary objective is to ascertain the intent of the legislature by looking at the language of the statute itself and giving it its plain, ordinary and commonly understood meaning." Subsection (3) of §2A-305 specifically states that "a buyer or sublessee from the lessee of goods that are subject to an existing lease contract and are covered by a certificate of title issued under a statute of this state or of another jurisdiction *takes no greater rights than those provided both by this section and by the certificate of title statute.*" (emphasis added) The certificate of title statute, §60-105, states that a buyer of a vehicle covered by the statute cannot obtain title to the vehicle until the buyer has physical possession *and a certificate of title.* Thus, the plain language of these statutes unambiguously supports the bankruptcy court's conclusion that a buyer of certificated goods must obtain the certificate of title to claim title to those goods, notwithstanding the buyer's status as a buyer in the ordinary course.

Neither *Dugdale* nor the comments to §§2A-304 and 2A-305 warrant a deviation from the plain language of the statute. The bankruptcy court declined to apply *Dugdale*'s interpretation of §2-403 to §2A-305 on several grounds, the most salient being that §2A-305(3) specifically incorporates the Nebraska certificate of title statute, whereas §2-403 is silent on the relationship between the two. The bankruptcy court explained: "To assume that *Dugdale,* which was not a lease case and which was not decided under a statutory provision that specifically makes the certificate of title act applicable to lease cases, is binding precedent would require the court to ignore a specific provision of the statute." The bankruptcy court's reasoning here is sound and will be affirmed.

The Debtor's suggestion that the comments to §§2A-304 and 2A-305 support interpreting those provisions in accordance with *Dugdale* is not wholly without merit, but courts are bound by statutes, not statutory commentary, and, as noted above, the plain language of §2A-305 compels the result reached by the bankruptcy court. Moreover, §2A-305 was enacted after the Nebraska Supreme Court ruled *Dugdale* (a fact the bankruptcy court also observed), and a legislature is presumed to have knowledge of judicial precedent relating to the subject matter under inquiry, so §2A-305's specific incorporation of the certificate of title act cannot be disregarded, even if the comments to the statute suggest a contrary interpretation. The Nebraska legislature might have intended to draft §2A-305 to incorporate the holding in *Dugdale*, but the statutory language does not reflect that intent. If anything, the specific incorporation of the certificate of title act into §2A-305 suggests that the Nebraska legislature intended to preclude the application of *Dugdale* to §2A-305.

For the reasons stated above, we affirm the bankruptcy court's decision.

B. Title with International Sales

As mentioned in Assignment 2, one of the major exclusions from the scope of the CISG is any issue regarding the rights of third parties to the goods that are the subject of the sale. CISG Article 4 provides that the CISG is concerned only with "the rights and obligations of the seller and the buyer" and that the CISG will not regulate "the effect which the contract may have on the property in the goods sold." The phrase "property in the goods sold" is a reference to the rights of third parties in the goods; therefore, the CISG has no provision comparable to the UCC's §2-403, which tells us how to determine which party has superior title to goods.

Interestingly, even though the CISG does not establish international rules regarding the resolution of competing claims to good title, it does include a provision creating a warranty of title on the part of the seller. CISG Article 41 requires that the seller "must deliver goods which are free from any right or claim of a third party, unless the buyer agreed to take the goods subject to that right or claim." This warranty is quite similar to UCC §2-312, which was discussed in Assignment 16. To determine the *validity* of the third party's right to the goods, however, the parties in an international sale are required to look to applicable domestic law rather than to the CISG.

C. Title with Real Estate

Much like the sale of goods, the sale of real estate includes an implied warranty of title. The one exception to the implied warranty is where the sale is by "quitclaim deed," in which the seller is promising to sell only whatever title the seller may have in the property. With real estate, the implied title warranty is generally created by statute and is implied with the transfer of a deed from seller to buyer. The warranty of title with real estate usually includes not only the present promise by seller that the title is good, but also two promises by seller that relate to the future: the warranty of quiet enjoyment and the warranty of further assurances. The warranty of quiet enjoyment promises that the buyer's future enjoyment of the premises will not be disturbed by either the seller or someone claiming through the seller. The warranty of further assurances promises the buyer that the seller will take steps to put the buyer in possession of the title that the seller warranted.

Keilbach v. McCullough

669 N.E.2d 1052 (Ind. Ct. App. 1996)

BAKER, J.

Today we revisit this court's decision in Rieddle v. Buckner, 629 N.E.2d 860 (Ind. Ct. App. 1994), in which we held that a grantee who was unsuccessful in defending his land from an adverse possessor could recover from the grantor reasonable attorney fees and expenses incurred in defending his title. Appellant-defendant Charles Keilbach contends that the trial court erred in interpreting *Rieddle* to allow appellee-plaintiff Dorothea McCullough, who was successful in her quiet title action, to recover her attorney fees and expenses from him.

Pursuant to a real estate contract dated December 19, 1978, and a warranty deed dated May 18, 1987, McCullough purchased approximately 120 acres of real estate from Keilbach. The real estate included a seven acre tract of land adjacent to property owned by Sid D. Martin. During 1993, when McCullough began attempting to sell her land, Martin recorded two affidavits in the Monroe County Recorder's office which provided that he was the owner of the seven acres as the result of his adverse possession of the land. Martin also approached a realtor representing McCullough and informed the realtor, while brandishing a firearm, that he owned the seven acres. In response to Martin's actions, McCullough filed a complaint to quiet title to the seven acres and for slander of title against Martin. Additionally, McCullough sought damages from Keilbach and from Lawyers Title Insurance Corporation, which had issued a title insurance policy to McCullough for the seven acres, for breach of their warranties of title and for their failure to defend her claim against Martin. Following a bench trial on November 21, 1994, the trial court entered its final judgment quieting title to the seven acres in McCullough. Further, the trial court found Martin liable to McCullough for slander of title and both Lawyers Title and Keilbach liable for breach of their warranties of title. With respect to Keilbach, the trial court specifically found:

12.4. Keilbach, in accordance with Rieddle v. Buckner, supra, breached his warranty deed when he refused to defend McCullough's title when challenged by Martin.

12.5. McCullough, in accordance with Rieddle v. Buckner, supra, is entitled to damages against Keilbach for the reasonable costs of her attorney fees and other expenses associated with the defense of her title.

Record at 83-84. As a result, the trial court found Martin, Lawyers Title, and Keilbach jointly and severally liable to McCullough for damages and attorney fees. Keilbach now appeals. Keilbach contends that the trial court erred as a matter of law in finding that he breached his warranty of title and in holding him liable for McCullough's attorney fees and expenses in quieting her title. Specifically, Keilbach argues that because McCullough was successful in quieting her title, he did not breach his warranty.

Keilbach transferred his property to McCullough pursuant to a warranty deed. A transferor, by means of a warranty deed, guarantees that the real estate is free from all encumbrances and that he will warrant and defend the title to the land against all lawful claims. In the instant case, McCullough initiated the proceedings against Martin to quiet her title and, in a literal sense, she was not "defending" her title. However, Martin's affidavits and actions forced McCullough to file her quiet title action and, in effect, required her to defend her title. Thus, we shall address whether Keilbach could be held liable, pursuant to *Rieddle*, for McCullough's attorney fees.

In *Rieddle*, this court held that a grantor, whose grantee was unsuccessful in defending her property against a claim of adverse possession, had breached his warranty of title to the grantee. As a result, we found that the grantee was entitled to reasonable attorney fees and expenses incurred in defending her title. According to Keilbach, the trial court erred in finding that *Rieddle* also stands for the proposition that a grantee can recover attorney fees and expenses in the successful defense of her title. We agree.

When a grantee successfully defends her title, the grantor has not breached his warranty of title and, therefore, cannot be held liable for expenses incurred in defending the title. We decline to extend the holding in *Rieddle* beyond situations in which a grantee is unsuccessful in defending her title. As a result, we must reverse the trial court's judgment against Keilbach for breach of his warranty of title and remand with instructions for the court to vacate the portion of its judgment holding Keilbach liable for McCullough's attorney fees and expenses.

Judgment reversed in part and remanded for proceedings not inconsistent with this opinion.

Most home buyers assume that the person in possession of the property must be the owner, but clearly that's not always the case. The immovable nature of real property, along with the various recording systems that have been created as a result of the immobile nature of real property, have made the title question in the real property sales system loom larger than it does in the personal property sales system.

The title insurance company is the primary institution that handles the complexities of the title issue in the real estate sales system. Whenever a prospective home buyer applies for a mortgage, the lender will inevitably require that the buyer purchase a title insurance policy on which the lender is the named beneficiary. The buyer may—or may not—choose to pay a nominal fee to buy a separate buyer's policy for its own protection, but almost no institution-financed home sale closing will take place today without a lender's title insurance policy.

Title insurance has evolved over time from a mere warranty of good title into a form of litigation insurance as well. Virtually every title insurance policy includes two different kinds of protection for the beneficiary: first, a promise to defend the insured against all lawsuits related to defects in title that are covered by the policy; and second, a promise to reimburse the insured up to policy limits for any losses sustained by the insured as a result of covered title problems that materialize.

Bad title can hurt a real estate buyer's interests in a number of ways. At worst, a defect in title can cause the buyer to lose the property that the buyer thought it owned. Some lesser title problems, generally known as "clouds" on title, may not dispossess the buyer but will prevent the buyer from selling the property to a new buyer for lack of a "marketable" title.

Most title insurance policies specifically protect against title defects, lack of access for the buyer, and the unmarketability of title. For a single payment at closing, the insured gets coverage for any future problem that relates to a defect in title that existed at the time the coverage was given.

Before writing a policy on a particular piece of property, title insurance companies will ordinarily make some effort to check the validity of title. The nature of this effort depends on the particular locale and the extent to which automation has put the relevant information online. The traditional approach was that the title company would compile abstracts of the property. These abstracts would consist of a record of various transfers of ownership going back in time to the first grant from the sovereign, all as shown on the public records. The title companies' discoveries in compiling the abstract would serve as a basis for listing any exception to a particular property's title policy.

In most major population centers today, title companies will maintain in-house their own set of information about local properties which is known as a "plant." Title companies that have sufficiently developed plants will issue title insurance based solely on the information at their own disposal without the need to avail themselves of the public records, which are often disorganized and hard to access. The most progressive title company plants will have all of the relevant information online so that a simple computer search can be the basis for issuing a title policy.

More often than not, in issuing residential policies title companies will find it cost-effective not to search records all the way back to the sovereign. Instead, they will often be satisfied with a much less complete search, sometimes for a fixed period of time (commonly in the range of 50 years), sometimes for even shorter periods. For example, in some developed urban areas, insurers check only to see that the current owners of the house received a valid warranty deed at the time of their own purchase. The idea is that if a reputable title company certified that there were no problems with title at the time of the most recent transfer, then there is very little likelihood that there is a problem now. The tremendous savings in time that the title company achieves by using this truncated approach is thought to outweigh the slight possibility either that the earlier warranty deed really did not convey marketable title or that some non-obvious problem with title has arisen since then.

In addition to the exceptions to coverage that title insurers identify in the course of researching the property's title, policies also come with a standard list of "exclusions" from coverage. Unlike the exceptions to coverage, the exclusions from coverage are typically not a function of the particular property whose title is being insured. Standard exclusions include such things as easements that do not appear in public records, mechanics' liens, and claims of parties that are currently in possession of the property.

Beyond exceptions and exclusions, buyers who purchase title insurance must also contend with denial of coverage based on the insurer's contract interpretation. As the following case demonstrates, title insurers are not in the business of construing ambiguities in coverage in favor of the insured.

Hatch v. First American Title Ins.

895 F. Supp. 10 (D. Mass. 1995)

Lasker, J.

When William and Melissa Hatch bought a home in Rowley, Massachusetts in April, 1986, they purchased a title insurance policy from First American Title Insurance Company. A little over a year later, the Hatches contracted to sell their Rowley property for $136,000 and, in anticipation of that sale, bought a home in Wayland, Massachusetts. To finance the purchase of the Wayland property, the Hatches borrowed $29,000, to be repaid with interest upon the sale of the Rowley property.

On November 30, 1987, the Hatches were notified by the prospective buyers of the Rowley property that there was an alleged defect in their title which rendered it unmarketable. In January, 1988, the Hatches terminated the Rowley land-sale contract and notified First American that their title to the Rowley property had been rejected as unmarketable.

First American admits that there was a "hole" in the Hatches' title to the Rowley property—the result of a very old town ordinance that provided for a long-unused right to graze cattle on the land. First American filed a "Petition for Registration" in the Massachusetts Land Court. In June, 1994, the Land Court entered judgment establishing the Hatches' title to the Rowley property. Soon thereafter, the Hatches sold the property, but for only $114,000, $22,000 less than the amount of their earlier contract.

After it was notified of the defect in title, First American voluntarily assumed payment of the interest due on the Rowley property, which was mortgaged; the Hatches, however, continued to pay interest on the loan that financed the purchase of their Wayland home. In 1993, the Hatches made a claim under the title insurance policy, demanding $136,000 for the loss of the value of their property and $20,000 for interest paid on the Wayland loan. First American denied liability under the contract. Now alleging a breach of contract, the Hatches sue First American. First American moves for summary judgment on the ground that the Hatches' claim is barred by a provision of the policy.

The facts are not in dispute. The question is one of contract interpretation. Paragraph 7 of the Hatches' title insurance policy provides:

> No claim shall arise or be maintainable under this policy (a) if the Company, after having received notice of an alleged defect, lien or encumbrance insured against hereunder, by litigation or otherwise, removes such defect, lien or encumbrance or establishes the title, as insured, within a reasonable time after receipt of such notice; (b) in the event of litigation until there has been a final determination by a court of competent jurisdiction, and disposition of all appeals therefrom, adverse to title, as insured, as provided in paragraph 3 hereof; or (c) for liability voluntarily assumed by an insured in settling any claim or suit without prior written consent of the Company.

First American contends that because it did undertake litigation to cure title in the Rowley property, and because that litigation did not result in a final judgment adverse to title, subsection (b) precludes the Hatches' claim. . . .

First American contends that a favorable court ruling—whether timely or not—precludes liability under paragraph 7(b). It asserts that paragraph 7(a), which bars claims when an alleged defect is cured "by litigation or otherwise . . . within a reasonable time," is irrelevant, because, as it says, "the Policy . . . limits liability of the insurer in each of three different scenarios, as evidenced by the use of the word 'or'."

The Hatches assert that clauses 7(a) and 7(b) must be read together and that, when so read, they bar a claim only where litigation is successfully concluded within a reasonable time. They contend that if the Land Court action, unresolved for five years, was unreasonably delayed by First American, paragraph 7 does not bar a claim for damages under the contract. If a final judgment in favor of title excused an insurer's indifference or negligence during litigation, they argue, the words "by litigation or otherwise" in paragraph 7(a) would be rendered meaningless. . . .

Paragraph 7 provides, in effect, that no claim shall arise under the policy (a) if any defect is cleared by litigation within a reasonable time; or (b) if any defect is cleared by litigation, ever. As First American has noted, the two provisions are not literally contradictory. Neither, however, are they absolutely compatible. Rather, the first provision implies what the second precludes: that an insurer must reasonably litigate any lawsuit which it undertakes on behalf of the insured. . . .

Massachusetts courts observe the frequently cited principle that ambiguities contained in an insurance policy are to be construed against the insurer, typically the drafter of the contract. See Falmouth National Bank v. Ticor Title Insurance

Co., 920 F.2d at 1061. The Falmouth Court noted one caveat to this rule: "[t]he rationale behind interpreting ambiguities against the insurer would not seem to apply as strongly when the transaction is between two parties of equal sophistication and equal bargaining power." Falmouth, 920 F.2d at 1062. Such was clearly not the case here. The Hatches bought the insurance policy from First American at the closing of their Rowley land purchase; it was not even delivered to them until 18 days later. The Hatches are entitled, therefore, to have the ambiguity contained in paragraph 7 construed against First American, the drafter of the language in question.

Accordingly, the contract at bar is interpreted to mean—as paragraph 7(a) suggests—that the Hatches may prevail on their claim if they can demonstrate that First American failed to cure the title defect in question within a reasonable time after its discovery.

The Hatches notified First American of the title defect in January, 1988. The Massachusetts Land Court action, commenced in early 1989, was concluded in June, 1994. Whether First American cured the defect within a reasonable time is a question of fact. . . .

Accordingly, First American's motion for summary judgment is denied.

In the *Hatch* case, the buyers were unable to consummate the sale of their home due to a cloud in their title that their title company had missed when issuing the policy. The buyers ended up losing that sale and had to settle for a significantly lower price in a later sale of their home.

The loss experienced by the buyers in *Hatch* was small, however, compared with that faced by some refinancing homeowners who dealt with a crooked title company in Missouri:

> In 1992, Michael and Rebecca Dolly decided to take advantage of falling interest rates and refinance the mortgage on their Kansas City home. Instead of a lower house payment, they ended up with two house payments. Their title agent pocketed the money to pay off their first mortgage. The Dollys are fighting in court to get it back.
>
> The Dollys are not alone. Others in Missouri have nearly lost their homes because of unscrupulous practices of title insurers and a state agency that has done little to regulate the industry. . . .
>
> How title insurance works is a mystery to many people. Most homebuyers pay more attention to choosing drapes for their new home than title insurance.
>
> They shouldn't. Title insurance offers homebuyers their only guarantee that their property carries a clear title—that they won't be unwittingly saddled with outstanding debt. Title insurance companies are supposed to make sure that bills have been paid before a homebuyer closes on property, and that the first mortgage is paid off after closing. If they don't do their job, the buyer can take on debts ranging from a few hundred dollars in unpaid taxes to tens of thousands from

a first mortgage. ("Title Insurance: Let Buyers Beware," *St. Louis Post-Dispatch*, October 1, 1995.)

Although title insurance companies are now a fixture in virtually every residential real estate sales system in this country, this was not always the case. For example, title insurance really did not exist in Oklahoma 40 years ago. But then mortgage lenders there began to require it because they needed it to sell their mortgages on the secondary market. Today title insurance policies are issued in nearly 98 percent of residential real estate transactions in Oklahoma.

Problem Set 17

17.1. a. Pierre, the art dealer from Problem Set 16, tells you that he feels especially embarrassed about his next problem, but he wants to try to make things right. A famous local art collector, Shelby Kostner, brought Pierre an original work, Caged Compassion, which she asked Pierre to frame for her. While the painting was still in Pierre's gallery, one of his associates signed an agreement with the local museum in which the museum paid $10,000 for the right to display the painting during the next year. Pierre wants to know whether Shelby can get Caged Compassion back from the museum immediately. What do you advise? UCC §§2-403(2), 2A-304(2), 2A-307(2); Official Comment 3 to §2A-304.

b. Same facts as part (a), except instead of taking the painting to frame, Pierre purchases Shelby's painting with a check that later bounces. Pierre then leases the painting to the museum for one year. If Shelby discovers that Pierre is broke and is not going to make good on his bad check, at what point can Shelby recover the painting from the museum? UCC §2A-304(1), Official Comment 2 to §2A-304, §2-403.

c. Same facts as part (a), except now when the museum receives possession of the painting pursuant to its one-year lease agreement, the museum leases the painting to a private art gallery for five years. What rights does Shelby have to recover the painting from the private art gallery? UCC §§2A-305(1) and (2), 2A-103(2), 2-104(1), Official Comment 2 to §2-104.

17.2. As if things were not bad enough for Pierre, he now tells you that his problems have taken on an international flavor. Three weeks ago, Pierre sold a $60,000 painting, Man of La Mancha, to a Mexican art gallery, Las Pinturas, located just across the Texas border. One week following the sale, when the owner of Las Pinturas brought the painting to be displayed at a Texas art show, local sheriffs seized the painting pursuant to a writ of attachment issued by a Texas state court in response to a title action brought by Texas resident Ronald Manson. It turns out that Manson used to own the Man of La Mancha painting, but sold it to Allison Wheeler, who paid for it with a check that bounced. Allison then sold the painting to Pierre, who sold it to Las Pinturas. Now Las Pinturas is threatening to sue Pierre in a Texas court for breach of the title warranty. Does Pierre have reason to be concerned? CISG Arts. 4, 41; UCC §2-403.

17.3. You represent Bobby Bailey, an Indiana resident who just bought a farm in Brown County, Indiana, a little over a year ago. The seller was a woman named Cindy Beecher. Now one of Bobby's eccentric neighbors, Pearl Maberly, has filed a suit in the county courthouse claiming that nine of the acres of Bobby's property actually belong to her by virtue of adverse possession. When Bobby contacted Cindy Beecher and the Hoosier Title Company, which was the title insurer at Bobby's closing, they both told him that Pearl was crazy and that they did not believe it was their duty to defend Bobby against frivolous title suits. Bobby is not sure whether or not there is any merit to Pearl's claims, but he is certain that he does not want to spend a lot of money defending Pearl's suit. Bobby, who is not a lawyer but likes to read local court opinions as a hobby, suggests to you the following strategy: let Pearl win the suit by default judgment and *then* sue Cindy and Hoosier Title for breach of their title obligations to Bobby. That way, says Bobby, not only will he be compensated for the loss of land, but he can also be reimbursed for his attorney's fees. Does Bobby have a viable strategy? Cf. UCC §2-607(5)(a), F.R.C.P. 14. Can you think of any strategies that are better than Bobby's?

17.4. Take a look at Paragraph 7 of the buyers' title insurance policy in the *Hatch* case, which appears in small print in the case excerpt above. Imagine that you are an in-house lawyer for the title insurance company, and you have been asked in light of the *Hatch* decision to prepare a proposal for the state insurance commission to revise the state's form insurance policy to protect insurance companies against similar litigation in the future. Your job is to re-draft that paragraph so that in a future case like *Hatch*, the insurance company's position will prevail. How would you re-draft the clause to avoid the result in the *Hatch* case?

Assessment Questions for Chapter 2

Question 1: Second Wind Sports is a sporting goods retailer that sells both used and new sporting goods equipment. Sam Sedentary visits the store one day and tells the manager on duty, Frieda Fitness, that he is looking to buy a new treadmill in the $3,000 price range because he has decided that he would like to improve his aerobic fitness. Frieda suggests for him a True Brand PS100 Model treadmill. Frieda tells Sam that in her many years of selling treadmills, she believes that the True PS100 is the best treadmill in that price range. Sam listens closely and decides to purchase the treadmill. Has Frieda made an implied warranty of fitness for a particular purpose in this sale to Sam?

(A) Yes, because Frieda is a merchant with respect to goods of this kind.

(B) Yes, because Sam was clearly relying on Frieda's skill or judgment to help select for him this particular treadmill.

(C) Yes, for both of the reasons stated in (A) and (B).

(D) No, because Frieda's express warranty about the treadmill supersedes any implied warranty that she might have made.

(E) No, because most people buy treadmills to improve their aerobic fitness.

Question 1 Answer: The correct answer is (E). In order for an implied warranty of fitness for a particular purpose to arise under §2-315, the seller must know of some particular (non-ordinary) purpose for which the goods are required. Buying a treadmill to improve one's aerobic fitness is not an unusual or special purpose for buying a treadmill. (A) is wrong because Frieda's status as a merchant with respect to goods of the kind is relevant to the creation of an implied warranty of merchantability under §2-314, but not with respect to an implied warranty of fitness for a particular purpose. (B) is wrong because Sam's reliance on Frieda's expertise is a necessary but not sufficient condition to the creation of an implied warranty of fitness under §2-315. (C) is wrong because both (A) and (B) are wrong. (D) is wrong because any express warranty that Frieda made under §2-313 is not inconsistent with and therefore would not supersede any implied warranty that she made here.

Question 2: Same facts as Question 1, except that Sam asks for a used treadmill in the $3,000 price range and tells Frieda that the most important feature for him in a treadmill is that it has excellent cushioning for shock absorption (due to Sam's history of tendinitis in both of his knees). As a result, Frieda recommends that Sam purchase a used NordicTrack Elite 9700 Pro treadmill for that purpose. When Sam purchases that used treadmill, has Frieda made an implied warranty of merchantability with that sale?

(A) Yes, because Sam was relying on Frieda's skill and judgment in buying this particular treadmill for his special purpose.

(B) Yes, because Frieda is a merchant with respect to goods of this kind.

(C) Yes, for both of the reasons stated in (A) and (B).

(D) No, because there is no implied warranty of merchantability with the sale of used goods.

(E) No, because an implied warranty of fitness for a particular purpose supersedes an implied warranty of merchantability.

Question 2 Answer: The correct answer is (B). Because Frieda is a merchant with respect to goods of this kind, she makes an implied warranty of merchantability under §2-314. (A) is wrong because Sam's reliance on Frieda's skill and judgment is not relevant to the creation of an implied warranty of merchantability under §2-314, but is only relevant with respect to an implied warranty of fitness for a particular purpose under §2-315. (C) is wrong because (A) is wrong. (D) is wrong because Official Comment 3 to §2-314 says that the implied warranty of merchantability applies to used goods as well as new goods. (E) is wrong because any implied warranty of fitness here would not be inconsistent with the implied warranty of merchantability (the two could be cumulative) and thus one warranty would not need to "supersede" the other.

Question 3: Buyer buys a new car from Car Dealer. The sales contract for the car does not include any disclaimers of warranty. Buyer's adult son ("Son"), who still lives at home, borrows Buyer's car. While Son is driving the car, the brakes on the car malfunction and Son suffers personal injuries in the ensuing accident. Son sues Car Dealer for damages for personal injuries on a theory of breach of implied warranty. Putting aside Magnuson-Moss and tort law, which of the following is true?

(A) In a §2-318 Alternative A jurisdiction, Son loses for lack of vertical privity.
(B) In a §2-318 Alternative A jurisdiction, Son loses for lack of horizontal privity.
(C) In a §2-318 Alternative A jurisdiction, Son wins because that Alternative allows him to overcome his vertical privity problem.
(D) In a §2-318 Alternative A jurisdiction, Son wins because that Alternative allows him to overcome his horizontal privity problem.
(E) In a §2-318 Alternative C jurisdiction, Son loses because he cannot show any property damage or economic loss.

Question 3 Answer: The correct answer is (D). But for §2-318, Son would lack horizontal privity in a warranty action against Car Dealer. However, Alternative A of §2-318 allows Son to overcome his horizontal privity problem by extending Car Dealer's warranty to Son. Son qualifies for the benefits of Alternative A because Son is "in the family or household" of Buyer, it is reasonable to expect that Son "may use, consumer or be affected by" the car, and Son was injured in person by Car Dealer's breach of the implied warranty of merchantability. (A) is wrong because Son does not lack vertical privity with Car Dealer, just horizontal privity. (B) is wrong because even though Son lacks horizontal privity in this lawsuit, Alternative A allows him to overcome that problem. (C) is wrong because Son does not lack vertical privity with Car Dealer, just horizontal privity. (E) is wrong because Alternative C gives Son greater rights with which to overcome privity problems than Alternative A, not lesser rights.

Question 4: Same facts as Question 3, except suppose Car Dealer's contract with Buyer includes a conspicuous and properly drafted disclaimer of the implied warranty of merchantability. Putting aside Magnuson-Moss and tort law, which of the following statements is true?

   (A) In a §2-318 Alternative A jurisdiction, Son wins because Car Dealer cannot successfully disclaim the implied warranty of merchantability vs. the intended beneficiaries of that Alternative.
   (B) In a §2-318 Alternative A jurisdiction, Son loses.
   (C) In an Alternative C jurisdiction, Son wins because Son suffered personal injuries.
   (D) Both A and C are true.
   (E) None of the above is true.

Question 4 Answer: The correct answer is (B). Even though the final sentence in Alternative A of §2-318 says that "[a] seller may not exclude or limit the operation of this section," that does not mean that a seller will always be liable for breach of warranty to those beneficiaries covered by these Alternatives. Rather, Official Comment 1 to §2-318 makes clear that when a seller excludes or limits warranties or remedies to the buyer, as Car Dealer did here, "such provisions are equally operative against beneficiaries of warranties under this section." All of the other answers are wrong because Son will not win here thanks to Car Dealer's inclusion of a conspicuous and properly drafted disclaimer of the implied warranty of merchantability.

Question 5: Same facts as Question 3, but now suppose that there is a written Five-Year Limited Warranty and that Magnuson-Moss applies. In this variation, Son suffers no personal injuries in the accident, but Son's new iPhone is destroyed in the accident. Son sues Car Dealer for loss of his $500 iPhone. Which of the following statements is true?

(A) In a §2-318 Alternative A jurisdiction, Son wins even without the help of Magnuson-Moss.

(B) In a §2-318 Alternative A jurisdiction, Son loses even with the help of Magnuson-Moss.

(C) In a §2-318 Alternative A jurisdiction, Son wins but only due to Magnuson-Moss.

(D) In a §2-318 Alternative C jurisdiction, Son loses even with the help of Magnuson-Moss.

(E) In a §2-318 Alternative C jurisdiction, Son wins but only due to Magnuson-Moss.

Question 5 Answer: The correct answer is (C). Without Magnuson-Moss, Son would lose in a §2-318 Alternative A jurisdiction because that Alternative removes Son's horizontal privity problem only if Son suffers personal injury, which here he did not. However, Magnuson-Moss and its broad definition of "consumer" under §101(3) (which includes any transferees of consumer products during the duration of an implied or written warranty on the product) would remove the horizontal privity problem for Son here even though Son did not suffer personal injuries from the breach of warranty. (A) is wrong because Alternative A will not help Son overcome his horizontal privity problem in the absence of personal injuries suffered by Son as a result of the warranty breach. (B) is wrong because Magnuson-Moss and its broad definition of "consumer" would remove the horizontal privity problem for Son even though Son did not suffer personal injuries from the breach of warranty. (D) is wrong because both Magnuson-Moss and Alternative C remove Son's horizontal privity problem even though Son suffered no personal injuries as a result of the warranty breach. (E) is wrong because Alternative C removes the horizontal privity problem for Son even in the absence of personal injuries suffered by the breach of warranty.

Question 6: Same facts as Question 5, but Son would like to use Magnuson-Moss to sue Car Dealer in federal court and to recover attorneys' fees if he wins his case. Regarding Son's prospects for prevailing on those two issues — federal jurisdiction and recovery of attorneys' fees if he wins — which of the following statements is true?

(A) Son can sue in federal court, but cannot recover attorneys' fees even if he wins.

(B) Son cannot sue in federal court, but can recover attorneys' fees if he wins.

(C) Son can sue in federal court, and can recover attorneys' fees if he wins.

(D) Son cannot sue in federal court, but he can recovery attorneys' fees whether he wins or loses.

(E) Son cannot sue in federal court, and cannot recover attorneys' fees even if he wins.

Question 6 Answer: The correct answer is (B). Magnuson-Moss §110(d)(3) limits federal jurisdiction for warranty suits to cases where the amount in controversy is at least $50,000. However, there is no minimum threshold amount for amount in controversy in order for a victorious plaintiff in a Magnuson-Moss suit to recover attorneys' fees under §110(d)(2). (A) is wrong because Son can recover attorneys' fees if he wins. (C) is wrong because Son cannot sue in federal court under Magnuson-Moss on a $500 claim. (D) is wrong because Son can only recover attorneys' fees under §110(d)(2) if he prevails in his lawsuit. (E) is wrong because Son can recover attorneys' fees if he prevails.

Question 7: Lessee needs a new widget production machine for its factory. Lessee approaches Seller and chooses a machine from Seller's inventory that suits Lessee's needs. Lessee then convinces Bank to purchase the machine from Seller and lease it to Lessee for 10 years. The machine has an expected useful life of 20 years. Lessee has final approval rights over the sales contract between Seller and Bank, which includes an express warranty that the machine will not require any maintenance for at least five years. Bank purchases the machine, which is delivered directly to Lessee's factory. After one month, the machine breaks down and needs extensive maintenance in order to function effectively. Lessee sues both Seller and Bank for recovery of the maintenance costs. What is the likely outcome of that lawsuit?

(A) Lessee will prevail vs. Bank for breach of implied warranty, but will not prevail vs. Seller because of lack of vertical privity.

(B) Lessee will not prevail vs. Bank for breach of implied warranty, and will not prevail vs. Seller because of lack of vertical privity.

(C) Lessee will prevail vs. Bank for breach of implied warranty, and will also prevail vs. Seller for breach of express warranty (subject to no double recovery).

(D) Lessee will not prevail vs. Bank for breach of implied warranty, but will prevail vs. Seller for breach of express warranty.

(E) None of the above.

Question 7 Answer: The correct answer is (D). Under §2A-212(1), Bank will not give Lessee the normal implied warranty of merchantability that is available with a standard lease because this lease is a finance lease. However, because this is a finance lease, under §2A-209(1) Lessee will get the benefits of the express warranty that Seller gave to Bank even though Lessee otherwise lacks vertical privity in a warranty action against Seller. (A) is wrong for the same reasons that (D) is correct. (B) is wrong because §2A-209(1) allows Lessee to overcome its lack of vertical privity in a warranty suit vs. Seller. (C) is wrong because §2A-212(1) does not allow Lessee to get the normal implied warranty of merchantability from Bank since this is a finance lease. (E) is wrong because (D) is correct.

Question 8: Same facts as Question 7, except suppose that the machine has an expected useful life of 10 years, and that Lessee has no right to terminate the lease. Now when Lessee sues both Seller and Bank for recovery of the maintenance costs, what is the likely outcome of that lawsuit?

(A) Lessee will prevail vs. Bank for breach of implied warranty, but will not prevail vs. Seller because of lack of vertical privity.

(B) Lessee will not prevail vs. Bank for breach of implied warranty, and will not prevail vs. Seller because of lack of vertical privity.

(C) Lessee will prevail vs. Bank for breach of implied warranty, and will also prevail vs. Seller for breach of express warranty (subject to no double recovery).

(D) Lessee will not prevail vs. Bank for breach of implied warranty, but will prevail vs. Seller for breach of express warranty.

(E) None of the above.

Question 8 Answer: The correct answer is (A). Under §1-203(b)(1), this transaction is necessarily a disguised sale since the lessee has no option to terminate, and the term of the lease is equal to the remaining useful life of the goods. Because this lease is no longer a true lease, it cannot be a finance lease. Therefore, Lessee will now prevail vs. Bank for breach of the implied warranty of merchantability under §2-314. Lessee will no longer prevail vs. Seller for breach of warranty because in the absence of a finance lease, Lessee now lacks vertical privity with Seller because Lessee did not purchase or lease the machine directly from Seller. (B) is wrong because Lessee will now prevail vs. Bank since this is no longer a finance lease. (C) is wrong because Lessee cannot prevail vs. Seller because Lessee's lack of vertical privity with Seller is now dispositive since this lease is no longer a finance lease. (D) is wrong for the same reasons that (A) is correct. (E) is wrong because (A) is correct.

Question 9: Merchant Seller (Seller) sells a drill press machine to Merchant Buyer (Buyer). Buyer makes it clear to Seller prior to the sale that Buyer needs this machine for the unique purpose of manufacturing custom-made widgets at Buyer's factory. Seller agrees orally that the machine being sold will be suitable for Buyer's special purpose. Seller and Buyer then both sign a written contract that includes an express warranty that the machine being sold will not require any maintenance for at least two years. The written contract also includes a conspicuous disclaimer that the machine is being sold "AS IS." There is no merger clause in the written contract. Which, if any, of the following warranties, does the "AS IS" term in the written contract effectively disclaim: the two-year express warranty, the implied warranty of merchantability, or the implied warranty of fitness for a particular purpose?

(A) None of those warranties.

(B) All three of those warranties.

(C) Only the implied warranty of merchantability and the implied warranty of fitness for a particular purpose.

(D) Only the implied warranty of merchantability and the express warranty.

(E) Only the implied warranty of fitness for a particular purpose and the express warranty.

Question 9 Answer: The correct answer is (C). Section 2-316(3)(a) says that all implied warranties are excluded by expressions like "as is" unless "the circumstances indicate otherwise." Perhaps one could argue that the oral conversation here about the special purpose of the machine was a "circumstance indicat[ing] otherwise," but that pre-contract conversation merely created the implied warranty of fitness which was then prominently disclaimed in the written contract. The parol evidence rule of §2-202 would seem to prevent Buyer from introducing evidence of that conversation since that evidence would not be a "consistent additional term" relative to the writing. Section 2-316(1) would seem to make the "as is" disclaimer ineffective to disclaim the express warranty that is part of the written contract. That is because §2-316(1) says that when a contract purports both to give an express warranty and then to disclaim all warranties, the "negation or limitation is inoperative to the extent that such construction is unreasonable." All four of the other answers are wrong for the same reasons that (C) is the correct answer.

Question 10: Same facts as Question 9, except now suppose that the written contract did not contain the "AS IS" clause, but it did contain a conspicuous merger clause. Suppose also that prior to both parties signing the written contract, Seller orally told Buyer, "I hereby disclaim all warranties, including merchantability, fitness for a particular purpose, and any express warranties." Now which of the three warranties have been effectively disclaimed by Seller?

    (A) None of those warranties.

    (B) All three of those warranties.

    (C) Only the implied warranty of merchantability and the implied warranty of fitness for a particular purpose.

    (D) Only the implied warranty of merchantability and the express warranty.

    (E) Only the implied warranty of fitness for a particular purpose and the express warranty.

Question 10 Answer: The correct answer is (A). Because of the conspicuous merger clause in the written contract, Seller will not be able to introduce evidence of his oral disclaimers of warranties under §2-202's parol evidence rule. Even if Seller could introduce evidence of those disclaimers, the only one that would work would be the disclaimer of the implied warranty of merchantability. Section 2-316(2) says that such a disclaimer must mention "merchantability" but does not have to be in writing. Putting aside the merger clause, §2-316(2) also says that any effective disclaimer of the implied warranty of fitness for a particular purpose must be in writing. Furthermore, even if there were no merger clause or even no parol evidence issue more generally, §2-316(1) would probably render ineffective the attempted oral disclaimer of the express warranty here. The other four answers are wrong for the same reasons that (A) is correct.

Question 11: Consumer Buyer (Buyer) purchases a used treadmill from Merchant Seller (Seller) and signs a contract that includes a description of warranty and remedy coverage that is entitled "LIMITED TWO-YEAR WARRANTY." Underneath that heading is a conspicuous statement that "Any implied warranties, including the implied warranty of merchantability, are hereby limited to three years." The contract also includes a conspicuous exclusive remedy that limits the buyer to repair or replacement of defective parts, and a separate conspicuous exclusion of consequential damages. If the treadmill ends up malfunctioning (and putting aside the possibility of personal injury and tort law), which of the various disclaimers and limitations in the contract—the limitation on duration of implied warranties, the exclusive remedy, and the separate exclusion of consequential damages—will be effective to limit Buyer's rights against Seller?

(A) None of them.

(B) Just the exclusive remedy and the limitation on duration of implied warranties.

(C) Just the exclusive remedy and the separate exclusion of consequential damages.

(D) Just the separate exclusion of consequential damages and the limitation on duration of implied warranties.

(E) All three of them.

Question 11 Answer: The correct answer is (E). Even with the inclusion of a limited written warranty, a seller is still allowed under Magnuson-Moss §108(b) to limit the duration of an implied warranty to a duration that is no shorter than the duration of the limited warranty itself. Here the implied warranties are limited to three years, which is longer than (and thus no shorter than) the two-year duration of the limited written warranty. Furthermore, a written warranty under Magnuson-Moss does not prevent a Seller from limiting or excluding remedies as was done here. All four of the other answers are wrong for the reasons that (E) is correct.

Question 12: Same facts as Question 11, except assume that Seller's warranty coverage was entitled "FULL TWO-YEAR WARRANTY," and further assume that in addition to the other conspicuous statements, Seller included a conspicuous statement that "This used treadmill is sold AS IS with all faults." Now if the treadmill ends up malfunctioning (and putting aside the possibility of personal injury and tort law), will the "AS IS" clause be effective to disclaim the implied warranty of merchantability, and will the limitation on duration of implied warranties be effective?

(A) Both will be effective.

(B) The "AS IS" clause will be effective, but not the limitation on duration of implied warranties.

(C) Neither will be effective, and the "AS IS" clause would not have been effective to disclaim the implied warranty of merchantability even if it had used the word "merchantability" as part of the disclaimer.

(D) Neither will be effective, but the "AS IS" clause would have been effective to disclaim the implied warranty of merchantability if it had used the word "merchantability" as part of the disclaimer.

(E) The limitation on duration of implied warranties will be effective, but not the "AS IS" clause.

Question 12 Answer: The correct answer is (C). With any written warranty, whether it is limited or full, the seller cannot disclaim completely the implied warranties under Magnuson-Moss §108(a)(1). Therefore, neither an "AS IS" disclaimer nor even a disclaimer that specifically mentioned "merchantability" would be sufficient here to disclaim the implied warranty of merchantability. As for the limitation on the duration of the implied warranties, even though such a limitation is allowed with a limited written warranty under Magnuson-Moss §108(b), it is not allowed with a full written warranty according to Magnuson-Moss §104(a)(2). (A) is wrong because the "AS IS" clause will not be effective under Magnuson-Moss §108(a)(1). (B) is wrong for the same reason. (D) is wrong because even using the word "merchantability" would not have overcome Magnuson Moss §108(a)(1)'s prohibition against disclaiming any implied warranties in a case where there is a written warranty. (E) is wrong because Magnuson-Moss §108(b) does not allow limiting even the duration of the implied warranties in a case like this where there is a full written warranty.

Question 13: Chicago Butcher ("Butcher") agrees to buy from Iowa Seller ("Seller") 200 pounds of filet mignon steaks for a total cost of $4,000. Seller is relying on obtaining the steaks for this contract from Nebraska Supplier ("Supplier"), a cattle farmer that has supplied steaks to Seller many times in the past. The day that Supplier's delivery of the steaks is supposed to take place, Supplier calls Seller to let Seller know that Supplier will not be able to supply the 200 pounds of steaks as promised. Given this short notice from Supplier, Seller is unable to obtain steaks from any other suppliers in time to deliver the steaks on time to Butcher. Assuming that Seller gives timely notice of this excuse to Butcher, will Seller thereby avoid any damages to Butcher for the delay or non-delivery of these steaks?

(A) Yes, as long as Butcher knew that Supplier was Seller's exclusive source of supply in this contract, and Supplier itself had a valid excuse for failing to perform its contract with Seller.

(B) Yes, as long as Butcher knew that Supplier was Seller's exclusive source of supply in this contract, even if Supplier itself did not have a valid excuse for failing to perform its contract with Seller.

(C) Yes, whether or not Butcher knew that Supplier was Seller's exclusive source of supply in this contract, and even if Supplier itself did not have a valid excuse for failing to perform its contract with Seller.

(D) Yes, whether or not Butcher knew that Supplier was Seller's exclusive source of supply in this contract, as long as Supplier itself had a valid excuse for failing to perform its contract with Seller.

(E) No, because failure of a source of supply cannot count as a grounds for excuse under UCC §2-615.

Question 13 Answer: The correct answer is (B). Official Comment 5 to §2-615 makes it clear that if a particular source of supply "is assumed by the parties at the time of contracting," then failure of that source can qualify as a valid excuse under §2-615 without regard to any valid excuse for the supplier's own failure. (A) is wrong because it adds the condition that Supplier itself had to have a valid excuse for failing to perform. (C) is wrong because the excuse only works where Butcher knew or assumed that Supplier was Seller's exclusive source of supply for this contract. (D) is wrong for the same reason as (C) and is also wrong by suggesting that Supplier itself had to have a valid excuse for failing to perform. (E) is wrong because failure of a source supply can indeed count as a grounds for excuse under §2-615.

Question 14: Same facts as Question 13, but now assume that the CISG rather than the UCC applies in this case. Assuming that Seller gives timely notice of this excuse to Butcher, will Seller thereby avoid any damages to Butcher for the delay or non-delivery of these steaks?

(A) Yes, as long as Butcher knew that Supplier was Seller's exclusive source of supply in this contract, and Supplier itself had a valid excuse for failing to perform its contract with Seller.
(B) Yes, as long as Butcher knew that Supplier was Seller's exclusive source of supply in this contract, even if Supplier itself did not have a valid excuse for failing to perform its contract with Seller.
(C) Yes, whether or not Butcher knew that Supplier was Seller's exclusive source of supply in this contract, and even if Supplier itself did not have a valid excuse for failing to perform its contract with Seller.
(D) Yes, whether or not Butcher knew that Supplier was Seller's exclusive source of supply in this contract, as long as Supplier itself had a valid excuse for failing to perform its contract with Seller.
(E) No, because failure of a source of supply cannot count as a grounds for excuse under CISG Article 79.

Question 14 Answer: The correct answer is (A). Unlike UCC §2-615, CISG Article 79(2)(b) requires that in order for a party to a contract to qualify for excuse (or "exemption" as Article 79 calls it) based on a third party's failure to perform, the third party's failure to perform must itself qualify for exemption under Article 79(1). (B) is wrong because Seller would not qualify for excuse under the CISG if Supplier itself did not have a valid excuse for failing to perform its contract with Seller. (C) is wrong for two reasons: first, because Butcher would have needed to know of Seller's exclusive source of supply in order for its failure to count under Article 79(1) as an "impediment" beyond Seller's control; and second, Seller would not qualify for excuse under Article 79(2) (b) if Supplier itself did not have a valid excuse for failing to perform its contract with Seller. (D) is wrong because Butcher would have needed to know of Seller's exclusive source of supply in order for its failure to count under Article 79(1) as an "impediment" beyond Seller's control. (E) is wrong because failure of a source of supply could, under appropriate circumstances, count as a grounds for excuse under CISG Article 79.

Question 15: Consumer Buyer ("Buyer"), who has never before owned a computer, goes to Merchant Seller ("Seller") and purchases a used computer for the posted price of $4,000. Buyer is not pressured to purchase this computer, nor does Buyer do any research about the product or even price computers at another store. The computer comes with no written warranty and in fact Seller emphasizes orally to Buyer that all sales in this store, including this sale of the used computer, are "as is." It turns out that this exact model of computer sells for $1,000 brand-new at any number of local computer discount stores. It further turns out that this particular used computer breaks down two weeks after Buyer purchases it. If Buyer wishes to rescind the sale on the grounds of unconscionability, what is the likely result in most courts?

(A) Buyer wins, because it is per se unconscionable to include an "as is" clause with the sale of used goods.
(B) Buyer wins, because there is clearly procedural unconscionability in this case.
(C) Buyer wins, because there is clearly substantive unconscionability in this case.
(D) Buyer loses, because although there may well be procedural unconscionability, there does not appear to be substantive unconscionability.
(E) None of the above.

Question 15 Answer: The correct answer is (E). As the casebook indicates, most courts hearing a §2-302 unconscionability case will require both procedural unconscionability ("an absence of meaningful choice") and substantive unconscionability ("unreasonably favorable terms"). In this case, it appears that Buyer was the victim of substantive unconscionability by significantly overpaying for a used computer that broke two weeks later, but not proce-dural unconscionability. Buyer, in effect, was a victim of Buyer's own failure to research the market or shop around. (A) is wrong because it is not per se unconscionable to include an "as is" clause with the sale of used goods. (B) is wrong because there probably has been no procedural unconscionability in this case. (C) is wrong because most courts will require both procedural and substantive unconscionability in order to allow for rescission on unconscio-nability grounds. (D) is wrong because even though it is correct that Buyer will lose here in most courts, it is not for lack of substantive unconscionability, but rather for lack of procedural unconscionability.

Question 16: Same facts as Question 15, except that the transaction is a lease rather than a sale. How might that affect the outcome?

(A) Lessee (as compared to Buyer) might receive attorneys' fees if she wins.
(B) Lessee (as compared to Buyer) might be liable for attorneys' fees if she loses.
(C) Lessor (as compared to Seller) might be liable for unconscionable con-duct in collecting from Lessee (as compared to Buyer) if the full price has not been paid up-front.
(D) None of the above.
(E) All of the above.

Question 16 Answer: The correct answer is (E). The two key differences between §2-302 and §2A-108 are first, that under §2A-108 (but not §2-302) attorneys' fees are possible in both directions, and second, that §2A-108 (but not §2-302) grants relief to a plaintiff when there is unconscionable conduct in the collection of a claim. (A), (B), and (C) are all true but incomplete, and (D) is wrong because (E) is correct.

Question 17: Thief breaks into Owner's house and steals Owner's antique clock. Thief then brings the clock into Merchant for repairs. Merchant is in the business of repairing and selling antique clocks, but Merchant has no reason to believe that Thief is not the owner of the clock. While the clock is in Merchant's store for repairs, one of Merchant's clerks accidentally sells the clock to Buyer, a buyer in the ordinary course of business. Owner is ultimately able to locate the clock in Buyer's possession. When Owner sues Buyer to recover the clock from Buyer, what is the most accurate statement of the likely outcome?

(A) Buyer wins, because Buyer was a buyer in the ordinary course of business that purchased the clock from a merchant who deals in goods of that kind.

(B) Buyer wins, because the clock was entrusted by Thief to merchant, thereby giving merchant voidable title.

(C) Buyer loses, because Buyer can only inherit the Thief's rights in this case.

(D) Buyer loses, because Buyer only has voidable title, which is not good enough to defeat Owner's title.

(E) Both (C) and (D) are true.

Question 17 Answer: The correct answer is (C). According to §2-403(2), Merchant had the power to transfer "all rights of the entruster" to Buyer, since Buyer was a buyer in the ordinary course of business and Thief entrusted possession of the clock to Merchant, who deals in goods of that kind. Since Thief only had void title, that is what Buyer inherits. (A) is wrong because Buyer only inherits Thief's title in this case under §2-403(2), and that was not good title. (B) is wrong because Merchant did not in fact have voidable title, but only void title. Due to Thief's theft of the clock, any later party following Thief could only have void title. (D) is wrong because Buyer has void title, not voidable title, given that there is a true thief (Thief) in the chain of title. (E) is wrong because (D) is wrong.

Question 18: Same facts as Question 17, except that there is no Thief and it is Owner who brings the clock in for repairs. After Buyer purchases the clock from Merchant, Buyer gives the clock as a birthday gift to Niece. Owner is ultimately able to locate the clock in Niece's possession. When Owner sues Niece to recover the clock from Niece, what is the most accurate statement of the likely outcome?

(A) Owner wins, because Niece does not qualify as a buyer in the ordinary course of business.

(B) Owner wins, because Niece only has voidable title to the clock, which is not good enough to defeat Owner's title.

(C) Niece wins, because Niece's voidable title is strong enough to defeat Owner's title.

(D) Niece wins, because as between Niece and Owner, Niece could not have done anything to prevent the mistake by Merchant, but it was Owner who chose to entrust the clock to Merchant.

(E) Niece wins, because Niece inherits whatever title that Buyer had, and that was good title to the clock.

Question 18 Answer: The correct answer is (E). Section 2-403(1)'s "shelter principle" says that a "purchaser" (which includes a donee such as Niece, see §1-201(b)(29) & (30)) inherits whatever title her transferor had. In this case, Niece's transferor, Buyer, had good title thanks to §2-403(2). Under §2-403(2), Merchant had the power to transfer Owner's rights to Buyer, a buyer in the ordinary course of business, since Owner had entrusted the clock to Merchant, a merchant who deals in goods of this kind. (A) is wrong because Niece does not need to qualify as a buyer in the ordinary course of business to have good title in this case; only Buyer needs to have that status under §2-403(2). (B) is wrong because Niece does not have merely voidable title; she has good title. (C) is wrong for the same reason (B) is wrong. (D) is wrong because the issue here is not relative fault between Niece and Owner, but instead the operation of the entrustment provisions of §2-403(2) with the "shelter principle" of §2-403(1).

Question 19: Owner sells his painting for $20,000 to Buyer, who purchases the painting with a personal check that is ultimately dishonored for insufficient funds in Buyer's checking account. Before Owner realizes that Buyer's check has been dishonored, Buyer leases the painting to Lessee, a good-faith lessee for value, in a two-year lease contract under which Lessee is obligated to pay Buyer $300 per month. When Owner is able to locate the painting in Lessee's possession just one month into the lease, Owner demands that Lessee return the painting immediately to Owner. Lessee refuses to turn over the painting to Owner, instead insisting that the lease with Buyer is valid. Because Owner has learned that Buyer is now insolvent, Owner sues Lessee for immediate return of the painting. What should be the outcome of that lawsuit?

(A) Owner gets immediate return of the painting because of §2-403(1).

(B) Owner gets immediate return of the painting because of §2A-304(1).

(C) Owner does not get immediate return of the painting because of §2-403(1), but Owner rather than Buyer gets the monthly rent and also return of the painting at the end of the lease term.

(D) Owner does not get immediate return of the painting because of §2A-304(1), but Owner rather than Buyer gets the monthly rent and also return of the painting at the end of the lease term.

(E) Owner does not get immediate return of the painting, nor does Owner get the monthly rent or return of the painting at the end of the lease term.

Question 19 Answer: The correct answer is (C). Section 2-403(1) rather than §2A-304(1) covers this case because Lessee here is not a "subsequent lessee" as would be required for §2A-304(1) to apply. Under §2-403(1)(b), Buyer has voidable title to this painting by purchasing it with a bad check. As a party with voidable title, Buyer has the power to transfer good title to a "good-faith purchaser for value." Under §1-201(b)(29) and (30), the term "purchaser" specifically includes a lessee. Owner does, however, have superior rights to the painting to Buyer. Therefore, Owner at least gets to inherit whatever rights Buyer has as lessor of the painting, which include monthly rent and return of the painting at the end of the two-year lease term. (A) is wrong because while it cites the right Code section it gives the wrong outcome. (B) is wrong both because it cites the wrong Code section and because it gives the wrong outcome. (D) is wrong because §2A-304(1) will not govern this case since Lessee is not a "subsequent lessee," and §2A-304(1) only covers voidable title cases where there is an initial lease and then a subsequent lease. (E) is wrong because it suggests that Owner's rights to the painting are not even superior to Buyer's.

Question 20: Music Store rents, sells, and repairs used musical instruments. Player, a lessee in the ordinary course of business, leases a rare antique cello from Music Store under a two-year lease term for $100 per month. One month into that lease, a string breaks on the cello and Player brings the cello into Music Store to have it repaired. After the string is fixed on the cello, a new clerk at Music Store makes a mistake and leases the cello to Singer, a lessee in the ordinary course of business, in a three-year lease for $100 per month. When Player comes to the store to get the repaired cello, Player is very upset to learn that the cello has been leased to Singer. Player manages to locate Singer and insists that Singer relinquish possession of the cello to Player, at least for the remainder of Player's two-year lease. If Player sues Singer in order to enforce its rights to the cello, what should be the outcome?

(A) Singer gets to enforce its three-year lease despite Player's existing lease, and the result would be the same even if Music Store were not a merchant with respect to goods of this kind.

(B) Singer gets to enforce its three-year lease despite Player's existing lease, but the result would be different if Music Store were not a merchant with respect to goods of this kind.

(C) Player gets to enforce its two-year lease only because it was entered into prior to Singer's lease.

(D) Player gets to enforce its two-year lease only because Music Store is a merchant that deals in goods of this kind.

(E) Player gets to enforce its two-year lease both because it was entered into prior to Singer's lease and because Music Store is a merchant that deals in goods of this kind.

Question 20 Answer: The correct answer is (B). This is a §2A-304 case, where a lessor with an existing lease makes a new lease of the same goods to a different lessee. The normal rule, under §2A-304(1), is that the later lessee must take subject to the existing lessee. But this case falls under the special rule of §2A-304(2) since Music Store is a lessor that is a merchant with respect to goods of this kind and the original lessee has entrusted the leased goods back to the lessor. In that scenario, if the lessor leases the goods to a new lessee (such as Singer here) who is a lessee in the ordinary course of business, the new lessee's rights will be superior to the original lessee. (A) is wrong because it says that the result would be the same even if Music Store were not a merchant with respect to goods of this kind. (C), (D), and (E) are all wrong for incorrectly stating that Player, the original lessee, has rights greater than Singer, the subsequent lessee. Although that would be true in the normal case under §2A-304(1), this is a §2A-304(2) case of entrustment by the original lessee.

Chapter 3. Performance

Assignment 18: Closing the Sale with Sales of Goods

Unlike in the real estate context, where the "closing" is a significant event that marks the point when the property is the buyer's problem rather than the seller's, the closing of a sale of personal property is perhaps as much a journey as it is a destination. The process of closing a sale of personal property begins with the buyer's physical receipt of the goods, but that is by no means the end of the story. The buyer is always given a reasonable opportunity to inspect the goods, before which time the buyer may "reject" the goods and put them back into the seller's possession.

Once the buyer's inspection time has passed and the buyer has accepted the goods, the buyer in many cases will have a second opportunity to unravel the transaction, a right known as revocation of acceptance. The buyer's right to reject or revoke acceptance, however, is not without limit. If the seller can tender a satisfactory cure of the non-conformity, then the buyer must keep the cured goods and the deal will proceed.

Even after the time for revocation has passed, the buyer has not lost all rights of recourse against the seller if a later problem with the goods arises. For example, any suit for breach of warranty by the buyer is premised on the assumption that the buyer has in fact already accepted the goods. UCC §2-714(1). Thus, the functional consequences for the buyer of acceptance under Article 2 are simply that the buyer has lost one particular remedy (rejection), the buyer now has the burden of proof on non-conformities, and the buyer must give timely notice of a breach in order to recover any damages from the seller.

In practice, buyers are not usually eager to reject shipments from sellers if there is any way in which the goods might be either repaired or replaced with conforming goods.

The general pattern in the sale of goods system is one in which sellers are fairly generous in responding to relatively late complaints by buyers, and buyers in turn are mostly amenable to seller's attempts to cure defects.

The law on the books dictates that there are three ways in which a buyer will be deemed to have "accepted" goods: (1) an affirmative signification that buyer has accepted, (2) a failure to reject the goods following a reasonable opportunity to inspect them, and (3) an act by the buyer that is inconsistent with the seller's ownership. UCC §2-606(1).

Discussions with parties in the field, however, suggest that in practice neither buyers nor sellers are thinking very much about the point at which the buyer satisfies this standard. If buyers truly worried about the consequences of acceptance, they would probably spend more time and energy on their inspection procedures. Some larger buyers have fairly formal and detailed inspection procedures in which the goods are checked for non-conformities right as they are received. Most smaller manufacturers, however, will not conduct formal inspections of the raw materials they purchase. Their inspections, such as they are, occur when they begin to use those materials for producing the finished product.

As one officer of a medium-sized plastics manufacturer described it, "We don't bother to inspect material as it comes in other than to count and weigh it. Anything more would be too expensive. Instead we just wait until we use the stuff for production to see if there's any problem with it. There has never been an issue about us waiting too long to complain. Sometimes material might sit around for a few months before we begin using it for production, but if what the supplier sent isn't right, then they know they have to fix it no matter when we discover the problem."

The in-house counsel for a Fortune 200 manufacturer echoed these sentiments: "We take the position as buyer that it's never too late to complain about a nonconformity, even if it's not discovered until after it's in a finished product, as long as we're in a position to prove that the problem existed with the material that we received from the supplier. Our quality assurance program would catch most of those problems before that point, but it may not catch all of them all of the time."

Much like manufacturers who buy raw materials from suppliers, wholesalers that buy from manufacturers believe that even if they do not end up discovering a problem with the goods until they have been shipped to retailers, it is still not too late to complain to the manufacturers. Similarly, wholesalers are generally willing to remedy complaints about the goods they sell to retailers for as long as the goods sit on the shelf in the retailer's store. Not surprisingly, retailers have come to expect this accommodation.

As the in-house lawyer for one major retail buyer put it, "Our stores typically don't follow formal inspection procedures when they get the goods. On the other hand, we'll know pretty quickly if there's a problem either because we'll see it when we put clothes out on the shelf or our customers will let us know. Clothes have a relatively short shelf life, but even with a longer-shelf item like a TV, we've never had an issue about it being too late for us to send goods back to our seller on the grounds that the goods were nonconforming."

The typically long period that sellers give buyers to complain about problems with accepted goods seems to work well generally, but there is occasional abuse. For example, an officer at a medium-sized furniture manufacturer is convinced that a few of his company's retail buyers would damage the goods themselves shortly before the 12-month warranty period expired as a way to return furniture that they had not been able to sell: "In some cases it was pretty obvious — the furniture had punctures in it but the box in which the furniture was shipped did not." Echoing this same desire to dispose of stale merchandise, a lawyer for a retail buyer admitted, "Generally, we'll give sellers a chance to cure, unless we've decided that the merchandise is a dog and we need a reason to justify giving it back to them."

The supplier certification program is a relatively new feature of the sales system that is likely reducing even further the amount of time that buyers spend inspecting the goods when they receive them. With a supplier certification program, the buyer devotes a significant amount of time only at the beginning of a relationship with a new seller to determine whether that seller has adequate quality control mechanisms in place. Thus, at the beginning of a relationship, a buyer may perform these supplier certification procedures. Such procedures involve intensive inspections of shipments a buyer receives along with visits to the seller's factory to insure the quality of the seller's entire operation. Once a particular supplier is certified by a buyer, the buyer will do only spot inspections of that supplier's deliveries.

Although in the vast majority of cases buyers and sellers are able to work out their differences concerning the quality of the goods shipped, there are occasions in which one or both parties will choose to resort to the legal system. In these situations, the buyer is given a couple of goods-oriented remedies under Article 2: rejection and revocation. Rejection authorizes, but does not require, the buyer to cancel the contract with the seller.

Rejection must occur within a reasonable time after delivery of the goods, and it is ineffective unless the buyer seasonably notifies the seller. UCC §2-602(1). If the buyer fails to state the specific grounds for rejection, then the buyer may lose the ability to use the unstated rejection grounds to justify the rejection. UCC §2-605(1).

The buyer's right to reject technically exists whenever the goods "fail in any respect to conform to the contract," §2-601, but there are a number of exceptions to this so-called perfect tender rule. First, if the contract is an installment contract (one in which the contract contemplates a series of separate deliveries), then the buyer may reject an installment only "if the non-conformity substantially impairs the value of that installment and cannot be cured." UCC §2-612(2). Second, the seller may have contractually limited the buyer's remedies, including the right to reject, thereby obligating the buyer to accept the seller's efforts to repair or replace defective parts.

Third, the seller's right to "cure" (more on this follows) can often reverse a buyer's rejection. And finally, concepts such as usage of trade, course of dealing, and course of performance may allow the seller some "commercial leeways in performance" that will preclude the buyer's rejection of a less-than-perfect tender. Official Comment 2 to UCC §2-106.

A buyer that does successfully reject the seller's delivery has very little responsibility for the rejected goods. Non-merchant buyers merely need to hold the goods with reasonable care for the seller for a time sufficient to enable the seller to remove them. UCC §2-602(2)(b). Merchant buyers have a slightly heightened duty with respect to rejected goods. When the goods are in the buyer's possession and the seller has no agent at the place of rejection, the merchant buyer must follow any reasonable instruction of the seller as to resale, storage, or the like. UCC §2-603(1). If the goods are perishable or will lose their value quickly, the buyer must sell them on the seller's behalf. UCC §2-603(1).

When a buyer has accepted the goods, which typically occurs by default when the buyer fails to reject the goods following a reasonable opportunity to inspect, the buyer has lost its legal right to reject the goods. UCC §2-607(2). This does not, however, mean that the buyer has lost all opportunity to return the goods to the seller. Aside from the practical likelihood that the seller will accept return of defective goods even if it is untimely, the buyer also has the legal right in some cases to revoke acceptance.

The buyer who wishes to revoke acceptance must overcome a number of hurdles that the rejecting buyer does not. First, with a revocation the non-conformity must "substantially impair" the value of the goods to the buyer. UCC §2-608(1). Second, the buyer may revoke its acceptance only in one of two circumstances: (1) where the buyer reasonably believed that the problem with the goods would be cured and it has not been, or (2) where the buyer was unaware of the problem because of seller's assurances or because the problem was too hard to discover before acceptance. UCC §2-608(1).

The revoking buyer also must deal with some time limits. The revocation must occur within a reasonable time after the buyer actually discovered or should have discovered the grounds for the revocation, and it must also occur before there is any substantial change in the goods that was not caused by their own defects. UCC §2-608(2). And, just as with rejection, revocation is not effective until the buyer notifies the seller of it. As the following case demonstrates, if a buyer is strung along by the promises of a seller to make things right, that standard gives the buyer quite a long window in which to effectively revoke acceptance of the goods.

North American Lighting, Inc. v. Hopkins Manufacturing Corp.

37 F.3d 1253 (7th Cir. 1994)

CUDAHY, C.J.

Hopkins Manufacturing Corporation (Hopkins) appeals from a judgment for North American Lighting, Inc. (NAL) for refund of the partial purchase price of a headlight aiming system. The district court held that NAL had timely revoked its acceptance of the system and was not liable for the rental value of the system during the period prior to revocation. We affirm in part and reverse in part.

Hopkins produces headlight aiming systems and other photometric quality control devices. NAL produces headlamp assemblies for most major automobile manufacturers, including replaceable bulb headlamps. NAL needs to conform its replaceable bulb headlamps both to individual car maker specifications and, as required under the Motor Vehicle Safety Act, to industry standards. 15 U.S.C. §§1391-1426. Consistent with the Act, the Society of Automobile Engineers (SAE) promulgated standards which were then adopted by Federal Motor Vehicle Safety Standard No. 108 (Standard 108). . . .

. . . NAL decided to purchase a [Machine Vision System] (MVS), based largely on Hopkins' ongoing promises that software could be added to correct problems experienced with the prototype. The permanent MVS was purchased in June 1989 for an invoice price of $79,548, ten percent of which NAL withheld pending completion of the promised software upgrades — including upgrades to allow testing of the two checkpoints about which NAL's engineer had expressed some concern. The permanent system, which arrived in August 1989, did not perform well. One NAL employee testified that the permanent system sometimes gave readings that varied more than 100% from the known light intensity properties of certified headlamps. On other occasions, the MVS would give a "zero" reading even though a light beam was present. Over the course of 210 days, 74% of the system's readings fell outside the required 10% accuracy range and the system failed to test at some of the checkpoints required by Standard 108. . . .

Both parties concede that NAL accepted the MVS. They disagree, however, on whether NAL could subsequently revoke its acceptance. Hopkins argues that, since NAL knew the existing capabilities and shortcomings of the MVS, there was no "non-conformity" upon which NAL could base its revocation. Hopkins relies on §2-607(2) of Illinois' version of the Uniform Commercial Code (UCC), which provides:

> (2) Acceptance of goods by the buyer . . . if made with knowledge of a non-conformity cannot be revoked because of it unless the acceptance was on the reasonable assumption that the non-conformity would be seasonably cured. . . .

810 ILCS 5/2-607(2). Hopkins relies on this provision, as well as cases from this Circuit and from Illinois, to suggest that goods "conform" to the contract whenever the buyer knows or has reason to know that goods will not serve the function for which he bought them.

We, like the district court, reject this argument. The language of §2-607(2) itself makes clear that the buyer can "know" of a non-conformity without destroying his right to revoke acceptance. Id. (buyer with knowledge of non-conformity may revoke where he accepted "on the reasonable assumption that the non-conformity would be . . . cured"). And the authorities Hopkins cites in support of its notion of "non-conformity" demonstrate, at most, that, where a buyer accepts goods with an understanding of what they can and cannot do, he cannot later undo the contract, under certain conditions resulting from his acceptance. The condition allegedly precluding revocation of acceptance here is that this preclusion is based solely on the fact that the goods, while performing to his expectations, nevertheless failed to serve the purpose for which the buyer claims to have bought the goods.

But NAL does not seek to revoke based solely on the failure of the MVS to test light intensities at the Standard 108 checkpoints. Rather, NAL seeks to revoke based on what it claims was its reasonable acceptance based on Hopkins' assurances that this failure would be rectified. Indeed, the notion that NAL fully understood the capabilities of the MVS defies common sense. There is no suggestion that NAL failed to make a good faith effort to comply with Standard 108. NAL has repeatedly demonstrated its willingness to comply with the standard: by sending its headlamps to a New York laboratory, by trying to obtain software upgrades on the MVS, by using its sensitive certification equipment to perform due care testing (and thereby risking damage to that equipment) and by attempting to procure a replacement for the MVS as soon as the promised upgrades failed to enable the system to perform the required tests. It would be nonsensical to conclude that NAL acquired the MVS and spent months trying to have it upgraded merely to have the opportunity to sue, as it did below, for a refund of the purchase price and related expenses.

More plausible is NAL's version of the facts, which the district court accepted. NAL claims not to have discovered the non-conformity of which it complains, as indicated by its reliance on [UCC] subsection [2-608(1)(b)]. This is entirely consistent with the record. NAL does not deny that it knew that the MVS was originally intended to serve as an aiming device and it admits that its engineer and other employees expressed at least some doubt as to Hopkins' ability to adapt the MVS for NAL's purposes. As we have indicated, however, these facts do not preclude the existence of a non-conformity. Rather, it follows that the undiscovered non-conformity NAL claims was not that the unmodified MVS could not perform the Standard 108 tests but rather that the system would not perform the tests even after modifications.

We are left, then, with the question whether, given NAL's failure for an extended period to discover that the MVS could not be modified to suit its purposes, NAL properly revoked. Specifically, we must determine whether NAL could, relying on Hopkins' alleged assurances, revoke its acceptance even after it had used the MVS for several months. We conclude that NAL could revoke. . . .

A seller may be found to have given "assurances" within the meaning of §2-608 based on either circumstantial evidence or the seller's explicit language and, where the seller has assured the buyer explicitly, revocation will be available whether or not the seller made the assurances in bad faith. There is ample evidence in the record that Hopkins assured NAL that the MVS could be modified for the purpose of satisfying its due care obligations under Standard 108. Hopkins' written materials support this point, as does testimony by both NAL and Hopkins employees. As indicated, moreover, it would strain credulity to think that NAL would accept the device and expend resources over several months to modify it unless it had been persuaded, presumably by Hopkins, that the device could eventually suit its needs. Further, given the sophistication of the technology involved, the district court did not err in finding that NAL behaved reasonably in relying on Hopkins' assurances. While NAL's engineer and other employees may have alerted it to some limitations of the MVS, it stands to reason that NAL would defer to Hopkins regarding the capabilities of its products, especially since NAL does not itself make headlight aiming or photometric devices.

Whether the value of the product has been impaired is determined subjectively, from the buyer's perspective. Whether such impairment is "substantial," however, is determined based on the objective evidence. There can be little disagreement that NAL purchased the MVS to perform daily testing of its headlight assemblies at sixteen critical checkpoints, a function required of NAL by federal regulations. Nor is there any dispute that the MVS was never able to carry out this function.

Indeed, the MVS eventually stopped working altogether. Thus, there was "substantial impairment" of the device's value within the meaning of §2-608.

Section 1-204(2) [1-302(b) as amended] of the UCC indicates that what is a "reasonable time" for revocation depends on the nature, purpose and circumstances of the transaction. In particular, the period where revocation is allowable may be extended where the seller gives continuous assurances, and where the seller fails, after repeated attempts, to repair defects of which the buyer complains. Here, there is substantial evidence that Hopkins made express written and oral assurances, with respect to both the loaned prototype MVS and the permanent system that arrived in August, 1989. These assurances—and Hopkins' failure to make good on them—were sufficient both to cause concern at Hopkins and to induce NAL to continue working with Hopkins to upgrade the system. NAL's responsiveness to such inducement was reasonable for much the same reason that NAL's acceptance of the system was reasonable: NAL could reasonably defer to Hopkins' superior expertise with the device's technology until the promised software upgrades failed to make the device viable. That NAL did not seek to revoke during the several months between delivery of the permanent system and the upgrades attests, perhaps, to NAL's desperation to find a more economical method of satisfying its due care obligations, but such delay did not make NAL's revocation untimely given Hopkins' repeated assurances and the other facts of this case. We reject Hopkins' argument that NAL could not revoke simply because it used the MVS. Consistent with the Code, Illinois courts have rejected the notion that any use by the buyer constitutes an irrevocable acceptance by the buyer, "hav[ing] tempered [this] absolute rule of acceptance with a consideration for the reasonableness of the buyer's conduct." Alden Press, Inc. v. Block & Co., 527 N.E.2d 489, 497 (Ill. App. 1988). It would be inequitable to require NAL to pay for the MVS in full if it reasonably delayed revocation in order to allow Hopkins to make good on its promises. Indeed, given the clear evidence that Hopkins assured NAL that the system could be adapted for due care purposes, Hopkins' product use argument comes dangerously close to suggesting a rule that would allow sellers to "lock in" purchasers of goods by promising them the moon—only to bring them back to earth when they attempted to revoke the acceptance that they were persuaded to give because of their failure to understand fully a substantial defect. Thus, there was timely revocation of acceptance here.

With respect to the [MVS,] we conclude that some compensation is due Hopkins. As indicated, where revocation of acceptance has been established, the aggrieved buyer's remedies are the same as those afforded a buyer who has rejected the goods. These remedies are set out at UCC §2-711, which does not specifically provide for an offset for beneficial use prior to revocation of acceptance. However, the Code does state: "Unless displaced by the particular provisions of this Act, the principles of law and equity . . . shall supplement its provisions." UCC §1-103. Such supplementary principles include quantum meruit recovery. In order to be successful on a theory of quantum meruit under Illinois law, a party must prove performance of the services, reasonable value of the services, and the receipt by the defendant from the plaintiff of a benefit which it would be unjust for him to retain without paying the complaining party.

As indicated, there is substantial evidence that NAL knew that there were problems in adapting the MVS to enable NAL to satisfy its due care obligations. Thus, even though it would appear that NAL was not aware that the MVS would not suit its needs even after the promised software upgrades were finally made, it seems equally clear that NAL purchased the device knowing that its performance would be, at least initially, suboptimal. That NAL continued to use the device instead of finding alternative methods of testing the bulbs—but, as we have indicated, there is no indication of bad faith on NAL's part—indicates that the device served some beneficial use. The fairness of this result is supported by the fact that NAL, at the time of its revocation, itself proposed that NAL pay rental fees through July, 1990 in exchange for a refund of the portion of the purchase price already paid. Further, Hopkins presented testimony that another of Hopkins' devices with similar capabilities was on lease for $3,300 per month and that, based on this figure and the amount that NAL was spending to send its assemblies to the New York laboratory, a reasonable rental figure for the MVS would be $1,600 per month. These facts, while sparse, seem to satisfy the general requirements for quantum meruit recovery. Thus, we remand to the district court to consider—based on these facts and whatever other evidence the district court, in its discretion, deems appropriate—what rental value would be reasonable compensation for NAL's use of the permanent MVS from the time of its arrival in August, 1989 until the time of NAL's timely revocation some months later.

———————

One revocation issue that the court in *North American Lighting* did not have to discuss is whether a seller has a right to cure in the case of a revoking buyer. Suppose, for example, that a buyer ordered a machine, used it for a while, and then discovered that the machine had a defect that could not have been discovered until the machine had been used for at least a short time.

At this point, it would probably be too late for the buyer to reject the machine, since the buyer has taken acts inconsistent with the seller's ownership of the machine and a reasonable time for inspection has seemingly passed. Nevertheless, the buyer could argue that it still had a right to revoke its acceptance under UCC §2-608(1)(b), since the buyer could argue that it accepted the goods without discovery of the non-conformity because of the difficulty of its discovery before acceptance.

Suppose that in response to the buyer's announcement that it intended to revoke its acceptance, the seller told the buyer that it wished to cure the problem by repairing the machine. Would the buyer in that case be obligated to accept the seller's cure attempt, or could the buyer decide that it simply wanted to undo the transaction for good?

UCC §2-508 makes it clear that where the buyer *rejects* the seller's tender, the buyer must allow the seller an opportunity to cure if either (1) the time for performance has not yet expired (e.g., there was a set delivery deadline and the seller delivered early) or (2) the seller had reasonable grounds to believe that its rejected tender would be acceptable to the buyer. What §2-508 is not clear about is whether the revoking buyer, as opposed to the rejecting buyer, has the same responsibility to give the seller a chance to cure.

A common point of contention in cure situations is determining what should count as an acceptable cure and who should define what that is. An officer for a medium-sized furniture manufacturer explains, "If furniture has minor defects, we authorize the retailers who have repair capabilities to repair the furniture themselves and then bill us according to an hourly rate that we have agreed to in advance. But we have one retailer who simply refuses to accept repair as a cure. For that retailer, we always have to send brand-new furniture. Most of the other buyers will accept repair as a valid cure as long as the defect is only minor."

Often the dynamics of the cure details come down to who has more leverage, buyer or seller. Although leverage can be a function of a number of things, one factor that can affect leverage in the cure setting is the schedule for the buyer's payment of the purchase price. One institutional buyer noted that he specifically arranges for a holdback just for the purposes of retaining leverage in cure situations: "I like to set up a payment system that holds back money until we've had a chance to test the machine that we've purchased, particularly an expensive piece of lab equipment. I might pay a quarter of the purchase price at the signing of the contract, a quarter more at delivery, and then hold back the other half until the researcher has had an adequate opportunity to really test the machine."

One argument that buyers sometimes make is known as the Shaken Faith Doctrine. The Shaken Faith Doctrine was first used in Zabriskie Chevrolet, Inc. v. Smith, 240 A.2d 195 (N.J. 1968), where an auto dealer attempted to cure the buyer's defective new car by replacing the transmission in that car rather than giving the buyer a new car. The court in *Zabriskie* said that the cure attempt was ineffective because the nature of the defect was such that the buyer's faith in that particular car was legitimately shaken.

Rather than viewing the "Shaken Faith" case as creating a new doctrine, one could also interpret the case as simply making the point that the seller cannot unilaterally define what constitutes an acceptable cure under §2-508. The cure that is tendered must be at least enough to satisfy a reasonable person in the buyer's position.

Sinco, Inc. v. Metro-North Commuter R. Co.
133 F. Supp. 2d 308 (S.D.N.Y. 2001)

HELLERSTEIN, J.

In this action for breach of contract, the parties filed cross-motions for summary judgment pursuant to Federal Rule of Civil Procedure 56. Oral argument was heard on December 14, 2000. For the reasons stated below, I grant the motion for summary judgment filed by Defendant Metro-North Commuter Railroad Company

("Metro-North") and deny the motion for summary judgment filed by Plaintiff Sinco, Inc. ("Sinco"). I refer the case to Magistrate Judge Frank Maas for an inquest as to damages.

I.   FACTUAL BACKGROUND

In early 1998, Metro-North determined that federal and state laws required the installation of a fall-protection system for certain elevated walkways, roof areas, and interior catwalks in Grand Central Terminal [(GCT)] before maintenance and renovation work could proceed in those areas. The system was necessary to ensure the safety of Metro-North employees during work performed at great heights on the interior and exterior of the Terminal. In order to conclude its extensive renovations of the Terminal and permit necessary ongoing maintenance work, the system had to be installed promptly.

Metro-North reviewed various bids, including Sinco's proposal for a system called "Sayfglida." This system involves a harness worn by the worker, a network of cables, and metal clips or sleeves called "Sayflinks" that connect the worker's harness to the cables. Metro-North awarded the contract to Sinco, agreeing to pay $197,325.00 for the construction and installation of the system by June 26, 1999.

The contract provided that Sinco deliver a reliable fall-protection system, a "fall protection system [that] will provide a safer work environment for maintenance personnel in various areas within GCT." See Contract at 146. The reliability of such a system was crucial; any failure of the fall protection equipment easily could result in injury or loss of life. The contract language reflected this emphasis on reliability. Article 14.01 provided:

> Contractor shall ensure that all goods, components, parts, equipment, accessories and material that shall be furnished have been tested, found compatible with each other and meet all applicable Federal, State and Local guidelines.

The "Contractor Quality Control Program Requirements" provided:

> Metro-North requires that Work under this Contract must be performed in conformance with a Quality Control (QC) Plan which complies with the Quality Control requirements in the Technical Provisions.

Article 1.02(9) of the contract terms defined the "contract" broadly, encompassing Sinco's proposal document as well as various other supporting documents. Sinco's proposal repeatedly stressed the reliability of the system; for example, Section 8(d) of the proposal stated that the system "will provide 100% Fall Protection for the users."

The contract also gave the contractor an opportunity to cure any alleged breach, following a notice of default by Metro-North. Article 7.02 of the contract provided:

If an Event of Default occurs, Metro-North may so notify the Contractor ("Default Notice"), specifying the basis(es) for such default, and advising the Contractor that, unless such default is rectified to the satisfaction of Metro-North within seven (7) days from such Default Notice, the Contractor shall be in default; except that, at its sole discretion, Metro-North may extend such seven (7) day period for such additional period as Metro-North shall deem appropriate without waiver of any of its rights hereunder. The Default Notice shall specify the date the Contractor is to discontinue all Work (the "Termination Date"), and thereupon, unless rescinded by Metro-North, the Contractor shall discontinue the Work upon the Termination Date.

After the award of the contract, Sinco performed installation work at Grand Central. On June 29, 1999, Sinco began a training session for Metro-North employees. During the session, a Metro-North employee was examining a Sayflink sleeve when the sleeve fell apart in his hands. The three other sample Sayflinks delivered by Sinco were found to have identical defects, and the training immediately was suspended. On June 30, 1999, Metro-North's representative wrote to Sinco, "Metro-North herewith puts Sinco, Inc. on notice, that the entire 'Fall Protection System' as currently installed by Sinco, Inc. at Grand Central Terminal pursuant to the subject contract is unacceptable."

Sinco's representatives, after a brief internal investigation, admitted that their quality control processes had failed. Specifically, they determined that there had been a failure of the metal "staking" that helped maintain the structural integrity of the Sayflink sleeve. In a June 30, 1999 letter, Sinco's representatives attributed the defective staking to the fact that the operator constructing the parts "was performing operations which he had not done recently," resulting in the metal staking being "off center."

Within two days, Sinco manufactured and delivered two types of replacement clips: four replacement clips were staked by machine; and four had additional metal welded across the end of the stake as reinforcement. Sinco also included a videotape of a stress test performed on a welded Sayflink. Metro-North timely rejected the proposed cure.

At meetings and in telephone discussions following the June 29, 1999 incident, Sinco also suggested other potential cures. Sinco offered to pay for an independent engineering firm to examine the fall protection system to determine its reliability. Sinco also offered to perform "drop tests" at Grand Central Terminal for observers, to pay for Metro-North employees to travel to Minnesota to inspect its manufacturing plant and undergo training on the equipment in question, to conduct on-site training and demonstrations at Metro-North offices, and to substitute sleeves manufactured by a different company in place of the Sayfglida sleeves. Metro-North did not accept any of these ideas.

On August 11, 1999, Metro-North sent a Notice of Default to Sinco, stating that the contract would be terminated on August 19, 1999, following the seven-day cure period provided in the contract. On September 16, 1999, following additional meetings and communications with Sinco, Metro-North terminated the contract. Following Sinco's termination, Metro-North awarded the work to another company, Surety, Inc., at a contract price of $347,896.99. The price of the

Surety, Inc. contract, therefore, was $126,360.99 more than the Sinco contract price of $197,325.00.

On October 19, 1999, Sinco filed its complaint in this action, alleging breach of contract. Metro-North counterclaimed for its alleged cost of cover, the difference between the Sinco contract price and the Surety, Inc. contract price.

II.   ISSUES PRESENTED

The parties have filed cross-motions for summary judgment, which raise three central issues. First, was Sinco's breach so egregious as to be total, without potential for cure? Second, by delivering replacement parts and an accompanying video-tape of stress testing, did Sinco cure its breach? Third, did any of Sinco's subsequent proposals constitute a cure of the breach?

Article 10.14 of the contract provides: "This Contract is to be construed and enforced pursuant to the laws of the State of New York." As the contract was for a transaction in goods, the substantive law of Article 2 of the New York Uniform Commercial Code governs this dispute. See N.Y. UCC §2-102. Summary judgment may be granted if the pleadings and written discovery, together with the affidavits, show that there is no issue of material fact and that the moving party is entitled to judgment as a matter of law. Fed. R. Civ. P. 56(c), Anderson v. Liberty Lobby, Inc., 477 U.S. 242, 249, 106 S. Ct. 2505, 91 L. Ed. 2d 202 (1986); Celotex Corp. v. Catrett, 477 U.S. 317, 322, 106 S. Ct. 2548, 91 L. Ed. 2d 265 (1986); Gallo v. Prudential Residential Servs., Ltd. Partnership, 22 F.3d 1219, 1223 (2d Cir. 1994). I find no issue of material fact precluding judgment as a matter of law for Metro-North.

III.   SINCO'S BREACH DID NOT RENDER CURE FUTILE

Metro-North alleges that Sinco's delivery of the defective Sayflinks was so material a breach that Metro-North was entitled to terminate the contract without even providing an opportunity for cure. This argument conflicts with both the language of the contract and the substantive law of New York.

Article 7.01 of the contract provides that a "material breach" by Sinco may be considered an "Event of Default." "The remedy of termination—or, more accurately, the 'right' to terminate—is available only where one party has materially breached the contract. . . . Where a breach is material, the party is justified in refusing to go on, and thus the law provides that party with the right to terminate." ESPN, Inc. v. Office of the Comm'r of Baseball, 76 F. Supp. 2d 383, 392 (S.D.N.Y. 1999). It is well-settled under New York law that in order to justify termination, "a breach must be . . . so substantial and fundamental as to strongly tend to defeat the object of the parties in making the contract." Babylon Assocs. v. County of Suffolk, 101 A.D.2d 207, 475 N.Y.S.2d 869, 874 (App. Div. 2d Dep't 1984) (quoting Callanan v. Keeseville, A.C. & L.C.R., 199 N.Y. 268, 284, 92 N.E. 747, 752

(1910)). Termination is an "extraordinary remedy" to be permitted only when the breach goes to "the root of the agreement." Septembertide Publishing, B.V. v. Stein & Day, Inc., 884 F.2d 675, 678 (2d Cir. 1989).

An injured party's right of termination, however, is limited by the doctrine of cure.

> Although a material breach justifies the injured party in exercising a right to self-help by suspending performance, it does not necessarily justify the injured party in exercising such a right by terminating the contract. Fairness ordinarily dictates that the party in breach be allowed a period of time—even if only a short one—to cure the breach if it can. If the party in breach does cure within that period, the injured party is not justified in further suspension of its performance and both parties are still bound to complete their performances.

E. Allan Farnsworth, Farnsworth on Contracts, §8.18 (2d ed. 1998). Here, in fact, Article 7.02 of the contract specifically provides Sinco with an opportunity to cure in the event of a material breach. Sinco's breach, although material, justifying Metro-North's exercise of its contractual and common-law right to declare Sinco in default and suspend performance, did not eliminate Sinco's right, under Article 7.02 and under New York common law, to cure its breach.

Nevertheless, Metro-North argues that the delivery of defective Sayflinks was so severe a breach that it irremediably undermined Metro-North's confidence in the fall-protection system, rendering futile any attempt at cure. Following the discovery of the defect, Metro-North's unions reported that their members would not use the system, and the unions repeatedly expressed a complete lack of confidence in Sinco and its products. Metro-North contends that nothing Sinco did—no curative performance of any sort—could restore this lost confidence. In other words, the breach could not be cured.

In support of this "shaken faith" or "loss of confidence" theory, Metro-North cites case law from states other than New York. I find these authorities not entirely applicable to the case before me.

Zabriskie Chevrolet, Inc. v. Smith, 99 N.J. Super. 441, 240 A.2d 195 (N.J. Sup. Ct. 1968) involved a car dealer's efforts to cure its delivery of new car with a faulty transmission by replacing the transmission with one removed from a showroom model. The court found that the substitution of a transmission "not from the factory and of unknown lineage" was "not within the agreement or contemplation of the parties." Id. at 458, 240 A.2d 195. In short, the cure did not conform to the terms of the contract. The court's discussion of "shaken faith" is not essential to its conclusion; it appears from the text of the opinion that the attempted cure was objectively unreasonable.

Hemmert Agricultural Aviation, Inc. v. Mid-Continent Aircraft Corp., 663 F. Supp. 1546 (D. Kan. 1987), decided under Kansas state law, better illustrates Metro-North's theory. The flaws in a "crop-duster" airplane purchased by the plaintiff created "fear and apprehension" in the pilot. The court held that, "[w]here the buyer's confidence in the dependability of the machine is shaken because of the defects and possible because of seller's ineffective attempts to cure, revocation appears justified." Id. at 1552.

There appear to be no New York cases treating the "shaken faith" theory articulated in *Hemmert* under Kansas law. I am not prepared to hold that Sinco's breach rendered futile any potential cure. A materially breaching party generally is entitled, subject to the relevant terms and conditions of the contract and the Uniform Commercial Code, to cure its breach within a reasonable period of time. Cure, in this case, required not only the timely delivery of conforming replacement parts, but a convincing showing of the reliability of the equipment. Such a showing would have required a description of Sinco's manufacturing methods and a precise explanation of the reasons why the demonstration parts failed in relation to such methods. If Sinco had timely tendered such a cure, Metro-North would have been able to assess the reasons for the failure and the reliability of the cure. If, objectively, the cure was shown to be reliably safe, Metro-North would have been obligated to accept the cure, despite, perhaps, any lingering subjective misgivings of its employees. Ultimately, however, Sinco failed to cure and Metro-North justifiably terminated the contract.

IV.   SINCO'S DELIVERY OF REPLACEMENT PARTS FAILED TO CURE ITS BREACH

Section 2-508(2) of the New York Uniform Commercial Code provides a seller with an opportunity to cure a non-conforming delivery by prompt tender of a conforming product:

> Where the buyer rejects a non-conforming tender which the seller had reasonable grounds to believe would be acceptable with or without money allowance the seller may if he seasonably notifies the buyer have a further reasonable time to substitute a conforming tender.

Therefore, any cure made by Sinco would have to meet all its contractual requirements, including the conditions regarding reliability.

It is undisputed that Sinco's attempted performance under the contract—its delivery of a fall-protection system that included the defective Sayflinks—did not satisfy its contractual obligations. Pursuant to the Code and the contract, Sinco had the opportunity following this breach to cure.

Sinco, as the party attempting to effect a cure, had the burden to show that its proffered cure did, in fact, conform to the terms of the contract. Those terms included stringent conditions regarding quality control and reliability. It is uncontested that the welded Sayflinks, manufactured and delivered within two days after the equipment failure, were not subjected to Sinco's internal quality controls. The contractual conditions regarding reliability also applied to the replacement Sayflinks that came from the regular assembly line that did not include the additional welding. Sinco had to show exactly what had caused the defect in the demonstration parts, that the underlying problem had been remedied, and that the defect would not recur. Furthermore, in order to conform to the contract, any replacement system had to be demonstrably reliable. In a situation such as this, involving the failure of vital safety equipment in front of the very individuals the equipment was designed to protect, the injured party did not have to accept at face value the word of the breaching party regarding the reliability of replacement equipment. Metro-North was entitled to objective evidence of such reliability.

Sinco did not satisfy that obligation by delivering to Metro-North a videotape of a welded and staked Sayflink surviving a single "pull test" of over 6200 pounds of stress. The replacement parts sent by Sinco included four Sayflinks that had been staked, and four that had been both welded and staked. The videotaped test was performed only on a Sayflink with the supplemental welding, not on a "standard" Sayflink that lacked the welding. Moreover, the test involved the application of stress in a different direction than the direction in which the failure occurred, and did not show reliability over time and frequent use. Finally, the videotape was produced by Sinco itself, not by a disinterested and objective third party. The videotaped stress test did not demonstrate the reliability of Sinco's attempted cure.

V.   NONE OF SINCO'S SUBSEQUENT SUGGESTIONS CONSTITUTED A "CURE"

When Metro-North did not accept Sinco's first attempted cure, Sinco proposed several ideas for other possible cures during discussions with Metro-North. However, these mere offers of potentially curative performance did not adequately cure Sinco's breach.

Pursuant to Section 2-508(2) of the New York Uniform Commercial Code, Sinco had to notify Metro-North of its intention to cure and had to make a "conforming tender." "This clearly entails *more than a mere offer,* but less than actual physical delivery." Allied Semi-Conductors Int'l, Ltd. v. Pulsar Components Int'l, Inc., 907 F. Supp. 618, 624 (E.D.N.Y. 1995) (emphasis added). The parties in *Allied Semi-Conductors* were wholesale suppliers of computer components, and the case involved the sale of defective computer chips by the defendant, Pulsar Components, to the plaintiff, Allied Semi-Conductors. At a bench trial before a magistrate judge, Pulsar sought to prove that it had made "an offer to cure" the shipment of defective chips. In deciding in favor of Allied, the magistrate judge held that even if Pulsar proved that it made such an offer, the offer was "not sufficient to constitute a cure." Id. at 625. The magistrate judge concluded, "Pulsar never communicated an unconditional intention to cure and never made or even tendered a conforming delivery." Id. Pulsar appealed to the district court.

In affirming the magistrate judge's decision, the district court closely reviewed the meaning of "conforming tender" under N.Y. UCC §2-508. The court held that, although tender does not require the seller to make "actual, physical delivery," "[t]ender of delivery under the Code requires the seller to put and hold conforming goods at the buyer's disposition and give the buyer any notification reasonably necessary to enable him to take delivery." Id. at 624 (citing H. Sand & Co., Inc. v. Airtemp Corp., 934 F.2d 450, 454 (2d Cir. 1991)). See also N.Y. UCC §2-503(1). The court distinguished cases such as T.W. Oil, Inc. v. Consolidated Edison Co. of

New York, Inc., 57 N.Y.2d 574, 457 N.Y.S.2d 458, 443 N.E.2d 932 (1982), cited by Sinco in the instant case. The court found that the seller seeking to cure in *T.W. Oil* "had a present ability to effect delivery"; here, Sinco did not have such ability, having failed to put conforming goods and evidence of their reliability at Metro-North's disposition. In sum, the court in *Allied Semi-Conductors* rejected the argument made by Pulsar, and similarly made by Sinco in this case, "namely, that an offer to make conforming goods available, without more, preserves the seller's rights under UCC §2-508." *Allied Semi-Conductors*, 907 F. Supp. at 625.

Sinco's bare offers of potentially curative performance were not enough. The contract called for reliable equipment to protect Metro-North's employees from grave injury or death, and Sinco's equipment had been shown to be unreliable. In order to effectuate a cure, Sinco was obliged to make a conforming tender—that is, to put a fall protection system and proof of its reliability at Metro-North's disposition, leaving it to Metro-North to accept the tender. In essence, Sinco had to take the initiative; it could not shift any part of its burden to Metro-North. It was not enough for Sinco merely to suggest possible solutions. Because Sinco failed to cure its breach, I deny its motion for summary judgment and grant Metro-North's motion for summary judgment on the issue of liability.

Problem Set 18

18.1. a. Kim McNicholas orders a home computer from Computers by Mail, Inc. When the computer arrives, she takes it out of the box and uses it for about 10 minutes before she discovers that the left side of the screen's frame is cracked. At this point, has Kim accepted the computer? UCC §2-606, Official Comment 4 to §2-606.

b. Same facts as part (a), except that as soon as Kim takes the computer out of the box, she drills several holes in its plastic base and screws it onto her desk. Then she uses it for about 10 minutes before she discovers that the left side of the screen's frame is cracked. At this point, has Kim accepted the computer? UCC §2-606.

c. Same facts as part (a), except that Kim sees the crack in the frame as soon as she takes the computer out of the box. Nevertheless, she proceeds to use the computer for 10 minutes. At this point, has Kim accepted the computer? UCC §2-606.

d. Same facts as part (a), except that Kim sees the crack in the frame as soon as she takes the computer out of the box. She immediately calls the seller, Computers by Mail, and tells them that she is rejecting the computer. Nevertheless, she proceeds to use the computer for 10 minutes. At this point, has Kim accepted the computer? UCC §2-606.

e. Same facts as (a), except that Kim's contract with Computers by Mail is for a series of four computers, one to be shipped at the beginning of each month. When the first computer arrives, Kim takes it out of the box and immediately notices a crack on the left side of the screen's frame. May Kim reject this installment? May the seller cure the defective installment? May Kim cancel the remainder of the contract? UCC §§2-612, 2-508; cf. §2-601.

f. Same facts as (a), except that Kim's contract with Computers by Mail is for a series of four computers, one to be shipped at the beginning of each month. When the first computer arrives, Kim takes it out of the box, plugs it in, and the computer explodes. Kim is frightened, but she is not injured by the blast. May Kim reject this installment? May the seller cure the defective installment? May Kim cancel the remainder of the contract? UCC §§2-612, 2-508.

g. As a general proposition, once Kim accepts the goods, has she precluded herself from any remedy for the computer's defects? UCC §§2-607(2) and (3)(a), 2-608(1).

18.2.   Arlene Ledger, president of Heavy Metal, Inc. (from Problem 3.2), has come to your office with what she describes as an "ethical dilemma." She also wonders whether her problem has legal implications. Last week Arlene received a shipment of raw steel from a new steel supplier, Nielson Steel. In conducting a spot inspection, Arlene discovered that the steel had a slight impurity that would make it somewhat more expensive for Heavy Metal to use in manufacturing the circular weight plates that Heavy Metal sells to sporting goods stores. Accordingly, Arlene immediately called Nielson and told its president that Heavy Metal was rejecting the 10-ton shipment of raw steel. Heavy Metal kept possession of the steel while it waited for Nielson to pick it up. Two days ago, the price of raw steel suddenly shot up, and now Arlene wants to know whether her company, which still has the steel, could simply begin using it in production and thereby effectively "un-reject" the goods so as to take advantage of what now seems like a good deal. Arlene also tells you that Nielson is on the verge of filing for bankruptcy, so the likelihood is slim that Arlene could recover damages from Nielson. What do you tell Arlene? UCC §2-606(1), Official Comment 4 to §2-606, §2-602(2)(a), Official Comment 2 to §2-601.

18.3.   Lou from Lou's Used Cars for Less (Problem 2.1) has come to you to talk about "quality control" problems he has been having with his used-car business. When Lou obtains a fresh "pre-owned" vehicle, his company's current procedure is to devote about six or seven hours of a mechanic's time to inspecting the car for any major problems. "Do you know what mechanics cost these days?" Lou asks you rhetorically. Lou's brilliant idea for saving money is to just wax and shine the cars as they come in, drive them around for 10 minutes, and then put them on the lot to sell. Lou explains that with the money he saves from mechanic inspection time, he will be more than happy to cure any problems that dissatisfied customers bring to him after they have owned the car for a time (these cars are not being sold "as is"). "I just need to know that I'll still have the right to fix the car, and that no buyer can kill the deal and get their money back just because of some problem we didn't discover," Lou tells you in earnest. What advice do you have for Lou about his new plan? UCC §2-508.

18.4. Your firm does occasional work for a local small college, Mammoth College, which has a full Division III sports program. Mammoth's athletic director, Shelly Stone, comes to see you about her school's purchase of a used bus last week for the purpose of transporting school teams to away games. Mammoth purchased the bus from Big Al's, a used-bus dealer in town, who promised in writing that the bus did not burn oil. After paying for the bus, the school learned that contrary to Big Al's warranty, the bus was a true oil guzzler: on its first team trip, a mere 100 miles away, the bus consumed six quarts of oil. One week following that first team trip, Shelly now has four questions about the bus purchase: (1) May the school void its deal with Big Al's and get its money back? (2) If so, can the school keep possession of the bus until Big Al's gives the school its money back? (3) Even though Shelly wants to undo the deal, she would desperately like to use the bus one last time this weekend, oil problems and all, for her school's conference track meet, which is about 150 miles away. Would this final use hurt her school's ability to give the bus back to Big Al's and undo the deal? (4) Would Shelly's school have to accept an offer by Big Al's, should he make one, to fix the oil guzzling problem as an alternative to voiding the whole deal? What do you advise? UCC §§2-508, 2-602, 2-606, 2-608, 2-711(3).

18.5. Hi Tech Corp. was a Chicago retailer in the business of selling office computers. Danker & Kodner was a 10-lawyer partnership that was also located in Chicago. Don Danker, managing partner of the law firm, negotiated a contract with Hi Tech for the purchase of six computers. The contract indicated that Hi Tech would deliver the six machines to the Danker firm for a total price of $16,000. The contract said that the computers would be installed at no extra charge. On the date of performance, the six computers arrived at the law firm's offices and Don paid the agreed-on purchase price. When Don called Hi Tech president Harold Scott to ask about installation, Harold said, "We'll get to it eventually." Disgusted, Don told Gretchen Giltner, a new associate who was the office computer whiz, to try to install the computers. Gretchen gave it her best shot, but during the next week both lawyers and secretaries at Danker experienced assorted difficulties with the computers. An angry Don once again called Harold, this time telling him that he was going to send back all of the computers and demand a refund of the purchase price. In response, Harold sent out one of his technicians, who concluded that the computers themselves each had a slight keyboard problem that existed at the time of delivery. The technician added, however, that almost all of the difficulties Danker workers had experienced the previous week were due to a faulty installation job. Discuss whether Danker & Kodner has the right at this point to send the computers back to Hi Tech for a refund. UCC §§2-508, 2-601, 2-602, 2-606, 2-608; Official Comments 3 and 4 to §2-606, Official Comment 2 to §2-106.

Assignment 19: Closing with Leases, International Sales, and Real Estate

A. Closing with Leases

The provisions in UCC Article 2A on acceptance, rejection, revocation, and cure mostly mirror the comparable provisions in Article 2. The one major exception is with the case of finance leases. Finance leases, you may recall from Assignment 11, are three-party deals in which the lessor's principal connection with the lease transaction is to provide the financing to make it happen.

In re Rafter Seven Ranches, L.P.

546 F.3d 1194 (10th Cir. 2008)

SEYMOUR, C.J.

Rafter Seven Ranches, L.P. (Rafter Seven) appeals a Bankruptcy Appeal Panel (BAP) decision upholding the bankruptcy court's rejection of Rafter Seven's objection to C.H. Brown Company's (Brown) claim that it was liable to Brown on certain equipment leases. *See* Rafter Seven Ranches, LP v. C.H. Brown Company (*In re Rafter Seven Ranches, LP*), 362 B.R. 25, 27 (10th Cir. BAP 2007) (*Rafter II*). We have jurisdiction pursuant to 28 U.S.C. § 158(d), and we affirm.

I

The facts and procedural history of this case have been fully reported in both *In re Rafter Seven Ranches, LP,* Case No. 05-40483, 2007 WL 2903200 (Bkrtcy. D. Kan. Oct. 3, 2007) (unpublished), and *Rafter II,* 362 B.R. at 27 (10th Cir. BAP 2007). We repeat here only what is necessary to explain the issues.

Rafter Seven was interested in purchasing used sprinkler systems for use on its farm property. Its general partner, Michael J. Friesen, contacted Ochs Irrigation (Ochs), a used system dealer. Because Ochs did not have the appropriate used sprinklers in stock, Kenny Ochs located the desired sprinklers from another source. Rafter Seven did not have the funds to purchase the sprinklers, so Mr. Ochs suggested it contact Brown, a Wyoming private agricultural and equipment lender, to finance the purchase of the sprinkler systems. At a meeting on April 20, 2001,

Brown agreed to a finance lease arrangement whereby Rafter Seven could acquire four used sprinkler systems which Ochs would supply and install.

Brown forwarded four equipment leases to Rafter Seven for execution, one for each sprinkler system. Rafter Seven's general manager executed the leases on behalf of the company. The leases were for a term of five years, required semi-annual payments, and were to be governed by Wyoming law. The leases each provided that the lease payments would be due with respect to each item of equipment "when Lessee has received Equipment which is equal to 50% of the value to Lessor of all Equipment to be leased." Aple. Sup. App. at 134. In addition, the leases made it plain that Brown, the lessor, was not warranting the sprinklers for any purpose:

> WARRANTIES: Lessee agrees that it has selected each item of Equipment based upon its own judgment, and disclaims any reliance upon any statement of representations made by Lessor. LESSOR MAKES NO WARRANTY WITH RESPECT TO THE EQUIPMENT, EXPRESSED OR IMPLIED, AND LESSOR SPECIFICALLY DISCLAIMS ANY WARRANTY OF MERCHANTABILITY AND OF FITNESS FOR A PARTICULAR PURPOSE AND ANY LIABILITY FOR CONSEQUENTIAL DAMAGES ARISING OUT OF THE USE OR THE INABILITY TO USE THE EQUIPMENT. Lessee agrees to make the lease payments required hereunder without regard to the condition of the Equipment and to look only to persons other than Lessor, such as manufacturer, vendor, or supplier thereof, should any item of Equipment for any reason, be defective.

Id. Upon Rafter Seven's authorization, Brown sent payment to Ochs to fund purchase by Ochs of the sprinklers.

The parties were aware that the sprinkler systems were needed as soon as possible for the corn planting season ending May 1. When the sprinkler systems did not arrive during May, Rafter Seven wrote to Brown informing it that it had received neither the money for the leases nor the equipment. Upon receipt of the letter, Brown contacted Kenny Ochs, apparently urging him to make delivery.

The first sprinkler system was delivered and installed in late July. It did not conform to any of the leases in terms of serial number or equipment characteristics. Despite the nonconformity and some serious defects, Rafter Seven made use of the sprinkler system. On August 15, 2001, Rafter Seven sent a letter to Ochs regarding the remaining three sprinklers:

> By casual checking, I have learned that apparently you have used the money provided by C.H. Brown and Co. as well as money from Rafter Seven, in an amount exceeding $100,000 for purposes other than the purchase of sprinklers, generators and underground pipe. In other words, it appears that Rafter Seven and/or C.H. Brown Co. may need to recover (from you) more than $50,000. If you have any information to the contrary, it would be greatly appreciated.
>
> In the meantime, it would be my suggestion . . . that you get ready to make the first annual payments on three sprinklers that aren't delivered or functioning. Additionally, I believe that you should provide us with some form of tangible security such as mortgages, titles, or assignments until this matter is cleared.

Unless I have the written response before August 23, to my home address . . . indicating the location of the sprinklers and generators, we will have to insist on a meeting to arrange a restructuring of your contract with Rafter Seven.

Aplt. App. at 127.

Sometime between mid-August and mid-September of 2001, two additional nonconforming sprinkler units were delivered to Rafter Seven. Friesen was in the fields when Och's employees made delivery. After examination, Friesen determined that the sprinklers were defective. He testified they were "rusty old stuff with flat tires that—it was just junk." Aple. Supp. App. at 186. He directed that the sprinklers not be installed. The equipment was left standing in the fields and was never completely assembled or made operational. The fourth sprinkler system was never delivered.

Approximately six weeks later, on November 1, 2001, Rafter Seven sent a letter to Brown stating that it would not honor the leases. This letter, which was sent before the first payments were due, stated:

> As we told Susie on the telephone last month, we have not insured the sprinklers—such as they are. *At that time, we mentioned that we might have to reject the sprinklers* and repudiate the lease. Nothing has happened since that conversation to change our minds.
>
> At the time of this writing, Mr. Ochs has partially installed one sprinkler. This sprinkler is not 1296 feet long, as promised, nor does it have a generator to provide power to the system. The sprinkler leaks to such an extent that the watering patterns are uneven. Additionally, two tower motors (or gear drives) are worn to the point that they are noisy. This sprinkler was delivered in July, after the crops were already stressed. We have tried to mitigate our damages by keeping our production costs low, but that alone did not prevent the yields from being a disaster.
>
> With respect to the other three circles, we can only say that there are no circles with crops underneath them, or operating sprinklers. *As this summer became fall, we continued to believe that the two antiquated, dysfunctional systems standing in the weeds would somehow become operational in time to plant wheat.* They have not. Not only has Rafter Seven lost 390 acres of irrigated row crops, but we have lost the benefit of timely planting the fall wheat crop. The minimum loss now exceeds the entire lease amount of $80,000. Rafter Seven cannot honor the lease agreement under these circumstances.
>
> *We are sorry to take this position and will be willing to work toward another agreement that might resolve this loss.*

Aplt. App. at 129-30 (emphasis added).

After receiving this letter, Brown phoned Friesen. Brown told him that it had no responsibility for breach of warranty, and that Rafter Seven was still liable under the leases. Hence, on November 23, 2001, Rafter Seven sent Ochs a letter saying it expected Ochs to pay Brown for the sprinkler systems. The letter also indicated Rafter Seven would try to hire someone to move or modify the existing systems to try to make them operational so as to mitigate further damages. Specifically, the letter states:

As you know, Rafter Seven Ranches, LP, has repudiated its lease agreement with C.H. Brown Co. The obvious reason was the failure of consideration, in that there was no performance on behalf of the lessee because the contracts (which were designated as true leases) were not fulfilled in a timely manner. As a result, Rafter Seven completely lost the production on three circles and suffered substantial losses on the fourth. A conservative loss estimate is $20,000-$25,000 per quarter. In other words, the failure of Rafter Seven to receive four sprinklers, (1985 or newer) 1296 feet long, in working order, so that irrigated crops could be planted and insured has caused us the value of the entire lease. This does not include approximately $25,000 in cash advances paid by Rafter Seven. It now appears that Rafter Seven will lose its FSA cost share grant unless the installation on the home quarter is completed within thirty days.

I have, of course, been in touch with Mr. Brown, who indicated that we would be contacting him with a date for a conference telephone call—which I assume to be an attempt to resolve this problem. I have not heard from you in this regard, therefore let me suggest the following approach: since you guaranteed payment of this indebtedness, I have enclosed a payment notification form and self-addressed envelope to the Brown Co. for the first payment. There will be seven more of similar amounts in the next 12 months. You can probably absorb these, but I'm sure that Mr. Brown would like this confirmed.

I anticipate that Mr. Brown will want a new agreement. Rafter Seven will want a release and some idea about repayment, restitution or presentment of four generators and a fourth sprinkler. Mr. Brown and I both agree that if you can not perform, as I just suggested, that you advise him promptly with the written answer to this question: "where is the money?" or "what happened to Mr. Brown's $80,000?"

I will proceed to further mitigate Rafter Seven's damages by hiring other contractors to move or modify the existing systems to try to make them operate and I will attempt to purchase another system, be it new or used. These additional costs should not be those of Rafter Seven so you should be advised that some recompense will be sought.

Aplt. App. at 45-46 (emphasis added).

No payments were ever made under the leases. Brown filed suit against both Rafter Seven and Ochs in Wyoming state court. It obtained a default judgment against Ochs, but the case against Rafter Seven was stayed when Rafter Seven filed for Chapter 12 bankruptcy. Brown filed a claim in the bankruptcy for payment on the leases, to which Rafter Seven objected. After a two day trial, the bankruptcy court overruled the objection, finding that Rafter Seven had accepted the goods and had failed to reject them seasonably as provided for in the Uniform Commercial Code (UCC), codified at Wyo. Stat. Ann. §34.1-1-109 *et seq.* Rafter Seven filed a Motion to Reconsider asserting that the right to inspect includes a right to test and that because Ochs never sent complete sprinklers, Rafter Seven had no opportunity to test them and hence was never required by the UCC to reject them. The bankruptcy court denied the motion, holding that the right to inspect did not include a right to test. Rafter Seven appealed to the BAP, which affirmed.

II

Rafter Seven contends on appeal that the bankruptcy court and the BAP erred in concluding Rafter Seven had no right to test the sprinklers before the obligation to notify Brown accrued. It also asserts the bankruptcy court erred in deciding the case on issues Rafter Seven claims were not included in the pretrial order or any other pleading. Finally, it argues that the bankruptcy court abused its discretion in denying Rafter Seven's Motion to Reconsider.

RIGHT TO TEST

Rafter Seven's appeal does not challenge the facts as gathered at trial and recounted by the bankruptcy court. Rather, it contends it had a right to test the equipment before it was required to reject it, implying there was no time frame within which it was required to test. The applicable statutes dictate otherwise. The right to inspect, synonymous with the right to test, is not separate from the obligation to notify the lessor of rejection within a reasonable time.

Under Wyo. Stat. Ann. §34.1-2.A-407, a commercial lessee's promises in a finance agreement become irrevocable and independent upon acceptance of the goods. Because this is a finance lease, acceptance of goods with the knowledge of nonconformity precludes revocation of acceptance. *Id.* at §34.1-2.A-516(b). Acceptance of goods is defined in §34.1-2.A-515(a).

> Acceptance of goods occurs after the lessee has had a reasonable opportunity to inspect the goods and: (i) [t]he lessee signifies or acts with respect to the goods in a manner that signifies to the lessor or the supplier that the goods are conforming or that the lessee will take or retain them in spite of their nonconformity; or (ii) [t]he lessee fails to make an effective rejection of the goods (section 34.1-2.A-509(b)).

Id. Under §34.1-2.A-509(b), "[r]ejection of goods is ineffective unless it is within a reasonable time after tender or delivery of the goods and the lessee seasonably notifies the lessor." If, as here, no time for rejection is prescribed by the relevant agreement, then a "reasonable time for taking any action depends on the nature, purpose and circumstances of such action." *Id.* at §34.1-1-204(b). An action is taken "seasonably" if it is taken "within a reasonable time." *Id.* at §34.1-1-204(c).

Rafter Seven contends it did not accept the sprinklers within the meaning of §34.1-2.A-515 because it never had an opportunity to test them given that they were not even delivered in usable form. Application of the law to the facts does not support Rafter Seven's position. Rafter Seven received the first sprinkler in late July. Knowing the sprinkler did not conform, Rafter Seven kept it and made use of it anyway. Use of a nonconforming good constitutes acceptance. *See* 34.1-2.A-515(a)(i). Although Rafter Seven did not use the second and third sprinklers, received between mid-August and mid-September of 2001, it failed to effectively reject them. It inspected the second and third sprinklers upon delivery, determined they were "junk," refused to have them assembled, and then let them sit in the fields for approximately six weeks before making what it argues is a rejection of the goods. Effective rejection of the goods did not occur until, at the earliest, November 1, 2001, when Rafter Seven wrote its letter to Brown. Even if we assume this letter constituted an unambiguous rejection of the sprinklers, six weeks was an unreasonable period of time to inspect given the facts of this case.

To convince us otherwise, Rafter Seven cites Capitol Dodge Sales, Inc. v. N. Concrete Pipe, Inc., 131 Mich. App. 149, 346 N.W.2d 535 (1983). In *Capitol Dodge,* a commercial company sought to buy a truck with a snowplow attachment. *Id.* at 537. During the test drive, the truck overheated. The seller represented that the overheating was the result of incorrect placement of the snowplow attachment. The buyer accepted the explanation and attempted to properly attach the snowplow per the seller's instructions. Over the next two days, the vehicle overheated several times and the buyer repeatedly contacted the seller, ultimately telling him he did not want to buy the truck. *Id.* at 537-38. Upon suit, the seller contended the buyer's use of the truck constituted acceptance, while the buyer claimed he was only exercising his right to a reasonable inspection period. The court held that approximately three days of inspection was not unreasonable. *Id.* at 540.

In Colonial Pacific Leasing Corp. v. JWCJR Corp., 977 P.2d 541 (Utah App. 1999), also cited by Rafter Seven, an auto shop purchased a computer and software system financed by Colonial Pacific. On the day of delivery, the debtor informed the creditor that the equipment was received but not yet operational. *Id.* at 543. On the second day, the creditor contacted the debtor and this time the debtor informed it that the software system was working. Later that same day, the system crashed. The debtor called the software company but was unable to get the system working. Soon after, the debtor contacted the software company to come and pick up the equipment. *Id.* The debtor also called the creditor twice within ten days of the system crashing to inform it that the equipment was not operational. *Id.* at 546. Through his conversations with the creditor, the debtor understood that he was no longer obligated on the lease due to his rejection of the goods. *Id.*

More than two years later, the creditor brought suit against the debtor to recover unpaid lease payments. The trial judge ruled for the creditor. The appellate court reversed, holding that the trial court failed to make factual findings about whether the debtor had a reasonable opportunity to inspect the system. In so doing, the court noted:

> Taking possession of the goods is not determinative of acceptance, nor is the signing of a form acceptance before receipt of goods, nor the making of a lease payment. A reasonable time to inspect under the UCC must allow an opportunity to put the product to its intended use, or for testing to verify its capability to perform as intended.

Id. at 545 (internal citations and quotation marks omitted). We agree with this interpretation of a reasonable time to inspect or test, but that does not change the outcome of this case.

The facts of both *Capitol Dodge* and *Colonial Pacific* diverge significantly from those here. With respect to the second and third sprinklers, Rafter Seven recognized immediately that the used sprinklers delivered to it were nonconforming to the leases and were "junk." No testing was necessary to determine nonconformance. Instead of notifying Brown, however, Rafter Seven left the sprinklers sitting in the field. This is in stark contrast to *Capitol Dodge* and *Colonial Pacific,* where the buyers attempted to put the purchased goods to use and immediately contacted the appropriate party upon finding the defects.

Seasonable rejection is intertwined with the concept of a reasonable time to inspect. *See* §34.1-1-204. For either concept, the reasonable time period is tied to the difficulty of discovering the nonconformity. *See* 1 James J. White & Robert S. Summers, Uniform Commercial Code §8-3 at 447-48 (4th ed.1996) (hereinafter White & Summers). In this case, Rafter Seven knew immediately on inspection that the second and third sprinklers were nonconforming because not all of the parts were delivered and the equipment was not operable. Case law supports the conclusion that Rafter Seven's time to reject was relatively short in these circumstances. *Compare* Pioneer Peat, Inc. v. Quality Grassing & Servs., Inc., 653 N.W.2d 469 (Minn. App. 2002) (one month lapse between acceptance and rejection not reasonable where company knew product was nonconforming); McClure Oil Corp. v. Murray Equip., Inc., 515 N.E.2d 546, 552 (Ind. App. 1987) (ineffective rejection where buyer did not give unambiguous rejection until nineteen days after receipt of product during which time he used product, claimed to be dissatisfied with product from first day of use, and ordered alternative equipment nine days after receipt of disputed equipment); EPN-Delaval, S.A. v. Inter-Equip, Inc., 542 F. Supp. 238, 243, 247 (S.D. Tex. 1982) (where defect is total and blatant, sixty-five days constitutes unreasonable rejection time); *with* Integrated Circuits Unlimited, Inc. v. E.F. Johnson Co., 691 F. Supp. 630, 631, 634 (E.D.N.Y. 1988) (one month reasonable where purchaser actively testing complex electronic equipment), rev'd on other grounds, 875 F.2d 1040 (2d Cir. 1989); Tri-Continental Leasing Corp. v. Law Office of Richard W. Burns, 710 S.W.2d 604 (Tex. App. 1985) (testing time of one month reasonable where equipment malfunctioned immediately and buyer was constantly working with seller to make equipment operable); Moses v. Newman, 658 S.W.2d 119 (Tenn. App. 1983) (one day not long enough to constitute reasonable time to inspect).

Rafter Seven knew upon inspection that the equipment was nonconforming, yet it did nothing to reject the second and third sprinklers for at least six weeks after they were delivered. According to the specific language of the statute, these actions are consistent with acceptance rather than rejection. *See* §34.1-2.A-515 (acceptance occurs when lessee does any of three things after a reasonable opportunity to inspect the goods: (a) signifies acceptance; (b) fails to make an effective rejection; or (c) does any act that signifies acceptance). While a reasonable opportunity to inspect and test is available under the UCC, six weeks was an unreasonable period in the circumstances of this case, given Rafter Seven's immediate recognition of the defective condition of the equipment.

White & Summers make clear why "speedy notification" is important:

> The policies for speedy notification are not mysterious. The obvious policies behind the notice provisions are to give the seller [here, the lessor] an opportunity to cure, to

permit the seller to assist the buyer in minimizing the buyer's losses, and to return the goods to seller early—before they have depreciated, rotted or worse. If the seller can cure the difficulty and so save the sale and prevent lost profits that the buyer might otherwise suffer, the policy has been fulfilled. Even if the seller's inspection discloses that the goods are defective and the seller agrees to take them back, the entire loss from the transaction may be minimized by early action, because the seller may be able to resell the goods to another party and at a higher price than the goods would command after they had depreciated.

White & Summers at 445-46.

The dissent does not believe "the Uniform Commercial Code [would] really leave a lessee in Rafter Seven's position to be so rooked without recourse," dissent at 5, and suggests we are ignoring the realities of the situation. To the contrary, as the lease agreements note, this is a case in which the lessee, Rafter Seven, chose the supplier, Ochs, and authorized the finance lessor, Brown, to pay the supplier for the cost of the sprinklers before the goods were delivered to the lessee. This is also a case in which Rafter Seven agreed that Brown would not be responsible for warranting the fitness of the equipment, and that Rafter Seven would look only to Ochs in the event that any item of equipment was defective. As one court has explained in a tripartite situation such as this:

> When the commercial context has been, as here, a financing lease, the weight of authority is that the consideration which flows from the financing lessor is money, not a functioning product. Accordingly a breach by the supplier of the equipment does not excuse the lessee from making lease payments to the finance-lessor, unless the equipment lease otherwise provides. Where, as in many lease documents with a finance-lessor (and in the instant case), there is an express disclaimer of liability for malfunctioning equipment, the position of the finance-lessor is that much stronger.

Patriot Gen'l Life Ins. Co. v. CFC Investment Co., 11 Mass. App. Ct. 857, 420 N.E.2d 918, 922 (1981) (footnote omitted) (citing cases). Given that Rafter Seven knew immediately, without testing, that the long-overdue sprinklers were non-conforming, it was clearly obligated by § 34.1-2A-515 to so inform Brown to whom it owed payments for financing the transaction. The bankruptcy court correctly determined that Rafter Seven had all the time it needed to inspect the facially nonconforming goods, and that its rejection was therefore not seasonable.

BANKRUPTCY COURT PROPERLY ADDRESSED TIMELINESS OF REJECTION

Rafter Seven claims the bankruptcy court incorrectly decided the case because Rafter Seven's objection to Brown's claim was based on Ochs' complete failure to deliver the sprinklers described in the leases, see Aplt. App. at 108 ("The debtor contends that the irrigation sprinklers which were the subject of the leases . . . were never delivered. . . . What was delivered to Rafter Seven was basically 'a pile of junk.' "), while the bankruptcy court's decision was based on Rafter Seven's failure to seasonably reject the sprinkler systems. Rafter Seven contends the bank-ruptcy court abused its discretion in deciding the case on an issue not identified in the pretrial order or other pleadings.

We do not agree. We are persuaded by our review of the record that the bank-ruptcy court's decision was based on the general issues and principles articulated by the parties in the pretrial order and the proceedings thereafter. The parties were well aware that the law governing this matter is Article 2A of the UCC, as codified in Wyoming. While Rafter Seven took the position that delivery of conforming goods was never made, the UCC makes clear that nonconforming goods may be accepted or rejected, and that any rejection must be done within a reasonable time with notice to the lessor. *See* Wyo. Stat. Ann. §§34.1-2.A-509(b) & 34.1-2.A-515.

The record clearly reveals that the trial of the matter revolved around accep-tance or rejection of the goods, and Rafter Seven did not object to that course of events. Under Fed. R. Civ. P. 15(b)(2) "[w]hen an issue not raised by the pleadings is tried by the parties' express or implied consent, it must be treated in all respects as if raised by the pleadings." The bankruptcy court clearly saw timeliness of rejec-tion as the key to this case, *see* Aple. Supp. App. 201-22, and Rafter Seven gives us no grounds to hold that the court abused its discretion in so doing.

For the foregoing reasons, we AFFIRM.

LUCERO, C.J., concurring in part and dissenting in part.

I agree with my respected colleagues that Rafter Seven Ranches accepted the first sprinkler system and used it in an attempt to mitigate its damages. But I can-not accept that by leaving sprinkler parts in Rafter Seven's field in September, Ochs "delivered" the second and third systems. Were we to assume delivery, as the majority does, a "reasonable opportunity to inspect" includes the ability to test, which Rafter Seven never had during the six weeks before it notified Brown on November 1. Because the majority applies an unduly inflexible view of the UCC that misapprehends the realities of this transaction, I respectfully dissent.

I

Let us be clear on what happened. As early as 2000, Ochs was promoting sprinkler systems to Rafter Seven and asked for and received "down payments" totaling about $25,000 for generators and nozzle packages to be part of a later sprin-kler delivery. In April 2001, after Rafter Seven discouraged Ochs because it could not afford the complete systems, Ochs arranged for Friesen to meet with Brown. Under the terms of the lease agreements with Brown, Ochs was to supply Rafter Seven with four functional sprinkler systems around May 2001, in time for the planting season. The leases specified the manufacturer, model, and serial number of each sprinkler system. The "Delivery and Acceptance" clause of each Brown lease allowed Rafter Seven to certify that the equipment was "delivered, inspected, installed, . . . in good working condition, and . . . accepted by [Rafter Seven] as sat-isfactory" before approving Brown's payment to Ochs. Rafter Seven signed these clauses at the same time the leases were signed—a time when all parties knew the equipment was undelivered. This fiction allowed Brown to pay Ochs immediately, thus enabling the nearly contemporaneous acquisition and delivery of the sprinkler systems. Yet, the *first* sprinkler system was not delivered until sometime in July. Apparently, Rafter Seven was expected to pray for rain in the interim.

Although it is undisputed that the first system was woefully inadequate, Rafter Seven had no alternative but to use it in an attempt to salvage some of its crop. As for the other three systems, the record is unimpeachable: Ochs never delivered any other complete sprinkler systems in working condition.

When Ochs attempted to deliver a second and third system apparently as late as mid-September—at or near the end of the growing season—Friesen immediately recognized that the equipment was incomplete and did not match the serial numbers or specifications in the lease agreements. He pronounced it "junk" and asked Ochs' delivery men to remove it. When they did not, Friesen decided to make the best of a bad situation by waiting to see if they would complete the installation so that the sprinklers sufficiently conformed to the terms of each lease. He awaited delivery of numerous missing and replacement parts. They never came. Now Rafter Seven is in bankruptcy, Ochs has Brown's $80,000, and Brown is attempting to recover lease payments from Rafter Seven for equipment that Ochs never supplied.

II

A

Engaging in analytical hopscotch, the majority skips to inspection without passing delivery. As the "Delivery and Acceptance" clause of each leases shows, all parties contemplated specific sprinkler systems delivered in good working condition. Such certifications are ordinarily signed at or after delivery. *See, e.g.,* Old Kent Leasing Servs. Corp. v. McEwan, 38 S.W.3d 220, 224-25 (Tex. App. 2001); Eaglefunding Capital Corp. v. Kamar, No. 011928, 2002 WL 1020663, at *1-2 (Mass. Super. Ct. April 17, 2002). Because Rafter Seven signed this clause before delivery—otherwise, Ochs would have been unable to acquire the equipment—it lost the ability to withhold payment from Ochs for unsatisfactory equipment. Nonetheless, the clause informs our understanding of the terms of the leases: installation of the sprinkler systems was part and parcel of the supplier's performance and, necessarily, a prerequisite to inspection. The majority assumes delivery occurred, Maj. Op. at 1200-01, a fatal oversight I cannot condone.

The idea that delivery is not effected willy-nilly any time a supplier dumps some parts on a lessee is hardly revolutionary. In Moses v. Newman, 658 S.W.2d 119 (Tenn. Ct. App. 1983), cited by the majority, a buyer purchased a mobile home that was later destroyed by a windstorm before the seller had completed installing it. *Id.* at 120. Despite the fact that the buyer had made multiple trips to see the house before purchasing it, and despite the fact that he had placed personal items in the trailer, the court held that the buyer had not yet had a reasonable opportunity to inspect it largely because the seller had contracted for delivery *and installation,* and "the seller had not completed the contracted installation at the time of loss." *Id.* at 121-22; *see also* Davis v. Vintage Enters., Inc., 23 N.C. App. 581, 209 S.E.2d 824, 828-29 (1974).

My colleagues imply that because "Rafter Seven left the sprinklers sitting in the field," Maj. Op. at 1201; *see also id.* at 1200-01, it somehow accepted a delivery. This is plainly contrary to Wyoming law. Rafter Seven, which had refused installation of the sprinklers after declaring them junk, did not bear the burden of removing them from its property. With language that could just as easily apply to the present case, the Wyoming Supreme Court has held:

> When [the buyer] told [the seller] that the machine was not workable without modifications, that can mean nothing else than that the machine which was delivered to the [buyer] was not successful, and hence the condition of a sale, if there was a sale, was not fulfilled. *It is difficult to see what further notice of the lack of success of the machine could have been given.* As already indicated, if [the seller] did not then want the [buyer] to retain possession, there was nothing at that time, or at any time thereafter, to prevent him from taking it back. *The fact that it remained in [the buyer]'s possession was [the seller]'s own fault, at least as much as that of [the buyer].*

Morgan v. Union Pac. R.R. Co., 346 P.2d 1071, 1077 (Wyo. 1959) (emphases added).

Rafter Seven's decision to await actual delivery is eminently reasonable. The leases each specify that lease payments "shall commence when Lessee has received Equipment which is equal to 50% of the value." I refuse to call a pile of sprinkler parts, incapable of watering anything, valuable under this lease. For these reasons, Rafter Seven's November 1 letter to Brown was a seasonable rejection of Ochs' ineffective delivery.

B

The majority concludes that Rafter Seven's obligation to Brown is independent of Ochs' failure. Does the Uniform Commercial Code really leave a lessee in Rafter Seven's position to be so rooked without recourse? In my view, the answer is "no." Wyoming law is unambiguous in requiring that a lessee have a reasonable opportunity to inspect goods. *See* Wyo. Stat. Ann. §34.1-2.A-515(a). As the majority recognizes, precedent requires that the opportunity to inspect must include a reasonable opportunity to test, and that reasonableness must be determined by the facts and circumstances of a particular transaction.

In asking what constitutes a "reasonable time" to inspect, we have a duty to look at the realities of the transaction rather than to simply count days. Rafter Seven was in an obvious bind. If it did not allow Ochs the opportunity to deliver and install sprinkler systems in working condition, it would assuredly lose its crops. Because Rafter Seven allowed Ochs a few more weeks to complete the systems, the majority holds that it failed to seasonably reject the sprinklers. This result is particularly odd because, although Rafter *rejected* the goods by telling the seller, Ochs, that the sprinklers were incomplete and refusing to permit their installation in that condition, the majority holds that Rafter Seven somehow, at the same time, managed to *accept* the same goods with regard to the lessor (under this approach, perhaps Schrödinger's cat *could be* both dead and alive at the same instant). We are not directed by the majority to a single case interpreting UCC §2A-515 to produce such an enigma, and I would not read the Code to allow this baffling and inequitable result. I therefore cannot accept that Rafter Seven, which never received delivery of the sprinklers for which it had bargained, can be said to have had an opportunity to inspect them.

To bolster its conclusion that Rafter Seven took an unreasonable length of time to inspect, the majority relies on a treatise which explains the policy rationales requiring "speedy notification" of rejection. Tellingly, none of these policies are furthered by my colleagues' disposition. For example, timely rejection gives a seller an opportunity to cure, Maj. Op. at 1202-03 (quoting James J. White & Robert S. Summers, Uniform Commercial Code §8-3 at 445-46 (4th ed.1996)), but there is no doubt that the *seller* in this case—Ochs, not Brown—was unambiguously on notice that it had not delivered goods that were fit for installation and testing. The party with an opportunity to actually deliver conforming goods was therefore immediately on notice that the sprinklers it had delivered thus far were not satisfactory. *See, e.g.,* EPN-Delaval, S.A. v. Inter-Equip, Inc., 542 F. Supp. 238, 247 (S.D. Tex. 1982) (observing that the "purpose [of notice of rejection] is to inform the seller that the buyer rejects the goods in sufficient time to give the seller opportunity to cure, and to assist in minimizing the buyer's losses").

This remains true even if, as a technical matter, Brown, not Rafter Seven, was the "buyer" with regard to Ochs. *See* Midwest Precision Servs., Inc. v. PTM Indus. Corp., 887 F.2d 1128, 1132 (1st Cir. 1989) (describing the role of the parties in a tripartite lease-finance arrangement). Ochs pitched the sprinklers to Rafter Seven, Ochs took its "down payments," Ochs set up the meeting between Brown and Friesen, and Ochs was paid. It only makes sense that Rafter Seven would demand performance from Ochs, not Brown. Brown had long ago paid Ochs for the sprinklers, so it was not in a position to pressure Ochs into delivering conforming equipment. Rafter Seven never received that equipment from Ochs and it never saw a penny of Brown's money.

Moreover, this delay must be viewed in perspective: Rafter Seven was promised sprinkler systems in May. If Brown had learned of Rafter Seven's definitive rejection in, say, early October instead of early November, it would have made little practical difference for the purposes of mitigating Brown's losses. (Unless I am sorely mistaken, there are no farmers in Wyoming who plant crops in October for calendar year production.) Indeed, Brown received a July 10 letter informing it that Ochs failed to deliver the sprinklers, and admits that thereafter it had no idea, one way or another, whether the sprinklers were ever shipped.

There is also little likelihood that the six-week inspection period compounded Brown's losses through "depreciat[ion], rot[ting], or worse. . . ." Maj. Op at

1202-03 (quoting White & Summers at 445-46). We are not dealing with a contract for refrigerated trucks filled with arugula, but rather one for non-fungible sprinklers. *See Moses,* 658 S.W.2d at 121 ("What is a reasonable opportunity varies, depending upon the type of goods involved."); Buckeye Trophy, Inc. v. S. Bowling & Billiard Supply Co., 3 Ohio App. 3d 32, 443 N.E.2d 1043, 1046 (1982) (trial court did not err in finding a 65-day delay before inspection reasonable when, among other things, the goods were "not perishable or subject to severe market fluctuations"). Brown does not dispute that the second and third sets of sprinklers not only failed to match the descriptions in the leases, they were also ancient, lacking in essential parts, and, as delivered, largely worthless. This is not a case where a lessor suffered some appreciable loss due to a few weeks' delay or where "the entire loss from the transaction [would have been] minimized by early action." Maj. Op. at 1202-03 (quoting White & Summers at 445-46). To the contrary, the incomplete sprinklers remained on Rafter Seven's property because no party considered them worth the expense of removing them.

III

Meanwhile, back at the ranch, Rafter Seven did what a reasonable rancher would do under these circumstances. Let us not forget, these sprinklers were to be delivered around May 2001, in time for the planting season; *tempus agrarius fugit*—time flies out on the farm. When Ochs delivered an incomplete mess of sprinkler parts three to four months after tender was due, Rafter Seven, already faced with the loss of its crops, afforded the seller six more weeks for delivery and installation of a testable sprinkler system. Because such a system was never delivered, I do not see how it can be said that Rafter Seven had a reasonable opportunity to test the sprinklers. Even assuming that the sprinklers were "delivered" at all, the six weeks taken for testing was not unreasonable in the circumstances. Consequently, I cannot fathom how Rafter Seven can be liable for the lease payments at issue.

Whenever a lease transaction is a finance lease, the finance lessee's ability to revoke acceptance of the leased goods is much narrower than the revocation rights of an ordinary buyer or of a non-finance lessee. In fact, the only situation in which a finance lessee may revoke acceptance of the leased goods is where the finance lessee's failure to discover the non-conformity before acceptance was reasonably induced by the *lessor's* assurances. Since the finance lessor is typically not going to be making many assurances (the finance lessee, after all, selects the goods), it will be an unusual case in which the finance lessee may revoke acceptance.

Given certain other attributes of the finance lease, however, failing to give the finance lessee broad revocation rights is not nearly as draconian as it might seem. For example, suppose that there is a finance lease for a drill press. Imagine that the finance lessee accepts the drill press and then later discovers a non-conformity that was virtually impossible to discover prior to acceptance. UCC §2A-517(1)(b) states clearly that the finance lessee may not revoke acceptance of the leased goods in this situation.

Is the finance lessee, then, stuck with no recourse? Although the finance lessee does not retain the goods-oriented remedy of revocation in this situation, it does nevertheless remain eligible for its breach of warranty rights against the supplier. As you may recall from Assignment 11, the finance lessee gets the benefit of all the warranties that were made by the supplier to the lessor. Thus, the finance lessee may demand that the supplier make things right or pay damages. As Official Comment 1 to §2A-516 notes about the narrowing of the finance lessee's revocation rights, "this is not inequitable as the lessee has a direct claim against the supplier."

B.   Closing with International Sales

Probably the broadest statement that can be made about the difference in "closing" concepts between the international sales system and the domestic sales system is that the international system is much more averse to letting buyers use goods-oriented remedies. This reluctance is perhaps understandable given that delivery costs are generally higher in international sales than in domestic sales and therefore there is more dead-weight loss that is suffered in an international sale if the sales transaction must be physically reversed.

The CISG recognizes only two situations in which the buyer may "avoid" its contract with the seller. CISG Art. 49(1). The first is where the seller has committed a "fundamental breach" of contract. CISG Art. 49(1)(a). A fundamental breach is a breach that amounts to a substantial deprivation of the aggrieved party's benefit of the bargain. CISG Art. 25. Where the buyer wishes to declare a fundamental breach, it must give notice to the seller no later than a reasonable period following the time when the buyer knew or ought to have known of the defect. CISG Art. 49(2)(b)(i).

Delchi Carrier SpA v. Rotorex Corp.
71 F.3d 1024 (2d Cir. 1995)

Winter, C.J.

Rotorex Corporation, a New York corporation, appeals from a judgment of $1,785,772.44 in damages for lost profits and other consequential damages awarded to Delchi Carrier SpA following a bench trial before Judge Munson.

The basis for the award was Rotorex's delivery of nonconforming compressors to Delchi, an Italian manufacturer of air conditioners. . . .

In January 1988, Rotorex agreed to sell 10,800 compressors to Delchi for use in Delchi's "Ariele" line of portable room air conditioners. The air conditioners were scheduled to go on sale in the spring and summer of 1988. Prior to executing the contract, Rotorex sent Delchi a sample compressor and accompanying written performance specifications. The compressors were scheduled to be delivered in three shipments before May 15, 1988.

Rotorex sent the first shipment by sea on March 26. Delchi paid for this shipment, which arrived at its Italian factory on April 20, by letter of credit. Rotorex sent a second shipment of compressors on or about May 9. Delchi also remitted payment for this shipment by letter of credit. While the second shipment was en route, Delchi discovered that the first lot of compressors did not conform to the sample model and accompanying specifications. On May 13, after a Rotorex representative visited the Delchi factory in Italy, Delchi informed Rotorex that 93 percent of the compressors were rejected in quality control checks because they had lower cooling capacity and consumed more power than the sample model and specifications. After several unsuccessful attempts to cure the defects in the compressors, Delchi asked Rotorex to supply new compressors conforming to the original sample and specifications. Rotorex refused, claiming that the performance specifications were "inadvertently communicated" to Delchi.

In a faxed letter dated May 23, 1988, Delchi cancelled the contract. Although it was able to expedite a previously planned order of suitable compressors from Sanyo, another supplier, Delchi was unable to obtain in a timely fashion substitute compressors from other sources and thus suffered a loss in its sales volume of Arieles during the 1988 selling season. Delchi filed the instant action under the United Nations Convention on Contracts for the International Sale of Goods ("CISG" or "the Convention") for breach of contract and failure to deliver conforming goods. . . .

The district court held, and the parties agree, that the instant matter is governed by the CISG, reprinted at 15 U.S.C.A. Appendix (West Supp. 1995), a self-executing agreement between the United States and other signatories, including Italy. Because there is virtually no caselaw under the Convention, we look to its language and to "the general principles" upon which it is based. See CISG art. 7(2). The Convention directs that its interpretation be informed by its "international character and . . . the need to promote uniformity in its application and the observance of good faith in international trade." See CISG art. 7(1). Caselaw interpreting analogous provisions of Article 2 of the Uniform Commercial Code ("UCC"), may also inform a court where the language of the relevant CISG provisions tracks that of the UCC. However, UCC caselaw "is not per se applicable." Orbisphere Corp. v. United States, 726 F. Supp. 1344, 1355 (Ct. Int'l Trade 1989).

We first address the liability issue. . . . Under the CISG, "[t]he seller must deliver goods which are of the quantity, quality and description required by the contract," and "the goods do not conform with the contract unless they . . . [p]ossess the qualities of goods which the seller has held out to the buyer as a sample or model."

CISG art. 35. The CISG further states that "[t]he seller is liable in accordance with the contract and this Convention for any lack of conformity." CISG art. 36.

Judge Cholakis held that "there is no question that [Rotorex's] compressors did not conform to the terms of the contract between the parties" and noted that "[t]here are ample admissions [by Rotorex] to that effect." We agree. The agreement between Delchi and Rotorex was based upon a sample compressor supplied by Rotorex and upon written specifications regarding cooling capacity and power consumption. After the problems were discovered, Rotorex's engineering representative, Ernest Gamache, admitted in a May 13, 1988 letter that the specification sheet was "in error" and that the compressors would actually generate less cooling power and consume more energy than the specifications indicated. Gamache also testified in a deposition that at least some of the compressors were nonconforming. The president of Rotorex, John McFee, conceded in a May 17, 1988 letter to Delchi that the compressors supplied were less efficient than the sample and did not meet the specifications provided by Rotorex. Finally, in its answer to Delchi's complaint, Rotorex admitted "that some of the compressors . . . did not conform to the nominal performance information." There was thus no genuine issue of material fact regarding liability, and summary judgment was proper.

Under the CISG, if the breach is "fundamental" the buyer may either require delivery of substitute goods, CISG art. 46, or declare the contract void, CISG art. 49, and seek damages. With regard to what kind of breach is fundamental, Article 25 provides:

> A breach of contract committed by one of the parties is fundamental if it results in such detriment to the other party as substantially to deprive him of what he is entitled to expect under the contract, unless the party in breach did not foresee and a reasonable person of the same kind in the same circumstances would not have foreseen such a result.

CISG art. 25. In granting summary judgment, the district court held that "[t]here appears to be no question that [Delchi] did not substantially receive that which [it] was entitled to expect" and that "any reasonable person could foresee that shipping non-conforming goods to a buyer would result in the buyer not receiving that which he expected and was entitled to receive." Because the cooling power and energy consumption of an air conditioner compressor are important determinants of the product's value, the district court's conclusion that Rotorex was liable for a fundamental breach of contract under the Convention was proper. . . .

Besides the "fundamental breach" scenario, the second situation in which the buyer may avoid the contract under the CISG is where the seller's delivery is later than the agreed-on due date plus any additional time that the buyer has agreed to give the seller to deliver. CISG Art. 49(1)(b). If a buyer agrees to give the seller additional time to deliver, the buyer does not thereby prejudice its right to damages for the delay. CISG Art. 47(2).

The functional consequences of avoidance by the buyer are that both parties are relieved of their obligations, but the buyer may sue for damages. CISG Art. 81(1). Either party may claim restitution if the partial performance has resulted in a benefit to the other party. CISG Art. 81(2). If the buyer has already received the goods, the buyer has an obligation to return the goods to the seller in substantially the same condition that they were received in. CISG Art. 82(1).

Where the seller's breach is less than "fundamental," the buyer must keep the goods but retains its rights to sue for any of the non-avoidance remedies under the CISG. These could include monetary damages, CISG Arts. 74-77, or a demand by the buyer that the seller cure the problem. CISG Art. 46. The seller is also given the right to cure any non-fundamental breaches. CISG Art. 48.

C.   Real Estate Closings

The Ritual Closing Ceremony

This is an important and highly traditional part of the home buying process, the last major hurdle you must clear before you become an official homeowner. Essentially what you must do, in the Ritual Closing Ceremony, is go into a small room and write large checks to total strangers. According to tradition, anybody may ask you for a check, for any amount, and you may not refuse. Once you get started handing out money, the good news will travel quickly through the real estate community via joyful shouts: "A Closing Ceremony is taking place!"

Soon there will be a huge horde of people — lawyers, bankers, insurance people, termite inspectors, caterers, photographers, people you used to know in high school — crowding into the closing room and spilling out into the street. You may be forced to hurl batches of signed blank checks out the window, just to make sure that everyone is accommodated in the traditional way.

Another ritual task you must perform during the Closing Ceremony is to frown with feigned comprehension at various unintelligible documents that will be placed in front of you by random individuals wearing suits.

Random Individual: Now, as you can see, this is the declaration of your net interest accrual payments of debenture.
You (frowning): Yes.
Random Individual: And this is the notification of your Pro Rata Indemnities of Assumption.
You: Certainly.
Random Individual: And this is the digestive system of a badger.
You: Of course.

Dave Barry, Homes and Other Black Holes, 45-47 (1988).

To anyone who has ever gone through the process, a real estate closing does seem to take on the aura of an ancient ritual. Much of what goes on passes for federally mandated "disclosure," but as the hypothetical story above suggests, disclosure and comprehension are two completely different things.

In the midst of all of the papers being signed at a typical house closing, the fundamental exchange taking place is the buyer giving a check for the purchase price and the seller giving the deed to the property. The legal transfer of ownership from the seller to the buyer takes place when the seller "delivers" the deed to the buyer. Delivery requires both a physical transfer of the deed from the seller to the buyer as well as an intent on the seller's part to create a present ownership interest in the buyer as a result of the physical delivery.

In contrast to the sales of goods system, there is a true functional significance to the moment of the "closing" in real estate sales. Following the closing, there is very little chance, absent some fundamental fraud or mistake in the transaction, that the buyer would be able to reject or revoke acceptance of the real estate and rescind the entire contract.

Gray v. First NH Banks

640 A.2d 276 (N.H. 1994)

BATCHELDER, J.

The plaintiffs appeal the decision of the Superior Court (O'Neil, J.) dismissing their suit for rescission of a real estate purchase. They argue that the trial court erred: (1) in finding that the defendants' violation of RSA 485-A:39 (1992) did not provide the basis for a cause of action; (2) in failing to rule that the lack of signatures on the site assessment study constituted per se liability; (3) in finding that the realtor was acting as an intermediary, rather than as the bank's agent; and (4) because its findings on each theory of recovery were clearly erroneous. We affirm.

In July 1990, the plaintiffs, Peter Gray, his wife, Sandra, and his parents, Henry and Shirley, learned of the availability of a bowling alley, Lakeview Lanes, on the shore of Little Squam Lake in Holderness. Defendant First NH Banks, formerly First Central Bank (the bank), had acquired title to the bowling alley by virtue of a deed in lieu of foreclosure against the previous owner. Peter Gray contacted the bank about the property. Shortly thereafter, Rod Donaldson, a real estate agent associated with defendant La-Sal Properties of New Hampshire, Inc. (La-Sal) who had worked with Gray in unsuccessful negotiations for another property, became involved in the negotiations for Lakeview Lanes on Gray's behalf. After viewing the property with Gwendolyn Davis, a bank representative, Peter Gray offered to buy it for $225,000. The bank made a counteroffer of $325,000, and the parties failed to reach agreement.

Following the initial offer, Peter Gray spoke with a co-worker, Philip Stone, who had worked for several summers at Lakeview Lanes. Stone told Gray that he "had heard that there were problems with the septic system," that the son of a former owner had been deterred from purchasing the property because "there were significant problems with the septic system," and that he should have the system checked. Gray responded that he intended to use the septic problems "as a negotiating tool with the bank to lower the purchase price." The system was never inspected.

On October 17, 1990, Peter Gray offered $275,000 for the property, requesting a warranty deed. The proposal to purchase contained the following paragraph: "4. Buyers and Sellers recognize that there is a present and potential problem with subject property's well and septic systems." The parties ultimately entered into a sales agreement on October 23, 1990, which provided that the property would be transferred by quitclaim deed and made no reference to the septic system. The Grays and the bank closed the sale and transferred title on November 16, 1990.

When the Grays began operating the bowling alley and restaurant, the septic problems surfaced. The system needed frequent pumping and emitted noxious odors. After learning that RSA 485-A:39 (1992) (current version at RSA 485-A:39 (Supp. 1993)) required the preparation of a site assessment study evaluating the sewage system of developed waterfront property before it could be offered for sale, Shirley Gray contacted Donaldson and requested a copy of the document. Although the Grays maintain that they had no knowledge of the site assessment until Shirley Gray received a copy from Donaldson in January 1991, the bank contends that the Grays were given a copy of the document at the closing.

The Grays filed suit against the bank and La-Sal, contending that the bank's failure to procure a site assessment until the day before the closing violated RSA 485-A:39, entitling them to rescission of the contract, and that the negligent or fraudulent misrepresentations of the bank and La-Sal entitled them to money damages. . . .

The plaintiffs' first two arguments raise the consequences of a violation of the site assessment statute. RSA 485-A:39 requires the owner of developed waterfront property, prior to offering it for sale, to procure a site assessment study on the sewage disposal system. In this case, the site assessment study was dated the day before the closing and was not signed by the buyers as required. That the requirements of the site assessment statute were not met is not in dispute. Rather, it is the remedy for failure to strictly comply with the statutory mandate that is at stake. The plaintiffs contend that the failure to comply creates per se liability, entitling them to rescission of the purchase. We disagree.

Although a violation of RSA 485-A:39 occurred, evidence at trial refuted the plaintiffs' argument that the violation in any way caused their injuries. The trial court found that "[t]he plaintiffs were aware of significant problems with the septic system prior to the sale." In addition to Stone's testimony that he had warned Peter Gray of the problems with the septic system, the initial proposal to purchase contained an express acknowledgement that there was "a present and potential problem with subject property's well and septic systems." Further, Gray testified that this language was included because "the bank wanted to be sure that I wouldn't come back later on and say I've got no water and my leach field is not working."

The evidence that is most damaging to the plaintiffs is Peter Gray's admission that he intended to use the septic problems "as a negotiating tool with the bank to lower the purchase price." The purpose of the site assessment study is "to determine if the site meets the current standards of sewage disposal systems established by the division [of water supply and pollution control, department of environmental services]." RSA 485-A:39, I; see RSA 485-A:2, III. Thus the statute serves to inform a prospective buyer of the condition of the sewage system, information not readily apparent from a site inspection of the property. Here, however, the plaintiffs knew of the problems yet chose to utilize them as a bargaining chip in negotiations for the purchase of the property. Accordingly, because the plaintiffs failed to prove that the statutory violation, rather than their chosen negotiation strategy, caused their injuries, the trial court's ruling was not contrary to the evidence or erroneous as a matter of law.

We recognize that the material required by the statute to be disclosed to the potential purchaser is broader than the information that the plaintiffs acknowledged they received. The trial court specifically found, however, that "[t]here was nothing new in the way of septic system information in the [site assessment] report." Because this factual finding was not clearly erroneous, we will not overrule it. We note that in future cases, the lack of strict compliance with the statutory mandate may give rise to the remedy sought by the plaintiffs here. . . .

The plaintiffs finally contend that the trial court's findings on each of its theories of recovery were so against the weight of the evidence as to constitute an abuse of discretion. With respect to the plaintiffs' count based on negligent or fraudulent misrepresentation, "[o]ne who fraudulently makes a misrepresentation . . . for the purpose of inducing another to act or to refrain from action in reliance upon it, is subject to liability to the other in deceit for pecuniary loss caused to him by his justifiable reliance upon the misrepresentation." Restatement (Second) of Torts §525 (1976). Similarly, "[o]ne who, in the course of his business . . . supplies false information for the guidance of others in their business transactions, is subject to liability for pecuniary loss caused to them by their justifiable reliance upon the information, if he fails to exercise reasonable care or competence in obtaining or communicating the information." Id. §552. The plaintiffs failed to meet their burden on both theories.

The trial court found that no misrepresentation occurred. Further, based on evidence that included Peter Gray's own testimony, the court found that the plaintiffs were aware of the problems with the sewer system early on in the negotiations, thus negating any argument that they relied on the bank's or realtor's statements. Finally, Peter Gray testified that he had no evidence that the value of the property is substantially less than that bargained for with the defendants. Because there was evidence on which the trial court could reasonably base its finding that no misrepresentation occurred, it did not err in dismissing this count.

Finally, the plaintiffs maintain that the trial court erred in dismissing its count seeking restitution by rescission for mutual mistake. "Where a mistake of both parties at the time a contract was made as to a basic assumption on which the contract was made has a material effect on the agreed exchange of performances, the contract is voidable by the adversely affected party." Restatement (Second) of Contracts §152(1) (1979). Because the trial court found that "[t]he plaintiffs were aware of significant problems with the septic system prior to the sale" and because there was ample evidence to support this finding, no mistake occurred. Consequently, we find no abuse of discretion in the trial court's ruling.

AFFIRMED.

In the real estate system, the buyer has an opportunity to inspect the property and negotiate for repairs during the executory period between the signing of the contract and the closing of the sale. Typically, the buyer will do a final "walk-through" of the property on the day before closing or the day of closing just to make sure that no changes have occurred following the buyer's earlier, formal inspection.

In the United States, many western states use escrow agents to take the place of a formal closing. In these states, the parties will agree on escrow instructions that will bind the escrow's ability to deliver the deed to the buyer and the purchase price to the seller.

Where the more standard closings take place, the parties that attend the closing will vary from state to state. Both the buyer and the seller will attend in person in some states; they may not in other states. The broker almost always attends in most states (perhaps to make sure it gets its commission check!). Lawyers are typically used by the two sides at a closing in some states, whereas in other states lawyers are rarely involved and most of the details and documents are handled by the title company.

As a future lawyer, consider the following:

Washington (AP)—Lawyers at the Justice Department and the Federal Trade Commission think a proposal to allow only lawyers to conduct real estate closings in Virginia is a rotten idea.

"It's difficult enough trying to buy a home," said Anne K. Bingaman, who heads Justice's antitrust division. "Let's not make it even more costly or difficult for those trying to grab a piece of the American dream."

She and Director William J. Baer of the Federal Trade Commission sent a stiff letter to Thomas A. Edmonds, director of the Virginia State Bar Association on Friday.

A committee of the association said in an opinion that real estate closings by anyone other than a lawyer should be considered an unauthorized practice of law. The committee stressed the risk that a lay person will make a mistake that a lawyer would not and that the consumer would be hurt.

The opinion eventually may see action by the legislature or the state Supreme Court or both. The Justice-FTC letter will become part of a comment package to be considered by the Virginia State Bar Council.

The Justice Department said lay settlement services and attorneys compete in real estate closings in many states, including in New Jersey, where the state Supreme Court ruled last year that non-lawyers may conduct closings and settlement.

The court found that in the southern part of the state, where lay settlements were commonplace, buyers paid $350 on average to non-lawyers and $650 to lawyers, the department said. In northern New Jersey, where lawyers handle most such transactions, sellers paid $750 in lawyers fees on average and buyers $1,000. (Harry F. Rosenthal, "Justice, FTC Oppose Lawyers-Only Real Estate Closings," September 20, 1996, Associated Press.)

Problem Set 19

19.1.   a. Not quite a month following her last visit to your law office, Mammoth College athletic director Shelly Stone (from Problem 18.4) is back to see you again — with more bus problems. After unloading Big Al's bus back to him, Shelly discovered that a local bank, First National, had a leasing division that leased buses. A leasing officer there, Mark Archer, had convinced Shelly of the benefits of a finance lease. Shelly had agreed to a five-year finance lease of a two-year-old bus that she had personally selected from the fleet at Little Sal's, a local bus dealer who happened to be Big Al's younger sister. Shelly had intended to have a mechanic check out the bus before accepting it, but Mark Archer convinced her that his bank's experience with Little Sal's was so consistently positive that Shelly should not waste her time and money getting a mechanic. Unfortunately, when the bus took its first long trip with the women's volleyball team, the bus turned out to be an even worse oil guzzler than the one Shelly had dumped back on Big Al's. The lease contract that Shelly signed with First National had a clause that said, "The lessee's promises under the lease contract become irrevocable and independent upon the lessee's acceptance of the goods, AND THERE SHALL BE NO EXCEPTIONS TO THE EFFECTIVENESS OF THIS CLAUSE." Shelly now wants to know if she can revoke acceptance of the bus and, if she cannot, what other recourse she has and against whom. What do you advise? UCC §2A-407, Official Comments 1 and 2 to §2A-407, §2A-517(1), Official Comment 1 to §2A-516, §1-302.

b. Same facts as part (a), except that the lease contract did not contain the clause that was quoted in part (a). Can Shelly revoke acceptance of the bus? UCC §2A-407, Official Comments 1 and 2 to §2A-407, §2A-517(1), Official Comment 1 to §2A-516, §1-302.

c. Same facts as part (a), except instead of a bus for Mammoth College, Shelly was leasing a van for her personal use, and the lease contract did not contain the clause that was quoted in part (a). Further, Mark Archer gave no assurances to Shelly in this case. When it turns out that the van is an oil guzzler, can Shelly revoke acceptance of the van? If not, what recourse does Shelly have and against whom? UCC §§2A-407(1), 2A-517, 2A-209(1), 2A-212(1).

d. Same facts as part (a), except instead of a bus for Mammoth College, Shelly was leasing a van for her personal use. The lease contract contained the same clause as in part (a), but Mark Archer gave no assurances to Shelly in this case. When it turns out that the van is an oil guzzler, can Shelly revoke acceptance of the van? If not, what recourse does Shelly have and against whom? UCC §§2A-407(1), 2A-517, 2A-209(1), 2A-212(1); Official Comment 6 to §2A-407.

e. Same facts as part (a), except that the problem with the bus was not oil guzzling but a defective steering wheel that Shelly discovered even before leaving Little Sal's lot (but after signing the lease with the bank). (1) Must Shelly go through with the lease? (2) What if the clause had said that Shelly's obligations under the lease became irrevocable and independent "upon the lessee's signing of the lease contract" instead of "upon the lessee's acceptance of the goods"? §§2A-515, 2A-108, 1-302.

19.2. a. Mal's Shop for Men, a Chicago suit retailer, made a contract to buy four dozen men's suits from Italy's Best, a suit manufacturer headquartered in Italy. Mal's received the suits on time and, as was the store's practice, simply put the suits on the racks. The suits sat there for a couple of months before anyone bought them. When customers finally started buying the suits, virtually every customer who had purchased those suits complained about the suit's "cheap material," which frayed significantly. At this point, which was about three months after the store had received delivery of the suits, Mal's announced to Italy's Best that Mal's was sending back all of the suits for a refund. Does Mal's have a right to void this contract? Does Italy's Best have a right to cure? CISG Arts. 25, 39, 49, 48, 46.

b. Same facts as part (a), except that the suit's material was fine, but the sleeves on a few of the suits were missing one or both buttons. Once again, Mal's does not discover these defects until customers start complaining later on. Does Mal's have a right to void this contract? Does Italy's Best have a right to cure? CISG Arts. 25, 49, 48, 46.

c. Same facts as part (a), except that Italy's Best delivers the suits three weeks before the contractual delivery date and Mal's discovers the fraying material by inspecting the suits immediately. Mal's then calls Italy's Best to complain about the material. Does Mal's have a right to avoid this contract? Does Italy's Best have a right to cure? CISG Arts. 25, 37, 49, 48, 46.

19.3. After three years of living in an apartment, Mike and Dayna Wellston had finally put together enough funds to purchase their first home in a modest section of Manchester, New Hampshire. Mike was an engineer for an environmental auditing firm and Dayna was a reporter for a suburban newspaper. Together their salaries were just enough to qualify for the mortgage necessary to finance the $170,000 home. Two months after the closing, Mike was digging a hole in his backyard to put in a pole for a basketball hoop when he happened upon a buried gas tank. Mike believed the sellers when they told him they knew nothing about the tank, but when Mike learned of the $40,000 cost of removal he and Dayna came to see you about a possible rescission action. Mike and Dayna had commissioned a standard inspection of the home that, not surprisingly, did not discover the tank. Mike was aware from his work that occasionally prospective home buyers would commission an environmental audit of the land they were going to buy, but such audits were rare given the tremendous expense. What do you say to Mike and Dayna about the likelihood of a successful rescission of their home purchase?

Assignment 20:   Risk of Loss with Sales of Goods

In Assignment 18, we explored the vagaries of the "closing" concept in the sale of goods system. An issue that is closely related to closing is risk of loss. Risk-of-loss rules define which party, between the buyer and the seller, is responsible for the destruction of or damage to goods that occurs between the time that the contract is entered into and the time that the buyer receives possession of the goods.

Risk-of-loss issues can arise in two-party cases where the seller itself delivers the goods or the buyer comes and picks up the goods at the seller's place of business. Most of the action in risk of loss, however, occurs in the very common three-party situation, in which the seller makes arrangements to have the goods delivered to the buyer by a third-party common carrier such as a truck, plane, or boat.

Before getting into some of the complicated rules governing risk of loss, a couple of more general points about the subject should be considered. The first point is that if the destruction or damage to goods occurs through the fault of either the buyer or the seller, then the negligent party must bear the loss, and the usual risk-of-loss rules do not come into play. In other words, the risk-of-loss rules were designed to cover only the cases in which the destruction or damage to the goods occurs in a way other than through the fault of either buyer or seller.

Second, risk-of-loss fights in actual practice tend to involve insurance companies, either against each other or against the buyer or seller. In three-party transactions where the seller uses a common carrier, the carrier will almost always have insurance to cover losses in transit. Similarly, the buyer and seller will usually each have their own backup insurance policies that may cover any losses that occur during the executory period between contracting and buyer acceptance. Some larger companies will effectively self-insure at the lower levels by having insurance policies with huge deductibles.

The purchasing agent for a medium-sized plastics manufacturer, which does not insure its orders in transit, described the risk-of-loss issue this way: "The real question in risk of loss situations is not which party, the buyer or the seller, will bear the loss. Rather, the issue is usually which party, the buyer or the seller, will have to deal with the hassle of going against the carrier's insurance company." The in-house attorney for a Fortune 500 seller that does insure its deliveries in transit described the risk-of-loss issue as involving little more than getting paid for the loss by its own insurance company, which then goes after the carrier's insurance.

The third, more general point to make about risk of loss is a point that we have made in other contexts as well: even where the legal rule would seem to dictate one result, business considerations may cause parties to agree to another result that is technically inconsistent with their legal obligations. For example, one medium-sized furniture manufacturer includes in its contracts a provision that shifts risk of loss to the buyer as soon as the furniture leaves the seller's factory, but when there is a problem in transit the seller almost always makes the buyer whole anyway. As the operations manager for this manufacturer explained, "Officially, we say that risk of loss passes from us to the buyer as soon as we load the goods onto the truck. In fact, though, if there is a problem that occurs during delivery our customers expect us to pay them and then go against the carrier ourselves. If they're good customers, we will almost always do that for them."

Most high-volume sellers have their own dedicated third-party carriers that they use to deliver shipments even when the buyer is contractually obligated to pay for the cost of freight. The seller in these cases will arrange for the transportation and then charge the buyer for use of the seller's captured carrier. In setting the delivery fee for buyers, sellers will charge not only for the actual cost of the third-party carrier but also a profit to account for the seller's time in arranging the delivery details. Some large buyers have their own dedicated fleets that come to the seller's place of business and pick up the goods.

Whenever there is a third-party carrier involved, seller and buyer will almost always specify when risk of loss passes. In practice, parties to domestic sales transactions almost always use just two basic delivery terms: FOB Seller's Place (a "shipment" contract) and FOB Buyer's Place (a "destination" contract). (FOB is short for "free on board" and means the seller must pay all charges necessary for the merchandise to arrive, on board, at the designated location, free of charge to the buyer.) If the parties fail to specify a delivery term, Article 2's default rule calls for a shipment contract. UCC §2-308(a), Official Comment 5 to §2-503.

With a shipment contract, risk of loss shifts to the buyer when the goods are delivered to the carrier, and the buyer is responsible for paying the cost of freight. §2-509(1)(a). With a destination contract, risk of loss does not shift to the buyer until the goods are tendered to the buyer at the stated destination, and the seller is responsible for paying the cost of freight. §2-509(1)(b). Whether the delivery ends up as a shipment or a destination contract will be a function of both negotiation and the relative leverage of the parties. Some sellers with significant leverage make it non-negotiable that all of their sales be shipment contracts so that those sellers never have to contend with insuring risk of loss in transit.

Most risk-of-loss cases probably involve goods that are damaged in transit, but there are also cases in which the goods are lost or stolen in transit. In the unusual case where there is loss or theft in transit, the losses involved can be significant, as the following case demonstrates.

Stampede Presentation Products, Inc. v. Productive Transportation, Inc.

2013 WL 2245064 (W.D.N.Y. 2013)

SCHROEDER, U.S. Magistrate Judge.

Plaintiff Stampede Presentation Products, Inc. ("Stampede"), brought this action in New York State Supreme Court, Erie County, against defendants Productive Transportation, Inc., Productive Transportation Carrier Corp. (collectively, "Productive"), and 1 SaleADay L.L.C., seeking money damages based on an alleged loss of an interstate shipment of 960 flat screen TVs. The case was removed to this court pursuant to 28 U.S.C. §1441 by Notice of Removal filed on May 24, 2012 by defendant Productive (as consented to by defendant 1SaleADay), alleging original federal jurisdiction under 49 U.S.C. §14706 (liability of carriers under receipts and bills of lading).

Pending for report and recommendation is defendant 1SaleADay's motion to dismiss the complaint against it for failure to state a claim upon which relief can be granted. Upon consideration of the pleadings and submissions presented, and for the reasons that follow, it is recommended that defendant's motion be granted.

BACKGROUND

As alleged in the original Verified Complaint, filed in state court on May 2, 2012, Stampede is in the business of distributing presentation equipment, including flat panel display units and projectors, to audio/visual, computer, and home theater resellers. Pursuant to a "Purchase Invoice" dated February 10, 2012, Stampede purchased 960 thirty-two inch flat screen TVs from 1 SaleADay, an Internet discount retailer, for a total price of $205,440.00. Stampede pre-paid the purchase price in cash by wire transfer on January 2, 2012.

Pursuant to a "Uniform Straight Bill of Lading" dated February 2, 2012, Stampede hired Productive for a fee of $3,475 to pick up the TVs at the manufacturer's warehouse in California, "FOB Origin," and deliver them to Stampede's customer, TigerDirect (also referred to as "SYX Distribution"), located in Naperville, Illinois. Productive in turn subcontracted with another carrier, MML Transport, Inc. ("MML") of Chicago, Illinois, to pick up the TVs in California and deliver them to Stampede's customer in Illinois. As alleged in the original Verified Complaint, "[t]he [TVs] were in fact picked up at the California warehouse, but they were never delivered to [Stampede]'s customer. Instead, they were stolen and/or lost by the trucker who picked them up at the warehouse." Stampede claims that Productive engaged MML as its agent to perform the obligations of the contract without authenticating MML's qualifications, resulting in the loss of the shipment and causing Stampede to suffer damages in the amount paid to 1 SaleADay, along with the profits it would have made in the resale of the TVs to its customer. Stampede asserts causes of action against Productive based on theories of breach of contract, negligence, fraudulent inducement, and tortious interference with contractual relations. Stampede also seeks recovery of the contract price and lost resale profits from 1 SaleADay based on theories of breach of contract, negligence, unjust enrichment, and money had and received.

On June 19, 2012, defendant 1 SaleADay filed a motion to dismiss the claims asserted against it, on the following grounds:

> 1. Stampede fails to state a claim against 1 SaleADay for breach of contract because, under the Uniform Commercial Code ("UCC"), the Purchase Invoice governing the sale of the TVs was a "shipment" contract, not a "destination" contract, and the risk of loss passed from the seller to the buyer upon delivery of the goods to the carrier;
> 2. Stampede fails to state a negligence claim against 1 SaleADay because there is no allegation of a legal duty independent of the duty imposed by the contract itself;
> 3. Stampede fails to state claims for unjust enrichment or money had and received because those quasi-contract doctrines do not apply where the parties' obligations are governed by a written contract for the sale of goods.

On July 9, 2012, following entry of a scheduling order for briefing on the motion to dismiss, Stampede filed an Amended Complaint containing new allegations in an effort to remedy the pleading defects addressed by 1 SaleADay's motion. Specifically, with regard to the delivery of the TVs to the carrier at the manufacturer's warehouse, Stampede now alleges in the Amended Complaint that:

> 20. Possession of the Goods was in fact turned over at the California warehouse. However, the Goods were not turned over to MML. Instead, SaleADay turned them over to an unauthorized stranger, to whom defendant Productive had apparently provided a bill of lading.
> 21. The Goods were never delivered to plaintiff's customer. Instead, they were stolen by the unauthorized stranger to whom defendant SaleADay delivered them.

With regard to the negligence claim against 1SaleADay, Stampede alleges in the Amended Complaint that 1SaleADay "had a duty to confirm that the person to whom [it] delivered the Goods was a carrier or person authorized by plaintiff to retrieve them. Defendant SaleADay failed to do so, and thus breached this duty." The "unjust enrichment" and "money had and received" causes of action against 1SaleADay remain unchanged as alleged in the original state court Verified Complaint.

In response to the motion to dismiss, Stampede asserts that the Amended Complaint has clarified the claims against 1 SaleADay by alleging that 1 SaleADay breached the contract by delivering the TVs to someone other than the carrier authorized by plaintiff. According to Stampede, 1SaleADay has mis-characterized the transaction at issue as a UCC "shipment contract/risk of loss" case, and the Amended Complaint sufficiently alleges that the breach occurred at the time the TVs were delivered by 1SaleADay to the "unauthorized stranger." Stampede also asserts that the Amended Complaint has clarified the negligence claim against 1SaleADay by specifying the independent legal duty breached by the delivery of the TVs to the "unauthorized stranger."

DISCUSSION AND ANALYSIS

* * *

BREACH OF CONTRACT

1SaleADay contends that Stampede has failed to state a breach of contract claim against it because the Purchase Invoice for the sale of the TVs is a "shipment contract" governed by §2-504 of New York's Uniform Commercial Code, pursuant to which to the risk of loss of or damage to the goods passed from the seller to the buyer upon delivery of the goods to the carrier at the warehouse in California. UCC §2-504 provides:

> Where the seller is required or authorized to send the goods to the buyer and the contract does not require him to deliver them at a particular destination, then unless otherwise agreed he must
> (a) put the goods in the possession of such a carrier and make such a contract for their transportation as may be reasonable having regard to the nature of the goods and other circumstances of the case; and
> (b) obtain and promptly deliver or tender in due form any document necessary to enable the buyer to obtain possession of the goods or otherwise required by the agreement or by usage of trade; and
> (c) promptly notify the buyer of the shipment.
> Failure to notify the buyer under paragraph (c) or to make a proper contract under paragraph (a) is a ground for rejection only if material delay or loss ensues.

N.Y. UCC §2-504. In contrast, a "destination contract" is covered by UCC §2-503; it arises where "the seller is required to deliver at a particular destination." N.Y. UCC §2-503(3).

Allocation of the risk of loss is addressed by UCC §2-509(1), which provides:

> Where the contract requires or authorizes the seller to ship the goods by carrier
> (a) if it does not require [the seller] to deliver them at a particular destination, the risk of loss passes to the buyer when the goods are duly delivered to the carrier . . . .
> (b) if it does require him to deliver them at a particular destination and the goods are there duly tendered while in the possession of the carrier, the risk of loss passes to the buyer when the goods are there duly so tendered as to enable the buyer to take delivery.

N.Y. UCC §2-509(1).

Based on this Court's reading of the documents governing Stampede's purchase of the TVs from 1SaleADay in this case, and considering the undisputed logistics of the transaction, it is clear that the contractual arrangement required or authorized 1SaleADay to ship the TVs by carrier, designated by Stampede to be Productive Transportation. The Purchase Invoice (submitted as Exhibit A to both the original and amended complaints) contains no express requirement that 1SaleADay deliver the TVs "at a particular destination." The invoice simply identifies 1SaleADay as the "Vendor," and directs that the purchased items are to be shipped to Stampede's resale customer, TigerDirect, in Naperville, Illinois. The Uniform Straight Bill of Lading, prepared on a "Productive Transportation" form designating Productive as the "delivering carrier," clearly indicates that the TVs were to be shipped "FOB Origin" by the "Shipper," identified as Stampede, from their origin at the warehouse in California to TigerDirect in Illinois.

As recognized by the Second Circuit, "[w]here the terms of an agreement are ambiguous, there is a strong presumption under the UCC favoring shipment contracts. Unless the parties 'expressly specify' that the contract requires the seller to deliver to a particular destination, the contract is generally construed as one for shipment." Windows, Inc. v. Jordan Panel Systems Corp., 177 F.3d 114, 117 (2d Cir.1999) (citing 3A Ronald A. Anderson Uniform Commercial Code §§2-503:24, 2-503:26; also citing Dana Debs, Inc. v. Lady Rose Stores, Inc., 65 Misc. 2d 697, 319 N.Y.S.2d 111, 112 (N.Y. City Civ. Ct. 1970) ("The word 'require' means that there is an explicit written understanding to that effect for otherwise every shipment would be deemed a destination contract."). Here, the terms of the agreement clearly express the parties' understanding that the buyer (Stampede) designated a carrier (Progressive) to make the shipment of the TVs from the manufacturer's warehouse to the customer. There is no express language anywhere in the contract documents specifying that the seller (1SaleADay) was itself required to deliver the TVs to a particular destination. Even if these terms of agreement were to be somehow construed as ambiguous, "the strong presumption favoring shipment contracts" would lead the Court to conclude that UCC §2-509(1)(a) should apply to allocate the risk of loss to Stampede upon 1SaleADay's delivery of the TVs to the carrier at the warehouse in California. Windows, Inc., 177 F.3d at 117; Dana Debs, 319 N.Y.S.2d at 112.

This conclusion is strengthened by the clearly printed indication on the Bill of Lading that the goods were to be shipped by Stampede, and delivered by Productive, "FOB Origin" from the warehouse in California to the resale customer in Illinois. "The general rule is that upon a sale 'f.o.b. the point of shipment,' title passes from the seller at the moment of delivery to the carrier, and the subject of the sale is thereafter at the buyer's risk." Sara Corp. v. Sainty Intern. America Inc., 2008 WL 2944862, at *7 (S.D.N.Y. Aug.1, 2008) (quoting Standard Casing Co. v. California Casing Co., 233 N.Y. 413, 416, 135 N.E. 834 (1922)). Under the ordinary application of this rule, "delivery to the carrier is delivery to the buyer." Chase Manhattan Bank v. Nissho Pacific Corp., 22 A.D.2d 215, 254 N.Y.S.2d 571, 577 (App. Div. 1964), aff'd, 16 N.Y.2d 999, 265 N.Y.S.2d 660, 212 N.E.2d 897 (1965); see also UCC §2-319(1)(a) ("Unless otherwise agreed the term F.O.B. (which means 'free on board') at a named place . . . is a delivery term under which . . . when the term is F.O.B. the place of shipment, the seller must at that place ship the goods in the manner provided in this Article (Section 2-504) and bear the expense and risk of putting them into the possession of the carrier").

Stampede contends that 1SaleADay's reliance on the UCC provisions dealing with allocation of risk of loss is a "pure red herring," since the facts pleaded in the Amended Complaint clearly set forth a plausible claim that 1 SaleADay breached the contractual arrangement by delivering the TVs to an unauthorized carrier. To the contrary, since the parties are merchants as that term is defined in UCC §2-104(1), and the transaction at issue is for the sale of goods as defined in UCC §2-105(1), it cannot be disputed that the allocation of the risk of loss to the goods during the transaction is covered by UCC Article 2. See, e.g., Suzy Phillips Originals, Inc. v. Coville, Inc., 939 F. Supp. 1012, 1017 (E.D.N.Y. 1996) ("In New York, [UCC] Article 2 governs disputes concerning the sale of goods between merchants."), aff'd, 125 F.3d 845 (2d Cir. 1997); Kabbalah Jeans, Inc. v. CN USA Intern. Corp., 907 N.Y.S.2d (Table), 2010 WL 1136511, at *2 (N.Y. Sup. Ct. 2010) (transactions between merchants for sale of goods covered by UCC Article 2).

Applying the UCC's allocation of risk of loss provisions, because the contract documents clearly identify Stampede as the party to the transaction responsible for hiring an authorized carrier to ship the goods from the point of origin to its customer in Illinois, and because there is otherwise no express indication that 1 SaleADay itself was required to deliver the goods at a particular destination, the contract governing the transaction at issue must be construed as a shipment contract under UCC §2-504(a), and the risk of loss passed to Stampede when the goods were delivered to the carrier, under UCC §2-509(1)(a). As indicated by the signatures on page one of the Bill of Lading, the TVs were picked up by the carrier on February 2, 2012, and there is nothing in the pleadings or in the contract documents attached as exhibits thereto to indicate that the goods were non-conforming or were otherwise not duly delivered within the requirements of UCC Article 2.

Accordingly, since 1 SaleADay had already fulfilled its contractual obligations, and Stampede had assumed the risk, at the time the goods were lost, there can be no set of facts pleaded that would allow the Court to draw the reasonable inference that 1 SaleADay is liable for breach of contract.

Based on this analysis, accepting the material facts alleged in the complaint as true and drawing all reasonable inferences in the plaintiff's favor, this Court finds that Stampede has failed to plead sufficient factual content to state a breach of contract claim against 1 SaleADay that is plausible on its face. It is therefore recommended that Stampede's breach of contract claim against 1 SaleADay be dismissed.

Negligence

It is a well-established principle of New York law that "a simple breach of contract is not to be considered a tort unless a legal duty independent of the contract itself has been violated." Clark-Fitzpatrick, Inc. v. Long Island R.R., 70 N.Y.2d 382, 389, 521 N.Y.S.2d 653, 516 N.E.2d 190 (1987), quoted in LaSalle Bank Nat. Assoc. v. Citicorp Real Estate Inc., 2003 WL 1461483, at *3 (S.D.N.Y. Mar. 21, 2003). Further, a negligence claim cannot be sustained against a contracting party if it "do[es] no more than assert violations of a duty which is identical to and indivisible from the contract obligations which have allegedly been breached." Metro. W. Asset Mgmt., LLC v. Magnus Funding, Ltd., 2004 WL 1444868, at *9 (S.D.N.Y.

June 25, 2004) (quoting Luxonomy Car, Inc. v. Citibank, N.A., 65 A.D.2d 549, 408 N.Y.S.2d 951, 954 (App. Div. 1978)).

Stampede alleges in the Amended Complaint that 1SaleADay breached its duty to confirm that the trucker to whom it delivered the goods was actually the carrier authorized by Stampede. Stampede contends that this duty arises from the degree of care that a reasonably prudent person would use upon tender of $220,000 worth of electronic equipment to a trucker for shipment from California to Illinois—a duty entirely independent of the contractual obligations in the Purchase Invoice.

However, as discussed above, it is undisputed that Stampede was the party to the transaction charged with arranging for an authorized carrier to pick up the goods at the manufacturer's warehouse and transport them to the customer. It is also undisputed that 1SaleADay delivered conforming goods to the carrier, and that the loss of goods sued upon occurred after that delivery. As discussed above, since 1SaleADay had already fulfilled its obligations under the shipment contract at the time the goods were lost, and Stampede had assumed the risk of loss, there can be no set of facts pleaded that would allow the Court to draw the reasonable inference that 1 SaleADay breached a duty that arose "from circumstances extraneous to, and not constituting elements of," the obligations of the contract itself. *Clark-Fitzpatrick*, 70 N.Y.2d at 389, 521 N.Y.S.2d 653, 516 N.E.2d 190. "Merely charging a breach of a 'duty of due care,' employing language familiar to tort law, does not, without more, transform a simple breach of contract into a tort claim." Id. at 390, 521 N.Y.S.2d 653, 516 N.E.2d 190.

Accordingly, the Court finds that plaintiff has failed to allege facts sufficient to support a facially plausible negligence claim against defendant 1SaleADay.

UNJUST ENRICHMENT/MONEY HAD AND RECEIVED

Likewise, Stampede has failed to state a claim upon which relief can be granted against 1SaleADay based upon quasi-contractual theories of unjust enrichment or money had and received. See Goldman v. Metropolitan Life Ins. Co., 5 N.Y.3d 561, 587, 807 N.Y.S.2d 583, 841 N.E.2d 742 (2005) ("The theory of unjust enrichment lies as a quasi-contract claim. It is an obligation the law creates in the absence of any agreement."); Hoyle v. Dimond, 612 F. Supp. 2d 225, 231 (W.D.N.Y. 2009) (cause of action for money had and received sounds in quasi-contract; citing Rocks & Jeans, Inc. v. Lakeview Auto Sales & Serv., Inc., 184 A.D.2d 502, 584 N.Y.S.2d 169, 170 (App. Div. 1992). As explained by the New York Court of Appeals:

> The existence of a valid and enforceable written contract governing a particular subject matter ordinarily precludes recovery in quasi contract for events arising out of the same subject matter. A "quasi contract" only applies in the absence of an express agreement, and is not really a contract at all, but rather a legal obligation imposed in order to prevent a party's unjust enrichment. *Clark-Fitzpatrick*, 70 N.Y.2d at 388, 521 N.Y.S.2d 653, 516 N.E.2d 190 (citations omitted).

As discussed above, it is not disputed that the subject matter of the transaction at issue in this case, and the essential terms and conditions of the relationship between the parties, was defined by a valid and enforceable written contract, precluding recovery in quasi-contract for events arising out of the transaction. Accordingly, the Court finds that plaintiff has failed to plead facts sufficient to sustain a facially plausible claim for relief against 1SaleADay based upon quasi-contractual theories of unjust enrichment or money had and received.

CONCLUSION

For the foregoing reasons, it is recommended that defendant 1SaleADay's motion to dismiss be GRANTED.

Both the destination contract and the shipment contract contain some additional requirements for the seller that are incorporated by reference to other provisions in Article 2. In a destination contract, the Code says that the seller must "tender" the goods to the buyer at the stated destination. The requirements of "tender," in turn, are set out in §2-503. Most significantly, tender requires that the seller (1) put and hold the goods at the buyer's disposition for the period necessary for the buyer to take possession, (2) give the buyer notice of tender, and (3) give the buyer any documents that are needed for the buyer to take delivery.

In a shipment contract, the seller must "deliver" the goods to the carrier in order for risk of loss to pass to the buyer. The specific requirements that the seller must meet in order to shift risk to the buyer are set out in §2-504. These requirements are that the seller must (1) put the goods in possession of the carrier, (2) make a reasonable contract for their transportation, (3) deliver any document necessary to enable the buyer to take delivery, and (4) promptly notify the buyer of shipment.

What counts as a "reasonable contract" for the goods' transportation under §2-504(a) is not always clear, as the following case demonstrates.

Cook Specialty Co. v. Schrlock

772 F. Supp. 1532 (E.D. Pa. 1991)

WALDMAN, J.

Defendant Machinery Systems, Inc. ("MSI") contracted to sell plaintiff a machine known as a Dries & Krump Hydraulic Press Brake. When the machine was lost in transit, plaintiff sued defendants to recover for the loss. Presently before the court is plaintiff's Motion for Summary Judgment and defendant MSI's Cross-Motion for Summary Judgment. . . .

Plaintiff entered into a sales contract with defendant MSI for the purchase of a Dries & Krump Press Brake in August of 1989 for $28,000. The terms of the contract were F.O.B. MSI's warehouse in Schaumburg, Illinois. Defendant R.T.L., also known as Randy's Truck Lines, ("the carrier") was used to deliver the press brake from the defendant's warehouse to the plaintiff in Pennsylvania. MSI obtained a certificate of insurance from the carrier with a face amount of $100,000 and showing a $2,500 deductible.

On October 20, 1989, the carrier took possession of the press brake at MSI's warehouse. While still in transit, the press brake fell from the carrier's truck. The carrier was cited by the Illinois State Police for not properly securing the load. Plaintiff has recovered damages of $5,000 from the carrier's insurer, the applicable policy limit for this particular incident. The machine was worth $28,000. . . .

The term "F.O.B., place of shipment," means that "the seller must at that place ship the goods in the manner provided in this Article (section 2-504) and bear the expense and risk of putting them into the possession of the carrier." [UCC §2-319]. Thus, MSI bore the expense and risk of putting the machine into the carrier's possession for delivery. At the time the carrier takes possession, the risk of loss shifts to the buyer. The UCC provides:

> Where the contract requires or authorizes the seller to ship the goods by carrier
> > (a) if it does not require him to deliver them at a particular destination, the
> risk of loss passes to the buyer when the goods are duly delivered to the carrier. . . .

[UCC §2-509.]

Goods are not "duly delivered" under §2-509, however, unless a contract is entered which satisfies the provisions of Section 2-504. [See UCC §2-509, Official Comment 2.] Section 2-504, entitled "Shipment by Seller" provides that:

> Where the seller is required or authorized to send the goods to the buyer and the contract does not require him to deliver them at a particular destination, then unless otherwise agreed he must
> > (a) put the goods in the possession of such a carrier and make such a contract for their transportation as may be reasonable having regard to the nature of the goods and other circumstances of the case.

[UCC §2-504.]

Plaintiff argues that the contract MSI made for the delivery of the press brake was not reasonable because defendant failed to ensure that the carrier had sufficient insurance coverage to compensate plaintiff for a loss in transit. Plaintiff thus argues that the press brake was never duly delivered to a carrier within the meaning of section 2-509 and accordingly the risk of loss never passed to plaintiff. . . .

The dearth of support for plaintiff's position is instructive. A leading UCC authority has remarked: "Under this subsection [§2-504], what constitutes an 'unreasonable' contract of transportation? Egregious cases do arise." See J. White and R. Summers, Uniform Commercial Code §5-2 (1988). The only such "egregious case" identified by White and Summers is [one in which] "the package was underinsured, misaddressed, shipped by fourth class mail, and bore a 'theft-tempting' inscription." White and Summers, supra, at §5-2.

The actions taken by the defendant in [that case] were utterly reckless. Moreover, unlike the defendant in that case, MSI did not undertake the responsibility to insure the shipment, and did not ship the press brake at a lower cost than the plaintiff expressly authorized it to pay.

Plaintiff also relies on Miller v. Harvey, 221 N.Y. 57, 116 N.E. 781 (1917). This pre-Code case is inapplicable. In *Miller*, by failing to declare the actual value of goods shipped on a form provided for that purpose, the seller effectively contracted away the buyer's rights against the carrier. Official Comment 3 to section 2-504 states:

> [i]t is an improper contract under paragraph (a) for the seller to agree with the carrier to a limited valuation below the true value and thus cut off the buyer's opportunity to recover from the carrier in the event of loss, when the risk of shipment is placed on the buyer.

Thus, a contract is improper if the seller agrees to an inadequate valuation of the shipment and thereby extinguishes the buyer's opportunity to recover from the carrier. That is quite different from a seller's failure to ensure that a carrier has sufficient insurance to cover a particular potential loss, in which case the carrier is still liable to the buyer.

Plaintiff's focus on a single sentence of Official Comment 3 ignores the explicit language of the statute which defines reasonable in the context of "having regard to the nature of the goods," [UCC §2-504], and the portion of the Comment which states:

> Whether or not the shipment is at the buyer's expense the seller must see to any arrangements, reasonable in the circumstances, such as refrigeration, watering of live stock, protection against cold . . . and the like. . . .

[UCC §2-504], Official Comment 3.

The clear implication is that the reasonableness of a shipper's conduct under §2-504 is determined with regard to the mode of transport selected. It would be unreasonable, for example, to send perishables without refrigeration. No inference fairly can be drawn from the section that a seller has an obligation to investigate the amount and terms of insurance held by the carrier.

The court finds as a matter of law that MSI's conduct was not unreasonable under section 2-504. MSI obtained from the carrier a certificate of insurance and did nothing to impair plaintiff's right to recover for any loss from the carrier. Accidents occur in transit. For this reason, the UCC has specifically established mercantile symbols which delineate the risk of loss in a transaction so that the appropriate party might obtain insurance on the shipment. The contract in this case was "F.O.B." seller's warehouse. Plaintiff clearly bears the risk of loss in transit.

There are no material facts in dispute and MSI is entitled to judgment as a matter of law.

There are other ambiguities in §2-504 besides what does or does not constitute a "reasonable" contract for shipment by the seller. Much of the additional uncertainty about the operation of §2-504 stems from the last sentence in the section: "Failure to notify the buyer under paragraph (c) or to make a proper contract under paragraph (a) is a ground for rejection only if material delay or loss ensues."

This sentence raises the question of whether the requirements for a proper shipment by seller under §2-504 are truly prerequisites for passing risk of loss to the buyer or whether instead they are merely requirements on which buyer can rely to recover damages that are directly related to seller's inability to fulfill them. For example, suppose that buyer purchased 12 dozen crystal vases from seller, "FOB Seller's Factory." Without consideration for the fragile nature of the goods, seller arranges delivery with a fly-by-night carrier that has a reputation for damaging goods in transit. Seller promptly notifies buyer that the vases are on their way.

Suppose that halfway to the buyer's destination, and with no damage yet to the vases, the delivery truck gets hit by lightning and all of the vases are destroyed. Can seller argue that buyer has risk of loss here since seller delivered the goods to the carrier and promptly notified buyer? Can buyer argue that seller still has the risk since seller did not make a reasonable contract of transportation for the vases, as seller is required to do under §2-504(a)? Can seller counter that even if it failed to fulfill that obligation, its failure to do so was not the cause of the loss and, therefore, under the "no harm, no foul" concept of the last sentence in §2-504, buyer cannot complain?

These questions have not met with clear answers in the case law. In one oft-cited case, the North Carolina Court of Appeals held that even though the parties in that case agreed to a shipment contract, risk of loss for the crates of wine being sold did not pass to the buyer after the carrier received them because the seller failed to give the buyer prompt notice of shipment. Rheinberg-Kellerei GmbH v. Vineyard Wine Co., 281 S.E.2d 425 (N.C. App. 1981). The court reasoned that, had the buyer received prompt notice of shipment, the buyer might have insured the wine and therefore avoided the loss that occurred when the wine was lost at sea by the carrier. In this sense, the court said, the seller's failure to notify the buyer caused the buyer's loss to "ensue," as is required by the last sentence of §2-504.

Up to this point, we have been looking at cases in which neither the buyer nor the seller is in breach of its substantive obligations under the sales contract, as opposed to its more procedural obligations related to delivery. In a case where either the buyer or the seller is in breach of the underlying contract, the various delivery codes created by Article 2 give way to a special set of rules governing risk of loss.

Section 2-510 covers the effect of a breach by either the buyer or seller on when the risk of loss passes from the seller to the buyer. Section 2-510(1) provides that "[w]here a tender or delivery of goods so fails to conform to the contract as to give a right of rejection the risk of their loss remains on the seller until cure or acceptance." Thus, for example, suppose the seller agrees to ship the buyer two dozen model 110Z stair climber aerobic machines, "FOB Seller's Factory." Imagine that the seller inadvertently sends two dozen model 104X stair climbers. If that delivery is destroyed in transit through no fault of either party, the seller keeps the risk of loss since the goods delivered "so failed to conform to the contract as to give a right of rejection."

Section 2-510(2) provides that when a buyer rightfully revokes acceptance, the buyer may treat the risk of loss as if it had rested on the seller from the beginning, but only to the extent of a deficiency in the buyer's insurance coverage. Therefore, suppose in the stair climber case above, with the same term of FOB shipment, the buyer received the machines, accepted them without discovery of the non-conformity (which was difficult to discern), and then revoked its acceptance by notifying the seller. While waiting for the seller to pick up the stair climbers, the machines were destroyed through no fault of the buyer. Under §2-510(2), if the buyer had insurance that covered the destroyed machines, the insurer would pay for the loss. If the buyer did not have insurance, then risk of loss would be with the seller even though this was a shipment contract that would normally put the risk with the buyer as soon as the seller delivered the goods to the carrier.

Section 510(3) covers the effect of breach by the buyer on risk of loss. This section says that, where the buyer repudiates as to conforming goods already identified to the contract, risk of loss will be on the buyer for a commercially reasonable time to the extent of any deficiency in the seller's insurance coverage. Thus, suppose our stair climber seller (with the same FOB shipment term) had identified to the contract two dozen machines that conformed to its contract with buyer. Imagine buyer called seller before the machines left seller's warehouse and told seller that the deal was off. If shortly after that call the stair climbers were destroyed in a fire at seller's warehouse, buyer would have the risk of loss if seller's insurance was deficient. This is true even though seller never delivered the goods to the third-party carrier, which would normally be required for seller to pass the risk to buyer, even in a shipment contract such as this one.

Clearly, there are going to be problems of proof in a system where risk of loss can sometimes hinge on the condition of goods while they are still inside of a box. For example, if goods in a shipment contract are destroyed while in transit, how will the buyer know, as it must under §2-510(1), whether the goods were so non-conforming when they reached the carrier "as to give a right of rejection"?

One possible answer is that many carriers will take their own inventory of the goods when they receive them from the seller. The nature of such an inventory is limited, of course, if the goods are sealed inside of a box, but at least a carrier can record things like color, style, or quantity that are indicated on the packaging. Any of these pieces of information might be sufficient for the buyer to claim that the goods did not conform to the contract while seller still had the risk, and therefore that risk of loss never passed to the buyer.

Also on the subject of proof, most sellers require the carrier to have the buyer sign an invoice upon receiving the goods that verifies that the goods in fact were delivered. The seller will then receive a copy of this invoice from the carrier in case the buyer later tries to claim that it never received the goods.

This fairly simple system of having the buyer sign an invoice upon receipt prevents fraud in most cases, but not all. Consider this tale from the general counsel of a computer hardware distributor: "We had a delivery scam recently where somebody called us with a real customer number but with what turned out to be a fictitious address. When the goods proved to be undeliverable because of the fictitious address, our carrier brought the goods back to the carrier's own trucking depot. Then the thief called the depot and said he would pick the goods up at the depot's will-call. After the carrier let the goods go to the thief and we learned about it, we pointed out to them that their contractual responsibility was to call us first whenever any goods proved to be undeliverable. They weren't too happy to hear that, but this was only a $50,000 loss for a carrier that we give $3 million worth of business every year."

Up to this point, our discussion about risk of loss has been limited to the common situation in which the contract requires or authorizes the seller to ship the goods by carrier. Risk-of-loss issues can arise in other situations as well, and Article 2 has special rules for those.

In a case where the seller is using a third-party bailee to hold the goods for the buyer, such as a meat seller that stores its goods in a refrigerated third-party warehouse, risk of loss passes to the buyer at the first of three events: (1) when the buyer receives a negotiable document of title covering the goods, (2) when the bailee acknowledges to the buyer the buyer's right to possession of the goods, or (3) when the buyer receives a non-negotiable document of title or other written direction to the bailee to deliver. UCC §2-509(2).

The default rule on risk of loss for cases involving neither a third-party carrier nor a bailee (such as a case where the buyer is coming to the seller's place to pick up the goods) is that risk passes to the buyer on receipt of the goods if the seller is a merchant. If the seller is not a merchant in these non-carrier/non-bailee cases, then risk passes to the buyer when the seller tenders delivery of goods to the buyer. §2-509(3).

Remember again that all of these risk-of-loss rules, just like the rules for risk of loss in cases involving a carrier, are subject to three important qualifications: (1) if the parties specifically agree when risk of loss will pass, that agreement governs; (2) if one of the parties causes the loss in question, the negligent party assumes that loss; and (3) if one of the parties is in breach of its obligations under the contract, then the special rules of §2-510 will determine when risk of loss passes from seller to buyer.

Problem Set 20

20.1.   Lou from Lou's Used Cars for Less (Problem 2.1) stops by your office with a problem that he says he has never encountered before. Two weeks ago, a new customer came in and agreed to buy a used Chevy Camaro that Lou had on his lot. The next day, the customer sent Lou a cashier's check for the full amount of the price and told Lou that he would be in during the next couple of days to pick up his car. Lou received the customer's check and cashed it. A week later, when the customer still had not picked up the car, Lou unsuccessfully tried to phone the customer several times. The car is still sitting on Lou's lot "taking up space," as Lou put it. Lou has a couple of questions for you. First, would Lou be responsible if the car were damaged or stolen? Second, what can Lou do in this case and in the future to ensure that customers pick up their cars after they purchase them? UCC §§2-509(3), 2-509(4), 2-103(1)(c), 2-509(2)(b), 2-510(3); Official Comment 3 to §2-509.

20.2.   Before Lou leaves your office, he has one more "problem customer" that he needs to discuss. It turns out that the customer, Karen Frederick, is a law student ("or so she tells me," says Lou). Karen had purchased a used Ford Taurus from Lou and brought the car back a couple of weeks later because of a major problem with the car's brake system. Karen (who still had not purchased insurance on the car) had told Lou upon returning the car, "If you don't fix the brake problem in two days, I will revoke my acceptance of the car and demand my money back." The next night, before the brakes were fixed, vandals entered Lou's lot after it closed (through no fault of Lou's) and caused $3,000 worth of body damage to the car. Lou tells you he has fixed the brakes but needs to know whether he is also responsible for fixing the extensive body damage. (1) What do you advise? (2) Would your answer be different if Karen had said, "I hereby revoke until you get the brake system working properly"? UCC §§2-510(1), 2-510(2), 2-608(2); Comment 3 to §2-510.

20.3.   Arlene Ledger, president of Heavy Metal, Inc. (from Problem 3.2), is having another run-in with Gold's Gym. Gold's had signed a contract for an order of 10 tons of assorted free weights, all painted gold, for one of its franchisees that is expanding the size of its operations. The contract said that the order would be sent "FOB Seller's Factory." Arlene had Heavy Metal's usual carrier, Dependo, come and pick up the weights, and Arlene had notified Gold's Gym of the shipment. The first problem was that Arlene neglected to tell her shipping department that these were to be gold-painted weights rather than the standard black-painted weights. Thus, the weights that were given to the carrier were black instead of gold, and the shipping boxes indicated that fact. The second problem was that the two trucks carrying the shipment were stolen during transit while they were parked overnight. The third problem was that the carrier's insurance, unknown to Arlene, had lapsed the previous month for failure to pay the premium. (1) What Arlene would like to know is who, between Heavy Metal and Gold's Gym, has the burden of pursuing the carrier for the loss? (2) Would your answer change if the sales contract had included a conspicuous exclusive remedy clause that limited Gold's Gym's remedies to repair or replacement of defective weights? UCC §§2-319(1)(a), 2-509(1)(a), 2-509(4), 2-510(1), 2-601, 2-719.

20.4.   Same facts as Problem 20.3, except now suppose the weights Heavy Metal sent were conforming, but Arlene had neglected to give notice to Gold's

Gym of the shipment when it was made. Gold's Gym was therefore not able to insure the goods in transit. (1) Which party, between Heavy Metal and Gold's Gym, would bear the risk of loss in this situation? (2) Would your answer change if Gold's Gym had happened to learn from third-party sources that the shipment was made, but still never bothered to insure the goods in transit? UCC §§2-319(1)(a), 2-509(1)(a), 2-504; Official Comment 2 to §2-509, Official Comment 6 to §2-504.

20.5. a. Frank Ziegler decided to sell his used rider lawn mower through the classified ads. Frank was asking $3,000 for the mower, which he had purchased ten years ago. Not long after the ad appeared, Frank had a potential buyer, Ed Kinman, out to see the mower. Ed told Frank he would buy it for $3,000, and Frank had Ed sign a handwritten contract that Frank had prepared. The contract said nothing about risk of loss. Ed promised Frank that he would be back with his pickup truck and a cashier's check for $3,000 "in the next couple of days." The next day, Frank discovered that the rider mower had been stolen from his garage. Who had risk of loss as to the stolen mower? UCC §§2-509(3), 2-503(1).

b. Same facts as part (a), except that a week passed with no word from Ed, and then the mower was stolen from Frank's garage. Who had risk of loss as to the stolen mower? UCC §§2-509(3), 2-503(1), 2-510(3).

c. Same facts as part (a), except that six months passed with no word from Ed, and then the mower was stolen from Frank's garage. Who had risk of loss as to the stolen mower? UCC §§2-509(3), 2-503(1), 2-510(3), 2-709(1)(a), 1-103.

d. Same facts as part (a), except that Ed paid Frank with a $3,000 cashier's check the first night that he looked at the mower, promising to come back with his pickup truck "in the next couple of days." When the rider mower was stolen the next day, who had risk of loss? UCC §§2-509(3), 2-503(1).

e. Same facts as part (d), except that after paying the $3,000 check, Ed never picked up the mower. Then, six months later, the rider mower was stolen from Frank's garage. Who had risk of loss as to the mower? UCC §§2-509(3), 2-503(1), 2-510(3), 2-709(1)(a), 1-103.

20.6. a. Grandma's Superstore in Boise, Idaho, decided to start carrying frozen steaks to complement its wide inventory of non-food items. Grandma's made a contract with Enos's Slaughterhouse in Missoula, Montana, in which Enos's was to ship 500 8-ounce filet mignons to Grandma's, "FOB Missoula." Because it was cheaper, Enos's had the goods shipped by a non-refrigerated truck from Dependo Carriers, Inc. Dependo, as its name suggests, had an excellent reputation for reliability. The steaks were fine when they were loaded on the truck for the 400-mile journey to Boise, but 10 miles into the journey the truck was run off the road and into a lake, where the steaks were destroyed. Enos's had given Grandma's timely and proper notice of shipment. Who had risk of loss as to the steaks? UCC §§2-319(1), 2-509(1), 2-504; Official Comment 2 to §§2-509, 2-510(1).

b. Same facts as part (a), except that Enos's did use a refrigerated truck and there was no accident on the way. However, 40 of the steaks were ruined during the trip when some rodents hopped aboard the truck midway through the journey. May Grandma's reject some or all of the steaks when they arrive? UCC §§2-319(1), 2-509(1), 2-601.

c. Same facts as part (a), except that Enos's did use a refrigerated truck and there was no accident on the way. However, 30 of the steaks were already bad when Enos's had them loaded on the truck, and another 40 were ruined during the trip when some rodents hopped aboard the truck midway through the journey. May Grandma's reject some or all of the steaks when they arrive? UCC §§2-319(1), 2-509(1), 2-601, 2-510(1).

d. Same facts as part (a), except that Enos's did use a refrigerated truck and there was no accident on the way. After Enos's had selected the steaks and was about to load them on the truck, Grandma's called and said that it was canceling its order. Enos's told Grandma's that Enos's was not waiving its right to sue for the breach. A week later, the 500 steaks that had been earmarked for Grandma's were destroyed in a fire at Enos's Slaughterhouse through no fault of Enos's. Enos's had insurance, but it came with a $1,000 deductible. Enos's lost a total of $15,000 worth of meat in the fire, including the 500 steaks that had been ordered by Grandma's, for which Grandma's had agreed to pay $6,000. Who had risk of loss as to the 500 steaks that had been earmarked for Grandma's? UCC §§2-510(3), 2-709(1).

e. Same facts as part (d), except Enos's insurance policy included the following clause: "Insurance Company reserves the right to recover any amounts paid under this policy from parties that would have had the risk of loss as to the destroyed goods, but for the existence of this policy." How would this clause affect Grandma's liability for the destroyed steaks? UCC §2-510(3), Official Comment 3 to §2-510.

Assignment 21: Risk of Loss with Leases, International Sales, and Real Estate

A. Risk of Loss with Leases

The passage of risk of loss with leases more or less tracks the system for passage of risk with sales of goods. There is, however, one important distinction. Article 2A sets out a default rule stating that risk of loss never passes from the lessor to the lessee except in the case of finance leases. UCC §2A-219(1). This is in contrast to the default rule on passage of risk in sales, where (at least in the absence of breach) risk eventually does pass to the buyer at some point, whether the seller is itself delivering the goods, a third party is delivering the goods, or the buyer is picking up the goods. Even with finance leases, however, risk of loss will not pass until the finance lessee has accepted the leased goods.

In re Jawad
2006 WL 6810985 (9th Cir. BAP 2006)

RUSSELL, J.

A lender entered into a finance lease with the debtor, which required the lender to make two payments to the equipment seller ($17,000.00 upon execution of the lease and $19,805.00 upon completion and delivery of the purchased equipment). As collateral for the transaction, the debtor pledged certain real property. The equipment was never delivered to the debtor, and the transaction was cancelled. The lender never paid the second installment of $19,805.00. Although it has now been repaid $23,744.65 by the debtor on its advance of $17,000, the lender sought to foreclose on the debtor's real property, contending that the debtor still owed the remainder of the lease payment obligations.

To avoid foreclosure, the debtor filed for chapter 13 relief and later objected to the lender's claim, and also sought avoidance of the lender's lien. Holding that there was a failure of consideration under the lease, that the lender had been fully compensated for its partial performance, and that the lender's conduct constituted bad faith, the bankruptcy court disallowed the claim and avoided the lien. We AFFIRM.

FACTS

In July 2000, Samey Jawad ("Debtor") (doing business as International Auto) agreed to acquire an air-conditioned modular office building (the "Equipment") from Francine Escobar, Abigail Escobar, Rudy Escobar and Thermal Dynamics (the "Vendors"). To finance this acquisition, Debtor entered into a transaction with appellant Michael R. White and Associates ("Lender") whereby Lender would purchase the Equipment and in turn lease it to Debtor.

On July 31, 2000, Debtor and Lender executed a business equipment lease (the "Lease") and a pre-delivery addendum to the Lease (the "Addendum"). The Lease and Addendum required Lender to advance $36,805.00 to purchase the Equipment from Vendors. In exchange, Debtor would pay $1,315.78 monthly to Lender for sixty months (for a total payment of $78,946.80). To secure payment of the Lease, Debtor executed a deed of trust in favor of Lender on certain real property located in Whittier, California (the "Property").

Pursuant to the Addendum, Lender disbursed $17,000 to Vendors upon execution of the Lease. Lender was to disburse the remaining $19,805.00 upon completion and delivery of the Equipment. It did not do so. This is because, as Lender acknowledges, the Equipment was never delivered or installed.

The Lease, a pre-printed form provided by Lender, states that the risk of loss was assumed by Debtor "[u]pon delivery of the Equipment to Lessee [Debtor]." Lease at ¶15. Thus, prior to delivery, the risk of loss was borne by Lender. Delivery never occurred.

The Addendum contained language contradictory to the Lease. It provided that Debtor was deemed to have accepted the Equipment upon execution of the Lease and not upon completion or delivery of the Equipment. The Addendum states in Paragraph 3 that the Lease "shall become effective upon execution and lease payments shall commence . . . notwithstanding that the [E]quipment may not have been completed, delivered, installed or tested by that date" and the Equipment is accepted "AS IS" and "WHERE IS" upon the start date [i.e., the effective or execution date] even without delivery or inspection. The Addendum also contains a waiver of warranties provision in Paragraph 4, which provides that Lessor is not responsible "for construction or completion of the Equipment" or for any breaches by Vendor in providing the Equipment.

When Vendors failed to deliver the Equipment, Debtor notified Lender promptly and Lender did not fund the remaining $19,805.00. Debtor was able to obtain $5,200 from the Vendors, which he then remitted to Lender in two checks (totaling $5,263.14) in November and December 2000. This amount was applied against Lender's first and only advance of $17,000.00.

Nevertheless, in September 2001, deeming Debtor to be in default, Lender prepared a Notice of Default and Election to Sell under Deed of Trust. Lender maintained that Debtor was in default in the amount of $11,610.58 as of September 7, 2001. Debtor then filed his initial Chapter 13 petition in 2002 and scheduled Lender as holding a disputed, secured claim in the amount of $36,505.00. Lender filed a proof of claim for $32,845.52.

Debtor obtained confirmation of a plan proposing to make monthly payments to Lender in the amount of $1,099.89 on a disputed principal amount of $32,843.52 with a 7% interest rate. Debtor explicitly reserved the "right to litigate the legitimacy" of the claim. Lender admits that it received $18,481.51 from Debtor through the Chapter 13 plan. Therefore, Lender has received at least $23,744.65 from Debtor.

Debtor's initial Chapter 13 case was dismissed because of his failure to complete plan payments. On October 7, 2004, Lender again noticed a Trustee's Sale, indicating that the amount due from Debtor was $27,011.24. In response, Debtor filed his second Chapter 13 case on November 3, 2004.

On December 20, 2004, Lender filed a proof of claim indicating that Debtor owed it $25,222.30 as of the petition date. According to the "Lease Payment Record" appended to the proof of claim, the original loan amount was $35,014.96. Even though the Lease does not provide an interest rate, Lender added a 7% interest rate to the outstanding balance, explaining that it used such rate because that was what was proposed in Debtor's initial Chapter 13 plan. Lender argues that the amount due in its proof of claim reflected a credit for the $19,805.00 which it did not advance (plus charges and interest associated with that amount), but then added approximately $15,000.00 in attorneys' fees to its claim. If Lender's proof of claim were allowed, Lender would receive $48,966.95 for its advance of $17,000.00.

Debtor objected to Lender's proof of claim and requested that the bankruptcy court avoid the lien securing the debt. Debtor argued that (1) Lender had assumed contrary positions as to the amount owed, (2) that enforcement of the lease and allowance of the claim would be unconscionable, and (3) that there was a failure of consideration by Lender. In response, Lender argued that the risk of loss for non-delivery of the Equipment was on Debtor and that the court should enforce all of the terms of the Lease.

At the claim objection hearing, the court ruled that Lender's attempted enforcement of the balance of payments due under the Lease was "unconscionable." It reasoned: "I've read all documents very carefully and I think under these circumstances that it would be unconscionable on [sic] the bankruptcy context to allow that claim to survive anymore. I think it's been paid considerably more than ever it was owed at a reasonable rate of interest."

The bankruptcy court thereafter signed an order disallowing the claim and avoiding Lender's lien. The order recites that Debtor "never received adequate consideration under the [Lease]," that Debtor "has paid much more to [Lender] than he was ever obligated to pay," and Lender's claim "was filed in bad faith and is without merit." This appeal followed.

ISSUE

Did the bankruptcy court err in disallowing Lender's claim and avoiding its lien?

DISCUSSION

Pursuant to section 502(b)(1), a bankruptcy court may disallow a claim to the extent it is "unenforceable against the debtor and property of the debtor, under any agreement or applicable law for a reason other than because such claim is contingent or unmatured. . . ." 11 U.S.C. §502(b)(1). To the extent a lien secures a claim that has been disallowed pursuant to section 502(b)(1), that lien is void. 11 U.S.C. §506(d)(1).

In deciding whether the court erred in disallowing Lender's claim and voiding its lien, we apply state law. Cossu v. Jefferson Pilot Securities Corp. (In re Cossu), 410 F.3d 591, 595 (9th Cir. 2005) ("The validity of a creditor's claim is determined by the rules of state law. . . ."); see also In re Jones, 72 B.R. 25, 26 (Bankr. C.D. Cal. 1987) ("State substantive law is applied to determine the existence and validity of a claim, unless the Bankruptcy Code provides otherwise.").

A.   THE RISK OF LOSS WAS IMPROPERLY SHIFTED TO DEBTOR

The Lease is a finance lease under the Uniform Commercial Code, because the lessor (here, Lender) is strictly acting as a financing entity (as opposed to the vendor or supplier of goods). Therefore, the lessee (here, Debtor) generally must look to a third party (the vendor) if the goods are defective or otherwise unsuitable for intended use. The lessee (as opposed to the lessor) bears the risk of loss once the goods are tendered for delivery. 2 White & Summers, Uniform Commercial Code §13-3 (4th ed.) (updated by 2005 Pocket Part).

The Uniform Commercial Code ("UCC") accords very few protections to a lessee under a finance lease. Perhaps recognizing the harms inherent in a commercial setting that permits a party to have all of the protections of a lessor (ownership of leased property as opposed to a security interest) without any attendant burdens (such as honoring warranties and ensuring performance of the leased goods), the UCC provides that finance lease lessors retain the risk of loss until delivery. Unlike in ordinary leases where the lessor retains the risk of loss throughout the lease term, risk of loss switches to the finance lease lessee upon acceptance of the leased goods. Under the UCC, acceptance occurs only after the lessee has had a reasonable opportunity to inspect the goods.

The Lease, at Paragraph 15, conformed to the UCC in that the risk of loss was on the Lender prior to delivery. If the Lease controls, the risk of loss did not pass to Debtor because the Equipment was never delivered. Thus, while Debtor was obligated to compensate Lender for amounts advanced to the Vendors, Debtor was not responsible to pay the balance due under the finance lease. This is consistent with section 10219(a) and (b)(3) of the California Commercial Code.

The Addendum, however, contains terms that appear to be inconsistent with the Lease, although no provision of the Addendum directly contradicts or voids the risk of loss provision stated in Paragraph 15 of the Lease. The Addendum provides that Debtor was deemed to have accepted the Equipment upon execution of the Lease and not upon completion or delivery of the Equipment. This is contrary not only to section 10515(a) of the California Commercial Code) but also to Paragraph 15 of the Lease itself. The Addendum states in Paragraph 3 that the Lease "shall become effective upon execution and lease payments shall commence . . . notwithstanding that the [E]quipment may not have been completed, delivered, installed or tested by that date" and the Equipment is deemed to have been accepted "AS IS" and "WHERE IS" upon the start date [i.e., the effective or execution date] even without delivery or inspection. The Addendum also contains a waiver of warranties provision in Paragraph 4, which provides that Lessor is not responsible "for construction or completion of the Equipment" or for any breaches by Vendor in providing the Equipment. Notably, however, the Addendum does not specifically state that the risk of loss passed to Debtor even before acceptance of the Equipment.

The Addendum's "deemed acceptance" clause effectively negates the Lease's risk of loss provision (as well as the risk of loss as allocated by the UCC and California law). While parties are able to contract around some statutory provisions, they may not do so unreasonably.

The effect of provisions of this code may be varied by agreement, except as otherwise provided in this code and except that the obligations of good faith, diligence, reasonableness and care prescribed by this code may not be disclaimed by agreement but the parties may by agreement determine the standards by which performance of such obligations is to be measured if such standards are not manifestly unreasonable. Cal. Comm. Code §1102(3). Shifting risks in a one-sided manner is unreasonable. See A & M Produce Co. v. FMC Corp., 135 Cal. App. 3d 473, 487, 186 Cal. Rptr. 114, 122 (1982) (disclaimer of warranties in contract was an unconscionable and unenforceable shifting of risks under the Uniform Commercial Code; "a contractual term is substantively suspect if it reallocates the risks of the bargain in a objectively unreasonable or unexpected manner").

In the Addendum, the Lender negated the few protections accorded to Debtor by law and the Lease itself, thereby rendering the inconsistent and one-sided "deemed acceptance" clause unenforceable under case law interpreting the UCC. Other finance lessors who have attempted to improve their position in a manner inconsistent with the acceptance provisions of the UCC have not been successful. Most of the courts facing clauses providing that acceptance occurs upon signature without a reasonable opportunity to inspect have refused to enforce them. See, e.g., JAZ, Inc. v. Foley, 104 Hawai'i 148, 85 P.3d 1099, 1104 (2004) (applying provisions identical to California Commercial Code sections 10407 and 10515, the court held that a written acceptance clause was ineffective because there must be a tender or delivery of goods for the risk of loss to pass to the lessee in the case of a finance lease).

Lender cites one case with a contrary holding: Stewart v. United States Leasing Corp., 702 S.W.2d 288 (Tex. App. 1985). As the *Foley* court notes, *Stewart* is unpersuasive and is inconsistent with the majority line of cases:

> Other cases dealing with signing an acceptance certificate before delivery are contrary to *Stewart*. In Colonial Pacific Leasing Corp. v. J.W.C.J.R. Corp., 977 P.2d 541

(Utah Ct. App. 1999), the Utah Court of Appeals stated that taking possession of the goods, signing a form acceptance before receipt of goods, and making a lease payment are not determinative of acceptance. Id. at 545. In Moses v. Newman, 658 S.W.2d 119 (Tenn. Ct. App. 1983), the Tennessee Court of Appeals held acceptance had not occurred despite purchaser's possession of the goods because affording a purchaser a reasonable opportunity to inspect does not imply possession. Id. at 121-22. In Tri-Continental Leasing Corp. v. Law Office of Richard W. Burns, 710 S.W.2d 604 (Tex. Ct. App. 1985), the Texas Court of Appeals held that there was no acceptance because the buyer must have a reasonable opportunity to inspect the goods. Id. at 608. In Information Leasing Corp. v. GDR Investments, Inc., 152 Ohio App. 3d 260, 787 N.E.2d 652 (2003), the Ohio Court of Appeals held that merely signing an acceptance certificate is not acceptance because the requirement of a reasonable time for inspection cannot be circumvented. Id. at 655-56. Under these cases, signing an acceptance certificate before delivery does not mean a lessee has accepted the goods. The lessee must have a reasonable time for inspection, which requires that lessee have actual possession of the goods.

Foley, 85 P.3d at 1104 (emphasis added). We also decline to hold that mere execution of an "acceptance" deprives the lessee of the right to reject the goods even before their receipt.

Under this case law, the bankruptcy court's decision not to allow Lender's claim was correct. The Addendum's efforts to impose a "deemed acceptance" (and thus a "deemed" disavowal of the express risk of loss provision of the Lease and of California law) upon Debtor is unenforceable. Therefore, the risk of loss provision (Paragraph 15) of the Lease and sections 10219, 10407 and 10515 of the California Commercial Code control and the risk of loss never passed to Debtor since the Equipment was never delivered or accepted. Debtor therefore was not required to pay for goods that he never received, and for which Lender also never paid. . . .

MONTALI, J., dissenting:

I believe the majority is refusing to honor the sanctity of contract and is rewriting the Lease to relieve Debtor of a bad bargain. That is not the proper role for a trial or appellate court. The majority treats the Lease as sacred and the Addendum as an inconsistent undermining of the Lease. The Lease and Addendum were executed at the same time and must be considered together as the agreement of the parties. The documents were executed when Debtor needed the Equipment and Lender was willing to advance the costs, with an appropriate shifting of the risks. The majority should not reverse that negotiated balance of rights and obligations.

The Lease is a finance lease under Article 2A of the Uniform Commercial Code (adopted at Cal. Comm. Code §10101 et seq.). A finance lease involves three parties: the lessor (Lender), the lessee (Debtor) and the supplier (Vendors). See Cal. Comm. Code §10103. The lessor retains title to the leased property and provides the financing. Because the lessor is not the supplier, it is not responsible for the fitness or merchantability of the property. See Cal. Comm. Code §10209. The lessee's obligation to pay rent under a finance lease is "irrevocable and independent upon the lessee's acceptance of the goods." Cal. Comm. Code §10515(1)(a). This is known as the "hell or high water" clause of the Uniform Commercial Code:

> The lessee under the statute must pay the finance lessor—come hell or high water. After all, the parties have actually entered into a financing transaction in which the lessor is really lending money and dealing largely in paper rather than goods. Put another way, the lessor as lender has no interest in how the lessee as debtor chooses to spend the money for goods. If the lessee should order [property] which is unsuitable or defective, this is not the lessor's problem. The lessor's responsibility is merely to provide the money, not to instruct the lessee like a wayward child concerning a suitable purchase. . . . This deprives the finance lessee of the argument that any defects in the goods as supplied by the supplier or manufacturer are somehow attributable to the lessor and in some way grant the lessee a right of setoff or of cancellation as against the finance lessor.

James J. White and Robert S. Summers, Uniform Commercial Code §13-3 (4th ed.) (updated by 2005 Pocket Part).

Here, Debtor signed an Addendum agreeing that acceptance occurred upon execution and prior to delivery. Therefore, the "hell or high water" provisions of the Lease and the Uniform Commercial Code came into play and Debtor is responsible for payments due under the Lease, even absent delivery. The majority seeks to relieve Debtor of his agreement by holding that the "deemed acceptance" clause of the Addendum is unconscionable or somehow otherwise unenforceable. This is not supported by the record. . . .

I look at this from a practical point of view: Debtor, who selected the Vendors, wants the Equipment and does not have the money. Lender, who is providing the money for Debtor to get the Equipment, is asked to provide the funds prior to delivery. Why would it not shift the risk? If Lender has to commit $17,000 for Debtor's benefit, Debtor should bear the risk. The economics of the deal are exactly like a third party purchase money finance, except it was styled as a lease here.

Unlike the majority, I would adopt the reasoning of the court in Stewart v. United States Leasing Corp., 702 S.W.2d 288, 290 (Tex. App. 1985), that parties who sign a "deemed acceptance" clause are bound by such clauses. *Stewart*, 702 S.W.2d at 290. The Stewart court noted that the lessee's execution of the acceptance certificate prior to actual delivery was part of the consideration for the lessor's agreement to provide financing. The same is true here; the parties agreed on the terms for the financing and Debtor must live by those terms.

I understand that the terms may seem unfair. The bankruptcy court even queried:

> Why would any sane person enter into an agreement as you say it is? You sign it. It doesn't matter if you get the stuff and even if you don't get it you'll pay for it for years rent [sic]. Why would anybody ever enter into that kind of agreement?

The answer is (1) this is a financing lease under the Uniform Commercial Code that statutorily grants lessors multiple protections and (2) Debtor did agree to accept the goods prior to delivery. Otherwise the Vendors would not have to deliver them. While it may seem unfair, it is the contract. This court should not rewrite it.

The majority also emphasizes that the "deemed acceptance" clause in the Addendum is contrary to the Lease itself. I believe that this demonstrates why it should be enforced. Hand-written or typed terms that differ from a pre-printed form govern. See Cal. Civ. Code §1651; Fid. & Deposit Co. v. Charter Oak Fire Ins. Co., 66 Cal. App. 4th 1080, 1087, 78 Cal. Rptr. 2d 429, 433 (1998) ("Where a contract is partly written or printed under the special direction of the parties, and the remainder is copied from a form prepared without reference to the particular contract in question, the parts which are original control those which are not.").

I have reviewed the transcript of the hearing and believe that the bankruptcy court started with an incorrect assumption, viz. that Debtor received nothing and, having paid Lender more than $23,000, that enough was enough. I believe the court failed to appreciate that the commercial realities are such that the parties were free to shift the risk of the vendor's breach, and Lender in fact parted with $17,000 which it was entitled to recover, either as a finance lessor or as an over-secured creditor, inasmuch as Lender held a lien on Debtor's residence. It is not "unconscionable" to do what the law permits. . . .

———————

After setting out the broad default rule of "no passage of risk to lessee in non-finance leases," the Article 2A drafters then mimic the provisions of §§2-509 and 2-510 for all those cases where "risk of loss is to pass to the lessee and the time of passage is not stated." §§2A-219, 2A-220. Thus, for example, if lessor and lessee agree to a five-year lease of a printing press, "FOB Lessor's Place of Business," then the provisions of §2A-219(2)(a) would dictate that risk would pass to the lessee at the point when the lessor delivers the goods to the carrier, just as would be the case under §2-509(1)(a) with a sale of the same goods.

B.   Risk of Loss with International Sales

The CISG has a fairly organized set of default rules to govern when risk of loss passes from seller to buyer in an international sale covered by its provisions. However, the most important pieces of information to know about passage of risk in an international sale are the standard "Incoterms," which, if included in the contract, will govern passage of the risk of loss. Recall that CISG Article 6 allows the parties to an international contract to vary the provisions of the CISG. As a result, parties can agree to use a standard shipping term to contract around the CISG's default rules for risk of loss. However, there are some cases in which the decision of whether to use an Incoterm instead of the CISG default rules is not an "either/or" proposition. As the following case demonstrates, the Incoterm included in a particular sales contract might work together with the default terms under the CISG to define exactly when and whether risk of loss has passed.

Citgo Petroleum Corp. v. Odfjell Seachem

2013 WL 2289951 (S.D. Tex. 2013)

Miller, D.J.

* * *

I.   BACKGROUND

This is a breach of contract claim stemming from a January 13, 2005, contract between YPF and Tricon Energy, Ltd. for the sale of 4,000 MT of cyclohexane. Dkt. 1. YPF sold the cyclohexane to Tricon and agreed to ship the cargo from Argentina to Houston, Texas, with a delivery window of February 15 through March 15, 2005. Id. Under the contract, YPF was required to load the cargo between February 15 and March 5, 2005. Dkt. 113, Ex. 2. Tricon sold the cyclohexane to Citgo under a sales agreement dated March 9, 2005, and agreed to ship the cargo to Freeport, Texas, with a delivery window between April 15 and 20, 2005. Dkt. 1. The agreements stated that the cargo would be shipped on board the BOW FIGHTER. See Dkt. 101, Exs. A, B. The BOW FIGHTER did not arrive in La Plata, Argentina until March 17, 2005. Dkt. 1; Dkt. 116, Ex. D. YPF sent Tricon an email on March 14, 2005, stating that the BOW FIGHTER would be delayed until March 18, 2005. Dkt. 116, Ex. E. YPF requested an extension of the load date until March 23, 2005. Id. YPF sent a separate email advising that it needed standby letters of credit. Id. On March 16, 2005, Tricon sent YPF amended letters of credit for the BOW FIGHTER. Dkt. 116, Ex. F. The amended letters replaced the previous load date of no later than March 17, 2005, with a load date of no later than March 23, 2005. Id.

YPF loaded the cargo, and the BOW FIGHTER set sail for Houston on March 19, 2005. Dkt. 1; Dkt. 116, Ex. D. Citgo claims the BOW FIGHTER was unseaworthy prior to the inception of the voyage due to pre-existing engine problems. Dkt. 1. While en route to Houston, the BOW FIGHTER suffered a major engine breakdown and deviated to Philadelphia for repairs. Id. The repairs delayed the arrival of the cargo in Houston and Freeport by nearly two months. Id. Citgo claims that the market price for cyclohexane had plummeted in the interim. Id.

Citgo settled with Tricon and, under the terms of the agreement, can pursue Tricon's claim for its loss of $450, 000. Dkt. 1. On September 13, 2007, Citgo brought claims against the BOW FIGHTER, Odfjell Seacem (the owner of the BOW FIGHTER), and YPF, as subrogee of Tricon, and against Odfjell Seachem and YPF in its own right. Id. Odfjell and the BOW FIGHTER (through Odfjell Asia) filed a motion to dismiss Citgo's claims against them because the arbitration provision in the charter party mandated arbitration of disputes in London. Dkt. 17. The court determined that the parties were bound by the arbitration provision and dismissed Citgo's claims against Odfjell and the BOW FIGHTER with prejudice. Dkt. 40. . . .

II.   MOTION FOR SUMMARY JUDGMENT

YPF moves for summary judgment Citgo's claim arguing that it is preempted by the United Nations Convention for the International Sale of Goods ("CISG"). Dkt. 101. YPF argues first that Citgo's claims should be dismissed because it pled a state law breach of contract claim rather than a violation of the CISG. Id. YPF argues next that, even if the court construes Citgo's complaint as alleging a claim under the CISG, the claim should be dismissed because the contract only required YPF to deliver the cyclohexane over the BOW FIGHTER's rails, which it did, and there is no duty under the CISG to engage a reasonable carrier. Id.

Citgo argues that summary judgment is inappropriate first because YPF breached the terms of the original contract between Tricon and YPF when it failed to load the cargo by the required date, and YPF has not shown that Tricon ever accepted the modified date that YPF proposed. Dkt. 112. Next, Citgo asserts that it does not matter if the CISG preempts Citgo's Texas state law claims, as the CISG recognizes a cause of action for breach of contract on terms essentially identical to Texas law. Id. Citgo claims that the CISG requires YPF to act reasonably and in good faith in the performance of a contract, and that YPF did not do so when it engaged the BOW FIGHTER, as it knew or could have discovered the problems with the BOW FIGHTER with reasonable effort. Id. Citgo contends that YPF knew or could not have been unaware that the BOW FIGHTER had issues before it delivered the cargo over her rails, and that YPF was therefore in breach of its duties under the CISG. Citgo requests that the court deny YPF's motion for summary judgment because there is a question of material fact as to whether YPF breached its duty by load-ing cargo onboard a vessel that was incapable of carrying the cargo. Id. Citgo urges the court to deny the motion for summary judgment as there are fact issues with regard to the vessel's nomination, the controlling agreement, and the extent of YPF's knowledge, and Citgo asserts that it is entitled to continue discovery to resolve these issues before finally presenting its case on the merits. . . .

B.   Preemption

YPF argues that the CISG preempts Citgo's state law contract claims. Dkt. 101. The CISG was ratified by the U.S. Senate in 1986. United Nations Convention on Contracts for the International Sale of Goods, opened for signature Apr. 11, 1980, 19 I.L.M. 668; see BP Oil Int'l, Ltd. v. Empresa Estatal Petroleos de Ecuador, 332 F.3d 333, 336 (5th Cir. 2003). It "creates a private right of action in federal court" and "applies to 'contracts of sale of goods between parties whose places of business are in different States . . . [w]hen the States are Contracting States.'"

Id. (quoting CISG art. 1(1)(a)). Here, the contract at issue is between citizens of Argentina and the United States, both of which are contracting states. See Forestal Guarani S.A. v. Daros Int'l, Inc., 613 F.3d 395, 397 (3d Cir. 2010) (noting that the United States ratified the CISG in 1986, Argentina ratified it in 1983, and it became effective in both countries in 1988). Thus, it appears the CISG applies.

Citgo contends that YPF's argument that Citgo's state law claims are preempted by the CISG is misleading and ultimately irrelevant because Citgo pled that YPF breached its contract with Tricon, and both the UCC and the CISG provide for liability for the breach of contract. Dkt. 112 at 12-13. Citgo argues that the CISG recognizes a cause of action for breach of contract on terms essentially identical to those employed by the UCC, so YPF's argument presents a distinction without a difference. Id. at 13.

YPF contends, however, that Citgo has not pleaded a cause of action under the CISG. Dkt. 116. YPF argues that Citgo is bound by its pleadings, has never asserted a claim under the CISG, and should not be allowed to do so now. Id.

Citgo's complaint asserts a general breach of contract claim against YPF. Dkt. 1. The CISG applies to contracts for the sale of goods between parties of signatory states. BP Oil, 332 F.3d at 336. "As incorporated federal law, the CISG governs this dispute so long as the parties have not elected to exclude its application." Id. Neither party argues that either contract at issue excludes the CISG's application. The court does not believe that the fact that Citgo did not mention the CISG in its complaint is fatal to its claim, since it asserted a breach of contract claim and the CISG is merely the law that governs that claim. Thus, the court finds that the CISG applies, a fact that the parties do not appear to dispute, and that Citgo may pursue its breach of contract claim against YPF under the CISG even though it did not specifically invoke the CISG in its complaint.

C. CISG

Under YPF and Tricon's contract, YPF was required to ship the cyclohexane CFR. "CFR," which stands for "Cost and FReight," is an International Commercial Term ("Incoterm") defined by the International Chamber of Commerce ("ICC"). BP Oil, 332 F.3d at 335. The ICC defines eleven different Incoterms to aid in the interpretation of "the most commonly used trade terms in foreign trade." Internal Chamber of Commerce, From 1936 to Today: The Incoterms Rules, http://www.iccwbo.org/products-and-services/trade-facilitation/incoterms-2010/history-of-theincoterms-rules/ (last visited May 13, 2013). The ICC Incoterms are incorporated into the CISG treaty through article 9(2). See BP Oil, 332 F.3d at 337. Under article 9(2),

> The parties are considered, unless otherwise agreed, to have impliedly made applicable to their contract or its formation a usage of which the parties knew or ought to have known and which in international trade is widely known to, and regularly observed by, parties to contracts of the type involved in the particular trade concerned.

CISG art. 9(2). The CFR Incoterm

means that the seller delivers the goods on board the vessel or procures the goods already so delivered. The risk of loss of or damage to the goods passes when the goods are on board the vessel. The seller must contract for and pay the costs and freight necessary to bring the goods to the named port of destination.

International Chamber of Commerce, The Incoterms Rules, http://www.iccwbo. org/products-andservices/trade-facilitation/incoterms-2010/the-incoterms–rules (last visited May 13, 2013).

YPF argues that according to the Incoterm, the risk of loss passed to Tricon as soon as YPF delivered the cyclohexane to the BOW FIGHTER's rails and that YPF, as a CFR seller, had no obligation under the CISG to engage a "reasonable carrier." Dkt. 101 at 8. Citgo argues that YPF had an obligation under the CISG to act reasonably and in good faith in the performance of its obligations under the sales contract. Dkt. 112. Citgo additionally argues that YPF had already breached the contract when it loaded the cargo, and the CISG articles pertaining to passing the risk do not impair its remedies for breach. Id.

1.   Duty to Act Reasonably and in Good Faith

Citgo argues that YPF had a duty to act reasonably and in good faith under the CISG and that it breached that duty when it placed the cyclohexane on a vessel that was not capable of delivering the cargo. Dkt. 112. It also argues that under article 32 of the CISG, YPF was required to arrange for carriage of the goods by a means of transportation "appropriate in the circumstances" and that YPF was thus bound to exercise reasonable care and good faith when it arranged for carriage of the cargo, ensuring that the vessel was appropriate. Id. Citgo additionally argues that under article 79 of the CISG, which states that a party is not liable for failure to perform if it proves failure due to an impediment beyond its control, YPF had an obligation to take into account reasonably foreseeable impediments to the delivery of the cyclohexane. Id.

YPF argues that Citgo has not pleaded a negligence claim against YPF, and the allegations that YPF should have exercised reasonable care sound in negligence. Dkt. 116. YPF claims that the purpose of a CFR contract is to place the risk of loss on the buyer, and that its obligation as a CFR seller was merely to place the cargo on a vessel of the type normally used for the transport of cyclohexane, which it fulfilled. Id. As far as Citgo's argument that the CISG required YPF to exercise reasonable care and good faith in arranging for the carriage of the cargo under article 32, YPF claims that article 32 is merely a "stop-gap" and only applies absent a contrary agreement of the parties. Id. According to YPF, the agreement to ship CFR and thus transfer the risk to the seller when the cargo was loaded was a contrary agreement. Id. YPF argues that article 79 is not on point as both Tricon and Citgo agreed to the use of the BOW FIGHTER.

Citgo relies first on *BP Oil* for its argument that YPF had a duty to act reasonably and in good faith under the CISG. In *BP Oil*, the Fifth Circuit considered whether a district court appropriately granted summary judgment on a breach of contract claim involving a contract for the purchase and transport of gasoline from Texas to

Ecuador. *BP Oil*, 332 F.3d at 334. BP Oil International, Ltd. ("BP") contracted with Empresa Estatal Petroleos de Ecuador ("PetroEcuador") for the purchase of 140,000 barrels of gasoline delivered CFR to Ecuador. Id. at 335. The gasoline was to have a gum content of less than three milligrams per one hundred milliliters, to be determined at the port of departure. Id. BP had the gasoline tested and loaded it aboard a ship at Shell's Deer Park refinery. Id. The ship sailed to Ecuador, and the gasoline was tested for gum content. Id. The gum content exceeded the contractual limitation when tested in Ecuador, and PetroEcuador refused to accept delivery. Id. BP resold the gasoline at a loss of about $2 million. Id. BP sued PetroEcuador for breach of contract and wrongful draw of a letter of guarantee. Id. The district court applied Texas choice of law rules and determined that Ecuadorian law governed the breach of contract claim. Id. It held that under Ecuadorian law, BP was required to tender conforming goods to the destination—in this case Ecuador—and granted summary judgment in favor of PetroEcuador. Id. BP appealed, arguing that the CISG applies and that, since it was a CFR seller, the risk of loss passed to PetroEcuador after BP delivered conforming goods on board the ship. Id. at 335-36.

The Fifth Circuit held that the CISG applied as incorporated federal law. Id. at 337. It then noted that the CISG incorporates Incoterms, including CFR, and that "[s]hipments designated 'CFR' require the seller to pay the costs and freight to transport the goods to the delivery port, but pass title and risk of loss to the buyer once the goods 'pass the ship's rail' at the port of shipment." Id. at 338. It held that BP fulfilled its contractual obligations if the gasoline met the contract's gum content requirement when it passed the ship's rail pursuant to article 36(1) of the CISG. Id. PetroEcuador argued that BP cut corners by buying the gasoline "as is" from Shell and failing to add sufficient gum inhibitor. Id. The Fifth Circuit, relying on article 40 of the CISG, noted that "BP could have breached the agreement if it provided goods that it 'knew or could not have been unaware' were defective when they 'passed over the ship's rail' and the risk shifted to PetroEcuador." Id. The court held that there was "a fact issue as to whether BP provided defective gasoline by failing to add sufficient gum inhibitor" and that the district court should permit discovery on this issue. Id. at 339.

The articles relied upon by the *BP Oil* court with regard to the "knew or could not have been unaware" standard—articles 38 through 40—have to do with whether the goods delivered were conforming goods. See CISG arts. 38-40. Citgo relies on this standard to argue that YFP had a duty to act reasonably and in good faith. Dkt. 112 at 2. Article 40 states that the "seller is not entitled to rely on the provisions of articles 38 and 39," which relate to the buyer examining the goods for conformity and giving notice to the seller about lack of conformity, "if the lack of conformity relates to facts of which [the seller] knew or could not have been unaware and which [the seller] did not disclose to the buyer." CISG arts. 38-40. Citgo argues that there is a fact issue with regard to whether YPF knew or should have known that there were issues with the BOW FIGHTER that would cause delays in the arrival of its cargo and that this fact issue precludes summary judgment. Articles 38 through 40, however, do not apply here because there is no contention that the cyclohexane did not conform to the contract specification. Id. These articles do not deal with whether YPF chose a reasonable carrier.

Next, Citgo argues that YPF had a duty under article 32 of the CISG. Under article 32(2), if "the seller is bound to arrange for carriage of the goods, he must make such contracts as are necessary for carriage to the place fixed by means of transportation appropriate in the circumstances and according to the usual terms for such transportation." CISG art. 32(2). According to Citgo, there is a material question of fact as to whether YPF knew the BOW FIGHTER was an inappropriate vessel, and thus summary judgment should not be granted in YPF's favor. Dkt. 112. YPF concedes that whether it had knowledge of the pre-existing breakdowns and should have conveyed these facts to Tricon is a disputed question of fact, but it argues that it is not *material* because Citgo cannot recover even if it had such knowledge under the CISG since the risk of loss transferred to Tricon when YPF loaded the cargo.3 Dkts. 101, 110. YPF asserts that article 32 only applies if there is nothing in the contract relating to the seller's delivery options. Dkt. 116. Since the contract used the Incoterm CFR, YPF argues that the requirements imposed on YPF as a CFR seller supersedes any requirements that would otherwise have been imposed by article 32 of the CISG.

Under the CFR Incoterm, a CFR seller is obligated to (1) provide goods that conform with the contract; (2) obtain export licenses or other official authorization to export; (3) "contract on usual terms at his own expense for the carriage of the goods to the named port of destination by the usual route in a seagoing vessel . . . of the type normally used for the transport of goods of the contract description"; (4) deliver the goods on board the vessel on the date agreed; and (5) bear the risks of loss until the goods have passed the ship's rails at the port. Dkt. 101, Ex. C at 202 (International Chamber of Commerce, Incoterms (2000)). YPF argues that it fulfilled all of these obligations when it loaded the cyclohexane aboard the BOW FIGHTER, which is a vessel of the type normally used for the transport of cyclohexane. Dkt. 116.

Citgo, however, argues that the article 32 of the CISG imposes an additional duty on a CFR shipper—namely, that YPF was bound to exercise reasonable care and good faith when it arranged for carriage of the cargo, regardless of whether the risk of loss passed when the cargo was loaded. Dkt. 112. YPF does not dispute that it arranged for the BOW FIGHTER to carry the cargo. Instead, it cites a secondary source indicating that article 32 applies only "'in the absence of contrary agreement between the parties'" and that "'[i]n practice, the agreement will spell out the seller's delivery obligations quite precisely by adopting an established shipment term . . . and less frequently by incorporating the INCOTERMS.'" Dkt. 116 at 6 (quoting Ziegel and Samson, Report to the Uniform Law Conference of Canada on Conventions for the International Sale of Goods 81 (1st ed. 1981)). However, even if the agreement spells out the seller's delivery obligations by denoting that it is a CFR contract, these delivery obligations are not necessarily contrary to a concurrent responsibility under article 32 to select an appropriate vessel. The court finds that article 32 applies here and that YPF had an obligation to secure a "means of transportation appropriate in the circumstances." There is a question of fact as to whether YPF met this obligation. YPF's motion for summary judgment on this ground is thus DENIED. . . .

Incoterms are international trade delivery terms that are understood well by any player in the system. These 11 codes, which delineate the respective responsibility of seller and buyer as to various shipping matters, are published periodically by the International Chamber of Commerce in Paris. They were first published in 1936 and most recently in 2010.

Buyers or sellers that engage in international transactions with ignorance of the Incoterms are proceeding at their own peril:

> An exporter who ignores Incoterms may watch a profitable export become a horrendous loss. Consider the case of the Kumar Corp., a Florida business that sold electronic goods to South America. Kumar's shipping documents included an Incoterm that required Kumar to provide transit insurance. Kumar failed to insure the shipment, and then it disappeared after it was delivered to the freight handler. By failing to provide insurance for that risk, as the Incoterm required, Kumar became the self-insurer for the loss. (Frank G. Long, "Shipments Often Vanish; Know if Buyer or Seller Pays," *Arizona Business Gazette*, September 19, 1996, p. 5.)

The 11 Incoterms can be divided into four functional categories based on the first letter in the code. An E Incoterm creates the lowest level of responsibility for the seller. For example, with the EXW term, the seller must merely pack the goods and store them at the point of origin. The buyer assumes the risk of loss from that point and must also pay for shipping and insurance.

An F Incoterm represents a slightly higher level of responsibility for the seller. With an FCA term, for example, the seller at least has the responsibility of delivering the goods to the carrier, after which point the buyer assumes risk of loss and responsibility for paying the cost of carriage.

The next level of Incoterm, C, often requires the seller to pay for certain shipping and insurance charges. With the CIP term, for instance, the seller has the responsibility of paying for the shipping and insurance charges to the port of destination, but risk of loss will still pass to the buyer once the goods are loaded onto the carrier.

The final category, D Incoterms, puts the greatest responsibility and risk on the seller. For instance, a DDP term requires that the seller must pay all insurance, delivery, loading, and unloading costs. Furthermore, with the DDP term, risk of loss does not pass to the buyer until the goods are tendered at the stated destination.

In setting out default rules for the passage of risk of loss, the CISG addresses three different situations: (1) where the goods are to be delivered to the buyer but the goods are not in transit at the time the contract is entered into, (2) where the goods are already in transit when the contract is made, and (3) where the buyer is to pick up the goods from the seller or from some third party.

For the first category, risk of loss passes to the buyer when the seller delivers the goods to the first carrier. CISG Art. 67(1). This is similar to the default rule of UCC Article 2, where the UCC presumes a shipment contract in the absence of anything stated explicitly. As the following case demonstrates, resolution of the risk-of-loss question often depends upon which party has the burden of proof as to when the alleged defect in the goods arose.

Chicago Prime Packers, Inc. v. Northam Food Trading Co.

408 F.3d 894 (7th Cir. 2005)

FLAUM, J.

Defendant-appellant Northam Food Trading Company ("Northam") contracted with plaintiff-appellee Chicago Prime Packers, Inc. ("Chicago Prime") for the purchase of 40,500 pounds of pork back ribs. Following delivery, Northam refused to pay Chicago Prime the contract price, claiming that the ribs arrived in an "off condition." Chicago Prime filed this diversity action for breach of contract against Northam. Following a bench trial, the district court awarded Chicago Prime $178,200.00, the contract price, plus prejudgment interest of $27,242.63. Northam appeals the award. For the reasons stated herein, we affirm.

I.   BACKGROUND

The district court found the following facts based on the stipulations of the parties and the evidence presented at trial. Because neither party contends that any of the findings of fact in this section are "clearly erroneous," we accept them as established for purposes of this appeal. See Fed. R. Civ. P. 52(a).

Chicago Prime, a Colorado corporation, and Northam, a partnership formed under the laws of Ontario, Canada, are both wholesalers of meat products. On March 30, 2001, Chicago Prime contracted to sell Northam 1,350 boxes (40,500 pounds) of pork back ribs. Northam agreed to pay $178,200.00 for the ribs, with payment due within seven days of receipt of the shipment. The contract also set forth a description of the ribs, the price, and the date and location for pick-up.

Chicago Prime purchased the ribs specified in the contract from meat processor Brookfield Farms ("Brookfield"). When a pork loin is processed at Brookfield, it is broken into various segments, one of which is the back rib. After processing, Brookfield packages back ribs "flat" (horizontally), layer by layer, in 30-pound boxes. The ribs are placed first in a blast freezer and then transferred to an outside freezer where they remain until shipped.

In addition to its own freezers, Brookfield stored the ribs at issue in this case in as many as two independent cold storage facilities: B & B Pullman Cold Storage ("B & B") and Fulton Market Cold Storage ("Fulton"). According to Brookfield's temperature logs and quality control records for its own facilities, the ribs were maintained at acceptable temperatures and were processed and maintained in accordance with Brookfield's procedures. Records presented at trial also indicate that the ribs were stored at or below acceptable temperatures during the entire time they were in B & B's possession. The parties offered no evidence regarding storage of the ribs at Fulton.

On April 24, 2001, Brown Brother's Trucking Company ("Brown"), acting on behalf of Northam, picked up 40,500 pounds of ribs from B & B. Chicago Prime, the seller, never possessed the ribs. When Brown accepted the shipment, it signed a bill of lading, thereby acknowledging that the goods were "in apparent good order." The bill of lading also indicated, however, that the "contents and condition of contents of packages [were] unknown." The next day, Brown delivered the shipment to Northam's customer, Beacon Premium Meats ("Beacon"). Like Chicago Prime, Northam, the buyer, never possessed the ribs. Upon delivery, Beacon signed a second bill of lading acknowledging that it had received the shipment "in apparent good order," except for some problems not at issue in this case.

Under the terms of the contract, Northam was obligated to pay Chicago Prime by May 1, 2001. Sandra Burdon, who negotiated the contract on behalf of Northam, testified that, on that date, Northam had no basis for withholding payment. In fact, she thought that a check had been sent to Chicago Prime prior to May 1, 2001, but subsequently discovered that the check had not been mailed. On May 2, 2001, Chicago Prime, not having heard from Northam, demanded payment.

On May 4, 2001, Beacon began "processing" a shipment of ribs and noticed that the product appeared to be in an "off condition." Beacon asked Inspector Ken Ward of the United States Department of Agriculture ("USDA") to examine the product. Ward inspected the ribs at the Beacon facility, found that the meat "did not look good," and ordered Beacon to stop processing it. Ward then placed a "U.S. Retained" tag on the shipment, noting "yellow, green, temp[erature], abused, spoiled," and had the ribs placed in Beacon's freezer. The same day, Northam and Chicago Prime learned of a potential problem with the ribs.

Inspector Ward returned to Beacon on May 7 and 8, 2001 and examined both frozen and thawed samples of the product. On May 23, 2001, Dr. John Maltby, Ward's supervisor, also conducted an on-site inspection of the ribs. When Dr. Maltby arrived, Beacon employees were "reworking" the ribs, trying to salvage any good portions. Dr. Maltby reviewed Beacon's shipping records and temperature logs from the relevant time period and found no "anomalies" or "gaps." In addition, he examined approximately 20 cases of ribs and prepared a written report. According to this report, Beacon gave Dr. Maltby two pallets of frozen ribs untouched by Beacon, as well as some of the product that Beacon had reworked. Looking inside the intact pallets, Dr. Maltby found ribs stacked both horizontally and vertically, with some frozen individually and others frozen together in larger units. The individually frozen ribs were "putrid," while the ribs frozen in larger units were "good."

Examining samples of the thawed, reworked product, Dr. Maltby found putrid, green, slimy ribs, but no sign of temperature abuse. He concluded in his report that the inspected product was rotten, that it arrived at Beacon in a rotten condition, and that it appeared to have been "assembled from various sources." Dr. Maltby also concluded that there was no opportunity for salvage and that all of the product should be condemned. The same day, the USDA issued a Notice of Receipt of Adulterated or Misbranded Product and the entire shipment of 1,350 boxes of ribs was condemned. After Northam informed it of the results of Dr. Malby's inspection, Chicago Prime continued to demand payment and eventually filed suit.

At trial, it was undisputed that the parties entered into a valid and enforceable contract for the sale and purchase of ribs, that Chicago Prime transferred a shipment of ribs to a trucking company hired by Northam, and that Northam had not paid Chicago Prime for the ribs. Northam argued that it was relieved of its contractual payment obligation because the ribs were spoiled when its agent, Brown, received them. The district court concluded that it was Northam's burden to prove nonconformity, and held that Northam had failed to prove that the ribs from Chicago Prime were spoiled at the time of transfer to Brown. The court went on to state alternative holdings in favor of Chicago Prime based on its finding that, "even if the ribs were spoiled at the time of transfer, Northam . . . failed to prove that it examined the ribs, or caused them to be examined, within as short a period as is practicable under the circumstances, or that it rejected or revoked its acceptance of the ribs within a reasonable time after it discovered or should have discovered the alleged non-conformity." Chi. Prime Packers, Inc. v. Northam Food Trading Co., 320 F. Supp. 2d 702, 711 (N.D. Ill. 2004). The court awarded Chicago Prime the contract price of $178,200.00, plus prejudgment interest of $27,242.63.

II.   DISCUSSION

The district court held, and the parties do not dispute, that the contract at issue is governed by the United Nations Convention on Contracts for the International Sale of Goods ("CISG"), reprinted at 15 U.S.C.A. Appendix (West 1997), a self-executing agreement between the United States and other signatories, including Canada. Under the CISG, "[t]he seller must deliver goods which are of the quantity, quality and description required by the contract," and "the goods do not conform with the contract unless they . . . [a]re fit for the purposes for which goods of the same description would ordinarily be used." CISG Art. 35(1)-(2). The risk of loss passes from the seller to the buyer when the goods are transferred to the buyer's carrier. CISG Art. 67(1). While the seller is liable "for any lack of conformity which exists at the time when risk passes to the buyer," CISG Art. 36(1), the buyer bears the risk of "[l]oss of or damage to the goods after the risk has passed to the buyer . . . unless the damage is due to an act or omission of the seller." CISG Art. 66. In other words, Chicago Prime is responsible for the loss if the ribs were spoiled (nonconforming) at the time Northam's agent, Brown, received them from Chicago Prime's agent, Brookfield, while Northam is responsible if they did not become spoiled until after the transfer.

The parties agree that the main factual issue before the district court was whether the ribs were spoiled at the time of transfer. On appeal, Northam makes two arguments: (1) that the district court erred in placing upon Northam the burden of proving that the ribs were spoiled at the time of transfer, and (2) that the evidence presented at trial does not support the district court's finding that the ribs became spoiled after Brown received them from Brookfield.

A. Burden of Proof

Northam asserts that Chicago Prime should bear the burden of proving that the ribs were not spoiled at the time of transfer because the quality of the goods is an essential element of Chicago Prime's breach of contract claim. Chicago Prime counters that nonconformity is an affirmative defense for which Northam, as the defendant-buyer, has the burden of proof. Proper assignment of the burden of proof is a question of law that we review de novo. Estate of Kanter v. Comm'r of Internal Revenue, 337 F.3d 833, 851 (7th Cir. 2003), rev'd on other grounds, Ballard v. Comm'r of Internal Revenue, ___ U.S. ___, 125 S. Ct. 1270, 161 L. Ed. 2d 227 (Mar. 7, 2005).

The CISG does not state expressly whether the seller or buyer bears the burden of proof as to the product's conformity with the contract. Because there is little case law under the CISG, we interpret its provisions by looking to its language and to "the general principles" upon which it is based. See CISG Art. 7(2); see also Delchi Carrier SpA v. Rotorex Corp., 71 F.3d 1024, 1027-1028 (2d Cir. 1995). The CISG is the international analogue to Article 2 of the Uniform Commercial Code ("UCC"). Many provisions of the UCC and the CISG are the same or similar, and "[c]aselaw interpreting analogous provisions of Article 2 of the [UCC], may . . . inform a court where the language of the relevant CISG provision tracks that of the UCC." *Delchi Carrier SpA,* 71 F.3d at 1028. "However, UCC caselaw 'is not *per se* applicable.'" Id. (quoting Orbisphere Corp. v. United States, 726 F. Supp. 1344, 1355 (Ct. Int'l Trade 1989)).

A comparison with the UCC reveals that the buyer bears the burden of proving nonconformity under the CISG. Under the UCC, the buyer may plead breach of the implied warranty of fitness for ordinary purpose as an affirmative defense to a contract action by the seller for the purchase price. See Comark Merch., Inc. v. Highland Group, Inc., 932 F.2d 1196, 1203 (7th Cir. 1991); Alberts Bonnie Brae, Inc. v. Ferral, 188 Ill. App. 3d 711, 135 Ill. Dec. 926, 544 N.E.2d 422, 423 (1989); see also 77a Corpus Juris Secundum Sales §287 (2004) ("[T]he buyer, when sued for the purchase price, may set up a breach of warranty as a defense to the seller's action."). In such an action it is the defendant-buyer's burden to prove the breach of the warranty. See *Comark Merch.,* 932 F.2d at 1203; *Alberts Bonnie Brae,* 135 Ill. Dec. 926, 544 N.E.2d at 424-425.

Section 2-314 of the UCC provides that a warranty that goods are "fit for the ordinary purpose for which such goods are used" is implied unless the contract states otherwise. Mirroring the structure and content of this section, Article 35(2) of the CISG provides that unless the contract states otherwise, "goods do not conform with the contract unless they . . . [a]re fit for the purposes for which goods of the same description would ordinarily be used." See Ralph H. Folsom, 1 International Business Transactions §1.15, at 39 (2d ed. 2002) (the CISG's approach "produces results which are comparable to the 'warranty' structure of the UCC"). Accordingly, just as a buyer-defendant bears the burden of proving breach of the implied warranty of fitness for ordinary purpose under the UCC, under the CISG, the buyer-defendant bears the burden of proving nonconformity at the time of transfer. See Larry A. DiMatteo et al., *The Interpretive Turn in International Sales Law: An Analysis of Fifteen Years of CISG Jurisprudence,* 24 Nw. J. Int'l L. & Bus. 299, 400 (2004) (Under the CISG, "[t]he buyer is allocated the burden of proving that the goods were defective prior to the expiration of the seller's obligation point."); see also Folsom, 1 International Business Transactions §1.15, at 41. The district court was correct to conclude that Northam bears the burden of proving that the ribs were spoiled at the time of transfer.

B. CONFORMITY OF THE RIBS AT THE TIME OF TRANSFER

The district court held that Northam failed to prove that the ribs were spoiled, or nonconforming, at the time of transfer. First, the court found that other evidence undermined Dr. Maltby's testimony that the ribs were rotten when they arrived at Beacon:

> Chicago Prime points out several problems with Northam's reliance on Dr. Maltby's conclusion. Most significantly, neither Dr. Maltby nor anyone else could confirm that the meat Dr. Maltby inspected was in fact the product that was sold to Northam by Chicago Prime, and evidence was produced at trial to suggest that they were not the same ribs. Even though the rib boxes were labeled with Brookfield establishment numbers, the evidence showed that Beacon had purchased and received other loads of ribs originating from Brookfield prior to April 25, 2001. Furthermore, some of the ribs examined by Dr. Maltby (from one of the Intact Pallets) were stacked both horizontally and vertically. Brookfield packages its loin back ribs only horizontally. Dr. Maltby had no personal knowledge of how or where the meat was stored from April 25, 2001 to May 23, 2001, and the first time any government inspector viewed the meat was on May 4, 2001. According to Dr. Maltby, loin back ribs, if kept at room temperature, could spoil in five to seven days. Surprisingly, Northam did not present any witness affiliated with Beacon to address those issues.

Chi. Prime Packers, 320 F. Supp. 2d at 710 (citations omitted). Next, the district court found that three witnesses had credibly testified that "the ribs delivered by Brookfield were processed and stored in acceptable conditions and temperatures from the time they were processed until they were transferred to Northam on April 24, 2001." Id. Despite Northam's attempts to discredit the testimony of these witnesses by pointing to deficiencies in Brookfield's record-keeping during the relevant period, the district court found "nothing in the evidence demonstrating that Brookfield, B & B or Fulton did anything improper with respect to the ribs or that the ribs were spoiled prior to being transferred to Northam." Id. Based on these factual findings, the district court concluded that Northam had not met its burden of demonstrating that the ribs were spoiled at the time of transfer. Id. at 711.

By highlighting Dr. Maltby's testimony and potential gaps in Chicago Prime's evidence, Northam suggests that the opposite holding is also supportable. This, however, is not the correct inquiry. On appeal from a bench trial, we will not set aside the factual conclusions of the district court "unless clearly erroneous." Fed. R. Civ. P. 52(a). "Under this standard, one who contends that a finding is clearly erroneous has an exceptionally heavy burden to carry on appeal." Spurgin-Dienst v. United States, 359 F.3d 451, 453 (7th Cir. 2004). This is especially true when the appellant argues that the district court erred in crediting or discrediting a witness's testimony. See id.

Northam argues that the district court erred in discrediting Dr. Maltby's testimony, and contends that Dr. Maltby's conclusion that the ribs were rotten before the transfer should be determinative. Even if the district court *could* have given Dr. Maltby's conclusion more weight, however, Northam has not shown that the court clearly erred in finding the evidence undermining his conclusion to be more persuasive.

The evidence supporting Northam's position was not so overwhelming that it was clear error to find in favor of Chicago Prime. Northam offered no credited evidence showing that the ribs were spoiled at the time of transfer or excluding the possibility that the ribs became spoiled after the transfer. In addition, it presented no evidence that Brookfield stored the ribs in unacceptable conditions that could have caused them to become spoiled before the transfer. Finally, Northam did not present a witness from Beacon to respond to the evidence suggesting that the ribs examined by Dr. Maltby were not those sold to Northam by Chicago Prime. Upon this record, the district court did not clearly err in finding that Northam did not meet its burden of proof as to its affirmative defense of nonconformity.

Because we hold that the district court correctly assigned to Northam the burden of proving nonconformity and did not clearly err in finding that Northam had not met this burden, we need not reach the district court's alternative holdings.

III.   CONCLUSION

We AFFIRM the district court's award to Chicago Prime.

If the goods in an international sale are already in transit when the parties enter into a contract for those goods, risk passes to the buyer at the time the contract is concluded. CISG Art. 68. However, risk in the transit case may pass to the buyer retroactively from the point when the goods were handed over to the carrier "if the circumstances so indicate" and if the seller did not know or have reason to know that the goods were lost or damaged at the time the contract was concluded. CISG Art. 68.

In a situation where the buyer is to pick up the goods from the seller's place or from some third party, risk passes to the buyer when it "takes over the goods" or when its failure to pick up the goods amounts to a breach of the contract. CISG Art. 69(1). In a case where the buyer's pickup will take place at a third-party location, the standard is stricter for the buyer: risk will then pass to the buyer "when delivery is due and the buyer is aware of the fact that the goods are placed at his disposal at that place." CISG Art. 69(2).

When the seller has committed a "fundamental breach" of its obligations under the contract, the buyer retains all of its remedies for the seller's breach, including the right to "avoid" the contract. CISG Arts. 70, 82. This result is similar to that in UCC Article 2, where nonconforming goods will prevent passage of the risk of loss to the buyer, even if the non-conformity has nothing to do with the damage or destruction of the goods that occurs. The difference between the CISG and the UCC on this score is that, in the UCC context, any non-conformity that gives the buyer a right to reject under the "perfect tender" rule also prevents the passage of risk to the buyer; in the CISG context, there must be a fundamental beach of the contract by the seller in order for the buyer to avoid the contract and effectively prevent passage of risk.

C.   Risk of Loss with Real Estate

With the sale of real estate, the common law default rule in most states today is that the risk of loss during the period between the signing of the contract and closing is on the buyer. The real estate risk-of-loss rule has been justified by reference to the obscure doctrine of equitable conversion, which says that once an enforceable sales contract has been signed by both parties, the buyer has equitable title in the property from that point forward and the seller is merely holding the property in trust for the buyer during the executory period.

The problem with this theory today as a justification for the risk-of-loss rule is that the modern real estate sales contract is rife with conditions and qualifications of various sorts that make the contract's true "enforceability" virtually coterminous with the closing itself. Accordingly, it should come as no surprise that the risk-of-loss default rule has only had a limited practical effect in modern real estate practice, for at least two important reasons.

First, and most important, courts almost always require the seller to hold any insurance proceeds in trust for the buyer, thus limiting the significance of the default rule to cases of inadequate insurance. Second, most standard real estate sales contract forms include an express provision contracting around the common law rule. Such a provision looks something like this in a simple residential transaction:

Risk of loss to the improvements on the property shall be borne by Seller until title is transferred. If any improvements covered by this contract are damaged or destroyed, Seller shall immediately notify Buyer in writing of the damage or destruction, the amount of insurance proceeds payable, if any, and whether Seller intends, prior to closing, to restore the property to its condition at the time of the contract. In the event Seller restores the property to its prior condition before scheduled closing, Buyer and Seller shall proceed with closing. In the event the property is not to be restored to its prior condition by Seller before closing, Buyer may either (a) Proceed with the transaction and be entitled to all insurance money, if any, payable to Seller under all policies insuring the improvements, or (b) rescind the contract, and thereby release all parties from liability hereunder. Buyer shall give written notice of his election to Seller or listing agent within ten (10) days after Buyer has received written notice of such damage or destruction and the amount of insurance proceeds payable, and closing will be extended accordingly, if required. Failure by Buyer to so notify Seller shall constitute an election to rescind the contract. A rescission hereunder does not constitute a default by Seller.

Commercial transactions frequently include similar provisions concerning allocation of the risk of loss. However, buyers in commercial transactions will often retain the right to walk away if the damage is severe, reflecting the subjectivity of damage assessment in this context.

Even when the parties specify in their agreement what should happen in the event of loss or damage to the property during the executory period, such carefully drafted provisions do not always prevent litigation, as the following case demonstrates.

Voorde Poorte v. Evans

832 P.2d 105 (Wash. Ct. App. 1992)

SWEENEY, J.

Art and Ann Voorde Poorte brought this action for damages against William and Jeannette Evans following a fire which resulted in the loss of their mobile home. The Evanses were in the process of purchasing the home when the fire occurred. On the Evanses' motion for summary judgment, the court dismissed the Voorde Poortes' complaint. The Voorde Poortes appeal. We affirm in part, reverse in part and remand for further proceedings.

In July 1987, the Voorde Poortes and the Evanses executed a real estate purchase and sale agreement for the sale of land and a mobile home owned by the Voorde Poortes. The mobile home was vacant and the utility services had been disconnected.

The sale agreement provided in part that: closing was to occur on or before August 15, 1987; the buyers (Evanses) were entitled to possession on closing; and if the property was destroyed by fire, the buyers (Evanses) could terminate the agreement. The sale was originally set to close on July 26, 1987, but closing was delayed by agreement of the parties because the Voorde Poortes could not provide clear title.

Prior to closing, the Evanses took possession, moved employees into the mobile home and restored electrical service to the mobile home. On September 16, 1987, after the Evanses' employees had just finished lunch in the mobile home, they noticed smoke coming from somewhere in the mobile home. The local fire department responded, but the mobile home was destroyed by the fire.

Following his investigation, Grant County Fire Marshall Sam Lorenz concluded that the fire probably started in the kitchen and most likely involved the electrical system. He did not know the exact cause of the fire. There was no evidence that the fire was caused by incendiaries, chemicals, lightning or smoking. Fireman Steven Mitchell helped extinguish the fire and also investigated its cause. He believed the fire was caused by an electrical device that overheated or shorted out. The employees occupying the mobile home were transient workers who could not be located and therefore were not questioned.

After the fire, the Evanses terminated the sale agreement. The Voorde Poortes brought causes of action based on contract, tort and trespass. . . .

Contractual provisions allocating the risk of loss will generally be enforced in Washington. In [one Washington Supreme Court case, for example,] the court enforced a contract provision placing risk of loss prior to closing on the seller. It held the seller liable for damage to an orchard which had occurred prior to closing.

The Voorde Poortes contend that risk of loss should follow possession. While their position has a certain equitable appeal, it is against the weight of authority.

Phillips v. Bacon, 267 S.E.2d 249 (1980), presents a fact pattern similar to the case before us. There, the sale contract gave the purchaser the option of canceling the contract if the property was destroyed prior to closing. The purchaser improved and occupied the property before closing. The closing did not occur as scheduled because of a problem with the title. Before the closing could be completed, the house was destroyed by fire. The Georgia Supreme Court affirmed a summary judgment dismissing the seller's action for specific performance concluding that the risk of loss provision controlled.

Here, there is a disagreement whether the Voorde Poortes knew or consented to the Evanses' early possession of the mobile home. However, that dispute is not a genuine issue of material fact. Risk of loss remained with the sellers even if we assume the Evanses' occupancy was nonpermissive. Early possession of the mobile home did not affect the contract provision that placed the risk of loss with the sellers.

If a contract is unambiguous, summary judgment is proper even if the parties dispute the legal effect of a certain provision. Interpretation of an unambiguous contract is a question of law.

Here, the only dispute involved the legal effect of early possession. The court correctly decided as a matter of law that the risk of loss remained with the sellers. . . .

In *Voorde Poorte*, the court stressed that even if the Evanses' early possession amounted to a breach of the sales contract, that would not affect the risk of loss since their early possession had nothing to do with the loss that occurred. Contrast this result with what UCC §2-510(1) provides in the sales system, where any non-conformity that would give the buyer a right to reject will delay the passage of risk to the buyer. Thus, in the UCC system, the seller can suffer a loss that occurs in transit merely because the goods were non-conforming, even though the non-conformity had no connection to the loss.

One aspect of the real estate risk-of-loss system that is raised but not discussed much in Voorde Poorte is that if the loss in question is caused by either party, then that party must suffer the loss despite what the usual risk-of-loss rule would be. Thus, had there been any evidence that the Evanses or their employees had started the fire negligently or otherwise, that would be a triable factual dispute that would bear on the risk-of-loss issue. Given what was reported by the fire department, however, the court in Voorde Poorte did not believe there was any evidence to support the notion that the Evanses or their employees were responsible for starting the fire.

Problem Set 21

21.1. a. State Law School leased a hi-tech photocopying machine for use in its mailroom. The lessor was Ted's Copy Shop. The lease was for five years at $2,000 per year, and the lease said nothing about the risk of loss. Steve Manion, a disgruntled mailroom employee, acts out his frustrations one night by taking an ax to the photocopying machine, which he thoroughly destroys. The parties were in the third year of the lease when the machine was destroyed. When Steve is caught, he loses his job and is more broke than ever. Neither the lessor nor the lessee had insured the goods. Who has risk of loss as to the destroyed machine? UCC §2A-219(1).

b. Same facts as part (a), except that the machine is destroyed by an accidental fire, and the lease is a finance lease. The lessor is First National Bank, and the supplier is Ted's Copy Shop. Who has risk of loss as to the destroyed machine? UCC §2A-219(1).

c. Same facts as part (a), except the machine is destroyed by an accidental fire, and at the time of the machine's destruction State Law School was two months behind in its lease payments. Who has risk of loss as to the destroyed machine? UCC §2A-220(2).

d. Same facts as part (a), except the machine is destroyed by an accidental fire, and State Law School had promised in the lease contract that it would insure the machine. At the time of the machine's destruction, State Law School had never taken out an insurance policy on the machine. Who has risk of loss as to the destroyed machine? UCC §2A-220(2).

21.2. Recall the facts of Problem 20.3: Heavy Metal signs a contract to sell Gold's Gym 10 tons of assorted free weights, painted gold. The contract said that the order would be sent "FOB Seller's Factory." Arlene had Heavy Metal's usual carrier, Dependo, come and pick up the weights, and Arlene had notified Gold's Gym of the shipment. However, the weights that were given to the carrier were black instead of gold, and the two trucks carrying the shipment were stolen during transit. Finally, the carrier had no insurance. Assuming that this shipment was to a Gold's Gym franchise in Canada, who would have risk of loss as to the stolen weights? CISG Arts. 66, 67, 70, 82, 49, 25, 58(3).

21.3. a. Take a look at the sample risk-of-loss real estate clause excerpted earlier in this assignment. Mary Russell and David Gavin, a newly married couple and your clients, signed a purchase contract with this clause on a house that was being sold by David's one-time neighbor, Mary Ellen O'Neill. Mrs. O'Neill is a widow who used to be a next-door neighbor to David when David was growing up. When Mrs. O'Neill decided that she needed to move to a retirement center, she gave David and Mary the opportunity to buy her house for $120,000, which David believed was at least $15,000 below market. In between the signing of the contract and the scheduled closing, there was an electrical fire at the house that caused $20,000 worth of damage. Mrs. O'Neill had fire insurance, but the policy had a $5,000 deductible. Mrs. O'Neill, through her lawyer, notified David and Mary that she would neither restore the property nor lower the price, although she was perfectly willing to proceed with the closing as scheduled. David and Mary come to you and ask you what their options are at this point, and which option you would advise them to take. What do you tell them?

b. Same facts as part (a), except that the electrical fire was caused after David went through the house to do some last-minute inspection. He left one of the lamps on, which normally would not cause a fire, except this lamp had a faulty cord. David was actually in the house without permission, but Mrs. O'Neill had already moved to the nursing home. David knew from growing up next door that Mrs. O'Neill always kept a spare house key under the bush near the front porch. How would these additional facts change the advice that you gave David and Mary in part (a)?

Assessment Questions for Chapter 3

Question 1: Corey Haney, owner of Gold's Gym fitness facility, orders a new commercial-grade elliptical aerobics machine for her gym from Heavy Metal. After one week of use by the gym's clients, the new machine's electronic heart-rate monitor starts to display inaccurate heart rates for the users of the machine. If Corey wishes to reject the machine at this point, which of the following factors will be LEAST relevant to her ability to do so?

(A) Whether her sales contract included a limitation of remedies to repair or replacement of defective parts.

(B) Whether Heavy Metal's time for performance in the sales contract has already expired.

(C) Whether the defect in the heart-rate monitor amounts to a "substantial impairment" of the machine's value to Corey.

(D) Whether Corey has had a reasonable opportunity to inspect the machine at this point.

(E) Whether Corey has done any act inconsistent with Heavy Metal's ownership of the machine at this point.

Question 1 Answer: The correct answer is (C). Whether the defect in the heart-rate monitor amounts to a "substantial impairment" of the machine's value to Corey is the least relevant factor for Corey's right to reject because the "substantial impairment" standard is the standard for revocation of acceptance under §2-608(1). The standard for rejection under §2-601's perfect tender rule is whether the goods "fail in any respect to conform to the contract." (A) is wrong because a limitation of remedies is specifically noted as an exception to §2-601's right to reject for a buyer such as Corey. (B) is wrong because whether Heavy Metal's time for performance has expired is relevant to Heavy Metal's right to cure under §2-508(1), and such a right to cure would remove Corey's right to reject. (D) is wrong because under §2-606(1)(b) Corey will be deemed to have accepted the machine if she fails to make an effective rejection after a reasonable opportunity to inspect has passed. (E) is wrong because under §2-606(1)(c) Corey will be deemed to have accepted the machine if she does any act inconsistent with Heavy Metal's ownership of the machine.

Question 2: Same facts as Question 1, except now assume that Corey accepted this machine the day after it arrived without knowing about the defective heart-rate monitor. For this question, assume also that this machine is the first installment in a series of five elliptical machines that Heavy Metal promises to deliver to Corey's gym every two weeks over the next two months. If Corey wishes to revoke her acceptance of the first machine at this point, which of the following factors will be LEAST relevant to her ability to do so?

(A) Whether this non-conformity substantially impairs the value of the whole installment contract.

(B) Whether there has been any substantial change in the condition of the machine that was not caused by the heart-rate monitor defect.

(C) Whether Corey's acceptance was reasonably induced by the difficulty of discovering the faulty heart-rate monitor.

(D) Whether Corey's revocation of her acceptance occurs within a reasonable time after she discovered or should have discovered the faulty heart-rate monitor.

(E) Whether Corey's acceptance was reasonably induced by Heavy Metal's assurances about the high quality of the machine.

Question 2 Answer: The correct answer is (A). Whether this non-conformity substantially impairs the value of the whole installment contract is not necessarily relevant to Corey's ability to revoke acceptance of this installment under §2-608(1). Instead, the relevant standard for revocation under §2-608(1) is whether the defect substantially impairs the value of this machine to Corey. The standard given in this answer would be relevant under §2-612(3) if Corey were seeking to show a breach of the whole installment contract rather than just this single installment. (B) is wrong because §2-608(2) says that an effective revocation must occur before any substantial change in the condition of the goods that is not caused by their own defects. (C) is wrong because under §2-608(1)(b), the only revocation route available here to Corey (because she was unaware of the defect when she accepted), requires that the buyer's acceptance was induced either by the difficulty of discovery before acceptance or by the seller's assurances. (D) is wrong because §2-608(2) says that revocation must occur within a reasonable time after the buyer discovers or should have discovered the defect. (E) is wrong for the same reason that (C) is wrong.

Question 3: Finance Lessee arranges with Seller and Finance Lessor to have Seller sell a custom-made drill-press machine to Finance Lessor, who will then lease it to Finance Lessee for Finance Lessee's factory. Finance Lessee meets with Seller to make sure that Seller understands the particular needs of Finance Lessee's factory operations. Finance Lessee explains that the factory where this machine will be used has a very high level of humidity, so the drill-press machine must be able to operate even under very humid conditions. Seller assures Finance Lessee that this custom-made drill-press machine will operate effectively even in the most humid climates. Seller delivers the machine to Finance Lessee, and Finance Lessee accepts the machine and begins using it in the factory's manufacturing operations. Two weeks into the finance lease, the drill-press machine breaks down because it turns out that in fact it is not able to function effectively in humid climates. At this point, may Finance Lessee revoke its acceptance of the drill-press machine?

(A) Yes, because Finance Lessee's failure to discover the non-conformity before acceptance was reasonably induced by Seller's assurances.
(B) Yes, even if the finance lease contains an explicit "Hell or High Water" clause.

(C) No, because Finance Lessee failed to give notice of the non-conformity soon enough to preserve its right to revoke acceptance.

(D) No, but only if the finance lease contains an explicit "Hell or High Water" clause.

(E) No, but Finance Lessee will still have recourse against Seller.

Question 3 Answer: The correct answer is (E). Section 2A-517 makes it clear that with a non-consumer finance lease like this one, the only situation in which the finance lessee may revoke its acceptance is under §2A-517(1)(b). That section says that revocation is still possible for the finance lessee if the finance lessee's acceptance of the goods was reasonably induced by the lessor's assurances. Here Finance Lessee's acceptance of the machine was reasonably induced not by Finance Lessor's assurances, but instead by Seller's assurances. However, even though Finance Lessee may not revoke its acceptance at this point, Finance Lessee will have a direct action for damages against Seller (the "supplier" in this case) under §2A-209. (A) is wrong because Seller's assurances are not what triggers Finance Lessee's revocation possibility under §2A-517(1)(b), and Finance Lessor made no assurances about the machine to Finance Lessee. (B) is wrong because even without an explicit "Hell or High Water" clause in the finance lease, one is implied under §2A-407, and furthermore, the "Hell or High Water" clause governs the finance lessee's liability for continued payments rather than its right to revoke. (C) is wrong because Finance Lessee's timing of revocation was fine under the standard given in §2A-517(4) ("within a reasonable time after the lessee discovers or should have discovered the ground for it and before any substantial change in condition of the goods which is not caused by the nonconformity"). (D) is wrong because Finance Lessee's ability to revoke here does not depend on whether the finance lease contains an explicit "Hell or High Water" clause.

Question 4: Seller, a Toronto-based seller of textbooks, makes a contract with Bookstore, based in Syracuse, New York, for the sale of 800 chemistry textbooks to be delivered to Bookstore by August 15. The contract states that "time is of the essence," since Bookstore needs to stock these books for its university's fall-semester Introductory Chemistry classes. The books are ultimately delivered to Bookstore on August 22, and each of the books is missing the same three pages from the middle of the book. When Bookstore receives this delivery of textbooks, may it avoid its contract with Seller?

(A) Yes, but if Bookstore chooses to avoid the contract, then it thereby waives its rights to recover damages for Seller's breach.

(B) Yes, and even if Bookstore chooses to avoid the contract, it retains its right to damages for Seller's breach.

(C) Yes, but only if the missing pages amount to a "fundamental breach" of the contract.

(D) Both (B) and (C) are true.

(E) Both (A) and (C) are true.

Question 4 Answer: The correct answer is (B). Given the lateness of delivery in a "time is of the essence" contract like this one, we don't even need to ask under Article 49 whether the missing pages amount to a fundamental breach of this contract. And even though avoidance means that both parties are relieved of any further obligations under the contract, Bookstore will still retain its right to sue Seller for damages under Article 81(1). (A) is wrong because Article 81(1) makes it clear that avoidance of a contract does not waive the avoiding party's right to recover any damages that are due to it. (C) is wrong because given the lateness in a "time is of the essence" contract, Bookstore will not need to prove that the missing pages amount to a "fundamental breach" of the contract. (D) is wrong because (C) is not true. (E) is wrong because (C) is not true.

Question 5: The Gainesville, Florida franchisee for Planet Fitness orders 10 complete sets of rubber-coated steel dumbbells from Heavy Metal's Chicago, Illinois, factory. Planet Fitness uses a purchase order that Heavy Metal signs and accepts, but the purchase order does not include any delivery term and does not otherwise address risk of loss. Heavy Metal makes a delivery contract with Dependo, a nationwide carrier that Heavy Metal has used with great success many times in the past. Heavy Metal promptly notifies Planet Fitness when it puts the goods into Dependo's possession. Unfortunately, the Dependo truck gets hijacked along the way and the dumbbells destined for Gainesville are stolen. Which party, as between Heavy Metal and Planet Fitness, has risk of loss in this case?

(A) Heavy Metal, because the UCC default mode for risk of loss is a destination contract.

(B) Heavy Metal, because the UCC default mode for risk of loss is a shipment contract.

(C) Planet Fitness, because the UCC default mode for risk of loss is a shipment contract.

(D) Planet Fitness, because the UCC default mode for risk of loss is a destination contract.

(E) The two parties will share the loss since neither side bothered to indicate what the risk of loss should be.

Question 5 Answer: The correct answer is (C). According to Official Comment 5 of §2-503, if the two parties fail to indicate a particular delivery term, then UCC Article 2's default rule is for a shipment contract. With a shipment contract under §2-504, the seller must deliver the goods to the carrier in order for risk of loss to pass to the buyer. Delivering the goods under §2-504 includes making a reasonable contract for their transport, putting them into the possession of the carrier, giving the buyer prompt notice of shipment, and tendering any documents necessary for the buyer to take delivery (not indicated here). Because Heavy Metal did all those things, then risk of loss had passed to Planet Fitness by the time the dumbbells were stolen en route to Gainesville. (A) is wrong because the UCC default mode for risk of loss is a shipment contract, not a destination contract. (B) is wrong because even though the UCC default mode for risk of loss is a shipment contract, that means that Planet Fitness gets stuck with the loss here, not Heavy Metal. (D) is wrong because the UCC default mode for risk of loss is a shipment contract, not a destination contract. (E) is wrong because the default mode for risk of loss under the UCC is not loss-sharing, it is a shipment contract.

Question 6: Same facts as Question 5, except that the purchase order that Heavy Metal accepted specifically indicated that this contract is "FOB Seller's Factory." Also, in this variation, Heavy Metal accidentally ships steel dumbbells that are not rubber-coated and therefore would not be suitable for the needs of Planet Fitness. When the dumbbells get stolen en route, which party, as between Heavy Metal and Planet Fitness, has risk of loss in this case?

(A) Heavy Metal, even though this was a shipment contract.
(B) Heavy Metal, unless the purchase order that Heavy Metal accepted included a limitation of remedies to repair or replacement of defective dumbbells.
(C) Both (A) and (B) are true.
(D) Planet Fitness, because this was a shipment contract.
(E) Planet Fitness, because Planet Fitness never actually rejected the steel dumbbells that lacked the rubber coating.

Question 6 Answer: The correct answer is (A). Whenever a particular delivery of goods so fails to conform to the contract as to give a right of rejection, §2-510(1) says that risk of loss remains with the seller until cure or acceptance, neither of which happened here. It does not matter that now we have a specific risk of loss term that indicates a shipment contract; Heavy Metal's breach by delivering the wrong dumbbells overrides what would be the usual risk-of-loss rule with an "FOB Seller's Factory" shipment term like this one. Under §2-601's "perfect tender" rule, there is no question that these dumbbells without the rubber coating are non-conforming enough to have given Planet Fitness a right to reject them, since they "fail in any respect to conform to the contract." (B) is wrong because a limitation of remedy to repair or replacement of defective dumbbells should not change the risk of loss in a case like this where the seller is in breach. Otherwise, such a limitation would "fail of its essential purpose" under §2-719(2) by denying Planet Fitness any remedy in this case. (C) is wrong because (B) is not true. (D) is wrong because under §2-510(1) this is a case where the seller's breach overrides what would be the usual risk-of-loss rules for a shipment contract under §2-509(1)(a). (E) is wrong because §2-510(1) does not require that the buyer actually reject the goods in order for risk of loss to remain with the seller. Instead, the standard is whether the tender or delivery of the goods "so fails to conform to the contract as to give a *right* of rejection" (emphasis added). An actual rejection by the buyer is not required.

Question 7: Lessor and Lessee enter into a finance lease under which Supplier will deliver a machine by third-party carrier to Lessee's factory for a five-year lease term. Nothing is said in the lease contract about the passage of risk of loss. Supplier puts a conforming machine into the possession of a reliable third-party carrier and gives timely notice to Lessee of the delivery, but Lessee fails to get insurance on the machine during transit. The machine then gets destroyed en route to Lessee through no fault of Lessor, Supplier, or Lessee. As between Lessor and Lessee, who has risk of loss as to the destroyed machine?

(A) Lessor, but only because this is a finance lease.
(B) Lessee, but only because this is a finance lease.
(C) Lessee, and that would be true even if this were not a finance lease.
(D) Lessor, because even with a finance lease the risk will not pass until Lessee has accepted the goods.
(E) Lessee, because Lessee should have insured the goods once it received notice of delivery from Supplier.

Question 7 Answer: The correct answer is (D). Section 2A-219(1) says that "[i]n the case of a finance lease, risk of loss passes to the lessee." Although that provision does not say when risk of loss passes to the lessee in a finance lease, case law has made it clear that in the absence of a specific risk-of-loss term in the lease contract, the finance lessee must first accept the goods before risk of loss will pass. Here the machine was destroyed in transit, and therefore Lessee never had an opportunity to accept the goods. (A) is wrong because even though Lessor does have the risk of loss here, it is not because this is a finance lease; rather, it is because Lessee never accepted the machine. (B) is wrong because even though risk of loss can pass to a lessee in a finance lease, the lessee still must accept the goods, which did not happen here. (C) is wrong both because Lessee does not have the risk of loss and because Lessee would not have the risk of loss even if this were not a finance lease. (E) is wrong because Lessee's failure to insure the goods does not affect risk of loss.

Question 8: Same facts as Question 7, except now assume that this lease is not a finance lease, and that the delivery term in the lease is "FOB Lessee's Factory" (since in a non-finance lease there will be no Supplier, and Lessor will be delivering the goods). When the machine gets destroyed en route to Lessee through no fault of Lessor or Lessee, who has risk of loss as to the destroyed machine?

(A) Lessor, because in a non-finance lease risk of loss does not pass to Lessee.
(B) Lessor, because this was a destination contract.
(C) Lessee, because this was a shipment contract.
(D) Lessor, and that would also be true if the delivery term in the lease were "FOB Lessor's Factory."
(E) Lessee, because Lessor did nothing to cause the loss.

Question 8 Answer: The correct answer is (B). Even though §2A-219(1) sets out a default rule that says risk of loss will not pass to the lessee in the case of a non-finance lease, that default rule can be changed by the parties. By using the "FOB Lessee's Factory" delivery term, which is a destination contract, Lessor changes §2A-219(1)'s default rule for risk of loss. Under §2A-219(2)(a)(ii), which covers destination contracts like this one, risk of loss does not pass to Lessee because the machine was never "duly so tendered" at Lessee's factory "as to enable the lessee to take delivery." (A) is wrong because although it correctly states the default rule of §2A-219(1), this case does not fall under the default rule. Instead, this case is handled under §2A-219(2)(a)(ii) because of the specific FOB delivery term that makes this a destination contract. (C) is wrong because this was a destination contract rather than a shipment contract. "FOB Lessee's Factory" requires the lessor to deliver the machine to a particular destination rather than simply deliver the goods to the carrier. (D) is wrong because if the delivery term in the lease were "FOB Lessor's Factory," that would be a shipment contract. Under §2A-219(2)(a)(i), risk of loss in a shipment contract would have passed to Lessee as soon as Lessor delivered the goods to the carrier. (E) is wrong because even though Lessor did not cause the loss, Lessor still has the risk in a destination contract until the goods are "duly tendered" at the stated destination under §2A-219(2)(a)(ii).

Chapter 4. Remedies

Assignment 22: Seller's Remedies with Sales of Goods

A. Why Do Legal Remedies Matter at All?

When thinking about remedies in the sales of goods system, two important but seemingly contradictory truths need to be kept in mind: (1) The players in the system rarely resort to the legal remedies available to them for breaches by the other side; and (2) the existence of the legal remedies is nevertheless a crucial feature of the system.

As to the first point, the general pattern in the system when there are disagreements about a particular transaction is that the business people work out those disagreements. If the disagreements arise in the context of a long-term relationship, both sides often realize that they have much to lose if they are unable to settle the problem — and for that reason, both sides have a great incentive to compromise. Even where the problem arises in a context where "relational" considerations are not as great, the parties still have to consider how costly and time-consuming it will be, if only in the short term, to fail to resolve the dispute.

Even where one or both sides finally conclude that the other side is being completely unreasonable and that the dispute cannot be resolved consensually, the most common remedies that are employed do not involve resort to the legal system. For the aggrieved seller, perhaps the most common remedy for a breach by the buyer is simply to refuse to sell to that buyer ever again. The seller may also take informal steps, short of business slander, that will make it more difficult for the buyer to transact business in the relevant trade community. Unless the stakes are very high and victory seems sure, the aggrieved seller will normally eschew resort to a litigation system that is costly, time-consuming, and uncertain.

Even though so few sales disputes make it to litigation, the formal legal remedy structure available to aggrieved parties is still a crucial feature of the sales system. One way to explain this seeming anomaly is to think of the legal remedies structure as a kind of shadow that lurks behind all negotiations involving disputes between buyers and sellers. As the general counsel for a computer hardware distributor described it, "When our business people get ready to meet with a customer with whom we have a dispute, they will always first come to the legal department just to know what their legal bottom line is coming into those dispute resolution meetings."

Another way to justify the significance of legal remedies is to say that, while access to formal legal remedies will not matter much in most disputes, the cases where they do matter tend to have very high stakes. It is true that with most disputes, either the stakes will be too low to justify litigation or there will be non-legal incentives, either relational or reputational, that will reduce the likelihood of advantage-taking by either side. On the other hand, there will be some cases where the amount in controversy is so large, or where the non-legal sanctions will be so small for a particular party, that the possibility of bad faith and opportunism would be much greater in the absence of a legal remedy for the aggrieved party.

In Professor Russell Weintraub's extensive survey of general counsels for major U.S. companies, one question he posed was, "If there were no legal sanctions for breach of contract and compliance depended on nonlegal sanctions (e.g., reputation in the business community, intra-corporate incentives for good performance), what is your estimate of how business operations would be affected?" Roughly two-thirds of the general counsel responded that there would be a "substantial detrimental effect." Russell J. Weintraub, A Survey of Contract Practice and Policy, 1992 Wis. L. Rev. 1, 24.

As one respondent put it: "Our conduct would change very little because our reputation is critical on a long term basis. My concern would be that smaller companies and start-up operations would be substantially disadvantaged. We would be less inclined to take service or products from them. They have no reputation and [there would be] no legal penalty for non-performance." Id.

Another respondent noted: "I suspect that business in general would tend to the lowest common denominator. Probably would be more uncertainty and sharp practices. Legal sanctions for breach of contract are absolutely essential to business. A contract sets the rules for virtually every transaction." Id. at 24-25.

It is perhaps a tribute to the default remedies for sellers set out in Article 2 of the UCC that few sales contracts in practice change those standard remedies. The main tinkering with remedies in sales contracts affects the buyer's remedies: limitations of remedies to repair or replacement of defective parts, or separate exclusions of consequential damages. A contract that includes a liquidated damages provision could affect the seller's remedies as well, but liquidated damages provisions (which we will discuss in greater detail in Assignment 28) are not prevalent in most sales contracts.

B. What Are a Seller's Legal Remedies?

Before exploring the standard seller's remedies under Article 2 in any detail, one needs first to consider two more general provisions in the UCC that relate to seller's remedies. The first of these is §1-305, a provision that one might think of as "the spirit of the remedies" section. Section 1-305(a) sets down two principles that are significant for a seller's remedies: (1) that the goal of all the remedy provisions in the Code is "that the aggrieved party may be put in as good a position as if the other party had fully performed," and (2) that consequential damages are not allowed unless there is specific provision made for them in the Code.

The first principle, the "benefit of the bargain" idea, can often be a useful gauge against which to measure conflicting interpretations of an individual seller's remedies in various contexts. The second principle means that sellers are not eligible for consequential damages under Article 2 since there is no provision in Article 2 that gives them such damages. Sellers are eligible for "incidental damages" under §2-710, and as the *Firwood* case demonstrates later in this assignment, sellers sometimes argue hard for a broad definition of incidental damages that becomes hard to distinguish from consequential damages.

In addition to §1-305, the other general Code section on seller's remedies that is worth noting at the outset is §2-703. Section 2-703 serves as a convenient catalog for two different aspects of contracts: (1) the various ways in which a buyer might breach its contract with the seller, and (2) the possible remedies available to the seller.

Section 2-703 gives four different ways in which a buyer might breach: (1) wrongfully rejecting goods, (2) wrongfully revoking acceptance, (3) failing to make a payment when due, or (4) anticipatorily repudiating the contract. The one characteristic that all four types of breach have in common is that the buyer is failing to timely pay the seller the full price for the goods purchased. Presumably the seller will not care much what the buyer does as long as the buyer has paid the full price on time and is not asking for its money back.

Section 2-703 lists seven different possible remedies that an aggrieved seller might pursue: (1) withhold delivery, (2) stop delivery by any bailee, (3) identify goods to the contract in the case of an anticipatory repudiation, (4) resell and recover damages under §2-706, (5) recover contract-market damages (or lost profits) under §2-708, (6) sue for the price under §2-709, or (7) cancel the contract. Note that the first three remedies listed are really just actions that the seller may take to limit damages; the last four remedies represent various measures of damages, which we will cover below in order. Specific performance and liquidated damages will be covered in Assignment 28's treatment of "special remedies."

The remedy possibilities that are set out in §2-703 are likely intended to encompass all of the seller's remedies but are clearly not meant to be mutually exclusive of one another. For instance, in a case where a buyer anticipatorily repudiates a contract with the seller before the seller even identifies the goods to the contract, the seller could theoretically pursue four of the listed remedies: (1) withhold delivery of the goods, (2) identify them to the contract, (3) resell them to a third-party buyer and sue for resale damages, and (4) cancel the original contract (since the "canceling" party always retains the right to sue for breach, §2-106(4)).

Whether the pursuit of one remedy by the seller should bar another is not always as simple as the above example suggests. For instance, if an aggrieved seller resells goods prior to the original performance date that were intended for the original contract, can the seller later choose to pursue contract-market damages rather than resale damages if the former end up being more lucrative than the latter? The guidance that the Code gives us on this issue, found in Comment 1 to §2-703, is cryptic at best: "This Article rejects any doctrine of election of remedy as a fundamental policy and thus the remedies are essentially cumulative in nature and include all of the available remedies for breach. Whether the pursuit of one remedy bars another depends entirely on the facts of the individual case."

1. Action for the Price

In discussing particular seller remedies, a good place to begin is the seller's action for the price under §2-709. This remedy is in effect the seller's right of specific performance: it allows the seller to file suit forcing the buyer to pay the agreed-upon price. It is not, however, universally available. The seller is eligible to sue for the price in any of the following three circumstances (all of which assume that the buyer has not yet paid the price): (1) where the buyer has accepted the goods; (2) where conforming goods, whether or not accepted, have been lost or damaged "within a commercially reasonable time after risk of their loss has passed to the buyer"; and (3) where the seller has identified goods to the contract and there is no reasonable prospect of reselling them to a third party for a reasonable price. UCC §2-709(1). If none of those three circumstances exists, the seller cannot sue for the price.

Sack v. Lawton

2003 WL 22682043 (S.D.N.Y. 2003)

Fox, J.

In this action, plaintiffs Shirley D. Sack ("Sack") and Shirley D. Sack, Ltd. ("Sack, Ltd.") (collectively "plaintiffs") allege breach of contract against Kenneth Lawton ("Lawton" or "defendant") and Salvatore Romero ("Romero"). Upon Lawton's failure to answer or otherwise respond to the complaint, United States District Judge Allen G. Schwartz ordered that a default judgment be entered against him. Judge Schwartz then referred the matter to the undersigned to conduct an inquest and to report and recommend the amount of damages, if any, to be awarded to plaintiffs against the defendant. . . .

Sack is a citizen of the state of New York and the president of Sack, Ltd. Sack, Ltd. is a corporation organized and existing under the laws of the state of New York. Lawton is a citizen of the state of North Carolina.

Plaintiffs are the owners of a drawing by the Italian Renaissance artist Raphael, entitled "St. Benedict Receiving Mauro and Placido." The drawing is referred to, by the plaintiffs and others, as the "Modello." Sack avers that the Modello is a unique work of art: an original drawing, with provenance proven beyond question, executed solely by Raphael, and dated 1503-1504 by New York's Metropolitan Museum of Art.

The plaintiffs acquired the work approximately ten years ago; in or about July 2000, plaintiffs offered the Modello for sale. At the time of the offering, the Modello was appraised and determined to be authentic. The work is insured for $12,000,000 by Lloyds of London. Several prospective buyers, including a museum, expressed interest in the Modello; in addition, the plaintiffs received several offers for the drawing. On August 23, 2000, the plaintiffs, acting through their agent, Alan M. Stewart ("Stewart"), entered into an agreement with Lawton whereby Lawton agreed to purchase the Modello for $12,000,000. According to Sack, there was no indication from Lawton that the sale was subject to any further agreement or conditions, and Lawton agreed that the purchase price would be transferred by wire to Stewart's International Capital Management ("ICM") account in New York City.

The sale of the Modello was memorialized in a document entitled "Bill of Sale," dated August 23, 2000, and executed by Stewart and Lawton. The Modello remained in the possession of the plaintiffs pending payment by Lawton of the purchase price. However, Lawton failed to pay any part of the purchase price, despite numerous demands by the plaintiffs, as well as representations by Lawton that the funds were, or would be, forthcoming.

According to Sack, when it became clear that Lawton would not pay the purchase price for the Modello, she attempted to find other buyers for the work. To this end, she displayed the work at a gallery in New York City and publicized its availability among art dealers and members of the art community. However, she was unable to find another buyer for the work at a price comparable to the price agreed upon by Lawton. In addition, Sack contends, since the bill of sale to Lawton is fully executed and has never been cancelled, she may be unable to convey clear title to the work, in the event that she finds a buyer and attempts to consummate an unconditional sale.

At the time Stewart was negotiating the sale of the Modello on behalf of the plaintiffs, Lawton offered to sell plaintiffs a work by the artist Giovanni Bellini, entitled "Madonna and Child." This work is referred to by the plaintiffs as the "Bellini." On or about August 30, 2000, Lawton entered into an agreement with Stewart whereby Stewart became his exclusive agent with respect to the sale of the Bellini. The terms of their agreement were set forth in a commission agreement dated September 18, 2000, and executed by Stewart and Lawton. The commission agreement stated, among other things, that Lawton and Romero were the sole lawful owners of the Bellini and, as such, possessed the legal right to sell, convey and transfer the work without restriction.

Sack states that it was her intention to resell the Bellini immediately after purchasing it, and that she agreed to pay Lawton $10,000,000 for the Bellini after ascertaining that she could resell the work to prospective buyers for $15,000,000. However, according to Sack, after Lawton agreed to sell the Bellini, she was informed that Lawton was not the owner of the work and was not authorized to offer it for sale, and, furthermore, that the true owner did not wish to sell the work to Sack. As a result, Lawton failed to surrender the Bellini to the plaintiffs or to accept payment in connection with their agreement to purchase the work.

Plaintiffs aver that Lawton breached his contract with them for the sale of the Modello and that, although they have reasonably attempted to resell the drawing in order to mitigate the damages caused by the breach, they have been unable to do so, in whole or in part. Plaintiffs also contend that Lawton breached his contract with them concerning the purchase of the Bellini and that they have sustained damages in connection with the breach in the amount of their anticipated profit upon resale of the work. Thus, plaintiffs seek damages in connection with the contract for the sale of the Modello in an amount equal to the purchase price, that is, $12,000,000, as well as interest, and consequential damages in the amount of $3,000,000. In connection with the contract for the purchase of the Bellini, plaintiffs seek damages equal to their anticipated profit, that is, $5,000,000.

Lawton has opposed plaintiffs' claims for damages. In a letter dated February 18, 2002, Lawton denied having breached the contracts at issue in this case and asserted that the Modello was "last traded publicly in London at a Christie's sale in 1989, for under $60K." Lawton also submitted what purports to be a declaration, setting forth essentially the same contentions concerning plaintiffs' damages claims as those contained in his earlier letter. However, the "declaration" is neither signed nor attested.

In support of their application for damages, plaintiffs submitted, *inter alia:* (i) a copy of the August 23, 2000 bill of sale conveying the Modello to Lawton for a sum of $12,000,000; (ii) a copy of the September 18, 2000 commission agreement setting forth the terms of Stewart's agency arrangement with Lawton with respect to the sale of the Bellini; (iii) the declaration of Stewart in support of plaintiffs' motion for a default judgment against Lawton; and (iv) a statement of the interest claimed to be due on plaintiffs' contractual damages. . . .

The general rule for measuring damages for a breach of contract is "the amount necessary to put the plaintiff in the same economic position he would have been in had the defendant fulfilled his contract." Indu Craft, Inc. v. Bank of Baroda, 47 F.3d 490, 495 (2d Cir. 1995). Under New York law, which governs this diversity action, in a case involving the breach of a contract for the sale of goods, a seller may recover the entire contract price, "if the seller is unable to resell [the goods] at a reasonable price or the circumstances reasonably indicate that such effort will be unavailing." Uniform Commercial Code ("UCC") §2-709(1)(b); see also Hyosung America, Inc. v. Sumagh Textile Co., Ltd., 137 F.3d 75, 80-81 (2d Cir. 1998); Creations by Roselynn v. Costanza, 189 Misc. 2d 600, 601, 734 N.Y.S.2d 803, 804-805 (App. Term 2d Dep't 2001).

An aggrieved seller may also recover incidental damages, that is, "commercially reasonable charges incurred in [for example] stopping delivery [or] in the transportation, care and custody of goods after the buyer's breach. . . ." UCC §2-710; see also UCC §§2-708 and 2-709. Since the purpose of providing incidental damages "is only to put the seller in as good a position as performance would have done," incidental damages under the UCC "are limited to out-of-pocket expenses." Ernst Steel Corp. v. Horn Constr. Div., Halliburton Co., 104 A.D.2d 55, 64, 481 N.Y.S.2d 833, 840 (App. Div. 4th Dep't 1984).

Although New York's commercial code provides for incidental damages in the event of a breach by a buyer, there is no comparable provision allowing an aggrieved seller to recover consequential damages. See Associated Metals & Minerals Corp. v. Sharon Steel Corp., 590 F. Supp. 18, 21 (S.D.N.Y. 1983) (citing Petroleo Brasileiro, S.A., Petrobras v. Ameropan Oil Corp., 372 F. Supp. 503, 508 [E.D.N.Y. 1974]). . . .

Based on a review of the parties' submissions in this case, the Court finds that plaintiffs have provided sufficient documentary proof to establish that they are entitled to the amount claimed to be owed for Lawton's breach of the contract for the sale of the Modello. Furthermore, plaintiffs are entitled to prejudgment interest under New York law. However, the Court is not persuaded that plaintiffs are entitled to recover the amount claimed to be owed as consequential damages.

The material submitted by plaintiffs in connection with this inquest establishes that plaintiffs entered into a contract with Lawton for the sale of the Modello for a sum of $12,000,000 and that Lawton failed to pay any part of the purchase price. There is no evidence that the Modello has been resold. Moreover, plaintiffs have established that, under the circumstances, they are unable to resell the Modello at a reasonable price. Accordingly, based on the record evidence, Lawton owes the plaintiffs $12,000,000, the contract price of the Modello. . . .

For the reasons set forth above, I recommend the plaintiffs be awarded damages in the amount of $12,000,000 on their claim for breach of the contract for the sale of the Modello, and prejudgment interest, to be calculated by the Clerk of Court at a rate of 9% per year, on $12,000,000, accruing on August 23, 2000. . . .

[The court denied the plaintiffs' claim for $5 million in lost profits because there was no evidence to indicate that damages for lost profits were within the parties' contemplation at the time the contract for sale of the painting was made.]

———————

If the seller sues for the price, not surprisingly, the seller must hold for the buyer the goods that are the subject of the contract. UCC §2-709(2). If the buyer ultimately pays the judgment for the price, the buyer is entitled to the goods. If while the seller is holding the goods for the buyer, resale becomes possible, then the seller may resell and must deduct from its action for the price any proceeds of resale. UCC §2-709(2).

The seller that sues for the price is also eligible to recover incidental damages. Incidental damages are defined under §2-710 to include "any commercially reasonable charges, expenses or commissions incurred in stopping delivery, in the transportation, care and custody of goods after the buyer's breach, in connection with return or resale of the goods or otherwise resulting from the breach."

2. Resale Damages

In addition to the seller's action for the price, a second standard seller's remedy available under the Code is the seller's right to resale damages. The seller is eligible for these damages whenever the buyer breaches, the seller reasonably identifies the goods being resold as referring to the broken contract, the seller gives the buyer notice of resale, and the seller resells the goods at either a public or private resale. UCC §2-706. The damages formula for the reselling seller that is given under §2-706(1) is KP – RP + ID – ES, where KP = contract price, RP = resale price, ID = incidental damages, and ES = expenses saved as a consequence of buyer's breach. To give the seller an incentive to obtain the highest possible price, the Code provides that the seller is not liable to account to the breaching buyer for any profit that it makes on a resale. UCC §2-706(6).

When the seller's resale takes place over an extended period of time, as in the following case, at least a couple of issues are raised: (1) May the seller's resale still be considered commercially reasonable? and (2) Will the seller be compensated for the time value of money lost to the delay?

Firwood Mfg. Co. v. General Tire

96 F.3d 163 (6th Cir. 1996)

Kennedy, C.J.

Defendant General Tire, Inc. appeals the District Court's . . . judgment . . . awarding plaintiff Firwood Manufacturing Company, Inc. $187,513 in resale damages and $100,476 in interest in this breach of contract dispute. . . . For the following reasons, we AFFIRM the liability award but REVERSE the award of interest.

This dispute arises from a contract between Firwood and General Tire in which General Tire allegedly agreed to purchase fifty-five model 1225 post-cure inflators (PCIs), thirty-thousand dollar machines used by General Tire in its manufacturing process. . . .

By April 1990, General Tire had purchased twenty-two PCIs from Firwood under the contract. General Tire closed its Barrie plant soon thereafter.

On April 11, 1991, Firwood wrote General Tire to remind it of its obligation to purchase fifty-five PCIs. Firwood informed General Tire that the thirty-three remaining PCIs were in the following stages of production: eight units, 100 percent complete; five units, 95 percent complete; and twenty units, 65 percent complete.

After learning that General Tire did not intend to complete the purchase of the remaining thirty-three PCIs at issue in this dispute, Firwood began looking for alternative buyers. Firwood contacted every major tire company in the United

States. General Tire also sought alternative buyers for the PCIs. After three years of searching for alternative buyers, during which it sold a few machines, Firwood was ultimately able to sell the balance of the thirty-three PCIs intended for General Tire, but at a price below that called for in the contract with General Tire.

While looking for buyers, Firwood filled some of its ongoing orders for spare parts with parts that already had been installed in the thirty-three PCIs intended for General Tire. Although the PCIs themselves were specially made for General Tire, the parts taken from the General Tire PCIs and sold as spare parts were fungible parts regularly sold in Firwood's spare parts business.

Following a jury trial, the jury awarded Firwood $287,989 in damages, of which $187,513 represented the difference between resale price and contract price, and $100,476 represented interest. Following trial, General Tire filed a motion seeking judgment as a matter of law, a new trial, or remittitur. The District Court denied General Tire's post-trial motions, and this appeal followed. . . .

General Tire argues that Firwood cannot recover under [UCC §2-706] because it did not comply with this section's requirements. General Tire argues that Firwood did not reasonably identify the goods under the contract because the thirty-three PCIs ultimately sold contained parts not originally included in the machines at the time of the breach. There is also a question whether the resale was commercially reasonable where twenty-nine of the thirty-three machines were sold three years after the breach.

We must first decide whether a seller may substitute fungible goods for those identified to the contract at the time of the breach. Here, identical parts were used to replace the parts which had been sold in the interim. On this question, we find persuasive the reasoning of those courts that allow sellers to substitute fungible goods for purposes of resale so long as the goods truly are fungible and the resale itself is commercially reasonable. In Servbest Foods, Inc. v. Emessee Indus., Inc., 82 Ill. App. 3d 662, 37 Ill. Dec. 945, 403 N.E.2d 1 (1980), the Court allowed a seller to recover damages under §2-706 of the UCC when the resale included different meat than that specifically identified to the contract at the time of the breach:

> the nature of fungible goods suggests no reason why, where a contract involving fungible goods is breached by the buyer, a seller could not recover a deficiency award under section 2-706 based upon a resale of goods other than those identified to the contract inasmuch as such a sale would not affect or alter the price received for the goods in either a private or public sale.

Servbest, 37 Ill. Dec. 945, 403 N.E.2d at 9. The Second Circuit adopted the *Servbest* rule in a case considering whether a heating oil seller could receive damages under §2-706 when the oil ultimately resold was different from the oil originally identified to the contract. Apex Oil Co. v. Belcher Co. of New York, Inc., 855 F.2d 997, 1005 (2d Cir. 1988). The resold model 1225 post-cure inflators remained reasonably identified to the contract. Thus Firwood is not barred from recovery simply because the PCIs it ultimately sold contained parts different than those at the time General Tire breached. The parts were fungible, and the PCIs into which they were placed were essentially the same PCIs specially made for General Tire.

However, *Apex Oil* and *Servbest* identified another important consideration for analyzing whether resales involving substituted fungible goods are commercially reasonable. In *Apex Oil,* the court noted that "[t]he most pertinent aspect of reasonableness with regard to identification and resale involves timing." *Apex Oil,* 855 F.2d at 1006. Noting that §2-706 is designed to provide the seller the difference between market value and the contract price, and that resale is designed to determine market price, the court cautioned that timely resale was particularly important in cases involving substituted goods:

> The rule that a "resale should be made as soon as practicable after . . . breach" should be stringently applied where, as here, the resold goods are not those originally identified to the contract. In such circumstances, of course, there is a significant risk that the seller, who may perhaps have already disposed of the original goods without suffering any loss, has identified new goods for resale in order to minimize the resale price and thus to maximize damages.

Apex Oil, 855 F.2d at 1007 (citation omitted); see also McMillan v. Meuser Material & Equip. Co., Inc., 260 Ark. 422, 541 S.W.2d 911, 913 (1976) (finding resale commercially unreasonable because "the resale of [a] bulldozer, in excess of fourteen months after the alleged breach, will be of 'slight probative value' as an indication of the market price at the time of the breach.").

We must decide whether Firwood's resale of PCIs may not serve as the basis of the damage award because sales three years after a breach are not commercially reasonable. There is significant support for the view that three years is unreasonable. See *Apex Oil,* 855 F.2d at 1006-07 (finding that six-week delay between breach and resale of heating oil, when market volatility over that period was considered, prevented resale from accurately reflecting the market value of the oil); *Meuser Material,* 541 S.W.2d at 913.

Nevertheless, as the Second Circuit recognized in *Apex Oil,* sellers ought not to be precluded from recovering damages in every case in which resale does not occur immediately:

> "If no reasonable market existed at [the] time, no doubt a delay may be proper and a subsequent sale may furnish the best test, though confessedly not a perfectly exact one, of the seller's damages."

Apex Oil, 855 F.2d at 1006, quoting 4 Anderson on the Uniform Commercial Code §2-706:25 (3d ed. 1983). Indeed, Comment Five to [UCC §2-706] notes that "[w]hat is such a reasonable time depends upon the nature of the goods, the condition of the market and the other circumstances of the case; its length cannot be measured by any legal yardstick or divided into degrees." Even though there was a three-year delay between breach and resale here, we cannot say that the jury was required to find that the resale was commercially unreasonable. At the time of the breach, there was no market for PCIs, machines costing over thirty-thousand dollars that have a very specialized use. Moreover, Firwood made a continuing good faith effort to locate other purchasers. While a three-year delay is suboptimal, we are mindful that UCC remedies are to be liberally construed to ensure that the aggrieved party is "put in as good a position as if the other party had fully performed. . . ." [UCC §1-305(a)]. Accordingly, we hold that the District Court did not err when it denied General Tire's motion for judgment as a matter of law.

Finally, defendant argues that the District Court erred in denying its remittitur motion to eliminate the interest portion of the damage award. Defendant argues that the District Court abused its discretion because, under the UCC, sellers are not entitled to interest damages when buyers breach the contract, and interest is a consequential, not incidental, damage. The District Court denied defendant's motion on the ground that, since courts have required breaching buyers to compensate sellers for extra interest payments made on loans as a result of a breach, plaintiff should be allowed to collect its lost use of money due to the breach. We review a district court's denial of a remittitur motion for abuse of discretion, reviewing the legal component of such denial de novo.

Resolution of this question rests on the distinction between incidental and consequential damages, for sellers are entitled to incidental, but not consequential damages, under the UCC. Michigan defines a seller's incidental damages to include any commercially reasonable charges, expenses or commissions incurred in stopping delivery, in the transportation, care and custody of goods after the buyer's breach, in connection with return or resale of the goods or otherwise resulting from the breach. [UCC §2-710]. The District Court held that "commercially reasonable charges . . . resulting from the breach" include interest on the lost use of money caused by the breach. The District Court drew support for its expansive interpretation of "commercial reasonable charges" from Bulk Oil (U.S.A.), Inc. v. Sun Oil Trading Co., 697 F.2d 481 (2d Cir. 1983), in which the seller, Bulk Oil, was awarded post-breach interest payments on a loan taken out to finance its $4,000,000 fuel oil purchase. 697 F.2d at 482. The District Court implicitly held that lost use of money was "related to the concept of interest paid on a loan that would not have been taken out absent breach." Since interest payments constituted incidental damages under *Bulk Oil,* the District Court reasoned, Firwood could recover an analogous incidental damage, viz. its lost use of money caused by General Tire's breach. . . .

Although New York has interpreted incidental damages broadly to include interest payments attributed to the breach under its version of the UCC, Michigan defines incidental damages much more narrowly. In S.C. Gray, Inc. v. Ford Motor Co., 92 Mich. App. 789, 286 N.W.2d 34 (1979), the Michigan Court of Appeals held that a seller could not recover "interest it paid on loans taken out to maintain the business when Ford failed to pay" as incidental damages because interest payments constitute consequential damages. *S.C. Gray,* 286 N.W.2d at 43.

Moreover, Michigan courts have impliedly rejected sellers' claims to the lost use of money by treating interest payments as consequential damages. In Sullivan Indus., Inc. v. Double Seal Glass Co., Inc., 192 Mich. App. 333, 480 N.W.2d 623 (1991), appeal denied, 441 Mich. 931, 498 N.W.2d 737 (1993), the Court of Appeals noted: "Examples of consequential damages include lost profits and interest paid on loans taken out to maintain business operations, see *S.C. Gray,* 92

Mich. App. at 811-812, 286 N.W.2d 34." *Sullivan Indus.*, 480 N.W.2d at 631 (citations omitted); see also id. 480 N.W.2d at 633 ("Interest paid on loans taken out to maintain the business, if foreseeable, falls within the category of consequential damages as prescribed by the UCC."). Since Michigan considers interest paid on loans to be a consequential damage, not an incidental damage, and since sellers may not seek consequential damages, Firwood could not have sought to collect interest payments on a loan to pay for the raw materials in the machines it was to build for General Tire. Nor could it seek the economic equivalent—its lost use of money. . . .

Moreover, even if lost use of money were somehow economically distinguishable from interest payments on a loan, we are inclined to agree with the Seventh Circuit's view that sellers are not entitled to the former as an element of the damage award because lost use of funds is a consequential damage. In *Afram Export Corp. v. Metallurgiki Halyps, S.A.*, the Seventh Circuit rejected a seller's claim for interest payments. 772 F.2d 1358 (7th Cir. 1985). Noting that

> a foregone profit from exploiting a valuable opportunity that the breach of contract denied to the victim of the breach fits more comfortably under the heading of consequential damages than of incidental damages

it held that "the interest or profit [plaintiff] could have obtained from investing, or using elsewhere in its business, the money that it would have gotten [if defendant had not breached]" was a consequential damage. *Afram Export,* 772 F.2d at 1369-70. Since sellers may receive only incidental damages, not consequential damages, and since the lost use of money is a consequential damage, Firwood was not entitled to receive interest as a measure of the damage award. . . .

Nevertheless, Firwood was entitled to claim statutory interest from the date on which suit was filed under Mich. Comp. Laws Ann. §600.6013 even if, as a seller, it was not entitled to interest as a measure of damages under the UCC.

For the foregoing reasons, the District Court is AFFIRMED in all respects except: the award of interest as an element of damages is VACATED, and the case is REMANDED to the District Court for calculation of prejudgment interest under Mich. Comp. Laws Ann. §600.6013.

The result in *Firwood* calls into question the wisdom of not allowing sellers to be eligible for consequential damages under Article 2. Suppose that instead of waiting around three years to ultimately find a buyer for these specialized machines, the seller in *Firwood* had chosen instead to sue immediately (or at least right after it failed to find a new buyer despite contacting all of the major tire companies) for the price under §2-709(1)(b) ("if the seller is unable after reasonable effort to resell [the goods] at a reasonable price or the circumstances reasonably indicate that such effort will be unavailing"). Given the very specialized nature of these expensive machines, the seller could have argued that circumstances reasonably indicate here that efforts to resell would be unavailing.

Had the seller in *Firwood* sued immediately for the price, then under Michigan law it would have been able to claim statutory interest on that amount from the date the suit was filed. Instead, the seller diligently tried for three years to sell all of the machines until it finally was able to. Yet despite these good-faith efforts that mainly benefited the breaching buyer, the Sixth Circuit was not willing to give the seller the time value of its money, a value that the seller certainly would have been able to capture in a successful action for the price. Given the Sixth Circuit's position on this matter, what incentive will a seller in Firwood's position have in the future when faced with a similar breach by a buyer: try long and hard to resell, or look for the first opportunity to sue for the price?

One reason that the incentives created by the *Firwood* case should be troubling for the larger sales system is that, as a general matter, the seller is in a much better position than the breaching buyer to dispose of goods for the highest possible price. If sellers are encouraged to immediately sue for the price rather than wait to resell, then it will be the buyer rather than the seller that will ultimately have to dispose of the goods in any case where the seller actually recovers the price from the buyer.

3. Contract-Market Difference (Without Resale)

In addition to the contract-resale difference and an action for the price, another basic seller's remedy is the contract-market difference under §2-708(1). Whenever the buyer repudiates or wrongfully fails to accept, the seller's damages under §2-708(1) equal KP – MP + ID – ES, where KP = contract price, MP = market price, ID = incidental damages, and ES = expenses saved as a consequence of buyer's breach.

The market price under §2-708(1) is measured as of the time and place for tender, both of which are defined by the contract. The time for tender will be the stated performance date in the contract, and the place for tender will be a function of the delivery term. Thus, an "FOB shipment" term would measure the market price at the seller's location; an "FOB destination" term would measure the market price at the buyer's location.

4. Lost Profits

The last major route that the aggrieved seller may pursue to recover damages is the "lost profits" measure of §2-708(2). This complicated formula will be the subject of Assignment 24. For now, think of the lost-profits seller (also called "lost-volume" seller) as one that, had the buyer not breached, would have made an additional profit. Because such a seller will have lost a profit as a result of the buyer's breach, neither the contract-resale nor contract-market damage measures truly puts this seller in the same position the seller would have been in had the buyer not breached.

Problem Set 22

22.1.   a. Specialty Dolls, Inc., is in the business of manufacturing children's dolls and stuffed animals. At the height of the "Beanie Baby" craze, Specialty Dolls made a contract to sell 2,000 Beanie Babies to a retailer, Kid Knacks, for a total price of $10,000. The contract said that the 2,000 Beanie Babies would come from "the stock of 8,000 Beanie Babies currently stored in the Specialty Dolls warehouse." When suddenly the Beanie Baby mania died out, Kid Knacks repudiated its contract with Specialty Dolls and told it not to ship the Beanie Babies. At this point, the dolls intended for the Kid Knacks contract had not been set apart from the other 6,000 dolls in the Specialty Dolls warehouse. Specialty Dolls spent lots of time during the next couple of days calling around for another buyer. The only one it found, however, was the Everything Is a Dollar store, which was willing to pay just $1,000 for a shipment of 2,000 Beanie Babies. If Specialty Dolls declines the offer from the Everything Is a Dollar store, may it recover the price from Kid Knacks? UCC §§2-704(1)(a), 2-709.

b. Same facts as part (a), except that after turning down the offer from Everything Is a Dollar, the goods are completely destroyed in a fire through no fault of Specialty Dolls. Unfortunately, Specialty Dolls has no fire insurance. May Specialty Dolls recover the price from Kid Knacks? UCC §§2-510(3), 2-709, 2-501(1); Official Comment 5 to §2-501, §§2-105(4), 1-201(b)(18).

c. Same facts as part (a), except that after turning down the offer from Everything Is a Dollar, Specialty Dolls sends one of its representatives to a local flea market in an attempt to sell its last stock of Beanie Babies, including those intended for Kid Knacks. The Specialty Dolls rep brings three identical boxes of 2,000 Beanie Babies each, including one that has Kid Knacks' name on it. The first buyer at the flea market agrees to pay $6,000 for one of the boxes, so the Specialty Dolls rep gives the buyer the box with Kid Knacks' name on it. The second buyer agrees to buy one of the two remaining boxes for $7,000, and the third buyer buys the last box for $4,000. Assuming that Specialty Dolls gave Kid Knacks proper notice of its intent to resell at the flea market, for what amount may Specialty Dolls recover from Kid Knacks? UCC §2-706.

d. Same facts as part (a), except suppose that originally the parties had two separate contracts: one for a box of 1,000 "Dobie Dog" dolls for $5,000 and the second for a box of 1,000 "Digger Frog" dolls for $5,000. When Specialty Dolls goes to the flea market to sell its last stock of these dolls, it ends up selling the box of Dobie Dogs for $8,000 and the box of Digger Frogs for $3,000. Assuming proper notice of the resale, for what amount may Specialty Dolls recover from Kid Knacks? UCC §2-706.

22.2.   a. Mel's Furniture for Less makes a contract with Kathy Levine to sell her an oak desk for her home office that she just had built in her basement. Payment was due a month after delivery. Kathy receives the desk and immediately notices that there is significant water damage on the surface of the desk. She intends to call Mel's to complain, but she gets busy with other things. When Mel's sends the bill a month later, Kathy announces to Mel's that she is not going to pay for the desk and Mel's should come and pick it up. Should Mel's be allowed to recover from Kathy in a suit for the price? UCC §§2-709, 2-606, 2-607(2) and (3), 2-602(1), 2-608.

b. Same facts as part (a), except that the desk was perfectly fine, but Kathy decided on the day that she received it that she did not like how it looked in her basement. She immediately called Mel's and told the manager there, "Come get your desk. I've decided I don't want it after all, and I'm not paying for it." Should Mel's be allowed to recover from Kathy in a suit for the price? UCC §§2-709, 2-606, 2-602.

c. Same facts as part (a), except that the desk was perfectly fine, but Kathy decided two weeks after she received it that she did not like how it looked in her basement. She then called Mel's and told the manager there, "Come get your desk. I've decided I don't want it after all, and I'm not paying for it." Should Mel's be allowed to recover from Kathy in a suit for the price? UCC §§2-709, 2-608; Official Comment 5 to §2-709.

22.3.   Shoe Works was a Boston manufacturer of athletic footwear. Foot Locker was a Chicago retailer that sold shoes of all kinds, including sports shoes. On May 1, Shoe Works and Foot Locker entered into a contract in which Shoe Works agreed to sell Foot Locker 500 pairs of "Sambas," a trendy brand of children's gym shoes. The price was $7,500, the delivery date was "on or before June 1," and the delivery term was "FOB Seller's Plant." Delivery costs from Boston to Chicago were $300, which the buyer paid in advance. Shoe Works put the shoes into the possession of a carrier in Boston on May 25, and the shoes arrived at Foot Locker on June 1. By that point, Foot Locker had concluded that Sambas were no longer "hot," so the Foot Locker manager immediately called the Shoe Works president and told her that the Foot Locker was rejecting the order. Shoe Works quickly arranged to have the shoes sold to Hermann's Sporting Goods in the Chicago suburb of Oak Lawn. Hermann's paid $6,000 for the shoes and picked up the shoes itself from Foot Locker. Unfortunately for Shoe Works, it forgot to give Foot Locker notice of this resale. The market price of 500 Sambas was $6,000 in Chicago on June 1 and $6,500 in Boston on the same date. On May 1, the market price was $7,000 in Chicago and $7,500 in Boston. On May 25, the price was $6,200 in Chicago and $6,700 in Boston. In a suit against Foot Locker, how much may Shoe Works recover (assuming Shoe Works is not a lost-volume seller)? UCC §2-509(1)(a), Official Comment 2 to §2-706; §§2-706, 2-708(1), 2-503(2), 2-504; Official Comment 1 to §2-708.

22.4.   a. Ben Farmer, a local cattle rancher, is visiting your office for the first time. It turns out that earlier this year Ben had agreed to sell 100 cattle (the last 100 Ben had available for sale) to Mel's Meat for Less (MMFL) for $50,000, "buyer to pick up on May 1." On May 1, MMFL called Ben and repudiated the contract. The market price for 100 cattle on May 1 was $45,000. On June 15, without ever giving notice to MMFL, Ben sold the 100 cattle to a third party for $49,000. It cost Ben roughly $400 per month to feed these cattle. Ben would like to know what his damages against MMFL will be. What do you advise? UCC §§2-708(1), 2-706, 1-305(a); Official Comment 1 to §2-703.

b. Same facts as part (a), except Ben's resale had been for just $40,000. What would Ben's damages be then? Official Comment 2 to §2-706.

c. If Ben's resale had been for $40,000, except this time he had given proper notice of the resale, what would Ben's damages be then? Official Comment 5 to §2-706.

d. Suppose now that MMFL had repudiated on March 1, and then on March 15 Ben gave MMFL notice of resale, identified the cattle as the subject of resale, and resold the cattle for $48,000. If the market price of the cattle on May 1 were $45,000, would Ben still be eligible for §2-708(1) damages? If not, why not? UCC §§2-708(1), 2-706, 1-305(a); Official Comment 1 to §2-703.

e. Suppose that MMFL had repudiated on March 1, and then on March 15 Ben identified the cattle as the subject of resale and resold the cattle for $48,000. But this time Ben, though he intended otherwise, completely forgot to give notice of the resale to MMFL. If the market price of the cattle on May 1 were $45,000, would Ben still be eligible for §2-708(1) damages? If not, why not? UCC §§2-708(1), 2-706, 1-305(a); Official Comment 1 to §2-703.

22.5. Super Dave's Ford Dealership in Waterloo, Iowa, was participating in a manufacturer's incentive program whereby Ford would give a $20,000 bonus to any dealership that sold 100 new Ford Aerostar mini-vans in one calendar year. In late November, Super Dave's had sold 87 new Aerostars when the Waterloo School District made a contract with Dave's to purchase 15 Aerostars for delivery on December 20. Immediately before the district signed the contract, Super Dave told the district representative, "The reason I am able to give you such a great price on these vans is that the 15 vans that you're buying brings our total Aerostar sales to 102 for the year, and we get a $20,000 bonus from Ford if we sell over 100 Aerostars for the year." On December 18, the superintendent of the school district calls Super Dave's to tell him that the district had found a different dealership with a better price on the mini-vans, and thus it would not be buying the vans from Super Dave's. On December 31, Super Dave's had sold a total of 91 Aerostars for the year and therefore did not qualify for the $20,000 incentive payment. When Super Dave's sues the school district for breach, may Super Dave's include in its damages the $20,000 manufacturer's incentive? UCC §§2-710, 1-305(a), 2-706(1), 2-708, 2-709(1); cf. §2-715(2)(a).

Assignment 23: Lessor's and Seller's Remedies with Leases, International Sales, and Real Estate

A. Lessor's Remedies

Although the UCC drafters clearly used the Article 2 remedy structure as a foundation for drafting the remedy provisions of Article 2A, there are a number of fundamental differences between a sale and a lease that in turn create major differences between the remedies for a seller and those for a lessor.

The most fundamental difference between a sale and a lease is that the lessor has a residual interest in the goods that are leased, but the seller has no continuing interest in the goods that are sold. As a result, the lessor and lessee realize at the outset that their contract is necessarily in the nature of a long-term relationship, whereas the seller and buyer may view their contract as a one-shot deal.

The functional significance of the long-term nature of the lessor-lessee relationship is that parties to a lease contract are more likely than buyers and sellers to specify in the lease contract just what the lessor's remedies will be in the event of a default. Similarly, the lessor and lessee are more likely to articulate in their contract exactly what constitutes an event of default. The seller and buyer, by contrast, will likely know that, ordinarily, the only way that the buyer can breach is by failing to pay the price.

Section 2A-523 categorizes both the lessor's remedies and the various ways in which the lessee can breach. In comparing §2A-523 with §2-703 (listing seller's remedies), two differences are apparent. The first is that the lessor, unlike the seller, is given the right to repossess the goods as one of its standard remedies in §2A-523. Unless the seller has a security interest in the goods it sells on credit, the seller will not normally have a right to repossess upon the buyer's failure to pay the price (and even then the right to repossess arises under Article 9 and the parties' agreement, not Article 2). Because the lessor has a residual interest, however, a default by the lessee can trigger the lessor's right to repossess, which helps the lessor preserve the value of its residual interest.

The second difference between the lessor's listed remedies and those of the seller is that §2A-523(1)(f) specifically mentions that the lessor may "exercise any other rights or pursue any other remedies provided in the lease contract." This recognizes the practice described above of the lessor and lessee often spelling out in their lease contract the various ways in which the lessee might be in default of its obligations to the lessor.

The lessor's action for the rent under §2A-529 is the analogous remedy to the seller's action for the price. The lessor's "price" equivalent consists of both unpaid past rent plus the present value of any future rent. UCC §2A-529(1). Once the lessor sues for the rent, it must hold the leased goods for the lessee for the remaining term of the lease. UCC §2A-529(2). If the lessor leases the goods to a new lessee before the end of the existing lease term, then the original lessee gets credit for the revenue gained on the new lease. UCC §2A-529(3). If the lessee pays the judgment for the rent, it is entitled to possession and use of the leased goods for the remainder of the term. UCC §2A-529(4).

The lessor who sues for the rent is also eligible for incidental damages under §2A-530.

The lessor's analogue to contract-resale damages is found in §2A-527. If the lessor enters into a new lease agreement that is "substantially similar" to the original lease agreement, the lessor is entitled to UR + (PVOL − PVNL) + ID − ES, where UR = accrued but unpaid rent on the original lease as of the date of the new lease term, PVOL = the present value, as of the same date, of the total remaining lease payments for the original lease, PVNL = the present value, as of the same date, of the total lease payments in the new lease for the term that is comparable to the remainder of the original lease, ID = incidental damages, and ES = expenses saved as a consequence of the lessee's breach.

Note the reason why the "substantially similar" limitation exists for new leases but not for resales: whereas with lease agreements the lease terms can vary in length, with sales agreements the transfer of ownership from seller to buyer is always intended to be final. If the lease agreement in the new lease is not "substantially similar" to the original lease, then the lessor must seek damages under §2A-528, Article 2A's contract-market measure. The formula under §2A-528 is UR + (PVOL − PVML) + ID − ES, where UR = accrued but unpaid rent for the original lease (measured as of the default where lessor has not repossessed or the date of repossession where the lessor has repossessed), PVOL = the present value, as of the same date, of the total remaining lease payments for the original lease, PVML = the present value, as of the same date, of the market rent for such a remaining term at the place where the goods are located, ID = incidental damages, and ES = expenses saved.

Section 2A-528(2) also provides a "lost profits" alternative for the aggrieved lessor when the lessor can show that the other measures of damages do not place it in the same position that performance by the lessee would have.

C.I.C. Corp. v. Ragtime, Inc.
726 A.2d 316 (N.J. App. 1999)

PRESSLER, J.

. . . Plaintiff C.I.C. Corp., a New Jersey corporation, appeals from a judgment entered upon a jury verdict awarding it damages of one dollar on its contract claim against defendants, Ragtime, Inc., and Donald Tabatneck. It also appeals from the subsequent order of the trial court denying its motion for a new trial on damages. We find plain error in the court's instructions to the jury respecting damages and accordingly reverse and remand for a new damages trial.

Plaintiff is in the vending machine business. Pursuant to written contracts with owners of various types of retail establishments, it places a variety of coin-operated machines, which it owns, on their premises, including cigarette machines, jukeboxes and game machines. If the machine sells a product, plaintiff keeps the machine stocked. It also services the machines on an on-call basis. The coins are removed by its collectors on a bi-weekly basis and the revenue is shared between plaintiff and the owner of the premises in accordance with the terms of their agreement. Defendant Donald Tabatneck is the proprietor of a so-called go-go bar in West Paterson owned by his corporation, 821 McBride Avenue Corporation, and operated under the trade name Ragtime. He had had plaintiff's coin-operated machines on his premises since the late 1970s or early 1980s under a series of consecutive contracts.

The controversy between the parties arose out of the five-year contract executed by them on October 13, 1994. The agreement covered a cigarette machine, a jukebox, a pool table, and a pinball machine, which had been on the premises for some time. Pursuant to the terms of the agreement, and at defendant's request, plaintiff also loaned defendant $3,500 by way of an advance on his portion of the future revenues at ten percent interest. In the following month, defendant repaid the loan and the four machines were removed. . . .

The problem here is only as to damages. Plaintiff's Office Manager Kathleen Strojny explained plaintiff's computerized record-keeping system and its printouts by which she was able to determine the average net monthly revenue earned by plaintiff from each of the four machines that it had placed in defendant's premises during the twelve-month period preceding the breach. Its net average monthly revenue from the cigarette machine, based on an average monthly sale of 242 packs, was $254. The arrangement with respect to the jukebox was a flat $15 weekly rental sum paid by defendant to plaintiff or, roughly, a monthly net revenue of $60. The monthly revenue from the pinball machine and the pool table was shared between the parties, and plaintiff's average total net for the two machines totaled $386. Strojny therefore calculated plaintiff's net lost monthly revenue over the life of the contract at $700. Over the course of the 59 months of the term remaining on the lease at the time of the breach, the total loss of net revenue was, therefore, $41,000. That was the sum plaintiff sought to recover.

Defendant did not dispute Strojny's calculations respecting the revenue earned by the four machines during the year prior to the breach. The thrust of his defense to the damages claim was his assertion that plaintiff was required to mitigate damages and had failed to do so. And therein lies the error that tainted this damages verdict. In sum, as a matter of law, plaintiff was not required to mitigate.

We consider that legal issue in the context of this record. First, defendant, on his cross-examination of Strojny, attempted to elicit from her information as to what had happened to the four machines after they were removed from his premises. All she could say is that they had been taken to plaintiff's warehouse and that another customer would, in the normal course of business, have been sought for them. She was unable to say, beyond speculation, if these machines had ever been placed with another customer and, if so, how long it had taken to do so. The mitigation issue was next referred to by the court in overruling defendant's objection to the admission into evidence of Strojny's computer printout respecting the average monthly revenue earned by each machine in the year preceding the breach. Although permitting its admission, the court noted that:

> It can be argued that there were very effective arguments made against it, for example, that the equipment was used by somebody else within a few months and the [defense] hasn't been able to say, you know, what happened to the equipment and whether it was used by another company or not.

Evidently, then, the judge was of the view that mitigation was an applicable doctrine here, and plaintiff did not take exception to these comments, perhaps because he had prevailed on the evidence issue that provoked those comments.

The mitigation issue was again referred to in both summations. Defendant's attorney told the jury that he believed the judge would instruct it on mitigation of damages and then referred to Strojny's testimony respecting her lack of knowledge as to the disposition of the equipment after its removal from defendant's premises. He concluded these remarks with this argument:

> Because they want $41,400 from Mr. Tabatneck, if you find he breached his contract, and it didn't work—didn't go as Mr. Tabatneck said. They want you to give them 41,000—what is it again? Four hundred dollars. But they don't tell you whether they made earnings and what earnings they made on those machines when they took them out of there or when it all started. They're going to ask you to take a shot in the dark. That's what they're asking you. Pick a number, pick 41,400, pick any number you want. Do you understand what I'm saying? Put in the position that this defendant is put in, he's asked to pay forty-one.

In his ensuing summation, plaintiff's attorney argued that there was no duty to mitigate. This is what he said:

> But let's assume that eventually we were able to do that [place the equipment elsewhere]. Does that mean that we don't have losses? Of course not. We have the right to have two establishments, Ragtime plus the next one, a thousand establishments. Now granted, we would have to buy a couple more machines to put into these other establishments, but he is asking you to believe that, if we found another establishment, that wipes out our monetary losses. His position is completely wrong. It's as wrong as, if somebody signs a contract to buy a television set and refuses to pay for it and doesn't want the TV set, if the television seller wants to sue him, they can't say, well, you probably sold your new TV set to someone else. The response is going to be the same as I'm telling you. But what if we did sell that TV to someone else? We have a right to sell TVs to two people, so we want our lost profits from your transaction, Mr. Tabatneck.

Unfortunately, neither attorney requested a charge respecting the duty to mitigate despite defendant's clear assertion that there was such a duty as a matter of law and plaintiff's equally clear assertion that there was not. The judge then instructed the jury generally as to the primary function of compensatory damages, namely, making the injured party whole, and then had this to say:

> The plaintiff presented the testimony of Miss Strojny with regard to the records of the corporation and what the losses were with regard to each machine. You have an exhibit that goes through that testimony, which reveals that testimony, that testimony as to what the end result was with regard to each machine. *You also have the cross-examination of the defendant, which pointed out ways which may or may not have mitigated or lessened those damages. So what those damages are is for you to decide, according to the law that I just described.* Now in arriving at an amount of any loss of profits sustained by the plaintiff, you may consider any past earnings of the plaintiff in its business, as well as any other evidence bearing upon the issue. So you—the testimony that you heard from Miss Strojny about what happened in the immediate past and you have to make a determination as to whether that can be projected reasonably into the future or not. That's the kind of determination that you have to make if you get to the issue of damages in this case. [Emphasis added.]

Thus, although not expressly instructing the jury with respect to the doctrine of mitigation or its applicability here, the court nevertheless clearly advised the jury that, in fixing damages, it could consider what plaintiff did or should have done to "mitigate or lessen damages."

That instruction was in error. This is clearly a "lost volume" situation or, at least, the jury could have so found. As explained by Restatement (Second) of Contracts §347 comment f (1981):

> Whether a subsequent transaction is a substitute for the broken contract sometimes raises difficult questions of fact. If the injured party could and would have entered into the subsequent contract, even if the contract had not been broken, and could have had the benefit of both, he can be said to have "lost volume" and the subsequent transaction is not a substitute for the broken contract. The injured party's damages are then based on the net profit that he has lost as a result of the broken contract. Since entrepreneurs try to operate at optimum capacity, however, it is possible that an additional transaction would not have been profitable and that the injured party would not have chosen to expand his business by undertaking it had there been no breach. It is sometimes assumed that he would have done so, but the question is one of fact to be resolved according to the circumstances of each case.

And as further explicated by the Restatement, supra, §350 comment d (1981):

> The mere fact that an injured party can make arrangements for the disposition of the goods or services that he was to supply under the contract does not necessarily mean that by doing so he will avoid loss. If he would have entered into both transactions but for the breach, he has "lost volume" as a result of the breach. See Comment f to §347. In that case the second transaction is not a "substitute" for the first one.

We adopted the Restatement view in Locks v. Wade, 36 N.J. Super. 128, 114 A.2d 875 (App. Div. 1955), a case involving the remarkably similar circumstance of a jukebox rental. Relying on the analogous section of the first Restatement of Contracts §336 comment c, we held that:

> We think the position plaintiff takes on the matter is sound. Where, as here, a plaintiff lessor agrees to lease an article of which the supply in the market is for practical purposes not limited, then the law would be depriving him of the benefit of his bargain if on the breach of the agreement, it required his claim against the lessee to be reduced by the amount he actually did or reasonably could realize on a re-letting of the article. For if there had been no breach and another customer had appeared, the lessor could as well have secured another such article and entered into a second lease. In case of the breach of the first lease, he should have the benefit of both bargains or not—in a situation where the profit on both would be the same—be limited to the profit on the second of them. Id. at 130-131, 114 A.2d 875.

As we further pointed out in *Locks,* the lost-volume rule has been recognized throughout the country. Id. at 132, 114 A.2d 875. . . . Moreover, although the parties have not raised the issue, we note that by L. 1994, c. 114, §1 effective January 10, 1995, the Legislature adopted the Uniform Commercial Code—Leases, N.J.S.A. 12A:2A-101 to -532. Its provisions are instructive here. We acknowledge that Chapter 2A of the Code is not applicable to leases of goods entered into prior to its effective date and is hence not applicable to this lease. Nevertheless, we note that the lessor's remedies in the event of default provided for by N.J.S.A. 12A:2A-528(1) expressly include the present value of the total rent for the remaining term. N.J.S.A. 12A:2A-528(2) further provides that:

> If the measure of damages provided in subsection (1) is inadequate to put a lessor in as good a position as performance would have, the measure of damages is the present value of the profit, including reasonable overhead, the lessor would have made from full performance by the lessee, together with any incidental damages allowed under 12A:2A-530, due allowance for costs reasonably incurred and due credit for payments or proceeds of disposition.

We think it plain that the proofs here would have supported a jury finding that plaintiff had a warehouse full of a variety of coin-operated machines and could have placed as many as it could have found customers for. Thus, even if it eventually placed with another customer the machines removed from defendant's premises, it still would have lost the benefit of its bargain with defendant since, in that case, it would have made two deals, not just the second. We also think it plain that the judge's charge, to the extent it referred to mitigation and failed to explain the lost-volume rule, clearly misled and misinformed the jury.

We recognize that plaintiff failed to request a lost-volume instruction and failed, as well, to object to the instructions given. The plain-error rule, therefore, applies, and we must determine whether the erroneous instructions produced an unjust result or prejudiced substantial rights. . . . Obviously a charge that has the capacity to mislead, misinform and confuse the jury with respect to the measurement of damages—and it evidently did so here—meets the plain-error standard. . . .

We need not speculate as to why the jury awarded plaintiff only one dollar in damages. We are, however, persuaded that the error in the instructions deprived plaintiff of its right to have a properly informed jury address the damages issue. It is, therefore, entitled to a new trial on damages.

A final remedy for the lessor, which has no analogue in Article 2, is found in §2A-532, entitled "Lessor's Rights to Residual Interest." This remedy, which is in addition to other remedies that the lessor may exercise, compensates the lessor for "any loss or damage to the lessor's residual interest in the goods caused by the default of the lessee." This remedy protects the lessor against, among other things, damage to the leased goods by the lessee. For example, if a lessee in a two-year lease failed to pay the final four months' rent as well as negligently damaged the leased goods, the lessor could sue not only for the unpaid rent but also for the value of the damage to its residual interest in the leased goods.

B.   Seller's Remedies with International Sales

To understand the world of a seller's remedies under the CISG, one must appreciate a major distinction that the CISG draws at the outset: the difference between the seller that "avoids" the contract and the seller that chooses not to avoid the contract. A seller may avoid a contract only when the buyer commits a "fundamental breach," CISG Article 64(1)(a), which is in turn defined by Article 25 as a breach that substantially deprives the other party of "what he is entitled to expect under the contract."

Under Article 81(1), avoidance of a contract by either party releases both parties of their obligations thereunder, although the avoiding party retains its right to sue for damages. This means that the seller that chooses to avoid the contract may no longer bring what we think of as "an action for the price," since the buyer is no longer obligated to pay the price. The avoiding seller may, however, sue the buyer for contract-resale damages under Article 75 or contract-market damages under Article 76. Under either article, the seller may also recover what is thought of in the UCC as either incidental or consequential damages. CISG Art. 74. Thus, in international sales, the seller can get both incidental and consequential damages, but only to the extent that they are reasonably foreseeable by the buyer at the time of contract formation.

There are two interesting features to note at this point about the CISG remedies structure. First, the CISG combines the buyer's "cover" remedy (more about this in Assignment 26) with the seller's resale remedy in a single article, Article 75; it also combines in Article 76 both the buyer's and the seller's contract-market damages. Second, the CISG combines in a single article, Article 74, the buyer's incidental and consequential damages with the seller's incidental and consequential damages (including "lost profit"). Article 74 describes the damages solely as consequential damages and contains the *Hadley v. Baxendale* limit on the foreseeability of the harm ultimately suffered by the aggrieved party.

If the seller in an international transaction wishes to sue the buyer for the price, the seller's ability to do so seems at first greater than that of a seller under the UCC. Article 62 says quite simply, "The seller may require the buyer to pay the price, take delivery or perform his other obligations, unless the seller has resorted to a remedy which is inconsistent with this requirement."

This right of the seller under the CISG to demand specific performance of the buyer does, however, come with some limits. First, Article 77 sets up a general mitigation rule by which a party that fails to reasonably mitigate the damages of the breaching party may see its own claim for damages reduced accordingly. Second, in the case where the seller is still in possession of the goods, Article 88(2) creates a duty on the seller's part to resell the goods for the buyer's benefit in any case where the goods are subject to rapid deterioration. Third, and most significantly, Article 28 says that in a dispute under the CISG, the forum court "is not bound" to require specific performance of a particular party unless the forum court's domestic sales law would similarly require specific performance of that same party. Thus, in a CISG case before an American court, the seller's action for the price might be limited, depending on the court's interpretation of Article 28, to the situations that are enumerated in UCC §2-709. As a practical matter, then, an international action for the price may not be significantly broader than a domestic one.

C. Seller's Remedies with Real Estate Sales

When a buyer breaches its agreement in a real estate sale, the breach will almost always take the form of an anticipatory repudiation. Typically, the seller will not deliver title to the buyer until the seller receives cash from the buyer. Thus, the classic case of buyer breach in a real estate transaction is where the buyer repudiates the contract after the parties have signed the contract but before the sale has closed. In most cases, the typical default remedy for the aggrieved seller in this situation is the seller's contractual right to keep the buyer's earnest money deposit. Some courts, however, are cautious about letting the seller keep the buyer's deposit, especially where the deposit is particularly large, where it is clear that the buyer breached for reasons beyond its control (such as inability to obtain financing), or where the seller is unable to show any actual damages sustained by the buyer's breach.

Depending on the terms of the particular sales contract, some states may allow the seller to recover contract-market damages against the buyer, but only where the seller can prove those damages exist (i.e., prove that the buyer agreed to pay a price that was above the market price for the property) and where the seller first returns the buyer's deposit. Sellers are generally not entitled to contract-resale damages as such, but, as the next case shows, an actual resale by the seller shortly following the buyer's breach will be persuasive evidence of the property's market value for the purpose of calculating contract-market damages.

Williams v. Ubaldo

670 A.2d 913 (Me. 1996)

WATHEN, C.J.

Defendant John L. Ubaldo appeals from a judgment entered in the Superior Court (Oxford County, Alexander, J.) awarding damages to plaintiffs Roger and Cynthia Williams for breach of a real estate contract. Ubaldo, the purchaser under the contract, argues that the failure to consummate the sale resulted from his inability to secure financing, and the court erred in finding that he had breached the contract. He also challenges the elements of damage included in the judgment. We conclude that the court erred only in calculating the damage award. Thus, we modify the judgment and affirm.

The facts as developed in a jury-waived trial are as follows: In January 1993, Ubaldo entered into a written contract to purchase the Williamses' home in Oxford. The purchase price was $450,000. In preparation for closing, the property was appraised at $480,000. The terms called for a down payment of $10,000, the remainder to be paid at closing, scheduled for May, 1993. The contract contained a financing provision, stating that Ubaldo's obligation to purchase was contingent on his ability to secure adequate financing. He was required to seek and accept financing in good faith. In the event of a breach by Ubaldo, the contract provided that the Williamses would retain the earnest-money deposit, while still reserving all available legal and equitable remedies.

A few weeks prior to the closing, the parties amended the original contract, extending the time for Ubaldo's performance. The amendment resulted from the fact that he attempted to secure financing with a bank, but was unable to qualify for a mortgage loan. Ubaldo's mother agreed to co-sign the promissory note, and the bank then agreed to extend financing for the purchase. The loan was for $360,000; the remaining $90,000 was to be supplied by his mother on or before closing. The parties attended a closing, but the sale was not completed because the mother failed to provide the $90,000 cash payment. Ubaldo later applied for another mortgage loan without his mother, and was denied.

After a few months, the Williamses filed a complaint against Ubaldo seeking specific performance of the contract, and an award of the $10,000 deposit. Ubaldo then filed a complaint against the Williamses seeking a return of the deposit. The court consolidated the two cases. Before trial was held, the Williamses sold their home to another purchaser for $430,000.

At the trial, the court found that Ubaldo had breached the contract. In assessing damages, the court compared the contract price, $450,000, and the eventual selling price, $430,000, and awarded the $20,000 difference. In addition, the court assessed $3,500 for real estate taxes paid by the Williamses from the time of the breach to the time of sale, and $500 for expenses plaintiffs incurred in connection with snow removal. The court assessed damages in the total sum of $24,000; judgment was entered for $14,000 after offsetting the deposit. Ubaldo appeals. . . .

The court awarded plaintiffs the $20,000 difference between the contract price and the subsequent sales price as compensatory damages. "The overriding purpose of an award of compensatory damages for a breach of contract is to place the plaintiff in the same position as that enjoyed had there been no breach." Marchesseault v. Jackson, 611 A.2d 95, 98 (Me. 1992), citing Forbes v. Wells Beach Casino, Inc., 409 A.2d 646, 654 (Me. 1979). In an action for breach of contract for the sale of real property, the claimant is entitled to the "benefit of the bargain," which equals the difference between the contract price and the fair market value at the time of breach. The reports of professional appraisers have been accepted as evidence of the fair market value of real estate. Evidence of the price resulting from a subsequent sale is also probative of a property's fair market value.

Ubaldo argues incorrectly that the only evidence as to fair market value at time of breach is the testimony of the broker that the house had been appraised for $480,000. In fact, no appraiser actually testified. The court had only the subsequent sale before it. There is no suggestion that that sale was unreasonable or made in bad faith. The court acted well within its discretion in finding that the subsequent sales price was an accurate measure of market value at the time the contract was breached.

Ubaldo argues that the court erred in granting $3,500 in damages for the property taxes paid by the Williamses for the period of time between the breach and sale. We agree. The Williamses retained ownership, use, and occupancy of a valuable asset during that time. There is no authority for the proposition that the avoidance of tax liability is part of the benefit of the bargain and may be included without considering corresponding financial benefits.

Finally, Ubaldo challenges the special damages awarded for the Williamses' costs in repurchasing winter-related equipment and the extra costs of snow removal. He argues that these special damages were not within the contemplation of the parties when they signed the contract. A claimant is entitled to "special damages" resulting from the unique needs and characteristics of the parties, if the parties were reasonably aware of those circumstances at the time the contract was created. . . .

It is not reasonable to conclude that the extra costs of snow removal and winter equipment are foreseeable consequences of a breach of a real estate contract in the ordinary case. People selling their homes in Maine are not necessarily in the process of moving to warmer climates: they could be staying in Maine, or moving to another northern state. There is no evidence in the record that Ubaldo was aware of the Williamses' plans after the sale. Neither is there any evidence that they communicated their intention to sell their winter equipment and move to a warmer climate.

The Superior Court did not err in finding that Ubaldo breached the sale contract, but it erred in awarding payment for taxes and snow removal.

The entry is: Judgment modified to $10,000, reflecting a total damage award of $20,000 minus the offset for the deposit. As so modified, judgment affirmed.

Some states, such as Maine in the above case, will permit the aggrieved real estate seller to recover consequential damages in addition to contract-market damages. However, when consequential damages are recovered by sellers, the damages tend to be for costs associated with resale that the seller would not have incurred had the seller proceeded with the original sale: for example, if the original sale was to be "by owner" but the seller ended up having to pay a real estate agent to assist with the resale.

Note that in *Williams* the seller had originally asked for specific performance from the buyer, although the seller eventually itself conducted a resale. A specific performance remedy for sellers in the real estate context would be extremely rare for several reasons but not out of the question. Because the most common reason for a buyer breach is lack of money, specific performance is ordinarily completely impractical: if Ubaldo, the buyer in the *Williams* case, had the $450,000 there never would have been a lawsuit, and a court order commanding him to pay the $450,000 doesn't do anything to remedy his lack of money.

Finally, note that the contractual remedies provision in *Williams* gave the seller the ability to retain the security deposit at the same time it was suing for other damages. That provision is rather unusual. Most residential form sales contracts force the seller to choose between retaining the security deposit and pursuing other remedies against the buyer. Consider the following:

REMEDIES UPON DEFAULT

If either party defaults in the performance of any obligation of this contract, the party claiming a default shall notify the other party in writing of the nature of the default and his election of remedy. The notifying party may, but is not required to, provide the defaulting party with a deadline for curing the default. If the default is by Buyer, Seller may either accept the earnest money as liquidated damages and release Buyer from the contract (in lieu of making any claim in court), or may pursue any remedy at law or in equity. If Seller accepts the earnest money, it shall be divided as follows: expenses of Broker and Seller in this transaction will be reimbursed, and balance to go one-half to Seller, and one-half divided equally between Listing Broker and Selling Broker (if working as subagent of Seller) in lieu of commission on this contract. . . . In the event of litigation between the parties, the prevailing party shall recover, in addition to damages or equitable relief, the cost of litigation including reasonable attorney's fees. This provision shall survive closing and delivery of Seller's deed to Buyer.

Take a look at the last few sentences of this provision. Notice first the inclusion of a contractual reversal of the "American rule" that both parties are liable for their own attorney's fees. Second, note that this form contract allows the real estate brokers a right to a partial commission even in the absence of a consummated sale. These two special provisions on attorney's fees and broker commissions are probably understandable when you recall that the form in question (like most such forms) was promulgated by a brokers' association in conjunction with the local bar association.

Problem Set 23

23.1.   Big Lou of Lou's Used Cars for Less (from Problem 2.1) had not seen you for some time, but he just stopped by your office with a new problem. Lou's problem stemmed from an experience he had had with a small fleet of used cars that he leased. A couple of years ago a new customer, Charlie Erker, had agreed to lease a used Cadillac for three years at $400 per month. Exactly one year into the lease, Charlie dropped the car off at Lou's and said, "I don't need it anymore." Even before dropping the car off, Charlie had missed the last two payments on the lease. At the point when Charlie repudiated his lease, Lou's lease fleet was all in use. Therefore, it took Lou three months and a $50 newspaper ad to re-lease the car to a different customer; the new lease was for two years at only $300 per month. Lou always uses the same standard lease form, which contains blanks for the length of the lease and the rental rate. Lou had, however, made a special allowance for Charlie only in which Lou agreed to have the car hand-washed every month for Charlie at Lou's expense (this had cost Lou $10 per month). Lou asks you what amount of damages he could claim against Charlie for Charlie's breach. What do you advise? UCC §§2A-527, 2A-530; Official Comment 7 to §2A-527. (In calculating damages for this problem, don't bother actually discounting any of the payment streams to present value, but note to yourself where that would normally be done.)

23.2.   Big Lou had one more problem that was lease-related, and this one, Lou said, was even worse than the first. Lou had leased a used Ford Taurus to Sam Miller, a single father with four children. That lease was for $250 per month for four years. One year into the lease, Sam missed two consecutive payments and Lou had the car repossessed. Much to Lou's horror, Sam's children had torn much of the upholstery off the seats inside the car. It cost Lou $800 to repair the upholstery damage, after which Lou sold the car for $14,000, since Lou had stopped leasing used cars the day after Sam had leased this one. Now Lou wants to sue Sam for his breach of the lease agreement. The $250-per-month lease payment was roughly equal to the market value of the lease at the time of the breach. For what amount of damages may Lou recover? UCC §§2A-527, 2A-528, 2A-529, 2A-530, 2A-532. (In calculating damages for this problem, don't bother actually discounting any of the payment streams to present value, but note to yourself where that would normally be done.)

23.3.   Steel Works, Inc., is a Des Moines, Iowa, manufacturer that contracts to sell to Canadian Brinks, a Toronto security firm, a set of 10 specially manufactured steel doors for $70,000. The delivery date is October 5, and the delivery term is "FOB Seller's Factory." Canadian Brinks was responsible for installing the doors. On October 1, Canadian Brinks calls Steel Works and repudiates the contract. In calling around to find other possible buyers, Steel Works gets two offers: the first is from an Iowa buyer that will pay $45,000 for the doors and will pick up and install the doors itself; the second is from a California buyer that will pay $60,000 for the doors if Steel Works ships them (at a cost of $3,000) and installs them (another $1,500). On October 1, the market price for these doors in Iowa is $45,000, and in Toronto it is $43,000. The president of Steel Works comes to you and asks what damage options are available to her company and which option would be the company's best alternative. What do you advise? CISG Arts. 25, 64(1)(a), 74, 75, 76, 62, 77, 28.

23.4.   Joe Thompson was a Portland, Maine sportswriter who was tired of maintaining a single-family home and was looking to move into a condominium. He listed his house "For Sale by Owner" at $200,000, and he ultimately accepted Brad Pearson's offer of $190,000, in large part because it did not contain a financing contingency clause. Joe required that Brad put down a $5,000 earnest money deposit. Unfortunately for Joe, Brad ended up being unable to secure financing and Brad ultimately breached the sales contract for lack of a mortgage. Joe returned Brad's security deposit with a letter in which Joe retained his right to sue Brad for any and all remedies. When the house failed to sell after several more months, Joe relented and got a real estate agent. The agent convinced Joe to spend $10,000 for central air-conditioning, and finally the house sold almost exactly one year after Brad failed to close on his contract. The selling price was $170,000, but Joe owed his agent 6 percent of that. Besides the $10,000 Joe spent for central air-conditioning, he ended up paying $18,000 in mortgage payments and $1,500 in property taxes while he continued to occupy the house during the last year. Now that he finally has sold the house, Joe comes to you to ask for what amount he can recover from Brad for Brad's breach of the earlier contract. What do you advise?

Assignment 24:   Seller's Remedies: Advanced Problems

A.   The Lost-Volume Seller

In Assignment 22, three standard seller's remedies were considered: an action for the price, contract-resale damages, and contract-market damages. We saw that only in limited circumstances are sellers eligible to sue for the price. Although the contract-resale and contract-market measures of damages are available to almost any aggrieved seller, oftentimes neither of these remedies will put the seller in the same position that the seller would have been in had the breaching buyer performed.

Consider, for example, the plight of a new-car dealer. Imagine that a buyer comes into the showroom, test-drives a new Honda Accord, and signs a contract to buy the car for $21,000. Imagine that the buyer is due to pick up the car the next day but overnight has a change of heart and repudiates its contract with the dealer. A day or two later, the dealer ends up selling the Honda Accord that was earmarked for the first buyer to a second buyer for $21,000. The market price for new Honda Accords of this type is (not surprisingly) $21,000.

If the car dealer wants to sue the first buyer for damages due to the buyer's breach of its contract to buy the car, none of the three remedies discussed in Assignment 22 would do the seller any good. The seller would be ineligible to sue for the price, given that the goods were not accepted, were not destroyed, and were clearly resalable. The seller would be eligible for contract-market or contract-resale damages, but both of these measures would yield the dealer a zero recovery.

Even though the dealer was able to resell the same car, the dealer knows at some level that it was nevertheless damaged by the first buyer's reneging on its contract to buy the car. In short, the first buyer's breach cost the dealer one more profit that the dealer would have made but for the breach. The drafters of the UCC were sympathetic to the plight of those in the position of the car dealer, and they created a special remedies provision in §2-708(2) to deal with this very common type of case.

The first question under §2-708(2) is to figure out which sellers can qualify for the special relief afforded there. Section 2-708(2) has limited the class of eligible sellers to those that can show that "the measure of damages provided in subsection (1) [the contract-market measure] is inadequate to put the seller in as good a position as performance would have done." To put it more simply, the seller must show that the buyer's breach caused it to lose a profit.

This rule requires the seller to make two separate but related showings: (1) that its ultimate sale to a third party of the goods as to which the buyer breached would have occurred even if the buyer had not breached, and (2) that the seller's ability to sell these goods was greater than the current buyer demand for them. Or, as White and Summers put it, the seller would need to show that, in the absence of the buyer's breach, it "would have made the sale to the breaching buyer and the sale to the party who purchased the buyer's goods."

As to the first showing, recall the seller in the *Firwood* case from Assignment 22 that took three years to resell specialized machines after the original buyer had repudiated the sales contract. That seller ended up suing the buyer for contract-resale damages. Why couldn't the *Firwood* seller have sued for lost profits? The most likely reason is that the *Firwood* seller would probably have been unable to show that the ultimate sale of those machines would have occurred absent the first buyer's breach. To the contrary, the only reason the subsequent sales were made is that the first buyer breached: this seller did not typically make this particular type of machine and probably would not have produced them at all were it not for the first buyer's contract.

As to the second showing, probably most sellers most of the time could persuasively argue that they were not operating at full capacity and, therefore, could have made additional sales even if the buyer had not breached. One common group of sellers that would not be eligible for lost-profit damages are retail toy stores around Christmas, if a particular parent breached a contract to buy that season's most popular toy. Since hardly any store in this situation is able to have its supply keep up with the demand, a retail store under these circumstances that loses a particular sale has not really lost a profit. Even if one buyer reneges, there are more than enough eager buyers to take its place, and not enough of the "hot" toys in stock to satisfy all of the willing buyers.

Once it is determined which seller qualifies for lost-profits damages, the next issue is figuring out exactly how these damages are measured. Section 2-708(2) describes the appropriate recovery as "profit (including reasonable overhead) which the seller would have made from full performance by the buyer, together with any incidental damages provided in this Article, due allowance for costs reasonably incurred and due credit for payments or proceeds of resale."

To create a formula from this statement, one must first know how to define "profit." Profit for the seller in any given sale will consist of the contract price minus the seller's direct costs for that item minus an allocable share of the seller's fixed costs or overhead: $KP - DC - FC$, where KP = contract price, DC = seller's direct costs for this item, and FC = allocable share of seller's fixed costs for this item.

The seller's direct costs are sometimes called "variable costs" — costs that vary with the sale or production of the particular item in question. In the case of our car dealer above, its direct costs for the Honda Accord would consist of what it paid the manufacturer for that car, any direct handling or servicing of that car once received at the dealer, plus any commission that the dealer agreed to pay the salesperson who sold the car.

Fixed expenses, by contrast, consist of things we tend to think of as "overhead": utilities, rent, property taxes, executive salaries, and the like. These are expenses that are not directly affected by whether or not one particular item is sold. You should note, however, that the line between variable and fixed costs is in some sense artificial. While it may be true that one fewer item sold will not reduce the seller's fixed costs, at some point perhaps (say, 100 fewer cars sold) it can be said that the seller in fact would have needed one fewer executive, one fewer building, and so forth in order to operate efficiently.

Arriving at a true profit figure also requires determining not just what the fixed costs are, but also what portion of those fixed costs can be attributed to the item as to which the buyer breached. Because, however, the §2-708(2) formula specifically says "profit (including reasonable overhead)" rather than just "profit" standing alone, there is no need to determine an item's allocable share of fixed costs. Thanks to the "including reasonable overhead" language in parentheses, the statute's formula adds back into the seller's damage measure an allocable share of the seller's fixed costs: (KP − DC − FC) + FC = KP − DC, since the FCs cancel each other out.

From the first part of the formula, all that remains is the rather simple KP − DC, and the next thing §2-708(2) requires is to add incidental damages, leaving KP − DC + ID. Before incorporating the last two items in the language of §2-708(2) ("due allowance for costs reasonably incurred and due credit for payments or proceeds of resale," which, as explained later, apply only to a limited class of lost-profits sellers), the formula that will apply to most lost-profits sellers is KP − DC + ID.

The concept of "contract price minus direct costs plus incidental damages" seems simple enough on its face, but the hidden complication that invariably arises in litigation is which of the seller's expenses qualify as direct costs and which qualify as fixed costs. As the following case shows, the seller's incentives in classifying costs for damage purposes will sometimes be quite different from the seller's incentives in classifying costs for tax purposes.

Sure-Trip, Inc. v. Westinghouse Engineering

47 F.3d 526 (2d Cir. 1996)

Cardamone, C.J.

Plaintiff Sure-Trip, Inc. appeals from a judgment entered on May 20, 1994 in the District Court for the Western District of New York (Curtin, J.) granting it damages against defendants Westinghouse Electric Corporation and its Westinghouse Engineering and Instrumentation Services Division (collectively Westinghouse). . . .

In one of his proverbs Benjamin Franklin capsulizes the truism that a little neglect can cause a good deal of mischief, saying that "for want of a Nail, the Shoe was lost; for want of a Shoe the Horse was lost; for want of a Horse the Rider was lost." The Prefaces, Proverbs, and Poems of Benjamin Franklin, in Poor Richard's Almanac for 1758, at 275 (G.B. Putnam's Sons 1889). The record on this appeal reveals Sure-Trip's neglect in presenting its financial records, for want of which, proof of expenses was lost; for want of proof of expenses, proof of damages was lost; for want of proof of damages, plaintiff's suit might well have been lost. Here however plaintiff will get a second chance to establish its damages, as we conclude the district court erred in granting summary judgment on the issue of liability. Accordingly, we reverse the order granting summary judgment insofar as it held Westinghouse liable for breach of contract, vacate the damage award to Sure-Trip, and remand for a new trial. . . .

The dispute centers on Paragraph I of the contract, which provides:

> a. [Westinghouse] agrees to purchase a minimum of 100 kits per month starting January 1, 1988 through December 31, 1988. The 100 kits per month minimum to be calculated on a three-month average. If in any three-month period [Westinghouse] does not meet this volume commitment, then Sure-Trip will invoice the difference to [Westinghouse] between the 1987 list price of $889 and the contract price specified below. . . .

[Sure-Trip officers James] Fitts and [William] Penniston insist they understood the writing [Westinghouse purchasing manager Raymond] Baranowski sent them as committing Westinghouse to purchase 1200 retrofit kits in 1988. They understood Paragraph I as guaranteeing Sure-Trip quarterly "cash-flow protection" by providing that at the end of any quarter in which Westinghouse's purchases fell below 300 units, Sure-Trip could invoice Westinghouse for the difference between the $889 list price and the $756 discount price for 300 of the lowest-priced units—the difference being $133 times 300 or a total of $39,900—regardless of the number of units actually purchased.

As it turned out, Westinghouse only purchased 75 kits in all of 1988, paying the discounted prices set forth in the contract. . . .

A bench trial on damages was held in December 1992. Sure-Trip elected to prove damages on a lost profits theory, as permitted by Pennsylvania's version of §2-708 of the Uniform Commercial Code. Its evidence on this issue was limited to the testimony of its principals, Fitts and Penniston. Penniston stated that Sure-Trip sold 621 retrofit kits in 1988, and that the material, labor and packaging costs per kit totaled $225.97. Based on the lowest contract discount price of $756, Penniston calculated that Sure-Trip's profit would have been $530.03 on each of the remaining 1125 kits Westinghouse would have needed to buy to meet its volume commitment of 1200 kits, for a total lost profit of $596,283.75.

In contesting Sure-Trip's calculations Westinghouse offered into evidence Sure-Trip's 1988 tax return. The return showed a net taxable income of $11,954 derived from the sale of 621 kits. Sure-Trip's damage calculations thus amounted to a roughly five thousand percent increase in profits based on the purported 200 percent increase in sales had Westinghouse purchased the additional 1125 kits. Moreover, Westinghouse declared, Sure-Trip failed to offer evidence as to those expenses that might reasonably have been expected to increase as a result of tripled production, such as utilities, overtime, new employee training and related administrative expenses, such as payroll.

To this argument, Fitts simply responded that none of these expenses would have gone up because the company was already operating at a "break-even" volume. Sure-Trip also offered testimony that Fitts' and Penniston's compensation would not have risen due to the company's increased profits, that no additional product testing would have been necessary, and that workers in the additional assembly shifts would be capable of operating without supervision. Fitts conceded that utilities might have increased slightly due to the increased production, but made no attempt to calculate the amount of such an increase.

On May 10, 1994 the district court held that the list price-contract price differential specified in the third sentence of Paragraph I.a. [of the parties' contract] was ambiguous, that neither party intended that sentence to be interpreted as a liquidated damages clause, and that nothing else in the agreement spoke to damages. The trial judge believed that Sure-Trip, as a seller asserting a loss in the volume of its sales, was entitled under Pennsylvania law to seek lost profits. But because it had not adequately accounted for increases in overhead attributable to its putative increased production, the trial court concluded the plaintiff had failed to meet its burden of calculating lost profits.

Plaintiff's estimate of nearly $600,000 in damages was accordingly rejected. Instead, the district judge estimated Sure-Trip's damages based on the company's 1988 tax return. Dividing Sure-Trip's net taxable income of $11,954 by the 621 units it sold in 1988, it arrived at an estimate of $19.25 profit per kit. It then multiplied that figure by 1125, the number of additional units Westinghouse was required to buy under Sure-Trip's interpretation of the contract, to arrive at a total lost profit of $21,656.25. Judgment was entered in that amount, plus interest, costs and disbursements, in Sure-Trip's favor. . . .

We turn first to plaintiff's contention that the district court erred in its calculation of damages. The governing principles of contract law are well settled in Pennsylvania. Damages for breach of contract are designed to put the non-breaching party in as good a position as it would have been in had the contract been performed. The notion behind this theory is that damages should make the plaintiff whole.

Where plaintiff is seeking to recover lost profits, such damages are equal to the revenue that would have been derived, less additional costs that would have been incurred, in performing the contract. Fixed overhead costs, as opposed to variable costs, are not properly deducted in calculating plaintiff's lost profits. Fixed costs represent the total dollar expense that occurs regardless of output.

In contrast, variable expenses, defined as those additional costs necessarily incurred in performing the contract, must be deducted from plaintiff's recovery so plaintiff is not put in a better position than it would have been had defendant performed. Thus, Sure-Trip's alleged lost revenue had to be offset by any additional costs it would necessarily have expended in performing the contract to arrive at its lost profits. It was obliged with respect to the issue of damages to produce evidence regarding its increased costs, as plaintiff—in a breach of contract suit for lost profits—has the burden of establishing its damages by a preponderance of the evidence.

Sure-Trip declared through its witnesses' testimony that its only increased costs would have been for labor, materials, and packaging, and that the company would have been capable of tripling production without any additional expenditures for administration, insurance, or machine repair, and only a minor increase in utility expense. Conceding that it would have been necessary to add at least one additional production shift to meet the increased demand, Sure-Trip insists it would have incurred no additional costs for payroll administration, overtime, or hiring and training new employees. The district court properly rejected this testimony as incredible. It found plaintiff had failed to meet its burden of accounting for and deducting increased expenses that would have been incurred in performance of the contract.

Given Sure-Trip's failure to meet its burden of proof, the district court would have been justified in awarding no damages. Instead, it turned to plaintiff's 1988 income tax return as the best available source of information regarding plaintiff's actual profit margin. Unlike the witnesses' testimony, the tax return reflected deductions for those items such as office supplies, utilities and machine repair that the company considered variable expenses. Pennsylvania law permits the court to "make a just and reasonable estimate of the damage based on relevant data." Such evidence need not be complete or mathematically certain, so long as it provides a "reasonable basis" for calculation.

Although the district court was entitled to rely on information included in plaintiff's tax return, it remains to be seen whether it incorrectly equated taxable income with profit. Sure-Trip maintains the trial court's approach conflated fixed and variable expenses because both are allowed as deductions from taxable income. In arriving at taxable income, Sure-Trip was permitted to deduct business expenses—such as rent and depreciation—that were part of its overhead, even though such expenses are not typically deducted in arriving at damages for lost profits. Sure-Trip goes on to say that to arrive at its estimated profits, its taxable income ought to have been increased by the amount of those deductions it took for fixed business expenses.

A cursory examination of Sure-Trip's tax return reveals the difficulties involved in recasting the tax return into a profit and loss statement. To separate the deductions representing only fixed costs would necessarily lead to a significant degree of speculation. The deduction for rent is perhaps one clear example of an expense that would not have been likely to increase due to contract performance. Other deductions, such as those for advertising, travel, "patent expense" and depreciation, might fall into the same category. But items such as office supplies, bank charges, insurance and legal expenses are more problematic. A finder of fact might conjecture that such costs would have increased. Yet, assaying by what degree, without more evidence than was presented here, would be completely speculative.

For example, some of the most substantial deductions represent disguised compensation to Sure-Trip's principals, Fitts and Penniston: these include "subcontractor fees" of over $100,000, and a $15,000 "engineering consultation" fee, which was revealed at trial to be a personal expense of Penniston's. No evidence was introduced as to whether any of these costs represented compensation for services that might have increased due to contract performance, other than the unsubstantiated assertions of these two witnesses.

In short, Sure-Trip, having failed to meet its own burden as to proof of damages, proposes shifting that burden onto the trial court, and would have us impose a requirement that the trial judge undertake an independent inquiry into such facts as it can unearth. The indefinite nature of this inquiry obviously is attributable in large part to Sure-Trip's failure to present reasonably reliable proof of its damages, transforming the difficulties of calculation, absent adequate proof, into an exercise of the finder of fact's imagination.

Also in the realm of fantasy was the rapacious damage figure that Sure-Trip's principals estimated at nearly $600,000. That outrageous figure was correctly set aside. Rather, the district court having nothing else before it used plaintiff's taxable income, which could be measured, instead of its lost profits, which could not. Any upward departure from taxable income based on setting aside those deductions held to represent fixed expenses would, as we have seen, be speculative. But plaintiff's taxable income does provide a useful "floor": the court could reasonably conclude that Sure-Trip's per-unit lost profits were no lower than its 1988 per-unit taxable income. Sure-Trip, having failed to meet its burden of proof, cannot now be heard to complain. . . .

Almost all courts, like the Second Circuit in *Sure-Trip*, will accept without discussion that a seller's damages under §2-708(2) equal the contract price less the seller's costs associated with performing the contract ("direct costs") plus incidental damages (although none were alleged in *Sure-Trip*). Thus, the formula that these courts are using is the one we arrived at above: KP − DC + ID.

What these courts do not bother mentioning is that this simple formula is inconsistent with the language of §2-708(2) in that it ignores the last two items of the damage statement in §2-708(2): "due allowance for costs reasonably incurred and due credit for payments or proceeds of resale." Thus, the 2-708(2) formula should read: KP − DC + ID + CI − RP, with "+ CI" representing "due allowance for costs reasonably incurred" and "− RP" representing "due credit for payments or proceeds of resale."

To understand why courts choose to ignore this language, consider our Honda Accord dealer above. Suppose that the dealer's direct costs in selling a Honda Accord consist of $18,000 to the manufacturer, $200 in handling fees attributable to each car, and $1,000 in sales commission. Thus, the direct costs total $19,200. Using the "full" version of the §2-708(2) formula, the dealer would receive: KP ($21,000) − DC ($19,200) + ID (0) + CI ($19,200) − RP ($21,000) = 0!

If the full version of the §2-708(2) formula were used, no standard lost-profits seller like the Honda dealer would ever recover any damages under that formula. Why, then, does §2-708(2) include the terms "due allowance for costs reasonably incurred and due credit for payments or proceeds of resale"?

Answering this question requires a little bit of history. When the Code drafters created the language of §2-708(2), they had three types of lost-profits sellers in mind. First, they were thinking of someone like the Honda dealer in our example: a seller of standard-priced goods that could show that the buyer's breach caused it to lose a sale.

Second, they considered a group of sellers known as "jobbers." Jobbers are middlemen that make contracts for sale and never themselves touch the goods. In effect, jobbers help sellers find buyers and take a profit for themselves. Thus, if a buyer repudiates its contract with the jobber, the jobber loses that profit.

Finally, the drafters of §2-708(2) had in mind a case in which a component-parts manufacturer makes a contract to specially manufacture and sell a product to a buyer. If the buyer repudiates the contract while the manufacturing is in progress, the manufacturer may choose to stop in mid-production and sell what it has completed at that point for scrap as allowed under §2-704(2).

The drafters of §2-708(2) put in the last two terms of the formula to cover the third class of lost-profits seller, and only in the case where such a component parts manufacturer has stopped production in midstream and sold what it has at that point for scrap. Unfortunately, as mentioned earlier, the last two terms in the formula must be ignored in the case of the first two classes of lost-profits sellers.

To give you an example of how the full formula works with the third class of lost-profits sellers, suppose you have a component-parts manufacturer who contracts with a buyer to sell a specialized machine that will be assembled by the seller. The price is $2,000. Parts will cost the seller $800 and direct labor another $300. Therefore, this seller's expected "profit (including reasonable overhead)" is $2,000 − $800 − $300 = $900.

The seller begins assembly and then, midway through, the buyer repudiates. At this point, the seller has purchased all $800 worth of parts and has incurred $200 worth of direct labor costs. Nevertheless, the seller reasonably concludes that there is no market for the finished product and therefore exercises its option under §2-704(2) to stop production and resell the scrap for $600 (the raw materials have actually decreased in market value due to the work done on them so far).

What is the seller's recovery? For this seller, the appropriate §2-708(2) formula is KP ($2,000) − ADC ($1,100) (note this term is now "anticipated direct costs" since, with a seller who stops in midstream, the first part of the equation measures anticipated profit, given that such a seller does not actually complete production and make an actual profit) + ID (0) + CI ($1,000, representing "costs incurred" by the time of the buyer's repudiation) – RP ($600, representing proceeds of the scrap sale) = $1,300.

At first blush, this seller's recovery of $1,300 might seem to overcompensate the seller, given that we said at the outset that this seller only expected a profit of $900. The $1,300 figure makes sense when the case is considered in the following way: at the time of the contract, the seller expected to spend $1,100 and to receive $2,000, a net gain of $900. As a result of the buyer's breach, the seller has actually spent $1,000 and actually received from the scrap resale $600, thus putting the seller in a net loss position of $400. To turn a $400 loss into a net $900 gain (seller's expectation at the start of the contract) requires compensation of $1,300, not just $900, in order to account for the $400 that the seller is now in the hole. Suppose that instead of using the full version of the §2-708(2) formula to calculate its damages, the seller above had simply measured its damages under §2-706(1) (assuming that the seller gave proper resale notice and otherwise conducted the resale in a commercially reasonable manner): KP ($2,000) – RP ($600, here resale proceeds of the scrap) + ID (0) – ES ($100 expenses saved, since seller expected to spend $1,100 but due to buyer's breach spent just $1,000) = $1,300. Since §2-706(1) will always come to the same result as the long version of §2-708(2), the drafters probably should have just gotten rid of that last troublesome phrase in §2-708(2) and let the one case it was meant to cover simply be covered by §2-706(1).

One explanation that has been offered to justify why the §2-706 route might not be appropriate for the component-parts seller who stops in midstream is that §2-706 was meant to cover the resale of a finished product, not scrap. Yet the §2-706(1) formula works perfectly well in the scrap case to come to the same result as §2-708(2). Furthermore, both §2-704(1)(b) and §2-704(2) seem to contemplate the component-parts manufacturer reselling unfinished goods. Section 2-704(1)(b) says that an aggrieved seller may "treat as the subject of resale goods which have demonstrably been intended for the particular contract *even though those goods are unfinished*" (emphasis added). Section 2-704(2) says that, where the goods are unfinished, one of the seller's options is to "resell for scrap."

In the discussion above concerning the remedies available to the component-parts manufacturer that stops production in midstream, one issue that was not mentioned was the reasonableness of that seller's decision to cease production rather than completing production and trying to resell the goods in their finished state. Section 2-704(2) gives the seller the right to either continue production or to stop as long as the seller exercises "reasonable commercial judgment" in making that decision.

As the following case demonstrates, whether or not the seller's decision will later be found "reasonable" will often come down to the fact that the breaching buyer, and not the aggrieved seller, has the burden of proof on this issue.

Young v. Frank's Nursery & Crafts, Inc.

569 N.E.2d 1034 (Ohio 1991)

WRIGHT, J.

Plaintiff-appellant, William G. Young, had been cutting evergreen boughs on Michigan farms and selling them in the Toledo area since 1971. In 1975, after he had built up a customer base of twenty-five to thirty, Young began selling boughs to defendant-appellee, Frank's Nursery & Crafts, Inc. From 1976 through 1987, Young dealt exclusively with Frank's. Young's sales to Frank's had grown from $10,224 that first year to an order for $238,332.85 issued in early 1987 that is the subject of this case.

After receiving the order, Young began preparations to carry it out, even though the boughs were not to be cut until the following fall. Young obtained cutting rights from Michigan farmers for all the boughs to fill the three-hundred-sixty-ton order from Frank's. He also repaired his machinery and made seventy-five new hand tyers with which to tie the evergreen bundles. On June 30, 1987, Frank's mailed a new purchase order to Young, reducing its requirements to about seventy tons. At trial, Young estimated that the reduction had the effect of cutting the contract price from the original $238,332.85 to under $60,000. Young subsequently called three other evergreen bough buyers and two brokers about purchasing some of the material that Frank's no longer wanted. Those attempts to find other buyers were fruitless, Young testified, because other potential buyers already had their fall orders set by the time Young inquired in July. He did cut enough material to fill Frank's reduced order.

On October 7, 1987, Young filed a breach of contract action against Frank's in Lucas County Common Pleas Court. Prior to the start of trial on November 7, 1988, the defendant admitted liability for breach of contract, leaving only the issue of damages. The jury returned a verdict of $132,902 in favor of Young and Frank's appealed. The court of appeals reversed, holding that the trial judge erred in instructing the jury that the defendant had the burden of proving that Young's decision not to cut all the boughs originally ordered was commercially unreasonable.

This is a case of first impression in Ohio, but the law under the Uniform Commercial Code is clear on the issue of a seller's remedies where the buyer commits an anticipatory breach. . . .

The better position is that where a buyer commits an anticipatory breach of a contract and the seller proceeds under UCC 2-704(2) and 2-708 for his remedy, the burden of proving that the seller acted in a commercially unreasonable fashion in deciding to cease manufacturing is on the buyer. UCC 2-704, Official Comment 2; 1 White & Summers, Uniform Commercial Code (3d ed. 1988) 377, Section 7-15. The appellate court appears to have overlooked [UCC §2-704] when it analyzed the argument of Frank's. That section deals with seller's rights and obligations regarding unidentified and incomplete goods, which is precisely the situation here.

At the time of the breach, in July 1987, Young had not begun to assemble the goods that he had contracted to sell to Frank's. [UCC §2-703], "Buyer's wrongful rejection, revocation of acceptance, or nonpayment: remedies of seller," lists the seller's principal remedies under the code. Because the goods in this instance were unidentified to the contract, [UCC §2-703(c)] directs the seller to the next section, [UCC §2-704], for his remedy. In turn, [UCC §2-704(2)] provides:

> Where the goods are unfinished an aggrieved seller may in the exercise of reasonable commercial judgment for the purposes of avoiding loss and of effective realization either complete the manufacture and wholly identify the goods to the contract or cease manufacture and resell for scrap or salvage value or proceed in any other reasonable manner.

The theme of this section is mitigation. White & Summers, supra, at 377, in analyzing the import of this section, contends that the official comments to the UCC ". . . make clear that the burden is on the buyer to prove that the seller failed to use reasonable commercial judgment."

These respected commentators view the entire section as placing the burden on the breaching buyer:

> "To read §2-704 as consistent with the general rules of mitigation, we would interpret it to mean that the seller must exercise commercially reasonable judgment not only when he decides to complete, but also when he decides not to. . . .

> * * *

> ". . . Of course to preserve the usefulness of §2-704, the courts will have to be careful to place the burden on the buyer and to insist that he come forward with persuasive evidence that the seller acted in a commercially unreasonable way before they foreclose [the] seller from the right to complete or not complete." Id. at 379-380.

Mitigation is an affirmative defense in Ohio. Thus, we must rule that the trial judge was correct in placing the burden on Frank's to show that Young's decision not to complete cutting all the evergreen boughs originally ordered was commercially unreasonable.

Next, Young would look to [UCC §2-708], "Nonacceptance or repudiation; seller's damages," to determine the nature of his damages. The trial judge succinctly and clearly spelled out for the jury its responsibilities in this area, apportioning the burden of proof between Young and Frank's as required by the UCC.

[UCC §2-708(1)] provides for damages based on the contract price less the market price, unless such a remedy falls short of putting the seller in as good a position as performance would have done. Here, the plaintiff had determined in July that there would be no market available for his boughs in the fall. The judge instructed the jury that if it believed that decision was not commercially reasonable, to award the plaintiff the difference between what he could have sold the boughs for—the market price—and the unpaid contract price. If the jury believed that Young had failed to mitigate his damages, this remedy would have taken that into account by awarding him no more, in theory, than he would have made by cutting the boughs and selling the portion Frank's did not want to other buyers.

[UCC §2-708(2)] was offered by the trial judge as an alternate measure if the jury found that Young's decision not to cut the boughs was appropriate. In that case, the jury would have had to conclude that there was no market, as Young contended, and therefore, according to the statute, he should receive the profits that he would have made had there been full performance by the buyer.

Logic and equity, as well as the law, sustain the jury's verdict. Therefore, we reverse the judgment of the court of appeals and reinstate the judgment of the trial court.

JUDGMENT REVERSED.

In focusing strictly on the issue of who had the burden of proof as to the reasonableness of seller's decision, the Ohio Supreme Court in *Young* never discussed the substantive issue of how a seller should decide whether it does or does not make sense to complete manufacture or production where the buyer breaches midstream.

The reasonableness of a seller's decision to complete or stop in these circumstances will necessarily be a function of three separate variables: (1) how much more it will cost the seller to complete from the point when seller learns of the breach (the "Marginal Cost of Completion," or MCC); (2) how much the seller could get for the scrap if it stopped and sold the scrap at the time it learned of buyer's repudiation (the "Scrap Value," or SV); and (3) how much the seller could likely get from a third party were it to complete production (the "Resale of Finished Product," or RFP).

Once the seller plugs in numbers for these variables, the formula that should drive the seller's decision is that the seller should complete production whenever MCC < RFP – SV. Put another way, the seller ought to complete production only when the extra expense in doing so is justified by the increase in proceeds that would come from a resale of a finished product compared to a resale of the scrap.

The problem with this formula, as with any formula that attempts to quantify decisions of this sort, is that rarely will the seller at the time of buyer's repudiation actually be able to plug in the variables with any degree of certainty. In particular, trying to decide what a resale of the finished product would yield is a very tricky business. On the other hand, this formula does give the seller (and ultimately, a court) a framework for trying to assess after the fact whether the seller, given whatever information it did have, indeed acted reasonably in attempting to mitigate the breaching buyer's damages.

Problem Set 24

24.1. a. Swing Time is a retail store that sold expensive wooden swing-sets. Swing Time caters to upper-income families with small children and markets itself as the "full-service swingset specialist." The purchase price on all of Swing Time's sets includes both installation and delivery. Swing Time has five full-time employees who do nothing but installations and two full-time employees who do nothing but deliveries. Swing Time's average net profit on its sales is about 10 percent. Swing Time's cost of materials for each set is about 50 percent of the retail price. Brian Kingsbury signs a contract to have Swing Time install an $8,000 wooden set in his family's backyard. A couple of days before the delivery and installation, Brian calls Swing Time and repudiates the contract because he found an identical set across town for just $7,000, including installation and delivery. Swing Time is able to sell Brian's set to a new buyer for $8,000, but Swing Time could have made the same sale to the new buyer even in the absence of Brian's breach. For what amount may Swing Time recover from Brian? UCC §§2-706(1), 2-708.

b. Same facts as part (a), except that instead of employing a full-time staff of workers who deliver and install the sets, Swing Time uses a third-party independent contractor that charges Swing Time $50 for each delivery and $400 for each installation of this $8,000 set. For what amount may Swing Time recover from Brian? UCC §2-708.

c. Same facts as part (a), except that for some reason this summer wooden swingsets are all the rage, and Swing Time is forced to turn away many of customers because it simply cannot keep up with the sudden demand. For what amount may Swing Time recover from Brian? UCC §§2-708, §1-305(a).

d. Same facts as part (a), except that due to lagging sales over the past year, Swing Time's average net "profit" on its sales during the past year has been a negative 12 percent, even though its cost of materials has remained constant at about 50 percent of retail price. For what amount may Swing Time recover from Brian? UCC §2-708.

e. Same facts as part (a), except that due to a sudden shortage of certain parts for this swingset, the materials for this set end up costing Swing Time $9,000. For what amount may Swing Time recover from Brian? UCC §2-708.

f. Same facts as part (a), except Brian repudiates as to the $8,000 set and agrees to buy instead a $5,000 set from Swing Time. For what amount may Swing Time recover from Brian? UCC §2-708.

g. Same facts as part (a), except Brian is the president of the state park district and his order, which he made two months ago, was for 100 $8,000 swingsets to be installed in all of the state parks over the next 12 months. Due to the impact of Brian's repudiation, Swing Time feels that it must lay off one of its five full-time installers, whose employment cost the company $45,000 per year. (Each full-time installation employee would install about 100 swingsets each year.) For what amount may Swing Time recover from Brian? UCC §2-708.

24.2. With the winter holiday season coming, Arlene Ledger, President of Heavy Metal, Inc. (from Problem 3.2), has her hands full with all of the orders pouring in to her factory from retail fitness stores. One major order has gone sour, however, and that is the subject of her visit to your office today. Four weeks ago, on November 1, the Fitness Palace signed a contract to purchase 500

"Treadwalkers," a new treadmill product that includes ski poles to work the exerciser's arms as well as the legs. The contract price for the 500 Treadwalkers was $600 each, FOB Seller's Factory, delivery date December 1. Two weeks ago the Fitness Palace called Arlene and announced it was repudiating the contract. When the Fitness Palace had originally called in its order, Heavy Metal already had in stock 300 Treadwalkers that had cost Heavy Metal its customary $400 each to produce. Arlene admitted to you, however, that since her factory was already working at full "normal" capacity, by the time of the Fitness Palace order it would have cost Heavy Metal about $450 each to manufacture any additional Treadwalkers by December 1. This is because of the overtime pay that would have been necessary to complete any new orders by that date. One week after the Fitness Palace had signed its order contract (but prior to its repudiation), another retailer, the Sport Shoppe, had signed a contract with Heavy Metal to buy 200 Treadwalkers for $600 each. The Sport Shoppe has not repudiated its contract, which also has a delivery term of FOB Seller's Factory and a delivery date of December 1. Arlene would like to know what the extent of her damage claim will be against the Fitness Palace. (There were no other orders for Treadwalkers during the month of November.) What do you advise? UCC §§2-708, §1-305(a).

24.3. Yesterday you got to meet a new client, Mark Rabid, who was president of Weapons Parts, Inc. (WPI). His company manufactures specially made parts for weapons systems. One of WPI's clients, McDonald & Sons Space Systems (MSSS), commissioned WPI to produce a custom-made missile delivery system (to be included in a massive fighter plane that MSSS was manufacturing) for a total price of $500,000. Mark calculated that the total direct costs of producing this device would be $240,000 worth of raw materials and $70,000 in direct labor costs. Early in the production process, MSSS called WPI and unambiguously repudiated the contract. At that point, WPI had completed only the frame of the delivery system, having so far purchased and used $110,000 worth of raw materials and having expended $30,000 in direct labor costs. Figuring that the market for this specialized system was rather limited, WPI reasonably opted to cease production at that point. A couple of weeks later, a different WPI client, Steve Schale of Schale Aerospace (SA), was touring WPI's plant when he noticed the frame for the uncompleted delivery system. After studying the frame for a few minutes, Steve told Mark Rabid that he would like to buy that frame for one of his company's planes in progress. "I never would have thought to buy this from you if I hadn't seen it sitting there," Steve said. "We generally make all of our own delivery systems in-house." Steve said he would pay $200,000 for the frame in its current state if WPI would simply have it painted to comply with applicable military specifications. Mark agreed to do so, and expended an additional $5,000 for paint plus $5,000 for labor. Mark then seasonably informed MSSS of this proposed resale of the uncompleted delivery system. Mark wants to know in light of all this, what the extent of WPI's damage claim is against MSSS. What do you advise him? UCC §§2-703(c), 2-704, 2-706, 2-708(2).

24.4. Statues of America, Inc. (SOA), is a Nevada manufacturer of custom-designed wooden statues. SOA enters into a written contract with Georgia Frontenac of Reno, Nevada, to specially manufacture a statue of a battering ram with hamburgers wedged on each horn for a total price of $60,000, which includes delivery to Reno. Georgia wants the statue to be displayed in front of her highly successful restaurant, the Ramburger. At the time the contract is entered into, SOA estimates that it would take $18,000 in parts and $30,000 in direct labor costs to build the statue. Midway through production of the statue, Georgia calls SOA and repudiates the contract. At that point, SOA has purchased $10,000 in parts and has expended $20,000 in direct labor costs for the partially completed statue. Shortly following the repudiation call from Georgia, SOA concludes that it could currently sell the scrap for $7,000 to a local buyer who would come and pick up the scrap for no delivery charge. As for other buyers, SOA learns from calling around that one other buyer, Bill Wellbid, of Phoenix, Arizona, thinks he might be interested in purchasing a finished statue of this type. Bill tells SOA that before making a decision, he needs to see the finished statue. Nevertheless, Bill says that his good-faith estimate of the odds that he would purchase the statue once it is complete is about 75 percent that he would. Bill said that if he does purchase the completed statue he would pay $41,000 for it, but that price has to include delivery to Phoenix. Delivery to Reno, Nevada, would have cost SOA $2,000; delivery to Phoenix would cost SOA $5,000. Assume that Bill Wellbid would be the only possible buyer of the finished statue, that the odds he gives of his purchasing the finished product are truthful, and that the finished statue would have zero scrap value (even though the currently unfinished statue, as noted earlier, has a $7,000 scrap value).

Given all of the above information, consider three different scenarios and separately describe SOA's damage claim against Georgia Frontenac under each of the scenarios:

a. SOA chooses to stop manufacture now, gives proper resale notice, and sells the scrap for $7,000. UCC §§2-703(c), 2-704, 2-706, 2-708(2); Official Comment 2 to §2-704.

b. SOA completes manufacture, gives proper resale notice, and is able to sell the finished product to Bill Wellbid for $41,000.

c. SOA completes manufacture but after diligent effort is ultimately unable to sell the finished product to Bill Wellbid or to any other buyer. UCC §2-709.

Assignment 25:   Buyer's Remedies with Sales of Goods

Just as with this book's coverage of seller's remedies, this assignment begins the subject of buyer's remedies by making the point that the vast majority of remedies exercised by aggrieved buyers are of the non-litigation variety. In many cases, buyers are even better situated than sellers to use nonjudicial remedies since often buyers will not have paid the entire purchase price at the time they discover the seller's breach. In these situations, the buyer always has as a last resort simply withholding the price, which at a minimum puts the burden on the seller rather than the buyer to file a lawsuit. This simple act can be surprisingly effective in getting a seller's attention, particularly when the seller has borrowed money to fund its production or acquisition of the goods sold.

Typically when a buyer is dissatisfied with the seller's product, the first step that the buyer will take is to inform the seller of the problem and ask the seller to make things right. More often than not, the seller's response to the buyer's complaint will be to repair or replace the defective goods, unless the seller has some reason to believe that the buyer's complaint is unfounded.

In those unusual cases in which the seller does not or cannot fix the problem, the buyer still retains some leverage if it has not yet paid the full purchase price. As noted above, this nonjudicial exercise of setoff can be a powerful tool for the aggrieved buyer. The in-house counsel for a Fortune 200 department store chain explains how the setoff right can be even more potent where the buyer has multiple accounts with the same seller: "The one remedies issue that we pay attention to in our standard forms is that we make sure the seller realizes that they are dealing with our larger company, not just the particular store that is making the purchase. In that way we can preserve our ability to set off if the same vendor has dealings with any other of our stores."

If refusing to pay or delaying payment is inadequate to solve the problem, the buyer can turn to the more serious remedy of terminating its relationship with the seller. As the purchasing agent for a medium-sized plastics manufacturer put it: "We have never had to go to litigation in the 15 years that I've been here. Buyer remedies in practice are really pretty simple: if the material we get is not good, then the supplier fixes it for us or they don't get any more of our business. Think of it from the supplier's perspective: if we've got a $3,000 problem with one of their products and we do $400,000 worth of business with them in a year, doesn't it make sense for them to fix it for us?"

Just as with seller's remedies, it is a tribute to the UCC drafters that very few sales contracts spend a lot of space changing the Article 2 standard remedies for buyers. The one exception to this is consequential damages, which sellers are always eager to disclaim when they can. On the other hand, buyers will fight hard to retain their right to sue for consequential damages caused by the seller's breach.

The in-house counsel who advises the purchasing department of a Fortune 200 manufacturer explained it this way: "Our starting point is that a seller should be responsible for all damage that is caused by their breach. Depending on the seller and the leverage they have, they might be able to get us to make exceptions to that, like liquidated damages or limitation of consequential damages, but we fight hard to keep all of our remedies intact at the outset."

When informal negotiations fail and the buyer has not set off or used other nonjudicial leverage to satisfy itself, Article 2 provides a laundry list of possible litigation remedies for the aggrieved buyer. The potential UCC remedies available to the buyer will initially be a function of whether or not the buyer has accepted the goods. If the buyer has accepted the goods and it is too late to revoke acceptance, the buyer's remedies are limited to an action for breach of warranty, as outlined in §2-714. If the buyer has either failed to receive the goods or has justifiably rejected them or revoked acceptance of them, the buyer's remedies are more varied, as described in §2-711. Both categories of aggrieved buyers are eligible for incidental and consequential damages as defined in §2-715.

In all cases, the underlying idea of the buyer's remedies sections, as with seller's remedies, is to try to put the buyer in the position that the buyer would have been in had the seller performed. UCC §1-305(a). For the buyer that has accepted the goods and may no longer revoke its acceptance, the damages formula for seller's breach of warranty is found in §2-714: VCG − VNCG + ID + CD, where VCG = the value of conforming goods, VNCG = the value of the non-conforming goods that buyer in fact received, ID = incidental damages, and CD = consequential damages. In order for the aggrieved buyer to be eligible at all for breach of warranty damages, the buyer must give the seller notice of the breach "within a reasonable time after [the buyer] discovers or should have discovered any breach." UCC §2-607(3)(a).

Oftentimes the difference between the value of what the buyer actually received and the value of what the buyer should have received can be as simple as whatever it costs the buyer to have the defect repaired. Although the cost of repair might in some cases exceed the VCG-VNCG difference, it is normally viewed as an acceptable surrogate for this value difference because repair is often the practical way to provide the buyer with its expectation. Where repair is not possible, however, a court would be forced to assess in other ways the diminution in value that the seller's breach of warranty caused to the buyer's goods.

T.Co Metals, LLC v. Dempsey Pipe & Supply, Inc.

592 F.3d 329 (2d Cir. 2010)

LIVINGSTON, C.J.

Petitioner-Appellant T.Co Metals, LLC ("T.Co") appeals from judgments of the United States District Court for the Southern District of New York (Crotty, J.) resolving two consolidated actions commenced by T.Co and Respondent-Appellee Dempsey Pipe & Supply, Inc. ("Dempsey"), in which the parties sought, inter alia, to vacate, modify, and correct an arbitration award pursuant to the Federal Arbitration Act ("FAA"), 9 U.S.C. §§10-11. Conducted according to the International Dispute Resolution Procedures of the American Arbitration Association's International Centre of Dispute Resolution ("ICDR"), the arbitration concerned a dispute over allegedly defective steel pipe that T.Co delivered to Dempsey pursuant to two sales contracts between the parties. Arbitrator Paul D. Friedland issued a final award on April 20, 2007 ("Original Award"). Both parties then petitioned the arbitrator to amend the Original Award pursuant to ICDR Article 30(1). On May 30, 2007, the arbitrator issued an order ("Amendment Order") accepting a small portion of the requested changes and ordering that the Original Award be amended accordingly. The arbitrator then issued an amended award on June 4, 2007 ("Amended Award"). Both T.Co and Dempsey filed petitions in the district court to modify or to vacate the Amended Award in part. The district court denied T.Co's petition and granted in part and denied in part Dempsey's petition.

T.Co raises two issues on appeal. First, T.Co argues that the arbitrator acted in "manifest disregard of the law" by awarding diminution-in-value damages to Dempsey despite the parties' contractual provision barring consequential damages. The district court's ruling to the contrary, T.Co contends, resulted from an erroneous interpretation of the Supreme Court's recent decision in Hall Street Associates, L.L.C. v. Mattel, Inc., 552 U.S. 576, 128 S. Ct. 1396, 170 L. Ed. 2d 254 (2008). . . .

BACKGROUND

I. THE COMMERCIAL DISPUTE

Pursuant to two sales contracts dated February 25 and April 25, 2005, T.Co agreed to sell Dempsey approximately 2440 metric tons (or 2690 short tons) of twenty-foot, plain-end steel pipe, to be produced in Chile and sent to Philadelphia in four shipments arriving over the spring and summer of 2005. Among other things, each contract provided that "Seller is not responsible for consequential loss or damage." J.A. 27, 30. The contracts also contained an arbitration clause, reading in part as follows:

> Any . . . dispute, claim or controversy between [T.Co and Dempsey] which cannot be resolved through negotiations within a period of 30 days . . . shall be referred

to and finally resolved by arbitration under the [i]nternational arbitration rules of the American Arbitration Association [(hereinafter "ICDR Articles")]. Arbitration will take place in New York, N.Y. USA and proceedings will be conducted in English. The award of the Arbitration tribunal will be final and subject to no appeal. The costs and expenses of the prevailing party (including, without limitation, reasonable attorney's fees) will be paid by the other party.

Id. The contracts designated the "Laws of the State of New York" as their governing law. Id.

Upon delivery, Dempsey discovered that a substantial amount of the pipe it received was bowed or bent to the point of being out of tolerance for straightness. Nevertheless, out of the four shipments of pipe it received Dempsey ultimately rejected only a small portion of the second shipment, choosing to keep the rest of the delivered pipe and to straighten the defective pipe itself. The contract price for the pipe was $780 per short ton. After straightening the defective pipe, Dempsey was able to sell it at $922 per short ton.

T.Co sent Dempsey an invoice for $1,993,145.53, of which Dempsey paid $1,655,105.81. In June 2006, T.Co commenced arbitration and claimed damages against Dempsey for $338,039.72, the amount of payment that Dempsey had withheld. Dempsey filed a counterclaim that included a demand for $1,895,052 in damages due to the diminished value of the defective steel pipe that Dempsey accepted. In response, T.Co argued that Dempsey's counterclaim was an attempt to recover lost profits, which it asserted are defined as consequential damages under New York law and thus are not recoverable pursuant to the parties' contract. In its written submissions to this Court, Dempsey acknowledges that it did ask the arbitrator to award Dempsey consequential damages in the form of lost profits, contending that the contractual exclusion of consequential damages had been superseded by an oral agreement between the parties. But Dempsey asserts it also argued in the alternative that, if the arbitrator decided that the consequential damages provision remained in force, Dempsey was still entitled to recover damages for the diminished value of the pipe, since those damages constituted "benefit-of-the-bargain" damages under section 2-714(2) of the New York Uniform Commercial Code ("N.Y. UCC"), which provides that "[t]he measure of damages for breach of warranty is the difference at the time and place of acceptance between the value of the goods accepted and the value they would have had if they had been as warranted, unless special circumstances show proximate damages of a different amount."

II.   The Original Arbitration Award

On April 20, 2007, the arbitrator issued the Original Award, which included an award of $338,039.72 to T.Co for the outstanding unpaid invoices, and an award of $420,357 to Dempsey for the diminished value of the defective pipe.

When analyzing Dempsey's claim for damages, the arbitrator agreed with T.Co that the consequential damages exclusions in the contracts remained in effect. Nevertheless, the arbitrator also concluded that N.Y. UCC §2-714(2) provided the appropriate measure of damages for nonconforming goods where, as here, the fair market value of the goods as accepted was ascertainable.

The arbitrator proceeded to apply §2-714(2)'s formula—i.e., that damages equal the value of the goods as warranted minus the value of the goods as accepted, measured at the time and place of acceptance. The arbitrator calculated the value of the pipe as warranted by looking both to invoices of steel pipe sellers that supplied entities like Dempsey and to evidence regarding the price at which pipe was being sold by firms similarly situated to Dempsey. On this basis, the arbitrator determined that the value of the pipe as warranted was $1000 per short ton. After additional calculations and evaluation of the evidence, the arbitrator determined the value of the nonconforming pipe at the time and place of acceptance to be $737 per short ton. Under §2-714(2)'s formula, then, Dempsey was entitled to $263 ($1000-$737) per short ton, or $420,537 total for the 1599 short tons of pipe that the arbitrator determined were nonconforming.

* * *

DISCUSSION

I.   STANDARD OF REVIEW

"When a party challenges the district court's review of an arbitral award under the manifest disregard standard, we review the district court's application of the standard de novo." Porzig v. Dresdner, Kleinwort, Benson, N. Am. LLC, 497 F.3d 133, 138 (2d Cir. 2007) (quoting Wallace v. Buttar, 378 F.3d 182, 189 (2d Cir. 2004)) (internal quotation marks omitted). With respect to the district court's decision to vacate the Amended Award as exceeding the arbitrator's powers, we review the district court's legal rulings de novo and its findings of fact for clear error. ReliaStar Life Ins. Co. of N.Y. v. EMC Nat'l Life Co., 564 F.3d 81, 85 (2d Cir. 2009).

II.   WHETHER THE AWARD OF DIMINUTION-IN-VALUE DAMAGES WAS MADE IN MANIFEST DISREGARD OF THE LAW

* * *

. . . T.Co errs by making the unwarranted assumption that the breach-of-warranty damages that the arbitrator calculated pursuant to N.Y. UCC §2-714(2) inescapably amount to an award of "lost profits," which in turn constitute consequential damages. There is a difference between the loss of the inherent economic value of the contractual performance as warranted, which N.Y. UCC §2-714(2) addresses, and the loss of profits that the buyer anticipated garnering from transactions that were to follow the contractual performance. The fact that the N.Y. UCC addresses consequential damages in a separate section from diminution-in-value damages supports the inference that these two measures of damages are not necessarily equivalent. See N.Y. UCC §§2-714(2), 2-715(2); see also id. §2-714(3) (noting that, in addition to breach-of-warranty damages under §2-714(2), "[i]n a proper case any incidental and consequential damages under the next section may *also* be recovered" (emphasis added)). New York case law similarly demonstrates that a buyer may recover the diminution in the value of the contractual goods as warranted even where there is a contractual exclusion of consequential damages. See, e.g., Carbo Indus. Inc. v. Becker Chevrolet Inc., 112 A.D.2d 336, 491 N.Y.S.2d 786, 790 (N.Y. App. Div. 1985). Our case law has also recognized in an analogous context that a contractual exclusion of consequential damages "does not foreclose liability for lost profits to the extent those profits merely reflect the value of the goods at destination." Jessica Howard Ltd. v. Norfolk S. Ry. Co., 316 F.3d 165, 169 (2d Cir. 2003).

T.Co's attempts to undermine the weight of this authority are unpersuasive. Moreover, the sources T.Co cites in favor of equating Dempsey's damages under §2-714(2) to consequential damages fall short of demonstrating that this result is conclusively established by New York law. For example, T.Co cites a Uniform Commercial Code treatise by James J. White and Robert S. Summers for the proposition that §2-714(2) damages are not appropriate where the contract excludes consequential damages. See Appellant's Br. 37. But the White and Summers treatise is more equivocal than T.Co acknowledges. It notes that "reasonable persons often differ whether an item of damage is 'consequential' or not," 1 James J. White & Robert S. Summers, UNIFORM COMMERCIAL CODE §10-2 (5th ed. 2006), available at 1 WS-UCC §10-2 (Westlaw), and it specifically recognizes that "[i]n many cases, the consequential damages that appear to be recoverable under 2-715(2) may overlap with the direct 'difference-in-value' damages recoverable under 2-714(2)," id. §10-4, available at 1 WS-UCC §10-4 (Westlaw). The legal distinction between diminution-in-value damages and consequential damages, therefore, resembles the kind of "ambiguous law" that eludes analysis under the manifest disregard doctrine. See *Stolt-Nielsen*, 548 F.3d at 93 (quoting *Duferco*, 333 F.3d at 390).

When assessing damages in the present case, the arbitrator properly looked not only to Dempsey's plans for the pipe, but also assessed a cross section of invoices from other companies that dealt in the pipe in order to determine the pipe's fair market value at the time and place of acceptance. In doing so, the arbitrator was engaged in determining "the value differential component of the buyer's total loss," not the subjective lost profits and lost business opportunities of Dempsey. See White & Summers, supra, §10-4, available at 1 WS-UCC §10-4 (Westlaw). This process of calculating damages constituted a reasonable interpretation of the legal distinction between the diminution-in-value damages that were available to Dempsey under the N.Y. UCC and the consequential damages that were excluded by the parties' contracts. Accordingly, we perceive no manifest disregard of the law under any understanding of the current status of that doctrine. Whatever the scope of the manifest disregard doctrine may be in the wake of Hall Street, therefore, the arbitrator's decision to award diminution-in-value damages does not qualify. We therefore affirm the district court's denial of T.Co's motion to vacate the award of diminution-in-value damages to Dempsey. . . .

Although the buyer that has accepted the goods and can no longer revoke acceptance has lost its ability to return the goods back to the seller, such a buyer is explicitly given the right in §2-717 to deduct from the price any damages that result from seller's breach. In order to exercise this right, the buyer must first notify seller of its intention to do so. The reason that this notice is important is that it gives the seller a chance to assess the validity of the buyer's complaint and respond to it accordingly. More important as a practical matter, the right of the buyer to deduct damages from the purchase price is only as useful as the amount of the purchase price that still remains unpaid.

As noted above, in addition to the buyer that is stuck with defective goods, the second category of aggrieved buyer is the one that will end up with no goods at all, either because the seller never delivered or because the buyer rightfully returned defective goods back to the seller. This aggrieved buyer's options are set down in §2-711, and include (in addition to the buyer getting its money back) the right to "cover" and the right to contract-market damages. Such a buyer may, in certain circumstances, be entitled to specific performance, but discussion of that remedy will be deferred until Assignment 28.

In some cases, the rightfully rejecting or revoking buyer will still have the goods in its possession. Where such a buyer has already paid all or part of the purchase price, §2-711(3) gives a special self-help remedy: the buyer may hold the goods as security for repayment of its purchase price as well as for any expenses the buyer incurs in holding or storing the goods. Ultimately, such a buyer can resell these goods "in like manner as an aggrieved seller" (under §2-706(1)) as a way to recover its damages.

The buyer's right to cover is described in §2-712. In order to cover, the aggrieved buyer must make "in good faith and without unreasonable delay any reasonable purchase of or contract to purchase goods in substitution for those due from the seller." UCC §2-712(1). The covering buyer's damages are then measured as RBPP + CC − KP + ID + CD − ES, where RBPP = return of any purchase price paid by buyer, CC = cost of cover, KP = contract price, ID = incidental damages, CD = consequential damages, and ES = expenses saved as a result of seller's breach.

To the extent that there are disputes in cover situations, they tend to involve one of three issues: (1) Did the buyer wait too long to cover? (2) Were the goods that the buyer purchased as a cover really the same as the contract goods? and (3) Did the buyer pay too much for the cover goods?

Section 2-712 and its Official Comments are quite clear that buyer's cover is strictly an optional remedy for buyer. Section 2-712(3) says that "[f]ailure of the buyer to effect cover within this section does not bar him from any other remedy." Official Comment 3 reinforces the optional nature of cover for the buyer by noting that "[t]he buyer is always free to choose between cover and damages for non-delivery under the next section."

The "next section" referred to in Comment 3 is §2-713, the aggrieved buyer's contract-market measure of damages. Section 2-713 can be thought of as a kind of "hypothetical cover" for the buyer. The actual cover remedy of §2-712 does a great job of effectuating the "spirit of the remedies" policy of §1-305(a), in that it almost always puts the buyer in exactly the same position that the buyer would have been in had the seller performed: the buyer ends up getting the goods, and the seller pays the buyer for any additional cost that the buyer incurred in order to get the substitute goods.

The contract-market measure of §2-713 is less likely to put the buyer in exactly the same position that the buyer would have been in had the seller not breached. One reason for this is that its damage measure sets the market price as of the time that the buyer learns of the breach, UCC §2-713(1), which may not end up being the market price of the goods at the time of seller's originally promised performance. Under §2-713, the place where the market price is measured is the place of tender, unless the buyer rejects or revokes acceptance of the goods after arrival, in which case the market price is measured as of the place of arrival. UCC §2-713(2).

The §2-713(1) formula itself looks strikingly similar to the cover formula, with the only difference being that the market price number substitutes for the cost of cover: RBPP + MP – KP + ID + CD – ES, where RBPP = return of any purchase price paid by buyer, MP = market price, KP = contract price, ID = incidental damages, CD = consequential damages, and ES = expenses saved as a result of seller's breach.

One remedies-related set of issues that arises for both buyers and sellers is when one party gets information prior to the performance date that calls into question the other side's ability to perform the contract. At this point, the insecure party is entitled to demand adequate assurance of future performance. If such assurance is not forthcoming, then the insecure party can declare that the other side has committed an anticipatory repudiation of the contract, which is a form of breach that entitles the aggrieved party to all of the usual remedies. While the two sections governing this situation, §§2-609 and 2-610, apply equally to buyers and sellers, buyers are more likely than sellers to utilize these sections. This may stem from the more complex nature of a seller's performance — manufacturing or procuring goods — than the buyer's, which is simply paying the price. A not uncommon situation that often leads to a demand for adequate assurance is when one of the contracting parties becomes insolvent or files for bankruptcy.

As noted earlier, the buyer in a sales-of-goods case can always recover, in addition to contract-market, contract-cover, or cost-of-the-defect damages, any incidental and consequential damages that it can show resulted from the seller's breach. As noted in Assignment 22, Article 2 sellers cannot recover consequential damages. It might seem odd at first blush that there should be such a difference between the treatment of sellers and buyers on this score.

When thinking about eligibility for consequential damages, consider the nature of the seller's performance and the buyer's performance and the ways in which either party can breach the contract. When the buyer breaches, the breach will almost always amount to the simple failure to pay the price. Failing to pay the price, however, will not cause someone to get physically injured, nor will it typically prevent a seller from fulfilling the seller's obligations to other parties. After all, an aggrieved seller will often be able to sell its goods to someone else or borrow the money that it expected to receive from the breaching buyer as a way to avoid consequential damages.

Consider, by contrast, the nature of a seller's breach. If the seller's goods are defective, many bad things can happen to the buyer as a direct consequence of that: the buyer might be injured, the buyer's property might be damaged, or third parties might be injured. In addition, there are all kinds of economic losses that a buyer is likely to suffer if the seller's goods fail to perform or if the seller fails to deliver the goods at all. If the buyer owns a business and buys a machine from the seller, the failure of the machine (or the seller's failure to deliver it) might impact the buyer's ability to successfully carry out its business.

There is a special but not uncommon form of consequential damages that the buyer might suffer as a result of the seller's breach, of which a detailed discussion will be deferred until Assignment 27. In brief, this is the case in which the buyer itself is a seller and thus may suffer a lost profit in its contract with its own buyer. This will happen in any case where the original buyer is intending to resell the goods that it has contracted to buy from the initial seller.

Section 2-715(2) sets down two different categories of consequential damages available to Article 2 buyers. Oftentimes, a particular consequential damage that the buyer suffers will qualify for either category. Section 2-715(2)(a) allows as buyer's consequential damages those damages resulting from a seller's breach: (1) of any kind, including purely economic loss; (2) of which the seller had reason to know at the time of contracting (*Hadley v. Baxendale* foreseeability limit); (3) that were "caused in fact" (mere but-for cause, rather than "proximate cause") by seller's breach; and (4) that could not be prevented "by cover or otherwise" (basic mitigation principle).

The consequential damages that are allowed in the second category, §2-715(2)(b), are broader in some respects and narrower in others than the first category. For a buyer to show §2-715(2)(b) consequential damages, those damages must be (1) personal injury or property damage (economic loss does not qualify here), and (2) proximately caused by seller's breach (mere but-for cause is not enough). The way in which the second category of consequential damages is broader than the first is that there is no *Hadley* foreseeability limit to qualify for damages under the second category, nor is there the explicit language concerning buyer's need to mitigate.

Thus, suppose that the buyer purchases a machine from the seller for use in the buyer's factory. Imagine that the machine explodes because of a defect, injures the buyer, and causes the buyer's operation to shut down for two days. The buyer, unknown to the seller, purchased this machine to increase production for the benefit of a new client who would have given the buyer enough business in the next year to produce $5 million in profits. Because of the delay occasioned by the explosion, the buyer's new client takes its business elsewhere.

For what consequential damages would this buyer be eligible? Certainly the buyer could recover for its personal injuries, under either §2-715(2)(a) or (2)(b). Under §2-715(2)(a), the personal injuries are "any loss," caused in fact, seller had reason to know (everyone knows that exploding machines can injure people), and buyer could not have prevented the loss "by cover or otherwise." This also qualifies under §2-715(2)(b) because it was an injury to person proximately caused by the seller's breach.

The economic losses will be more difficult for the buyer to recover as consequential damages. They clearly will not fit under §2-715(2)(b), since that category is restricted to injuries to person or property. Even §2-715(2)(a) will be problematic, however, because of the *Hadley* foreseeability limit. It would be one thing if buyer were merely trying to recover "normal profits" in a case where seller knew that buyer was purchasing the machine for buyer's factory. But a $5 million profit that hinged on the performance of this machine seems to be a "particular" requirement or need of the buyer's that the seller had to have reason to know in order to be held responsible for it.

The buyer's incidental damages under §2-715(1) are a little more straightforward. Incidental damages for the aggrieved buyer are expenses that the buyer incurs in inspecting, transporting, storing, or reselling rejected goods, or in effecting cover as a result of the seller's breach, or "any other reasonable expense incident to the delay or other breach."

Despite their characterization as "incidental," §2-715(1) damages can sometimes be quite large for buyers. In one case, for example, a seller that disclaimed liability for consequential damages was nevertheless found liable for incidental damages of $293 million. These damages represented the buyer's storage costs for the radioactive nuclear fuel that was the subject of the breached contract. Commonwealth Edison Co. v. Allied Chemical Nuclear Products, Inc., 684 F. Supp. 1434 (N.D. Ill. 1988).

Problem Set 25

25.1. Jack's Industrial Tile for Less installs tile for schools, businesses, and other institutions with large buildings. Jack Kost, president of Jack's, has come to see you to discuss a couple of problem jobs that he has encountered during the last few weeks. The first involves Lakeside School, whose gymnasium Jack's had contracted to re-tile. The $40,000 contract called for a very hard grade of tile that would have cost Jack's $30,000 to obtain and install. Because of a mix-up at Jack's office, his workers installed a softer, but more expensive vinyl tile that cost Jack's $45,000 to obtain and install. Because of the various purposes for which the Lakeside School gym was used, the hard but cheaper tile was the only floor surface that would work for the school. The softer vinyl tile was essentially worthless for the school's purposes, at least in its original form. However, the vinyl could be treated with a special coating for $5,000 that would harden it and make it just as suitable for Lakeside's purposes as the tile that should have been installed. Removing the tile is not an attractive option, since it would cost Jack's more to remove the tile than the used tile could command in a resale. What would be the proper measure of Lakeside's damages if it chose to sue Jack's on a breach of warranty theory? UCC §§2-714(2), 1-305(a).

25.2.   Another school that Jack's had a contract with, Beasley Prep, was a victim of the same mix-up as Jack's involving Lakeside's order. Beasley paid Jack's $55,000 to have the more expensive vinyl tile for its gym, which was the same size as Lakeside's. Instead, Beasley ended up getting the cheaper, hard tile that was intended for Lakeside. In fact, however, this foul-up on Jack's part turned out to be a blessing in disguise for Beasley. The Beasley principal had not realized at the time she ordered the softer tile that it would simply not work for the various purposes for which the Beasley gym was used. Indeed, the softer tile that Beasley had ordered would have proven worthless for that school's purposes. The cheaper, harder tile, by contrast, was in fact perfect for the several uses to which the Beasley gym was put. What would be the proper measure of Beasley's damages if it were to sue Jack's on a breach of warranty theory? UCC §§2-714(2), 1-305(a).

25.3.   Joe Fortino owned a tennis specialty store. Two weeks ago he sold for $1,000 a custom-made, hand-strung racket to an up-and-coming pro player, Chrissie Austin. Chrissie had told Joe that she would be using this racket in an upcoming weekend tournament in Las Vegas that offered a $60,000 first prize. On that weekend, Chrissie cruised her way to the semifinal round of the tournament, at which point the frame cracked on her new racket while she was leading the match 6-2, 5-1. The cracked frame rendered the new racket worthless and clearly constituted a breach of the sales contract. Chrissie was able to borrow a racket from another player, but the new racket was a disaster for her. She ended up losing the next 12 games of the semifinal match, eventually dropping the match by scores of 2-6, 7-5, 6-0. The Vegas odds had made Chrissie a 4-1 favorite to win the tournament, and Chrissie can produce convincing evidence that she probably would have won the tournament if the racket had not cracked. Chrissie asks you for how much she can recover from Joe Fortino. What do you advise? UCC §§2-714(2) and (3), 2-715(2)(a); Official Comments 2 and 3 to §2-715.

25.4.   Arlene Ledger, President of Heavy Metal, Inc. (from Problem 3.2) comes by your office looking glum. Today, she says, she is not here to ask you about problems she is having with a breaching customer. Rather, she says, this time her company is the breacher. A large retailer, Company Fitness, had contracted to purchase from Heavy Metal an industrial-sized multi-station weight machine for $35,000. Company Fitness was planning to display (but not sell) the machine at a major trade show in order to attract possible future customers in the burgeoning business of supplying on-site office exercise facilities. The week before the trade show, Arlene realized that her production department had dropped the ball on this order and there was no way that Heavy Metal could fill the order in time for Company Fitness's appearance at the trade show. When Arlene informed Company Fitness of this fact, Company Fitness sought to cover.

a. Suppose that Company Fitness could not find a precisely comparable machine on such short notice and instead paid $42,000 for a slightly better machine. What would its cover damages be against Heavy Metal? UCC §2-712, Official Comment 2 to §2-712.

b. Suppose that Company Fitness could have purchased for $40,000 a machine exactly comparable to the one Heavy Metal promised to make. Instead, it covered by purchasing a much better machine that happened to be on sale for $40,500 (this machine normally sold for $50,000). What would its damages be against Heavy Metal? UCC §§2-712, 2-713.

c. Imagine under scenario (a) above that Company Fitness was intending to sell rather than just display the machine. Suppose that Company Fitness expected to sell the original machine for $45,000, but thanks to the additional features in the machine it purchased, it was able to sell it for $48,000. What would Company Fitness' cover damages be then? UCC §§2-712, 2-715(2)(a).

25.5.   a. Henry Brock was a collector of sports memorabilia, including baseball cards. On September 1, Henry made a contract with a store called Sports Collectibles to purchase an original 1909 Ty Cobb baseball card for $1,700. The contract said that Henry could come in and pick up the card on November 11, at which point he would also pay the purchase price in full. On October 1, a different buyer offered Sports Collectibles $2,500 for the same card (on the theory that an upcoming ESPN special on Cobb would increase the value of Cobb cards), and the store sold it on the spot to the new buyer for that amount. That afternoon, the manager of Sports Collectibles called Henry to inform him that the Ty Cobb card deal was off. Stunned by this unexpected development, Henry replied, "Not so fast. I'm not going to let you off on this one. I think you'd better reconsider." Two weeks later, on October 15, Henry called Sports Collectibles to ask if his Ty Cobb card would be ready on November 11. The clerk who answered the phone politely explained to Henry that the Cobb card had been sold to someone else two weeks ago. "Well," said Henry, "you had better tell your boss to buy it back, because I will be there with my check on November 11." True to his word, Henry shows up with his check on November 11, but the store does not have the Cobb card to sell him. If the market price of the card was $2,500 on October 1, $2,700 on October 15, and $3,000 on November 11, to what amount is Henry entitled in damages from Sports Collectibles? UCC §§2-713(1), 2-610, 2-609(4).

b. Same facts as part (a), except suppose that Sports Collectibles did not sell the Ty Cobb card to a different buyer. However, one month after Henry purchased the card from the store, Shelly Lopez sues Henry to recover the card on the grounds that she was the true owner and the card was stolen from her last year. Henry spends $800 in attorney's fees defending the suit, but ultimately loses the suit (and the card) to Shelly. Even though the card had a market value of $3,000 on November 11, its value had increased to $4,000 by the time Henry lost the lawsuit. For what amount may Henry recover in a lawsuit against Sports Collectibles? UCC §§2-312(1)(a), 2-714, 2-715(2), 1-305(a).

25.6.   a. Miles Gurney is a hog farmer, and for that reason he keeps a ready stock of hog feed in a warehouse on his farm. Miles had a contract with Mabel's Feed 'n Seed to purchase eight tons of hog feed for $6,400, which Mabel promised to deliver to Miles' farm on May 1. On May 1, Mabel fails to deliver the feed and announces to Miles that she is breaching the contract. On May 1, the market price for comparable hog feed is $1,000 per ton. Over the next month, as the market price for hog feed declines, Miles purchases three separate eight-ton loads of hog feed from other suppliers. The first load, purchased on May 20, costs Miles $7,000; the second, purchased on May 25, costs $6,500; and the third, purchased on May 30, costs $6,300. On June 15, Miles files suit against Mabel for breach of contract. To what amount is Miles entitled in damages? UCC §§2-712, 2-713; Official Comment 3 to §2-712, Official Comment 5 to §2-713.

b. Same facts as part (a), except that the May 1 market price is $800 per ton, and Miles makes the same three purchases on the same dates at the same prices as part (a). To what amount is Miles entitled in damages? UCC §§2-712, 2-713; Comment 2 to §2-712.

c. Same facts as part (a), except Miles does not purchase any additional hog feed during the month following the breach. Instead, he takes 8 tons from the stock of 20 tons in his warehouse. The average price of the 20 tons of hog feed, which Miles had purchased through several deals during the past year, was $1,200 per ton. To what amount is Miles entitled in damages? UCC §§2-712, 2-713.

25.7.   a. Rhonda Lewis, a traveling salesperson, buys a new Chevy Malibu for $22,000 from Jack Pollard's Chevy City, but the car's engine catches fire during the first week Rhonda drives it. Rhonda was not hurt, but she was so disgusted that she called Jack to revoke her acceptance and to get him to send out a tow truck to take the Malibu back to Chevy City. She then demanded her $22,000 back from Jack, who gave it to her. After getting her refund, Rhonda intended to search for another new Malibu at a different dealer. In the meantime, Rhonda rented a Malibu for $400 per month, plus 20 cents a mile for each mile over 1,000 per month. Because of her heavy travel schedule, Rhonda took four months to purchase a new Malibu, for which she ultimately paid $24,000. During the four months she used the rental Malibu, Rhonda put 2,500 miles on it per month, which added a total of $1,200 to her final rental bill. If Rhonda sues Jack Pollard's Chevy City for breach of contract, for what amount may she recover? UCC §§2-712, 2-715; Comment 2 to §2-712, 1-305(a).

b. Same facts as part (a), except that Rhonda had only paid $3,000 of the purchase price. Further, when Rhonda called to complain about the engine fire and give notice of her revocation, Jack Pollard failed to send out a tow truck and failed to tender a refund of Rhonda's $3,000. After a couple of days, Rhonda paid a towing firm $100 to take the car to a local storage company, which agreed to hold the car for Rhonda for $10 per day. Four months later, after Rhonda had rented the Malibu and then paid $24,000 for a different new Malibu, Jack Pollard called and said he wanted his car back and that he was willing to refund Rhonda's $3,000 in order to get it. To what extent may Rhonda hold out for still more money from Jack as a condition to her returning the car to him? UCC §2-711(3).

25.8.   a. Pro Roofing, Inc., an Atlanta residential roofing firm, made a contract with Industrial Shingles, a Nashville manufacturer, to purchase 20 tons of shingles for $50,000, "FOB Nashville." The stated delivery date was "on or before July 20," and the cost of delivering the shingles from Nashville to Atlanta was $1,500. On July 20, the shingles had not yet arrived to Pro Roofing, causing the president of Pro Roofing to call Industrial Shingles and learn that the seller was not going to perform. The market price of 20 tons of shingles on July 20 was $56,000 in Nashville, and $54,000 in Atlanta. Assuming that Pro Roofing does not cover, to what amount is it entitled in damages? UCC §§2-713, 2-319(1), 2-509(1).

b. Same facts as part (a), except that the delivery term is "FOB Atlanta." Assuming that Pro Roofing does not cover, to what amount is it entitled in damages? UCC §§2-713, 2-319(1), 2-509(1).

c. Same facts as part (a), except that the contract contains no delivery term whatsoever. Assuming that Pro Roofing does not cover, to what amount is it entitled in damages? UCC §§2-713, 2-509(1), 2-308(a); Official Comment 5 to §2-503.

d. Same facts as part (a), except that the shingles arrive on July 20, prove to be obviously and horribly defective, and Pro Roofing immediately rejects the shingles. Assuming that Pro Roofing has already paid for the goods and their delivery, and that Pro Roofing does not cover, to what amount is it entitled in damages? UCC §2-713.

e. Same facts as part (a), except that Pro Roofing learns on July 10 that Industrial Shingles had defaulted on its major bank loan and was threatening to file Chapter 11 bankruptcy unless its lender agreed to restructure the loan. In light of this news, what course of action should Pro Roofing pursue? UCC §§2-609, 2-610.

f. Same facts as part (a), except that Pro Roofing gets an e-mail from the Industrial Shingles president on July 10 that says the following: "I just got a call from a different buyer who is willing to pay $57,000 for 20 tons of the same shingles as yours. I guess this has become like an auction for those shingles. I hope that you can match that price if you still want the shingles." How should Pro Roofing respond to this message? UCC §§2-609, 2-610.

g. Same facts as part (a), except that on July 10, Pro Roofing gets a fax from the Industrial Shingles president that says, "Our deal is off. We're just not making that type of shingles anymore." On July 15, Pro Roofing covers by buying the same type of shingles from a different seller for $60,000 plus $2,000 in delivery costs. Then on July 16, Pro Roofing gets a voicemail message from the Industrial Shingles president that says, "You can ignore my July 10 fax. That just wouldn't be the right thing for us to do. You can expect to receive your shingles order as scheduled." Where does Pro Roofing stand now with respect to the original contract? UCC §§2-610, 2-611.

Assignment 26: Buyer's and Lessee's Remedies with Leases, International Sales, and Real Estate

A. Lessee's Remedies

The lessee's remedies under Article 2A very closely track the buyer's remedies outlined in Article 2. The translation is not perfect, of course, given the fundamental difference between a sale and a lease. Unlike a sale, a lease by definition will not give the lessee possession for the entire life of the goods. As discussed with the lessor's remedies in Assignment 23, this difference creates some special obligations of care on the lessee's part as to the leased goods that the buyer does not have with respect to goods that it purchases.

The difference between a sale and a lease also creates some additional responsibilities for the lessor. Section 2A-508, which gives the laundry list of lessee's remedies, includes one remedy that has no counterpart in Article 2: the possibility that the lessor may be "otherwise in default under a lease contract." UCC §2A-508(3). This is a reference, for example, to the not uncommon duty of a lessor in a lease agreement to keep the leased goods in good repair. When a lessor fails in this duty, the lessee may pursue remedies under the lease or may look to §2A-519(3), which would at a minimum give the lessee a right to recover from the lessor the cost of putting the leased goods back in working order.

The rest of the lessee's remedies more or less track those available to the aggrieved buyer. Section 2A-518 is the lessee's analogue to §2-712, the right to cover. The two differences between §2A-518 and §2-712 are ones that were discussed before in the context of a lessor's remedies: (1) §2A-518(2)'s formula speaks in terms of discounting future streams of rent to present value, a concept that we do not see in Article 2 damage sections; and (2) for a new lease to qualify as a valid cover under §2A-518, it must be "substantially similar" to the original lease.

While the goods purchased in a valid sales cover must also be similar to the originally promised goods, the "substantially similar" concept for lease covers is intended to encompass not just the leased goods themselves, but also the terms of the lease such as purchase options, lease covenants, and services to be provided by the lessor. Official Comment 5 to §2A-518. This is not to say that Article 2A denies damages to a lessee that covers with a new lease that is not substantially similar. Rather, as with Article 2, the statute merely remits such a lessee to its contract-market measure of damages. UCC §2A-518(3).

Subsections 2A-519(1) and (2) set out the lessee's contract-market damages, which are mostly analogous to §2-713 except again with the addition of the "present value" and "substantially similar" concepts. Subsections 2A-519(3) and (4) provide a remedy for the lessee that does not reject or revoke acceptance, which is much like the position of the buyer stuck with defective goods in §2-714. Much like the sales counterpart provision, the lease remedy section here allows the lessee to recover the difference between the value of the use that the lessee was promised and the value of the use that the lessee actually received given the lessor's default. UCC §2A-519(4).

Section 2A-520, defining the lessee's incidental and consequential damages, is almost an exact replica of §2-715. The final two lessee's remedies are specific performance (see §2A-521) and the right to recover goods on the lessor's insolvency (see §2A-522). These two lessee remedies also closely mimic the comparable Article 2 buyer's remedies, which will be covered in Assignment 28.

B. Buyer's Remedies with International Sales

There is a certain attractiveness to the simplicity of the damages provisions in the CISG. The CISG says all that there is to say about damages, for both aggrieved sellers and aggrieved buyers, in just four Articles. In the final analysis, these four articles end up coming to essentially the same results that Article 2 achieves. Unlike the CISG, however, Article 2 achieves these results with substantially more than just four sections on damages.

For the buyer's damages, the CISG once again relies (as it does with seller's damages) on a dichotomy between contracts that have been "avoided" by the buyer and those that have not. This is quite similar to the Article 2 dichotomy for buyer's damages between the buyer who has accepted the goods and can no longer reject or revoke acceptance of them, and the buyer who has never received the goods or who has rejected or revoked acceptance of them.

The buyer under the CISG may declare the contract "avoided" only if the seller's breach is "fundamental" or if the seller fails to deliver the goods on time or within any grace period that the buyer chooses to give the seller beyond the originally scheduled delivery date. CISG Art. 49(1). Recall that the effect of contract avoidance is that both sides are relieved of their contractual obligations, but the avoiding party retains its right to sue for damages. CISG Art. 81(1).

First, consider under the CISG the plight of the aggrieved buyer that has not avoided the contract. If this buyer does not yet have the goods because of the seller's non-delivery, the buyer may have a right to specific performance. Article 46(1) gives the buyer who has not received the goods a right to specific performance "unless the buyer has resorted to a remedy which is inconsistent with this requirement." However, Article 28 allows a court to restrict any party's right to specific performance to whatever right would exist with the forum court's own sales law. Thus, in any case brought before a U.S. court, the buyer's right to specific performance might be no greater than that given in the UCC, which will be discussed in Assignment 28.

Alternatively, the non-avoiding buyer might already have the goods and be aggrieved because the goods are non-conforming. If the non-conformity amounts to a "fundamental breach," that buyer can ask for specific performance, CISG Art. 46(2), subject again to the limitation in Article 28 about the forum court's law regarding specific performance. For a buyer that receives non-conforming goods and does not wish to pursue or is ineligible for specific performance, its damages are measured in much the same way as a similarly aggrieved buyer's damages are measured under the UCC: it is entitled to the "loss suffered . . . as a consequence of [seller's] breach." CISG Art. 74. This would presumably amount to the difference between the value of the goods that were promised and the value of the goods actually received given the non-conformity, plus incidental and consequential damages.

Next let us consider the buyer in an international sale who avoids the contract either because it got the goods and there was a non-conformity amounting to a fundamental breach, or because the goods were not delivered on time or within whatever grace period the buyer chose to give. This buyer, just like the Article 2 buyer, gets its choice between contract-cover damages (under Article 75) and contract-market damages (under Article 76). Both measures also include the broadly defined consequential damages of Article 74, which likely encompass what would be known as "incidental damages" under Article 2.

The buyer's cover rights under CISG Article 75 very closely track the comparable rights of a buyer under UCC Article 2. In order for the buyer's cover to be valid, it must be done "in a reasonable manner and within a reasonable time after avoidance." CISG Art. 75. The properly covering buyer is also eligible for "further damages recoverable under Article 74 [consequential damages]." Id.

The buyer's contract-market damages under Article 76 also look very much like the UCC Article 2 buyer's rights under §2-713. In order for a buyer to use the contract-market measure in the CISG, there must first be "a current [market] price for the goods." CISG Art. 76(1). Under the CISG, the market price is measured at the time the buyer avoided the contract (unless the buyer avoided the contract after "taking over the goods," in which case the market price is measured at the time the buyer took over the goods rather than at the time of avoidance). CISG Art. 76(1).

Under UCC Article 2, the market price should be measured at the place for tender, or if there is a rejection or revocation after arrival, then at the place of arrival. UCC §2-713(2). Under the CISG, the market price is measured at the place "where delivery of the goods should have been made." CISG Art. 76(2). Under both codes, the idea of this remedy is to create a hypothetical cover. The CISG contract-market measure, just like the UCC version, also gives the buyer the right to recover consequential (and, effectively, incidental) damages.

Article 74 of the CISG defines consequential damages as "the loss, including loss of profit, suffered by the other party as a consequence of the breach." Article 74 then contains a sentence limiting such damages by the *Hadley* "reason to know" standard. Thus, even property damage must have been reasonably foreseeable for the buyer to claim them under the CISG, unlike the UCC, where only economic damages contain the foreseeability limit. This is perhaps not so surprising when one considers that the CISG expressly provides that it does not cover the sale of goods bought for consumer use. CISG Art. 2(a). Further, the CISG expressly excludes from its coverage "liability of the seller for death or personal injury caused by the goods to any person." CISG Art. 5.

The only other limit on the CISG's broad definition of consequential damages, apart from the *Hadley* "reason to know" standard, is the CISG's general mitigation policy contained in Article 77. Article 77 simply says that if a party could have reasonably mitigated its damages but did not, then its damages must be reduced by the amount that the damages could have been mitigated. This is tantamount to the limit in UCC §2-715(2)(a)'s category of consequential damages, which are not available to the Article 2 buyer to the extent that the damages could have been "reasonably . . . prevented by cover or otherwise."

C.   Buyer's Remedies with Real Estate

With regard to remedies that are available to an aggrieved buyer in a real estate transaction, consider once more a division of the world into the two common situations in which the buyer might be aggrieved: first, there is the classic case of the seller who simply refuses to deliver title to the buyer; and second, there is the case in which the buyer has possession of and title to the property but discovers some defect of which the buyer was unaware at the time of closing.

As to the first situation, where the seller simply refuses to close, the buyer's standard remedy is an action for specific performance. In order to obtain specific performance, the buyer must make a couple of different showings. First, the buyer must demonstrate that money damages are inadequate, but this is typically an easy showing with real estate since most courts presume land to be unique.

Second, the buyer must show that the buyer itself is fully capable of performing its side of the bargain. Because the buyer's main obligation in most cases is to pay for the real estate, this ordinarily requires nothing more than a showing that the buyer has adequate financing or assets to complete the transaction.

If the buyer does not want specific performance in the case of the seller's refusal to deliver the title, the buyer can choose to sue for money damages instead. These will include at least the buyer's out-of-pocket damages. In about half of the states, the buyer can also ask for benefit-of-the-bargain damages if it can show that the price it agreed to pay was less than the market price for that property. One situation in which courts normally bar benefit-of-the-bargain damages is the case where the seller's breach is a result of the seller's own title being defective. Courts rationalize this rule as a limitation of the damages imposed on a seller whose breach is beyond its control.

All buyers that are aggrieved by a seller's refusal to close, even if they choose to demand specific performance, will also be eligible for consequential damages resulting from the delay in receiving title, as long as such damages were reasonably foreseeable. For example, if the seller wrongfully refused to close and the buyer ended up having to pay a higher mortgage rate when it finally forced the seller to close, the buyer could sue the seller for the difference between the buyer's original mortgage costs and the higher mortgage. Even if the higher rate was not necessarily predictable, it is nevertheless the sort of risk that a breaching seller must expect its buyers to face.

Unlike in the sales-of-goods context, it is not especially common in residential real estate transactions to have a buyer already in possession of the house sue the seller for some defect that the buyer discovers following the closing. The reason for this is that most standard residential real estate sales contracts have an "as is" clause that disclaims all warranties by the seller and also invites the buyer to have a professional inspection done as a condition to the effectiveness of the contract.

Thus, courts will not generally look favorably upon complaints by buyers that allege they discovered a material defect in the property following consummation of the sale. Generally, for a buyer to prevail in this situation, the buyer will have to show fraud: not only that something ended up being wrong with the house, but also that the seller affirmatively misrepresented a material fact that induced the buyer to purchase the house.

Jue v. Smiser

28 Cal. Rptr. 2d 242 (Cal. Ct. App. 1994)

Anderson, J.

The case at bench requires this court to resolve the following question: May a purchaser of real property who learns of potential material misrepresentations about the property after execution of a purchase agreement — but before consummation of the sale — close escrow and sue for damages? Our answer is, "yes."

On April 1, 1992, Kenn and Victoria Smiser (respondents) listed their home at 636 Hillgirt Circle in Oakland for sale with Tabaloff & Company, a realtor (Tabaloff). Tabaloff then began active marketing of the home. On April 22, 1992, an article about the home appeared in the *San Francisco Chronicle*. The article indicated that the home had been designed by Julia Morgan, a celebrated architect whose credits include Hearst Castle. Geoffrey and Charlene Jue (appellants) saw the article and called Tabaloff to make arrangements to see the home. When they toured it appellants were given a brochure which indicated that it was an "Authenticated, Julia Morgan Design, built 1917."

Appellants made a full price offer for the home, contingent on the sale of Geoffrey Jue's home. Respondents countered, requiring that the purchase agreement for their home not be contingent on the sale of Mr. Jue's home. Appellants accepted the counteroffer, and the parties agreed that the sale of respondents' home would close on June 11. Geoffrey Jue immediately listed his home for sale with Tabaloff, and he accepted an offer to sell it on May 5.

On June 8 appellants went to First American Title Company (apparently the escrow company for the sale) and signed the documents required for completion of the sale on June 11. After signing a note and deed of trust, as well as other closing documents, appellants were asked by Tabaloff to sign a contract supplement/addendum with two insignificant provisions and the following disclaimer: "BUYER AND SELLER ACKNOWLEDGE THAT THE RESIDENCE AT 636 HILLGIRT CIRCLE IS COMMONLY KNOWN TO BE A JULIA MORGAN DESIGN AND THAT THERE ARE NO PLANS AVAILABLE AT THE OAKLAND CITY HALL VERIFYING SAME." Appellants signed off on (agreed to) the other two provisions in the supplement/addendum but did not sign off on the disclaimer.

Over the next two days appellants spoke to Sara Boutelle, the author of a book on Julia Morgan homes, who told appellants that she was convinced the home was designed by Morgan; they also spoke to Lynn Stone, Morgan's goddaughter, who indicated that she was unaware of any proof that the home was designed by Morgan.

On June 9 respondents signed the supplement/addendum, as modified by appellants. Escrow closed, and title to the home passed to appellants on June 11.

On November 24, 1992, appellants filed a complaint seeking damages from Tabaloff, two of Tabaloff's agents and respondents. The claims against respondents were based on a number of different theories: fraud, concealment, negligent misrepresentation, negligence, mutual mistake of fact, unilateral mistake of fact (on the part of appellants), intentional infliction of emotional distress, negligent infliction of emotional distress, and various common counts.

In February 1993 respondents filed a motion for summary judgment or, in the alternative, summary adjudication of each cause of action asserted against them. The motion was based on respondents' assertion that appellants' claims were barred as a matter of law because it was "undisputed that [appellants] had actual knowledge of all material facts before the close of escrow and nevertheless voluntarily elected to proceed with the purchase of the property in the face of such knowledge."

Respondents' motion for summary judgment was granted. In its written order of April 6, 1993, the trial court stated its reason for granting the motion: "The bottom line is that [appellants] knew, before the close of escrow, that there were no official records to authenticate 636 Hillgirt Circle as a Julia Morgan design. They chose to proceed anyway; thus they did not purchase the property in justifiable reliance on the alleged fraud. All [appellants'] causes of action fail for the same reason."

Thereafter, respondents moved for entry of judgment under Code of Civil Procedure §437c and for an award of attorney fees under the purchase agreement between the parties. Both motions were granted, and the court awarded respondents $43,118.59 in fees and costs. . . .

"When a party learns that he has been defrauded, he may, instead of rescinding, elect to stand on the contract and sue for damages, and, in such case his continued performance of the agreement does not constitute a waiver of his action for damages. [Citations.]" (Bagdasarian v. Gragnon (1948) 31 Cal. 2d 744, 750, 192 P.2d 935.)

Appellants urge us to follow *Bagdasarian* and our decision in Storage Services v. Oosterbaan (1989) 214 Cal. App. 3d 498, 262 Cal. Rptr. 689 and rule that the trial court erred in granting summary judgment predicated on appellants' supposed lack of "justifiable reliance" on respondents' fraud when appellants closed escrow. Respondents, in turn, argue (a) that reliance is an essential element in any fraud claim and (b) that California law does not permit a buyer who acquires knowledge of a seller's alleged fraud while the purchase agreement is executory to close escrow and sue for damages. . . .

In the case at bench respondents argue that our decision in *Storage Services* was "expressly limited" to the "specific facts" of that case. Respondents also argue that our decision should be read as "reconfirm[ing] the general rule [that] a party discovering fraud while the contract is still executory cannot complete performance and still sue for fraud." Respondents' reading of our decision in *Storage Services* is incorrect.

First, the only part of our opinion which could be construed as limiting its application to the facts of that case is our analysis of whether or not Storage Services should be deemed to have "purchase[d] or otherwise acquire[d]" the subject property so as to come within the provisions of Civil Code §3343, subdivision (a)(4). (*Storage Services,* supra, 214 Cal. App. 3d at p. 510-511, 262 Cal. Rptr. 689.) Our analysis of whether or not Storage Services could maintain an action for fraud against the realtors, when Storage Services learned of the fraud after execution of the original purchase agreement and before escrow closed, was not so limited.

Respondents' second argument constitutes a distortion of our opinion in *Storage Services.* We specifically noted that any party who learns of a fraud before a contract has been completed will not complete it in "reliance" on the fraud. (*Storage Services*, supra, 214 Cal. App. 3d at p. 511, 262 Cal. Rptr. 689.) However, we noted that under *Bagdasarian*, a party's continued performance of the agreement does not constitute a waiver of his action for damages. . . .

In sum, we see no reason to deviate from or limit our decision in *Storage Services* here. The trial court erred in determining that appellants' (apparent) knowledge that the home at 636 Hillgirt Circle could not be confirmed as a Julia Morgan design prior to the close of escrow precluded their advancement of claims against respondents. The relevant issue was (is) whether or not appellants relied on respondents' (alleged) misrepresentations when the purchase agreement was struck on April 27, 1992. No evidence was presented in support of respondents' motion for summary judgment which served to negate the appellants' claim that they did rely on those (alleged) misrepresentations at that time.

Sound public policy considerations support our decision. The Legislature has enacted a series of statutes designed to foster honesty and full disclosure in real estate transactions. Our decision should encourage sellers and their representatives to investigate and learn the "true facts" pertaining to real property before it is offered for sale. Possession and communication of such knowledge will be of benefit to all parties in the course of negotiations leading to execution of a sales agreement.

In addition, if we were to adopt the rule urged upon us by respondents, a buyer of real property who learns of a misrepresentation or a potential misrepresentation after a purchase contract is struck but before escrow closes would be faced with an extraordinarily difficult choice: (a) consummate the purchase and waive any claim for damages or (b) rescind and deal with the consequences of that choice. Among those consequences may be (1) problems in securing a return of moneys deposited with the escrow holder; (2) the loss of moneys spent to secure a loan and to meet other costs of acquisition, such as escrow fees; and (3) the risk of being sued by the seller and/or the seller's representatives. One who may be the victim of another's fraud should not be forced to make such a choice. That policy is especially strong where, as here, it is unclear whether or not a particular representation was (is), in fact, false at the time a choice is required, and the time period in which to choose is extraordinarily short.

The judgment is reversed. Respondents are to bear costs on appeal.

Another way to view the *Jue* case, besides as a decision that gives the buyers the remedies they deserve, is as a precedent that discourages sellers from relying on the time-honored "bait and switch" technique to lure potential buyers. After all, what the realtors in *Jue* appeared to be engaged in was a classic bait-and-switch: brag in advertisements and marketing literature that this was an "Authenticated Julia Morgan Design" as a way to get buyers in the door; then, once the buyers were in the door and it turned out they *really* cared a lot about this fact, just hem and haw and ultimately admit that you don't in fact know whether this is a true Julia Morgan.

Problem Set 26

26.1.   a. Lou from Lou's Used Cars for Less (from Problem 2.1) has recently gone back into the business of leasing used cars, and is he ever sorry about that. He has a number of problem leases that he needs to ask you about. The first problem lease was a four-year, $100-per-month lease of a used Ford Taurus Wagon that Lou knew had an engine that suffered from hesitation problems. Lou had disclosed that fact to the lessee, and indeed the $100-per-month lease rate clearly reflected the car's shaky engine. Two months into the lease, however, the engine stopped working completely. When the lessee called Lou to complain, Lou told him to have the engine problem fixed and to send Lou the bill. Yesterday Lou got a bill for $2,500, which indicated that a brand-new engine had been installed to replace the dead one. "The lessee tells me the car works great now and the engine doesn't even hesitate," says Lou, "But what do you expect with a brand-new engine? I could probably lease that car for $150 per month with the new engine." Lou wants to know whether he must pay the entire $2,500 for the new engine or, alternatively, whether he can raise the lessee's monthly rate to reflect the addition of a new engine in the car. What do you advise Lou? UCC §§2A-519(4), 1-305(a).

b. Lou's second problem arose when Lou made too many lease contracts with not enough cars to lease. Thus, he was forced to breach a lease that he had made on a used Honda Odyssey. That was a three-year, $300-per-month lease with a purchase option at fair market value at the end of the lease. This lease also provided that Lou's would give the car a complete tune-up every six months during the lease at no extra charge. The aggrieved lessee has gone out and leased a different used Honda Odyssey from another dealer. The new lease was a four-year, $400-per-month lease with an end-of-the-lease purchase option at fair market value minus 10 percent of the total lease payments made. The new lease required the lessee to have the car tuned up every six months at the lessee's expense, which Lou estimated would cost about $150 per tune-up. Both Lou's lease and the new lease could be terminated by the lessee at any time by paying a $500 liquidated damages fee. The aggrieved lessee had told Lou that she was planning to sue him for his breach of their lease contract. Assuming that the lessee seeks contract-cover damages, for what amount of damages may she recover from Lou? UCC §2A-518, Official Comments 3 through 7 to §2A-518. (In calculating damages for this problem, don't bother actually discounting any of the payment streams to present value, but note to yourself where that normally would be done.)

c. Lou's third problem lease involves a used full-sized Dodge van that was leased to Larry Moppet, an unemployed cook who had just founded a new business that delivered food from popular local restaurants to people's homes. This van had given Larry so much trouble that he had been unable, due to the van's unreliability, to deliver meals on five evenings during the first two months on the job. Larry had brought the van in for repairs on three or four occasions during these first two months, but the van kept breaking down nevertheless. After revoking his acceptance of the van, Larry was suing Lou for the $300 that Larry was not paid for the delivery jobs he missed on those five evenings when the leased van failed to perform. Larry was also suing Lou for $100,000, representing what Larry claimed was the lost good will for his young business that was caused by the faulty van. Lou admits to you that Larry did tell Lou's salesperson about the intended use of the van. To what extent will Lou be liable to Larry? UCC §2A-520(2)(a).

26.2. The Fun Factory is a Minneapolis-based toy manufacturer that had a contract to buy three tons of raw plastic from a Canadian plastics distributor, Toronto Works. The Fun Factory was going to use the plastic to make 5,000 figurines to fulfill a contract that it had with a major retailer, Statues 'R' Us. Fun Factory agreed to pay Toronto Works $36,000 for the three tons of plastic, "FOB Buyer's Factory." A week before delivery was due, Toronto Works repudiated the contract. If the Fun Factory had made reasonable cover efforts, it could have purchased substitute plastic from a Seattle distributor for $45,000, "FOB Seller's Plant." Delivery costs from Seattle to Minneapolis would have been $500. (Cover was not available at all in Minneapolis.) Because the Fun Factory did not cover, it was unable to perform its contract with Statues 'R' Us. Although Statues 'R' Us has indicated it will not sue the Fun Factory, the Fun Factory did lose an expected profit in its Statues 'R' Us deal of $14,000. For what amount may the Fun Factory recover from Toronto Works? CISG Arts. 74, 75, 76, 77.

26.3. Last night you received a call from your cousin, Edgar, with whom you had not had contact since you were both children. It turns out Edgar heard that there was now a lawyer in the family, and you were it. Edgar's problem is that he was supposed to close on a house purchase deal four months ago, but he did not close until yesterday. The seller of the home had gotten "cold feet" the first time around, and only after much pleading from the seller's agent and many threats from Edgar's agent did the closing finally take place four months later. The four-month delay had a number of effects on Edgar's position, some negative and one positive: (1) he lost a $200 down payment that he had given to the movers whose job he had to cancel at the last minute; (2) he had to continue renting his apartment on a month-to-month basis, which cost him $700 per month compared to the $500 per month he had been paying under his annual lease; and (3) he had originally locked in an 8.5 percent rate on a 30-year, $100,000 mortgage, which would have had monthly payments, including taxes and insurance, of $950. By the time of the closing, rates had gone down during the four-month delay so that he ended up getting a 7.75 percent rate on the same mortgage. On a $100,000 mortgage, Edgar's bank would generally charge a borrower $1,000 for every quarter of a point that the borrower wished to "buy down" the 30-year rate for its loan. Edgar wants to know for what amount he can sue the seller for damages due to the delay. (Assume that the sales contract simply says that an aggrieved buyer may pursue "any remedy at law or in equity.") What would you advise Edgar?

26.4. Mike and Carol Vilchuck were both big Frank Lloyd Wright fans, which is why they bothered to come look at an $800,000 house for sale in Palo Alto, California, that was advertised as a "Frank Lloyd Wright Original." Mike and Carol were both quite impressed in their walk-through of the house, and they began to talk seriously about making an offer on the house. Before making an offer, the couple called their friend, Barry Swedeen, who was the most knowledgeable Frank Lloyd Wright expert the Vilchucks knew. Barry told them that there was a real question whether Frank Lloyd Wright himself ever designed any Palo Alto homes, even though it was generally accepted that several architects who were trained in Wright's studio had designed Palo Alto homes. Despite this uncertainty, the Vilchucks went forward and signed a sales contract to buy the house for $800,000. Three weeks after closing on this sale, the Vilchucks get a call from Barry, who managed through extensive research in the local real estate records to uncover definitive proof that their house was *not* designed by Frank Lloyd Wright. In light of this information, the Vilchucks come to you and tell you that they want to rescind this sales contract. What are the chances that they will be successful in a suit for rescission?

Assignment 27: Buyer's Remedies: Advanced Problems

A. The Lost-Profits Buyer

Whenever an aggrieved buyer exercises its cover remedy under §2-712, normally it can be said with confidence that the "spirit of the remedies" section, §1-305(a), is being achieved: the buyer is being put in the position that the buyer would have been in had the seller performed. If the buyer is purchasing a reasonable substitute and the seller is compensating the buyer for any additional cost of the substitute, this is usually about as close as the buyer can come to replicating actual performance by the seller.

Similarly, when an aggrieved buyer accepts non-conforming goods and chooses to sue the seller for breach of warranty damages under §2-714(2), it is fairly clear that the result will do a good job of achieving the buyer's expectancy damages. In most cases under §2-714(2), the buyer will simply be compensated for the cost of repair, which will put the goods in roughly the condition that they would have been in had they been conforming. If the buyer in the §2-714(2) case suffers additional damages owing to the non-conformity of the goods, Article 2 allows the buyer to recover for those as well, in the form of incidental or consequential damages.

However, there is one situation in which there is much more doubt as to whether the Article 2 remedies will put the buyer in the position that the buyer would have been in had the seller performed. This is the case in which the buyer never receives the goods or validly rejects or revokes acceptance of them, *and* the buyer is unable or unwilling to cover. In this situation, the buyer is left to claim damages under §2-713, the contract-market measure.

Consider, for example, a consumer that makes a contract on January 1 with a local car dealer to purchase a new Honda Accord for $23,000, with a performance date of May 1. On March 15, the car dealer calls and tells the consumer that it will not be able to fill the consumer's order. On the date of repudiation, the market price for a new Honda Accord is $23,500. On the date of performance, May 1, the market price has risen to $24,000. By the time of the March 15 repudiation, however, the consumer is just as happy not to purchase the Honda Accord and, therefore, does not go out and buy another one at that time.

The consumer's damages in this case under §2-713 would be $500, the difference between the contract price and the market price on the day that the buyer learned of the breach. Does $500 do a good job of approximating the position that the buyer would have been in had the seller performed? Not in this case. Had the seller performed, the buyer would have received a car on May 1 that was worth $24,000 for a price of $23,000, a net "gain" of $1,000. In this sense, the §2-713 damages undercompensate the buyer.

In another sense, however, the §2-713 damages in the case above actually overcompensate the buyer. As noted above, the buyer really did not care to go through with the deal by the time that the seller repudiated. In this sense, the buyer was not damaged at all, and paying the buyer $500 is a windfall for the buyer.

The problem with trying to put consumer buyers in the position that they would have been in had the seller performed is that, whenever aggrieved buyers are planning to use the goods themselves, it is difficult to quantify the loss they suffer in not getting the goods. There is, however, a not uncommon category of buyers for whom it is easier to quantify the loss felt from not receiving the goods: a group of buyers that might be called "lost-profits buyers." Perhaps the most common lost-profits buyers are the "jobbers" that were discussed briefly in Assignment 24. These buyers will not buy goods until they themselves have a buyer. They have no intention of keeping or using the goods, and their sole purpose in making the purchase is to make a profit on resale.

For these lost-profits buyers, it is easy enough to put them in the position that they would have been in had the seller actually delivered the goods: simply give them their lost profits. The following case provides a good example of how this works out in practice.

Jetpac Group, Ltd. v. Bostek, Inc.

942 F. Supp. 716 (D. Mass. 1996)

O'Toole, D.J.

The plaintiff, Jetpac Group, Ltd., a Louisiana corporation based in Shreveport, Louisiana ("Jetpac"), seeks damages from the defendant, Bostek, Inc., a Massachusetts corporation with its place of business at Hanover, Massachusetts ("Bostek"), that it says were caused by Bostek's having sold defective computers to Jetpac. . . .

Jetpac is an export/import trading company formed in 1988. Its business generally involves selling food products, such as frozen chicken, in various countries around the world, including Russia. In the years 1989 through 1992, Jetpac shipped about $17 million worth of food products to Russia. In April, 1992, Jetpac's president, James Duke, saw an advertisement that had been placed in the Journal of Commerce by a company in Montreal, Canada, called Natashquan Korotia Systems ("NKS"), seeking a supplier of computers for a Russian customer of NKS. At the time, shortly after the breakup of the Soviet Union, many people were trying to take advantage of the "opening up" of business opportunities in Russia. There was a particularly "hot" market in personal computers, so much so that an especially desired configuration actually acquired a common nickname: "Russian 286's." In the heated market, demand often outstripped supply. NKS had a customer in Russia that was interested in buying Russian 286's. That was the reason for NKS's advertisement in the Journal of Commerce; it had a customer, but it needed a source of computers.

Duke responded to the advertisement and as a result met NKS's president, Nowshade Kabir. Kabir, a Canadian citizen, originally hailed from what had been the Soviet Republic of Georgia and was experienced in doing business in Russia. In 1992, NKS sold approximately $4 to $5 million worth of computers within Russia. Duke and Kabir discussed an arrangement whereby Jetpac would supply several hundred Russian 286's that NKS would sell to its customer. Kabir told Duke that NKS had the opportunity to sell between 3,000 and 5,000 computers to its customer. In about May, NKS entered into a written contract with the Russian buyer for 3,000 "Russian 286's" at a price of $1,050 each. The customer was a cooperative named "Harmony."

Jetpac had never sold computers before, but it had recently hired a person, Al Konrad, who had been involved in computer systems trading since 1978. Duke assigned Konrad the task of locating computers that could meet the business opportunity presented by NKS. Konrad began to look to arrange a "test" shipment of about 100 computers. In early June, 1992, he contacted CNS Trading, Incorporated of Norwell, Massachusetts ("CNS"), a broker that obtained a quote from Bostek for personal computers meeting Konrad's specifications.

Bostek is a supplier of computer hardware, software, and consulting services. Among other things, it builds integrated systems to customers' specifications, buying the components from various sources, assembling the system, and then reselling it. On June 9 and 10, 1992, CNS relayed to Konrad Bostek's price quote of $605 per unit for a minimum of 1,000 systems, meeting Konrad's specifications, plus shipping charges. CNS also sent some information about Bostek.

Konrad flew to Boston on June 11, 1992, to visit the Bostek facility in Hanover. He wanted to assure himself that Bostek would be a suitable supplier of the large number of systems that Jetpac was contemplating buying and then, with NKS, reselling in Russia. Konrad met Mark Hanson, Bostek's president. Konrad described to Hanson that he was interested in finding a source for "Russian 286's" and that Jetpac expected to be able to sell between 3,000 and 5,000 systems in Russia. He did no identify either NKS or the anticipated customer in Russia, because he did not want Bostek and NKS to deal directly with each other, thus leaving Jetpac out of the business opportunity. Hanson also gave Konrad some literature about Bostek and gave him a tour of the Hanover facility. Konrad ran a test on a system similar to the one he wanted to buy and was satisfied with its performance.

Hanson assured Konrad that Bostek could build between 100 and 200 systems per day if given five to ten days notice. Konrad told Hanson that while Jetpac was looking to buy perhaps 3,000 to 5,000 systems over time, it wanted to make a test shipment of 100 computers to its Russian customer the following Monday, June 15. For this smaller number of computers, Bostek's price was $630 per unit, rather than $605 per unit for the larger quantity. Hanson indicated that Bostek could build 100 systems for shipment on Monday, June 15, but that they might have to be assembled in California. Bostek's literature contained a reference to "Bostek's worldwide presence with offices in Boston, Los Angeles, Calgary-Canada and London-England."

The parties agreed on the terms for the 100 computers, and Bostek issued to Jetpac an invoice dated June 11, 1992, reflecting those terms. The invoice described the systems to be sold as follows:

BOSTEK 286/16 MOTHERBOARD CONSISTING OF: DESKTOP CASE & 220 VOLT POWER SUPPLY, 40MB HARD DRIVE IDE, 1.2 & 1.44 FLOPPY DRIVES, 2 SER, 1 PAR, HARD FLOPPY CONTROLLER, 1MB RAM, VA CARD W/256K VGA MONITOR. 39, 800X600 CAPABLE, MOUSE 3 BUTTON SERIAL, M.S. COMPATIBLE 287 MATH CO PRO, 101 CYRILLIC/ENGLISH KEYBOARD NEW, CONFIGURED, TESTED, IN SHIPPING BOX FOB BOSTON

The price for the 100 systems was $63,000, and on June 12, Jetpac wired Bostek that amount. The units were to be shipped directly to the customer in Russia. Jetpac was to pay the freight costs for shipping from Boston, which would amount to $8,184.

Bostek was unable to assemble the systems in Hanover, and Hanson flew to California over the weekend to try to find systems to fill the order. Despite what one might have concluded from Bostek's literature, Bostek had no physical office or facility in California. Rather, it had a California representative who worked out of his home. After some searching, Hanson found a supplier, American Computer Systems ("ACS"), to provide the systems to fill Jetpac's order. Hanson did not tell Jetpac that Bostek was not assembling the systems but that they were rather being assembled by ACS. Hanson did not test any of the systems. He relied on ACS to have properly assembled the systems.

There was a delay in making the shipment, and the goods were not shipped until Thursday, June 18. The delay was partly due to Hanson's search for computers to fill the order, and it was partly due to a dispute between Bostek and Jetpac over which one should be responsible for the increased freight costs occasioned by the shipment from California rather than Boston, as originally agreed. Hanson had earlier agreed that Bostek would pay any difference in shipping costs, but he balked when the occasion actually arose, and Jetpac eventually paid freight charges that were $2,781.20 more than previously contemplated.

When the computers arrived in Russia, the customer notified NKS that there were significant problems. Not all the specified components were included. For example, no "mice" were shipped, though the specifications called for them, and there was no documentation for the major components. In addition, some of the wiring in the central processing unit was either missing or disconnected. Further, the monitors did not switch automatically from 110 to 220 volts, and as a result several of them "blew up" when they were initially switched on. Hanson had to send specific instructions about how to perform an internal adjustment on each monitor to permit it to operate with 220 volt electric current.

When the problems with the shipment appeared, Duke was in Europe on other business. He went to Moscow and met with the very dissatisfied customer. He also examined some of the computers and personally observed the problem of improper wiring. He tried to turn on five separate systems that had been in the shipment, only one of which "booted up."

In short, the "test shipment," designed to impress the new Russian customer and open the way to more sales, was a disaster. In an effort to convince the Russians that they could in fact fulfill its contract to supply specified computers, NKS and Jetpac bought an additional 200 computers and shipped them to the Harmony cooperative. Nonetheless, Harmony was still dissatisfied because of the problems with the first 100 computers supplied by Bostek. It refused to pay NKS fully for that first shipment, and NKS charged back to Jetpac its share of the shortfall, or $23,517.

In addition, as a direct consequence of the failure of the shipment to conform in significant material respects to the specifications given by Jetpac to Bostek, Harmony refused to buy the balance of the 3,000 systems called for by its agreement with NKS. Thus, reasonably probable sales of an additional 2,700 computers at the price of $1,050 each were lost, along with such profit as Jetpac would have earned if it had acted with NKS to fulfill the Russian order for those computers, as agreed between Jetpac and NKS.

The price in the contract between NKS and the Russian customer included a printer. Jetpac's agreement was to produce all the components of a system except the printer. The reason apparently was that printers suitable to the Russian market were difficult to obtain in the United States and relatively easy to obtain in Russia. NKS planned to acquire the printers in Russia and combine them there with the systems procured by Jetpac. According to Kabir, who had experience purchasing such printers in 1992, suitable printers could be purchased for about $235 per unit.

The cost of the systems sold to the Russian buyer was thus the total of the cost of the system procured by Jetpac, the cost of the printer, and the necessary shipping costs. Each of these costs would vary somewhat at different times and under different circumstances. For example, Jetpac paid Bostek $630 per unit for the shipment of 100 systems, but Bostek had quoted $605 per unit if Jetpac ordered a minimum of 1,000 systems. Similarly, the freight costs per unit for shipment from Boston had been quoted at $81.84, but the actual cost per unit for the shipment from California had been $111.65.

Taking these facts into account, it is possible to approximate the cost of systems to be sold under the NKS-Harmony contract as follows: First, a unit price of $605 for large quantities seems appropriate as a starting point, and it is not unfair to use the price Bostek itself quoted. Second, since it cannot be determined where all the systems would be shipped from and since the shipping point apparently has an effect on the costs, it seems appropriate to estimate shipping costs at about

$100 per unit, that is, in the middle of the range of shipping costs disclosed by the evidence. Finally, there was no evidence other than Kabir's about the cost of Russian printers, so it is appropriate to use that evidence to establish this cost element at $235 per unit. The total of these costs is $940. Given the contract sale price of $1,050, the profit on each unit would be $110. That figure is consistent with Kabir's estimate of a per unit profit in the range of $100 to $115. Because Jetpac and NKS had agreed to split the profits evenly, Jetpac's unit profit would have been about $55. For the 2,700 computers not sold under the NKS-Harmony contract because of the defects in the "test shipment," Jetpac's profit would have been $148,500.

Jetpac incurred other expenses as a direct result of the defects in the computers sold to it by Bostek. Duke incurred travel expenses of $3,997.13 in going to Moscow to try personally to mollify the unhappy customer. And, as noted, Jetpac incurred shipping expenses of $2,781.20 more than it had agreed with Bostek.

Jetpac and Bostek entered into a valid and binding contract for the sale of 100 computers conforming to the specifications set forth in the Bostek invoice of June 11, 1992. The contract was one for the sale of goods, and the implied warranty of merchantability imposed under the Uniform Commercial Code ("UCC") applied.

Bostek committed a breach of the contract by failing to furnish goods that conformed to the contract description. In addition, the goods furnished were defective, in breach of the warranty of merchantability.

For the breach of contract Jetpac is entitled to damages in the amount of any loss that resulted "in the ordinary course of events from the seller's breach as determined in any manner which is reasonable." [UCC §2-714(1).] For breach of the warranty, Jetpac is entitled to damages in the amount of the difference "between the value of the goods accepted and the value they would have had if they had been as warranted." Id. at §2-714(2). In both cases, the damages can be determined by Jetpac's share of the loss incurred by NKS when the customer in Russia refused to pay the full price for the goods. Jetpac's share, as described above, was $23,517.

In addition, "[i]n a proper case any incidental and consequential damages under [§2-715] may also be recovered." Id. at §2-714(3). Under §2-715, recoverable consequential damages include "any loss resulting from general or particular requirements and needs of which the seller at the time of contracting had reason to know and which could not reasonably be prevented by cover or otherwise." [UCC §2-715(2)(a).] Such damages include "prospective profits lost as the natural, primary and probable consequence of the breach."

In this case, Konrad had told Hanson at Bostek that the shipment of 100 computers was only the initial one in a prospective sale of 3,000 units to the buyer in Russia. Bostek thus had reason to know that a defective shipment could jeopardize that business opportunity and bring about a loss of the profits that could reasonably be earned if the full 3,000 units were to be shipped. To be sure, there was no assurance that for some other unforeseen reason the full 3,000 would not ultimately be sold. There was a firm contract for that number, however, and it is a reasonable inference that if the initial shipment had conformed to the contract specifications and the warranty of merchantability, the contract would have been fulfilled. Damages cannot be assessed upon conjecture or surmise, but by the same token the reasonable prospect of damages—such as is shown by the existence of NKS's contract with the Russian buyer—should not be defeated by conjecture or surmise, either. The plaintiff's burden is not to demonstrate its damages with mathematical certainty but only to a "fair degree of certainty." The calculation of lost profits set forth above meets that test.

Jetpac is also entitled under §2-715(1) to incidental damages, which include the increased shipping costs and the cost of Duke's trip to Moscow to try to solve the problem caused by the defective goods and thus to mitigate potential damages.

Accordingly, on its claim of breach of contract, Jetpac is entitled to damages for the direct loss in the transaction in the sum of $23,517, for consequential damages for lost prospective profits in the sum of $148,500, and for incidental damages in the sum of $6,778.33, for a total of $178,795.33. . . .

For the reasons set forth above, judgment shall be entered in favor of the plaintiff and against the defendant, awarding damages in the sum of $178,795.33, together with applicable interest and costs.

It is SO ORDERED.

The *Jetpac* case presents perhaps the simplest situation involving a lost-profits buyer. Because Bostek was contractually obligated to ship just 100 computers rather than the full 3,000 that were ultimately contemplated, the court was able to approach the case strictly in terms of §2-714. By using the §2-714 damage formula, the lost profits on the 3,000 computers could be captured neatly by the consequential damages part of the equation. The reason that the *Jetpac* court was able to use the §2-714 damage formula is that the buyer actually received and accepted the test shipment rather than rejecting it or never receiving it in the first place. Therefore, the buyer's damages could be measured under §2-714's formula for "Breach in Regard to Accepted Goods" rather than §2-713's formula for "Non-Delivery or Repudiation."

By contrast, had Bostek promised to sell 3,000 computers to Jetpac and not delivered, then Jetpac would have been forced to have its damages measured under §2-713 (assuming that Jetpac either could not or would not have covered). The difficulty with calculating a lost-profits buyer's damages under §2-713 is that, depending on changes in the market price of the goods in question, the contract-market difference might exceed the profits that the buyer would have made had the seller performed. In this case, a court would be forced to decide whether to follow the literal language of §2-713 and put the lost-profits buyer in a better position than the buyer would have been in had the seller performed, or to ignore the literal language of §2-713 and try to follow the more general "spirit of the remedies" policy that is embodied in §1-305(a).

TexPar Energy, Inc. v. Murphy Oil USA, Inc.

45 F.3d 1111 (7th Cir. 1995)

REAVLEY, C.J. [sitting by designation]:

In this contract dispute, appellant Murphy Oil USA, Inc. complains of the jury charge and the damages awarded to appellee TexPar Energy, Inc. Finding no reversible error, we affirm.

On May 29, 1992, TexPar contracted to purchase 15,000 tons of asphalt from Murphy at an average price of $53 per ton. On the same day, TexPar contracted to sell the 15,000 tons to Starry Construction Company at an average price of $56 per ton. Hence, TexPar stood to profit by $45,000 if both contracts were performed.

During the first half of 1992, the price of asphalt varied widely. Evidence was presented of prices ranging from $40 to $100 per ton. The wide range of prices reflected volatile market forces. From the supply standpoint, asphalt is one of the end products of petroleum refining, and must be sold or stockpiled to accommodate the production of more valuable petroleum products. Demand depends in large measure on the availability of government funding for highway construction. Weather also affects asphalt supply and demand. The price rose rapidly in June of 1992, and consequently, the sale price of $53 per ton lost its attractiveness to Murphy.

In May and early June TexPar took delivery of 690 tons of asphalt; but, on June 5, Murphy stopped its deliveries and notified TexPar that its sales manager lacked authority to make the contract. By then, the price of asphalt had risen to $80 per ton. Starry insisted that TexPar deliver the full 15,000 tons at $56 per ton as TexPar and Starry had agreed. Ultimately, with TexPar's approval, Starry and Murphy negotiated directly and agreed on a price of $68.50 per ton. This arrangement was reached several weeks after the repudiation by Murphy. By this time the market price had dropped, according to TexPar. TexPar agreed to pay Starry the $12.50 difference between the new price of $68.50 per ton and the original $56 per ton price. TexPar therefore paid Starry approximately $191,000 to cover the price difference.

The jury found that the difference between the market price ($80) and the contract price ($53) of the undelivered asphalt (14,310 tons) on the date of repudiation (June 5), amounted to $386,370. The court entered judgment for this amount.

The parties agree that Wisconsin law, and particularly Wisconsin's version of the Uniform Commercial Code, applies to this dispute. The district court applied UCC §2-713, which provides a measure of the buyer's damages for nondelivery or repudiation:

> Subject to [UCC §2-723] with respect to proof of market price, the measure of damages for nondelivery or repudiation by the seller is the difference between the market price at the time when the buyer learned of the breach and the contract price together with any incidental and consequential damages provided in [§2-715], but less expenses saved in consequence of the seller's breach.

Murphy does not dispute that if this provision is applied, the damages awarded are proper, since Murphy does not dispute the quantity of goods, the market price or the date of notice of repudiation used by the jury to calculate damages. Instead, Murphy argues that the general measure of damages in a breach of contract case is the amount needed to place the plaintiff in as good a position as he would have been if the contract had been performed. Murphy argues that since TexPar's award—$386,370—far exceeds its out-of-pocket expenses ($191,000) and lost profits ($45,000) occasioned by the repudiation, the court erred in instructing the jury merely to find the difference in market price and entering judgment in that amount.

We cannot quarrel with Murphy that the general measure of damages in contract cases is the expectancy or "benefit of the bargain" measure. The UCC itself embraces such a measure in §1-106 [§1-305 as amended], providing that the UCC remedies "shall be liberally administered to the end that the aggrieved party may be put in as good a position as if the other party had fully performed. . . . "

Nevertheless, we do not believe that the district court erred in awarding damages based on a straightforward application of [§2-713]. That provision is found in the article on the sale of goods, and specifies a remedy for the circumstances presented here—the seller's nondelivery of goods for which there is a market price at the time of repudiation.

We can see no sound reason for looking to an alternative measure of damages. Murphy argues that TexPar shouldn't be awarded a "windfall" amount in excess of its out-of-pocket damages. Since it depends on the market price on a date after the making of the contract, the remedy under [§2-713] necessarily does not correspond to the buyer's actual losses, barring a coincidence. Our problem with Murphy's suggested measure of damages is that limiting the buyer's damages in cases such as this one to the buyer's out-of-pocket losses could, depending on the market, create a windfall for the seller. If the price of asphalt had fallen back to $56 per ton by the time Starry and Murphy had arranged for replacement asphalt, TexPar's damages would have been zero by this measure, and Murphy could have reaped a windfall by selling at the market price of $80 in early June instead of the $53 price negotiated with TexPar.

Murphy argues that it did not in fact realize a windfall, since its cost of production was $70 per ton and it eventually agreed to sell to Starry for $68.50. We find this argument unpersuasive. Applying the market value measure of damages under UCC §2-713, as the district court did, is expressly allowed under the Code. Since §2-713 addresses the circumstances of a seller's nondelivery of goods with a market price, we see no error in applying this specific provision over the more general remedies provision found at §1-106. See Tongish v. Thomas, 251 Kan. 728, 840 P.2d 471, 474 (1992) ("[B]ecause it appears impractical to make [§1-106] and [§2-713] harmonize in this factual situation, [§2-713] should prevail as the more specific statute according to statutory rules of construction."). The UCC §2-713 remedy serves the purpose of discouraging sellers from repudiating their contracts as the market rises, if the buyer should resell as did TexPar, or gambling that the buyer's damages will be small should the market drop. It also has the advantage of promoting uniformity and predictability in commercial transactions, by fixing damages on the date of the breach, rather than allowing the vicissitudes of the market in the future to determine damages. Id. 840 P.2d at 476 ("Damages computed under [§2-713] encourage the honoring of contracts and market stability."). . . .

AFFIRMED.

The Seventh Circuit in *TexPar* seemed to rest its decision in large part on the idea that if shifting market prices are going to give somebody a windfall, it ought to be the non-breaching party rather than the breacher. This is a particularly understandable sentiment in light of the facts of this case, where it appears that Murphy could have performed the contract but simply chose not to because the price of asphalt had risen so dramatically.

Imagine, however, a case in which a good-faith seller is simply unable to obtain and deliver the promised goods to the buyer due to a shortage of that product. Imagine further that the ultimate purchaser is not going to sue the initial buyer. Finally, imagine that the "market price," such as there is one, is now three times what it was when the seller and buyer initially made their contract. Under these facts, does it make sense to allow the seller to give the buyer only the buyer's lost profits rather than an amount under §2-713's contract-market formula which could be several times that much?

The situation described above is essentially what happened in the widely discussed case of Allied Canners and Packers, Inc. v. Victor Packing Co., 209 Cal. Rptr. 60 (1984). The California appellate court in that case decided that the §2-713(1) contract-market formula was merely a hypothetical cover, and that the more general policy of §1-305(a) should prevail whenever the seller could prove, as here, that the buyer's actual loss was less than the contract-market differential.

Not all courts are persuaded by the wisdom of the decision in *Allied Canners,* as the next case demonstrates. This case also reminds us that the tension between §1-305(a) and the Code's more specific damage formulas can arise not only in the case of §2-713(1)'s contract-market measure, but also in certain unusual cases of cover under §2-712(1).

KGM Harvesting Co. v. Fresh Network

42 Cal. Rptr. 2d 286 (Cal. Ct. App. 1995)

COTTLE, J.

California lettuce grower and distributor KGM Harvesting Company (hereafter seller) had a contract to deliver 14 loads of lettuce each week to Ohio lettuce broker Fresh Network (hereafter buyer). When the price of lettuce rose dramatically in May and June 1991, seller refused to deliver the required quantity of lettuce to buyer. Buyer then purchased lettuce on the open market in order to fulfill its contractual obligations to third parties. After a trial, the jury awarded buyer damages in an amount equal to the difference between the contract price and the price buyer was forced to pay for substitute lettuce on the open market. On appeal, seller argues that the damage award is excessive. We disagree and shall affirm the judgment. . . .

In July 1989 buyer and seller entered into an agreement for the sale and purchase of lettuce. Over the years, the terms of the agreement were modified. By May 1991 the terms were that seller would sell to buyer 14 loads of lettuce each week and that buyer would pay seller 9 cents a pound for the lettuce. (A load of lettuce consists of 40 bins, each of which weighs 1,000 to 1,200 pounds. Assuming an average bin weight of 1,100 pounds, one load would equal 44,000 pounds, and the 14 loads called for in the contract would weigh 616,000 pounds. At 9 cents per pound, the cost would approximate $55,440 per week.)

Buyer sold all of the lettuce it received from seller to a lettuce broker named Castellini Company who in turn sold it to Club Chef, a company that chops and shreds lettuce for the fast food industry (specifically, Burger King, Taco Bell, and Pizza Hut). Castellini Company bought lettuce from buyer on a "cost plus" basis, meaning it would pay buyer its actual cost plus a small commission. Club Chef, in turn, bought lettuce from Castellini Company on a cost plus basis.

Seller had numerous lettuce customers other than buyer, including seller's subsidiaries Coronet East and West. Coronet East supplied all the lettuce for the McDonald's fast food chain.

In May and June 1991, when the price of lettuce went up dramatically, seller refused to supply buyer with lettuce at the contract price of nine cents per pound. Instead, it sold the lettuce to others at a profit of between $800,000 and $1,100,000. Buyer, angry at seller's breach, refused to pay seller for lettuce it had already received. Buyer then went out on the open market and purchased lettuce to satisfy its obligations to Castellini Company. Castellini covered all of buyer's extra expense except for $70,000. Castellini in turn passed on its extra costs to Club Chef which passed on at least part of its additional costs to its fast food customers.

In July 1991 buyer and seller each filed complaints. . . . Seller sought the balance due on its outstanding invoices ($233,000), while buyer sought damages for the difference between what it was forced to spend to buy replacement lettuce and the contract price of nine cents a pound (approximately $700,000).

Subsequently, seller filed suit for the balance due on its invoices, and buyer cross-complained for the additional cost it incurred to obtain substitute lettuce after seller's breach. At trial, the parties stipulated that seller was entitled to a directed verdict on its complaint for $233,000, the amount owing on the invoices. Accordingly, only the cross-complaint went to the jury, whose task was to determine whether buyer was entitled to damages from seller for the cost of obtaining substitute lettuce and, if so, in what amount. The jury determined that seller breached the contract, that its performance was not excused, and that buyer was entitled to $655,960.22, which represented the difference between the contract price of nine cents a pound and what it cost buyer to cover by purchasing lettuce in substitution in May and June 1991. It also determined that such an award would not result in a windfall to buyer and that buyer was obligated to the Castellini Company for the additional costs. The court subtracted from buyer's award of $655,960.22 the $233,000 buyer owed to seller on its invoices, leaving a net award in favor of buyer in the amount of $422,960.22. The court also awarded buyer prejudgment interest commencing 30 days before trial. . . .

In the instant case, buyer "covered" as defined in section 2-712 in order to fulfill its own contractual obligations to the Castellini Company. Accordingly, it was awarded the damages called for in cover cases—the difference between the contract price and the cover price. . . .

In this case, however, none of these typical [cover] issues is in dispute. Seller does not contend that buyer paid too much for the substitute lettuce or that buyer was guilty of "unreasonable delay" or a lack of "good faith" in its attempt to obtain substitute lettuce. Nor does seller contend that the lettuce purchased was of a higher quality or grade and therefore not a reasonable substitute.

Instead, seller takes issue with section 2-712 itself, contending that despite the unequivocal language of section 2-712, a buyer who covers should not necessarily recover the difference between the cover price and the contract price. Seller points out that because of buyer's "cost plus" contract with Castellini Company, buyer was eventually able to pass on the extra expenses (except for $70,000) occasioned by seller's breach and buyer's consequent purchase of substitute lettuce on the open market. It urges this court under these circumstances not to allow buyer to obtain a "windfall." . . .

Although the contract does not recite this fact, seller was aware of buyer's contract with the Castellini Company and with the Castellini Company's contract with Club Chef. This knowledge was admitted at trial and can be inferred from the fact that seller shipped the contracted for 14 loads of lettuce directly to Club Chef each week. Thus, seller was well aware that if it failed to provide buyer with the required 14 loads of lettuce, buyer would have to obtain replacement lettuce elsewhere or would itself be in breach of contract. This was within the contemplation of the parties when they entered into their agreement.

As noted earlier, the object of contract damages is to give the aggrieved party "as nearly as possible the equivalent of the benefits of performance." In the instant case, buyer contracted for 14 loads of lettuce each week at 9 cents per pound. When seller breached its contract to provide that lettuce, buyer went out on the open market and purchased substitute lettuce to fulfill its contractual obligations to third parties. However, purchasing replacement lettuce to continue its business did not place buyer "in as good a position as if the other party had fully performed." This was because buyer paid more than nine cents per pound for the replacement lettuce. Only by reimbursing buyer for the additional costs above nine cents a pound could buyer truly receive the benefit of the bargain. This is the measure of damages set forth in section 2-712. . . .

Despite the obvious applicability and appropriateness of section 2-712, seller argues in this appeal that the contract-cover differential of section 2-712 is inappropriate in cases, as here, where the aggrieved buyer is ultimately able to pass on its additional costs to other parties. Seller contends that section 1-106's [§1-305 as amended] remedial injunction to put the aggrieved party "in as good a position as if the other party had fully performed" demands that all subsequent events impacting on buyer's ultimate profit or loss be taken into consideration (specifically, that buyer passed on all but $70,000 of its loss to Castellini Company, which passed on all of its loss to Club Chef, which passed on most of its loss to its fast food customers). . . .

With these prefatory comments in mind, we look to the *Allied Canners* case. In [Allied Canners and Packers, Inc. v. Victor Packing Co., 209 Cal. Rptr. 60 (1984)], Victor Packing Company breached [a] contract to sell raisins in 1976. The buyer, Allied Canners, had contracts to resell the raisins it bought from Victor to two Japanese companies for its cost plus 4 percent. Such a resale would have resulted in a profit of $4,462.50 to Allied. When Victor breached the contract, Allied sued for the difference between the market price and the contract price as authorized by section 2-713. As the market price of raisins had soared due to the disastrous 1976 rains, the market-contract price formula would have yielded damages of approximately $150,000. Allied did not purchase substitute raisins and did not make any deliveries under its resale contracts to the Japanese buyers. One of the Japanese buyers simply released Allied from its contract because of the general unavailability of raisins. The other buyer did not release Allied, but it did not sue Allied either. By the time Allied's case against Victor went to trial, the statute of limitations on the Japanese buyer's claim had run.

Under these circumstances, the court held that the policy of section 1-106 (that the aggrieved party be put in as good a position as if the other party had performed) required that the award of damages to Allied be limited to its actual loss. It noted that for this limitation to apply, three conditions must be met: (1) "the seller knew that the buyer had a resale contract"; (2) "the buyer has not been able to show that it will be liable in damages to the buyer on its forward contract"; and (3) "there has been no finding of bad faith on the part of the seller. . . ." (Allied Canners & Packers, Inc. v. Victor Packing Co., supra, 162 Cal. App. 3d at p. 915, 209 Cal. Rptr. 60.)

The result in *Allied Canners* seems to have derived in large part from the court's finding that Victor had not acted in bad faith in breaching the contract. The court noted, "It does appear clear, however, that, as the trial court found, the rains caused a severe problem, and Victor made substantial efforts [to procure the raisins for Allied]. We do not deem this record one to support an inference that windfall damages must be awarded the buyer to prevent unjust enrichment to a deliberately breaching seller."

We believe that this focus on the good or bad faith of the breaching party is inappropriate in a commercial sales case. As our California Supreme Court recently explained, courts should not differentiate between good and bad motives for breaching a contract in assessing the measure of the non-breaching party's damages. Such a focus is inconsistent with the policy "to encourage contractual relations and commercial activity by enabling parties to estimate in advance the financial risks of their enterprise." "'Courts traditionally have awarded damages for breach of contract to compensate the aggrieved party rather than to punish the breaching party.' [Citations.]" (Foley v. Interactive Data Corp., supra, 47 Cal. 3d at p. 683, 254 Cal. Rptr. 211, 765 P.2d 373.)

The *Allied Canners* opinion has been sharply criticized in numerous law review articles and in at least one sister-state opinion. In Tongish v. Thomas (1992) 251 Kan. 728, 840 P.2d 471, the Kansas Supreme Court rejected the *Allied Canners* approach and instead applied the "majority view [which] would award market damages even though in excess of plaintiff's loss." . . .

As the foregoing discussion makes clear, we have serious reservations about whether the result in *Allied Canners,* with its emphasis on the good faith of the breaching party, is appropriate in an action seeking damages under section 2-713. We have no reservations, however, in not extending the *Allied Canners* rationale to a section 2-712 case. As noted earlier, no section 2-712 case has ever held that cover damages must be limited by section 1-106 [§1-305 as amended]. The obvious reason is that the cover-contract differential puts a buyer who covers in the exact same position as performance would have done. This is precisely what is called for in section 1-106 [§1-305 as amended]. In this respect, the cover/contract differential of section 2-712 is very different than the market/contract differential of section 2-713, which "need bear no close relation to the plaintiff's actual loss." (White & Summers, supra, at p.295.)

In summary, we hold that where a buyer "'cover[s]' by making in good faith and without unreasonable delay any reasonable purchase of . . . goods in substitution for those due from the seller, . . . [that buyer] may recover from the seller as damages the difference between the cost of cover and the contract price. . . ." (§2-712.) This gives the buyer the benefit of its bargain. What the buyer chooses to do with that bargain is not relevant to the determination of damages under section 2-712. . . .

The *KGM* court points out that the *Allied Canners* case has been sharply criticized by several law review articles and that it is still the minority view on the issue of whether the more general policy of §1-305(a) should ever serve as a cap of the more specific damages formulas given in Article 2. What the *KGM* court does not point out is that White and Summers, whose treatise was quoted liberally in the *KGM* opinion, "are at least tentatively persuaded that *Allied . . .* should be followed." James J. White & Robert S. Summers, Uniform Commercial Code 207 (4th ed. 1995).

Problem Set 27

27.1.   a. Tarpit, Inc. (TI) is an Austin, Texas, company that buys and sells asphalt. TI signed a contract on February 1 with Paving the Way (PTW), an

Austin, Texas, driveway contractor, in which TI promised to sell PTW 10,000 tons of asphalt for a price of $55 per ton, delivery March 5 of the same year, "FOB Seller's Place." The cost of delivering 10,000 tons of asphalt from TI to PTW is $3,000. On February 2, TI signed a contract with Blackrock, Ltd. (BL), a Tulsa, Oklahoma, company, to purchase from BL 10,000 tons of asphalt for a price of $52 per ton, delivery March 4 of the same year, "FOB Seller's Place." The cost of delivering 10,000 tons of asphalt from BL to TI is $12,000. On March 4, BL announced to TI that BL was breaching its contract to sell the asphalt. It is too late for TI to arrange suitable cover, and the market price for 10,000 tons of asphalt is now (on March 4) $94 per ton in Tulsa, but $86 per ton in Austin. Assuming that PTW will sue TI for whatever damages the UCC allows PTW once TI breaches its contract with PTW, what damages can TI claim against BL for BL's breach? UCC §§2-713, 2-715(2)(a), 1-305(a); Official Comment 6 to §2-715. In this part and all of the variations below, consider how the result might differ depending on whether the court follows *TexPar* rather than *Allied Canners*, or vice versa.

b. Same facts as part (a), except suppose that PTW decides it will not sue TI and executes an enforceable waiver to that effect. What damages can TI claim now against BL?

c. Same facts as part (a), except suppose TI covers with a "great cross-border buy" by purchasing 10,000 tons of asphalt in Mexico City, Mexico, on March 4 at $53 per ton, plus $12,000 in delivery costs from Mexico City to Austin. What damages can TI claim now against BL? UCC §2-712.

d. Same facts as part (a), except assume that TI clearly could have covered by purchasing 10,000 tons of asphalt in Mexico City, Mexico, on March 4 at $53 per ton, plus $12,000 in delivery costs from Mexico City to Austin, but it failed to do so. What damages can TI claim now against BL?

e. Same facts as part (a), except suppose that TI covers by purchasing 10,000 tons of asphalt in Mexico City on March 4 at $54 per ton, "FOB Buyer's Place." What damages can TI claim now against BL? UCC §2-712.

f. Same facts as part (a), except assume that TI clearly could have covered by purchasing 10,000 tons of asphalt in Mexico City on March 4 at $54 per ton, "FOB Buyer's Place," but it failed to do so. What damages can TI claim now against BL?

27.2.   Garden-Aid (GA) was a distributor of fertilizer. On June 1, GA entered into a contract to purchase 3,000 tons of fertilizer from LawnCo, Inc. (LCI), a local manufacturer of fertilizer, for a price of $20 per ton, delivery date August 1, "FOB Buyer's Place." On June 2, GA entered into a contract to sell 3,000 tons of fertilizer to Flowers 'n' Stuff (FNS), a local garden retail chain. FNS agreed to pay $27 per ton for the fertilizer, delivery date August 2, "FOB Seller's Place." GA made the mistake of pre-paying the entire contract price of $60,000 to LCI. On July 20, LCI called GA and said that its promised fertilizer shipment would be delayed until August 10. GA said that such a delay would be unacceptable given GA's contract with FNS, and so GA proceeded to arrange for the purchase of 3,000 tons of fertilizer from a third-party supplier in the same city as LCI for $22 per ton, "FOB Buyer's Place." After GA fulfilled its contract with FNS, LCI shipped the 3,000 tons of fertilizer to GA on August 10, despite GA's earlier conversation with LCI about the effect of the delay. Five days later, GA found a buyer for the 3,000 tons of fertilizer it had on hand and sold it to this new buyer for $23 per ton, "FOB Seller's Place." What amount may GA recover from LCI for the delay in delivery? UCC §§2-712, 2-715(2)(a), 1-305(a), 2-711(3), 2-706(6).

27.3. Carl Cautious was not fond of taking risks. Therefore, he started to worry when he began to hear reports on the news that a famous seismologist, Iben There, was predicting a major earthquake in Carl's hometown of St. Louis on July 10 of that year. Carl lived in an old brick house in south St. Louis, and he feared that the house would never withstand the force of a break in the mighty New Madrid fault. Accordingly, Carl determined that he needed to have constructed for himself a special earthquake shelter for his backyard in which he could confidently take refuge on that day. In addition, Carl wanted built for the shelter a special compact multi-purpose, single-unit appliance that included a refrigerator, a TV, and a microwave, not to exceed a total cubic space of three feet by four feet by two feet. Carl figured he might have to live in the shelter for a couple of weeks after July 10 to avoid the effects of the likely aftershocks.

On May 10 of the same year, Carl entered into contracts with two separate manufacturers. His first contract was with Shelters 'R' Us, an Atlanta manufacturer of sturdy, portable, and prefabricated mini-shelters. Carl entered into a written contract with Shelters 'R' Us in which Shelters agreed to construct for Carl's backyard in St. Louis an eight-foot by ten-foot by eight-foot portable shelter that was made of galvanized, earthquake-proof steel. The contract price was $12,000, the delivery date was July 5, and the delivery term was "FOB Seller's Place of Business." Delivery of the shelter from Atlanta to St. Louis would cost $500. In entering into the contract with Shelters, Carl told the representative he dealt with there about Carl's purpose for the shelter and about Carl's "master plan" for protection from the earthquake, including Carl's intent to commission the separate manufacture of a multi-purpose, single-unit appliance.

Carl's second contract was with Gizmoes 'N Such, a Chicago manufacturer of appliances. In a written contract, Gizmoes agreed to specially manufacture for Carl the combination refrigerator-TV-microwave device that Carl envisioned. The contract price was $2,000, the delivery date was July 8, and the delivery term was "FOB Buyer's Backyard." Gizmoes's direct costs in manufacturing the appliance were expected to be $600 in raw materials and $700 in direct labor. Delivery of the appliance from Chicago to St. Louis would cost $100.

On July 1, someone from Shelters 'R' Us called Carl and told him that Shelters definitely was not going to perform its contract with Carl. The market price of similar shelters in Atlanta on that day and on July 5 was $14,000; in St. Louis it was $18,000. The problem was, in neither location nor anywhere else could Carl, despite his best efforts, get a seller to agree to build such a special shelter for him by July 10. Accordingly, on July 2, Carl called Gizmoes 'N Such and told the representative there that regrettably, Carl would have to call off the manufacture of the special appliance unit. Gizmoes's representative told Carl to expect that Carl would be held accountable for all of Gizmoes's damages from Carl's breach. At that point, Gizmoes had purchased all of the raw materials for the project but had spent just $400 in direct labor. After spending $75 in employee time searching for possible buyers of either a completed unit or the partially completed unit in its current form, Gizmoes made the commercially reasonable decision to cease manufacture. Gizmoes then gave proper notice to Carl and resold the partially completed unit for $800 to a Chicago buyer who agreed to come and pick it up.

July 10 came and went with no earthquake. With that worry behind him, Carl now comes to your law office and wants to know for what amount he can sue Shelters 'R' Us for its breach. (Carl notes that he has made no payments so far to either seller.) In light of all of the above facts, what do you advise him? UCC §§2-713, 2-319(1) 2-509(1), 2-715, 2-708(2), 2-706(1), 1-305(a).

Assignment 28:   Special Remedies

A.   Specific Performance

This casebook has already explored the remedy of specific performance in a couple of different contexts. Assignment 26 showed how specific performance was the real estate buyer's primary remedy for the seller's breach. Assignment 22 considered, among other seller remedies, the seller's action for the price, which is in effect the seller's right to specific performance from the buyer.

Here, the focus shifts to the buyer's right to specific performance when the seller breaches a contract for the sale of goods. Specific performance as a buyer's remedy is a venerable common law option for the aggrieved buyer. The traditional common law rule says that the aggrieved buyer is entitled to specific performance only when it can demonstrate to the court that its remedies at law (i.e., monetary damages) are inadequate.

Article 2's specific performance section, §2-716, rejects the common law's fairly limited approach to awarding specific performance to the buyer, significantly broadening the circumstances when it is available. Section 2-716(1) says that "[s]pecific performance may be decreed when the goods are unique or in other proper circumstances." Official Comment 1 to §2-716 elaborates on this language by noting that "[t]he present section continues in general prior policy as to specific performance and injunction against breach," but "this Article seeks to further a more liberal attitude than some courts have shown in connection with the specific performance of contracts of sale."

The alternative requirement of §2-716(1) that the goods be "unique" seems more or less to account for the situation in which the remedy at law is inadequate, and therefore does not by itself change the common law standard very much. A number of buyers, in fact, have failed in their attempts to fit into the "unique" language the case in which the only thing that is unique about the goods is their very low price. In this situation, courts have had no trouble holding that the aggrieved buyer should be entitled only to the usual contract-cover or contract-market damages. Of course, if price is the only item of uniqueness, a decree for the appropriate damage remedy should mimic closely the effect of specific performance.

The "other proper circumstances" language of §2-716(1) has arguably created an expansion in the number of situations where courts have been willing to grant the buyer specific performance. In particular, courts have been willing to grant specific performance to aggrieved buyers in long-term output or requirements contracts involving fuel or other natural resources. In these situations, the goods involved are not "unique" in the traditional sense that courts have required for specific performance. Nevertheless, the tremendous disruption that effecting cover would cause to the buyer in these circumstances has caused many courts to conclude that specific performance is an appropriate remedy for the buyer.

Courts that allow specific performance for the buyer in a long-term contract of this sort can rest their decision not only on the "other proper circumstances" language but also on an expanded concept of "uniqueness" that is suggested in Official Comment 2 to §2-716: "The test of uniqueness under this section must be made in terms of the total situation which characterizes the contract. Output and requirements contracts involving a particular or peculiarly available source or market present today the typical commercial specific performance situation, as contrasted with contracts for the sale of heirlooms or priceless works of art which were usually involved in the older cases."

Section 2-716(3) is something of a mystery. It gives a buyer a right to replevin whenever cover is reasonably unavailable and the goods have been identified to the contract. Replevin is a doctrine based in property law; it enables the rightful owner of the goods to recover them from one who has wrongfully taken or held them. Yet a buyer that could show the impracticability of cover would seemingly qualify for specific performance anyway under §2-716(1). Since specific performance would seem to give an aggrieved buyer the same rights as replevin would, it is not surprising that there are virtually no reported cases on the use of §2-716(3).

There is a second part to §2-716(3) that does offer a possible independent benefit to the buyer from that subsection: It offers the buyer a replevin right in the case where "the goods have been shipped under reservation and satisfaction of the security interest in them has been made or tendered."

Thus, for example, suppose the seller ships goods by truck to the seller's agent in Reno, Nevada. The goods have already been identified to a particular buyer in Reno. The seller reserves for itself a security interest in the goods. When the goods arrive in Reno, the buyer is notified to come and get them, but then the seller tells its agent to hold the goods and sell them to a different buyer. In this case, the original buyer can pay the price for the goods (thereby "satisfying the security interest" of the seller) and demand the goods from the seller's agent, whether or not the goods are unique.

Section 2-716(2) says that a court's specific performance decree "may include such terms and conditions as to payment of the price, damages, or other relief as the court may deem just." The practical effect of this provision is to carry forward the common law requirement that a buyer requesting specific performance must demonstrate that it, the buyer, is ready, willing, and able to perform its side of the agreement. In the following case, the buyer attempts to use the specific performance doctrine as a device to increase the size of his monetary damages.

Bander v. Grossman

611 N.Y.S.2d 985 (N.Y. Sup. Ct. 1994)

Lᴇʙᴇᴅᴇꜰꜰ, J.

Following a jury trial on a claim that the defendant, a sports car dealer, repudiated plaintiff's contract to purchase a rare Aston-Martin automobile, plaintiff moves for judgment on its alternative request for monetary specific performance in the form of a judgment approximately ten times greater than the breach of contract damages awarded by the jury. In opposition, defendant moves to set aside the breach of contract jury verdict in favor of plaintiff. Both motions are consolidated for purposes of this decision. . . .

The attack on the verdict requires an amplification of the underlying facts. In the summer of 1987, plaintiff looked for a sports car to purchase for interim personal use and to sell when the price rose (a practice in which he had previously engaged). The defendant had in his inventory the subject 1965 DB5 Aston-Martin convertible with left hand drive. Plaintiff learned this particular model was one of only twenty in existence, with only forty having been made, although those twenty cars seem to turn over with more frequency than their number might suggest. Plaintiff testified he thought the car was undervalued, based upon his knowledge of sports car prices, and anticipated a price rise. A contract of sale was reached with a purchase price of $40,000, with plaintiff depositing $5,000.

The commercial agreement proceeded to unwind thereafter. The dealer could not obtain the title documents from the wholesaler from whom he had agreed to purchase the vehicle; the deposition testimony of the out-of-state wholesaler was read into evidence and confirmed that the title had been misplaced. The defendant did not transmit this explanation to plaintiff, but instead told a story about problems of getting title from a different individual. In August of 1987, the defendant attempted to return the deposit, but advised that he would continue to try to resolve the title problems. Plaintiff pursued the purchase until, ultimately, in December of 1987, plaintiff's lawyer wrote defendant that the contract had been breached and plaintiff would commence litigation. However, no further action was taken by plaintiff until this case was commenced in 1989, four months after defendant sold the car.

There was no dispute that the contract had been canceled. It was agreed that contract damages were to be given to the jury under the standard of UCC §2-713, applicable to a buyer who does not cover the difference between the market price when the buyer learned of the breach, and the contract price. The jury did not accept the defendant's claim that he could not deliver title, which would have excused his performance under the concept of "commercial impracticability" and the defendant does not challenge this aspect of the jury verdict.

The jury fixed plaintiff's knowledge of the breach as the time his attorney announced it, and did not accept plaintiff's insistence that the contract remained in effect thereafter. Given the continued assurances of defendant that he would pursue title, which proved to be a hollow promise, it was a fair view of the evidence that plaintiff could no longer claim ignorance of breach after his attorney proclaimed one.

The jury concluded that the market price had increased $20,000 by December, which defendant urges is unsupported. The jury was presented with evidence that the price remained basically flat at $40,000 throughout 1987, and by January of 1988 was in a range from $70,000 to $100,000. The jury clearly rejected the proposition that there was no upward curve in value toward the end of 1987. Accordingly, as of December of 1987, $60,000 was a fair and logical assessment of the value of the car and the jury, as it was instructed to do, deducted from the value the purchase price of the car, to reach an award of $20,000.

Plaintiff's final protest is that there was no specific car on the market in December of 1987. It cannot be ignored that the evidence before the jury fully portrayed an intimate community of Aston-Martin enthusiasts, linked by membership in an Aston-Martin club and supported by an Aston-Martin specialty dealer located in New Jersey. The jury's verdict is soundly premised on the conclusion that, had plaintiff attempted to offer to purchase a comparable Aston-Martin within this community, one would have surfaced with a price of $60,000. After all, the same seller who sold a vehicle in January would only have to be lured into the market a month earlier, somewhat before the market price ascent. . . .

The request for specific performance raises a novel issue under the Uniform Commercial Code concerning entitlement to specific performance of a contract for the sale of unique goods with a fluctuating price. Section 2-716(1) of the Uniform Commercial Code, which is controlling, provides that "specific performance may be decreed where the goods are unique or in other proper circumstances." The jury's advisory determined that the Aston-Martin car at issue was unique.

As noted above, the car was sold prior to the commencement of this litigation for a price of $185,000 more than the $40,000 contract price, and plaintiff requests that he be granted specific performance in the form of a constructive trust impressed upon the proceeds of sale, plus interest from the date of sale. As it developed, the defendant had not sold at the "top of the market," which peaked in July of 1989, approximately two years after the original contract, when the car had a value of $335,000, which was $295,000 over the contract price. Thereafter, collectible automobile values slumped and the sale price of a comparable Aston-Martin vehicle by January of 1990 was $225,000 and, by the time of trial, was $80,000.

Clearly, plaintiff's request for an award of specific performance monetary damages is legally cognizable, for every object has a price and even rare goods are subject to economic interchangeability (Van Wagner Advertising Corp. v. S & M Enterprises, 67 N.Y.2d 186, 191-194, 501 N.Y.S.2d 628, 492 N.E.2d 756 [1986]; compare, no other opportunity, Triple-A Baseball Club Associates v. Northeastern Baseball, Inc., 832 F.2d 214 [1st Cir. 1987]). Plaintiff urges that specific performance is particularly appropriate here for UCC §2-716 has been viewed as a statute enacted to liberalize the availability of specific performance of contracts of sale as a buyers' remedy (Ruddock v. First National Bank of Lake Forest, 201 Ill. App. 3d 907, 914, 147 Ill. Dec. 310, 559 N.E.2d 483 [App. 2 Dist. 1990]; Chadwell v. English, 652 P.2d 310 [Okla. App. Div. 2 1982]; Tower City Grain Co. v. Richman, 232 N.W.2d 61 [Sup. Ct. N.D. 1975]). Nonetheless, this change does not lessen the UCC's "emphasis on the commercial feasibility of replacement" as the most desirable approach (Comment 2, UCC §2-716), nor does it mean that typical equitable principles are inapplicable to consideration of the remedy (Massey v. Hardcastle, 753 S.W.2d 127 [Tenn. App. 1988]).

However, both on the facts and the law, the court determines that, if equitable monetary damages are to be awarded here, that award must be based upon value at the time of trial, rather than on an earlier valuation. Traditionally, equity "give[s] relief adapted to the situation at the time of the decree" (Union Bag & Paper Co. v. Allen Bros. Co., 107 App. Div. 529, 539, 95 N.Y.S. 214 [3d Dept. 1905]; Schaefer v. Fisher, 137 Misc. 420, 423, 242 N.Y.S. 308 [Sup. Ct. N.Y. Co. 1930]). This position is consistent with the explicit goal of the Uniform Commercial Code that its remedies are to "be liberally administered to the end that the aggrieved party may be put in as good a position as if the other party had fully performed" (UCC §1-106[1]) [§1-305(a) as amended], which, in the case of specific performance, has to confining the remedy to restoration of the equivalent of the subject goods to a plaintiff's possession (see Dexter Bishop Co. v. B. Redmond & Son, Inc., 58 A.D.2d 755, 396 N.Y.S.2d 652 [1st Dept. 1977]). Here, if plaintiff were to be awarded enough to be able to acquire another Aston-Martin at current prices, he would achieve the requisite equivalent.

Plaintiff has fervently, but ultimately unconvincingly, argued that the larger amount is his due. While every litigant wishes to gain a maximum economic benefit, a court of equity should not grant an award which would be "disproportionate in its harm to defendant and its assistance to plaintiff" (Van Wagner Advertising Corp. v. S & M Enterprises, supra, 67 N.Y.2d at 195, 501 N.Y.S.2d 628, 492 N.E.2d 756, quoting Matter of Burke v. Bowen, 40 N.Y.2d 264, 267, 386 N.Y.S.2d 654, 353 N.E.2d 567 [1976]). On the plaintiff's side of this equation, a higher award would give plaintiff more than the current equivalent of the automobile. On the defendant's side, the court found credible the dealer's testimony that he put the funds derived from the sale into his stock, which then decreased in value in the same measure as the car in question, so that a higher award would cause a disproportionate harm. This testimony was uncontroverted by plaintiff and it was undisputed that neither party saw a rise in price of the dimensions present here. The court rejects the request for monetary specific performance to the extent that more than the current market price is sought.

This conclusion limits the debate to the current price of the automobile, which is approximately $40,000 more than the contract price. As to interest in an equitable matter, generally, where damages are fixed as of the date of trial, interest is to commence as of the date judgment is entered, although the court must consider the facts of the case in determining the calculation of interest (Begen v. Pettus, 223 N.Y. 662, 119 N.E. 549 [1918]; see, for example, Frey Realty Co. v. Ten West 46th Street Corp., 1 Misc. 2d 371, 145 N.Y.S.2d 670 [Sup. Ct. N.Y. Co. 1955, Tilzer, J.]). There is a certain factual irony in that, by reason of market factors, the contract remedy plus interest would result in a specific performance monetary damages award only somewhat short of the current price.

The issue of monetary specific performance remains, despite this conclusion, because such an award would be somewhat higher than the contract measure of damages. Plaintiff's position that specific performance must follow a determination that an object is "unique" misperceives the law.

First specific performance rests upon the discretion of the trial court, reviewable under an abuse of discretion standard (Van Wagner Advertising Corp. v. S & M Enterprises, supra, 67 N.Y.2d at 192, 501 N.Y.S.2d 628, 492 N.E.2d 756). The use of a permissive "may" in the text of UCC §2-716 does not modify that standard in any way or change the accepted concept, as set forth in Da Silva v. Musso, 53 N.Y.2d 543, 547, 444 N.Y.S.2d 50, 428 N.E.2d 382 (1981), that specific performance may be declined if it is concluded such relief "would be a 'drastic' or harsh remedy." It should be noted in relation to price fluctuations that even an extreme rise in price is an insufficient reason, as a matter of law, to decline to consider this equitable remedy (Willard v. Tayloe, 75 U.S. (8 Wall.) 557, 19 L. Ed. 501 [1869]), but, on the other hand, neither does a mere "increase in the cost of a replacement . . . merit the remedy" (Klein v. PepsiCo, Inc., 845 F.2d 76, 80 (4th Cir. 1988), citing Hilmor Sales Co. v. Helen Neuschalfer Division of Supronics Corp., 6 UCC Rep. Serv. 325, 1969 WL 11054 [Sup. Ct. Queens Co. 1969]).

Second, a factual determination that an object is "unique," as the jury determined here in an advisory verdict, is an ingredient which has the greatest significance when an action for specific performance is commenced immediately after the breach, and is more complex when other factors or delays are present. In cases concerning the sale of goods promptly commenced after the breach, specific performance is frequently granted and turns primarily upon uniqueness (see, Schweber v. Rallye Motors Inc., N.Y. L.J. August 10, 1973 at p. 12, col 5, 12 UCC Rep. Serv. 1154, 1973 WL 21434 [Sup. Ct. Nassau County 1973], a Rolls-Royce Corniche, 100 sold each year in the United States, unique; Sedmak v. Charlie's Chevrolet, Inc., 622 S.W.2d 694 (Mo. App. 1981), new "Indy 500 Pace Car" Corvette unique; Copylease Corp. of America v. Memorex Corp., 408 F. Supp. 758 [S.D.N.Y. 1976], quality of chemicals unique; compare, Klein v. PepsiCo, Inc., supra, three comparable airplanes for sale within limited period of time, not unique; Scholl v. Hartzell, 20 Pa. D. & C.3d 304 [Ct. Comm. Pl. 1981], 1962 Corvette not unique; and Pierce-Odom, Inc. v. Evenson, 5 Ark. App. 67, 632 S.W.2d 247 [1982], mobile home not unique).

Once beyond this simple factual threshold, under New York law, "uniqueness" must be considered as it bears upon the adequacy of the legal remedy (Van Wagner Advertising Corp. v. S & M Enterprises, supra, 67 N.Y.2d at 193, 501 N.Y.S.2d 628, 492 N.E.2d 756). It is noted that not all jurisdictions take this view (see, King Aircraft Sales, Inc. v. Lane, 68 Wash. App. 706, 712, 846 P.2d 550 [Ct. App. Div. I, 1993], reciting a split of authority on this point).

With the passage of time, specific performance becomes disfavored. For example, because goods are subject to a rapid change in condition, or the cost of maintenance of the goods is important, time may be found to have been of the essence, and even a month's delay may defeat specific performance (see, delayed transfer of cattle, Ziebarth v. Kalenze, 238 N.W.2d 261 [N.D. 1976]; and Putnam Ranches, Inc. v. Corkle, 189 Neb. 533, 203 N.W.2d 502 [1973]), notwithstanding that risk of loss under title concepts is generally irrelevant under the UCC, which considers whether an item has been identified to a contract (see Tatum v. Richter, 280 Md. 332, 336-377, 373 A.2d 923 [1977], replevin of a Ferrari; and William F. Wilke, Inc. v. Cummins Diesel Engines, Inc., 252 Md. 611, 250 A.2d 886 [1969]). Even absent such special circumstances, with a greater delay, where a defendant has changed position or taken any economic risk, the court may conclude that "the plaintiff will lose nothing but an uncontemplated opportunity to gather a windfall" (Concert Radio, Inc. v. GAF Corp., 108 A.D.2d 273, 278, 488 N.Y.S.2d 696 [1st Dept. 1985], aff'd 73 N.Y.2d 766, 536 N.Y.S.2d 52, 532 N.E.2d 1280 [1988]). Particularly where some other transactions are available, it has been held that a "customer [for resale] may not . . . refuse to cover . . . and thereby speculate on the market entirely at the risk of the [defendant]" (Saboundjian v. Bank Audi [USA], 157 A.D.2d 278, 284, 556 N.Y.S.2d 258 [1st Dept. 1990], referring in part to UCC §1-106 which limits damages under UCC §2-713 to a buyer's expected profit where the purchase is for resale, quoting Brown v. Pressner Trading Corp., 101 A.D.2d 761, 762, 475 N.Y.S.2d 405 [1st Dept. 1984]).

Turning to the facts in the instant case, the plaintiff did not sue in December of 1987, when it is likely a request for specific performance would have been granted. At that point, the defendant had disclaimed the contract and plaintiff was aware of his rights. The plaintiff was not protected by a continued firm assurance that defendant definitely would perfect the car's title (see Telmark, Inc. v. Ayers, 80 A.D.2d 698, 436 N.Y.S.2d 458 [3d Dept. 1981]), and it was established that New York is an automobile "title" state, so that title is a specific impediment upon which complete legal possession must turn (compare, lease to be effective only upon lessor obtaining title, 7 Doyer St. Realty Corp. v. Great Cathay Development Corp., 39 A.D.2d 896, 333 N.Y.S.2d 941 [1st Dept. 1972]). The court does not accept plaintiff's protest that he believed the commercial relationship was intact; the parties had already had a heated discussion and were communicating through attorneys. A more likely explanation of plaintiff's inaction is that he proceeded to complete the purchase in April of 1988 of a Ferrari Testarrosa for $128,000 and a Lamborghini for $40,000 in 1989.

In short, the plaintiff abandoned any active claim of contract enforcement by late spring of 1988. Moreover, to the extent that his two sports cars constituted "cover," he did not present any evidence as to his treatment of those cars such that the court could evaluate damages or quantify what profits he expected to make on the Aston-Martin which he regarded, in significant part, as a business transaction (compare Fertico Belgium, S.A. v. Phosphate Chemicals Export Association, Inc., 70 N.Y.2d 76, 517 N.Y.S.2d 465, 510 N.E.2d 334 [1987], and Harper & Associates v. Printers, Inc., 46 Wash. App. 417, 730 P.2d 733 [App. Div. I 1986]). Finally, the court determines, as a matter of credibility, that plaintiff would not have pursued this matter had the price fallen below the contract price.

On this point, it is helpful to note that the initial burden of proving the proper remedy remains on the buyer (UCC §2-715, Official Comment 4). In this instance, plaintiff's very attempt to prove qualifiable specific performance damages has also proved: (a) the value of the disputed automobile was readily established by expert sources; (b) the adequacy of legal contract damages; and (c) the availability of "a substitute transaction [which] is generally a more efficient way to prevent injury than is a suit for specific performance . . . [and gives] a sound economic basis for limiting the injured party to damages" (see, comment c, Restatement [Second] of Contracts §360).

In closing, the court does not fault plaintiff for his valiant attempt to reach for a higher level of damages. As two leading commentators have pointed out, in relation to the use of uniqueness as a basis for specific performance, the "exact dimensions [of the concepts] are not fully known" (3A William D. Hawkland and Frederick Moreno, Uniform Commercial Code Series §2A-521:03 [Clark Boardman Callaghan 1993]). If only in the interest of commercial certainty, there is great wisdom in a rule of thumb that "uniqueness continues to cover one-of-a-kind goods and items of special sentimental value, [and] goods that have particular market significance, such as goods covered by an output contract or which are being specially manufactured" (Ibid.; footnotes omitted).

After full consideration of these factors, the court is satisfied that it would be inequitable and improper to grant specific performance in the form of a constructive trust upon the proceeds of sale.

Accordingly, the motion to fix the specific performance damages and the motion to vacate the jury verdict are denied.

B. Liquidated Damages

Much like specific performance, the special remedy of liquidated damages is one that is not unique to the UCC. The traditional dichotomy in the common law is that reasonable liquidated damages clauses are enforced, but "penalties" or "forfeitures" are not. This statement by itself is little more than conclusory, although courts love to cite it. Under the traditional common law rule, courts would generally disallow liquidated damages clauses in sales-of-goods cases unless the liquidated damages proved reasonable in light of the harm anticipated at the time the contract was entered into and there would be difficulties showing proof of loss.

Section 2-718(1), by contrast, allows liquidated damages clauses to be enforced whenever those damages are in an amount "which is reasonable in the light of the anticipated *or* actual harm caused by the breach, the difficulties of proof of loss, and the inconvenience or nonfeasibility of otherwise obtaining an adequate remedy." (Emphasis added.) Liquidated damages that are unreasonably large will be held void as a "penalty," §2-718(1), whereas liquidated damages that are unreasonably small may be struck down as unconscionable. Official Comment 1 to §2-718.

California & Hawaiian Sugar Co. v. Sun Ship, Inc.

794 F.2d 1433 (9th Cir. 1986)

NOONAN, J.

Jurisdiction in this case is based on the diversity of citizenship of California and Hawaiian Sugar company (C and H), a California corporation; Sun Ship, Inc. (Sun), a Pennsylvania corporation; and Halter Marine, Inc. (Halter), a Louisiana corporation. Interpreting a contract which provides for construction by the law of Pennsylvania, we apply Pennsylvania law. The appeal is from a judgment of the district court in favor of C and H and Halter on the main issues. Reviewing the district court's interpretation of the contract anew as a matter of law and respecting the findings of fact of the district court when not clearly erroneous, we affirm the judgment in all respects.

C and H is an agricultural cooperative owned by fourteen sugar plantations in Hawaii. Its business consists in transporting raw sugar—the crushed cane in the form of coarse brown crystal—to its refinery in Crockett, California. Roughly one million tons a year of sugar are harvested in Hawaii. A small portion is refined there; the bulk goes to Crockett. The refined sugar—the white stuff—is sold by C and H to groceries for home consumption and to the soft drink and cereal companies that are its industrial customers.

To conduct its business, C and H has an imperative need for assured carriage for the raw sugar from the islands. Sugar is a seasonal crop, with 70 percent of the harvest occurring between April and October, while almost nothing is harvestable during December and January. Consequently, transportation must not only be available, but seasonably available. Storage capacity in Hawaii accommodates not more than a quarter of the crop. Left stored on the ground or left unharvested, sugar suffers the loss of sucrose and goes to waste. Shipping ready and able to carry the raw sugar is a priority for C and H.

In 1979 C and H was notified that Matson Navigation Company, which had been supplying the bulk of the necessary shipping, was withdrawing its services as of January 1981. While C and H had some ships at its disposal, it found a pressing need for a large new vessel, to be in service at the height of the sugar season in 1981. It decided to commission the building of a kind of hybrid—a tug of catamaran design with two hulls and, joined to the tug, a barge with a wedge which would lock between the two pontoons of the tug, producing an "integrated tug barge." In Hawaiian, the barge and the entire vessel were each described as a Mocababoo or push boat.

C and H relied on the architectural advice of the New York firm, J.J. Henry. It solicited bids from shipyards, indicating as an essential term a "preferred delivery date" of June 1981. It decided to accept Sun's offer to build the barge and Halter's offer to build the tug.

In the fall of 1979 C and H entered into negotiations with Sun on the precise terms of the contract. Each company was represented by a vice-president with managerial responsibility in the area of negotiation; each company had a team of negotiators; each company had the advice of counsel in drafting the agreement that was signed on November 14, 1979. This agreement was entitled "Contract for the Construction of One Oceangoing Barge for California and Hawaiian Sugar Company By Sun Ship, Inc." The "Whereas" clause of the contract identified C and H as the Purchaser, and Sun as the Contractor; it identified "one non-self-propelled oceangoing barge" as the Vessel that Purchaser was buying from Contractor. Article I provided that Contractor would deliver the Vessel on June 30, 1981. The contract price was $25,405,000.

Under Article I of the agreement, Sun was entitled to an extension of the delivery date for the usual types of force majeure and for unavailability of the Tug to Contractor for joining to the Vessel, where it is determined that Contractor has complied with all obligations under the Interface "Agreement." (The Interface Agreement, executed the same day between C and H, Sun, and Halter provided that Sun would connect the barge with the tug.) Article 17 "Delivery" provided that "the Vessel shall be offered for delivery fully and completely connected with the Tug." Article 8, "Liquidated Damages for Delay in Delivery" provided that if "Delivery of the Vessel" was not made on "the Delivery Date" of June 30, 1981, Sun would pay C and H "as per-day liquidated damages, and not as a penalty" a sum described as "a reasonable measure of the damages"—$17,000 per day.

On the same date C and H entered into an agreement with Halter to purchase "one oceangoing catamaran tug boat" for $20,350,000. The tug (the "Vessel" of that contract) was to be delivered on April 30, 1981 at Sun's shipyard. Liquidated damages of $10,000 per day were provided for Halter's failure to deliver.

Halter did not complete the tug until July 15, 1982. Sun did not complete the barge until March 16, 1982. Tug and barge were finally connected under C and H's direction in mid-July 1982 and christened the Moku Pahu. C and H settled its claim against Halter. Although Sun paid C and H $17,000 per day from June 30, 1981 until January 10, 1982, it ultimately denied liability for any damages, and this lawsuit resulted.

Sun contends that its obligation was to deliver the barge connected to the tug on the delivery date of June 30, 1981 and that only the failure to deliver the integrated hybrid would have triggered the liquidated damage clause. It is true that Article 17 creates some ambiguity by specifying that the Vessel is to be "offered for delivery completely connected with the Tug." The case of the barge being ready while the tug was not, is not explicitly considered. Nonetheless, the meaning of "Vessel" is completely unambiguous. From the "Whereas" clause to the articles of the agreement dealing with insurance, liens, and title, the "Vessel" is the barge. It would require the court to rewrite the contract to find that "the Vessel" in Article 8 on liquidated damages does not mean the barge. The article takes effect on failure to deliver "the Vessel"—that is, the barge.

Sun contends, however, that on such a reading of the contract, the $17,000 per day is a penalty, not to be enforced by the court. The barge, Sun points out, was useless to C and H without the tug. Unconnected, the barge was worse than useless—it was an expensive liability. C and H did not want the barge by itself. To get $17,000 per day as "damages" for failure to provide an unwanted and unusable craft is, Sun says, to exact a penalty. C and H seeks to be "paid according to the tenour of the bond"; it "craves the law." And if C and H sticks to the letter of the bond, it must like Shylock end by losing; a court of justice will not be so vindictive. Breach of contract entitles the wronged party only to fair compensation.

Seductive as Sun's argument is, it does not carry the day. Represented by sophisticated representatives, C and H and Sun reached the agreement that $17,000 a day was the reasonable measure of the loss C and H would suffer if the barge was not ready. Of course they assumed that the tug would be ready. But in reasonable anticipation of the damages that would occur if the tug was ready and the barge was not, Article 8 was adopted. As the parties foresaw the situation, C and H would have a tug waiting connection but no barge and so no shipping. The anticipated damages were what might be expected if C and H could not transport the Hawaiian sugar crop at the height of the season. Those damages were clearly before both parties. As Joe Kleschick, Sun's chief negotiator, testified, he had "a vision" of a "mountain of sugar piling up in Hawaii"—a vision that C and H conjured up in negotiating the damage clause. Given the anticipated impact on C and H's raw sugar and on C and H's ability to meet the demands of its grocery and industrial customers if the sugar could not be transported, liquidated damages of $17,000 a day were completely reasonable.

The situation as it developed was different from the anticipation. The barge was not ready but neither was the tug. C and H was in fact able to find other shipping. The crop did not rot. The customers were not left sugarless. Sun argues that, measured by the actual damages suffered, the liquidated damages were penal.

We look to Pennsylvania law for guidance. Although no Pennsylvania case is squarely on point, it is probable that Pennsylvania would interpret the contract as a sale of goods governed by the Uniform Commercial Code. Belmont Industries, Inc. v. Bechtel Corp., 425 F. Supp. 524, 527 (E.D. Pa. 1976). The governing statute provides that liquidated damages are considered reasonable "in the light of anticipated or actual harm." 12A Pa. Cons. Stat. Ann. 2-718(1) (Purdon 1970) (Pennsylvania's adoption of the Uniform Commercial Code).

The choice of the disjunctive appears to be deliberate. The language chosen is in harmony with the Restatement (Second) of Contracts §356 (1979), which permits liquidated damages in the light of the anticipated or actual loss caused by the breach and the difficulties of proof of loss. Section 356, Comment b declares explicitly: "Furthermore, the amount fixed is reasonable to the extent that it approximates the loss anticipated at the time of the making of the contract, even though it may not approximate the actual loss."

Despite the statutory disjunctive and the Restatement's apparent blessing of it, the question is not settled by these authorities which must be read in the light of common law principles already established and accepted in Pennsylvania. Carpel v. Saget Studios, Inc., 326 F. Supp. 1331, 1333 (E.D. Pa. 1971); 13 Pa. C.S.A. §1103. Prior to the adoption of the Uniform Commercial Code, Pennsylvania enforced liquidated damage clauses that its courts labeled as nonpenal, but equitable considerations relating to the actual harm incurred were taken into account along with the difficulty of proving damages if a liquidated damage clause was rejected, e.g. Emery v. Boyle, 200 Pa. 249, 49 A. 779 (1901). We do not believe that the UCC overrode this line of reasoning. Indeed, in a lower court case, decided after the UCC's enactment, it was stated that if liquidated damages appear unreasonable in light of the harm suffered, "the contractual provision will be voided as a penalty" Unit Vending Corp. v. Tobin Enterprises, 194 Pa. Super. 470, 473, 168 A.2d 750, 751 (1961). That case, however, is not on all fours with our case: *Unit Vending* involved an adhesion contract between parties of unequal bargaining power; the unfair contract was characterized by the court as "a clever attempt to secure both the penny and the cake" by the party with superior strength. Id. at 476, 168 A.2d at 753. Mechanically to read it as Pennsylvania law governing this case would be a mistake. The case, however, does show that Pennsylvania courts, like courts elsewhere, attempt to interpret the governing statute humanely and equitably.

The Restatement §356 Comment b, after accepting anticipated damages as a measure, goes on to say that if the difficulty of proof of loss is slight, then actual damage may be the measure of reasonableness: "If, to take an extreme case, it is clear that no loss at all has occurred, a provision fixing a substantial sum as damages is unenforceable. See Illustration 4." Illustration 4 is a case of a contractor, A, agreeing to build B's race track by a specific date and to pay B $1,000 a day for every day's delay. A delays a month, but B does not get permission to operate the track for that month, so B suffers no loss. In that event, the Restatement characterizes the $1,000 per day as an unenforceable penalty. Sun contends that it is in the position of A: no actual loss was suffered by C and H because C and H had no tug to mate with the barge.

This argument restates in a new form Sun's basic contention that the liquidated damage clause was meant to operate only if the integrated tug barge was not delivered. The argument has been rejected by us as a misinterpretation of the contract. But in its new guise it gains appeal. If Illustration 4 is the present case, Sun is home scot-free. The Restatement, however, deals with a case where the defaulting contractor was alone in his default. We deal with a case of concurrent defaults. If we were to be so literal-minded as to follow the Restatement here, we would have to conclude that because both parties were in default, C and H suffered no damage until one party performed. Not until the barge was ready in March 1982 could C and H hold Halter for damages, and then only for the period after that date. The continued default of both parties would operate to take each of them off the hook. That cannot be the law.

Sun objects that Halter had a more absolute obligation to deliver than Sun did. Halter did not have to deliver the integrated tug, only the tug itself; it was not excused by Sun's default. Hence the spectacle of two defaulting contractors causing no damages would not be presented here. But Sun's objection does not meet the point that Halter's unexcused delivery would, on Sun's theory, have generated no damages. The tug by itself would have been no use to C and H.

We conclude, therefore, that in this case of concurrent causation each defaulting contractor is liable for the breach and for the substantial damages which the joint breach occasions. Sun is a substantial cause of the damages flowing from the lack of the integrated tug; Sun cannot be absolved by the absence of the tug.

Sun has a final argument. Even on the assumption that it is liable as a substantial cause of the breach of contract, Sun contends that the actual damages suffered by C and H for lack of the integrated tug boat were slight. Actual damages were found by the district court to consist of "interest on progress payments, unfavorable terms of conversion to long-term financing, and additional labor expense." No dollar amount was determined by the district court in finding that these damages "bore a reasonable relationship to the amount liquidated in the Barge Contract."

The dollar value of the damages found by the district judge is, to judge from C and H's own computation, as follows:

Additional Construction Interest	$1,486,000
Added Payments to J.J. Henry	161,000
Added Vessel Operating Expenses	73,000
C and H Employee Costs	109,000
	$1,829,000

But "actual damages" have no meaning if the actual savings of C and H due to the nondelivery of the integrated tug barge are not subtracted. It was clearly erroneous for the district judge to exclude these savings from his finding. These savings, again according to C and H's own computation, were:

Transportation savings	$ 525,000
Lay-up costs	936,000
	$1,461,000

The net actual damages suffered by C and H were $368,000. As a matter of law, Sun contends that the liquidated damages are unreasonably disproportionate to the net actual damages.

C and H urges on us the precedent of Bellefonte Borough Authority v. Gateway Equipment & Supply Co., 442 Pa. 492, 277 A.2d 347 (1971), forfeiting a bid bond of $45,000 on the failure of a contractor to perform a municipal contract, even though the loss to the municipality was $1,000; the disproportion was 45 to 1. But that decision is not decisive here. It did not purport to apply the Uniform Commercial Code. Rules appropriate for bids to the government are sufficiently different from those applicable between private parties to prevent instant adoption of this precedent. A fuller look at relevant contract law is appropriate.

Litigation has blurred the line between a proper and a penal clause, and the distinction is "not an easy one to draw in practice." Lake River Corp. v. Carborundum Co., 769 F.2d 1284, 1290 (7th Cir. 1985) (per Posner, J.). But the desire of courts to avoid the enforcement of penalties should not obscure common law principles followed in Pennsylvania. Contracts are contracts because they contain enforceable promises, and absent some overriding public policy, those promises are to be enforced. "Where each of the parties is content to take the risk of its turning out in a particular way" why should one "be released from the contract, if there were no misrepresentation or other want of fair dealing?" Ashcom v. Smith, 2 Pen. & W. 211, 218-219 (Pa. 1830) (per Gibson, C.J.). Promising to pay damages of a fixed amount, the parties normally have a much better sense of what damages can occur. Courts must be reluctant to override their judgment. Where damages are real but difficult to prove, injustice will be done the injured party if the court substitutes the requirements of judicial proof for the parties' own informed agreement as to what is a reasonable measure of damages. Pennsylvania acknowledges that a seller is bound to pay consequential damages if the seller had reason to know of the buyer's special circumstances. Keystone Diesel Engine Co. v. Irwin, 411 Pa. 222, 191 A.2d 376 (1963). The liquidated damage clause here functions in lieu of a court's determination of the consequential damages suffered by C and H.

These principles inform a leading common law case in the field, Clydebank Engineering & Shipbuilding Co. v. Yzquierdo y Castaneda, 1905 A.C. 6. The defendant shipyard had agreed to pay 500 pounds per week per vessel for delay in the delivery of four torpedo boat destroyers to the Spanish Navy in 1897. The shipyard pointed out that had the destroyers been delivered on schedule they would have been sunk with the rest of the Spanish Navy by the Americans in 1898. The House of Lords found the defense unpersuasive. To prove damages the whole administration of the Spanish Navy would have had to have been investigated. The House of Lords refused to undertake such a difficult investigation when the parties had made an honest effort in advance to set in monetary terms what the lack of the destroyers would mean to Spain.

C and H is not the Spanish Navy, but the exact damages caused its manifold operations by lack of the integrated tug boat are equally difficult of ascertainment. C and H claimed that it suffered $3,732,000 in lost charter revenues. Testimony supported the claim, but the district court made no finding as to whether the claim was proved or unproved. The district court did find that the loss of charter revenues had not been anticipated by the parties. But that finding has no bearing on whether the loss occurred. Within the general risk of heavy losses forecast by both parties when they agreed to $17,000 per day damages, a particular type of loss was pointed to by C and H as having happened.

Proof of this loss is difficult—as difficult, perhaps, as proof of loss would have been if the sugar crop had been delivered late because shipping was missing. Whatever the loss, the parties had promised each other that $17,000 per day was a reasonable measure. The court must decline to substitute the requirements of judicial proof for the parties' own conclusion. The Moku Pahu, available on June 30, 1981, was a great prize, capable of multiple employments and enlarging the uses of the entire C and H fleet. When sophisticated parties with bargaining parity have agreed what lack of this prize would mean, and it is now difficult to measure what the lack did mean, the court will uphold the parties' bargain. C and H is entitled to keep the liquidated damages of $3,298,000 it has already received and to receive additional liquidated damages of $1,105,000 with interest thereon, less setoffs determined by the district court. . . .

———————

Section 2-718(2) creates a statutory liquidated damages clause for the seller in the case where the breaching buyer has made pre-payments to the seller and the seller has justifiably withheld delivery of the goods. Section 2-718(2)(b) puts the issue in terms of the breaching buyer's entitlement to "restitution" from the seller of the buyer's pre-payment. It says that the breaching buyer is entitled from the seller to any amount by which the buyer's pre-payments exceed "twenty percent of the value of the total performance for which the buyer is obligated under the contract or $500, whichever is smaller."

The formula for the breaching buyer's restitution for its pre-payments under §2-718(2)(b) may be expressed as follows: R = P − (< of .2t or $500 or P), where R = the pre-paying buyer's right to restitution, P = the sum of the pre-payments made by the buyer, and t = the value of the total performance for which the buyer is obligated under the contract (normally the contract price).

Thus, suppose that the buyer pre-pays a deposit of $1,000 to purchase a $2,000 boat. Before the seller delivers the boat, the buyer repudiates the contract and asks for its deposit back. The repudiating buyer's entitlement to a refund under §2-718(2)(b) would be R = P ($1,000) − (< of .2t[.2($2,000 = $400] or $500 or $1,000) = $1,000 − $400 = $600. Ultimately, the repudiating buyer should get $600 back from the aggrieved seller, who is entitled by virtue of §2-718(2)(b) to keep $400 of the breaching buyer's pre-payment.

Section 2-718(3) adds a couple of more wrinkles to this formula, in that it says that the buyer's right to restitution as defined in §2-718(2) is "subject to offset" to the extent that the seller establishes: (a) actual damages occasioned by the buyer's breach, or (b) any benefits that the buyer has received "directly or indirectly by reason of the contract."

Expanding the formula of §2-718(2) to include the content added by §2-718(3) yields: R = P − (< of .2t or $500 or P) − SD − BB, where the first three variables are the same as above, SD = seller's actual damages, and BB = buyer's benefits from the contract. Thus, suppose that our boat seller above could show that it suffered $450 in lost profits as a result of the buyer's breach. The breaching buyer then would be entitled to R = P ($1,000) − (< of .2t [.2 ×$2,000 = $400] or $500 or $1,000) − SD ($450) − BB (0) = $1,000 − $400 − $450 = $150. Under this formula, then, the breaching buyer should get back $150 of its $1,000 deposit, and the seller should get to keep $850.

Although the above formula is clearly what the literal language of §2-718(2) and (3) yields, at least one court believed that the literal formula was too generous to the seller. In that case, Neri v. Retail Marine Corp., 334 N.Y.2d 165 (1972), a consumer buyer made a deposit on a boat purchase and then repudiated the contract. The seller successfully demonstrated that it was a lost-profits seller and therefore could show actual damages as a result of the buyer's breach. The seller, pointing to the literal language of §2-718(2) and (3), argued that it ought to retain from the buyer's deposit its actual damages plus the statutory liquidated damages of §2-718(2)(b). The court disagreed and said that despite the literal language, the seller could only retain the greater of its actual damages or the statutory liquidated damages.

Because there are so few litigated cases involving §2-718(2) and (3), it is hard to say whether the *Neri* approach or the literal approach is the proper or "majority" approach. Thus, probably the safest course for students is to know that both approaches exist and to understand the formulas for each. The literal formula is presented above. The *Neri* formula, by contrast, would look like this: R = P – (> of [< of .2t or $500 or P] or [SD]) – BB, with the variables all defined as they were above.

To take once again the situation of a breaching boat buyer who pre-pays $1,000 on a $2,000 boat, assume that the seller could show actual damages of $450 as a result of the buyer's breach. Under the *Neri* approach, the buyer would be entitled to R = P ($1,000) – (> of [< of .2t (.2 × $2,000 = $400)) or $500 or $1,000] or [SD][$450]) – BB(0) = $1,000 – (> of $400 or $450) – 0 = $1,000 – $450 = $550. Under *Neri*, then, the buyer is entitled to a refund of $550 from the seller rather than just $150, and the aggrieved seller gets to keep just $450 of the breaching buyer's pre-payment instead of $850.

Section 2-718(2) and (3) covers the breaching buyer's right to restitution of its pre-payments not only when the parties have failed to create their own liquidated damages clause, but also when the parties have included a liquidated damages clause that is valid under §2-718(1). In the case where the buyer has pre-paid some or all of the price and the parties have a valid liquidated damages clause, the breaching buyer's right to restitution would be defined as follows under §2-718(2)(a): R = P – LD, where R = buyer's right to restitution, P = buyer's pre-payment, and LD = seller's liquidated damages. If we add the literal language of §2-718(3), we get R = P – LD – BB, where BB = buyer's benefits from the contract. The reason that a court should not allow the seller to keep its actual damages in addition to its liquidated damages in this case is that now we are talking about a situation in which the parties themselves agreed to the terms of the liquidated damages clause.

C.   Special Remedies When the Breaching Party Is Insolvent

In many cases where a buyer or seller is breaching its sales contract, the breacher is at the same time reneging on its obligations to many other parties as well. In short, it is not uncommon for a breaching party in a sales contract to also be a party that cannot pay its debts as they become due. Therefore, an aggrieved seller or buyer often will not care as much about the monetary amount of its damage claim as it will care about the ability to get possession of goods that are the subject of the sales contract. Put another way, the biggest damage claim in the world will not amount to much against a party that cannot pay it.

Article 2 sets out a number of special remedies for aggrieved sellers and buyers who are dealing with insolvent parties. There are two sections, §§2-702 and 2-705, that protect a seller who sells goods on unsecured credit to a buyer who is insolvent. Realize, of course, that the seller's best protection in a situation like this is to have bargained for a security interest from the buyer in the goods that were the subject of the sale. Not all sales on credit will be of the secured variety, however, so the drafters of Article 2 gave even sellers on unsecured credit some protection in case their buyers turned out to be insolvent.

Where the seller discovers the buyer's insolvency prior to delivery, the seller can refuse delivery except for cash, "including payment for all goods theretofore delivered under the contract." UCC §2-702(1). In a case where the seller does not discover the buyer's insolvency until the goods are in transit, §2-705 governs. Section 2-705(1) provides that a seller that discovers the buyer's insolvency while the goods are in transit can stop delivery of the goods whether or not the buyer has breached. However, when a buyer has breached by repudiating the contract or failing to make a payment but the buyer is not insolvent, a seller may only stop delivery of "carload, truckload, planeload or larger shipments of express or freight." UCC §2-705(1). The seller's right to stop delivery in transit ends when the buyer either receives the goods or is given acknowledgement by a third-party carrier or bailee that the buyer now has the right to possession of the goods. UCC §2-705(2).

In a case where the seller discovers that the buyer has received the goods while insolvent, the seller is given a right to reclaim the goods under §2-702(2) as long as the seller makes the reclamation demand upon the buyer within 10 days of the buyer's receipt of the goods. There is no 10-day time limit on the seller's demand in a case where the buyer has misrepresented its solvency in writing to the seller within three months of the delivery in question.

The seller's reclamation right under §2-702 is not nearly as beneficial as it sounds on the surface. Section 2-702(3) makes the seller's reclamation right subject to the rights of a good-faith purchaser for value, and courts have held that a secured lender of the buyer that has a lien on the buyer's after-acquired property will count as a good-faith purchaser for value. Thus, a commercial buyer purchasing inventory will typically have a secured loan that would cover most goods that it would purchase from a seller on unsecured credit. The secured lender would therefore defeat the reclamation rights of an aggrieved unsecured seller in this situation.

A further limit on the seller's reclamation right occurs when the buyer files bankruptcy. Section 546(c) of the Bankruptcy Code recognizes the seller's state law reclamation right in bankruptcy as against the bankruptcy trustee, but attaches some limitations to that right. First, the seller's reclamation demand must be in writing. Second, the bankruptcy time limit for the seller's written reclamation demand (45 days from receipt of goods by the buyer) is not relaxed even where the buyer has misrepresented its solvency in writing. Section 546(c) does, however, extend the 45-day time limit to at least 20 days after the filing of the case whenever the 45-day period expires after commencement of the case. Finally, the §546(c) right of a seller to assert a reclamation claim in bankruptcy is specifically subject to the prior rights of a holder of a security interest in the goods in question.

Prior to the 2005 amendments to the Bankruptcy Code, the bankruptcy court had the option to satisfy the seller's valid reclamation right with a lien on other property of the bankruptcy estate or even with an unsecured administrative expense priority claim in lieu of the goods themselves. Amended §546(c) removes that discretion from the bankruptcy court but still gives the aggrieved seller the possibility of an administrative expense claim in a case where the seller loses its reclamation right for "failure to provide notice in the manner described" in §546(c). But even this consolation prize of an administrative expense claim will not be available to the seller unless the goods in question were received by the buyer within 20 days of the commencement of the bankruptcy case.

The seller is not the only party to a sales contract that might be adversely affected by the insolvency of the other side. A buyer who has pre-paid all or part of the purchase price could be left with little recourse in a case where the seller to whom it paid the price has become insolvent. Section 2-502(1) gives a buyer that has paid all or part of the purchase price a right to recover goods from the seller "if the seller becomes insolvent within ten days after receipt of the first installment on their price." In order for the buyer to have this right, the goods must have been identified to the contract under §2-501, which requires in most cases that the goods have been "shipped, marked or otherwise designated by the seller as goods to which the contract refers."

Problem Set 28

28.1.   a. Special Toys is a retail toy seller that sells high-end toys and gym sets to a mostly affluent clientele. Denise Daly, president of Special Toys, has come to your law office to ask you some questions. Her first question concerns a customer, Arnold Sinbad, who deposited $5,000 toward the purchase of a $36,000 Deluxe Disney Fort for his four-year-old son. Arnold called yesterday to repudiate the contract, and he wants all of his deposit back. Because there was such a high demand for these forts, Arnold had not yet received his fort at the time he repudiated. The purchase contract did not include a liquidated damages clause. Denise admits that she did not really lose a profit from Arnold's breach, since at this point there are many more eager buyers for these forts than she has forts to sell. What Denise wants to know is whether she can keep any or all of Arnold's deposit. What do you advise her? UCC §2-718(2).

b. Same facts as part (a), except assume that Denise could show actual damages of $3,000 as a result of Arnold's breach. How much of Arnold's deposit could Denise keep now? UCC §2-718(2) and (3).

c. Same facts as part (a), except suppose that Arnold's deposit was just $100. Would either party owe money to the other? UCC §2-718(2).

d. Same facts as part (b), except suppose that Arnold's deposit was just $100. Would either party owe money to the other? UCC §2-718(2) and (3).

e. Same facts as part (a), except suppose that the parties had included a valid liquidated damages clause of $3,000 in the event of buyer breach. How much of Arnold's deposit could Denise keep now? UCC §2-718(2).

f. Same facts as part (b), except suppose that the parties had included a valid liquidated damages clause of $2,500 in the event of buyer breach. How much of Arnold's deposit could Denise keep now? UCC §2-718(2) and (3).

g. Same facts as part (a), except suppose that Arnold had made no deposit and the parties had included a liquidated damages clause of $3,000 that may or may not be valid. Suppose at the time the parties entered into the contract, Denise's supply of forts could not keep up with demand. However, several weeks later when Arnold breached, Denise had more forts on hand than she knew what to do with, and at that point she could show actual damages of $2,900. Should the liquidated damages provision be upheld as valid? To what extent does it matter? UCC §2-718(1).

h. Same facts as part (g), except suppose at the time Arnold entered into the contract, Denise had more forts on hand than she knew what to do with, and at that point she expected to make a $3,000 profit on the sale. Several weeks later, however, when Arnold breached, Denise's supply of forts could not keep up with demand, and she had plenty of other buyers willing to buy Arnold's fort. Should the liquidated damages provision be upheld as valid? To what extent does it matter? UCC §2-718(1).

28.2. Denise Daly has one more problem concerning the Deluxe Disney Fort. She had signed a contract with one of her suppliers, FortCo, to ship her 100 of these forts for $25,000 each. When shortly thereafter these forts became the "in" toy for high-income parents to buy their children for the holiday season, FortCo decided that it would rather get more money for the forts from some other retailer. Accordingly, FortCo announced to Denise that it was repudiating the contract. Denise is now beside herself with worry. She tells you that she cannot order these forts from any supplier at any price now, because the short-term demand has simply outstripped the ability of manufacturers to make these forts. Denise said that she is particularly concerned not just about losing the profit on these forts, but about all of the future business she would have gained by being the only store in town to have some of these forts in stock. Denise wants to know if she can force FortCo to honor its agreement with her. Can she? UCC §2-716, Official Comment 2 to §2-716, §2-501(1)(b).

28.3. Wayne Geary comes to your office in a panic. He is the owner of one of the handful of factories in the country that has a contract with the U.S. mint to make pennies. Wayne's factory has been hovering on the brink of insolvency, but he is convinced that if his factory can complete this latest order from the government, it will finally be in a decent financial position. The problem is that the factory currently cannot make pennies because the penny-press machine that it just purchased has not been working. Wayne's pleas to the machine's manufacturer to repair it have so far fallen on deaf ears. The worst part, Wayne said, is that his factory does not even have enough spare cash to get the machine repaired by a third party. Wayne wonders if he can force the machine's manufacturer to live up to its contractual repair obligations. Can he? UCC §2-716.

28.4.   You are still the junior member of the Uniform Law Commission's Article 2 revision committee, which still includes senior member David Flanders (from Problem 2.4). David says he has another one of those stupid questions that he is afraid would embarrass him if he raised it before the more seasoned members of the committee.

"I don't get it," David tells you. "The current Article 2 seems to go out of its way to expand the situations in which a court may award a buyer specific performance, but some of my law and economics friends tell me that specific performance can be just plain inefficient. Suppose, for example, that you make a contract with me to buy my painting for $1,000. Then my mailman comes along and tells me he'll pay me $5,000 for the same painting. If Article 2 lets you demand specific performance, then we end up with a very inefficient result: I'm forced to sell the painting to someone who values it less than the highest-valuing buyer. I think maybe we should just get rid of specific performance as a remedy for the buyer." What response can you give to David in defense of specific performance?

28.5.   a. Gourmet Creations, a meat retailer, agrees to buy 1,500 pounds of top-grade salami for $4,000 from the Oscar Meyer Company. The terms are that Oscar Meyer will deliver the salami on June 10 to Gourmet Creations, "cash on delivery." The Oscar Meyer carrier accepts Gourmet Creations' check for $4,000, which is returned unpaid to Oscar Meyer's bank on June 23. Upon receiving the bounced check, Oscar Meyer investigates and discovers that although Gourmet Creations has not filed for bankruptcy, it has not been paying its suppliers on time for about the last month or so. Does Oscar Meyer have a right to demand its salami back from Gourmet Creations? UCC §§1-201(23), 2-702, 2-507, 2-511; Official Comment 3 to 2-507.

b. Same facts as part (a), except the payment term is not cash on delivery, but "full payment within 30 days of receipt." Oscar Meyer delivers the goods on June 10, and then discovers on June 18 that Gourmet Creations has been insolvent for the last month. Oscar Meyer also discovers that Gourmet Creations filed bankruptcy on June 16. Is it too late for Oscar Meyer to assert its reclamation rights? What form should its demand take? UCC §2-702, Bankruptcy Code §546(c).

c. Same facts as part (b), except that Oscar Meyer did not learn about Gourmet's June 16 bankruptcy until July 10. Is it too late for Oscar Meyer to assert its reclamation rights? UCC §2-702, Bankruptcy Code §§546(c), 503(b)(9).

d. Same facts as part (b), except it turns out that Gourmet Creations had a perfected secured lender, First National Bank, that had a lien on all of Gourmet's inventory, including after-acquired. If Oscar Meyer pursues its reclamation rights in bankruptcy, what will it be entitled to? UCC §2-702, Bankruptcy Code §§546(c), 503(b)(9).

e. Same facts as part (d), except that First National Bank fails to assert its security interest against the 1,500 pounds of salami. If Oscar Meyer pursues its reclamation rights in bankruptcy, what will it be entitled to? UCC §2-702, Bankruptcy Code §§546(c), 503(b)(9).

Assessment Questions for Chapter 4

Question 1: Heavy Metal in Chicago makes a contract to sell to a Holiday Inn hotel in Detroit one commercial-grade multi-station weightlifting machine for $20,000 for use in the hotel's fitness room. The contract provides that the goods will be delivered on or before June 1, "FOB Seller's Place." On May 20, Heavy Metal has Dependo, a reliable third-party carrier, come pick up the machine for delivery after Heavy Metal gives timely notice of this fact to Holiday Inn. Dependo picks up the machine but severe flooding on the highways from Chicago to Detroit end up ruining the machine by rusting the metal parts. When Holiday Inn receives the machine on May 21, it immediately rejects the machine because of the severe rust. Will Heavy Metal be able to recover from Holiday Inn in an action for the price of the weightlifting machine?

(A) No, because Holiday Inn never accepted the goods.

(B) No, because Heavy Metal failed to deliver conforming goods to Holiday Inn.

(C) No, for both of the reasons given in (A) and (B).

(D) Yes, and the result would be the same even if the delivery term had been "FOB Buyer's Place."

(E) Yes, as long as Heavy Metal sued within a commercially reasonable time after risk of loss had passed to Holiday Inn.

Question 1 Answer: The correct answer is (E). Under §2-709(1)(a), the seller may recover the price "of goods accepted or conforming goods lost or damaged within a commercially reasonable time after risk of loss has passed to the buyer." In this case, Holiday Inn did not accept the machine, but under §2-509(1)(a) (which designates this as a "shipment contract") risk of loss had passed to Holiday Inn once Heavy Metal placed the machine in Dependo's possession. (A) is wrong because even though Holiday Inn never accepted the goods, Heavy Metal could still have an action for the price under §2-709(1)(a) as long as risk of loss had passed when the goods were damaged. (B) is wrong because the delivery term here only required Heavy Metal to deliver conforming goods to its third-party carrier under §2-509(1)(a), as long as the carrier was reliable and Heavy Metal gave adequate notice to Holiday Inn of the delivery under §2-504. (C) is wrong because both (A) and (B) are wrong. (D) is wrong because the result would not be the same here if the delivery term had been "FOB Buyer's Place." If that had been the delivery term, then under §2-509(1) (b) risk of loss would not pass to Holiday Inn until the machine was tendered to Holiday Inn to enable Holiday Inn to take delivery. In that case, Heavy Metal would no longer qualify for an action for the price under §2-709(1)(a) since the damage to the goods would have occurred while the risk of loss was still with the seller.

Question 2: Houston Seller ("Seller") agrees to sell a drill-press machine to Los Angeles Buyer ("Buyer") for $450,000, "FOB Buyer's Place of Business." The cost of delivering the goods from Houston to Los Angeles is $15,000. The machine arrives to Buyer on the stated delivery date, and Buyer wrongfully rejects the machine. A week later, Seller is able to resell the machine in a commercially reasonable and procedurally proper resale for $360,000 to a different Los Angeles buyer that agrees to pick up the machine at its own expense. The market price for this drill-press machine on the date of tender is $390,000 in Houston and $375,000 in Los Angeles. Assuming that Seller is not a lost-profits seller, for what amount may Seller recover from Buyer?

(A) $45,000.
(B) $60,000.
(C) $75,000.
(D) $90,000.
(E) $105,000.

Question 2 Answer: The correct answer is (D). Under §2-706(1), the damages formula for a reselling seller like this one is KP – RP + ID – ES, where KP = contract price, RP = resale price, ID = incidental damages, and ES = expenses saved. In this case, we would get KP ($450,000) – RP ($360,000) + ID (zero) – ES (zero) = $90,000. Incidental damages end up being zero because the new buyer agreed to pick up the machine at its own expense. Expenses saved are zero because Buyer waited until the machine was shipped to reject it, thereby causing Seller to spend the shipping costs that Seller would have spent if Buyer had performed. Had Buyer repudiated prior to shipment, then Seller potentially would have saved the $15,000 in shipping costs (which are Seller's responsibility under this §2-509(1)

(a) destination contract). (A) is wrong because its damages figure uses contract-market damages under §2-708(1), uses a Houston market price (even though the place of "tender" is Los Angeles because of the FOB term), and subtracts $15,000 for expenses saved for delivery costs: $450,000 – $390,000 – $15,000 = $45,000. (B) is wrong for the same reason as (A) except that the answer in (B) does not subtract any expenses saved for delivery costs: $450,000 – $390,000 = $60,000. (C) is wrong because its figure uses contract-market damages under §2-708(1) (even though it does use the correct market price, Los Angeles): $450,000 – $375,000 = $75,000. (E) is wrong because while it correctly uses the contract-resale measure under §2-706(1), it adds $15,000 in incidental damages for the delivery costs incurred by Seller: $450,000 – $360,000 + $15,000 = $105,000. The reason that the delivery costs are not an incidental damage for Seller here is that if Buyer had performed as promised, Seller still would have incurred the $15,000 in delivery costs given the "FOB Buyer's Place of Business" delivery term here.

Question 3: Lessor and Lessee enter into a three-year lease of a drill-press machine for $10,000 per month. Fourteen months into the lease, Lessee has missed two lease payments and Lessor repossesses the machine according to its rights under the contract. Lessor spends three months and $2,000 in advertising costs from the point of repossession trying to re-lease the machine, and finally is able to enter into a substantially similar lease with a new lessee. The new lease is for five years at $9,000 per month. The old lease, but not the new one, required Lessor to do an annual maintenance treatment midway through each lease year that cost Lessor $2,000 for each treatment, one of which was performed under the old lease. Assuming that Lessor is not a lost-volume lessor and putting aside discounting to present value, for what amount of damages may Lessor recover from Lessee?

(A) $67,000.
(B) $37,000.
(C) $71,000.
(D) $65,000.
(E) None of the above.

Question 3 Answer: The correct answer is (A). Under §2A-527(1), if a lessor re-leases goods in a lease agreement that is "substantially similar" to the original lease agreement, the lessor is entitled to UR + (PVOL – PVNL) + ID – ES, where UR = accrued but unpaid rent on the original lease as of the date of the new lease term, PVOL = the present value, as of the same date, of the total remaining lease payments for the original lease, PVNL = the present value, as of the same date, of the total lease payments in the new lease for the term that is comparable to the remainder of the original lease, ID = incidental damages, and ES = expenses saved as a consequence of the lessee's breach. In this case, that gives us UR ($50,000 from two missed payments plus three months of searching for new lessee) + (PVOL – PVNL) (19 months left on original lease times [$10,000 minus $9,000] equals $19,000 of contract-resale damages) + ID ($2,000 in advertising costs) – ES (2 times $2,000 = $4,000 in maintenance costs saved by Lessee's breach) = $67,000. (B) is wrong because its damages figure ignores the $30,000 in additional missed payments that accrued during the three months when Lessor was searching for a new lessee. (C) is wrong because its figure fails to subtract the $4,000 in expenses saved as a result of the breach. (D) is wrong because its figure fails to include the $2,000 in advertising costs as an incidental expense. (E) is wrong because (A) is correct.

Question 4: Shortly before the new year, Toronto Seller (Seller) and New York City Buyer (Buyer) enter into a contract for the sale of 20 new Cadillac Convertible cars for $800,000, "FOB Seller's Place of Business." Seller explains to Buyer before signing the contract that by selling these 20 cars before the end of the fiscal year, Seller will be receiving a $100,000 incentive bonus from its manufacturer for reaching an overall sales goal for the year. The day before the delivery date, Buyer repudiates the contract. The cost of shipping the cars from Toronto to New York City would have been $20,000. Upon learning of Buyer's repudiation, Seller chooses to avoid the contract and resells the 20 cars to a local Toronto buyer for $770,000. In the resale contract, Seller has to spend $5,000 to deliver the cars to the local buyer. However, because the resale takes place just after the new year, Seller is no longer eligible for the $100,000 incentive bonus from its manufacturer. Assuming that Seller is not a lost-volume seller, for what amount of damages may Seller recover from Buyer under the CISG?

(A) $35,000.
(B) $135,000.
(C) $115,000
(D) $15,000
(E) None of the above.

Question 4 Answer: The correct answer is (B). After Seller avoids this contract, it still retains its right to sue for damages under CISG Article 81(1). In this case, Seller is suing for contract-resale damages under Article 75. Seller is also eligible for any incidental or consequential damages that it can show under Article 74. In this case, Seller's basic contract-resale damages would be $800,000 – $770,000 = $30,000. Seller could add to that amount the consequential damages of $100,000 in incentive bonus foregone as a result of Buyer's breach. These damages should qualify under Article 74 because in this case Buyer "foresaw or ought to have foreseen [these damages] at the time of the conclusion of the contract." Seller should also qualify for $5,000 in incidental damages because under the original contract with the "FOB Seller's Place of Business" delivery term, Seller would not have had to pay any transportation charges since those would have been Buyer's responsibility. So total damages are $30,000 + $100,000 + $5,000 = $135,000. (A) is wrong because its damages figure ignores Seller's legitimate consequential damages of $100,000. (C) is wrong because its figure subtracts $20,000 as "expenses saved" in delivery due to Buyer's breach, when in fact Seller did not save any transportation expenses as a result of the breach in light of the delivery term in the original contract. (D) is wrong because its figure ignores Seller's consequential damages and also includes $20,000 in expenses saved by Seller. (E) is wrong because (B) is correct.

Question 5: Buyer makes a contract to purchase 10 widgets from Seller for a total cost of $100,000. Buyer wrongfully repudiates that contract, and Seller resells the widgets to a new buyer for $100,000. The market price of the widgets at the time and place for tender is $98,000. Seller has fixed annual expenses of $100 million overall, and in addition spends $5,000 in direct labor costs and $3,500 in direct material costs for each widget produced. Assuming that Seller is a lost-volume seller, for what amount of damages may Seller recover from Buyer for Buyer's breach?

(A) Zero.
(B) $2,000.
(C) $15,000.
(D) $17,000.
(E) None of the above.

Question 5 Answer: The correct answer is (C). This problem requires an application of the "simple version" of §2-708(2)'s lost-volume seller damages: namely, KP – DC + ID, where KP = contract price, DC = seller's direct costs for this item, and ID = incidental damages. In this case, there are no incidental damages, so the damages formula ends up as simply KP ($100,000) – DC (10 x [$5,000 + $3,500] = $85,000) = $15,000. (A) is wrong because even though Seller is able to resell the widgets to a new buyer for the same price as Buyer agreed to pay, Seller is a lost-volume seller and therefore does incur damages as a result of Buyer's breach. (B) is wrong because its damages figure uses the contract-market formula under §2-708(1), even though in this case that measure of damages "is inadequate to put the seller in as good a position as performance would have done." (D) is wrong because its figure combines contract-market damages under §2-708(1) with lost-volume damages under §2-708(2). (E) is wrong because (C) is correct.

Question 6: Buyer and Seller enter into a contract in which Seller agrees to build a custom-designed drill-press machine for Buyer for a total price of $3.2 million. Seller plans to spend $1.2 million in direct labor costs and $800,000 in direct materials costs. Buyer repudiates the contract in mid-production, at which point Seller has purchased and used $400,000 in raw materials and has expended $800,000 in direct labor costs. Seller reasonably opts to cease production at that point. By spending an additional $80,000 in direct labor costs, Seller is able to sell the scrap for $1.4 million in a sale that Seller never would have made had Buyer not breached. For what amount of damages can Seller recover from Buyer?

(A) $1.2 million.
(B) $1.28 million.
(C) $1 million.
(D) $1.88 million.
(E) None of the above.

Question 6 Answer: The correct answer is (E). This is a case where we must use the "full version" of §2-708(2) because we have a component parts manufacturer who reasonably stops in midstream production and sells for scrap after the buyer repudiates. The damages formula for this case is KP – ADC + ID + CI – RP, where KP = contract price, ADC = seller's anticipated direct costs for this item, ID = incidental damages, CI = due allowance for costs reasonably incurred, RP = due credit for payments or proceeds of resale. Plugging in our numbers, we get KP ($3.2 million) – ADC ($1.2 million + $800,000 = $2 million) + ID ($80,000) + CI ($400,000 + $800,000 = $1.2 million) – RP ($1.4 million) = $1.08 million, which is none of the above figures. Another way to get to the same answer is using §2-706(1)'s resale formula: KP – RP + ID – ES, where KP = contract price, RP = resale price, ID = incidental damages and ES = expenses saved. As applied here, that would be KP ($3.2 million) – RP ($1.4 million) + ID ($80,000) – ES ($800,000 in costs saved by not having to complete) = $1.08 million. (A) is wrong because its damages figure simply takes the contract price minus anticipated direct costs, and ignores costs reasonably incurred, incidental damages and resale proceeds. (B) is wrong because its figure adds incidental damages to the wrong answer in (A) but still ignores costs reasonably incurred and resale proceeds. (C) is wrong because its figure ignores incidental damages. (D) is wrong because its figure uses the contract-resale measure but fails to include expenses saved.

Question 7: Seller, a Chicago company, agrees to sell to Buyer, a Houston company, a shipment of six dozen widgets for a contract price of $430,000, "FOB Chicago." Delivery date in the contract is July 9. Buyer arranges and pays for shipment, and on July 9 the widgets arrive in Houston on time. However, they are clearly defective and Buyer immediately rejects them. The cost of shipping six dozen widgets from Chicago to Houston is $25,000. The market price of six dozen widgets on July 9 is $395,000 in Chicago and $460,000 in Houston. Assuming Buyer has not pre-paid any of the purchase price and Buyer chooses not to cover, for what amount of damages may Buyer recover from Seller?

(A) $30,000.
(B) $5,000.
(C) Zero.
(D) $55,000.
(E) None of the above.

Question 7 Answer: The correct answer is (A). Under §2-713(1), the buyer's contract-market damage formula is KP – MP + ID – ES, where KP = contract price, MP = market price at the time buyer learned of the breach, ID = incidental damages, and ES = expenses saved as a result of seller's breach. Section 2-713(2) gives further guidance by noting that market price is determined "as of the place of tender or, in cases of rejection after arrival or revocation of acceptance, as of the place of arrival." The place of tender here would be Chicago given the FOB shipping term, but in this case the relevant market price will be Houston because Buyer rejected the goods after arrival. Thus, our formula yields MP ($460,000) – KP ($430,000) + ID (0) – ES (0) = $30,000. (B) is wrong because its damages figure assumes that there were $25,000 in "expenses saved" here for Buyer, whereas in fact Buyer had to pay for the delivery to Houston per the FOB term and thus did not save those delivery costs due to Seller's breach. (C) is wrong because its figure assumes that Chicago is the relevant market price rather than Houston. (D) is wrong because its figure adds $25,000 as "incidental expenses" to reflect the fact that Buyer had to pay for delivery charges from Chicago to Houston. However, even if Seller had not breached, Buyer would have had to pay those same $25,000 in delivery charges. (E) is wrong because (A) is correct.

Question 8: Super Cater is a high-end catering business that prepares and delivers gourmet dinners for fancy corporate events. Earth Dance, a not-for-profit organic farm, makes a contract with Super Cater to purchase dinners for 200 guests for Earth Dance's annual fund-raising event. Tickets to the dinner are $100 each, and Super Cater agrees to serve the 200 guests for a total price of $8,000. On the morning of the big dinner, Super Cater calls Earth Dance to say that it will not be able to serve the dinners that night. Earth Dance frantically calls around and is unable to locate another caterer who can handle such a big job on such short notice. Earth Dance reluctantly has to cancel this year's fund-raising dinner and refunds everyone's ticket price. When Earth Dance sues Super Cater for $12,000 in damages, what should be the result?

(A) Super Cater wins, unless Earth Dance can show that Super Cater's prices were significantly below the market.

(B) Super Cater wins, because Earth Dance cannot recover consequential damages when there is no injury to person or property.

(C) Earth Dance wins, even if Super Cater did not know that these dinners were for Earth Dance's annual fund-raising event.

(D) Earth Dance wins, but only if Super Cater had reason to know of Earth Dance's annual fund-raising event.

(E) Earth Dance wins, and would still win even if cover had been possible.

Question 8 Answer: The correct answer is (D). Section 2-715(2)(a) allows Earth Dance to recover these purely economic consequential damages here as long as Super Cater had reason to know "of the general and particular requirements and needs" of buyer at the time of contracting, and these damages could not be prevented "by cover or otherwise." In this case, then, the breach by Super Cater was clearly the "but for" cause of the lost profits that would have been made on the dinner ($20,000 in ticket sales minus $8,000 in costs equals $12,000 in consequential damages). Furthermore, these damages could not have been avoided by "cover or otherwise." So the only issue is whether Super Cater had reason to know of the purpose of this dinner and thus the financial ramifications of a last-minute breach. (A) is wrong because consequential damages under §2-715(2)(a) is a different category of damages for the aggrieved buyer than the contract-market measure of §2-713(1). (B) is wrong because injury to person or property is only required when the consequential damages are being sought under §2-715(2)(b). (C) is wrong for the same reason that (D) is correct. (E) is wrong because one of the elements for consequential damages under §2-715(2)(a) is that the damages could not reasonably be prevented "by cover or otherwise."

Question 9: Mexico City Buyer (Buyer) made a contract with Houston Seller to purchase five brand-new dump trucks for $750,000, "FOB Buyer's Factory." Two weeks before delivery of the trucks was due, Houston Seller wrongfully repudiated the contract. The reason that Buyer had made this contract with Houston Seller was that Buyer had arranged to sell to Mexico City Construction Company five brand-new dump trucks for $950,000. Buyer was going to use the trucks from Houston Seller to fulfill its own contract with Mexico City Construction, which had agreed to pick up the trucks from Buyer once Buyer had the trucks. If Buyer had made reasonable cover efforts, it could have purchased the same trucks from Dallas Seller for $800,000, "FOB Seller's Factory." Delivery costs from Dallas to Mexico City would have been $30,000. No cover was available in Mexico City, and Dallas was the closest place that offered a feasible cover. Because Buyer did not make these reasonable cover efforts, Buyer was unable to fulfill its own contract with Mexico City Construction Company. Fortunately, Mexico City Construction Company has made it clear that it would not be suing Buyer for Buyer's breach in failing to supply the dump trucks. For what amount may Buyer recover from Houston Seller?

(A) Zero.
(B) $200,000.
(C) $80,000.
(D) $50,000.
(E) None of the above.

Question 9 Answer: The correct answer is (C). Since Buyer did not cover here under CISG Article 75, Buyer will recover under the contract-market measure of Article 76: MP ($800,000 + $30,000 in delivery costs) – KP ($750,000) = $80,000. Article 76(2) tells us that the normal market price should be the price at the place where delivery of the goods should have been made. Article 76(2) also says, however, that "if there is no current price at that place," the market price should be "the price at such other place as serves as a reasonable substitute, making due allowance for differences in the cost of transporting the goods." In this case the Dallas price of $800,000 would be the market price, plus $30,000 in delivery that Buyer would have had to pay to buy the substitute trucks because of the "FOB Seller's Factory" delivery term. Recall that in the original contract the purchase price included delivery to Buyer because of the "FOB Buyer's Factory" delivery term. (A) is wrong because Buyer's failure to cover does not deprive Buyer of all damages here, only any damages that would have been avoided by cover (such as a portion of the $200,000 in profits that Buyer expected to make, see next under answer (B) explanation). (B) is wrong because Buyer's lost profits of $200,000 are not separately recoverable here under Article 74 as consequential damages. The $80,000 damages figure already captures the portion of that $200,000 that was truly unavoidable even if Buyer had covered: Had Buyer covered, Buyer still would have made a profit of $120,000 ($950,000 contract price minus $830,000 in Buyer's cover costs), but Buyer still would have been out the remaining $80,000 of the $200,000 profit that it originally expected to make. (D) is wrong because its damages figure fails to include the $30,000 in extra delivery costs from the Dallas market price. (E) is wrong because (C) is correct.

Question 10: Same facts as Question 9, except now Mexico City Construction successfully recovers $140,000 in damages from Buyer due to Buyer's breach of its contract with Mexico City Construction. For what amount may Buyer recover from Houston Seller?

(A) Zero.
(B) $140,000.
(C) $200,000.
(D) $220,000.
(E) None of the above.

Question 10 Answer: The correct answer is (E). The $140,000 in damages that Buyer is forced to pay Mexico City Construction cannot be added to Buyer's damages claim of $80,000 under CISG Article 76. Even though this additional $140,000 might normally qualify as a consequential damage for Buyer under Article 74, Article 76 makes it clear that Buyer's failure to mitigate by covering with a purchase of the Dallas dump trucks will make Buyer ineligible for this consequential damage. So Buyer is still eligible for just $80,000 in damages, the contract-market measure of Article 76. (A) is wrong because Buyer's failure to cover only makes Buyer ineligible for damages that cover would have avoided, rather than making Buyer ineligible for any damages. (B) is wrong because its damages figure suggests that Buyer is eligible for these consequential damages and not for the contract-market damages. (C) is wrong because $200,000 represents Buyer's expected lost profits alone, but those are still not separately recoverable as consequential damages under Article 74 because a portion of those lost profits could have been captured by Buyer had Buyer covered. (D) is wrong for the same reason that (E) is correct: $220,000 wrongly suggests that Buyer should get both its contract-market damages plus consequential damages for the amount Buyer has to pay to Mexico City Construction.

Question 11: On September 22, San Francisco Seller makes a contract with San Diego Buyer to sell 1,000 widgets on October 9 for a total price of $320,000, "FOB Seller's Place." The cost of delivering 1,000 widgets from San Francisco to San Diego is $20,000. On September 23, San Diego Buyer makes a contract to sell to Los Angeles Buyer 1,000 widgets for $380,000, "FOB Seller's Place," delivery date October 10. The cost of delivering 1,000 widgets from San Diego to Los Angeles is $10,000. On October 8, San Francisco Seller announces to San Diego Buyer that it will breach its contract to sell the widgets. It is too late for San Diego Buyer to arrange suitable cover, and from October 8 to October 10 the market price for 1,000 widgets is $450,000 in Los Angeles, $410,000 in San Diego, and $420,000 in San Francisco. Assuming that Los Angeles Buyer will recover from San Diego Buyer whatever damages the UCC allows and that no buyers here have pre-paid any of the purchase price, for what amount of damages may San Diego Buyer recover from San Francisco Seller under the approach in the *Allied Canners* case?

(A) $170,000.
(B) $100,000.
(C) $70,000.
(D) $80,000.
(E) None of the above.

Question 11 Answer: The correct answer is (C). The way to approach this problem is to begin with the formula. Here the appropriate damages formula is that which is found in UCC §2-713(1): RBPP + MP – KP + ID + CD – ES. Since San Diego Buyer did not prepay the price here, then RBPP = 0. The MP figure, according to §2-713(2), is to be determined at the time that the buyer learned of the repudiation and at the place for tender. The place for tender is San Francisco, given the "FOB Seller's Place" delivery term in the San Francisco Seller/San Diego Buyer contract. Thus, MP = $420,000. KP, the contract price, is $320,000 (this is the contract price between San Diego Buyer and San Francisco Seller, not the price of San Diego Buyer's contract with Los Angeles Buyer).

There do not seem to be any incidental damages here, so ID = 0. CD, consequential damages, will consist of two elements: (1) San Diego Buyer's lost profits in its contract with Los Angeles Buyer ($380,000 - $320,000 = $60,000, less the $20,000 in delivery costs that San Diego Buyer would have had to pay to get the widgets from San Francisco Seller [given the "FOB Seller's Place" delivery term in that contract], for a total lost-profits figure of $40,000) (Official Comment 6 to §2-715 leaves little doubt that a buyer's lost profits will count as a consequential damage of seller's breach: "In the case of sale of wares to one in the business of reselling them, resale is one of the requirements of which the seller has reason to know within the meaning of subsection (2)(a)."); and (2) The damages that San Diego Buyer will have to pay to Los Angeles Buyer for San Diego Buyer's failure to deliver the widgets to Los Angeles Buyer. This second element of consequential damages, the damages that San Diego Buyer will owe for its own breach, would be calculated as RBPP (0) + MP ($410,000) (in the San Diego Buyer/Los Angeles Buyer contract, San Diego was the place for tender given the "FOB Seller's Place" delivery term in that contract) – KP ($380,000, the price of the San Diego Buyer/Los Angeles Buyer contract) + ID (0) + CD (maybe Los Angeles Buyer has lost profits of its own to claim, but we are not given information to know this, so we'll assume 0) – ES (0, since §2-713 assumes a hypothetical cover at the place of tender, here San Diego per the delivery term, which means that Los Angeles Buyer would still have paid the $10,000 in delivery charges if it had effected such a cover in the San Diego market) = $30,000.

Thus, a literal reading of San Diego Buyer's §2-713(1) damages against San Francisco Seller would look like this: RBPP (0) + MP ($420,000) – KP ($320,000) + ID (0) + CD ($40,000 in lost profits + $30,000 in damages owed to Los Angeles Buyer) – ES (0, not $20,000, since the $20,000 "saved" in delivery costs has already been subtracted in calculating San Diego Buyer's lost-profits figure of $40,000 that appears in the consequential damages variable) = $170,000. The court in *Allied Canners*, however, said that the party in San Diego Buyer's position should be limited to a damages award that would put it in the position that it would have been in had San Francisco Seller performed. Such a figure would consist simply of its lost profit, $40,000, plus the damages that it will owe to Los Angeles Buyer, $30,000, for a total expectancy damages figure of $70,000.

(A) is wrong because it uses the contract-market formula in its literal form, even though *Allied Canners* rejected that approach in a case where it would have overcompensated the buyer relative to the buyer's expectancy. (B) is wrong because it simply takes the contract-market difference without including consequential damages, and still ends up overcompensating the buyer's expectancy interests, contrary to the *Allied Canners* approach of §1-305's "spirit of the remedies." (D) is wrong because it uses the contract-market difference without including consequential damages, and then subtracts the $20,000 in delivery costs that are saved by San Diego Buyer as a result of the breach, still overcompensating San Diego Buyer relative to its expectancy. (A) is wrong because (C) is correct.

Question 12: Same facts as Question 11, except that San Diego Buyer is able to cover by purchasing 1,000 widgets in Oakland for $320,000 plus $30,000 in delivery costs that it incurs to get the widgets to San Diego. As a result, San Diego Buyer is able to fulfill its contract with Los Angeles Buyer. For what amount of damages may San Diego Buyer recover from San Francisco Seller under the approach in the *Allied Canners* case?

   (A) $20,000.
   (B) $10,000.
   (C) $30,000.
   (D) Zero.
   (E) None of the above.

Question 12 Answer: The correct answer is (B). The cover formula of UCC §2-712(1) is RBPP + CC – KP + ID + CD – ES. Here, RBPP = 0; CC = $350,000 (counting the $30,000 in delivery costs); KP = $320,000; ID = 0; CD = possibly $10,000 in lost profits, since due to San Francisco Seller's breach San Diego Buyer made just $30,000 profits ((380,000 revenue – 350,000 cover cost = $30,000) in its contract with Los Angeles Buyer rather than the $40,000 it expected to make from the original contract (but see below); ES = $20,000, since if we count the $30,000 in delivery costs from Oakland as part of the cost of cover, we should also consider as an "expense saved" the $20,000 delivery costs that San Diego Buyer would have had to pay in the contract that San Francisco Seller breached. Any court, but especially one following the *Allied Canners* "spirit of the remedies" expectancy approach, should say here that San Diego Buyer should get no consequential damages, since its $10,000 in "lost profits" is already accounted for by the contract-cover difference of $30,000 (even after subtracting $20,000 for "expenses saved"). Thus, TI's §2-712 damages should be RBPP (0) + CC ($350,000) – KP ($320,000) + ID (0) + CD (0) – ES ($20,000) = $10,000. (A) is wrong because it adds consequential damages of $10,000 for lost profits even though the lost profits are already accounted for in the contract-cover differential. (C) is wrong because it does a contract-cover differential that includes as part of the cover cost the $30,000 in delivery expenses, but then it fails to subtract the $20,000 in delivery expenses saved by San Diego Buyer on the original contract as a result of the breach. (D) is wrong because it looks at a contract-cover differential without considering the difference in delivery costs occasioned by the breach. (E) is wrong because (B) is correct.

Question 13: Buyer makes a $15,000 deposit toward the purchase of a $108,000 widget and then wrongfully repudiates her contract before the delivery date. Seller could show actual damages of $9,000 as a result of the breach. Under a literal approach to UCC §2-718(3), how much of Buyer's deposit will Seller have to return to Buyer?

(A) Zero.
(B) $14,500.
(C) $15,000.
(D) $6,000.
(E) $5,500.

Question 13 Answer: The correct answer is (E). The formula for the literal approach to UCC §2-718(3) restitution damages for the breaching buyer who pre-pays looks like this: R = P − (< of .2t or $500 or P) − SD − BB, where R = the pre-paying buyer's right to restitution, P = the sum of prepayments made by the buyer, t = the value of the total performance for which the buyer is obligated under the contract (normally the contract price), SD = seller's actual damages, and BB = buyer's benefits from the contract. Plugging in the numbers here, we would get R = P ($15,000) − (< of .2($108,000) or $500 or $15,000) − SD ($9,000) − BB (0) = P ($15,000) − $500 − SD ($9,000) − 0 = $5,500. (A) is wrong because it assumes that Buyer is not entitled to any restitution here. (B) is wrong because it ignores Seller's actual damages in calculating Buyer's right to restitution. (C) is wrong because it fails to subtract from Buyer's restitution either the statutory liquidated damages or Seller's actual damages. (D) is wrong because it subtracts only the greater of statutory liquidated damages or Seller's actual damages rather than using the literal formula given in §2-718(3).

Question 14: Same facts as Question 13, except now Buyer's deposit is $20,000 and Seller's actual damages are $11,000. Under the approach taken by the court in *Neri v. Retail Marine Corp.*, how much of Buyer's deposit will Seller have to return to Buyer?

(A) $11,000.
(B) $20,000.
(C) $8,500.
(D) $9,000.
(E) None of the above.

Question 14 Answer: The correct answer is (D). Under the approach in *Neri*, the seller is not allowed to keep from the buyer's deposit both the statutory liquidated damages of §2-718(2)(b) plus the seller's actual damages, despite the literal language to that effect found in §2-718(3). Instead, the *Neri* court allowed the seller to keep the greater of statutory liquidated damages or the seller's actual damages. In this case, Seller's actual damages of $11,000 well exceed the statutory liquidated damages of $500. So Seller would get to keep $11,000 of Buyer's $20,000, meaning that Seller would have to return $9,000 to Buyer under the *Neri* approach. (A) is wrong because it tells us how much Seller would get to keep from Buyer's deposit rather than how much Seller will have to return to Buyer. (B) is wrong because it assumes that Seller does not get to keep any of Buyer's deposit. (C) is wrong because it uses the literal approach to §2-718(3) that the *Neri* court rejected, namely that Seller gets to keep both Seller's actual damages and the statutory liquidated damages of §2-718(2)(b). (E) is wrong because (D) is correct.

Table of Cases

Italics indicate principal cases.

Table of Statutes

Index